A WORLD FEDERATION
OF CULTURES:
AN AFRICAN PERSPECTIVE

PREFERRED WORLDS FOR THE 1990'S

Saul H. Mendlovitz, General Editor

On the Creation of a Just World Order
Preferred Worlds for the 1990's
edited by Saul H. Mendlovitz

Footsteps into the Future
Diagnosis of the Present World and a Design
for an Alternative
Rajni Kothari

A World Federation of Cultures
An African Perspective
Ali A. Mazrui

A Study of Future Worlds
Richard A. Falk

The True Worlds
A Transnational Perspective
Johan Galtung

A program of the World Order Models Project.
Sponsored by the Institute for World Order, Inc.
New York, New York.

A WORLD FEDERATION OF CULTURES: AN AFRICAN PERSPECTIVE

Ali A. Mazrui

THE FREE PRESS
A Division of Macmillan Publishing Co., Inc.
NEW YORK

The Free Press
A Division of Macmillan Publishing Co., Inc.
866 Third Avenue, New York, N.Y. 10022

Collier Macmillan Canada, Ltd.

Library of Congress Catalog Card Number 75-37318

Printed in the United States of America

printing number
1 2 3 4 5 6 7 8 9 10

This publication has been made possible by collaboration among the following:

The Free Press
A Division of Macmillan Publishing Co., Inc.
New York, N.Y.

Ghana Publishing Corporation
Accra, Ghana

Permission has been granted to reprint the extracts which are listed below: Lines from *The Modern Traveller,* by Hillaire Belloc, appearing on p. 40. Reprinted from H. Belloc, *Complete Verse,* 1970. With permission from Duckworth, London. / Portions of the poem, "Song of Lawino," by Okot p'Bitek, appearing on pp. 85–86, 169–170, and 172. With permission from East African Publishing House, Nairobi. Copyright © East African Publishing House, 1966. / Lines from the poem, "White Man's Burden," by Rudyard Kipling, appearing on pp. 156–157, 387, and 388. Reprinted from R. Kipling, *The Five Nations.* With permission from Mrs. George Bambridge, Macmillan of London & Basingstoke and Macmillan Co. of Canada. / Lines from the poem, "The English Flag," by Rudyard Kipling, appearing on p. 338. Reprinted from R. Kipling, *Barrack Room Ballads.* With permission from Mrs. George Bambridge and Eyre Methuen Ltd. / Lines from the poem, "If," by Rudyard Kipling, appearing on p. 343. Reprinted from R. Kipling, *Rewards and Fairies.* With permission from Mrs. George Bambridge, Macmillan of London & Basingstoke and Macmillan Co. of Canada. / Lines from the poem, *Return to My Native Land,* by Aime Cesaire, appearing on p. 405. Translated by Emil Snyder. Published by Présence Africaine, Paris, 1968. With permission from Présence Africaine. / Lines from the poem, "Vietnam," by Jonathan Kariara, appearing on p. 468. Reprinted from ZUKA, no. 2, Oxford University Press, Eastern Africa, 1968. Copyright © Jonathan Kariara.

Contents

v

Section Four
ECONOMIC CULTURE AND THE LURE OF DEVELOPMENT

Section Five
INTELLECTUAL CULTURE AS A MEDIUM OF DISSEMINATION

Section Six
CULTURAL CONVERGENCE AND ENLARGEMENT OF EMPATHY

General Introduction

Scholars and intellectuals, like human beings in other walks of life, need to interpret and come to grips with the crises plaguing the contemporary global political and social system. Indeed their obligation to do so may be a particularly special and important one. They are, or are supposed to be, able to discern trends, detect signals warning us of emerging social problems, think seriously and critically about alternative solutions and possible future worlds, as well as recommend strategies for achieving those solutions and worlds. One would think that this somewhat crucial albeit relatively precious sector of the world's population, more than others, is capable of avoiding too firm an anchor in the particulars of what is. "Reality" may, for a number of reasons, constrain and overwhelm the thinking and imagination of those who have to struggle for daily existence. But surely professional thinkers and analysts have a mandate to look beyond the obvious, the immediate, and to see the possibilities open for reform and improvement.

For reasons that I suspect to be familiar to most of us, social scientists have yet to meet this challenge adequately. There is, initially, the bias in the social sciences against work that explicitly utilizes preferences and values as a way of defining problems to be investigated, and as a standard to be used for what will be considered an adequate solution to the problems. Research that deviates from the confines of a perspective that is viewed by its adherents as empirical and scientific is either dismissed as ideological or as being an exercise in wishful thinking. In this view, description is a proper social science concern, while prescription is not. Second, the same tradition's narrow sense of realism and empiricism operates quite decisively to inhibit futuristic thinking and orientation. If one wants maximum certainty and minimum speculation, concern with what prevails is preferable to what might or will be. If some social scientists manage to get over their reluctance to engage in futuristic thinking, their work generally confines itself to relatively simple extrapolations of current trends. The future then becomes a mere extension of the present, as though humanity has little or no ability to shape the future in preferred directions.

Two additional factors are also to blame for the lack of creative thinking about the contemporary world order system and its major crises—e.g., war, social injustice, widespread poverty, ecological imbalance, and alienation—as well as alternative systems more compatible with a humane and just world order. The crises are global in scope, yet most social scientists who pay attention to them are wedded to an analysis in which the nation-state system informs their definitions and solutions to global problems. At the same time it is becoming increasingly clear that most of the major problems confronting humankind defy national solutions and perspectives, and are generally aggravated, if not directly caused, by the imperatives of national sovereignty.

Finally, creative thinking about the globe, its crises, and future is hindered by an element which is inherent in the nature of social knowledge itself and the extent to which it is culture-bound and geographically circumscribed. Even the most sympathetic and globally-minded scholar can only perceive the world from a particular angle and perspective; his (or her) roots in a particular nation, race, or class help determine and shape the choice of the problems—and the proposed remedies to them—that concern that person. Certain cultural assumptions, values, and concerns may sensitize a person to some problems at the same time they cause the individual to neglect a number of different problems that other people in other places deem important. Or, the same global problem or phenomenon is frequently interpreted in different ways by observers from different cultures. Given the global dimensions of our major world order concerns, these truisms of the sociology of knowledge recommend in favor of transnational and cross-cultural perspectives being brought to bear upon the questions and problems that concern us. In short, it speaks against ethnocentric knowledge and research. While this point has long been well known, there has been much too little social science research carried out in this fashion. The work of other scholars may be available, but collaborative research across cultures and world views is yet to be widely practiced.

II

A World Federation of Cultures is one book in the series of volumes entitled *Preferred Worlds for the 1990's* resulting from a transnational research enterprise, the World Order Models Project. Because the

World Order Models Project (WOMP) is likely to be the forerunner of many more such transnational and global enterprises, it seems appropriate to say something about its genesis, development, and future.

WOMP was initially conceived in response to pedagogical needs related to the study of the problem of the elimination of war as a human social institution. The individuals involved at the outset of this program brought to it a seriousness one associates with those individuals and groups who, between the eighteenth and nineteenth centuries, advocated and participated in the global movement to abolish slavery, or with those persons in this century who have been participating in the dismemberment of colonialism and imperialism.

To put the matter forthrightly, it was a conscious "political" act, based on a theory of social change which reasoned that most individuals in the globe, including political leadership, were encapsulated in a view of the world in which war, while perhaps unfortunate, was a necessary and permanent ingredient of human society. Thus the decision to enlist the energies of educational structures throughout the globe was partially based on the notion that the seriousness of the idea might be legitimated if the academic community throughout the world were to give it the status of a subject matter of discipline, or at least admit it was the kind of social problem which was amenable to rational analysis. Concomitantly and certainly as important as legitimation, was the possibility of enlisting the talent and skills of the academic community in the research and education necessary for a successful global peace movement.

And so it was in 1966 that we began to examine how to enroll volunteers so that our educational effort would merit serious attention by scholars and educators throughout the globe. WOMP emerged as an answer.

The notion which we began to pursue was that if we were to get outstanding scholars as well as thoughtful individuals throughout the globe to become involved in the problem of war prevention, it would be necessary that they contribute actively in the inquiry. We decided to invite groups of scholars in various parts of the world to direct nationally or regionally based inquiries into the problem of war prevention. We did not proceed very far in our recruitment of individuals for the project when it soon became clear that the subject matter would have to be expanded to include the related problems of economic well being and social justice, if we were to generate a world interest in this inquiry.

There were two reasons advanced for the inclusion of these problem areas. To begin with, there were many persons who argued that it was impossible to deal adequately with war prevention without taking into account poverty and social injustice; that as an empirical matter, these matters were so inextricably interwoven, they should be seen as part of the definition of the problem of war prevention. More importantly, however, it became increasingly clear that while peace, in the sense of the elimination of international violence, might have a very high priority with individuals in the industrialized sector of the globe, economic well being and social justice received a much higher rating in the Third World. When we discussed these three problems, war, poverty, and social injustice, as they persisted in national, regional, and global context, and proposed examining them in the light of the next three decades, with particular reference to the countervailing values of peace, economic well being and social justice, virtually all the scholars we approached agreed to participate in the project.

We held the first meeting of the World Order Models Project in New Delhi in February 1968. At that time five research groups had been organized, representing West Germany, Latin America, Japan, India, and North America. Groups representing Africa, the Soviet Union, and some Scandinavian scholars who preferred to present a non-territorial perspective, joined in subsequent years. More recently we benefited from the involvement in the project of a Chinese as well as a Middle Eastern scholar. One meeting was held with a group of economists organized by Jagdish Bhagwati of the Massachusetts Institute of Technology. This resulted in the first WOMP book, *Economics and World Order, From the 1970's to the 1990's* (Macmillan, 1972). A second book, *Africa and World Affairs* (The Third Press, 1973) edited by Ali Mazrui and Hasu Patel resulted from a conference organized by the African research group. All together, some nine meetings have been held in various parts of the world: India, Japan, East Africa, Western Europe, United States, and Latin America.

The results of nearly seven years of individual and collaborative work are only partially represented by this and the other WOMP volumes. We set out to create the basic instructional materials needed for a worldwide educational movement whose ultimate thrust would be global reform. No one is more aware than we are today of how many more and different materials still need to be created and disseminated. We set out to do normative social research that was at one and the same time oriented to the future, interdisciplinary, and focused on the design of social change actions, policies, and institutions. No one realizes more than the WOMP research groups how difficult it is to do this task with competence, combined with true imagination and intellectual power.

The project has fundamentally affected the personal and professional commitments of virtually everyone who participated in it. It is fair to say that what started out for almost all the participants as a short term and secondary interest has now become a lifetime scholarly and political vocation. At a meeting of the Directors of the World Order Models Project in Bogotá, Colombia, over the New Year period in 1974, the group decided to collaborate on a series of enterprises which they hope will continue to promote research, education, and a genuinely transnational social movement to realize the world order values of peace, economic well being, social justice, and ecological stability. The first of these ventures will be a transnational journal, *Alternatives,* of which Rajni Kothari will be editor, with a distinguished editorial board of some two dozen scholars throughout the globe.

Second, a number of the individuals associated with WOMP have assumed the responsibility for issuing an annual State of the Globe Message. This Message will attempt to evaluate local, regional, and global trends, rating the extent to which the world order values have been diminished or realized during the preceding year, and to make recommendations as to what ought to be done in the coming years. The State of the Globe Message, issued by a group of transnational scholars independent of any formal structures of authority, should be seen as complementary to the messages which are now coming from such formal sources.

Third, we have embarked upon a modest but significant research program for measuring world order indicators based on our values, which we hope will support the State of the Globe Message and provide alternative ways for social scientists to think about and measure the quality of social life. In addition, there will be a series of transnational seminars for scholars, public figures in all professions, expanded formal educational programming, and the beginning of a mass public education movement on a global basis. All of this programming has already begun in some form and we hope will involve constructive criticism, support, and participation by many people throughout the globe.

III

The world order images and change strategies presented in these WOMP books are strikingly diverse, reflecting the different methods, intellectual styles, and cultural/political backgrounds of their authors. Although we were able to agree on a way of stating world order problems, and establish a framework of value criteria for what we considered to be appropriate solutions, as well as devise a common methodology, it certainly would be premature to attempt to provide a consensus statement for these various manuscripts. There were, however, a set of guidelines which were stated with some precision early in the project; despite repeated critical examination and elaboration they have remained essentially intact. It seems appropriate to summarize these guidelines so that the volumes might be read and evaluated in their proper context.

WOMP was not principally a "utopian" undertaking, despite our refusal to succumb either to a complacent or a doomsday view of reality. Where our thinking is utopian, it advances what we call *relevant utopias,* that is, world order systems that make clear not only alternative worlds but the necessary transition steps to these worlds. In fact, each author was asked to attempt a diagnosis of the contemporary world order system, make prognostic statements based on that diagnosis, state his *preferred future* world order and advance coherent and viable *strategies of transition* that could bring that future into being. A stringent time frame, the 1990's, served to discipline and focus thought and proposals.

While easy to list, this set of steps impose severe demands on our methodological and creative capacity. It is probably fair to say that we discovered more methodological problems than we were able to solve to our satisfaction. Some of these problems are associated with how to do each of the steps, while others arise from trying to link different steps and to integrate the normative, descriptive, and theoretical modes of thought. In the end, most of the WOMP research groups chose to adopt the more traditional analytic interpretive style of research, rather than the more methodologically sophisticated behavioral science approach. The reasons for this choice varied from outright rejection of the presumed conservative biases of strictly data-based methods to pragmatic considerations of limited time and resources. In essence, we decided it was more important at this time to prepare full world order statements involving an integrated treatment of all the steps than it was to do a more rigorous investigation of only one or two of them.

While a full report on the methodological difficulties we faced shall have to await another occasion, it might be useful if I were to outline here the major problem areas and some questions that arose in the course of our investigation. Let me begin, however, by reiterating that we were able to agree that humanity faced four major problems: war, poverty, social injustice, and environmental decay. We saw these as social problems because we had values—peace, economic well being, social justice, and environmental stability—which, no matter how vaguely operationalized, we knew were not being realized in the real world. Our task then was to develop an analytic frame of reference that would provide us intellectual tools for coming to grips with these problems so as to realize world order values.

There was also general agreement that we should go beyond the nation–state system, at least in terms of the traditional categories applied to it, namely the political, military, economic, and ideological dimensions of foreign policy. Instead of asking how states manipulate their foreign policies along these four dimensions, or even, how they might move the present system to a world order value system, there was general agreement that we would have to use a much broader range of potential actors, including world institutions, transnational actors, international organization, functional activities, regional arrangements, the nation–state, subnational movements, local communities, and individuals. Even here, however, each of the groups placed different emphases, diagnostically, prognostically, and preferentially on the roles of this range of actors.

Second, far more effort than I anticipated was put into clarifying the values implied by these problems and into making some ordered value agenda from which operational strategies or policies could be formulated. Among the points to emerge from these efforts are:

1. The crucial importance of developing global social indicators or operational definitions of value goals.

2. The difficulty and necessity of preparing a set of decision rules for dealing with value conflicts.

3. The need for a unified approach to these problem/value areas and for more data and theory on the interrelationships among them.

4. The extent to which one's personal position on the value questions influences every other aspect of the world order research process.

5. The importance of maintaining a tension between some operational notions of "world interest" and the deeply-felt value agenda of one's particular social group and geographic region.

Third, a number of issues not associated with standard empirical research emerged because of our emphasis on constructing preferred worlds. In this connection it should be noted that the term *preferred world* came to have a relatively rigorous meaning. Building on the concept of relevant utopia previously stated a preferred world is an image of a reformed world stated in fairly precise behavioral detail, including a description of the transition process from the present to the new system. Since it is possible to depict a range of reformed systems and transition paths, a preferred world is the relevant utopia selected by a proponent because it is most likely to realize his or her value goals. Each of these issues that arose in this context requires separate examination, conceptual and methodological advances, and the testing of a variety of integrated research strategies before we will really be able to move systematically through the steps of world order research to preferred world statements that meet rigorous tests of workability and feasibility. To illustrate:

1. What are appropriate criteria for evaluating workability and feasibility and what are the appropriate testing procedures for each?

2. Notions of time and time horizons are critical to both feasibility and workability, yet both are far more complicated than the simple notion of years and decades. Assumptions about time seem to play a critical role in one's optimism or pessimism about the possibility of fundamental change. Also, time, as a key variable, is surprisingly easy to forget or discount when thinking about such things as value and attitude shifts, or reorientations in bureaucratic objectives and procedures.

3. Equally perplexing is the problem of adequately defining the relevant environment and its dynamics within which one's desired changes must take place. The tendency is to define the environment as the nation–state system itself, and to ascribe relatively little destabilizing or fundamental dynamics to it. As noted earlier, this can severely restrict creative thinking about alternative futures and transition processes. But it is not easy to come up with equally detailed and useful alternatives to the nation–state image, so rooted is it in our consciousness. To really examine this question is to open oneself to the most fundamental philosophical and methodological search.

4. On a more mundane level, the presentation of a preferred world in a way that is compelling and persuasive is far more difficult than it might appear. Like good fiction or poetry, utopia writing is an art attempted by many but achieved by few. It involves crucial choices of style and form. For example, how much and what kind of behavioral detail should be used to describe the workings of the preferred world? What are the differences between revolutionary and reformist rhetoric, and more importantly, what bearing does this answer have on concrete strategies and programs? How much attention is paid to immediate public issues and how are they made to relate to the preferred future, to explicate the method and perspective of the author?

Finally there was a set of issues which arose from my guidelines that each of the groups be as explicit as possible about the kinds of authority structure, about the formal constitutive order of the world community, that would be needed and preferred, both during the transition period, as well as at the end of this century. That is to say, there was a distinct weighting of institutional–constitutional issues and approaches in my original definition of our task.

I emphasized this approach despite the obvious dangers of formalism essentially for three reasons: first, an institutional approach requires a high degree of specificity and precision and focuses attention on procedures as well as principles; second, this approach leads readily to statements in the form of models with all that that implies for comparability across models and manipulation of parts within them; third, as a form of presentation, constitutional–institutional models can be easily, even powerfully, communicated.

In this connection I should like to acknowledge formally my debt to the book *World Peace Through World Law* (Harvard University Press, 1956, 1962, 1966) by Grenville Clark and Louis B. Sohn. My use of this book as an instructional model and as a source of research hypotheses leads me to conclude that many social scientists, as well as lay people, underestimate the extent to which formal constitutional models can lead to clarification of issues, and perhaps even more important, become a mobilizing instrument for social and political action. I remain convinced of the value of this way of thinking about world order, but the extent to which this view has been resisted, revised and ignored by the WOMP groups will be apparent in these volumes. Within this context, it should also be noted that the individual authors resolve the actors–levels–authority process questions differently. Some of the issues that surfaced during our discussions in this context included:

1. The extent to which an institutional or single actor-oriented conception of the world political system is useful either for understanding how the system is operating, how it might be made to change, or how it could or should operate. Such conceptions seemed to some to stultify imaginative thinking about alternatives and to mask important change potentials in the current system.

2. In thinking about transition, some argued for the "primacy of the domestic factor," i.e., fundamental reform in national societies, particularly within the major countries, preceding global social change. Others argued for the primacy of the global agenda and the critical role of transnational functional and political movements and institutions. This debate identified two further issues needing more attention.

3. Which problems require policy making and review at what level of social organization from the individual to the global? How much centralization and decentralization was appropriate in various substantive arenas? What are the relevant criteria for deciding the appropriate level or mix of levels?

4. What are and what might be the linkages between these levels for purposes of analysis, policy making and practical implementation?

IV

Finally, I wish to state my own view as to the significance of these manuscripts. As I see it, it is necessary to accept seriously not only the rhetoric but the reality of the term "the global village." The fact that the overwhelming majority of humankind understands for the first time in history that human society encompasses the entire globe is a phenomenon equivalent to humankind's understanding that the globe is round rather than flat. This knowledge is having an enormously dramatic impact on the images and attitudes we have with regard to the authority structures of the international community, as well as those of our domestic societies. I should like to state here a conclusion, for which I will not fully argue, but which I believe needs to be articulated for an understanding of the significant global political processes that are now taking place.

It is my considered judgment that there is no longer a question of whether or not there will be world government by the year 2000. As I see it, the questions we should be addressing ourselves to are, how it will come into being—by cataclysm, draft, rational design—and whether it will be totalitarian, benign, or participatory (the probabilities being in that order).

Since the so-called "age of discovery" (a Eurocentric concept which sorely needs modification in this global community), three major historical processes, or if you will, revolutions, have propelled humankind toward global community, and now toward global governance. These processes are the ideological revolution of egalitarianism, the technological and scientific revolution and the closely allied economic-interdependent revolution. It might be noted in passing that of these three, the egalitarian revolution has been least appreciated in recent times, but in fact may account for much of the disorder, dislocation, and social tensions throughout the globe.

These three processes or revolutions have converged in such a fashion that five problems have emerged and been identified as global in nature. War, poverty, social injustice, ecological instability, and alienation or the identity crisis, are recognized as having a planetary scope. It is now generally understood by policy elites and observers of world community processes generally that these problems are closely interrelated and that "solutions" in one area affect the other four areas. Furthermore, despite gross inadequacies if not outright failure of the recent global conferences run by the United Nations around the issues of environment, economic order, food and population, it is now obvious that governance processes and structures will become increasingly a focus of international and global politics.

In short, I believe that global community has emerged and global governance is not far behind. To my mind, this book and the other volumes in the *Preferred Worlds for the 1990's* series is a contribution to the serious dialogue about what will be the normative basis and constitutive structure of the global community. We hope these volumes will contribute to creating the social processes needed for a peaceful and just world order.

September 1974

Saul Mendlovitz
Director, World Order
Models Project

Special Acknowledgment

The Institute for World Order, Inc., would like to thank the Carnegie Endowment for International Peace and the Rockefeller Foundation for the financial support they gave to specific research within the World Order Models Project.

Acknowledgments

This book would not have been written without the obstinate, irritating, affectionate and often stimulating encouragement the author received from Saul Mendlovitz of the Institute for World Order. The work emerged out of the author's involvement in the World Order Models Project, a world-wide research enterprise committed to the study of global trends and their moral implications. The other colleagues in the enterprise helped to broaden the author's horizons in the process of joint periodic working sessions held in different parts of the world. As World-Chairman of the group as a whole, Saul Mendlovitz had the potentially creative but basically "thankless" job of prodding the different regional teams to complete their research and write their manuscripts. Now that the job is done, this author at least has found adequate detachment to appreciate more fully Saul's indispensable role in this whole enterprise.

The actual writing of the manuscript in its present form took place when I was a Fellow at the Center for the Advanced Study of the Behavioral Sciences at Stanford. I am greatly indebted to the Center for unstinting secretarial and xeroxing support during this period, as well as for a research climate which was paradoxically at once restful and energizing, relaxed as well as stimulating.

Specially involved in the secretarial work was Ms. Jean Crace. I am greatly indebted to her for her role in the preparation of this manuscript.

Much of the original research for the book was done when I was still at Makerere University, Kampala. My colleagues there provided an intellectual infrastructure for the enterprise. Special thanks are due to Professor John S. Mbiti, to Professor A. G. G. Gingyera-Pinycwa, Dr. Yashpal Tandon, Dr. Ahmed Mohiddin and Mr. John Anguma for their contributions to the evolution of this book. Quite often their influence came through strong criticism or in the course of sustained intellectual debates at Makerere.

Colleagues in other parts of Africa were also involved in stimulating aspects of this venture, sometimes without their realizing it. I am particularly indebted to Dr. Ilunga Kabongo of Zaire, Dr. Jonah Elaigwu and Dr. Okwudiba Nnoli of Nigeria, Mr. Nathan Shamuyarira of Zimbabwe, Dr. A. H. Rweyemamu of Tanzania, and Mr. Benjamin Bol Kok of the Sudan.

This book concerns itself with the Black Diaspora, as well as with Africa. *I am grateful to the Center for Afro-American and African Studies at the University of Michigan for moral and material support in the final stages of preparing the manuscript for publication.* Black scholars *elsewhere* in the Diaspora who have influenced this work include Dr. Locksley Edmondson of Jamaica, Dr. Selwyn Ryan of Trinidad, Dr. Walter Rodney of Guyana, and Dr. J. Henrik Clarke of the United States.

It is with a book of this magnitude that one realizes more fully the importance of one's own critics in one's intellectual evolution. I hereby acknowledge my debt to them—both when the critic and the author have finally found a point of academic convergence and when we have decided to maintain our intellectual distance from each other.

Finally, I must mention a critic of a different kind. This is my wife, Molly, with whom I have had debates ranging from the role of languages in world politics to the relevance of religion in economic behavior.

I would like to conclude with a grateful tribute to two foundations which helped to launch the project in the first place and to an editorial team which helped to finalize this particular product.

The research grant came from Carnegie Endowment for International Peace and the Institute for World Order. Research for this book and other supportive research in East Africa could not have been carried out without the generous support of these two foundations.

The editorial team which helped to give final shape to this book consisted of Ian Baldwin, and Nancy Silber of the Institute for World Order.

Whatever residual faults this book continues to bear have persisted inspite of its benefactors and critics.

Ali A. Mazrui

Nairobi and Ann Arbor

A Cultural Perspective on
World Order: An Introduction

The perspective of this book rests on three basic values. We accept as a premise that the world needs to be reformed in the direction of greater social justice, more widely distributed economic welfare, and reduced violence, actual or imminent. How do we get there? The answers we will suggest rest, in turn, on two major theories—a theory of normative convergence and a theory of dependency.

Purposeful world reform is a quest for the realization of new *values* through defining *new moral preferences*. The question therefore arises: Under what conditions do people begin to share values and moral preferences?

Our reasoning has a number of stages. To have new values accepted in this way is, by definition, a problem of mobilizing *consensus*. We must therefore begin to understand the nature of consensus and the conditions which make it possible.

Our position is that consensus behind a specific set of new reforms can best be obtained where people share a framework of social reasoning and social calculation. The ability to convince another person about a new idea requires a common universe of discourse. Persuasion itself is the art of exploiting mutually familiar predispositions. And this in turn is what normative convergence is all about.

To get mankind to agree to a new world system, we need to give mankind that shared framework of social reasoning and social calculation. Consensus behind three or four world values will need consensus behind many more *supporting values and perspectives*. To get Americans to agree to busing children away from neighborhood schools, one needs prior agreement among Americans on a number of other values as well.

In summary, we see world reform as a problem of mobilizing consensus; we see consensus as a problem of building up supporting values; and we see this latter as an outgrowth of cultural convergence.

1

Values are inseparable from culture. Indeed, what is culture but a system of interrelated values and social perspectives, active enough to condition the behavior of its adherents?

World Government versus World Culture

It is a postulate of our perspective therefore that the transmission of ideas and their internalization are more relevant for world reform than the establishment of formal institutions for external control. In other words, when members of world reform enterprises talk in terms of disseminating their proposals to the reading public, they are nearer to the heart of the issue than when they discuss what type of Security Council or what type of Agency for Environmental Control the year 1990 ought to have.

Yet even the transmission of ideas might require some institutions, though it is more concerned with *process* than with structure. When we talk of transition stages, we should be thinking of stages in the evolution of human values and human opinion, rather than stages in the evolution of human organization.

It is indeed true that even the process of opinion formation needs some types of structures for its promotion. It might need a Bureau of Information, or an Agency for Distribution of Books, or an Agency for the Facilitation of Inter-Regional Travel. But the main ambition should be to promote the right values and consolidate the right inhibitions in the behavioral orientations of human beings. The controls we should be aiming for are internalized controls, based on new human inclinations, rather than external controls by organizational mechanisms. Here the whole concept of *cultural engineering* looms into relevance. Engineering does itself connote an enterprise of building up new structures. But the main purpose of the exercise is not to build up structures of external coercion, but structures of internalized constraints. The aim should not be a world government but a world culture.[1]

At first sight, the evolution of a world culture seems to be even more distant than the evolution of a world government. But a closer look at human history so far would dispel this misconception. In reality, we are no nearer a world government than we were a century ago; but we are much nearer a world culture. Today there are more governments in the world, fewer empires, and a wider distribution of formal jurisdiction in the international scene. In fact, it is even arguable that since World War II we have moved further away from a world government than we were before World War II. The disintegration of empires has multiplied sovereignties. It is true that we have something called the United Nations, but even the United Nations has declined in power as it has grown in membership. By the beginning of the 1970's the United Nations had become, in some ways, a less powerful and even less influential organization than it was at the end of the 1950's. The influx of large numbers of small countries, exercising parity of voting in the General Assembly, and activated by issues not always understood by the bigger powers, has created a credibility gap between United Nations' resolutions and its performance. If, therefore, the weakening of the United Nations is itself an indication that we are moving away from world government, it must be concluded that we are further away in the 1970's than we were in the 1950's. However, if we look not at institutions designed for external coercion but at the phenomena of cultural dissemination and internalized cultural constraints, the picture is different. We are definitely much nearer to a world culture in the 1970's than we were in the 1940's. The increased spread of literacy, the effect of technology on life styles, the acceleration and facilitation of international travel, the internationalization of books, newspapers, television programs and films, the impact of the radio and the consolidation of external broadcasting services to other parts of the world as an aspect of foreign policy, have all combined to introduce the beginnings of shared values, shared tastes, and shared images among the peoples of this planet.

This is no more than an initial phase of cultural convergence. At one level the homogenization manifests itself in the cruder forms of pop culture. Certain American singers and musicians are heroes to teenagers in Iboland, Hong Kong, Bombay, Mombasa, and Rio de Janeiro. In other words, certain tastes in music, films, sports, magazines have become almost globalized.

Another area of cultural convergence is more directly political in its implications—that of shared political emotions, prejudices, and sensibilities. The American war in Vietnam illustrated this at its most dramatic. Protest against the war in Vietnam came from people drawn from diverse cultures, in different parts of the world. Anger at some of things which had happened in the war had a wider distribution on the globe than anger about any other war in human history. Never had a war in one part of the world been more widely reported in other parts of the world. Many of those who protested might not have known all that much about the background of the war, or about the issues involved, or about the actual unfolding of the conflict; but that so many knew about it at all was itself an indication both of the communications revolution in the world and of the resultant rudimentary homogenization of political sensibilities.

It is true that we still have wars, and the threat of war in interstate relations. It is true that we are nowhere near controlling man's capacity to prepare for destruction. It is true that we are nowhere near an interna-

3

tional police force strong enough to keep the Americans out of places like Vietnam, or the Russians out of countries like Czechoslovakia, or even the Israelis out of Arab lands. But it would be a mistake to conclude that just because there are no external mechanisms of coercion with global authority in the international system, there are no internalized mechanisms of constraint. And the mechanisms of constraint in the behavior of the big powers, fallible as they are, are themselves an index of the beginnings of political integration in the world. But the integration is at the level of values and their acceptance as a basis of inhibition, rather than at the level of organizational structures.

It is out of this recognition of the critical relevance of cultural convergence for world reform that we propose cultural engineering as the most promising approach towards that reform. How people view the world, and how they respond to events, are states of perception which have been deeply conditioned by cultural variables acting upon human material.

The political system of the world has sometimes been compared with "primitive" political systems—especially those variously described as systems of "ordered anarchy" or systems of "balanced opposition of political segments" or systems of "stateless societies".[2]

Roger D. Masters has enumerated four elements shared between politics within a certain type of "primitive society" on one side and international relations on a global scale, on the other side.

> First, the absence of formal government with power to judge and punish violations of law; second, the use of violence and "self help" by the members of the system to achieve their objectives and enforce their obligations; third, the derivation of law and moral obligations either from custom or from explicit, particular bargaining relationships (i.e., the absence of a formal legislative body operating on the basis of—and making—general rules); and fourth, a predominant organizational principle which establishes political units serving many functions in the overall social system.[3]

But when Masters goes on to concede the *differences* between "primitive political systems" and international political systems, one major factor stands out in its stark implications: "there is a marked tendency toward cultural homogeneity in primitive stateless societies, since most individuals accept without question the established way of life." The application of traditional rules for specific instances in traditional societies may be frequently disputed, but the "relative stability of culture limits the kinds of change occurring in most primitive systems."[4]

Masters concedes that the homogeneity of some ethnic groups is often exaggerated, but the factor of a shared cultural universe at some levels

4

remains an important characteristic differentiating such systems from the international system as it has so far evolved.

> As Almond has shown, national political systems which face the task of integrating different political cultures are subject to strains that are absent in more homogeneous societies; *a fortiori* the problem is even greater in a system which permits many antagonistic political cultures to organize themselves into nation-states. In general, therefore, it could be argued that self-help and structural decentralization tend to produce a greater degree of instability in world politics than in most primitive stateless societies.[5]

But in the meantime diverse cultures in the world have been coming closer together and have become a little more aware of each other than they had once been. These contacts themselves have had potentialities for stress and tension. When the new disparities between cultures include conspicuous differences in affluence and standards of living, that old ghost of "revolution of rising expectations" could itself release destabilizing forces among the more "backward" communities:

> Even in a primitive world, the contact of a more "advanced" people with a society without governmental institutions has often produced a rapid domination of the latter by the former. It is all the more to be expected, therefore, that the present structure of the international system is essentially transitional, and that quite considerable changes must be expected in the next century.[6]

What Masters underestimates are the integrative factors which would follow this initial instability arising from cultural interaction. It is true that the impact of Western civilization on many societies has included sheer disruption, but cultures have a habit of absorbing some of the new after a while and seeking some kind of *modus vivendi* with their cultural rivals. Because technology facilitates mobility and interaction between cultures, one major difference between "primitive" stateless societies, on the one hand, and the international system, on the other, will be narrowed. The stateless societies, by having a shared cultural universe, have created an infrastructure for consensus. They have found a basis of agreement and cooperation even in the face of periodic eruptions of feuds. A shared culture mitigates some of the harsh consequences of not having a shared government. Cultural convergence in the international system should also evolve into an infrastructure for consensus.

What all this means is that the way towards creating a more just, more comfortable, and less violent world is through creating a world *community*. We do often use the term "international community" in a loose sense, but more often what is implied is an aspiration rather than an accomplished fact. Yet even the aspiration has to be more squarely recognized—for it is an aspiration to evolve real communal relations, and not merely shared authoritative structures. The road towards creating a world community is primarily through a global convergence of cultures. Out of such a convergence we might look for the minimum degree of consensus which might make other fundamental world reforms feasible at last.

Dependency and World Culture

If we are nearer today to a world culture than we were a hundred years ago, we are also a little nearer to having a world community than we were then. The impact of the West on the rest of the world has resulted in widespread dissemination of Western tastes, values, techniques, and perspectives. Moral relativists have observed often enough that the ideas of "righteousness" are not stationary but capable of endless expansion, that "men may get scruples in the future that they have no thought of now."

Certainly many men in Africa and Asia today are getting scruples now that they, or their parents, had no conception of in the past. What must be emphasized is that it would be naive to attribute this merely to some metaphysical force called "moral progress". In the final analysis, the relative and gradual standardization of ethics in the world is to be attributed to the political and technological impact of the West, rather than to anything else. With that impact have come new ways of looking at things, new perspectives, new intellectual horizons, new values, and new types of jealousies, including those arising from Western concepts of sovereignty and Western definitions of territorial jurisdiction. John Plamenatz, the Oxford political philosopher and historian, has observed that "the vices of the strong acquire some of the prestige of strength."[7]

The vices of the West have certainly acquired some of the prestige of Western power. We use the term "West" in the older sense of "the Occident"—including North America, Eastern Europe, as well as Western Europe. Marxist communism itself becomes a branch of Western intellectual tradition, to be distinguished from oriental and Afro-Asian indigenous traditions.

The influence of Western civilization on the lives of peoples very far from the original fountain of that civilization brings us to the second major theory underlying much of the discussion in this book. Alongside the theory of cultural convergence in relation to *consensus* must be placed the theory of cultural convergence in relation to *dependency*.

The phenomenon of dependency may itself further be divided into two dimensions—*structural dependency* and *cultural dependency*. Structural dependency concerns the organizational aspects of political, economic, and technological imbalance. A lack of symmetry in power relations, captured in an institutional framework, lies at the heart of structural dependency. The phenomenon of multinational corporations constitutes one of the latest structures of dominance emanating from the Western world and operating elsewhere. Financial institutions, certain types of technological transfers, as well as large-scale military alliances involving major powers, are all forms of dependency structurally defined.

Much of the recent discussion in the Third World concerning dependency has in fact been an analysis of structural dependency. Preeminent among the tools of analysis have been Marxist concepts and techniques of interpreting social and international phenomena. Much of the work within the Third World has been done in Latin America, but theories of structural dependency have been emerging elsewhere in the Third World as well. Those addressing themselves primarily to African conditions include Samir Amin, Justinian Rweyemamu, and Walter Rodney.

What has been grossly underestimated has been the phenomenon of *cultural dependency,* affecting two areas of human behavior especially— motivation and social stratification. What people aspire to in the Third World, what tastes they develop, what expectations they begin to have, and what aversions they manifest, are all areas of response which are greatly conditioned by cultural variables. The impact of the West on the motivational patterns of the peoples of the Third World is a major dimension of dependency. The structural analysts do often refer to interlocking elites between the developed and the developing world. What the structural analysts do not always realize is that those elites that identify with metropolitan countries, and reinforce dependent structures, have been captured *culturally* by the West. The nature of their ambitions, the directions of their aspirations, the boundaries of their tastes and desires, are important factors behind their entire behavior. Their ambitions and aspirations have to undergo a change before they can evolve the *will* to break the structures of dependency.

A major stumbling block in the way of Third World assertiveness is the absence of the political will for change. And absence of that political will is substantially attributable to normative and cultural conditioning.

The other great domain of cultural dependency concerns domestic stratification within Third World countries. In much of Asia and Africa, credentials for leadership, and qualifications for becoming a national decision maker, have to include competence in certain Western metropolitan skills. In Africa there is in fact a high premium put on Western literary and verbal skills. The first wave of great African leaders consisted disproportionately of people who had acquired verbal or literary skills in either English or French. The Kwame Nkrumahs, the Nnamdi Azikiwes, the Julius Nyereres and the Tom Mboyas, the Jomo Kenyattas and the Hastings Bandas, have all been people who could demonstrate literary and verbal skills in the English language. In French-speaking Africa the same phenomenon has been observable with regard to competence in the French language as a precondition for political success. Almost no electoral code in Africa stipulated that a member of Parliament had to be able to speak at least one indigenous African language; but the great majority of electoral codes stipulated that a candidate had to be competent in English or French.

Access to political careers meant access to other privileges. People became not only powerful by virtue of the office they held, but also rich by virtue of what they acquired in addition. Nkrumah once urged "Seek ye first the political kingdom, and all else will be added unto it." He meant that *nations* should first seek the political kingdom; but it was even truer that individuals who first acquired power within the political kingdom then succeeded in having "all else added unto them". Literary and verbal skills borrowed from the West became necessary for attaining the commanding heights of the polity; and this in turn helped the new elite to share the commanding heights of the economy. Structures of dependency were reinforced by a system of domestic stratification which gave special advantages to those who had been culturally Westernized.

The avenues of European cultural infiltration into Africa were, first, modern education; second, metropolitan languages, with special reference to English and French; third, Western religion, primarily Euro-Christianity; and fourth, demonstration effect through Western control of mobility and communications.

The modern school in Africa became a major carrier of Western values, as well as Western techniques. The skills acquired from these schools became credentials for entry into the arena of national competition for privilege. Especially important among the skills acquired from schools was the metropolitan language itself. Political stratification in the country became profoundly conditioned by linguistic considerations of alien derivation.

Education, language, and communications all facilitated the urge to imitate. Religion reduced any inclination to rebel. The kind of Christianity which came into Africa made a virtue of obedience, and urged the colonized people to give unto Caesar that which was Caesar's, and sometimes unto Caesar that which was God's. At a time when the West itself was becoming secularized, and religion in the West was becoming less self-righteous, the missionaries in Africa were propagating a form of

Christianity which was already anachronistic in Europe. "Shut your eyes and pray," "Turn the other cheek"—these were doctrines of "pacification" in Africa, designed in part to end the warrior tradition and encourage subservience to the new white Caesar. The missionaries became important allies of colonizers. The stage was set for cultural dependency.

Regional Autonomy and World Culture

Our approach now appears to have contradictory aims: Consensus behind much-needed world reforms is impossible without substantial cultural convergence on a global scale. And yet the cultural convergence which the world has so far attained carries with it the evil of dependency. A global stratification system is maintained partly because Europe and her extensions have created relationships of structural and cultural dependency with other sections of the human race. This conflict we propose to solve as we turn recurrently to the problem of creating cultural parity as a basis for mutual respect. The trend towards the emergence of a world culture has to be maintained, and yet at the same time solutions have to be found to the accompanying problems of dependency which have so far emerged.

Europe has often argued that her impact on Africa has been in the direction of both declining violence and enhanced economic welfare. Two of our three world order values seem to have been historically realized as a result of Europe's impact on the African continent. The argument on declining violence rested on the assumption that the European presence in Africa reduced tribal warfare and initiated a process of general pacification. Concepts like Pax Britannica rested on the premise that colonialism was itself an umbrella of tranquility, a shade of peace for peoples who would be otherwise torn assunder in violent confrontations among themselves. The colonial process itself created new modes of production, which in turn seemed to be increasing the productive capabilities of the African people. Infant mortality was declining, people seemed to live longer, standards of living appeared to be on the rise. The second world-order value of maximization of economic welfare seemed to be well and truly served by the colonial experience itself.

Some analysts of dependency deny that economic development took place in Africa, for example, as a result of colonialism. On the contrary, so the argument goes, a process of retardation was what colonialism was all about. It interrupted normal directions of social change, reduced the self-confidence of the peoples over whom it exercised authority, exported for a while millions of slaves to plantations overseas, and distorted the motivational patterns of the societies it ruled. Development was distorted, and in some respects retarded, by the paralyzing consequences of racial and cultural subjugation.[8] But for the time being let us even accept the colonial power's self-image as an agency for development and positive transformation in Africa. We might allow ourselves to concede, at least for purposes of argument, the imperial claim that violence in Africa decreased and economic welfare rose as a result of the colonial experience while it lasted. We are still left with the third world order value of social justice, implying a relationship of balanced humanity, a reprobation of exploitation, and a system of mutual respect.

Mutual respect is the high-water mark of a slope which begins at the bottom with mutual toleration. And mutual toleration between peoples that are different from each other has to include a basic toleration of each other's values, that is, their cultures. The entire colonial experience started from a premise of cultural arrogance on the part of the colonizer. The belief that nonwhite peoples were fair game for colonial exploitation was derived from a web of normative arrogance. We shall be discussing later such concepts as "the white man's burden" and "the yellow peril". These, along with the whole idea of "civilizing the heathens", were perspectives saturated with the white man's vanity and self-righteousness.

If colonialism then did succeed in reducing violence and enhancing economic welfare, it also succeeded in perpetrating a variety of forms of social injustice. Racial groups were subjugated, cultural values were violated, indigenous religions were suppressed, and colonized peoples were exploited in the wake of the colonial experience.

And then colonialism retreated. In many former colonies, it is true violence has increased in the wake of decolonization and in some the pace of development and enhancement of economic welfare has declined. Those two world order values—reduced violence and increased welfare—which had been served well by colonialism, were shrinking after independence.

But with regard to the value of social justice, the imperial withdrawal has definitely enhanced it, by providing opportunities for self-management in the former colonies, with all the risks of self-mismanagement. We shall discuss later the process of political integration more fully, and indicate the role of conflict in that process. The pacification which came with the imperial presence had an artificiality about it. It denied the people themselves the chance to accumulate direct experience in conflict resolution. But one major role of imperialism was to expand the scale of political organization in Africa by bringing together communities and resources into bigger national entities. The new states of Africa, in spite of the artificiality of the boundaries which the colonial powers arbitrarily imposed, provide more effective units of political and economic organization in a world of nation-states than the original precolonial ethnic entities could, on the whole, have hoped to do.

Even more enduring in its consequences than the boundaries it imposed is the cultural impact of colonialism. African systems of values and beliefs have been disrupted beyond conceivable repair. Not that the masses of African peoples have become Westernized, but the general coherence of traditional values and beliefs has been seriously damaged. Those indigenous cultural aspects have been on the defensive ever since the intrusion of the conquering culture. The damage may get worse unless the process is slowed down soon.

The restoration of balance in the cultural arrangements of the world requires a combination of two approaches. First, the formerly colonized societies must seek to protect more effectively their own cultural heritages. Second, Western culture must be infiltrated by non-Western values to help make the global pool of shared culture less Eurocentric and more diversified.

In the case of Africa, ways have to be devised not simply for the preservation of ancestral ways, but also for the promotion of new indigenous innovation and experiment. Indeed, going back to ancient Africa is not only impossible; it would be undesirable. Africa was once vulnerable to both slave raiders and colonizers partly because Africa was slow in changing. A retreat to ancestral ways, even if it were feasible, would now be an act of cultural suicide. What is required is the creation of conditions which will make it possible for Africa to draw from within itself new cultural and intellectual directions. Africa's past should become a resource for the present and the future. But in order to use that resource effectively, Africa has to develop a new attitude towards it, less defensive, perhaps less apologetic.

Here, the principle of regional autonomy asserts its relevance. At its most obvious this autonomy is political and diplomatic. International law as it now stands seems to be intended to govern relations between states in general, and makes no coherent distinction as between continental locations of states. But in politics African diplomacy so far has recognized two levels of law. One level is indeed that of international law to govern relations between nations. The other level is a kind of Pan-African law to govern relations between African states themselves, much less codified than is traditional international law and with a future less assured. So far the ultimate documentary expression of Pan-African law is the charter of the Organization of African Unity. Yet, as in the case of traditional international law at large, documents normally emerge essentially as confirmation of preexistent consensus on canons of interstate behavior. Not all rules which are supposed to govern intra-

11

African relations are as yet documented; nor is the fact that such rules are not always obeyed evidence that they do not "really" exist. Just as a recurrent violation of traditional international law by Western countries did not completely deprive that law of some kind of a role in Western diplomacy, so repeated violations of the Pan-African code of interstate behavior has not entirely deprived that code of political significance in Africa. Such a code provides African states at least with a frame of reference for their complaints against each other. Sometimes it provides the basis for mediation by other African states towards easing tensions between diplomatic or military combatants.[9]

The central principle is that of *continental jurisdiction,* which simply asserts that there are certain African problems which should only be solved by Africans themselves, "Africans" being defined as citizens of member countries of the Organization of African Unity. The principle of continental jurisdiction concedes legitimacy to continental supranationality.

To a certain extent this does sound like an African Monroe Doctrine, but it should be noted that the analogy is with the Monroe Doctrine as it was intended to be, that is, to exclude intervention from outside the Americas, and not the Monroe Doctrine as it came to be, that is, to legitimate intervention in Latin America by the United States. From an African perspective the trouble with the Monroe Doctrine in the Americas was that it was hemispheric, giving the colossus of North America an unnatural jurisdiction over the affairs of the rest of the hemisphere. It would make better sense, in African terms, if the unit of noninterference were not a hemisphere but a continent tying Canada and the United States together, instead of tying the United States with Latin America. The individual U.S. citizen is indeed a foreigner both in Canada and in Latin America, but when all is said and done, he is more conspicuously a foreigner in Latin America than he is in Canada.[10]

By implication U.S. interference in Latin America must also be more conspicuously foreign interference than a similar activity in Canada. It should be made clear here that we are not recommending that there should be American interference in Canada. We are only defining different levels of foreignness in intervention, different levels of eternality. The cultural convergence which has taken place between Canadians and Americans is an important aspect behind the emergence of North America as a coherent cultural entity. The cultural convergence of Latin America, a result especially of the impact of Spanish and Iberian cultures, has also made the area a coherent entity.

Continental jurisdiction would help to consolidate cultural interaction within those areas themselves. In the case of Asia the approach has to be subcontinental because of the sheer size of the landmass, and the millions of its peoples. The Asians themselves will have to define which regions make best cultural sense. Problems of overlap are inevitable whenever limits of human organizations are being specified.

In the case of Africa, the overlap is particularly significant in relation to the Middle East. North African states are members both of the Arab League and of the Organization of African Unity. How much interplay there ought to be between the Middle East and Africa politically is something which is already part of practical politics. The readiness of the Organization of African Unity to appoint a special committee on the Middle East, and attempt to find the elusive breakthrough that would end the Arab-Israeli impasse, was one manifestation of this interaction between the Middle East and Africa. In the course of 1972 some half a dozen African countries broke off relations with Israel. More immediately, the Middle East crisis overflowed into the Nile Valley, intermingling with the problem of southern Sudan, Uganda, and separatist movements in Eritrea.

It might well be that one day Africa and the Middle East could constitute one region. This would be a happier situation for a country like Israel than to belong to a formally sovereign region in which almost everybody else was an Arab. Though Israel does indeed have critics and enemies within Black Africa itself, she also has more friends among Black Africans than she can claim among Arabs. A merger of the two regions would not only ease the problem of dual loyalties among North African states, but would also mitigate Israel's isolation.

But that is a matter for the future. For the time being a more strict continental jurisdiction makes better sense for Africa. Regional African autonomy, with limited interference from beyond the continent, and certainly from the major powers, would help to provide a climate for both cultural and structural independence in the years ahead.

Such independence would provide new credentials for parity of esteem with Europe and her extensions. It would also provide the basis of genuine cultural interdependence, in which European civilization will no longer be far and away the senior and dominant partner.

A Cultural Methodology

This book attempts to exemplify its own general thesis—regional autonomy with genuine participation in a world culture—by combining African problems and African perspectives with continual reference to the world cultural picture. In turn, the Euro centrism of world culture is illustrated by the author's repeated acknowledgment of his debt to Western writers and analysts, Western philosophers and scientists.

13

Much of the debate within the book is a debate with major thinkers within the intellectual tradition of the West.

But underlying this constant acknowledgment of the author's debt to Western civilization is an attitude of partial ideological agnosticism. The partial agnosticism of the author is itself an attempt to live out the general thesis. An African who embraces too completely a Western system of values, be it liberal or Marxist, is denying himself a chance to break loose from the intellectual dominance of Western ideas. An African Marxist is not a rebel against Western intellectual hegemony; he is more often a victim of that hegemony. After all, Marxism itself is a Western intellectual tradition. A partial ideological agnosticism on the part of Third World scholars, especially in Asia and Africa, is a precondition for the realization of a genuine world federation of cultures.

To some extent much of this book will appear politically Afro-centric and intellectually still Euro-centric. Our preoccupation with issues of autonomy and dignity for Africa continually relies on conceptual tools and ideas which draw considerably from European intellectual traditions. This contant tension between political Afro-centrism and cultural Euro-centrism must again be seen as part of the living evidence of the book itself in support of some of its own general arguments concerning the painful struggle against dependency. Some chapters may echo Marxian ideas; others may embrace capitalist assumptions about the nature of national development. A partial ideological agnosticism will persist throughout. Some Western readers may expect particular stereotypical positions or a certain kind of radical rhetoric from Third World intellectuals. This book will sometimes satisfy, but at other times disappoint, such expectations. In this case the problem is not the author's.

Transcending both the cultural Euro-centrism and the political Afro-centrism of this book is the larger ambition of a more viable world order for mankind as a whole. We see normative convergence as a precondition for the emergence of a global human community. Shared culture as an infrastructure for consensus is a basic component of our approach to world reform. The following pages should help to indicate, approximately, the case for such an approach. The story which is about to unfold should also help to indicate, on a modest scale, how far man has got on the road towards the ideal of a shared and *balanced* universe of culture, and how far his weary feet have yet to go before final arrival.

Footnotes

1. For a related if still divergent perspective consult W. Warren Wagar, *Building the City of Man: Outlines of a World Civilization* (New York: Grossman, 1971)
2. A favorite example is that of the Nuer, an African community in the Sudan and

Ethiopia. Consult E. E. Evans-Pritchard, *The Nuer* (Oxford: Clarendon Press, 1940) p. 181, and Evans-Pritchard "The Nuer of the Southern Sudan" in M. Fortes and E. E. Evans-Pritchard (editors) *African Political Systems* (London: Oxford University Press, 1940) p. 293. Consult also John Middleton and David Tait (editors) *Tribes Without Rulers* (London: Routledge & Paul, 1958) and Lucy Mair, *Primitive Government* (Baltimore: Penguin Books, 1962).

3. Masters, "World Politics as a Primitive Political System," *World Politics,* Volume XVI, July 1964, pp. 595, 597. Consult also Y. Tandon, "Diplomatic Anthropology: Impact of African Ethnography on the Study of International Relations," Makerere University, Kampala (mimeo).

4. Masters, *ibid.,* pp. 615–619. Masters cites Fortes and Evans-Pritchard, *African Political Systems,* pp. 9–10.

5. Masters, *ibid.;* see also Almond, "Comparative Political Systems" *Journal of Politics,* Volume XVIII, August 1956, pp. 400–402.

6. Masters, *ibid.*

7. John Plamenatz, *On Alien Rule and Self-Government* (London: Longmans, 1960).

8. One black analyst who belongs to this school is Walter Rodney. See his *How Europe Underdeveloped Africa* (Dar-es-Salaam: Tanzania Publishing House, 1972).

9. Consult also Mazrui, "African Diplomatic Thought and Supranationality," in Ali. A. Mazrui and Hasu H. Patel, *Africa in World Affairs: The Next Thirty Years* (New York: The Third Press, 1973) pp. 121–133.

10. Consult also Mazrui, *Towards A Pax Africana: A Study of Ideology and Ambition* (London: Weidenfeld and Nicolson and Chicago: University of Chicago Press, 1967).

Section I

ORIGINS AND OBJECTIVES

CHAPTER 1

Religion and the Origins of
World Culture

The evolution of the concept of a world culture owes a good deal to the emergence and spread of the great world religions. To the extent that a world culture presupposes an area of shared inhibitions, shared prejudices, and a narrowing gap between the different schools of morality, the world religions played a particularly significant part in promoting the idea of the Universal Man.

We have on one side this idea of the Universal Man and, on the other side, the concept of empathy. We shall discuss empathy more fully later. Suffice for the moment to define it as a capacity to identify with another. What connects the idea of empathy with the idea of the Universal Man is the whole process of *ecumenicalism,* which denotes the universalization of empathy.

Here we should distinguish between competitive ecumenicalism and compassionate ecumenicalism. Competitive ecumenicalism is a rivalry between two visions of the Universal Man, intensely held, and tending towards intolerance. The crusades in the Middle Ages and, at the more secular level, the cold war in our times at the period of its most intense ideological self-consciousness are instances of competitive ecumenicalism. Different visions of the Universal Man were not only seeking acceptance, but were fighting each other in the process. Competitive ecumenicalism rests on a deep-seated contradiction. When two visions of the Universal Man are at daggers drawn, how universal is their concept of Man? Competitive ecumenicalism sometimes verges on being a crusade to destroy humanity in the name of humanity.

Compassionate ecumenicalism, on the other hand, rests on a principle that allows for alternative visions of the Universal Man; it is prepared to coexist with those visions without abandoning its own. We discuss in a later chapter the three T's of nation building—tolerance, toil, and teamwork. Competitive ecumenicalism has certainly mobilized the resources

19

of toil and teamwork, but has been found wanting on the principle of toleration. Puritanism as a creed has been very important in the history of the economic culture of, for example, the United States. But while profoundly animated by principles of toil and teamwork within the puritan community itself, the creed was not strikingly conspicuous for its capacity to tolerate rival visions. When the world reaches the stage of compassionate ecumenicalism, the moment of empathetic fulfillment would be at hand. People could thus cling with passion to their own, and relate to others with compassion at the same time.

The most important great religions from the point of view of the emergence of ecumenicalism have been Christianity and Islam. This is partly because these two religions went further than almost any other of the world religions in the direction of *competitiveness*. Religions like Hinduism, Buddhism, and Confucianism, though ambitious at one stage of their history, later ceased militant proselytizing. To that extent they were not competitive in our sense. They settled for the converts they already had. In like manner, though on an even narrower basis, religions like Judaism and Shintoism have been basically not only national religions, but even nationalistic religions, and tending towards exclusiveness. It is true that in the earlier phases of Judaism especially the ecumenical component was present. Later Judaism became a religion inseparable from Jewish nationalism. We shall explore this more fully a little later in this chapter.

Islam and Christianity differed both from the multinational but noncompetitive religions like Hinduism and Confucianism, and from the nationalistic religions like Judaism and Shintoism. Islam and Christianity had a commitment to convert the world to their own image, and they became competitive precisely because of that desire.

Our analysis is based on two sets of hypotheses. First, religions which insist on the oneness of God have, in the short run, been more intolerant than religions which have accepted divine multiplicity. Belief in the oneness of God has, in the short run, led to behavior which militated against the principle of the oneness of man. Islam and Christianity have therefore a record of less toleration of rival visions of the ultimate than does Hinduism or many of the African traditional religions. The other side of this coin is that religions which admit of many gods tend to be more tolerant of others on religious grounds than monotheistic religions have been.

Again Judaism stands in a special relationship. It is indeed a monotheistic religion, and one which helped to shape the monotheism of Christianity and Islam. The intolerance of Judaism in the last twenty centuries or so has not been in terms of crusading for converts, but in terms of a self-sufficiency, a sanctified form of cultural autarky.

The second set of hypotheses underlying this chapter is that the Middle East was the cradle of ecumenicalism and Africa is likely to be the continent of its fulfillment in this religious domain. The Middle East, by producing Islam and Christianity, helped to bequeath to the world its most important experiments in competitive ecumenicalism. We hope to show how competitive ecumenicalism could gradually mature into compassionate ecumenicalism where conditions favor this. From the Middle East then came the competitive version; in Africa there is likely to be a compassionate fulfillment.

An alternative way of putting forward this hypothesis is to say, quite simply, that religious ecumenicalism in our sense was born in the Middle East and will be consummated in the African continent.

Both in Islam and in Christianity there were seeds for the moderation of monotheistic intolerance, for the emergence of an ecumenical spirit should other circumstances permit. Christianity in origin was a religion of the underdog, and its doctrines grew up with the notions of martyrdom and weakness. The founder of the religion died before he could himself build an empire. He retained to the end a humility which Muhammad later lost, because Muhammad had to run a political community.

In Islam the responsiveness to ecumenicalism lay not in the oneness of God, but in the multiplicity of His prophets. And this is where Islam steals a march on Christianity in terms of potential compassionate ecumenicalism. From the start, the religion admitted that the other monotheistic religions known to it were valid, in their own way. Islam has always accepted Christians and Jews as people of the book, an earlier version of the Islamic religion itself. Moses and Jesus Christ are recognized as Islamic prophets. ("Islam" means submission to God.) And yet although Islam has insisted that there is only one God, and that even the idea of a Trinity verges too dangerously on polytheism, the God of Islam has always had many messengers. At the time the religion was being revealed, at least twenty-four messengers were announced to the believers as having preceded Muhammad. There was a firm reluctance to concede new messengers after Muhammad, but the admissibility of older versions of religion, valid in their own right, was itself a potential seed for compassionate ecumenicalism.

Muslims in other parts of the world extended that toleration beyond the Jews and Christians. Muhammad did not know much about the Hindus or Buddhists to the east of him, but when Islam got to India, the issue arose as to whether the toleration conceded to the Jews and Christians by Islam admitted of extension to others. Some of the Moghul Emperors went so far in their compassionate ecumenicalism that they sought to create a fusion of Islam and Hinduism. The greatest of these attempts was undertaken by Akbar, who hoped to see in India a system of different interpretations of the ultimate.

The famous *millet* system of the Islamic Ottoman Empire, conceding religious autonomy to all the different groups scattered within the empire, was certainly an exercise in compassionate ecumenicalism, however imperfect it was. This essentially theocratic empire conceded to dissenting groups, including the Jews, far more freedom than the Jews have had in Europe from that time right up to this century. Again, it may be that the absolutism of Islamic monotheism was moderated by the plurality of the messengers of God allowed in Islam. And what started basically as a religion of competitive ecumenicalism stood a chance of evolving into a doctrine of compassionate empathy with the Universal Man.

The Middle East and Universal Man

In 1962 a painting of Jesus Christ, depicting him as a "black Christ", found its way to England from South Africa. St. Paul's Cathedral became its new home for the time being. Worshippers, as well as visitors, went in large numbers to see the painting. The British Press covered the event meticulously.

What was significant about the idea of a black Christ was the very fact that it was deemed to be so novel. In reality, Africa had already known messianic movements which had thought of Jesus as a black man. South Africa itself, as well as places like Zaire, had known such movements for many years before independence although they had always been considered heretical, on at least decidedly eccentric. There are a number of reasons why they were considered idiosyncratic, but one important reason was derived from the very notion of a black Jesus.

This issue is connected with the central aspects of this chapter—the concept of the Universal Man and its relation to the history of religion. The Middle East was the cradle of the Universal Man in our sense—and the idea of a Universal Man postulates expanding empathy and the acceptance of the villagization of the world with the collective responsibilities among men which arise therefrom.

If Jesus was a white man, it would make sense for all Christians to ask why He chose to be born white. Why was He not born brown to identify Himself with the massive humanity of parts of Asia and Africa? Or why was He not born yellow and Chinese? Mahatma Gandhi used to think of Jesus Christ as a fellow "Asiatic"—a brown man who would have been discriminated against had He found Himself in South Africa in the twentieth century. Not long before he died, Gandhi had occasion to refer once again to the Golden Rule, "Do unto others as you would that they should do unto you." Gandhi then went on to ask:

> Or, do [the white men] take in vain the name of Him who said this? Have they banished from their hearts the great coloured Asiatic who gave the world the above message? Do they forget that the greatest of the teachers of mankind were all Asiatics and did not possess a white face? These, if descended on earth and went to South Africa, will have to live in segregated areas . . . unfit by law to be equals of whites.[1]

Yet the very fact that it is possible to debate whether Jesus was a colored or a white man is itself symptomatic of the Middle East and its pigmentational ambiguity. One cannot help feeling that if Jesus wanted to emphasize the oneness of mankind, He could not have been born in a better place than where He was actually born. The Middle East was the very center of the known world at the time Jesus was born, and derives its very name partly from that fact. Of course other continents have been discovered since then—but at no other point on the globe do three major continents converge as they do in the Middle East. Even the name "Mediterranean" denotes the center of the world.

And if Jesus went about seeking the appropriate people among whom to be born, He could hardly have made a better choice than the Semites. There is a profound racial ambivalence about the Jews; and there is a profound pigmentational ambivalence about the Arabs who range in color from the white Arabs of the Lebanon and Syria, the brown Arabs of the Hadhramout, to the black Arabs of the Sudan and parts of Saudi Arabia. Large sections of the Arab populations of the Middle East are indistinguishable in physical features from Greeks, Spaniards, Italians, and other Mediterranean people. On the other hand, many Arab Sudanese are as black as the non-Arab Sudanese, and would certainly be indistinguishable from Hausamen and Jamaicans.

The Jews, a much smaller sector of the Semitic peoples, number only 14 million in the world as a whole. But racial ambivalence has also been a major factor in the history of the Jews. Raphael Patar has pointed out that Jews tend to share the physiological traits of their immediate non-Jewish neighbors, rather than the traits of other Jews in distant geographical areas.

Eighty-four per cent of the world's Jews are, according to some estimates, Ashkenazic Jews. It was in the tenth century that this group, settled in the Rhineland, began to assume general importance for the future of the world Jewry. It would seem that the group's name is derived from the medieval Hebrew word for "Germany," Ashkenaz. The Ashkenazim then spread to other parts of Europe, and to the new world in both North and South America.

The remaining 16 percent of the world Jewry is made up mainly of Sephardic and Oriental Jews. Sephardim were important in the history of Islamic civilization in the Mediterranean, assuming positions of influence in scholarship and the arts. They then became influential in de-Islamized Spain, until they were expelled in 1492 in the wave of intolerance in Iberia which also swept out the Moorish population. The language of the Sephardim has been Ladino, and apparently there is strong evidence of a partial Spanish ancestry. The oriental Jews are scattered from North Africa to the Indian sub-continent. There are also small groups of Jews such as the Falasha Jews of Ethiopia. It is because of this general racial ambivalence that it is possible to say, as an American magazine recently said: "As the Jewish homeland, Israel has Jews of almost every kind, color and Judaic language, although the Sephardic pronunciation of Hebrew has been made standard for Israel.[2]

The racial ambivalence of the Jews and the Arabs has led to a number of theories which form an important part of that side of intellectual history which has been concerned with speculations about the races of man. There is certainly a school of thought among black people which regards all Semitic peoples as having been originally part of the colored world. A branch of these broke off and gradually won their way into the bosom of whitehood, and became white men. These were the Jews. The other wing of the Semitic peoples remained in the fold of Afro-Asianism, militantly opposed to white domination, and politically aligned to the other colored races of the globe. The Arabs constituted this other Semitic wing. The Semites, the Hamites, and the black races have, it is known, interacted in a variety of ways. What has been in dispute among scholars is the nature of that interaction. The attachment of the Somalis to a Semitic civilization, the points of similarity between Amharic and the written language of pre-Islamic Southern Arabia, the impact of the Arabs on the racial mixture of northern Africa, the penetration and infiltration of Islamic values and cultural mores among diverse peoples in West and East Africa, the role of the Hamites in African civilizations and their relationship to Semitic groups, are all part of the total picture of a massive interaction between Semites, Hamites, and black peoples. There is even an important theory that a large section of the black population of Africa can be traced back to the Arabian peninsula. Research into Fulbe origins and their role in West African history led to theories which link the populations of Africa and the Arabian peninsula as basically one continental unit. Many eighteenth- and nineteenth-century Western historians had such a low opinion of Negro capabilities that they tended to attribute any great achievement in Africa to the influence of the Fulbe or, later, the Hamites. But one does not have to share these racialistic prejudices to emphasize the racial intermixture and cultural interaction among these different groups.

Among nineteenth-century historians, H. Barth was in many ways the most modern in his methodology. As Philip D. Curtin has put it "the questions [Barth] posed and the way he went about answering them were closer to the methods of the 1960s than to those of the 1830s." Barth noted that the Fulbe were related in language and culture to the Wolof but were racially distinct. He explained these facts and the peopling of West Africa generally by what Curtin calls "a two-stream theory". One stream of intrusive population into West Africa was deemed to be of Berber origin and to come from the region of Libya; the other stream, a deeper black in color, was deemed to have originated in southern Arabia. The two streams met in the western Sudan and intermingled for centuries, but the racial mixing did not homogenize into a single group. The Fulbe were one branch of the mixed race which had stabilized itself into a distinct entity; other sections were to be found in the Western Sudan with varying shades of color.[3]

Not all theories which black peoples have about a joint ancestry with the Semites or Hamites are attributable to works like the one by Barth. Questions of historical identification among black peoples, especially in the western hemisphere, are sometimes substantially affected by sociological factors and their impact on psychological perspectives. But historical evidence is not entirely hostile to the view that the Semites split into two groups, one of which intermingled with the whites and became part of the white world and the other which identified with Afro-Asian forces and became part of the colonized group. Among the colonized groups are indeed some colored Jews. But the most important Jewry became semi-assimilated into the northern hemisphere of the world, made an impact on the history of the globe partly through their participation in the European evolution, and sometimes suffered hardships as a minority group in white lands. Where they were not suffering these hardships, the white Jews of the northern hemisphere have sometimes been seen by black militants in the western hemisphere as renegades to the cause of black peoples. As Eric Lincoln observed in relation to the attitudes of black Muslims especially in the United States:

> There is a feeling in some quarters that the Jews, as Semites, are "not quite white" and should be grouped with the Arabs as members of the Black Nation. "How can we be accused of being anti-Semitic," one Muslim minister asked, "when our Arab brothers are Semitic?" For those who accept this implication, the Jews are traitors; black men who reject their true identity, scorn their black brothers and pass themselves off as white.[4]

The other aspect of the Jewish racial predicament which differentiates the Jews from the black people is, quite simply, the concept of *the chosen people*. This runs counter to the principle of the Universal Man. The concept of the chosen people has been both the strength of the Jews and their weakness. It has enabled the Jews to survive as a culturally distinctive entity in spite of generations of intermingling with other groups in different parts of the world. It has also sharpened the areas of enterprise and certain skills among the Jews. And yet the fact remains that the cultural exclusiveness of the Jews, and their self-conception as a group endowed by God with a special destiny, has made their racial predicament very different from that of the black people. What the black people are fighting against is precisely racial exclusiveness. They are asserting areas of maximum intermingling, including permissive intermarriage. It is true that in black America nowadays there is an ethic of anti-miscegenation, a distrust of black people who marry white people. But black anti-miscegenation in the United States for the time being is basically a *protesting* form of anti-miscegenation. It is not inherent in the cultural values of the group but arises substantially out of a posture of militancy in a given period of time. Jewish anti-miscegenation, on the other hand, is culturally sanctioned, and is at the core of Jewish values of identity. This is another great difference between the Jews and that other wing of the Semites, the Arabs. While the Jews owe their survival in part to their reluctance to marry outside their group, the Arabs are perhaps the most mongrel race on earth, as we have already suggested.

In the kind of religion they bequeathed to the world, there is also an important difference. Judaism is an exclusive religion in a way Islam is not. The religious heritage of the Jews is monopolistic and exclusive; whereas the religion which came with the Arabs aspires to universal validity and to accommodating diverse groups within it.

Bildad Kaggia, who later became a symbol of the Kikuyu wing of radical thought in Kenya, was a preacher for a while in the colonial period and became involved in the Mau Mau insurrection. He stood trial with Jomo Kenyatta and spent some years in detention. In the course of a cross-examination about a letter which Kaggia had written to Kenyatta in 1950, the following exchange took place between the prosecution and Kaggia:

> *Prosecution:* I am suggesting that in paragraph 4 of that letter [to Kenyatta] you are saying three things: That when you went to Europe you abandoned the CMS religion and all those other religions which had been brought here; I understand you to say that you only meant denomination?
>
> *Kaggia:* Yes.
>
> *Prosecution:* Then you say that when you returned to this country in 1946 you refused to have anything to do with any of the religions of the Europeans and you were left simply standing on the Bible?
>
> *Kaggia:* Yes.
>
> *Prosecution:* And in the last paragraph, did you say that the third stage of your spiritual development was to abandon the whole of the Bible?
>
> *Kaggia:* If you read the last paragraph properly you will see it says that I came to find that the Bible contained the customs and laws of the Jews and that I abandoned those.
>
> *Prosecution:* But that is not what the letter says. I will read it again. "I realise it contained the laws of the Jews and so I abandoned the teaching of the Bible?"
>
> *Kaggia:* Yes, as far as the laws and customs were concerned which are in the Bible. That is my meaning. I would like to explain the parts of the Bible. The Bible contains one part prophecy; one part Moses' laws; and another part is of Jewish customs; and the fourth is the teaching of Jesus Christ. And when I talk of laws and customs which are abandoned, those are the things which were meant solely for the Jewish people; but when we come to prophecies and the teachings of Jesus Christ, they are meant for the whole of mankind, which I, too, believe and practice.*

Kaggia later became a leading radical in Kenya and the Deputy Leader of the Kenya Peoples Union before the party ran into the political troubles of 1969 and was banned by the Kenya Government. But what is interesting in this earlier stage of Kaggia's career is, partly, his rejection of the Judaic part of the Bible on the grounds that it was an ethnocentric code of laws, intended only for the Jews, and therefore irrelevant for the African. It is true that Kaggia's rejection was a form of intolerance in itself. But more significant was the fact that it was an intolerance of someone else's cultural autarky, the doctrine of the chosen people and the culture of self-possessiveness that had characterized the Jews for so many centuries.

Nevertheless, it remains true that it was the Jews who produced Jesus Christ, and the Arabs who produced Muhammad. And from Jesus and Muhammad descended the *two most ecumenicalist* religions in world history. The impact of the two Semitic peoples on the evolution of world culture is therefore in some ways unparalleled. It is because of this that we have designated the Middle East as the cradle of ecumenicalism, and must now turn to Africa as the area of its final consummation.

Africa and the Universal Man

African scholars have themselves often debated whether or not traditional religions had a High God. The controversy has touched at times on the issue of whether traditional African religions were also basically monotheistic. But while there is a considerable body of scholarly opinion that interprets certain gods in African traditional religions as having been the nearest approximations to a High God in Africa's experience, only a few black Christian apologists are willing to hazard the more ambitious claim that these religions were literally monotheistic. That there should be one god higher than all others is one doctrine. But that there should be one God with no others whatsoever is another. The former doctrine implies a hierarchy of gods; the latter doctrine, divine monopoly and absolutism concentrated in one single Almighty.[5]

The African continent has produced no major religion, nor have its creeds proselytized among people outside the continent. On the contrary, the African continent has been overwhelmed by missionaries in recent years. Perhaps no other continent has faced such massive attention by those who have had religions or sacred wares to propagate. In the eighteenth, nineteenth, and much of the twentieth centuries Christianity found its greatest number of dedicated volunteers within the African continent. Europe exported not just administrators and businessmen but also peddlers of religious beliefs.

Even before the Christians, the Muslims had come to disseminate their religious ideas in various parts of the continent. Empires in West Africa grew up animated by the ideals of Islam. Trade, politics, and war promoted continuous contacts between West Africa and North Africa, and the Muslim heritage was part of this experience.

What we have then is a variety of indigenous African religions, coexisting and interacting with Islam and European Christianity. This is the tripartite soul of Africa which Nkrumah perceived so astutely: indigenous traditional life; the Islamic tradition; and "the infiltration of the

*This rendering of the exchange occurs in Montagu Slater *The Trial of Jomo Kenyatta* (London: Mercury Books, 1965), pp. 195–196. The exclusiveness of "being Jewish" was tested in a new way in Israel early in 1970 when the Israeli Supreme Court decided to allow two children of a Jewish father and a non-Jewish mother—both of them atheists—to be registered as of Jewish nationality. The Israeli Government decided to change the law which had made such a court ruling possible. The orthodox rabbinic law which said that only converts and children born of Jewish mothers were Jews was to be reaffirmed after all. See Ivan Yates, "Who shall define a Jew?" *The Observer,* (London) February 1, 1970.

Christian tradition and the culture of Western Europe into Africa, using colonialism and neo-colonialism as its primary vehicles." Continuing, Nkrumah groped for a principle which, in our terms, would certainly be akin to compassionate ecumenicalism. Nkrumah suggested that a new synthesis was needed to lend coherence to the tripartite nature of Africa's soul:

> With true independence regained . . . a new harmony needs to be forged, a harmony that will allow the combined presence of traditional Africa, Islamic Africa and Euro-Christian Africa, so that this presence is in tune with the original humanist principles underlying African society. Our society is not the old society, but a new society enlarged by Islamic and Euro-Christian influences.

Nkrumah urged a new synthesis of these three elements, to produce what he called "Philosophical Consciencism":

> The theoretical basis for an ideology whose aim shall be to contain the African experience of Islamic and Euro-Christian presence as well as the experience of traditional African society, and, by gestation, employ them for the harmonious growth and development of that society.[6]

The success of such an exercise in ecumenicalism would depend a good deal upon the attitudes of the three segments to each other. Particularly important would be that of traditional Africa, which could decide the temper of the merger, or at any rate of compassionate coexistence.

Fortunately, experience repeatedly reveals that African traditional religions are much more tolerant of other religions than the two imported religions of Islam and Christianity. If one examined the record of the degree to which religion is politicized in African societies, the conclusion is inescapable that the least politicizable of these three segments is the indigenous one. African parties have not been formed on the basis of tribal gods, nor African wars waged to gain converts to African traditional religions. On the contrary, African parents who still cling to traditional religions themselves are notoriously agreeable to the idea of their children being brought up as Christians in missionary schools. There are families in Africa which include in their membership Christians, Muslims, and followers of traditional beliefs. And among Christians, Catholic and Protestant coexist with each other, and with other denominations, on a scale unknown in other parts of the Christian world.

In political behavior, such as the choice of a leader, we might say that the least tolerant are precisely the African Christians. There is hardly any impressive illustration of a majority of African Christians electing a non-Christian for President; but there are a number of illustrations of a majority of non-Christian Africans electing a Christian for their President. While the American electorate in 1960 was wondering whether to elect its first Catholic President in the history of the Union, the Muslims of Senegal had already elected Leopold Senghor as their own Catholic President. And the preponderant Muslims of Tanganyika, later Tanzania, had been following enthusiastically the leadership of Julius K. Nyerere, another Roman Catholic.

A Christian nation in Africa has yet to get a Muslim President by popular vote. But by a military coup in January 1971, Uganda found itself with the Presidency of General Idi Amin Dada, a Muslim. Among the Baganda he was, for a while, much more popular than President Obote had been, although Obote was a fellow Christian.

What the picture as a whole illustrates is that the scale of toleration in the religious sphere in Africa starts with adherents of traditional religions as the most tolerant, followed by Muslims, and finally, by Catholics and Protestants. But the fact that the basic indigenous groups, followers of African traditional religions, are the most tolerant helps to improve the responsiveness of African Islam and African Christianity to the same general temper of compassionate ecumenicalism that is implicit in African traditional religions.

The polytheistic nature of African traditional religions has been largely responsible for the degree to which African parents have let their children belong to new gods without undue pangs of conscience. What is one more god between relatives? President Obote, on the day Akena Adoko's child was baptized, proudly claimed that he belonged to a family which was part Catholic, part Protestant, and part Muslim. He might also have added that all three parts had probably synthesized elements from traditional Langi beliefs.

President Obote's successor as President of Uganda was reported by his own Chief Justice to be planning to train two of his sons as Roman Catholic priests—although General Amin himself was a devout Muslim, observing the fast of Ramadam amidst all the hectic pressure of his first year in office. General Amin also adopted quite early the principle of ecumenicalism as the basis of relations between the church and the state in Uganda. He held conferences with religious leaders, and sometimes bullied them in the direction of national unity in religious affairs. Under Amin, Uganda was beginning to learn to distinguish between, first, a religious state with an established church like the United Kingdom or Pakistan; second, a secular state that insists that church and state shall not participate in each other's affairs, like the United States; and third, the ecumenical state. This last not only does not insist on state withdrawal from religious affairs but, on the contrary, is committed to the promotion of collaboration among the different denominations.

Here contact between Africa's experience and the experience of the Middle East is reflected. The most interesting ecumenical state in the world is Lebanon, which allocates political offices among religious denominations. The Lebanese are terrified of mutual religious hostility, because they know it is ready to erupt at any time. And so they have devised a political process which ensures that each of the major denominations has what is regarded as proportional representation in parliament, and each is eligible for the offices that are distributed, in pursuit of ecumenical justice. General Amin's Uganda seemed to be moving, under very different conditions, towards the Lebanese type of ecumenical principle. But whereas the Lebanese succeeded in making their system work because of a fear of each other, Africans may learn to achieve ecumenicalism because of tolerance in the religious sphere. Africans are mutually brutal on ethnic lines, but singularly tolerant across religious lines.

Finally, Africa is a remarkable arena for the consummation of compassionate ecumenicalism because the black man was for so long the ultimate underdog. We mentioned earlier that black Africans have not been among the most brutalized of the world communities in recent times. The Jews have a better claim to that painful distinction under Nazi Germany. Black Africans are also not among the most indigent and most poor of the communities of the world; there are Indians who experience a degree of squalor and poverty almost unknown in the African continent. The distinctiveness of the fate of the black people is that they have been the most *humiliated* in recent times, they were the most humiliated in slavery until its abolition in the last century; and have been the most humiliated by racialism and discrimination.

The restoration of black dignity is almost the ultimate measure of racial equality. It was Prime Minister Pandit Nehru of India who told his countrymen: "Reading through history, I think the agony of the African continent . . . has not been equalled anywhere.[7] And it was because of what Nehru called "the agony of the African continent", the unparalleled pangs of degradation the black man had sustained, that Kwame Nkrumah was so movingly persuasive when he said: "The emancipation of the African continent is the emancipation of man".[8]

And so the history of ecumenicalism, conceived competitively in the Middle East, may find its most moving consummation in the African continent. The heritage of the Semitic peoples, interacting with the polytheistic inheritance of African tribes, should provide in the years ahead a striking fulfillment of the ideal of the Universal Man.

But whatever the final conclusion to the story of competitive religion in

31

world history, what we do know already is that it has been a major factor behind the rise of world culture. Those religions which had the arrogance to believe that every member of the human species should embrace them, and which set out on their travels to convert the world, helped to promote a shared morality between societies which once diverged more sharply. The genesis of world culture may converge with the origins of the universe—"In the beginning was the word, and the word was of God" ... and the God was of culture.

Footnotes

1. *Harijan* (Ahmedabad), June 30, 1946. See also Haridas T. Muzumdar, (editor) *Sermon on the Sea* (Chicago: Universal Publishing Company, 1954).
2. "What's what in Jewry," Cover page, *Time* Magazine, April 10, 1972. This article, pp. 54–63, seems to be the most comprehensive on the Jews to have been published in a magazine of such great circulation for many years. The article has used a number of scholarly sources, including Patar's book referred to earlier, *Tents of Jacob.*
3. H. Barth, *Travels and Discoveries in North and Central Africa,* (London: 1857–1858), vol. 4, pp. 146–156. Cited by Philip D. Curtin, *The Image of Africa: British Ideas and Action, 1780–1850* (London: MacMillan, 1965) pp. 411–412. See also Barth, "A General Historical Description of the State of Human Society in Northern Central Africa," *Journal of the Royal Geographical Society,* XXX (1860), pp. 112–128, pp. 115–119.
4. *The Black Muslims in America* (Boston: Beacon Press, 1961), p. 165.
5. The debates among African scholars have included such writers as Professor John S. Mbiti, Professor of Religious Studies at Makerere University Kampala; Professor B. A. Ogot, Professor of History at the University of Nairobi in Kenya; and Mr. Okot P. Bitek, of the Institute of African Studies at the University of Nairobi. Mbiti's works on such themes include *African Religions and Philosophy* (London: Heinemann, 1969), *Concepts of God* and other works. Okot P. Bitek's works on the subject include *African Religions and Western Scholarship,* (Nairobi: East African Literature Bureau, 1970) and *Religion of the Central Luo* (Nairobi: East African Literature Bureau, 1971).
6. Kwame Nkrumah, *Consciencism* (London: Heinemann, 1964), pp. 68–70.
7. Jawaharlal Nehru, "Portugese Colonialism: An Anachronism," *Africa Quarterly* (New Delhi), vol. I, no. 3, Oct./Dec. 1961, p. 9.
8. Nkrumah, Consciencism (London: Heinemann, 1964), p. 78.

CHAPTER 2

Science and the Origins of
World Culture

In terms of the origins of world culture the roles of science and religion
are not too far apart. In different civilizations science was quite often
mobilized to serve the purposes of the ultimate; and the ultimate was
often defined in religious terms. In the last chapter we paid special attention to Christianity and Islam as agents in the dissemination of those
ideas which have been converging towards a world culture. As universalistic religions, these two—with their forebear, Judaism—have been exceptionally important in this regard.

Scientific contributions to world culture from other civilizations than
the Western have also been substantial. The work of Joseph Needham of
Cambridge University has revealed to English-speaking readers the impressive scientific experience of China. In volume after volume,
Needham and his colleagues have put before the world the history of a
scientific civilization of considerable implications.[1] The link between religion and science was as present in China as elsewhere, though Chinese religion was in any case less "other-worldly" than Hinduism and Christianity once were. Indeed, Needham's work on science in China was undertaken specifically "to correct the grievously distorted western notion
of the Chinese as other-worldly, unscientific, antitechnological." A study
which started primarily as a contribution to a debate on China developed
into what has been called "one of the most remarkable works of our
time."

Of the two universalistic religions we discussed in the last chapter, it
was at first Islam rather than Christianity which married itself to
science. The golden age of Arab Islam witnessed one of the most instan-
taneous civilizations in history. Hordes of horse riders and camel drivers,
bursting forth from the deserts of the Arabian peninsula, took on two
major empires of their time, the Persian and the Byzantine Empires, and
defeated both. Out of that first wave of conquest grew a civilization

33

oriented towards Mecca spiritually, but for a while also oriented towards the universe scientifically. Later conquests consolidated the scientific pursuits of the early Islamic era, and converted Arabic into the leading scientific language of its day.

In the Middle Ages Europe was still relatively asleep under centuries of intellectual stagnation. The Latin West had experienced the so-called "dark ages" from the sixth to the eleventh century. But then the West began to respond to the Arabian influence in the twelfth century, and through that influence came the renewed impact of Greek civilization. One part of what later came to be known as Europe learned from another part of Europe through the intermediate services of Islamic civilization.

In our own time of course Europe, and Europe's extensions in the New World, have preeminently been the strong fortresses of science and learning, technique and organization, industry and business enterprise. Even the Arab world, in spite of its political hostility to certain aspects of Western ways, does look today to Europe and the United States for standards of technology, medicine, and science at large. But Western science today is no longer Christian, the link between religion and science having been broken. This was not the case when Islam was supreme in the scientific field. The spiritual and the material, the normative and the scientific, were for a while fused.

> The Westerner knew full well that Islam held the learning and science of antiquity. Moslem proficiency in arms and administration had been sufficiently proved—the Occidental belief in them is enshrined in our semitic words "arsenal" and "admiral," "tariff," "douans," "average." There was a longing, too, for the intellectual treasures of the East, but also the same fear and repugnance to its religion that the East now feels for the West.[2]

Charles Singer reminds us of the question which is often asked as to why in the Middle Ages it was the practise to translate work from the Arabic rather than from the Greek, and why this tendency affected the works originally written in Greek. Singer advances the following reasons: First, before about 1200 A.D. Muslim learning was better organized, more original, and more vital than Byzantine. Second, because Byzantine Greek is far distant from the classical tongue, the language of Aristotle was incomprehensible to the monastic guardians of his manuscripts. But classical Arabic was intelligible to every well-educated man who spoke and wrote Arabic. Third, the whole trend of Byzantine learning was towards theology and away from philosophy and science. Fourth, the channels of trade with the West were either directly with Islam or through Western enclaves within the Byzantine Empire. Fifth, in the

Middle Ages languages were learned by speaking and not from grammars. Spoken Arabic was more accessible than spoken Greek. Sixth, Latin Christendom made little progress in occupying Byzantine territory. On the other hand, Islam was in retreat in the West. Seventh, Jewish help could be obtained through Arabic, but seldom through Greek.[3]

The relationship between science and religion remained a tense one in the Christian world until very recently. The history of university institutions in the Western world was not only intimately connected with religion but seemed to suffer unduly from the constraints imposed by religion. Scholarship itself was overwhelmingly oriented towards theological issues, or restrained by theological considerations. Science had to serve God *directly*—or be charged with the sin of heresy. Scientists had to be careful about what they did. Often those scientists were deeply religious themselves, and shrank from lines of thought which appeared to lead towards irreligious conclusions.

The link between religion and academic life remained strong. But the tensions between complete scientific objectivity and considerations of inherited religion entered a new era with the Copernican Revolution in the sixteenth century.

From the point of view of world culture, the Copernican theory that the planets, including the earth, moved in orbits surrounding the sun which was at the center must be counted a significant milestone. This is not simply because of the triumph of the scientific spirit in its first dramatic and cosmic confrontation with a religion in the Western world. It is also because it was a milestone in the long struggle against autocentrism in human thought specifically as represented by the Ptolemaic theory that had asserted that the sun and the planets moved around the earth. The older theory was indeed based on the arrogant notion of autocentrism. We define autocentrism as a tendency in man to see himself as the center of all things, and then to work out institutions and belief systems starting from that premise. The forms which autocentrism have taken range from Ptolemy's theory of the universe to ethnocentrism among aboriginal tribes in Australia.

In the following century, Galileo also got into trouble for promoting the Copernican theory. In 1633 he was compelled to renounce and repudiate the Copernican theory and was sent to prison. The fate of Galileo became a moving experience for many scientists in the succeeding generations. The scientists sometimes longed for greater intellectual liberation—but at that time many decided to avoid the danger of being accused of heresy, or even witchcraft, and then burned at the stake.

The interplay between the Reformation and the Renaissance was an important moment in the history of freedom of thought. The arts were being liberated from religion, and science had no longer to spend all its time proving that science was not Satan in disguise. But antiscientism was still an important feature of European civilization. Although Luther was rather hostile to certain sectors of the scientific world, Calvinism began to transform the fortunes of science in Europe. The importance of Calvinism for the growth of capitalism has long been debated, following Max Weber's brilliant thesis in *The Protestant Ethic and the Spirit of Capitalism.* But the link between Puritanism and the growth of the scientific spirit has not been discussed quite as extensively, though it has already found its champions among historians of science and technology. In England, the Royal Society, overwhelmingly Protestant by the seventeenth century, was also overwhelmingly *Puritan.* The men of science were basically nonconformists—the majority being neither Catholic nor Anglican.

The Puritan fascination with science had influenced Cromwell to establish a new university at Durham, the only new English university to be established between the Middle Ages and the nineteenth century. Durham University committed itself from its birth to the promotion of "all the sciences".[4] Cambridge University became more scientifically oriented than Oxford partly because it was more nonconformist in its religious composition. The origins of the scientific bias of Cambridge in the modern period may well lie in that period of high Puritan influence at Cambridge in the seventeenth century.[5]

In the United States too, the Puritan influence on the growth of the scientific spirit was considerable. Part of the influence came through Cambridge University in England which was described in that period as the *alma mater* of the Puritans. Of twenty leading Puritan clergymen in New England, seventeen were graduates of Cambridge, and only three of Oxford. Harvard's educational program also felt this Puritan influence. The sciences in the United States were certainly upheld better in Protestant than in Catholic institutions; within Protestant circles the Puritan bias towards scientificity stood out.[6]

In this period there was not a complete break between religion and science, not even a secularization of science. What was really happening was the scientification of religion. Not until the second half of the eighteenth century did the full wave of the secularization of science in the western world begin to be felt. Jeremy Bentham's establishment in the nineteenth century of University College, London, as an institution where scholars did not have to subscribe to the nine articles of the Anglican faith, was itself part of this new assertion in England of academic freedom and the scientific spirit.

The secularization of science was an important event for world culture. For as long as science was tied to particular religions, and designed to serve the purposes of these religions, science itself was to some extent culture-bound in the narrow sense. Science as a culture-bound entity was by definition less universal than science liberated from religious dogma.

Charles Singer has reminded us that science is not "a body of knowledge"; it is "an active process." By this definition, a body of scientific knowledge which ceases to develop soon ceases to be science at all. The science of one period of history can become the nonsense of the next, as witness alchemy, astrology, and the idea that certain numbers are lucky and others unlucky.

> Science, then, is no static body of knowledge but rather an *active process* that can be followed through the ages. . . . By derivation scientific implies *knowledge making,* and no body of doctrine which is not *growing,* which is not actually *in the making,* can long retain the attributes of science.[7]

The release of science from religion accelerated the growth of science. More scientific progress has been made since science was liberated from religion in the nineteenth century than in all the centuries of man before that put together.

The secularization of science has not only resulted in its genuine universalization but also in its dramatic expansion. Both factors have been quite fundamental for the evolution of a world culture. And the supremacy of the Western world in this new science has been a critical factor in the reasons behind the Euro-centrism of world culture as it has so far evolved.

Technology and World Culture

Science as an assembly of principles or a body of abstract knowledge did not alone bring forth these major transformations in human arrangements. Even more important than the link between religion and science is the link between science and technology. What technology owes science is all too obvious. What science owes technology has not always been as immediately perceived. In the words of Charles R. Walker:

> Without the telescope, a technological invention, the science of modern astronomy would have been impossible. Without the microscope, the modern sciences of zoology, biology, and bacteriology would not have developed. . . . One of the latest and most striking debts of science to technology lies in the fields of mathematics and physics. Progress in both is now dependent in part on the high speed automatic computer. The computer in turn owes its development to information theory, and the researches of the mathematician.[8]

37

Other writers have attempted to periodize the history of interaction between science and technology. Charles Singer has argued that up to the sixteenth century, and perhaps even later than that, technology was more often the parent than the offspring of science. It was not until the Renaissance that natural phenomena came to be more and more systematically observed, and the use of experiment, and the recession of empiricism to science, became increasingly evident.[9]

Alfred North Whitehead, though writing earlier than Singer, took the analysis further. He argued that the greatest invention of the nineteenth century was the invention of the method of invention. One element in the method was the discovery of how to set about bridging the gap between scientific ideas, and between these and the ultimate products of technology. Whitehead suggests that though England led in the Industrial Revolution, she did not lead in the reduction of technology to its ultimate principles. It was, according to Whitehead, the Germans who abolished "haphazard methods of scholarship". In their technological schools and universities the Germans did not let progress wait for the occasional genius or the occasional lucky thought, but set about to transform academic amateurs into scientific professionals.[10]

Both in situations of scientific discovery and technological invention cultural factors are once again at play. It is not mere necessity which is the mother of invention, but a culturally defined "necessity". That is the essence of the sociology of invention. The definitions of what is necessary may in turn change along with other aspects of culture. A certain predisposition in favor of innovation, a preliminary cultural preparation for discovery and change, are always necessary. Lewis Mumford has drawn our attention to "the wish before the scientific fact". Technology and civilization are the result of "human choices and aptitudes and the strivings, deliberate as well as unconscious". Choice reveals itself in society in small increments and day to day ad hoc decisions as well as in loud dramatic movements:

> ... and he who does not see his choice in the development of the machine merely betrays his incapacity to observe cumulative effects until they are bunched together so closely that they seem completely external and impersonal. No matter how completely technics relies upon the objective procedures of the sciences, it does not form an independent system, like the universe: it exists as an element in human culture and it promises well or ill as the social groups that exploit it promise well or ill.[11]

Behind the great milestones of science and technology, and the great material inventions, was what Mumford calls "a change of mind". Mumford sometimes exaggerates the autonomy of ideas, but his central thesis concerning cultural readiness for scientific discovery and technological invention is persuasive and critically significant for the history of world culture.

The first great cultural innovation of man was probably the taming of fire for human purposes. The use of fire has been described as the first great technological revolution, "the only open-and-shut difference between man and other animals". Carleton Coon argued that fire was man's first source of power which did not come from the conversion of food and air into energy inside his own body. "Fire made him a more efficient animal, and during the last 8,000 years he has found increasing uses for it, and burned even greater quantities of fuel. Fire has been the key to his rapid rise in mastering the forces of nature, his conquest and partial destruction of the earth, and his current problems."[12]

There are, of course, societies in the world today which have not fully exploited fire as a source of energy. Africa, which has until recently lagged behind so painfully in technological innovation, still has scattered communities that create and use fire in little more than the original prehistoric sense. Colin M. Turnbull, in his recent book about the Ik of Uganda, draws our attention to the elementary ways in which the Ik make fire and also their relative lack of interest in either mobilizing it for greater purposes or controlling it to prevent its destructive potential:

> The Ik still use the fire-drill to make fire, twirling one stick rapidly between both hands as it rests in a notch on another stick held firm by one foot. In a matter of seconds the friction produces smoke, and a little dry tinder poured over the stick on the ground bursts into flame with one puff. Fires were lit like this everywhere, with no attempt to control them.[13]

It was preeminently the technological lag which made Africa such an easy prey to European expansionism. Indeed, Europe's capacity to steal so much of the world was ultimately attributable to those cumulative choices in Europe which finally resulted in unprecedented technological power. Two forms of this technological power were particularly important for the whole history of Europe's expansion and the consequences of this for world culture. One form of power rested on the capacity to be *mobile*. We shall discuss this more fully later, but the impact of technology on communications and imperial mobility was a major ingredient in the transformation of much of the world into a periphery of Europe.

Another form of technology important for annexation was, quite simply, military technology. Europe's capacity to reduce to military impotence millions of people in different parts of the world was a major precondition for the unprecedented sizes of empires which grew up in the eighteenth, nineteenth, and twentieth centuries. In the words of the English writer, Hilaire Belloc, referring to the position of Europeans in Africa:

Whatever happens we have got
The Maxim gun, and they have not.

We shall also discuss later the interaction between the imperial mission and creative literature, with special reference to Rudyard Kipling. Again the critical variable of technological superiority was converted into a cynical justification for world dominance.

That they should take who have the power
And they should keep who can.[14]

Europe's expansion was itself a major element in the evolution of a world culture, and the main cause of the Euro-centrism of that culture. The longer-term effects include the emergence of the concept of "modernization" and Western leadership in that process. Modernization in our sense means change in a direction which is positively compatible with the present stage of human knowledge, and which does justice to man's capacity as an innovative being. In specific terms, the process has three levels. There is the modernization of techniques, the modernization of the motives behind men's actions, and the modernization of political and social stratification as an area of man's relations with man.

We shall discuss more fully the modernization of motivation and stratification in Chapters 13 and 14. What we have noted here is the West's leadership in recent times in the modernization of techniques. The capacity to produce in order to meet human needs more efficiently, the increased competence in exploiting nature, the principles of effective human organization, the methods of studying the universe—all these are important elements within that greatest of all bags of tricks, technological and scientific know-how. The concept of modernization outside the Western world has had to use the West's experience in these techniques as a reference point.[15]

But European technology did not only result in the exploitation of much of Asia and Africa. It also resulted more directly in the exploitation of nature. And in this latter phenomenon we have once again a link between autocentrism in human affairs and the rape of the environment. Also linked to this entire global experience is the possibility of a new cultural convergence that takes its starting point in the Copernican revolution and continues to manifest itself in African animism. It is to this complex of interlocking phenomena that we must now turn.

From Copernicus to the New Totemism

We have referred earlier to the Copernican revolution as a milestone in man's struggle against autocentrism. Let us now look a little more closely at the implications of this phenomenon.

A large number of societies in distant parts of the world have based their identity on a myth of origin. Many relate the origins of their own society to the origins of man as a species, the most extreme form of ethnocentrism. The Americas may have been the periphery of the ancient world from the point of view of those who knew only of Asia, Europe, and Africa. But the natives of the Americas had elaborate myths of their origin which were strikingly ethnocentric. Many of the tribes claimed to have been created at "the heart of the world". A number of them insisted that they were created first, and the other tribes came into being as an afterthought, sometimes almost as an accident. "The Jicarilla Apache of the Southwest say that one tribe only—their own—existed when the world was new."[16]

In Africa, a large number of different tribes are classified as "Bantu". The word merely means "people". The utilization of the word "people" for a collection of related tribes is partly the fault of the early European scholars, but is also connected with highly ethnocentric concepts of the people they studied.

The Jews, as we indicated in the previous chapter, have also seen themselves as "the chosen people". While Adam himself is not explicitly described as a Jew, he and his immediate offspring are made to carry Jewish names. And the entire story of mankind is linked to the history of the Jewish prophets. The very division of the world between Jews and Gentiles underlines the ethnocentric features of Jewish identity in historical perspective.

The Chinese in their history have also seen themselves as the center of the world, and have had their own equivalents of the term "Gentiles" to refer to the non-Chinese sections of the populations of the globe. At the height of their civilization the rest of the world became to the Chinese "barbarian".

But these direct manifestations of ethnocentrism are by no means the only manifestations which this human tendency takes. Many racial theories in history have been related in some sense to a kind of autocentrism. The white man especially worked out an elaborate pyramid of racial gradation, placing himself firmly at the pinnacle. Social Darwinism as a movement in Europe and white America also included within it a good deal of emphasis on credentials for leadership commanded by the white man.

The relevance of Copernicus to autocentrism lies in his challenge to the very roots of Christian autocentrism. To regard the world as the center of the universe was a special kind of arrogance, perhaps greater than that of regarding any particular group of inhabitants of this world as being in some sense central to this world. Copernicus struck at the collective planetary autocentrism of the human race as a whole, and provided foundations for the kind of humility which might then humble the human race.

Stavrianos sees Charles Darwin as another great figure who cut man down to size.

> ... just as the Copernican system of astronomy had deposed the earth from its central place in the universe, so Darwinism seemed to dethrone man from his central place in the history of the earth. Such was the natural conclusion of the churchmen when Darwin published another book, *The Descent of Man*, in 1871. In this work he marshalled the evidence that man is related to all animal life. . . .[17]

Many in his own time denounced Charles Darwin for insulting the dignity of man by making him a relative of the apes. "Benjamin Disraeli solemnly declared that if it were a choice between apes and angels, he was on the side of the angels."[18] Darwin was making a claim for the unity of nature which many of his contemporaries found quite unacceptable. But Darwin was wrong in assuming that his critics had more in common with the beliefs of "savage societies" than he had. He reprimanded his critics for clinging to primitive ideas of an unconnected world of nature. In Darwin's own words: "He who is not content to look, like a savage, at the phenomena of nature as disconnected, cannot any longer believe that man is the work of a separate act of creation."[19]

What Darwin did not adequately realize was that he was himself helping to bridge the gap between science and the beliefs of the very societies which his contemporaries tended to describe as "savage" and "primitive". The idea of the oneness of nature lay at the heart of totemism as a system of values. Curiously enough, the first debates about totemism among scholars in England were taking place at the same time as the debates about the descent of man. The terms totem and totemism entered general circulation in the English language when J. G. Frazer published his studies *Totemism* just one year before Darwin published his *Descent of Man*. Frazer gave to totem its classical definition: "a class of material objects which a savage regards with superstitious respect, believing that there exists between him and every member of the class an intimate and altogether special relation."[20]

Of course the oneness of nature which Darwin was trying to sell to the scholarly world was not of the same kind as the oneness of nature which underlay many totemic belief systems. But the great breakthrough here in cultural convergence was the very postulate of a natural unity, even if the basis of that unity differed as between Darwinism and totemism. A whole movement has got under way in more recent times, manifesting a deep and sincere *ecophilia*. We define ecophilia as an affectionate concern for nature and the environment, tending towards their preservation. Because of the massive dangers of pollution and dissipation of natural resources today, ecophilia has entered a new level of militancy. It is no longer satisfied simply with preserving the beauties of the countryside, and conserving animal species that are endangered by the prospect of extinction. Ecophilia is now concerned about the very survival of the human species if the present trend towards dissipating the resources of this world is not soon reversed.[21]

The linkage of ecophilia with questions of survival does echo totemic predispositions. As Bronislaw Malinowski put it almost two generations ago:

> In totemism we see ... a blend of a utilitarian anxiety about the most necessary objects of [early man's] surroundings, with some preoccupation in those which strike his imagination and attract his attention, such as beautiful birds, reptiles and dangerous animals. With our knowledge of what could be called the totemic attitude of mind, primitive religion is seen to be nearer to reality and to the immediate practical life interests of the savage, than it appeared to its 'animistic' aspect emphasized by Tylor and the earlier anthropologists.[22]

A major difference between totemic schools of thought and religions like Christianity and Islam lay in the distribution of the soul. Islam has sometimes wrongfully been accused of limiting the possession of the soul not just to human beings alone, but to the human male alone. Many Western critics of Islam have made this assumption, though not always with any evidence from Koranic scriptures to substantiate this interpretation. It is certainly not true that Islam denies women the soul. Women have duties to God that are almost as rigorous as those imposed on men, and women know that they are held accountable to God when they die. The Islamic meaning of soul (*ruh*) rests on this concept of ultimate accountability after death. If women are accountable after death, they are by definition different from cows, trees, and fish. They are, in other words, classified in the same category as the male of their own species—and not relegated, as some critics would have it, to join the ranks of the "silent animals".

43

A major reason why Islam has been misunderstood in this regard is the absence of an adequate description of what life would be like for women in the hereafter. This in turn is due to the strikingly earthy interpretation of the hereafter in Islam. More than a thousand years before Freud, Muhammad seemed to have grasped the striking efficacy of sex as a factor in human motivation. Paradise in Islam became a place of abundance for the flesh, including availability of beautiful women for the male faithful. Capturing the idea of novelty as a compelling aspect of sex, Islam portrays these particular women as having been created specially for the enjoyment of the faithful after death. They are not women who aged and died, and then were resurrected. They were the equivalent of women in a foreign country, hiding in their very novelty extra-sexual compulsiveness.

But what about those women who had lived in this world, and then aged and died? If they were faithful, what kind of paradise awaited them? That women too enjoyed sex was something which every Bedouin knew. Muhammad was preaching to people aware both of the ecstasies of the male and the thrills of the female. But the idea of defining too closely what kind of paradise awaited the faithful women would have offended certain canons of delicacy and good taste. If women sometimes had dreams of being in the arms of strong he-men, it was indelicate to point that out as a promise to the faithful. More by omitting to describe paradise for the women, than by any explicit statement denying the soul to women, Islam gave the impression that the world beyond the grave was not for the female of man's own species. But this impression was carried only by non-Muslims. I have yet to meet a single Muslim in any part of the world, either orthodox or reformist, who believes that Islam denies the soul to women.

What is clear is that Islam, as well as Christianity, does limit the possession of the soul to *homo sapiens*. In that lay the special danger of autocentrism once again. If only man as a species possessed a soul, the rest of creation could be taken to be entirely for the pleasure of man, almost without restraint. Autocentrism of this kind carried the seeds of peril for other animals, and peril for the rest of the environment. The actuation of such dangers is what has more recently been called "ecocide"—the murder of ecology.

In his passionate plea at the 1972 Stockholm conference of the United Nations on problems of the environment Richard Falk asked for special penalties against those who perpetrated the sin of ecocide. And yet Falk's position sometimes links too closely the value of nature to the value of man. If nature is important only because man is important, autocentrism is still with us. If ecocide is wrong only because it

44

endangers "this planet", and creates doubts about *man's* survival, the environment is still denied a soul of its own. The value of ecology is still *derivative,* linked too directly to the needs of man. Ecophiles of this persuasion have made a good deal of progress since the days before Copernicus and Darwin, but there may still be one more step to take.

The step does imply going back to totemism, and investing in the environment a value independent of man. In the words of Father Placide Tempels:

> Herein is to be seen the fundamental difference between Western thought and that of Bantu and other primitive people. . . . We can conceive the transcendental notion of "being" by separating it from its attribute "Force," but the Bantu cannot. "Force" in his thought is a necessary element in "being," and the concept of "force" is inseparable from the definition of "being." There is no idea among the Bantu of "being" divorced from "force". . . . It is because all being is force and exists only in that it is force, that the category "force" includes of necessity all "beings": God, men—living and departed—animals, plants, and minerals.[23]

Driberg, in an earlier work, defines the Nilotic concept of "Jok" in terms which sees it once again as the force which unifies the whole of nature: "Jok then, like wind or air is omnipresent, and like the wind, though its presence may be heard and appreciated, Jok has never been seen by anyone. . . . His dwelling is everywhere: in trees it may be, or in rocks and hills, in some springs and pools . . . or vaguely in the air."[24]

A Kenyan Nilote, B. A. Ogot, has helped to confirm this interpretation of a force permeating all things:

> The spiritual part of man, the only part which survives death, is *Jok,* and it is the same power which is responsible for conception as well as for fortunes and misfortune. Hence to the Nilote Jok is not an impartial universal power; it is the essence of every being, the force which makes everything what it is, and God Himself, "the greatest Jok" is life force in itself.[25]

Strictly speaking, the Nilotes are not as elaborately totemic as, say, their neighbors, the Baganda. Totemism is divisible into two parts—the philosophical and the social. The philosophical does carry with it notions of the unity of nature, and power operating within the different sections of it. The social functions of totemism usually involve identification between clans and specific sections of nature, either species, like lions or cattle, or even snakes along the coast of East Africa, or sometimes, categories of plants or non-growing objects. Kiganda culture does include both philosophical and social aspects. Each of the four dozen or so patrilineal exogamous clans among the Baganda carries a principal and a secondary totem, usually an animal or plant, neither of which is killed or eaten by the clan. Totemism in this sense is a selective kind of animism. Animism—which is widespread in Africa—blurs the distinction between the living and the dead, between the human and the nonhuman, between the animate and the inanimate. Both nature worship and ancestor worship have made some contribution to animism.

Chinese and Indian civilizations also have borrowed from both nature worship and ancestor worship. Vegetarian doctrines in India are special kinds of ecophilia, an empathic identification with at least the animal part of the ecology. Hindu beliefs in the transmigration of souls postulate a constant interchange between human and nonhuman identities. The Brahmin of today may become an ape in his next incarnation. Hinduism gives Darwin the possibility of reverse descent. Underlying much of Hindu philosophy is a theme of naturalism, which was once very important for the pre-European approaches to science in India.[26]

In Europe the nearest approaches to naturalism of this kind came with pantheism. Under this doctrine lay an even wider concept of Monism, the assertion that the universe is one single whole of closely interconnected parts, God Himself being either the whole of this entity or the force which animates it.

Pantheism had considerable influence on English literature. Alexander Pope's "Essay on Man" was pantheistic in many of its philosophical outlines, sometimes in spite of Pope himself who preferred to be a more orthodox Christian. William Wordsworth was preeminently a poet of nature, one of the most important literary ecophiles in history. He combined this with a theory of diction drawn from the "natural speech" of the average man. Both his theory of diction and his fascination with nature provided Wordsworth with a sense of immediacy to the simple things of life.

Through primrose tufts in that green bower
The perrywinkle trailed its wreaths
And it's my faith that every flower
Enjoys the air it breathes.
The birds around me hopped and played
Their thoughts I cannot measure
But the least motion which they made
It seemed a thrill of pleasure.
The budding twigs spread out their fans
To catch the breezy air
And I must think, do all I can,
That there was pleasure there.
If this belief from heaven be sent

If such be nature's holy plan,
Have I not reason to lament
What man has made of man?[27]

Wordsworth is not only seeing a grand design of *joy* in nature; he also laments man's incapacity to fulfill that design.

Spinoza was the most complete of the pantheist intellectuals of Europe. He was of course earlier than Wordsworth (Spinoza influenced the seventeenth century; Wordsworth enchanted the eighteenth). But pantheism in Europe was at that time always a heresy. And in Catholic Europe pantheism carried the risk of excommunication.

Our preference for the principle of totemism—selective as it is when compared with either pantheism in Europe or animism in Africa—hinges on the degree of identification with what is nonhuman. The pantheist interprets the universe, often in highly intellectualized styles, but does not necessarily recognize any important duty towards the holistic universe of which he is a part. Indeed, pantheism has often been accused of recognizing no distinction between good and evil, of being too deterministic, of deciding to be neutral as between destruction and preservation.

Even animism sometimes can be somewhat neutral as between questions of destroying nature and of preserving it. Describing the universe as one interconnected whole does not by itself carry the duty not to destroy any part of it. Indeed, when the distinction between life and death is blurred, what does it matter who dies when? And if nothing is ever totally destroyed, but is simply transformed, does it matter if we transform green fields into barren deserts, clear rivers into dark streams of pollution?

A commitment is needed somehow to *preserve*. Totemism, in spite of its selectivity, provides this massive commitment to preserve. There are communities along the coast of East Africa who would not kill a snake because of a bond of brotherhood. The lion clan of the Baganda has the eagle as secondary totem. Kintu, the royal ancestor of the clan and indeed of the nation, killed a lion and an eagle, and turned their skins into royal rugs; the lion and the eagle thenceforth became sacralized. Members of the leopard clan may not eat meat which has been torn or scratched by an animal. A sense of identification so deep that one shrinks from abusing the totem is what is probably needed as a foundation to the new ecophilia.[28]

Of all the continents of the world, Africa has, per capita, the largest number of people who still refrain from drawing any sharp distinction between nature and man. Animists and totemists are still numerically stronger than the followers of either Islam or Christianity. And even among Christians and Muslims one finds strong continuing traditions of either wider animism or more selective totemism as a specialized form of naturalism.

It is therefore fitting that the first United Nations agency ever to be placed in Africa should be in fact that concerned with ecology and environmental problems. The decision by the United Nations in 1972 to make Nairobi the headquarters of the specialized agency on the environment was, in philosophical terms, a fitting recognition of a continent which has departed least from a doctrine linking man with nature.

The streams of divergent cultures continue to converge towards the global pool. Hindu belief in transmigration of souls, the interplay between Taoism, Confucianism, and Buddhism in China, the philosophical and literary pantheism of post-Renaissance Europe, the totemism of Melanesia and Polynesia, the totemism of native North America, and the animism of Africa, all pour forth into the new global pool of environmental concern.

Behind them all is still the figure of Copernicus, who challenged this planet's right to regard itself as the center of the universe, and struck a scientific blow against man's inclination to be dangerously autocentric.

Conclusion

We started this chapter by indicating that the link between science and religion is an important one from the point of view of the history of world culture. There were times when religion more explicitly promoted science, and some of the most striking successes of this kind of marriage are to be found in the history of Islam and of Puritanism. Both Islam and Puritanism evolved a scientific commitment which, at least for a while, indicated an impressive synthesis. But on balance it was not until the secularization of science that the dramatic expansion of scientific knowledge took place, as well as its transformation into technology. For as long as science was married to religion, science was relatively culture-bound in the narrow sense. The divorce from religion put the stamp of universalism on the scientific spirit, and gave that spirit added stature in the entire historical movement towards a world culture. Technology has remained relatively culture-bound since it relates to the fulfillment of defined cultural needs. Europe's supremacy in science in the modern period resulted in her supremacy technologically and this in turn prepared the way for her successful expansionism. The Euro-centric nature of world culture as so far inherited remains substantially due to Europe's scientific and technological preeminence. And in the sense we use it here "Europe" includes Europe's extensions—the United States, Canada,

Latin America, the European part of the Soviet Union, Australia, and New Zealand.

Technological change has its costs, among those just recently been discovered being the cost to the environment. The depletion of natural resources, the pollution of lakes and oceans, the pollution of the very air we breathe, add up to a technological cost that is only just beginning to be adequately apprehended.

A new religion seems to be called for, adequately sensitive to the claims of nature for protection, preservation, and nourishment. In a subsequent chapter we shall speak more positively about homocentrism, when by this we mean the concern with man as an immediate end in himself, rather than man as a means to God. But even homocentrism is a form of autocentrism, that persistent and very often pernicious tendency in man to see himself, or his tribe, or his nation, or his race, or his species, as the ultimate center of the universe. He even made God in his own image, and then pretended that God had made him in His. It became worse when man destroyed man in the name of God. This was an inversion of ultimate purposes. Homocentrism becomes a more tolerant commitment when it is contrasted with a fanatical subordination of the well-being of man to the presumed dictates of the Almighty. But even homocentrism has to be tempered with greater sensitivity to the claims of the nonhuman parts of our environment.

Can the poorer nations ever hope to catch up with the richer if ecophilia has its way? Is there not a danger that the protection of the environment, the safeguards against pollution and depletion of resources, would hit those who are starting afresh in their technological development, and simply maintain if not increase the gap between them and the more affluent sectors of the human race? That hazard is real, and has to be borne in mind in all calculations concerning ecological safeguards. Those who are already affluent may have to make certain sacrifices to accelerate the development of those who have not yet arrived in a manner which would do least violence to man's environment.

Social justice has to be linked to totemic justice. The promotion of equal dividends from nature's heritage among men has to be mated to the protection of nature itself. Relations between the different clans of mankind have not only to find a basis of justice among themselves, but also a basis of fairness to their joint totems in the universe as a whole.

Wordsworth was seeing the beginnings of the Industrial Revolution in England. Would he not now have reason to lament in his grave what man has since made of *nature*?

The stream of experience meanders on
In the wide expanse of the valley of time;

The new is come and the old is gone,
And life abides a changing clime.

The changing clime includes a resacralization of science in the face of its environmental costs. Freud traced totemism to patricide. The sons came to the father, obtained a momentary release from their Oedipus complex, substituted totem as a father symbol, and nevertheless observed the taboos of incest and exogamy. The new totemism of environmental protection requires a new *Oedipus complex,* involving a deep attachment to mother nature as a whole. Ecocide would then become matricide—and must at all cost be averted.[29]

The steps towards preventing this ultimate form of matricide must include a readiness to link science once again with some form of religion. Belief in totemic justice involves a major sacred value. While science once expanded by releasing itself from the embrace of religion, it must now discipline itself by reestablishing contact with ultimate moral principles. Because the moral principles are now oriented towards preserving mother nature itself, the resacralization of science need not now mean a retreat away from universalism. On the contrary, the new totemism is a reaffirmation of both universalism and the balanced dignity of everything that shares existence with man.

Footnotes

1. *Science and Civilization in China* (Cambridge, England: Cambridge University Press, 1971). The latest is part 3 (on civil engineering and nautics) of volume 4 on physics and physical technology.
2. Charles Singer, *A Short History of Scientific Ideas to 1900* (Oxford: The Clarendon Press, 1959), p. 157.
3. *Ibid.,* pp. 159–161.
4. Consult I. H. Hayward, *The Unknown Cromwell* (London: G. Allen & Unwin, 1934), pp. 206–230, p. 315.
5. James B. Mullinger, *Cambridge Characteristics in the Seventeenth Century* (London: 1867), pp. 180–181 *et passim.*
6. Consult Robert K. Merton, *Social Theory and Social Structure,* (New York: The Free Press, 1967), pp. 574–605.
7. Singer, *op. cit.,* pp. 1–2.
8. Charles R. Walker (editor), *Modern Technology and Civilization* (New York: McGraw-Hill Book Company, 1962), p. 14.
9. Singer, *et al., A History of Technology* (New York: Oxford University Press, 1956), p. 274.
10. A. N. Whitehead, *Science and the Modern World* (New York: Macmillan, 1925), pp. 137, 292.
11. Lewis Mumford, *Technics and Civilization* (New York: Harcourt Brace & Co., 1934), pp. 6–7.
12. Carleton S. Coon, *A Reader in General Anthropology* (New York: Holt, Rinehart and Winston, 1948), pp. 62–63.
13. *The Mountain People* (New York: Simon and Schuster, 1972), p. 142.

14. L. S. Stavrianos links this cynicism, and the literature of self-righteous power, to Social Darwinism as an ideological movement. The concept of the survival of the fittest was simply transposed from biology to politics, with important consequences both for racism and imperialism. See L. S. Stavrianos, *Man's Past and Present: A Global History* (Englewood Cliffs, N.J.: Prentice Hall, 1971), pp. 270–273.

15. Consult also Raymond Aron (editor), *World Technology and Human Destiny* (Ann Arbor: The University of Michigan Press, 1963); Albert H. Teich (editor), *Technology and Man's Future* (New York: St. Martin's Press, 1972); David S. Landes, *The Unbound Prometheus: Technological Change and Industrial Development in Western Europe from 1750 to the Present* (Cambridge: Cambridge University Press, 1969); and Walter Rodney, *How Europe Underdeveloped Africa* (Dar-es-Salaam: Tanzania Publishing House, 1972).

16. "Ethnocentrism", *Dictionary of Folklore, Mythology and Legend,* vol. 1 (New York: Funk and Wagnalls, 1949), pp. 351–352.

17. L. S. Stavrianos, *Man's Past and Present,* p. 271.

18. *Ibid.*

19. Charles Darwin, *The Descent of Man and Selection in Relation to Sex* (New York: Appleton, 1888), pp. 630–631.

20. Frazer, *Totemism* (London: 1887), "The Origin of Totemism", *Fortnightly Review* (London), April and May, 1899, and "Beginnings of Religion and Totemism among the Australian Aborigines", *Fortnightly Review,* July and September, 1905. These three essays were later published in Frazer's book, *Totemism and Exogamy.*

21. An eloquent ecophile who has related nature to man in a new way is Richard Falk. See his *This Endangered Planet* (New York: Random House, 1971). Consult also the more technical books emanating from the Massachusetts Institute of Technology, including *Man's Impact on the Global Environment* and *Man's Impact on the Climate,* along with the Club of Rome sponsored study by Meadows, *et al.* on *The Limits to Growth.*

22. See Malinowski, *Magic, Science and Religion,* with an Introduction by Robert Redfield (New York: Doubleday Anchor Books, 1954), p. 21. The original publication of this essay by Malinowski took place in 1925.

23. *Bantu Philosophy* (English translation) (Paris: Presence Africaine, 1959), pp. 35–36.

24. J. H. Driberg, *The Lango,* cited by Okot p'Bitek, *Religion of the Central Luo* (Nairobi: East African Literature Bureau, 1971), p. 50.

25. "Concept of Jok", *African Studies,* vol. 20, 1961.

26. See D. P. Singhal, *India and World Civilization,* Vol. 1 (Ann Arbor: Michigan State University Press, 1969), pp. 153–188.

27. "Lines Written in Early Spring".

28. I am indebted to Johan Galtung for further stimulation on the issue of denying nature a soul, which has been so characteristic of the dominant forms of Christianity. This theme was touched upon in Galtung's opening address, at the conference on "Dependency and Development in Africa", organized by the Canadian African Studies Association and the School of International Affairs, Carleton University, February 16–18, 1973.

29. Consult Sigmund Freud, *Totem and Taboo* (1950); Emile Durkheim, *The Elementary Forms of Religious Life,* translated by J. W. Swain (1947), and James G. Frazer, *Totemism and Exogamy.* It should be remembered that the so-called totem poles, carved with symbols of the royal North Pacific Coast families, are not totemic. They were originally made as grave posts, and the animals depicted are either heraldic or narrative. See, *Dictionary of Folklore, Mythology and Legend,* p. 1120.

CHAPTER 3

The Process of Cultural Convergence

The history of both religion and science reveals the immense possibilities of culture as a language through which one century speaks to another and as a system of ideas by which one society influences another. The phenomenon of acculturation, of transmission of values and ideas across primordial cleavages, has been one of the great forces of human history.

We have to understand this process further if we are to tap its resources for the sake of a new world order. We have to grasp the dynamics of social integration as an aspect of cultural change before we can adequately use the process as part of the pursuit of social justice, of economic welfare, and minimization of violence.

Towards Global Integration

The necessary process of integration in this regard would involve four stages of interrelationship between diverse racial, national, and cultural groups in the world. The minimum degree of integration is a relationship of bare *coexistence* between distinct social identities. Such groups need not even know of each other's existence. Even within single countries in the African continent, for example, there are tribal communities which have no idea where the boundaries of their country end, which other communities are their compatriots and which are not. Their coexistence with a number of other groups in the same national entity is not always a conscious coexistence, but it is there all the same.

On a world scale, bare coexistence is of course an even more striking phenomenon. Africa and Latin America, for example, though very similar to each other, know very little about each other. Such countries share a world, but not a consciousness of that world's extent.

The second degree of interrelationship between social groups is a relationship of *contact*. This means that the groups have at least some minimal dealings or communication among each other. These groups need not be on friendly terms. Tribes or nations at war are often in a relationship of contact. And by that very reason they are at a higher stage of integration, as compared with groups that merely coexist.

A third degree of integration between social groups is a relationship of *compromise.* By this time the dealings among the groups have become sufficiently complex, diverse, and interdependent to require a climate of peaceful reconciliation among the conflicting interests. The groups or nations still have clearly distinct identities of their own, as well as distinct interests. But the process of national integration has now produced a capacity for a constant discovery of areas of compatibility.

Between this stage of compromise to the fourth stage of *coalescence* starts the process of convergence. *From a cultural point of view, convergence is a process which either creates or discovers a growing sector of shared tastes, emotions, images, and values.* Cultural convergence need not result in total coalescence of systems which were previously distinct. The convergence may combine cultural diversity with cultural sharing. But when convergence goes beyond a certain point, the stage of coalescence is reached.

What should be borne in mind is that whereas coexistence, contact, compromise, and coalescence are *stages* in the process of integration, convergence is the subprocess which takes groups or systems from the stage of compromise towards the stage of coalescence. This last stage is a coalescence of cultural systems or ethnic identities, rather than a merger of economic interests. The diversity of interests would continue. Indeed, should the society become technically complex and functionally differentiated at the same time as it becomes culturally integrated, the diversity of interest would increase as the distinctiveness of group identities become blurred. Capacity for compromise would still be needed at the stage of coalescence. But the conflict of interest is no longer a conflict between total identities or autonomous cultural systems, but between identities that have gone far in the process of interpenetration.

By what mechanism does the process of integration move from stage to stage? Two factors are critically important in this—one is *conflict* and the other is *mobility.* Let us take each of these in turn.

A relationship of bare coexistence has little conflict potential. Somehow *contact* has to be established with other groups before conflict situations can seriously arise. The move from coexistence to contact might be caused by a number of different factors. Among the most important is simply the factor of mobility. Migrant trade, or movements of population, or a newly built road, could convert bare coexistence into contact. It is mobility rather than conflict which *initiates* the process of integration.

54

But then conflict as a mechanism begins to assume its relevance once the relationship of contact has been established. Conflict plays a crucial part in the movement from a relationship of contact to a relationship of compromise, and then from compromise to coalescence. It is the cumulative experience of conflict *resolution* which deepens the degree of integration in a given society. Conversely, unresolved conflict creates a situation of potential disintegration. The groups within the society could then move backward from a relationship of compromise to a relationship of hostile contact.

At what points in this four-stage process of integration is violence at its most pronounced? There are occasions when violence erupts at first contact, as when a tribal community feels imperilled by the arrival of foreigners, and proceeds to take violent steps of defense. But the move from coexistence to contact *need not* be accompanied by violence, though it sometimes is.

It is the move from contact to a relationship of compromise that almost invariably entails an intervening period of violent confrontations. Much of the interethnic and even international violence in recent human history has occurred between the stage of contact and the stage of compromise. Political analysts have sometimes assumed, for example, that racial intermingling would itself result in reduced racial tensions. In effect, ethnic intermingling at large first results in increased tension before it finally reaches a plateau of normalization and ultimate ethnic integration. Social scientists often underestimate the tension-generating effects inherent between the stage of contact between groups and the future stage of compromise capability.

Yet the four stages of coexistence, contact, compromise, and coalescence, do not operate in precisely the same way between nation-states as they do between ethnic groups. The factors which initiate change from one stage to another are different in a multistate region, for example, from what they are within a single territorial state. Whereas in relations within a single country it is indeed the stage between contact and compromise which has a high potentiality for conflict between ethnic groups that are compatriots, in relations between nation-states it is very often the stage between compromise and coalescence. In other words, the subprocess of convergence is precisely the one which carries both the greatest promise and the highest tensions. It is not without significance, as we indicate elsewhere, that the two most ghastly wars experienced by the human race so far started off as European wars. Of the three older continents of the world—Africa, Asia, and Europe—Europe is indeed the most deeply integrated, more so than Latin America, in spite of the greater diversity of languages in Europe than in Latin America. And yet it is from within the tensions of this very integrated continent that major conflagrations have erupted.

On balance Europeans cross each other's borders more often than any other peoples within a single continent. Hence it is in Europe that we can begin to sense the implications of mobility as a device for growing interpenetration, and the growing interpenetration as gradually both a factor which could lead to war—as it did in the past—and a factor that could lead to the formation of new regional organizations, as it has done in the case of the birth of the European Economic Community. Conflict and mobility once again play their part in the integrative process.

At the same time a cultural core of values about how best to resolve conflicts in the future is growing. Mobility creates not only physical interpenetration between groups, but also interpenetration in terms of ideas. And the constant search to find solutions to problems which have arisen among groups consolidates one aspect of culture—that concerned with the norms of handling disputes.

The final basis for a world of social justice, economic welfare, and minimum violence, therefore, must be a cultural core of such shared norms. The world must find a way to facilitate the process of convergence towards a shared human culture.

The Tensions of Cultural Coalescence

Can we be sure that even the achievement of cultural coalescence itself would help to minimize violence, let alone extend the boundaries of social justice and economic welfare? World history reveals not only the tensions of cultural differences, but also the tragedies of high cultural convergence.

The worst domestic sin of Hitler's Germany was the sin of genocide against the Jews. Yet the German Jews were the most culturally assimilated, in relation to their own immediate society, of almost all Jews in the West. German Jews were indeed deeply German. A large proportion of them were no longer practicing Jews religiously. Nor did Hitler care whether a Jew was now a Christian, or still went to the Synagogue. German Jews who were no longer Jews by religion should surely have been deemed to be more German than ever, if one insisted on viewing Judaism as "unGermanic". Yet clearly, not even the adoption of German Christianity as an approach towards "assimilation" saved the cultural aspirants.

Africa too has had its own examples of cultural convergence accompanied by violent tensions. The two most convulsive social revolutions in Africa took place in the two relatively homogenous little states of Zanzibar and Rwanda. There was perhaps a greater degree of brutalization in both Rwanda and Zanzibar than that experienced anywhere else in modern Africa. And yet these two countries were also culturally among the most deeply integrated of all the new states on the continent. Arabs and Africans in Zanzibar shared a language (Swahili), a religion (Islam) and other aspects of culture. They had also intermarried considerably. The Tutsi and Hutu of Rwanda also shared a language, a religion, and other important aspects of culture. They too had intermarried. They too had difficulty quite often in drawing a line between where a Hutu ancestry ended and a Tutsi descent began. The two communities had experienced biocultural assimilation.

Yet in 1959 in Rwanda an uprising of the Hutu occurred with devastating consequences for the Tutsi. This was before independence, which was finally granted on July 1, 1962. In January 1964, a month after Zanzibar's independence, both countries almost simultaneously experienced further agonies of convulsive acculturation. In Zanzibar, the Arab Sultanate was overthrown at a cost of thousands of lives, as yet only vaguely calculated. In the same month several thousand Tutsi were massacred by the Hutu in Rwanda, and an exodus of yet another 12,000 Tutsi joined the ranks of the 150,000 refugees who were already scattered among Rwanda's neighbors.

Burundi, a third eastern African country with considerable cultural integration, for a while experienced intra-Tutsi violence, as the different ruling clans of the Tutsi competed for authority, till the Republicans finally succeeded in deposing the Mwami from his throne.

But in 1972 Burundi too experienced its hour of convulsion. Amid mutual recriminations as to who started the massacres, there seems little doubt that many thousands across the country were butchered, the majority of whom were Hutu. Again, in spite of a shared language, a shared culture, and significant racial interpenetration, Burundi joined with Zanzibar and Rwanda as countries with the worst levels of mutual brutalization in the recent history of eastern Africa. And all three were at the same time countries of remarkable cultural integration.

Does the experience of these three countries indicate a logical validity to the policy of *apartheid* in South Africa? As we shall further explore in a later chapter, *apartheid* is an elaborate attempt to prevent cultural integration. The Bantustans as an idea, the establishment of "native universities", the discouragement of cultural as well as racial interaction, are all ultimately designed to avert cultural convergence. Would this aversion of cultural convergence also delay the moment of violent explosions? I now believe that the experience of Zanzibar, Rwanda, and Burundi does lend a respectable logic, though not a respectable morality, to what the racist regime in South Africa is trying to do. Given that the

57

white people want to remain in power unchallenged, the pursuit of cultural and social distance makes sense as an aspect of a strategy for the time being.

If the aim of the white people was simply racial harmony, this could have been acquired through economic justice and social equality. But economic justice and social equality could not at the same time ensure that the whites would remain privileged. Could the whites remain privileged and still pursue a policy of cultural contact, of meeting non-whites at sherry parties, of educating Africans in Westernized schools and universities? Was racial privilege compatible with cultural integration?

The experience of Burundi, Rwanda, and Zanzibar was emphatically negative. All those three countries sought to maintain some degree of racial privilege (for the Arabs in Zanzibar, for the Tutsi in Rwanda and Burundi), but accompanied by considerable cultural integration. The cultural integration simply accentuated the violence which later occurred. Because the peoples were so much alike, they were the more brutal against each other.

And yet, we have adopted the premise that the ultimate solution to problems of world order at large is the promotion and consolidation of a shared culture for the human race as a whole. How could a shared culture on a world scale help if it has led to such convulsions in smaller societies?

Consensus and Stratification

Assuming that a desirable world is a world of social justice, economic welfare, and minimum violence, the search for such a world is bedevilled by two crises—the crisis of dissensus and the crisis of stratification. For our purposes dissensus is the negation of consensus. And consensus in turn is definable in the following terms:

> Consensus exists when the members of social systems are in a state of affirmative agreement about normative and cognitive matters relevant to their action towards one another, towards the central persons or roles in the system, and towards persons, roles, and collectivities outside the system. Consensus is, then, agreement about the rules which should govern their conduct concerning the goals of the system and the allocation of roles and rewards within the system. There is another element present in consensus: this is a solidarity formed by a sense of common identity arising from ties of personal affection, of primordial (ethnic, kinship, or territorial) characteristics, of a shared relationship to sacred things, of a membership in a common culture or in a common civil community.[1]

It would be premature to think of the whole world as a social system in this sense, but there is little doubt that a viable world order which could guarantee economic welfare, social justice, and minimum violence would indeed require a wide degree of consensus on a wide range of values.

Consensus has been known to grow out of the experience of shared fear. Consensus on the preconditions of such a viable world order could only be obtained either through fear or through a shared culture. But basing a new world order merely on fear would not only make that order more fragile and possibly transient; it would also distort the quality of human life. Even the fear of world destruction as the sole basis of a new world order could not be sustained without psychological costs to man.

Shared culture is then the only effective alternative to shared fear. Culture thus becomes an infrastructure for consensus. Consensus on fundamentals needs the foundation of a shared outlook on a number of other issues as well. Consensus in a void is a contradiction in terms, unless it is exacted by brute force. And yet our experience in a culturally homogenized Europe, and culturally homogenized Zanzibar, Rwanda, and Burundi, tells us explicitly that a wide area of shared values is not by itself an adequate safeguard against large-scale violence.

What might be needed therefore is a further analysis of the problem of consensus in relation to social and political change. It is clear in some fundamental sense that the human community needs new types of policies. Yet consensus on policies is secondary consensus, subject to fashionable fluctuations. Primary consensus, on the other hand, is consensus behind a new system of stabilized values, from which policies may be derived or on which social action may be based.

And yet even that is not adequate to avert convulsion. What should a people in a social system be especially agreed upon? In order to avert violence, it is ultimately imperative that they be agreed on criteria of *stratification*. Stratification in our sense is that part of the social system which allocates differential rewards and distributes power and influence hierarchically. A stratification system includes both the Marxian class system and the Weberian status system. It encompasses castes as well as estates. In the words of Talcott Parsons, social stratification is "the differential ranking of the human individuals who compose a given social system and their treatment as superior and inferior relative to one another in certain socially important respects."

Karl Marx was right in assuming that social inequalities have a propensity towards social antagonisms. But he was wrong in assuming that, first, all class differences imply class inequalities; and second, that class inequalities always do erupt into class struggle. The propensity in the direction of struggle is not the same thing as the realization of that struggle. We know only too well that systems of gross social inequalities have often lasted much longer without tension than systems of relative egalitarianism. A good deal might indeed depend upon the degree of consensus behind the inequalities, rather than the degree of the inequality itself. The Hindu caste system, because of the sanctification and legitimacy derived from sacred validation, has survived longer without widespread challenge than some of the more minor inequalities between groups in modern Europe. Even more startling is the almost universal inferior status of women as compared with men through much of human history. Both the Hindu caste system and the relative subordination of women owe their long durability to the consensus behind them. Both the privileged and the underprivileged groups have for very long accepted in the main the legitimacy of the criteria of stratification.

When that legitimacy begins to be eroded, despite considerable shared values in other spheres, the moment of violent challenge may indeed be at hand. The Arabized Waswahili and the Swahilized Waarabu of Zanzibar might indeed have shared a language, a religion, a style of life—but the criteria of stratification in Zanzibari society were now undergoing a process of erosion. The relatively privileged position of the Swahilized Arabs within the system was no longer accepted as fully legitimate by the Arabized Waswahili, in spite of the fact that these latter had once indeed accepted the legitimacy of Arab preeminence.

Similarly in Rwanda and Burundi, the Hutu, who had for a long time not only acquiesced in but accepted Tutsi preeminence, were now no longer convinced of its legitimacy. In a situation of widespread shared perspectives on other issues, dissensus on stratification carries heavy possibilities of violence. There are occasions when a ruling group which is completely foreign and distinctive can command easier submission than a ruling group which is otherwise too intimately linked to the ruled. Certainly the white man in Africa, by the mystique of the very distance, culturally and pigmentationally, between him and his subjects, confronted less compulsive challenges to his legitimacy than did his successors—the black Presidents of new African republics. The problem of political legitimacy in Africa is partly a problem connected with power in the hands of an elite too close ethnically and culturally to the masses, and yet deprived of the sanctity of validated stratification.

It should be clear from this that the issue of the precise relationship between consensus and stratification has direct bearing on problems of containing violence, promoting social justice, and enhancing economic welfare. The stratification system colors conceptions of social justice, and when challenged, begins to demand a redefinition of that form of justice. Social stratification as a system of differential allocation of rewards also concerns issues of differential allocations of economic welfare.

Where the criteria of stratification are still widely accepted, violence would be minimized without economic welfare being widely distributed. But where those criteria are undergoing the pressures of a new scepticism, violence would rise.

Social justice as an ideal is more relativistic, more culture-bound, than either economic welfare or the question of what constitutes a reduction of violence. It is relatively easy to get people from different cultures to agree on what sorts of services or facilities would constitute improved economic welfare. Incomes can be assessed, proteins can be measured, housing can be evaluated, medical facilities computed. Economic welfare in this sense is quantifiable. Quantifiable also is violence to a considerable extent. Casualties can be counted, riots tabulated, the destructive power of weapons measured.

It is when we come to the ideal of social justice that a new problem arises. How do we measure social justice? How do we get agreement on such issues as women's rights, polygamy, attitudes to foreigners, attitudes to other races? All such rights and attitudes are circumscribed by different traditions and cultures. And within each culture the concept of social justice could change from generation to generation. The militant scepticism in Zanzibar concerning the legitimacy of Arab dominance was in part a call for a new definition of social justice.

Yet, in a sense, social justice is prior to economic welfare and minimization of violence. Welfare will not be equitably distributed nor violence be averted unless justice is done or is in prospect. From the point of view of evolving a more desirable world order, a basic clash which needs to be resolved is precisely this one between the primacy of social justice as a value and the extent to which it is culturally relative.

Since it is not possible to divorce social justice from culture, the only solution lies in making culture itself less "relative". In short, the solution lies in promoting some degree of cultural homogenization on a world scale, with a system of stratification capable of yielding both widespread economic welfare and widespread retreat from violence.

A Euro-centric World Culture

Fortunately, we are not starting from scratch. A world culture has already begun to emerge. International law itself is a herald of world culture, consisting precisely of those core values designed to handle disputes. Starting as a system of rules to govern relations between European states, international law has since been virtually globalized as a diplomatic code. We might therefore place international law alongside such phenomena as the Bible, computer technology, the plays of William Shakespeare, the music of Mozart, the modern school, and Scotch whisky—as elements which have entered the mainstream of world culture.

We must distinguish cultural convergence from cultural conquest. Convergence implies a "marriage of true minds", some minimal mutual borrowing between cultures. But the trouble with world culture as it has so far evolved is that it is disproportionately Euro-centric, Western derived. International law itself heavily bears the marks of its ancestry. The very name it bears manifests the original European preoccupation with nation-states as the ultimate units of diplomatic restraint. "Aggression" under that law became virtually definable as the wanton violation of the sovereignty of another *state*. The idea of committing aggression against another race or another tribe was somehow remote from the canons of international law.

For a while this Western international law worked, as the basis of stratification in terms of ruling races and subject races. It had yet to feel the full challenge of the scepticism of the underprivileged. Even as late as the 1960's, India's invasion of Goa was denounced as aggression against *Portugal*. A well-meaning and otherwise broadminded Adlai Stevenson passionately denounced India's invasion in the United Nations as a violation of the principles of sovereignty and aggression against Portugal. The fact that the Portuguese presence in Goa might itself have been a violation of the racial sovereignty of the Indian subcontinent seemed quite incomprehensible to Western critics.

New definitions of "aggression" were being sought in the 1960's, partly because the older international law was too protective of both colonialism and racism, and regarded both as fair game provided that the sovereignty of no nation-state was violated. Krishna Menon denounced colonialism itself as "permanent aggression". Clearly international law as a part of world culture needed to be reexamined, so that the overwhelming preponderance of Western norms could be diluted through the introduction of a few of the more passionately held principles of the Third World.

The global cultural scene contained a hierarchy of cultures—with Western culture enjoying preeminence at the top. In literature, as in international law, there continues to be a disproportionate Western presence in the shared global pool. Western literary classics are read throughout the world—but Asian and African classics tend to be limited to their own regions. No Asian or African author can ever hope to be a world literary figure unless he makes a particularly strong impact on the West. But a Western writer can shoot into world fame before a single Indian, Chinese, or African reader has seen a single work of his. Even the world prizes for excellence are Western-based and Western-awarded.

The Nobel Prize winner for the non-Western world is, by definition, someone who has first to convince a collection of northern Europeans, usually of Nordic stock, of the value of his work.

In Africa, a head of state—Nyerere of Tanzania—has translated two of Shakespeare's plays, *Julius Caesar* and *The Merchant of Venice,* into Swahili. It would be staggering if a British Prime Minister were ever to be interested in translating into English the much shorter Swahili poetic work, *Utenzi Wa Mwana Kupona.* Another African head of state—the younger Obote of Uganda—had given himself the first name "Milton" out of admiration for the author of *Paradise Lost.* No British politician in the foreseeable future is likely to adopt a name from Uganda in admiration of a local African poet there. No king or premier would so enthuse.

These examples—in their very hyperbolic dimensions—bring out the sharp contrast between Britain alone on one side and the whole of Africa on the other as contributors to world culture as so far evolved. Instead of genuine cultural convergence, we continue to have cultural conquest or cultural imperialism. When to this is added the even more startling Western leadership in technology, the case for better balance and better symmetry in human arrangements for the 1990's becomes inescapable.

Through mobility, the expansion of imperialism, and the whole process of the villagization of the world, much of human race has indeed moved from bare coexistence to contact, and from there onwards to an uneasy compromise of cultures. But the compromise is vulnerable precisely because of the imbalance. A cultural world with the Western heritage at the top is a world of a cultural hierarchy, when what is really needed is a world *federation of cultures.*

Two problems continue to be at the heart of it all—first, an *uneven creativity* between races and nations; and secondly, *uneven dissemination* of what has been created. In some fields, especially in technology, the West in recent times has been disproportionately creative. Even particular groups in the Western world—like the Jewish people—have been staggeringly innovative in relation to their numbers.

But while the West has definitely been in the lead in technology, we cannot be quite as certain that it has also been in the lead in the arts and philosophy. All we know is that Western art and Western philosophy have been *disseminated* more efficiently and more widely than any other intellectual heritage in the modern world. It may well be that the imbalance in both creativity and dissemination is in turn connected with an imbalance in mobility. We shall return to this more fully later. The physical mobility of people and the intellectual mobility of ideas are not only agents of dissemination, but may also be sources of creative stimulus. The tremendous mobility of Americans intercontinentally and intranationally, and of Europeans in terms of crossing each other's boundaries must be contrasted with the immobility of the great majority of people in Africa and Asia who have not yet been one hundred miles from the village in which they were born. A world of more balanced mobility is clearly called for, if the imbalance in creativity and cultural dissemination is to be redressed. And only a redressing of that imbalance can ever stabilize the emergent compromise relationships in world integration that have so far been achieved.

Certainly much of racism in the world assumes that certain cultural ways are inferior to others. The theory of apartheid in South Africa claims parity of esteem among different cultures, and seeks to institutionalize their separateness. The reality of apartheid in South Africa rests in fact on an assumption that African cultures and African ways are inferior to the ways of the civilized white man. A lack of equilibrium in mutual conceptions at the cultural level has helped to deepen the tensions between the races in South Africa.

It seems probable that a really symmetrical world culture would be both a cause and an effect of growing egalitarianism in the world, and help to consolidate balanced conceptions between peoples. Out of this should grow consensus behind a form of stratification that does not entail gaps that are too glaring. An egalitarian system of stratification is basically a contradiction in terms, but there can be no doubt that some stratification systems are further away from egalitarianism than others. As we indicated earlier, consensus could grow behind a very elaborate stratification system that has big gaps and inequalities, as witness the Indian caste system.

We are inclined to believe that consensus behind glaring inequalities can survive in very large states, but can never indefinitely survive either in very small states or in the world community at large. Zanzibar was a small political community, and the convulsion which occurred was partly connected both with the size of the community and the tensions of cultural integration. Rwanda and Burundi are also compact states in Africa, having achieved a high degree of cultural integration partly because of that compactness, but vulnerable to violent eruption again because the society is small enough to have a large sector of face-to-face public relationships.

India, the United States, the Soviet Union, are very large entities. The largeness militates against rapid cultural integration, though given the century that India has had, a depth of integration has indeed been attained. But consensus behind special types of inequalities in the United

States, in India, and in the Soviet Union is a little more tenable than could now be conceivable in a compact little community elsewhere.

But what is even more fundamental is that inequalities in India, the United States, the Soviet Union, can more readily command acquiescence than inequalities within an evolving world community. Cultural convergence on a global scale must therefore carry with it the seeds of counterassertion, and the possibility of the underprivileged being nonacquiescent.

Conclusion

A central premise of our approach is that the three world order values of maximization of welfare, maximization of social justice, and minimization of violence, are themselves values which are subject to modification according to the cultural perspectives of those seeking to realize them. We have mentioned before that the most culture-bound of all these values is the value of social justice. What is social justice to a German in Bonn need not be social justice to a Karamajong in Moroto; what is social justice to an American Indian in Peru need not be social justice to a Korean peasant.

But economic welfare is more easily shared as a value. And both the Korean and the Peruvian Indian may know the difference when they have more to eat, or newer clothes to wear, or a better house to live in. The quantification of economic welfare is a more manageable ambition than the quantification of social justice.

Violence also is a concept subject to some extent to ideological and cultural differences. Concepts like structural violence have already entered even in the general discourse of the existing world languages. What is violence? The answer varies to some extent according to the ideological position of the person defining it. Ideology is an aspect of culture or subculture. In fulfilling all these three aims therefore cultural variations have to be allowed the opportunity to interplay and seek acceptability.

Our perspective on world order puts a special premium on cultural convergence, partly derived from the conviction that a shared pool of values constitutes consensus. The reform of the world in the direction of greater social justice, enhanced economic welfare, and diminishing prospects for violence, requires human consensus behind some core values. The world of tomorrow can either be tamed through outright force or through shared values. And the shared values are what constitutes cultural convergence.

However, our analysis pointed up the paradox of violence emerging precisely out of cultural convergence. Case illustrations drawn from recent African political experience, in societies small enough to offer opportunities of discerning the dynamics of human relations, have in fact revealed the tension-generating defects of cultural integration.

The viable world order we are pursuing is not only one of reduced violence, but also of economic welfare and social justice. The cases of Zanzibar, Rwanda, and Burundi, revealed the agonies of violence. But why did violence take place? Mainly because the stratification systems within those countries were no longer viable. Cultural convergence was therefore helping to reveal more glaringly the injustice of a stratification system that was too unequal. The Arabized Waswahili of Zanzibar therefore rose up against their cultural kinsmen, the Swahilized Waarabu. The rebellion was in part a rebellion against a system of inadequate social justice and asymmetrical economic welfare.

The successful Hutu rebellion against the Tutsi oligarchy in Rwanda, and the unsuccessful Hutu rebellion against the Tutsi militariat in Burundi, were again convulsions connected with the pursuit of social justice. But all three have been very expensive rebellions in terms of the violence which accompanied them, as compared with the modest returns of egalitarianism achieved in Zanzibar and Rwanda. And even these returns are very fragile, tending at times in the direction of a reversed hierarchical tyranny.

Cultural convergence on a world scale, however, has happier egalitarian prospects, mainly because of the scale of the unit of integration. It would be unlikely that consensus would be obtained on a world scale behind a system of gross inequalities between nations, states, races, and cultures. Cultural convergence globally must therefore carry the seeds of human equalization. The consensus which would emerge would be consensus behind a global stratification system which is not too glaringly unequal.

Cultural hierarchy converts one culture into the dominant culture of the world, and yet the culture is primarily drawn from a specific subsection of the human race. The great change which needs to be made in the days ahead is to establish a principle of cultural ecumenicalism. In our sense this would mean a World Federation of Cultures, with the constituent cultures coordinating their status, and with the joint pool consisting of borrowing from a number of regional and racial cultural contributions. The principle of regionalism combined with a creative utilization of the languages of the world could gradually help to cope with the imbalance of contemporary arrangements, and solve the problem of uneven creativity and uneven dissemination. Mobility in both the intellectual and physical domain could be critical in directing the human race toward that globalized community of cultures.

Whatever the precise mechanisms used, the world does need a more equitable distribution of both creativity and its dissemination. Because of these considerations, we see world order in terms of a federation of human cultural contributions, combining a global pool of shared achievement with local pools of distinctive innovation and tradition.

It is this principle of cultural federalism that we must now proceed to define more fully.

Footnote

1. *A Dictionary of Sociology,* G. Duncan Mitchell, (editor) (London: Routledge and Kegan Paul, 1968), pp. 40–43.

CHAPTER 4

The Concept of Cultural Federalism

Paul F. Kress has argued that political analysis and creative literature are, on some levels, comparable: "at least in that they are two symbols systems, each possessing some coherent arrangement of internal characteristics, and consequently certain possibilities and limitations."[1]

Kress also draws our attention to Murray Edelman's work. Edelman has argued: "We may be able to learn something about expressive political symbols from aesthetic theory, for an art form consists of condensation symbols. Its function, like that of the abstract political symbols discussed here, is to serve as a vehicle of expression. . . ."[2]

Elsewhere in this book we discuss more fully the relationship between aesthetics and world order. But for the time being we need only grasp this crucial idea of "condensation symbols"—symbols which try to capture and condense a world of implications and associations. Like aesthetic theory, political analysis has to resort at times to the use of analogy and metaphor. The strength of metaphor lies in its comparative utility. It brings forth the associations of one category of life to illuminate a different area of observation. It is with those remarks in mind that we must now introduce the concept of a "federation of cultures" as an elaboration and systematization of the concept of cultural convergence.

As in many discussions of federalism, especially in the British Commonwealth, we may here begin, in condensed form, with K. C. Wheare's classical definition of federalism. What emerges from Wheare is that federation is a constitutional arrangement based on a division of powers between one central and several regional authorities, each of which is in its own sphere coordinate with the others, and each of which acts directly on the peoples through its own machinery of implementation. Wheare included as an important requirement that each government in the federation shall be independent of the others. In this case the modification made by A. H. Birch is both more realistic as to political federations as we have known them so far and more useful for analytical transference to this new concept of cultural federations. In the words of Birch:

> The relations between governments and modern federations are characterized by interdependence rather than by independence which would now be undesirable in view of the need for cooperation in many services. What is essential is not that the governments should be strictly independent of one another, but that they should be co-ordinate in their powers, so that none of them is able to dominate the others.[3]

Toward Defining Cultural Federalism

A cultural federation in our sense is not a neatly institutionalized arrangement but a pattern of cultural relationships based ultimately on three principles. These principles are, first, an acceptance of cultural interdependence among the constituent parts; second, an acceptance of the principle of parity of esteem among the constituent cultural units, "co-ordinate in their powers, so that none of them is able to dominate the others"; and third, a promotion at a federal level of "cultural fusion" which is the equivalent of sharing the central powers of sovereignty in a political federation. In a cultural federation, we might call the federal level the shared culture or joint culture; and call the lower units simply constituent cultures.

Interaction among constituent cultures often leads to an expanding scale at the level of the shared culture. In other words distinctiveness among the constituent elements might remain, but a pool of shared values and ideas might be growing at the same time. A classic case is that of the history of Europe in the last 400 to 500 years. There was an evolving but not yet consolidated French culture, an English culture or English "way of life", an evolving Swedish culture, and a fragmented German culture. But linking these different constituent cultures was a growing pool which came to be called "European civilization" and, later still, "Western civilization". The pool of shared values and shared prejudices and shared techniques began as relatively modest, deriving sustenance from shared wars, conquests, and general historical interaction. There was never full parity of esteem among the constituent cultures of European civilization. The English despised the Germans in some things; the Germans looked down upon the English in others; the French were contemptuous of both. But cultural domination by any constituent unit was, at least by the eighteenth century, rapidly on the decline. There was a time when the relationship between Ango-Saxon culture and Norman French culture was not really coordinated in the federal sense. The prestige and power of Latin and the classics in certain periods of European civilization were also a case of the negation of the coordinate principle, at least for as long as the Latin civilization was at once a constituent culture and a shared dominant culture. But when the French cultural power over the rest of Europe began to decline, and non-French Europeans began to be as selective in what they honored of the French heritage as the French had been in what they revered of others, a neo-federal principle was introduced in inter-European cultural relationships. The shared level of European civilization became a pool of contributions from the different constituent units, and no longer the imposed bequest from one constituent unit to all the others.

In the field of philosophy and social theory, names like Hegel, Hume, Locke, Rousseau, Machiavelli, and Kierkegaard have in their greatness been elevated to the federal level of the joint culture—European civilization. In literature, names like Tolstoy, Dostoevsky, Shakespeare, Moliere, and Goethe, have also been part of the shared federal civilization of Europe. In the field of politics, Europe shared institutions like political parties, parliaments, a cabinet system, the popular vote. In music, European civilization echoes with the grand sounds of Beethoven, Tchiakovsky, Chopin, Brahms. In the economy there have come some shared characteristics of industrial civilization itself.

As in the case of a political federation, cultural federation may start from the looseness of confederal relationships and then through a process of integration move gradually toward the unitary end of the spectrum of relationships. The growth of executive power in the United States, and the continuing spatial interpenetration derived from sophisticated means of domestic mobility, have made the present-day federal level much more powerful than the constituent units, and much nearer to the dominance of a unitary government than it is to the casual looseness of a confederate system. Likewise, the present-day level of European civilization is approaching unity, having started from pluralism and diversity.

What creates conditions hospitable to cultural federalism? Here again it may be worth our while to refer to the original model of political federalism, and seek to understand from that what it has to tell us about the nature of its cultural counterpart. K. C. Wheare discusses what he calls "prerequisites" of federal government. Let us look at these more closely and determine whether they are at all helpful in evaluating cultural relationships between units:

A sense of military insecurity and of the consequent need for common defence; a desire to be independent of foreign powers, and a realization that only through union could independence be secured; a hope of economic advantage from union; some political association of the communities concerned prior to their federal union either in a loose confederation, as with the American states and the Swiss Cantons, or as parts of the same Empire, as with the Canadian and Australian colonies; geographical neighbourhood; and similarity of political institutions—these half-dozen factors all operated in the United States, Switzerland, Canada and Australia, to produce a desire for union among the communities concerned.[4]

Framed in this manner, Wheare's prerequisites do not seem to be particularly relevant for cultural federalism in our sense. But some of the factors Wheare mentions might be useful for our purposes if, like S. W. Springer, we first divided Wheare's six factors making for unity into two classes—a class which may be called "predisposing conditions" and another which may be called "inducements".[5]

The predisposing conditions are the ones which Wheare describes as, first, geographical neighborhood; second, similarity of political institutions; and third, some political association prior to federal union either in a loose confederation or as part of the same empire.

The predisposing conditions turn out to be, in a sense, as relevant for cultural federalism as for political federalism. Certainly among the major factors for cultural homogenization in human history has precisely been "some previous political association", especially in the form of empire. British expansionism, and French imperialism to a lesser extent, have been among the great carriers of culture in the history of man. Aspects of Western civilization have been spread to social groups and geographical locations far removed from the West in distance and cultural points of departure. The world has made significant strides toward an evolution of a world culture precisely because of imperialism.

Geographical neighborhood as another predisposing condition for federalism is again as relevant for political as for cultural federalism. What ought to be borne in mind is that in any case the revolution of mobility in the world has transformed the concept of geographical neighborhood. Culturally, this transformation is even more striking. Cultural neighborhood is attained, in spite of large distances, where there is intellectual and cultural interaction from media, written, oral, and visual. The radio, television, newspapers, books, technical assistance in terms of teachers for schools, can all add up to cultural neighborhood. The whole trend toward McLuhan's concept of the global village is in part the villagization of the world in the cultural sphere, perhaps even more dramatically than in the spatial sphere.

Similarity of political institutions is another predisposing condition for cultural federalism, assuming that the similarity is not an outcome of prior cultural interaction. Accidental similarity of political institutions could create an atmosphere of potential political empathy. The

72

phenomenon of empathy is central to this book, but in this case we need only note that a discovery of cultural congruence, of areas of similarity between cultures otherwise different in origin, could itself foster smoother cultural relationships between the groups, and even lead to cultural fusion in due course.

The Crisis of Cultural Dominance

The British were fascinated by the Baganda from quite early partly because they recognized in the Baganda culture aspects reminiscent of their own, a case of cultural congruence between the colonizer and the colonized. And though their relations were at times tense, there were bonds of cultural empathy between the Baganda and the British, perhaps greater than between the British and any other African group. The monarchical tradition, the capacity to combine innovation with traditionalism, the cultivated air of reserve in personal relations, the reliance on special forms of training for the elite with an orientation toward a modernizing aristocracy, all combined as factors to make the Baganda almost natural cultural allies to the British. But since the Baganda were a subject people, this situation resulted in Ganda receptivity to Anglicization in a manner which did not shock the group out of its own traditional values. Indeed, the capacity of the Baganda to be deeply Anglicized and at the same time profoundly traditionalist has remained one of the fascinating aspects of the history of these people. If we look at the African continent as a whole, we see that it is very often those Africans who completely abandoned their roots who have later become particularly hostile to foreign influences and western ways. Their abandonment of their roots creates a sense of insecurity, and a struggle starts to recapture a little of the mystique of the past. Some of us turn to a form of dress which is clearly less Western, in our bid to reassure ourselves that we are indeed different from and more than mere black Europeans. Others use alternative devices, like libation in Ghana at a ceremony which is otherwise Western, or like an extra-mural lecture based on aggressive cultural anti-imperialism. Many of these elements, ranging from the wearing of colourful *kitenge* shirts to writing a poem of lament like Okot p'Bitek's *Song of Lawino,* are indications of a cultural complex among Westernized African intellectuals who are not yet adequately at peace with themselves.

But, on balance, the Baganda have been different. They have shown neither great evidence of Anglophobia nor ritualistic rejection of British ways. On the contrary, a study of the sociology of dress in Uganda would reveal that Ganda taste in dress is, by African standards, singularly British. Professor Lloyd A. Fallers, former Director of the East African

Institute of Social Research at Makerere and later Professor of Anthropology at the University of Chicago wrote:

> One of the striking characteristics of the Baganda is their ability to wear western clothing with a real feeling for style. Over much of Africa, western clothing is worn like an uncomfortable ill-fitting uniform, but Baganda men and women have penetrated sufficiently into the inner recesses of western style that many of them can wear Western clothes with real taste. . . . The Kabaka himself is an elegantly-tailored Cambridge-educated young gentleman who speaks flawless English.[6]

Because of the nature of imperial relationships, the Baganda have, of course, borrowed much more from Britain than Britain has borrowed from the Baganda. When cultural relationships are blatantly asymetrical, they do not amount to cultural federalism. We will remember that it is a precondition of the concept of cultural federalism that the constituent cultures should be "coordinate" and that "none of them is able to dominate the others". A preexistent cultural similarity between the Baganda and the British has helped to lead the Baganda toward the evolving world culture, but the world culture itself at the moment is of a kind which has a preponderance of Western contributions.

At the federal level of the joint culture in a world federation of cultures, no single heritage should be disproportionately represented if it can be helped. At the moment the situation is one where, partly because of the disseminating functions of Western imperialism, partly because of Western leadership in science and technology, and partly because of the preponderance of Western languages as lingua franca in world communications, the cultural currency of global exchange continues to bear the minting insignia of the West.

Our concept of cultural federalism here then must borrow to some extent the language of input and output used in other branches of the social sciences. In this case we see the joint culture as being a level which receives inputs from the different constituent cultures. These inputs determine which of the hundreds of cultural systems in the world are represented in the evolving world culture. The outputs of the system consist of fertilization from the joint pool to the smaller constituent cultures. Conceptually the different elements are so interconnected that it is the cross-fertilization among different smaller cultural systems which actually defines the very notion of a joint culture.

The principle of parity of esteem among constituent cultures demands that systematic attempts be made to facilitate diversity of inputs into the joint culture. In reality the common pool can probably never reflect a fair representation of all the cultural systems of the world. Indeed, since the representation is unlikely to be measurable in the way we count the number of representatives from a particular state, no complete parity of inputs from the different cultural systems is likely ever to be attained. What a world federation of cultures ought to aim at is ultimately a combination of two principles—the principle of cultural pluralism and the principle of a shared civilization. It is true that these two principles, to the extent that they are supposed to be both present, imply a profound paradox. But the paradox is not very dissimilar from the whole paradox of federalism, with its theoretical anomalies of divided sovereignty, and with the combination of one shared central government and several smaller regional governments at once interdependent and autonomous.

The emergence of just one culture in the world, with the disappearance of all others, would constitute a serious process of human impoverishment. Some degree of continuing plurality of cultural systems would therefore appear to be inseparable from optimum human versatility and diversity. On the other hand, the mere presence of hundreds of little cultural systems, each revolving round its own axis, would continue to deprive mankind of an adequate universe of shared discourse. That is why the symbolism of cultural federalism is so attractive as an aim for future human arrangements, since it concedes at once the desirability of pluralism and the imperative of global cultural integration.

The Four Dimensions of Culture

Culture has a number of dimensions or constituent elements which add up to a coherent social whole. We shall focus on four dimensions which we regard as the most fundamental of any sociocultural system. Within each such system there is, first, a *kinship culture* concerned with issues of dissent, marriage, succession, and kinship loyalties, obligations, and entitlements. The second subunit of the sociocultural system might be called, for lack of a more satisfactory terminology, the *intellectual culture* of the society. The intellectual culture is that part of the system which provides the framework of reasoning, the *presuppositions* of *inference and deduction,* the basic ideas of intellectual discourse, and the boundaries of analytical capability and abstract thought. It will be seen from this definition that the intellectual culture of a people has to determine and define areas of artistic creativity, scientific innovation, and the orientation of the society in relation to the past, the present, and the future. The degree to which a society approves or disapproves of change, promotes experimentation, and facilitates enlargement of empathy, are all deeply rooted in the intellectual culture of that people.

The third major subunit of a cultural system is the economic dimension. The *economic culture* of the people defines the means of production and livelihood in society, the techniques of economic distribution and exchange, and the *values* and *norms* underlying and motivating economic behavior. In some societies the economic culture is much more closely tied to the kinship culture than in others. In all societies the economic culture is partly conditioned by the horizons of the intellectual culture already available. Psychological change in society is one important area of interaction between intellectual culture and economic culture. The system of thought and analysis, in relation to innovation and experimentation, can profoundly determine the pace and direction of economic change. How people produce their food, how they construct their shelter, how they manufacture their other requirements and how they distribute them all, can be determined by the balance between a people's attitudes toward the past and their orientation toward the future.

The fourth subunit of culture important for us is *political culture.* By political culture we mean, quite simply, the values, prejudices, inhibitions, and ideas which condition political behavior in a given society and help to determine the nature of political institutions and the direction of political change. Again, kinship culture can be profoundly relevant for political culture in one society and less so in another. But economic culture and political culture are invariably interrelated in any society partly because politics is to a considerable extent concerned with the distribution of economic resources (the proverbial "Who gets what, when, how"). We shall indeed pay special attention to that area of contact between economic change and political behaviour, and discuss the whole process of economic development and modernization. We shall also be concerned with the phenomenon of violence in societies in relation to both political and economic areas of culture. In some cases violence as an outcome of deficiencies in the economic arrangements is precisely the connecting arm between economics and politics. Not all violence, of course, is economically inspired even when it is clearly violence concerned with social issues. After all, not all social issues are concerned with economics, whatever the Marxian intellectual system might presuppose. There are ethnic tensions in Africa, for example, which cannot easily be explained in economic or class terms. And yet all violence connected with social issues has to be seen in the context of political culture.

If there is to be a world federation of cultures, the balance of contributions from the different societies of the world will vary according to the dimension of culture. It is quite clear, for example, that Africa has much more to learn about efficient economic organizations from the West than the West has to learn from Africa. In the field of technology and science the Indians have more to learn from, say, the Japanese than the Japanese have to learn from the Indians. The representation of the different societies in the federal pool of cultures is for the time being bound to be heavily uneven in some spheres.

We mentioned that intellectual culture includes not only the framework of scientific reasoning but also the context of artistic creativity. That part of intellectual culture concerned with scientific progress will again be asymetrical when we are comparing the western world with the Third World. But that part of intellectual culture which is concerned with artistic creativity should provide a more balanced basis of cultural interaction. Reciprocal musical influences, reciprocal stimuli for sculpture and painting, reciprocal inspirations for poetry, are among the possibilities awaiting a more balanced federal pool in a world federation of cultures.

On balance, kinship culture tends to be more rigidly localized and more subject to the jurisdiction of constituent cultures than the other dimensions of culture we mentioned. In other words, although political, economic, and other intellectual ideas could be rapidly disseminated, transferred, and assimilated in spite of other cultural differences, kinship culture tends to be defiantly parochial. The norms and values conditioning relationships among kins are more resistant to dissemination than other values and norms.

And yet this is only in relative terms. Kinship culture is not untransferable—it is just less readily transferred than other subunits of a cultural system. In this book we hope to demonstrate that kinship culture has a profound bearing on race relations and the whole problem of color prejudice and tensions. Kinship culture could also seriously interfere with the quest for an enlarged empathy. Whether or not a people is capable of responding to humanitarian considerations, whether or not they disapprove of "miscegenation", whether or not politics and sex interact centrally in a given system, are questions which are substantially determined by the texture of the kinship cultures involved in a given situation.

What transpires from all these questions is the profound relevance of kinship culture to certain aspects of race relations. We hope to show in the next series of chapters that kinship culture has immense underlying implications for certain problems of world order.

We shall then address ourselves to the interplay between violence and political culture, and between development and economic culture, and the extent to which all these factors in turn affect the quest for a world of minimized violence, maximized social justice, and optimum economic welfare.

And at the end of that tunnel of man's groping may lie a world of cultural relationships which facilitate both cultural diversity and cultural synthesis, both individual innovation and human empathy.

Footnotes

1. "Self, System and Significance: Reflection on Professor Easton's Political Science," *Ethics,* Vol. 77, No. 1, October 1966, p. 3.This point is used in a related context in Mazrui, *Cultural Engineering and Nation-Building in East Africa* (Evanston, Illinois: Northwestern University Press, 1972). The use of analogy in political science is now all-pervasive. Eastonian political science, for example, heavily relies on metaphors like "input," "out-put," "parapolitical," "feedback" etc., and among modernization theorists in political science neologisms like "political goods," "political decay" have been creatively utilized.
2. *The Symbolic Uses of Politics* (Urbana: University of Illinois Press, 1964), p. 11. Consult also Ernest Cassirer, *The Philosophy of Symbolic Forms,* 3 vols. (New Haven: Yale University Press, 1953, 1955, 1957).
3. See K. C. Wheare, *Federal Government* (London: Oxford University Press, 1946). Birch, in a perceptive essay written for guidance to East African federation, discussed and elaborated on Wheare, as well as introduced important new perspectives. See Birch, "Opportunities and Problems of Federation," chapter 1, in Colin Leys and Peter Robson (editors) *Federation in East Africa: Opportunities and Problems* (London and Nairobi: Oxford University Press, 1965) pp. 6–29.
4. *Federal Government,* p. 37.
5. For more, see S. W. Springer, *Reflections on the Failure of the First West Indian Federation.* (Harvard University: Occasional Papers in International Affairs, 1962) p. 46.
6. "Ideology and Culture in Baganda Nationalism," *American Anthropologist,* Volume 63, (1961), pp. 677–686. This point is discussed more fully in the chapter comparing the Baganda with the Japanese as examples of precedence of confident response to the western impact.

Section II

KINSHIP CULTURE AND PROBLEMS OF IDENTITY

CHAPTER 5

Monogamy and Descent in Black-White Relations

Any scheme to restructure the political universe has to take cognisance of the problem of sexual mating as a world order issue. Sex is at once a profoundly private experience and a deeply social phenomenon. Some of the most far-reaching impulses and inhibitions in the human person as a social being are related to those aspects of intimacy between the sexes.

Formerly sexual issues impinged more directly on diplomacy. England's break with the Roman Catholic Church under Henry VIII was the outcome of an interaction among politics, religion, and sexual appetites. Indeed, the whole institution of dynastic marriages through the ages was a utilization of personal mating for international and diplomatic purposes. In our own age sexual issues enter world politics less through the marriage arrangements of monarchs than through the dynamics of race relations. It is therefore necessary to understand the nature and implications of interracial mating and interracial systems of descent as part of our attempt to diagnose the defective world order which faces us. In the next chapter we shall address ourselves to the impact of differential kinship culture on relations between black and brown races, with special reference to relations between Indians and Africans. What we propose to examine in this chapter is, first, the relationship between monogamy and racism and, second, the impact of differential miscegenation on systems of descent.

Because of the nature of this analysis, a wide comparative approach is essential. In order to understand the effect of Christian monogamy on black-white relations we shall also examine the impact of Islamic polygamy on black-Arab relations. The kinship culture of Islamic civilization has to serve as a foil to the kinship culture of the Christian heritage.*

Sexual Puritanism and Racial Intolerance

Would it be true to say that polygamy is more conducive to toleration of mixed marriages than is monogamy? The Germanic Europeans are among the most monogamous of the westerners. In the more literal meaning of the word, all westerners are, of course, monogamous: the laws of their countries do not permit more than one *wife*. But when we discuss monogamous *attitudes,* we are referring to *inclinations* even outside marriage. We see polygamy and monogamy as two points on a continuum. In general, the Germanic-speaking Europeans are more monogamous in their sexual moralism than the Latin-speakers are known to be. The French, Italians, and the Latin-Americans, are, in other words, less moralistic in their attitude to promiscuity than are Teutons and Anglo-Saxons. The case of the Iberian Peninsula is complicated by the direct, massive influence of the Catholic Church. Were the church as weak in the peninsula as it is in, say, France, it is probable that Spain and Portugal would have shared the sexual broadmindedness of their fellow Latins.

Given then that the Germanic peoples are more monogamous in their attitudes, is it merely a coincidence that they also happen to be more racialistic in their attitudes to intermarriage? Perhaps no Latin country could have produced a racist maniac like Hitler dedicated to "the purity of the blood". Perhaps only the Germans proper could have worked themselves up into such a frenzy about miscegenation. But theirs was an extreme case of something shared by other Germanic peoples. As Dame Margery Perham put it in her Reith Lectures:

> The Germanic-speaking Europeans—the British, the Germans, the Americans, the Dutch—share a deep bias against intermarriage with the Negro race. . . . This conscious, or sometimes subconscious, fear of race mixture accounts both for the [Germanic] white man's innermost ring of defence and also for all his outer ring of political, social and economic ramparts.[1]

Dame Margery does not go on to say it, but it is not entirely a coincidence that both Hitlerism and apartheid are outgrowths of Germanic kinship cultures.

What is being suggested here is that there is something about monogamy which probably encourages endogamy. On the other hand, we

---

*In this chapter we shall limit ourselves to polygeny, but we prefer the word "polygamy" because of its more general familiarity.

might say as a generalization that an attitude which permits a person to acquire a number of wives permits him at the same time to look beyond his own group for at least some of those wives. Monogamy as a limitation of matrimonial choice encourages group protectiveness, and seeks to assure that the girls in that particular society have adequate opportunities for honorable marriages with their own kind. But where a man is permitted to have more than one wife, the matrimonial opportunities of the women of his own society need not be imperilled, and the inner defensiveness in kinship relations is relaxed.

Of course intermarriage can be accepted without two societies really regarding each other as equals, with total racial toleration and reciprocal esteem. But it does mean that one important dimension of intergroup relations is, at least partially, depoliticized.

This is also connected with the basis of descent for the offspring of mixed marriages. To which of the parents does a child of racial mixture belong? Does it belong to the mother regardless of her race, or to the father irrespective of who the mother is? Or is descent determined by which of the two groups is higher or lower in the stratification of the given social situation?

Underlying this whole web of relationships is a connection between sexual puritanism and racial intolerance. Christianity played an important part in forging this connection. "Primitiveness" became partly defined in terms of sexual laxity. The white man's burden as understood by the missionaries included the ambition to tame the sexual appetites of "less civilized peoples". From this point of view, the Christian impact on Africa has to be seen as two-pronged. Africa witnessed what might be called the *Christianization of sexual relations;* and Africa also witnessed the *politicization of Christianity.* The Christianization of the world of sex prepared the ground for moral puritanism; the politicization of Christianity in Africa initiated the theocratic process by which imperialism ruled the continent in the name of the Christian God.

The Christianization of sexual relations arose out of the widespread belief among the early missionaries that the world of sex in African societies was a little too loose; that inadequate discipline was exercised over sexual appetites. The missionaries were bringing the Gospel to "heathen communities" steeped not only in superstition but also in sinful desires. The first behavioral imperative therefore was to control those areas of African life which helped to whet those appetites and desires. Discipline was of the first order, and a new regularity needed to be imposed. Even when the missionaries accomplished successfully the excellent mission of rescuing victims of slave-traders, and establishing settlements for them pending their rehabilitation, they took the opportunity

to transform the moral ways of these liberated victims. In the words of
the British historian, Roland Oliver:

> Within the enclaves there was no social ostracism to be endured for Christ's
> sake. . . . There were no sexual initiation rites and no ceremonial debauches
> to enflame the passions beyond their normal vigour. Instead, there was a
> new social solidarity calculated to support the ethical doctrines of Chris-
> tianity. Monogamy, the greatest stumbling block, was a condition of res-
> idence (in these enclaves), and polygyny in the new economic conditions lost
> much of its significance as the only means to wealth and power.[2]

The new schools which came into being proceeded to discourage important areas of African cultural life, on the assumption that these
contributed to moral laxity and sinful appetites. Africa experienced its
own interrupted symphony—the interruption of certain kinds of dance,
music, and drama as these were banned by missionary intervention.

A moral liberal and deeply Afrophile modern missionary who worked
in Uganda, F. B. Welbourn, cited the lament of a pious Christian English
woman: "We are told to make friends with Africans and to invite them
to our houses. But I cannot bring myself to regard as social equals men
who are polygamists. Perhaps I'm out of date and ought to go back to
England for good."

Trying to understand both sides, Welbourn attempted to define the di-
lemma for the Church in Africa, arising from the clash between western
Christianity and firmly rooted African customs. In the words of
Welbourn:

> The first missionaries . . . found a society that was polygamous by convic-
> tion. Bride wealth was an important aid to the stability of marriage. . . .
> They found a society where drunkenness was rife. Dances not only were an
> essential contribution to social well-being but often ended in unrestrained
> sexual promiscuity. . . . The first impact of Christianity on Buganda led to
> the banning of all traditional dances as potentially obscene. All African
> music was felt, in some way or other, to be connected with paganism and
> were therefore 'of the devil'.[3]

The banning of certain traditional forms of dancing and music has
remained in many East African schools to the present day. Some
changes have indeed taken place in some respects. Increasingly attention
is given to the possibility of using some traditional music for church
services. Welbourn referred to the adoption of the traditional Royal
Dance of Acholi, with suitable modifications, for use at Christian festivals. Today it is possible to see, on Uganda Television, Acholi dancing
by Acholi girls from schools which bear names like "The Immaculate
Virgin". Of course the girls are covered from neck to toe quite often, and

not just across their breasts and between navel and knee. But the movements of the traditional dance are now actually being permitted, duly covered up, on television under the sponsorship of a religious school.

And yet it was an Acholi poet, Okot p'Bitek, who put into the words of Lawino the lament concerning Africa's interrupted dances. Okot captured the clash of interpretations concerning what kind of dancing was obscene. Ocol, a westernized Acholi husband, apparently Christianized in his inhibitions, denounced to his wife, Lawino, traditional dances as "mortal sins". Lawino's own description of these dances does reveal why missionaries had reservations about them. The dances according to Lawino are held in broad daylight so that things can be seen openly.

All parts of the body
Are clearly seen in the arena,
Health and liveliness
Are shown in the arena!

When the daughter of the Bull
Enters the arena
She does not stand there
Like stale beer that does not sell,
She jumps here
She jumps there.
When you touch her
She says "Don't touch me!"

The tattoos on her chest
Are like palm fronds
The tattoos on her back
Are like stars on a black night;
Her eyes sparkle like the fireflies,
Her breasts are ripe
Like the full moon.

When the age mate of her brother sees them,
When, by accident,
The eyes of her lover
Fall on her breasts
Do you think the young man sleeps?
Do you know what fire eats his insides?

But Lawino then moves on to indicate how the ballroom dancing which her Christian husband approves of is to her more shameful than anything performed in a traditional Acholi arena. In the words of Lawino:

My husband laughs at me
Because I cannot dance white men's dances;
He despises Acholi dances

He nurses stupid ideas
That the dances of his People
Are sinful,
That they are mortal sins.

I am completely ignorant
Of the dances of foreigners
And I do not like it.
Holding each other
Tightly, tightly
In public
I cannot.
I am ashamed.
  . . .

Each man has a woman
Although she is not his wife,
They dance inside a house
And there is no light.[4]

What we have here are competing Acholi and western interpretations of obscenity.

But we also have in this section of the imperial experience, recurrent examples of the link between Christian versions of puritanism and European racial intolerance. The Africans were held in contempt partly because the styles of their sexual life offended the monogamous ideals of Christian morality. The fact that many white immigrants into Africa were at least as promiscuous as their native subjects did not make the white man more humble. A slave owner in the United States complained about the sexual looseness of the "Niggers" as he undressed to go to bed with one of his own slave girls. The monogamous theme in this case took the form of highly idealized morality. The white man's self-image fell short of self-recognition.

We must not make the mistake of many students of race relations and forget that the sexual act is a process of impregnation as well as of pleasure. We do not accept that inhibitions about intercourse itself across the racial boundary are the central variable relevant to the understanding of race relations. In this chapter we now proceed to emphasize the status of the child, rather than the nature of the act between the parents. It may well be true that the source of inhibitions may ultimately lie in the attitude toward the offspring of mixed marriages, rather than the attitude toward interracial intercourse. Residual disapproval of sexual intimacy across the racial boundary may still be compatible with a significant elevation of the status of the children of mixed marriages. And since descent is a matter of longer-term generational consequences than copulation, the central issue for cultural modification is the issue of miscegenation.

This inevitably brings into play additional factors of kinship culture, with all the conditioning of custom and religion. Interracial mating becomes in part an intercultural transaction. The principle of tolerance becomes inseparable from the mode of acculturation which is operating in a given situation.

In discussing the spread of Islam in the Nuba Mountains of the Republic of the Sudan, R. C. Stevenson referred to two parallel processes of social change: "one linguistic and cultural, by which the people of the land acquired Arabic as their language and certain Islamic cultural conceptions and became connected with the Arab tribal system; and the other racial, by which the incoming Arab stock was absorbed in varying degrees, so that today a modicum of Arab blood flows in their veins."[5]

It is this combination of acculturation and intermating between races which might be called a process of *bicultural assimilation.* Some degree of integration between groups is achieved by the process of mixing blood and fusing cultural patterns.

Symmetry in Bicultural Assimilation

Two concepts need to be further refined: symmetrical acculturation and symmetrical miscegenation. Symmetrical acculturation arises when a dominant group not only passes on its culture to the groups it dominates but is also significantly receptive to the cultural influence of its subjects or captives, that is, when cultural transmission is a two-way affair. Complete symmetry is impossible to achieve, and even if achieved, would be impossible to measure. What needs to be approximated is a significant reciprocal influence.

There have been occasions in history when acculturation has been asymmetrical, and yet the receiving group has been the politically dominant. The classic example is that of the Greek influence on the Roman conquerors. After the decline of Greece and the rise of Rome, Greek subjects succeeded in partially Hellenizing the Roman conquerors.[6] A more common example is the kind of asymmetry in which the politically dominant culture transmits itself to its subjects and captives and receives little in return. The British cultural influence in much of Africa has been of this type. We might call this descending asymmetry, and call the Greco-Roman example a model of ascending asymmetry.

Symmetrical miscegenation would arise in a situation where two racial communities intermarry and produce a comparable number of both men and women who crossed the racial boundary to seek partners from another community. In very isolated circumstances, and even there with some qualifications, such symmetry is conceivable. It may be conceivable in a situation where one race or ethnic group is patrilineal and the other is matrilineal. The matrilineal group might not mind its women crossing the border and marrying men from the other country. The patrilineal group, in like manner, might permit the men to be exogamous. But in such situations claims as to whether the mother or the father has priority in rearing the children, and how descent is to be determined, might become issues as soon as the married couple appear to be on the verge of separating. For as long as they are together, it is conceivable for a child to enjoy dual racial citizenship. To the matrilineal race, the child is regarded as sharing the race of its mother; while the patrilineal wing recognizes the child's racial affinity to its father. Tensions in such situations are conceivable, precisely in the duality of citizenship and the pulls of potentially conflicting loyalties. Symmetrical miscegenation in such an instance could indeed be approximated.

A much more prevalent phenomenon is that of *asymmetrical* miscegenation. Certainly, in the great majority of cases where black people have intermarried with non-black people, lack of symmetry has been a continuing characteristic.

Although in this chapter we are paying special attention to racial mixture as between white and black races, we are doing this in a broad comparative perspective, relating the issue to the Afro-Arab experience as well as to the different histories of racial mixture in the United States, Latin America, and South Africa. These latter three, when combined with the Afro-Arab model, provide four distinct patterns of the relationship between miscegenation and social structure.* And the types of miscegenation correlate closely to different nuances of monogamous culture.

All four models of miscegenation are asymmetrical, but in significantly different ways. In each case the dominant ethnic group has produced many more husbands than wives in the racial mixture. Seventy-five percent of the so-called black population of the United States has white blood, but overwhelmingly the white blood has come through white males rather than white females. Until recently, mating between whites and blacks in North America usually meant white men and black women.

*In this chapter we use the word "miscegenation" in the full realization that its origins are racialistic. The whole concept implied by it is based on a disapproval of racial mixture. Our own use of it is, in spite of the origins of the word, intended to be value free. By miscegenation we mean mating between different races, in or out of wedlock, resulting in children of mixed parentage.

The Latin American model is less straightforward, but it is still basically asymmetrical. It is the fairer-skinned males who have easy access to darker-skinned females, rather than the other way round. A factor which has in some respects accentuated the asymmetry in Brazil is the sexual prestige of the mulatto girl among white Portuguese.

> Gilberto Freyre has written that prolonged contact with the Saracens led to the idealization among the Portuguese of the type of the "enchanting Mooress", a seductive ideal with dark eyes, enveloped in sexual mysticism. ... Freyre suggests that dark-skinned women were preferred by the Portuguese for love, or at least for physical love.[7]

Within the African continent the asymmetry in miscegenation originated partly in the phenomenon of slavery itself. Both in South Africa and in Arabized black Africa, slavery was the breeding ground of asymmetrical miscegenation. The Boers in the Cape, and the Arabs in Zanzibar and the Sudan, helped themselves to female African slaves and produced children. The transmission of Afrikaner blood in South Africa and of Arab blood in Zanzibar and the Sudan was definitely through the dominant Afrikaner or Arab male.

In spite of the fact that all the four models of race relations that we are going to discuss are based on asymmetrical miscegenation, the fate of the children varies in fundamental ways among those four models. Do the children of a mixed marriage between a dominant race and an underprivileged race follow the father into the amenities of dominance or do they follow the mother into the handicaps of underprivilege? Or do they in fact become a class apart?

The answers to these questions are different in each case, depending on whether we are looking at the North American, the Latin American, the South African, or the Afro-Arab models. The precise fate of children in mixed unions has a great deal of relevance for the whole issue of a biological approach to national integration. Does racial mixture reduce cleavages between groups and in what way? The answers differ in the four models, and their pertinence to the integrative process has to be correspondingly differentiated.

Miscegenation: Descending, Ambivalent, and Divergent

We must again remind ourselves that acculturation and intermarriage do not necessarily result in social intermingling between the races or even in a system of desegregation. It very much depends upon the precise systems of descent observed by the race in question, and the general racial attitudes of the dominant race in a particular society.

One might say that there are four active models of relationship between blood mixture and social structure at large. One is the North American model. Within this model, whenever there is mating between a white person and a black person, the offspring is invariably "black". We may call this the model of *descending miscegenation*. Over threequarters of black Americans have Caucasian blood flowing in their veins, and yet they are categorized as Negroes or Blacks. Some states in the United States presumed to characterize a person's race by a calculation of how much Negro blood the person had. As recently as the 1960's, the law of white-dominated Florida defined a Negro as a person with "one-eighth or more of African or Negro blood". Further, the laws of Florida, like the laws of eighteen other states in the American union in 1963, specifically prohibited "miscegenation".* The correlation with monogamous puritanism was strong here. American rhetoric was full of the virtues of the happy family defined in terms of strict sexual faithfulness—though American practise fell short of that.

The second model, *ambivalent miscegenation,* is that of Latin America. In Brazil especially, the mating of a black person and a white person produces a mulatto or mestizo. Depending partly on the actual color he inherited from his parents the mestizo could either enjoy the same rights as the white person or the same handicaps as the black person. In other words, much of the prejudice in Latin America is color prejudice rather than race prejudice. Class stratification in Brazil does correlate substantially with the shades of skin color—the fairer the child, the better its chances of social success in the future.

The picture as a whole contrasts with the North American model in levels of puritanism, as well as in other respects. The idea of a married man having a mistress is treated with greater indulgence in Brazil than in the United States. That same toleration of extra-marital lapses among the Latins is extended to interracial "lapses".

The North American model of descent puts an emphasis on purity of blood, regardless of how fair the child is. Indeed, a person might have an indisputably white skin, but if the legal calculators of blood in Florida were to discover that one eighth of this white man's blood was "Negro blood", the white-skinned person would be reclassified as a black man. What this line of reasoning implies was disapproval of racial mixture *as*

---

*For quite a while, the United States Supreme Court had avoided a direct ruling on the constitutionality of laws which forbade mixed marriage. But those laws began to disappear in the 1960's in spite of the Supreme Court's inhibition. Enough changes were emerging from the political scene to make reforms in this direction inevitable. For a useful background article see Arthur Krock, "Miscegenation Debate", *The New York Times,* (Review of the Week), September 8, 1963. See also the article by Charlotte G. Moulton, published in *The Nationalist* (Dar-es-Salaam), November 11, 1964.

mixture. All one has to prove is that the child is of mixed parentage—and promptly the child descends to the status of the less privileged group. The Brazilian model by contrast does not condemn mixture *as mixture.* It may be indisputable that a child is of mixed parentage—but if the child is relatively fair its chances in life are improved accordingly. The Brazilian model is a purer case of *color* prejudice—a man is judged by his own skin color and not by the sexual tastes of his parents.[8]

During the colonial phase of Brazil's history, Francisco Manuel de Melo noted that "Brazil is the Inferno of Negroes, the Purgatory of White Men, and the Paradise of Mulattoes of both sexes."[9] It is unlikely that de Melo was ever right in this formulation. Brazil might indeed have been, and to some extent still remains, an inferno for Negroes. But it is clearly the white men that are in paradise, and the mulattoes that are in purgatory. The mulatto, a person of mixed parentage, could either find himself in the hell of black people or in the paradise of white people, depending upon the precise shade of his color.

Census figures in Brazil have tended to adopt the three categories of whites, Negroes, and "mestizos," the mixed group that allows also for the inclusion of Indian blood. But Brazilian census figures in these terms have always been bedevilled precisely by this phenomenon of racial mobility—the capacity of a person to move upward in race classification if his physical features and skin-color permitted it. Many light mulattoes, refined, educated, and of good appearance, must appear to be white. Mestizos appearing to be white are included as white, contrary to the practise in the United States, where one-eighth of Negro blood classifies one as Negro.[10]

This important distinction has struck other writers too. Donald Pierson has noted that while the American criterion was based on racial descent, the Brazilian was based on physical appearance. Pierson draws attention to the phenomenon of many Negro grandparents having grandchildren who are "white".

It is this consideration which leads to the conclusion that while in the United States the progeny of mixed marriages is classified as belonging to the less privileged group, the progeny of mixed marriages in Brazil could be classified either with the privileged or with the underprivileged depending upon physical features and color of skin.

In the white group, then, one finds not only true whites but also white phenotypes, that is, Afro-white and Indian-white mestizos reverting to white type. In the Negro group there are Negroes and Negro-phenotypes, mulattoes and *cafuzos* [Indian-Negro] reverting to Negro type. Finally, the mestizo classification shows the greatest lack of precision, for mulattoes, mixtures of Negro and white, are not distinguished from *caboclos,* mixtures of Indian and white.[11]

In South Africa we see a third category in which the progeny of mixed marriages between white and black are neither automatically black, as they are in the United States, nor entitled to upward mobility if physical features permit, as they are in Brazil. The South African model decrees that the progeny of a mixed marriage between white and black belongs to a group apart: the Coloreds. We might call this the model of *divergent miscegenation.* Like descending miscegenation, this third model is characteristic of conditions of sexual puritanism and racial bigotry.

Over threequarters of the Colored population of South Africa live in the Cape. The concentration of this mixed population coincides roughly with the settled districts of the western Cape during the slave period. The Coloreds have been defined as "the product of a dual process of westernization and miscegenation between whites, Hottentots, and slaves".

The puritanical streak again correlates with racial intolerance. The particular Christian denomination of South African Afrikanerdom, the Dutch Reform Church, is basically more puritanical than the major religious denominations of the United States. South Africa's dominant political culture bears the stamp of the Dutch Reform Church—and sexual intolerance within that culture intermingles with racial intolerance. The Immorality Laws of South Africa—forbidding sexual mating across racial boundaries—constitute a legal monument to this dual intolerance. Yet, as in the case of the American slave owner, monogamous ideals did not always result in monogamous behavior. And the very offspring were often relegated to the ranks of the underprivileged. The total subordination of the woman slave to the whims of her master, and the interest of the master in producing highly prized mulatto slaves, promoted a good deal of racial intermingling. In culture the bulk of the Colored population is a sub-group of the Afrikaner culture. Indeed, the great majority are native Afrikaans-speakers.

In the United States the Coloreds would have belonged more firmly to the "black" population, since any mixture of blood follows the line of less privilege. Under Latin American conditions the Colored population of South Africa would have been divided between the Blacks and the Whites, according to physical features inherited from the parental groups. Some Coloreds would definitely have been accepted fully as part of the Afrikaner population. But since South Africa is neither the United States nor Latin America, the Coloreds have remained a group apart, distinct both from the pinnacle of racial privilege and from the base at the bottom of that pyramid.[12]

Ascending Miscegenation

Our fourth model of the Afro-Arab polygamous culture can be studied in places like the Sudan and Zanzibar. The population of the Sudan as estimated on January 17, 1956, was 10,262,536, of which 39 percent was deemed to be racially Arab. The racial definition of Arab was in terms of membership, or claimed membership, of an Arab tribe. This constituted biological intermingling between the races, real or claimed.

But in a country like the Sudan there is also the linguistic definition of Arab to be taken into account, that is, a person is an Arab if his mother tongue is Arabic. Muddathir Abdul Rahim has estimated that 51 percent of the Sudanese speak Arabic as their first language and must, according to the census figures, be deemed to be Arabs. The linguistic definition hinges not on biological integration but on cultural or linguistic assimilation.

Although Abdul Rahim emphasizes the linguistic definition of Arab, he also draws attention to the remarkable racial intermingling in many parts of the Sudan. The two southern provinces of Bahr al-Ghazal and the Upper Nile are almost exclusively populated by Nilotics. There are also relatively unmixed communities, in the biological sense, in parts of northern Sudan. The central parts of the country illustrate considerable genetic mixture.

> Although Arab tribes predominate in the provinces of Khartoum, Blue Nile, Kordofan, and Northern Province, the Beja in Kasala, Westerners in Darfur, and the Nilo-Hamites in Equatoria, it is obvious that considerable racial mixing has taken place, particularly in the central parts of the country. A clear indication of this is the wide range of colours and features among the Sudanese Arabs (over half of the total population) who are, on the whole, much darker than other Arabic speaking peoples north of the Sahara and across the sea in Arabia.[13]

If in the Sudan the utilization of the linguistic definition of Arab increases the number of Arabs from 39 percent to 51 percent of the population, in revolutionary Zanzibar a linguistic definition of Arab would have nearly *halved* the Arab population. In other words, while the Sudan has more native Arabic speakers than it has people with Arab blood, pre-revolutionary Zanzibar had more people with Arab blood than it had native Arabic speakers. Many Arabs in pre-revolutionary Zanzibar were native speakers of Swahili, a Bantu language.

These differences indicate that the distinction between Arabs and black Africans is not dichotomous but has the complexity of a continuum. That was one reason why the Organization of African Unity was born as a multi-pigmentational enterprise. The Arabs as a race defy straight pigmentational classification, as we noted earlier. Within Africa itself the range of color among the Arabs runs indeed from white to black; even within Egypt, the range of color is virtually as wide as it is in the Arab world as a whole.

Afro-Arab intermingling contrasts sharply with the model of Afro-Saxon intermingling in the United States, Afro-Latin intermingling in Brazil, and Afro-Afrikaner intermingling in South Africa. To the Arabs the idea of "half-caste" is relatively alien. If the father is Arab, the child is Arab without reservation. If we visualize an Arab marrying a Nilotic woman in the fourteenth century and producing a son, the son would be Arab. If we imagined in turn that the son again married a Nilotic woman who bore a son—this son, too, would be an Arab. If we then assumed the process repeated, generation after generation, until a child is born in the second half of the twentieth century with only a drop of his blood still ostensibly of Arab derivation and the rest of his blood indubitably Nilotic, that twentieth-century child would still be an Arab.[14] It is this phenomenon which has saved the Arab-Negro division in Africa from being a dichotomous gulf—and converted it instead into a racial continuum of merging relationships.

In Pan-African literature it has been more the Afro-Americans than either the Arabs or the black Africans who have grasped this fact of the racial continuum. Edward Blyden, the nineteenth-century Liberian intellectual of West Indian birth, put it in the following terms:

> With every wish, no doubt, to the contrary, the European seldom or never gets over the feeling of distance, if not of repulsion, which he experiences on first seeing the Negro. . . . The Arab missionary, on the other hand, often of the same complexion as his hearer, does not "require any long habit to reconcile the eye to him." He takes up his abode in Negroland, often for life, and, mingling his blood with that of the inhabitants, succeeds in the most natural manner, in engrafting Mohammedan religion and learning upon the ignorance and simplicity of the people."[15]

Blyden here captures the paternalism which characterized missionary work both by Arabs and by Europeans. Nevertheless the social distance purposefully created by European missionaries in the areas in which they worked contrasts with the more integrative approach to proselytism adopted by Muslim missionaries. The Christian missionary even today may indeed walk among the people to comfort the sick, educate the ignorant, convert the heathen, and reform the sinner. But he does not mix his blood with them. If he is a Catholic, and has already been ordained, then he has taken the vow of celibacy, in any case. If he is a Protestant, and has been ordained, he has probably taken the precaution of getting himself a wife from home prior to coming to Africa.

By contrast, Muslim missionaries did not have to be monogamous, and were hardly ever celibate. Nor did they regard it as necessary to arm themselves with a wife from their own community before venturing into the darkness of Africa. In the words of by Blyden: "The Muslim missionary often brought to the aid of his preaching the influence of social and domestic relationships—an influence which in all efforts to convert a people is not to be entirely ignored."[16] What Blyden here is suggesting is the efficacy of biological integration as a method of cultural assimilation. He even quotes Dean Stanley's assertion: "The conversion of the Russian nation was effected, not by the preaching of the Byzantine clergy, but by the marriage of a Byzantine princess."[17]

It is arguable that the three most important ways of spreading a culture to other lands are, first, by purposeful cultural transmission and proselytization; second, by the flow of trade and its incidental consequences in the field of culture contact; and third, by actual migration of people from one land to settle in another. Imperialism is a means toward a means, helping to determine the magnitude of trade, cultural transmission, or migration.

Traders, Farmers and Marriage

Special emphasis needs to be placed on the phenomenon of trade and the incidence of cultural contact caused by trade. In the impact of Europe on Africa, the missionary and the trader were distinct specimens, though often in alliance. But in the case of the impact of Islam and Arab civilization on Africa, the missionary and the trader were often the same person.

Islam very often spread casually as a result of contact between individuals, and as a result of ordinary social intermingling between a Muslim and a non-Muslim. The Arab shopkeeper in a small town in Tanzania or the Sudan could converse about Islam to his animistic customers, and sometimes influence them toward conversion. The Arab shopkeeper may marry among the same alien people he served commercially, and through the influence of kinship and marriage he may at the same time unofficially proselytize for Islam. Or the Arab trader may be a nomadic businessman, moving from town to town selling his wares, while functioning also as a mobile mission for Islam. In the European penetration of Africa the missionary tended to precede the trader, and both in turn helped to prepare the way for the flag.

William C. McLeod, discussing the trader and intermarriage in colonial North America, put forward the hypothesis that a trading man was more ready than a settler to marry into groups other than his own. Concurrently, he disputed the theory that there were differing "Latin" and "Germanic" attitudes about interracial marriage:

> In contrasting the French and the English, [popular writers] make the cardinal error of comparing French traders not with British traders but with British agriculturists; and the needs of a French colonial regime which never developed to the point where the trading interests lost control with the needs of dominantly agricultural British settlements. French and British traders alike married Indian women and gave rise to numbers of half-breeds; and both groups were able to adapt themselves to Indian ways of life and the Indian manner of thinking.[18]

The Spaniards and the Portuguese, McLeod asserts, are indeed capable of intense racial prejudice. But their attachment to religion has tended to make the religious differences a greater barrier to adequate social intercourse than racial differences. The Moor and the Jew in Spain and Portugal were hated only so long as they refused to become Christians; Christianized they were racially absorbed by both the aristocratic and the commoner strata of the population.[19]

McLeod is here exaggerating the Iberian tolerance of Christianized Moors and Jews. And yet, in conceding the relevance of Iberian Christianity to their racial attitudes, McLeod was beginning to concede the relevance of Latin culture at large for differential behavior as between the Latin and the Germanic peoples.

McLeod emphasized the relevance of those aspects of culture which have to do with cooking, keeping house, and making general domestic arrangements. He insisted that these very mundane aspects of culture, often determined by whether the man has settled in one place for good or regards himself as a transient, have been far more important in determining racial orientations in matrimonial matters than the wider concepts of culture concerned with God and values.

> Farmers needed wives who knew the ways of European housekeeping and husbandry, who knew how to milk cows, fry eggs, and so on. Indian women would not do. The farmer, even in Virginia, so late as 1632, often preferred to pay the expense of importing women of questionable repute from the European cities, at considerable cost, than to take Indian women who would be helpless on a farmer's homestead. Champlain offered one hundred and fifty francs as a dowry to each French-Canadian farmer who would marry an Indian girl, but his offer was in vain.[20]

Herbert Moller, writing more than a decade later, reaffirmed McLeod's thesis. Moller took the position that the greater extent of interracial mingling in Spanish and Portuguese America could not be attributed to an inherently different attitude on the part of the Latin peoples in their relations with "the natives". The history of race relations in New France would, according to Moller, be an effective witness against such a position. During the second half of the seventeenth century, when the early French colonists were mostly males, there was no prejudice against alliances with Indian women. Only four marriages between French men and Indians were recorded at the time, but "left-handed marriages are known to have been frequent". But by the turn of the century, the sex ratio in the eastern parts of Canada was beginning to be fairly balanced, partly because the number of males was not radically increased by new immigration. With the balance came a decline in mixed marriages in Canada. On the other hand, the western parts of Canada still remained strongly masculine, and so did Louisiana. "Their concubinage with young Indian squaws was the rule through the eighteenth century."

Similarly, argues Moller, British colonists had relatively easy ideas about miscegenation for as long as there was a great shortage of white women, and moral attitudes had not been deeply influenced by white women. In addition, Moller suggests that the predicament of the new North American colonists, still unsure of the future and even of survival in very strange new circumstances, is sociologically comparable to the position of the trader settling in a village and being guided by the likely impermanence of his abode.

Once the agricultural pattern of life began to gain roots and the people were at last settlers, the aversion to mixed marriages began to rise perceptibly among North American colonists. Moller asserts that the kind of racial prejudices which grew up in North America were not imported from Europe. Such antipathies were, according to the writer, virtually nonexistent in the Europe of the seventeenth and eighteenth centuries. Racial aversions of the form which was found in subsequent decades of North American history, were, so to speak, native to the American experience.

> The most plausible explanation, so far, for the increasing avoidance of interracial marriage in the British colonies has been the need of agriculturalists and tradesmen for wives "who know the ways of European housekeeping and husbandry"; whereas traders, both French and British could afford to marry Indian women.[21]

Moller's own important contribution to the debate was his thesis regarding the influence of the white women on racial attitudes. Usually, the emphasis was on sexual insecurity in the white male as a major reason for his aggressive response to any suggestion of interaction between a black man and a white woman. Moller, on the other hand, argues that it was to some extent the sexual insecurity of the white woman combined with fears of unknown worlds of interracial sexuality which sharpened racial repugnance among certain sections of white colonists in North America. He also argued that women as a rule refrain from matrimonial and social relations with men of a lower social class or stratum than their own—female hypogamy. The majority of women persist in this attitude even if the price is life as an old maid and complete celibacy. Significant here is the tendency of women to identify themselves completely with their husbands or lovers, while men do not share this urge to any comparable degree. Hypogamy, as marriage beneath one's station, is considered with greater aversion by women than by men:

> Whereas in Europe this feminine attitude prevented women from marrying beneath their social status, it worked in America against their marrying into culturally socially inferior races. Moreover, through their enhanced influence on family and community life, women became more or less unintentionally the foremost agents in the establishment of racial barriers. Thus the development of aversion to racial miscegenation in the thirteen colonies can be traced to the invasion of feminine sentiments into colonial society.[22]

Valuable as McLeod's and Moller's contributions to theories of race relations might be, they both overemphasized white attitudes to the relations between men and women and did not pay enough attention to white attitudes to the *offspring* of mixed mating. It is true that disapproval of mixed marriage profoundly conditions subsequent attitudes to the children produced by mixed marriages. But that very attitude to the children is itself a changing phenomenon and has to some extent to be treated as an important additional variable in its own right.

It may be true that traders are more tolerant of mixed marriages than settled agriculturalists. It may also be true that much of the initial success of mixed marriages between Arabs and black Africans was partly attributable to the fact that the Arabs were structurally nomadic in the sense of being engaged in trade in eastern Africa and the Sudan. Yet this is not the whole story. Many Arabs settled in Zanzibar permanently, and still intermingled biologically with the black societies among whom they had established residence.

Similarly, in the Sudan, migrations of Arab tribesmen often resulted in Arab settlements, and involvement in trades and agriculture rather than commerce as such. There was a significant process of migration with whole populations settling in new areas. Fadl Hasan has even suggested that until the end of the fifteenth century the processes of Arabization and Islamization were "almost entirely accomplished by tribal migration". Inhabitants of the Sudan became Arabized and assimilated into the Arab tribal system.

> . . . the dominance of Arabic culture suggests, among other factors, that the Arab invaders arrived in large numbers and came to exercise a considerable influence over the life of the local population. Indeed, when Bruce travelled the country of the Ja'aliyyin towards the end of the eighteenth century, he saw no distinction between the indigenous population, who were already Arabized, and the Arabs (probably meaning nomads), except that the former continued to live in mud houses beside the river bank, while the latter lived in tents.[23]

Not all those who claimed Arab descent, or who included themselves more specifically in a particular tribal genealogy, did in fact have Arab blood flowing in their veins. The fluidity of genealogies and tribal affiliations exaggerated the degree of biological Arabization. What is clear is that the distinction which McLeod and Moller made between attitudes to miscegenation among agriculturalist settlers and such attitudes among traders was much less vindicated in the field of Afro-Arab relations than it might have been in North America.

An important differentiating characteristic is the much stronger patrilineal principle in Islam and Arab culture as contrasted with the culture of the Germanic peoples. The idea that the father determined the tribal affiliation of the descendants was the critical difference between the Afro-Arab model of ascending miscegenation and the North American tendency to regard the offspring of mixed marriages as belonging to the race of the underprivileged—that is, descending miscegenation.

Black Slaves and White Masters

Critical in the comparative histories of our models is the attitude to the offspring of slave girls mated to their masters. In the case of the American experience the law in the slave states asserted that if one of the parents was a slave, the offspring would follow the status of the mother rather than the father. The American historian Herbert Aptheker adds the following: "Generally, of course, where the parents were slaves and free, the mother was a slave and the father was a white man, often a slave owner, who, thus in accordance with the law had both pleasure and profit."[24] In his book, *Black Reconstruction in America*, W. E. B. DuBois refers, in parenthesis, to the consequences of that law in more vivid terms: "The law declares that the children of slaves are to follow the for-

99

tunes of their mother. Hence the practise of planters selling and bequeathing their own children."[25]

Perhaps because they knew of this rigid prejudice against miscegenation in the Germanic section of the New World (our first model), black Americans who went to Africa were impressed by the Afro-Arab racial continuum. In the United States the divide was dichotomous—it was between white men and Negroes. And a person could not pass as "white" if he was mixed enough to be "brown". In Africa, however, the division was between Arabs and black Africans—and yet there were many Arabs who were as black as black Africans. And so W. E. B. DuBois could make the following observation:

> Anyone who has traveled in the Sudan knows that most of the "Arabs" he has met are dark-skinned, sometimes practically black, often have negroid features, and hair that may be almost Negro in quality. It is then obvious that in Africa the term "Arab" . . . is often misleading. The Arabs were too nearly akin to Negroes to draw an absolute color line.[26]

Religion again played a part. Because Islam was polygamous, it was easy to legitimize concubinage and the offspring of such a union. A Christian slave owner, on the other hand, subscribed to a religion which permitted him the sexual services of only his single lawfully wedded wife. Concubinage, though practised, was stigmatized as immoral and the resulting children, illegitimate. Against the background of pre-twentieth-century prejudices, it was a short step from illegitimacy to exploitable orphanhood. The children of a white master were not necessarily his *descendants*.

Slavery helped create the mixed populations in the Sudan, Zanzibar, South Africa, Latin America, as well as the United States. But there was this persistent and fundamental difference between the mating of black slaves to white masters, and the mating of black slaves to Arab masters.

Within our first model of descending miscegenation based on experience in North America, we have already discussed the phenomenon of white masters making love to their slave girls, partly with a view to improving the quality of the offspring so that their own children may later be sold at a higher price. After all, lighter colored slaves often fetched a better price than very black ones.

Experience in Latin America, with special reference to Brazil, was somewhat less straightforward. It varied to some extent historically, depending partly upon the decrees of the government of the day. At certain times some families accepted the offspring derived from the mating of slave girls to white masters into the very body of the family, to be brought up as members thereof. But there was always an important section of opinion, sometimes triumphant in the legal process, which regarded the practise of accepting mixed children as members of white families as erosive of the essential basis of the caste society. In the words of Florestan Fernandes:

> The incorporation of the element of color in the legal nucleus of a great family would bring with it the formal recognition of social equality between the *white man* and the *Negro* or *mulatto*. In order to avoid this, petitions were drawn up opposing intermarriage and subordinating marital relations to endogamic standards. . . . The prohibitions did not affect sexual relations but only marital relations. Not only were the slave sex partners not elevated to the social position of the masters, but children born of these unions remained in the same condition as their mothers.[27]

Through much of the colonial period of Brazil, the Crown disapproved of concubinage, and the Brazilian church declared itself against such practises. Yet concubinage in Brazil remained alive for a long time, and was practised not only by masters but sometimes even by priests. Also widespread was a situation whereby children born of such unions assumed the status of their bonded mothers. For as long as slavery continued there was a strong tendency in Latin America, as in North America, toward *descending* miscegenation.

In this respect the experience of South Africa was similar. A slave woman who won the favor of her master in bed, and produced fair-skinned children, could indeed quite often improve her own status and the status of her children. But this would be an improvement within the slave system, being relieved of some chores, enjoying extra privileges, and perhaps even having supervisory power over other slaves. The children also perhaps were better fed than the children produced of unions of slave with slave. But the persistent pattern in South Africa, as elsewhere in the world of white slave-ownership, was to regard the children of slave girls as being themselves slaves, regardless of whether the father was free or not. Descending miscegenation continued to be the rule in conditions of slave-ownership. As Van den Berghe put it in relation to South Africa's experience:

> The close symbiosis of masters and slaves, and the total subordination of the female slave to her male owners made for extensive intermixture. Other incentives accelerated the process. Through miscegenation the female slave could improve her condition and the status of her children. The White Master, on his side, had, apart from sexual gratification, an economic interest in increasing and "improving" his human stock by producing highly priced mulatto slaves.[28]

Later on, when slavery was abolished, the idea of colored people in South Africa being a group apart both from whites and blacks began to consolidate itself. Divergent miscegenation became the new pattern. But in the background was the whole experience of regarding children born of a union between a master and a slave girl as being themselves slaves.

Black Slaves and Arab Masters

The differences between this phenomenon of slavery in the white world and in the Arab world have had important consequences for the status of the children of mixed mating. In Islam any child born to a slave girl by her master is legitimate: the legitimacy in this case confers upon the child descent from his father, including the status of a free-born and rights of inheritance; and this descent confers upon the child links with the father's tribe. In slave conditions, Islam insists on ascending miscegenation. If the father is Arab the child is Arab, regardless of whether the mother is a wife or concubine, and regardless of the nationality of the mother.

If a similar system of descent had been operative in the United States, the majority of those who are now called "blacks" would, in fact, have belonged to the "white" community. They would have acquired this paternal descent simply because most of the children of mixed unions in the United States have issued from white fathers and black mothers. If the Germanic and Anglo-Saxon cultures had had as sharp a principle of paternal descent as the Arabs, the population of underprivileged black people in the United States today would have been much smaller. The bulk would have been assimilated *upward* into the dominant and privileged community.

In South Africa, the application of the Arab principle that the father's tribe determines the child's tribe would have tilted the balance of population as between English-speaking whites and Afrikaans-speaking whites, as well as affecting attitudes to gradation of color within the system as a whole.

The racial prejudice of the whites is solely responsible for the social existence of a distinct Cape Colored group, a fact recognized by many "moderate" Afrikaners today, and indeed by some Hertzogites as early as the twenties. Except for the concern with color of South African "Whites" (many of whom have themselves "Colored blood"), Afrikanerdom would be nearly twice as large as it is today, and would outnumber the English-speaking whites by well over two to one. For every six white Afrikaners there are approximately five Colored Afrikaners and four English-speaking Whites. In the entire population there are four non-Whites to one White, if color is the criterion; but, if the mother tongue is taken as the criterion, there are only two non-Europeans to one European.[29]

In the Latin American model of racial mixture the application of the Arab principle of paternity would have made another kind of difference—it would have obliterated to some extent the categories of mestizo and mulatto. Given that the child follows the father in tribal or racial affiliation, the so-called white population would have become more varied in skin color; and conceivably also the non-white would also have had a variety of colors. But the balance between the groups—white, black, Indian would have had a different basis. Variations in color would still have been significant but the relative populations of the different groups would have been substantially changed, reducing in the process the number of those who were relatively underprivileged.

In Islam, however, the color of the offspring is certainly no reason for denying its paternity and descent, even in a situation where the mother is a fair-skinned Arab and so is the father. Reuben Levy, a Cambridge professor, draws our attention to the following hadith: "The extreme case is quoted, or invented, of a Bedouin Arab who came to the Prophet declaring that his wife had given birth to a negro child, and hinting that he wished to repudiate it. Muhammad, however, refused him permission to do so. . . ."[30]

Levy also draws our attention both to the legitimacy of children born in concubinage and to the concern of the tribe as a whole in ascertaining the paternal link with the tribe.

> In Islam it is sufficient for the father to acknowledge cohabitation with his wife or slave to establish the legitimacy of the child. . . . Seeing that concubinage is lawful in Islam, it is not necessary for the mother of a child to be married to its father in order for it to be declared legitimate. . . . The powers of the father over his children are very great [but] He cannot sell them into slavery. . . . [Normally], indeed, the legitimacy of a boy is a matter of some concern to the father's family or tribe. . . .[31]

Arab patrilinealism in Zanzibar, reinforced by Islamic prescriptions, resulted on the one hand in the cultural assimilation of the Africans into Islam, and on the other into the biological Africanization of the Arab immigrants. The local indigenous populations imbibed imported culture to a considerable extent, while the future composition of the Arab population in the island absorbed genetically important African strains.

When, in addition, the racial intermingling led to the emergence and consolidation of the Swahili language as the national language of Zanzibar, problems of differentiating Arab from non-Arab became compounded. The result was considerable ethnic fluidity. We know that

103

social mobility is the capacity of a person to move from one class to another; but Zanzibar had in addition racial mobility in the sense of the capacity of a person or even whole subgroups to move from one racial category into another.

Before the revolution, the Arab minority in Zanzibar was described as "Sub-Saharan Africa's second largest alien oligarchic minority"—in proportional size second only to the white community of South Africa. But if the South African method of descent had been applied to Zanzibar, and the Zanzibari method of descent had been applied to South Africa, South Africa's proportion of whites would have been greater than it is today, and Zanzibar's proportion of Arabs would have been much smaller than it was at the time of the revolution.

The substantial issue to be borne in mind is precisely the ethnic fluidity which was characteristic of Zanzibar's racial situation. In the 1930's and 1940's the Arab population in Zanzibar increased significantly, not because new immigrants had arrived from the Persian Gulf, nor because the Arabs' natural rate of reproduction had suddenly taken a sharp upward turn. In 1924 the Arabs constituted 8.7 percent of the total population of Zanzibar, by 1948 the Arabs were up to 16.9 percent.

A small fraction of this increase was doubtless Arab. But the vast bulk of the increase in the Arab population had to come from within Zanzibar society, from among segments of the population which had previously opted for categories of self description other than Arab. Between 1924 and 1931 large numbers of former non-Arabs changed their minds, as it were, about the ethnic category most suited to their own descent and decided to "join" the Arab community.[32]

On the coast of Kenya during the colonial period similar shifts in racial categorization took place. The Arab population of the coast of Kenya was barely 20,000 by the 1948 census. The population rose by a few thousand in the early 1950's simply because groups of Arabized coastal tribes, previously designated as non-Arabs, were at last given recognition by the British colonial authorities as Arabs. They had themselves been pressing for such recognition from the British colonial authorities, though their credentials were challenged by those who were already recognized as Arabs. The British colonial authorities, perhaps partly influenced by the bewildering fluidity of intermingling between Arabs and Africans, decided to confer the more prestigious title of Arab upon the new claimants from the coast.

The advantages which Kenya coastal Arabs enjoyed as against Kenya coastal Africans were sometimes more than just prestige. Terms of service for jobs were, during the period, categorized as European, Asian, and African terms of service, in descending wage levels. The Arab sector, by its racial ambivalence, was sometimes eligible for the Asian terms of service, and sometimes not. Certain banks in Mombasa classified all Arabs as Africans, and paid them accordingly. East African Railways and Harbours also classified many Arabs as Africans and paid them accordingly. And yet in much of the civil service within Kenya, Arab civil servants were often regarded as being eligible for Asian terms of service. The pigmentational and racial ambivalence of the Arabs converted them into marginal men.

In the entertainment world there were also differentials in privileges among the groups. A symbolic differential concerned films which were given the grade of X by the censors in colonial Kenya. X-films in Kenya meant "Not to be shown to Africans and children under sixteen." The term "African" at the initial introduction of the censorship law encompassed Arabs, and so they too for a while were kept out of film shows rated X. It took a demonstration organized by a prominent Mombasa Arab, Shariff Abdulla Salim, to force the Majestic Cinema in Mombasa to admit a group of militantly defiant local Arabs. Once the breach was made at the Majestic Cinema, gradually the term X as a category of censored film excluded only Africans and children under sixteen, but accepted the Arabs.

This resulted in conferring significant powers of racial categorization on the gatekeepers and ticket-sellers at the cinemas. An African could indeed acquire the privilege of seeing an exciting sex film, or a film involving violence, if he could convince the booking-office clerk or the gatekeeper at the Regal Cinema that he was an Arab and not an African. On the other hand, a black Arab might have to argue his way, or even bribe his way into the cinema, if the clerk insisted in regarding him as an African.

In the Sudan, ethnic fluidity has also been a persistent feature of the whole process of acculturation. It is true that the initial impetus toward Arabization was given by the coming of large numbers of Arabs and Arab immigration continued in varying volume over many years. But Sudanese Arabs themselves often grossly exaggerate the numbers of Arabs who came in. Much of the population of northern Sudan is a population of Arabized Africans, rather than Arabs as such. Whole groups began to identify with particular Arab tribal names, and genealogies grew up, of varying authenticity, establishing the Arabness of the different groups.

Unfortunately we know remarkably little of the way in which Arabization was accomplished. The whole of our knowledge is derived from two different types of sources: the first, a limited number of contemporary medieval

Arabic writings and the second, a large body of Sudanese genealogical traditions which in their present form were compiled at a much later date.[33]

Fadl Hasan admits that the genealogical traditions which are at the moment current in the northern Sudan indicate a high degree of Arabization. But he warns: "However, any conclusions that are drawn from these genealogies as to tribal origin, must be accepted with some reserve."[34]

The sheer fluidity of ethnic affiliations, and the cultural pull of the dominant identity, have resulted in a high degree of integration in northern Sudan. Denominational differences in religion assumed a greater political significance in the Sudan than the racial categories of the northern population. Disputes as to whether such and such a family is really Arab by descent or not, and evaluations of family prestige partly in terms of lighter shades of color, have all remained an important part of the texture of Sudanese life in the north. Prejudices based on color have by no means disappeared. There are black Arabs, deeply black, whose credentials are fully respected in relation to their Arab genealogies. There are others who may be a shade lighter, and yet have their Arab credentials disputed by at least some families. The political sociology of shades of color remains a part of the Sudanese scene; but the phenomena of intermarriage and miscegenation on the basis of patrilineal descent have resulted in a more integrated model of racial mixture than that afforded by either the North American, the Latin American, or the South African experience.

Arab Arrogance and White Apartheid

The gradual conversion of the Sudan today to Arabism and its culture is in part a repetition of what went on in Egypt earlier. The Sudanese process appears noticeable partly because the majority of Arabs in the world are fairer than black Africans. What is often overlooked is that Egypt was conquered by the Arabs from the deserts of the Peninsula who were darker than the Egyptians they subjected. The Arabs from the Peninsula were also darker than the Syrians whom they converted to Islam in that first wave of conquest. The Fertile Crescent and Egypt, partly because of their diplomatic prominence over the centuries, began to be identified with the leadership of the Arab world. Because their inhabitants were fair, it was assumed that the very origins of Arabness implied light Mediterranean skin. If the Sudanese Arabs are dark, so are many of the inhabitants of Mecca and Medina. They may not be as dark as the Sudanese, though some of them are. The Arabs of Mecca and Medina are a blend of Asia and Africa, while the Lebanese and Syrians, for example, are a blend of Europe and Asia.

In their expansionism the Arabs have insisted on asymmetry both in culture and in miscegenation. This is the essence of Arab arrogance. It is certainly true also with regard to the Arab impact on the Sudan. Arabic is a conquering language, sometimes absorbing a little of the local languages, but in its very pride tending toward ultimate triumph. Patrilinealism, as we shall indicate, operates in terms of permitting and even encouraging Arab men to marry women from other communities, but forbidding or discouraging Arab women from similar unions.

The example of Zanzibar, on the other hand, is distinct. The Arabs in Zanzibar stood for asymmetrical miscegenation, but they also stood for symmetrical acculturation. The Arabic language was not an irresistible conqueror, flattening out local linguistic opponents. On the contrary, many Arabs of Zanzibar actually ceased to be Arabic speakers, and became instead native speakers of Swahili, a basically Bantu language. The Arabs of Zanzibar had allowed themselves to become less "Arab" than the Egyptians and Sudanese had done—and yet at the time of the revolution, the Zanzibar Arabs were regarded as less native to their part of Africa than northern Sudanese were to theirs.

The passionate hatred of the Arabs at the time of the revolution within Zanzibar was, in some ways, one of the most remarkable anomalies in contemporary African history. There seems to have been more passionate hatred of the Arabs in Zanzibar than there was hatred of the white man in Tanganyika. It is true that there were differences in situations. Some of the worst brutalities committed by white people against local Tanganyikans were committed by the Germans, before the British assumed control after World War I. The British, the new rulers, were also exclusive in their social habits, but they were not as arrogant or as cruel as the Germans in Tanganyika. Nevertheless, there is no escaping the fact that the British were a small minority of people, conferring privileges on local Indians and local Europeans, exercising considerable hegemony over Africans, and clearly demanding separate treatment.

The Arab oligarchy in Zanzibar, on the other hand, mixed socially with the Africans, called many Africans uncle or cousin, shared the same religion with them, prayed shoulder to shoulder in mosques, appreciated the same jokes, sometimes frequented the same brothels. Yet, by 1958, it was already clear that a deep anti-Arab animosity had consolidated itself in large sectors of the African population in Zanzibar. When race riots erupted in 1961, there was no doubt that all the years of mixed marriages and reciprocal acculturation had not resulted in minimizing hostility.

The question which arises is whether that hostility may have been partly due to the very interpenetration which had taken place between the groups. Had the British, by keeping themselves completely apart, averted in the short run those depths of feeling? It is true that in Kenya there was sufficient anti-British hostility to erupt into a Mau Mau insurrection, but again was it significant that the Mau Mau movement took place among the Kikuyu, the most acculturated of Kenya's peoples at that time, partly because of their very nearness to the British authorities? Elsewhere in Kenya there was resentment of the white man, but nothing of the depth manifested against the Arabs on that tragic island of Zanzibar in January 1964. The problem which this raises is whether tension and hostility increases rather than diminishes when the dominant group narrows the cultural gap between itself and the underprivileged group.

According to this thesis, the Arabs of Zanzibar expedited their vulnerability to African challenge as they themselves became more culturally African. Were the Arabs not arrogant enough? The adoption of the Swahili language as the dominant language of Zanzibar, and the decline of Arabic except in a section of the Arab population was, in some ways, an establishment of cultural parity between Arabian culture and the Bantu linguistic cultures. But did this bring the revolution nearer? Are there occasions when economic imbalance is indeed stabilized precisely by cultural compartmentalization? Where a dominant group looks and speaks differently, and displays a very different way of life, it may perhaps have to face less of a challenge than if it mixes more fully with the population and reduces the social and cultural distance.

In the latter situation where the cultural differences are fading, the economic imbalance becomes more conspicuous. By becoming almost the only residual difference between the privileged and the underprivileged, the economic disparity becomes the more exposed.

It might, therefore, be said that those who worked out the philosophy of apartheid were basing their experiment, at least in the short run, on sound sociological grounds. If the economic imbalance between the whites and the non-whites was to be stabilized for a while, it made sense to attempt to keep the cultures apart.

And yet such stability can only be a short-term achievement. It is true that Zanzibar remains a tragic case of biocultural assimilation. The population was becoming a relatively homogeneous Swahili-speaking people, sharing the same religion as well as the same language. It may also be true that the situation became revolutionary precisely because an economic imbalance based largely on land-ownership persisted in spite of cultural homogenization.

But the tragedy of Zanzibar may have been the tragedy of a premature racial revolution. Sudan may remain unsure as to whether it is part of the Arab world or black Africa, but independent Zanzibar could not have sustained its Arab identity for much longer. The mixture of the population internally, the retreat of the Arabic language, the emergence of a Swahili culture, and the links which this forged between the island and the black East African mainland, were almost bound to accelerate the de-Arabization of Zanzibar. Indeed, the anti-colonial movement itself had already divided the Arab community between those who continued to take pride in their Arab descent and those who were emphasizing their Zanzibari identity. By the year of independence it was the latter who were winning. Independent Zanzibar would have been the most culturally integrated of all countries south of the Sahara, with the possible exception of Swaziland, Rwanda, Burundi and Somalia. Just as many Africans in colonial Zanzibar had found it expedient to claim Arab descent, so many Arabs after independence would have found it expedient to emphasize their African descent.

It should not be forgotten that the "minority" government which was overthrown in January 1964 had obtained 46 percent of the popular vote only a few months earlier—by no means a "small" minority. In an election seven years before that (in 1957), the school of thought represented by this minority government—"ours is Zanzibar nationalism"—won less than a quarter of this support. In other words, support for this concept of the *Zanzibar nation* was growing rather than diminishing when the revolution took place. But these trends were never tested under conditions of independence since the Zanzibar revolution took place within less than four weeks of the attainment of independence.

But what if Arabism had remained strong in Zanzibar in spite of independence? In such a case the long-term solution would have had to lie in the *ascending* nature of Afro-Arab miscegenation. Let us assume that the Arabs had remained dominant, had continued to intermarry, and had still recognized all children with Arab fathers as Arabs. In such circumstances, and given no sharp differences in fertility between Arabs and Africans, the proportion of local Arabs to local Africans could have continued to increase. It had certainly been increasing for the previous three generations, both because of ascending miscegenation and because the racial composition of Zanzibar was fluid enough to make it possible for some unmixed Africans to claim Arab descent.

It is precisely this principle of ascending miscegenation which makes a fundamental difference between prospects for racial mixture in the Sudan today as against such prospects in southern Africa. Claims that the Sudan and southern Africa afford examples of similar racial situations are at best naive, or more likely propagandist.

The Portuguese territories in southern Africa are an imperfect illustration of the *ambivalent miscegenation* of Brazil, but with greater discouragement of mixed unions than is now characteristic of Brazil.[35]

Rhodesia, with its Anglo-Saxon background, started with *descending miscegenation*. The population of Eur-Africans had been increasing. They were the offspring of European fathers and African mothers. In the villages they were accepted in the communal way of life and brought up according to the custom and language of the mother. But the disintegration of village life, and the drift toward the cities, have brought to the surface the problem of these racially mixed people. While fellow Africans in the villages had readily assimilated the "half-castes", the Africans in the cities have shown greater distrust of these lighter-colored members of the lumpenproletariat.

The Eur-African has also had problems with European employers. As one observer put it some years ago: "He goes to a prospective employer, but owing to his light skin the white man expects him to know English (as all 'Coloreds' do) and generally be more sophisticated than an African straight from the kraal, which is all he feels himself to be. He is again rejected.[36]

But how many Eur-Africans are there in Rhodesia? The exact numbers are as obscure as they were when the following observation was made: ". . . the total Eur-Africans in the Native Reserves can scarcely be less than 10,000; it might be even ten times that number. Nobody knows. But it is growing faster than ever.[37]

But even at that stage the situation showed signs of future transformation from descending miscegenation (as in North America) to *divergent miscegenation* (of the South African "Colored" Model). Eur-Africans in Salisbury had begun to appeal to the government for recognition as a distinct community, for compulsory registration as such, and for rights of compulsory education.[38]

Since its Unilateral Declaration of Independence, the chances have increased for Rhodesia to drift toward the South African system of apartheid, complete with divergent miscegenation. Ian Smith's own views about Africans displayed early symptoms of sexual repugnance and racial stereotyping. He told 200 journalists at a news conference in London on the eve of U.D.I. that he had regular confidential reports of the "sordid happenings" in some countries in Africa with black governments. In some places, Mr. Smith asserted, European parents dared not let their daughters go to school without escorts. "This is the kind of conduct which Rhodesia is resisting!"

When asked if Africans in Rhodesia should be denied universal franchise because one minister in a black African state had tried to seduce a stenographer, Mr. Smith retorted angrily: "It was not a case of seduction. It was attempted rape. How would you feel if that had happened to your wife or daughter?"*

It seems doubtful that Rhodesia will succeed in working out an apartheid system which will go to the extent of creating Bantustans. What is more likely is that Rhodesia is evolving a system intermediate between the old American model of descending racial mixture and the current South African model of more rigid compartmentalization.

This contrasts sharply with the problem of southern Sudan. The war in the south flared up precisely because the Khartoum Government was *opposed* to the idea of maintaining the south as a separate Bantustan. For as long as the south was kept separate, and assumed that it would remain separate, tension was minimized. But the very attainment of independence in the Sudan created fears among southerners that they would no longer be left alone, and subsequent policies of deliberate cultural assimilation increased those anxieties. Again, precisely because the Sudan does not practise apartheid, the danger of tensions between groups is coming sooner. Converting the south into a Bantustan, as the missionaries had done, delayed for quite a while the outbreak of hostility, though memories of prior interaction and slave-raiding remained vivid. And as the Sudanese now intermarry, and as Arabic acculturation gathers momentum, the price which will be paid will be in terms of increased social tension, at least for a while.

It is unlikely that asymmetrical miscegenation in the Sudan will ever come to an end. The Sudanese, as well as black Africans like the Dinka, are too patrilineal to evolve a system where both men and women may marry as they wish across racial boundaries without incurring certain social reservations. But the system of *ascending miscegenation* guarantees a form of upward mobility which has no equivalent in any other type of racial mixture.

Symmetry in acculturation is more feasible in the Sudan than elsewhere in the Arab world, and has, to some extent, already taken place. The recency of cultural contact has produced varieties of Arabic in the Sudan which bear the strong imprint of non-Arabic African languages. The cultural symmetry in the Sudan is not quite of the level attained in Zanzibar or Persia where the local subjugated group profoundly influenced the conqueror culturally, as well as permitted itself to be

---

East Africa and Rhodesia (London) October 14, 1965, p. 95. Disapproval of mixed *marriages* in Rhodesia is even stronger than disapproval of casual mating between the races. A distinguished United Nations official was once denied a job at the University College in Salisbury because he had a white wife. The man was himself a black Rhodesian.

influenced thereby. Nevertheless, the degree of reciprocity in the Sudan is greater than farther down the Nile, or elsewhere in the Arab world now that Zanzibar is no longer part of it.

But the most stable of all interactions is a combination of cultural symmetry and economic balance. Where the groups learn from each other as well as teach each other, without creating a society of vast disproportion in economic advantages, the prospects for a stable society are good.

The emergence of socialist ideas in the Sudan may reinforce the levelling tendencies of race mixture. The Sudanese Communist party is certainly the largest in independent Africa and one of the oldest south of the Mediterranean African countries. The party's political fortunes have varied from regime to regime, but it has played a part in disseminating more moderate socialist values to other groups in the Sudan which are less explicitly Marxist.

The triumph of an egalitarian ethic seems likely in the Sudan in the long run. Northern Sudanese intellectuals are disproportionately left of center, however anticommunist some of them may be. If the country survives intact, the Sudan may be the first modern nation in Africa to have creatively used a combination of socialism and sex for national integration. It remains to be seen whether the polygamous origins of both Arab and African cultures of the Sudan would add an additional relevant ingredient to that exciting political chemistry.

Conclusion

In our attempt to demonstrate the relevance of kinship culture to world order problems, we have examined in this chapter the political sociology of patterns of matrimony and descent across racial boundaries. Afro-Arab relations were used as a foil to Afro-European relations in exploring this domain of human experience.

We sought to demonstrate that strict monogamous attitudes correlated with other forms of intolerance. Those who are sexually puritanical tend also to be contemptuous of cultures which are more promiscuous. A Germanic white man may tolerate an individual member of his own society who is sexually lax—but would find it difficult to respect a foreign culture he suspects of honoring permissiveness. Strict monogamous puritanism tends to correlate with racial intolerance, including a disapproval of racial mixture at large.

Indigenous black African cultures are on the whole polygamous. Attitudes to those cultures among early Christian missionaries were strongly conditioned by a sexual premise. Civilizations which were polygamous were, ipso facto, "primitive". Christianity in Africa was therefore more culturally arrogant in its attitude to native custom than Islam had been.

But the real importance of interracial mating from a sociological point of view is less in the sexual divide and more in the ranking of the children. It is because of this that we categorized miscegenation as ascending, descending, ambivalent, and divergent.

The beginnings of social treatment must lie in social diagnosis. Man must understand himself before he can attempt to cure himself. The issue of racial gradation is a fundamental world order problem. An understanding of the kinship cultures involved in that gradation must therefore be deemed to be a precondition of success in man's most formidable task—autotherapy in the political domain.

From our analysis, ascending miscegenation has emerged as a particularly promising approach to the long-term difficulties of racial cleavage. But even this approach—though still better than the other three—falls far short of equity and parity of esteem between races. The very qualification, "ascending", signifies a hierarchy of relationships. But whatever solution may emerge in an ideal federation of cultures on this issue of sexual compromise, the federal pool of values in such a federation would do well to borrow more from the experience of ascending cultures than from the other systems of cultural constraints on sexual behavior.

What ought to be maintained is the quest for symmetry in biocultural assimilation for the sake of both equality between races and parity between the sexes in the years ahead.

Footnotes

1. *The Colonial Reckoning,* (Collins Fontana Library, 1963) pp. 64–65. Consult also Ali. A. Mazrui, "Political Sex," *Transition,* No. 17, 1964.
2. *The Missionary Factor in East Africa,* 2d ed. (London: Longmans, 1965) p. 64.
3. *East African Christian* (London: Oxford University Press, 1965) pp. 104–105; 114–115.
4. Okot p'Bitek, *Song of Lawino* (Nairobi: East African Publishing House, 1966) pp. 34–35, 41.
5. "Some Aspects of the Spread of Islam in the Nuba Mountains (Kordofan Province, Republic of the Sudan)", in I. M. Lewis (editor), *Islam in Tropical Africa* (London: International African Institute, 1966) p. 209.
6. Consult for example H. Bamford-Parkes, *Gods and Men: The Origins of Western Culture* (New York: Alfred A. Knopf, 1959) Section 3; William H. McNeill, *The Rise of the West* (Chicago and London: The University of Chicago Press, 1963) especially Chapter VI.
7. *Casa Grande E. Senzala,* 9th ed. (Rio de Janeiro, 1958), pp. 12–13. Cited by Jose Monorio Rodrigues, *Brazil and Africa,* translated by Richard A. Mazzara and Sam Hileman (Berkeley & Los Angeles: University of California Press, 1965) p. 55.
8. This distinction between race prejudice based on color and race prejudice based on

purity of blood is also discussed in Mazrui, "Political Sex", *Transition*. The article is reprinted as Chapter 15 in Mazrui, *Violence and Thought: Essays on Social Tension in Africa* (London: Longmans, 1969), pp. 306–318.

9. See Rodrigues, *Brazil and Africa,* p. 64.

10. *Ibid.,* p. 75.

11. *Ibid.* Consult also Donald Pierson *Brancos e Protos ma Bahia,* (Sao Paolo: Companhia Editora Nacional, 1945, pp. 186, 188–189.

12. See Pierre Van den Berghe, *South Africa: A Study in Conflict,* (Berkeley and Los Angeles: University of California Press, 1967) pp. 39–40.

13. Muddathir Abdel Rahim, *Imperialism and Nationalism in the Sudan: A Study in Constitutional and Political Development, 1899–1956* (Oxford: Clarendon Press, 1969) pp. 4–5. See also the Republic of the Sudan, Ministry for Social Welfare, *First Population Census of the Sudan: Twenty-One Facts about the Sudanese* (1958) pp. 13, 23.

14. This point is discussed in similar terms in Mazrui, *Towards a Pax Africana: A Study of Ideology and Ambition* (London and Chicago: Weidenfeld and Nicolson and University of Chicago Press, 1967) p. 113. See also Yusuf Fadl Hasan, *The Arabs and the Sudan: From the Seventh to the Early Sixteenth Century* (Edinburgh: Edinburgh University Press, 1967) especially chapter 5, pp. 135–176.

15. *Christianity, Islam and the Negro Race* (London, 1888) reprinted in the African Heritage Books, edited by George Shepperson and Christopher Fyfe (Edinburgh: Edinburgh University Press, 1967) pp. 24–25.

16. *Ibid.,* p. 19.

17. Dean Stanley, *Eastern Church,* p. 34. Cited by Blyden, *ibid.,* pp. 19–20.

18. William C. McLeod, *The American Indian Frontier* (New York: Alfred A. Knopf Inc., 1928) pp. 359–361.

19. *Ibid.*

20. *Ibid.*

21. Herbert Moller, "Sex Composition and Correlated Culture Patterns of Colonial America," *The William and Mary College Quarterly,* Vol. II, April 1945, pp. 131–133; 136–137.

22. *Ibid.,* p. 137.

23. Hasan, *The Arabs and the Sudan,* p. 175.

24. Herbert Aptheker (editor), *One Continual Cry: David Walker's Appeal to the Colored Citizens of the World, 1829–1830.* (New York: Humanities Press, 1965) p. 41.

25. *Black Reconstruction in America, 1860–1880* (first published 1935) (Cleveland and New York: The World Publishing Company, 1962), p. 35.

26. DuBois, *The World and Africa* (first published 1946) (New York: International Publishers, 1965) enlarged edition p. 184.

27. See *Ordenacoes Filipinas,* Book 5, Titles XXIII to XXX. Cited by Rodrigues, *Brazil and Africa,* p. 61.

28. *South Africa: A Study in Conflict,* p. 41.

29. *Ibid.,* p. 42.

30. *The Social Structure of Islam* (Cambridge: Cambridge University Press, 1962), p. 137.

31. *Ibid.,* pp. 136, 143 and 138. Consult also Asaf A. A. Fyzee, *Outlines of Muhammadan Law.* (London: Oxford University Press 1964 Edition), especially chapters 2 and 5.

32. Michael F. Lofchie, *Zanzibar: Background to Revolution* (Princeton University Press and Oxford University Press, 1965), pp. 73–75.

33. Hasan, *The Arabs and the Sudan,* p. 135.

34. *Ibid.*

35. For a general historical background see C. R. Boxer, *Race Relations in the Portuguese*

Colonial Empire (Oxford: Clarendon Press, 1963). See also Rodrigues, "Influence of Africa on Brazil", *Journal of African History,* Vol. III, No. 1, 1962; Institute of Race Relations *Angola:* A Symposium (London: Oxford University Press, 1962).
36. See *Manchester Guardian,* April 28, 1956.
37. *Ibid.*
38. *Africa Digest,* Vol. III, No. 8, May–June, 1956, pp. 38–39.

CHAPTER 6

Suttee and Levirate in Black-Brown Relations

In August 1972 General Idi Amin Dada, President of Uganda, staggered the world with a series of measures designed to remove or drastically reduce the Asian presence in Uganda. The term "Asian" in this context referred to people who came from the Indian sub-continent as a whole, from Pakistan and Bangla Desh, as well as from the Indian Republic. What was involved was the ethnic or racial identity of a relatively prosperous minority group in Africa.

Both kinship culture and economic culture are involved in the issue of the Indian presence in Africa as a whole. There are significant Indian communities in southern Africa and central Africa as well as eastern Africa. The Ugandan experience dramatized an issue which was bigger than Uganda itself, and more widespread than might have been realized.

In international affairs Asians and Africans have had moments of solidarity. Milton Obote, the former President of Uganda, has described the late Jawahahal Nehru as "the founder of nonalignment"; and nonalignment has formed the cornerstone of the foreign policies of most African states. A number of African leaders have been influenced by both Nehru and Mahatma Gandhi. Kwame Nkrumah, the first President of Ghana and himself a major figure in African history, said: "We salute Mahatma Gandhi and we remember in tribute to him that it was in South Africa that his method of non-violence and non-cooperation was first practised."[1]

There is no doubt that Africa was partly apprenticed to India in the arts of nationalist agitation before independence and the arts of diplomacy afterwards. The black man and the brown man formed an alliance to fight the arrogance of the white man. And yet why could they not live together themselves? How symptomatic of a deeper global malaise was

117

the behavior of that African soldier in Uganda in 1972 against an Asian minority in his country?

We shall address ourselves in this chapter to aspects of kinship culture insofar as they conditioned the dynamics of Indo-African relations in that particular East African society. We shall later also examine economic culture and differences in performance between Africans and Asians. But, first, a brief word about the historical background of the Asian presence in East Africa.

Asians became significant in mainland East Africa in the eighteenth century, but their influence was limited to the coastal areas until the end of the nineteenth century. Their numbers and impact on the East African economy were consolidated more slowly. They did indeed help in building the railway line from Mombasa to the lake in the interior, but contrary to popular belief, the bulk of the Indians are not descended from those railway builders. On the contrary, a sizeable section of those who helped build the railway returned to India, and much larger numbers of immigrants who had nothing to do with the railway line settled in East Africa over the years.

In Uganda, as in Kenya, measures were taken by the colonial authorities to keep the Asian immigrants off the land and encourage them to enter the commercial world, the liberal professions, and the clerical, managerial, and administrative areas of specialization. They became successful—perhaps too successful for their own safety in the long run. Certainly not long after independence, measures were being considered by the new African government of Uganda to reduce the Asian factor in the national economy.

It soon became clear that three distinct elements were involved in this entire endeavor. First, there was the deep race consciousness which had been building up for half a century, and which emphasized people's awareness of each other's color of skin; second, the fragile but growing territorial nationalism attached to the new states of Kenya and Uganda; and third, a genuine desire to create an effective African entrepreneurial culture and a successful African business class.

The race consciousness made Asians vulnerable, whether or not they adopted local citizenship. The territorial nationalism exposed black Africans from neighboring countries working in Uganda, while at the same time protecting those Asians who had adopted citizenship. In other words, when Ugandans adopt policies based on territorial nationalism, Rwandese, Kenyans, and Tanzanians, however black they may be, are more exposed than Asians who have adopted local citizenship. This was certainly the case in the last eighteen months of Obote's rule, when his new labor policies resulted in a large exodus of black Kenyans, many of whom had lived and worked in Uganda for many years. President Obote seemed to be embarking on policies similar to those which had been adopted by Busia when he was Prime Minister of Ghana. Busia in 1969 and 1970 initiated a series of measures which resulted in the expulsion of thousands of Nigerians and other non-Ghanaian West Africans, who trekked forth, uprooted from their normal areas of residence, often impoverished in the very act of removing themselves from Ghana. Similarly in Uganda under Obote, cooks, porters, houseboys, large numbers of whom were from Kisumu and surrounding areas in Kenya, were forced out of the country, while the future of Asians who were citizens remained secure for the time being.

The third factor in this entire Asian question is the ambition to create a local entrepreneurial system. Independence had brought very effective African participation in government, administration, university life, managerial work, clerical professions, law and, increasingly, medicine and other professions. But African participation in the higher reaches of the commercial life of the country was still modest. Again Obote's government, partly following Kenya's lead, initiated a series of measures to promote the Africanization of commerce in Uganda, ranging from special loans to enable Africans to enter the commercial world, to a request by the Uganda government to Makerere University that a School of Business be established as quickly as possible. In 1969 the Trade Licensing Act and a new Immigration Act were passed under Obote's government, both of which were designed to contain and circumscribe the Asian presence in business, and to promote more rigorously an effective African entry into this area of national endeavor. In short, General Amin's measures to expel Asian citizens of Britain, Pakistan, and Bangla Desh within 90 days from August 9th, 1972, was an acceleration of the policies of his predecessor Milton Obote, and a dramatization of somewhat similar policies in Kenya and Zambia.

Lesser political figures in East Africa since independence have certainly expressed strong opinions about Asians, both as to their relative social exclusiveness and their relative economic prosperity. But the top man in each of the three countries of East Africa had, on the whole, refrained from direct denunciation of the Asian community. In some cases, the top man had even gone as far as to counter the wave of racism inherent elsewhere, in an attempt to guard the interests of the immigrant communities. But General Amin opted for a policy of confrontation with the Asian question, sometimes laying even greater stress on problems of social exclusiveness than on problems of economic preeminence.

Within the issue of racial exclusiveness lies no less a subject than sex itself. The eternal worry concerning sex across racial boundaries received

119

presidential articulation in the first year of Uganda's Second Republic. Asians were accused of being excessively concerned about the purity of their blood, inclined to protect their sons and more militantly their daughters from sexual or matrimonial attentions across the racial divide. The number of Uganda Asians who had ever married Africans was somehow discovered. It was pitifully below a dozen, and the majority of those preferred to live abroad for as long as possible. President Amin also received personal communications from other Indo-African lovers under a cloud of persecution from the Indian side of the racial divide.

A number of questions arose out of the debate concerning the endogamous tendencies of the Indian community in Uganda and the response of Africans toward it. From an academic point of view we could even ask whether the real issue was Freudian or Marxian. Was the debate concerning the place of sex in racial integration a manifestation of class struggle in Uganda, however disguised, or was it a manifestation of primeval forces concerning identity and sex? If the ultimate issue lay in the economic prosperity of Asians and their dominance in the exchange and commercial sectors of the economy, then it is Karl Marx rather than Sigmund Freud to whom we should turn for guidance. But if the sexual issue has had an independent political significance in its own right, then we must look further than the Indian *duka* for a clarification of the deeper issues. For our purposes here, Freud poses issues of kinship culture; Marx poses questions of economic culture.

A major premise of this book is that sex is a distinctive variable in its own right in race relations. As we have already tried to show, sex is not merely a disguised rationalization of class struggle and economic motivation. This is partly because sex, with all its taboos and prescriptions, remains central to many of the *mores* and values of the different cultures of the world. If race relations are not merely a matter of economic relations but are also a matter of cultural differences, then sex cannot be divorced from racial tensions. Much of culture is derived from the *mores* acquired in family life, and the central aspect of family life is indeed sex, and the values governing it.

In approaching the question of sex and Indophobia in East Africa, we must therefore first take a broader social and philosophical view. We should indeed place General Idi Amin in a broad context which touches other continents, and involves culture and literature as well as politics. We shall then return to focus more explicitly on the East African scene.

Suttee versus Levirate

In the year 1829, the British in India banned the practise of suttee, the cremation of the wife on her husband's funeral pyre. Across the Indian

Ocean within the continent of Africa an alternative practice, in some ways fundamentally different, continued to hold sway. This was the custom of levirate, in which a wife was inherited by her husband's brother upon the death of her husband. It is a basic premise of this chapter that the difference between suttee and levirate is to some extent at the heart of the debate on sex and Indophobia in Uganda in the 1970's.

The records would seem to show that suttee began in the fourth century B.C. as an ad hoc sacrifice undertaken by a disconsolate widow who could not bear the thought of being left behind by her husband. The word indicated a kind of virtuous renunciation by the woman. By the sixth century A.D. suttee had received religious approval in Hinduism. The woman attained sainthood by burning herself with the corpse of her husband. She also helped to cleanse her own family and the family of her husband of evil.

Suttee became absorbed into the general mores governing the Indian caste system as a whole. The preservation of the purity of caste became a central aspect of Hindu social organization. The higher the caste the stricter were the rules governing the chastity of women. Child marriage developed as part of this quest for the preservation of caste and the protection of chastity. But what if the husband of the child died? Remarriage of the widow rapidly became untenable, even if the widow was an infant. The extreme method of avoiding this acquisition of a new husband was precisely the burning of the widow—suttee.

In theory, the practise was a voluntary expression of devotion by the widow to her husband—the husband having been, in orthodox Hinduism, a god to his wife. She was now going to join her husband partly because it was through her sins that he had died at all. But in reality by the beginning of the nineteenth century, suttee was no longer a voluntary exercise. Relatives of the widow, or of her late husband, exerted considerable pressure on the woman to burn herself on the funeral pyre. The Brahmins in the Ganges Valley, especially Bengal, led the way numerically in this custom. The British recorded several hundred burnings every year up to the year 1828. The practise was also extensive among the Rajputs particularly in Rajasthan, and also in the Punjab. In south India it had been largely suppressed by Muslim rulers before the British took control.

From the point of view of our analysis, the significance of suttee lies simply in the fact that it was an extreme form of a custom which is still deeply embedded in Indian psychology—that a wife was not inherited, that a widow could not remarry.

The impact of British and of Western culture generally has tended to modify this strong aversion toward female remarriage. But basically the underlying value-pattern which tied the woman so closely to the man she married has proved to be a resilient aspect of Indian culture,[2] even among those people of Indian origin who have been converted to Islam.

In contrast to this rigid discouragement of female remarriage in Hindu custom, especially among the upper castes, is the widespread custom of levirate in Africa. In many societies a widow is indeed inherited by the brother of the deceased. But what if the deceased has no brother? Professor John S. Mbiti reminds us that such a situation is unlikely:

> By brother it should be understood to mean not only the son of one's mother but any other close relative. We pointed out earlier on that a person has literally "hundreds" of brothers, due to the extensive kinship system found in most African societies. The brother who inherits the wife and children of his deceased relative, performs all the duties of the husband and father. The children born after this inheritance generally belong to the deceased man; though in some societies they are the children of the "new" father.[3]

Mbiti tells us that in some societies in Africa if a son dies before he has been married, the parents arrange for him to get married in absentia, so that the dead man is not cut off "from the chain of life". Leaving children behind is the path to immortality, and procreation by proxy is feasible in some societies.

All these factors concern a situation where a young man has already died. But occasionally one finds traces of anticipatory levirate, whereby a husband permits his younger brother limited sexual privileges with his wife, simply in view of the fact that the younger brother might well inherit her eventually.

Although suttee was unique to India, the levirate has by no means been unique to Africa. The idea of widows being inherited by a brother or other close male relative is discernible in societies outside the African continent. The levirate marriage is still strong in Africa but it is being slowly undermined by Euro-Christian influences.

Leadership and Levirate

But although the levirate is mentioned in the Bible as part of the culture of the ancient Hebrews, its attraction in Africa is being eroded by the impact of Christianity. Western religion has gradually undermined certain areas of African sexual spontaneity. If we took Catholicism, Protestantism, and Islam as three distinct religious intrusions into Africa, we might say that Islam interfered least and Catholicism most with the sexual aspects of the African cultural universe. In between Islam and Catholicism lay the different schools of Protestantism.

These factors impinged on the lives of individual African leaders. The meeting point among matrimony, sex and politics was influenced by the religious denomination of Africans in positions of authority after independence. And some of the influences at play antedated independence by several decades, going back to formative periods in the lives of these leaders. An interesting example in this regard is Kwame Nkrumah and his early sexual inhibitions.

In his autobiography, Nkrumah refers to the terror he had of women in his younger days. He talks about a young girl who was apparently in love with him, and who used to wait for hours in a lane near his home. Whenever she tried to start a conversation with him as he passed her in the lane, he would look at her like a frightened animal. One day the girl gathered up enough courage to whisper into his ear "I love you." Nkrumah's religious sensibilities were horrified. He ran into his mother's house and complained about the wickedness of the girl. Nkrumah's mother laughed and said: "You should be flattered, my boy, what is wrong with somebody being fond of you?"

Nkrumah's mother herself later became subject to the levirate customs of the tribe. Nkrumah's father died while the boy was still at school. Those traditions that had once governed the marriage customs of the Hebrews were still operative among the Nzima. As Nkrumah himself delicately and perhaps euphemistically tells us: "According to our custom, when a man dies, his wife and children become the responsibility of his successor and they automatically move to the house of the deceased man's next of kin. And so my mother left Half Assini and went to live with my uncle at the mouth of the Ankrobra River."[4] But although Nkrumah was a child of a levirate culture, the Roman Catholic Church had begun to blunt his own sexual spontaneity. Curiously enough his first sexual test outside his country was encouraged by an Indian. It is often assumed that Indians are more sexually inhibited than Africans, and this may be the case in general. But the generalization does not hold with regard to that day in the 1930's when Nkrumah was venturing out of West Africa for the first time on his way to the United States. On board the ship he struck up a friendship with an Indian passenger. At the Canary Islands the Indian invited Nkrumah to accompany him ashore, and see the sights of Las Palmas, the capital. He accepted the invitation and they ventured forth into the town. "Not knowing anything of life outside my native country I followed him in all innocence into a building which looked like a hotel." Nkrumah and his friend sat at a table. Nkrumah himself had never drunk alcohol, but his Indian friend insisted on ordering beer. The beer arrived, followed soon after by "two elegant Spanish girls in negligées." Nkrumah was at once morally horrified and psychologically terrified. He kept his eyes glued to the legs of the *table*.

123

He prayed to the Virgin Mary that these two specimens of womanhood should vanish as quickly as they had come.

> But to my utter horror and embarrassment one of them came over, planted herself on my knee and began stroking my hair and generally enveloping me with her limbs. I had only seen white women from a distance and the fact that one of them should approach me at such uncomfortably close quarters completely unnerved me. I uttered a cry, jumped up, spilling both the woman and the beer onto the floor and ran as fast as my trembling legs would carry me back to the ship.[5]

For the rest of the trip Nkrumah's Indian friend would not let him forget the episode. He laughed and laughed at the other's sexual naiveté. Two young people, one drawn from a levirate culture in Ghana and the other from the land of the suttee, were cast briefly in an amusing episode on the Canary Islands on their way to Liverpool. A moment of sexual mirth was the meaning of the episode to the Indian; but to the young African it was at once a moment of sexual terror and a phase in his racial maturation. The sheer availability of white women had one kind of pull on an African from colonial conditions; and yet the fear of sin was itself a consequence of imperial Christianity at a particular moment in history. In Nkrumah's own words:

> Probably it was the same fear that my aspirations might be held in check by the Roman Catholic Church that made me afraid of getting myself tied up with women. In those days my fear of women was beyond all under-standing. . . . I have never outgrown that feeling towards women. It is not fear today, but something deeper.[6]

Nkrumah himself never seemed to have fully understood the ramifica-tions of these inhibitions. In later life he thought it was perhaps a dread of being trapped, of having his freedom taken away, of being overpowered. And yet even these rationalizations did not seem to be fully convincing to him. The secret lay in the interaction between Christian teaching and personal psychology as they worked themselves out in the growing personality of Kwame Nkrumah at a formative period in his life.

Pollution versus Oblivion

What are the wider cultural and spiritual ramifications of the suttee syndrome and the levirate complex? In what way does the prohibition of female remarriage differ in its significance from the idea of inheriting wives? In the ultimate analysis the distinction may lie in what differen-tiates fear of pollution from fear of oblivion. At the heart of Hindu cul-ture lie the Laws of Manu governing caste. And at the heart of the caste system lies the fear of pollution. The idea of spiritual cleanliness in Hinduism is inseparable from the physical idea of touching and not touching. An elaborate system governing food which may or may not be touched by others, utensils which may or may not be touched, and hands which may not be shaken, grew up as part of the entire apparatus of protection against pollution.

The link between this Brahminic fear of pollution on the one hand and the color black on the other seems to have matured among the Indus peoples when fair minorities met very dark majorities for the first time in urban centers. The *Brahmin,* the priests and teachers, became identified as white. The *Kshatriya,* the secular rulers and fighters, acquired the symbolic color of *red.* The *Vaishya,* the cultivators, traders, and artisans, found an identity in the symbolic color of *yellow.* But black was the colour symbolically reserved for the *Sudra,* the servants, slaves, and menial workers.

There seems to be little doubt that these associations of color exerted some influence on Indian attitudes to black Africans. The rules governing relations between colors in the Indian caste system were, in their very essence, inegalitarian. "A Brahmin white might kill a Sudra black for the cost of a cat. The reverse offence would entail immediate as well as eternal punishment."[7]

What should be remembered is that Indian color prejudice started as a prejudice of one Indian against another, and should not therefore be confused with pure racial prejudice. To regard the black color as less attractive than fairer shades is by no means unknown among Africans themselves. Some African societies mistook the first white men to arrive in the last century for gods simply because their belief systems had already lent divine qualities to the color white in certain circumstances. In Uganda, for example, certain aspects of anti-Nilotic feeling among Bantu people are connected with the simple fact that the Nilotes tend to be significantly blacker than the average Bantu.

Color prejudice within Indian society is definitely more elaborate than color prejudice among African peoples. All that we are seeking to establish here is that *varna,* or the system of symbolic colors in social relations in India, is a form of color prejudice that should not be directly equated with radial prejudice. But it has had consequences for the system of marriage in India and for patterns of descent, and leads us back to the phenomenon of suttee and the militant possessiveness it implies. The Laws of Manu have enforced breeding within each caste, and have forbidden breeding or marriage between castes. Thus, endogamy has been at the heart of the status of women in Indian society, helping to encourage child marriage and a form of purdah after marriage, and the principle of eternal widowhood upon the death of the spouse.

In reality, it is not simply the prohibition of literal suttee which has affected the situation. Processes of westernization and modernization have also helped to relax some of these Laws of Manu and their consequences. The idea of a second marriage for widows is slowly gaining acceptance, though not as yet respectability. But the ghost of suttee continues to exert its influence on the matrimonial and social values of Indian society.

Nor is it only the Hindus who show these inclinations. Indian Muslims are as much Indian as they are Muslims. Many of the pre-Islamic norms of Indian culture have remained resilient among Islamized Indians in spite of the passage of time. Among the more resilient are precisely norms governing family relations and attitudes to marriage.

The principle of suttee as compared with the principle of levirate emphasizes some of the differences between the system of matrimonial values which Indians brought to Africa, and the system of matrimonial values which seemed dominant among the indigenous majorities they encountered there. Suttee as a matrimonial principle is spouse-oriented. If the spouse is a wrong spouse, then the children are dishonored. The very idea of a half-caste in Kiswahili, for example, is directly borrowed from the Indians. The Indians came with the concept of *chotara,* half-caste, to denote in that instance a progeny of a racially mixed marriage. And *chotara,* when one of the parents was Indian, were basically children dishonored because a parent was disgraced. The levirate is progeny-oriented, rather than spouse-oriented. Instead of children being disgraced because the mother belonged to the wrong caste or wrong race, the levirate permits a mother to be honored because she was the mother of her husband's children. Suttee as a prohibition of female remarriage was an extreme form of monogamy. A woman once married was never to marry again, even if her husband died. The levirate, on the other hand, was a fusion of polygamy and reincarnation. A dead brother's widow could join the household of the living brother, even if the living brother already had several wives.

Both suttee and the levirate implicitly deny the Christian matrimonial principle of "Till Death Do us Part." In both the Hindu and the indigenous African systems death need not nullify the bonds of matrimony. In the case of suttee, continued widowhood was continued matrimonial commitment beyond the hour of death. In the case of the levirate, we have also an affirmation that marriage is a bond between the living, the dead, and those who are yet to be born. The widow passes on to the next of kin.

While both suttee and levirate imply an indissolubility, there is a fundamental difference between them. Suttee is a denial that the husband can be represented by another, least of all a close kinsman. Suttee in its distrust of incest converts levirate into a double sin. The husband is not only represented, which is bad enough, but he is represented by a brother or other close relative, which adds incest to injury. Levirate by contrast is an affirmation of the representability of a matrimonial partner. In some African societies the representability is feasible even while the husband lives, provided it has the husband's permission.

Nor must it be forgotten that African marriages are not indissoluble in either the Christian or the Hindu sense. An African marriage is indissoluble by death because neither the man nor the woman has assented to such a dissolution. The bond can therefore be deemed to continue for as long as there are kinsmen to inherit the widow. But a marriage can be ended by an act of will on the part of either partner. Certainly an act of will by the man can terminate the partnership. But in many African societies the woman also has at least the ultimate resort of walking out and going back to her parents. The divorce, if willed by the woman rather than the man, may then simply necessitate suitable compensation for the man. While African societies often deny death the power of terminating what was entered into by the living, the living themselves may readjust certain arrangements as they deem fit.

Finally, there is a fundamental distinction in the very fact that suttee is ultimately individualistic, while levirate is basically a collective bond. Suttee as a form of female commitment to the individual man she has married, focusses the bond directly between the particular woman and the particular man. Of course relatives are involved on both sides, but the matrimonial loyalty is between two individuals. Levirate, on the other hand, is a collectivization of the marriage principle in the face of death itself. Brother can represent brother, and the widow retains sexual rights, as well as economic subsistence rights, within the family.

Behind it all there continues to be a distinction between the fear of pollution and the fear of oblivion. The fear of pollution generates complexes regarding endogamy, and stiffens into possessiveness about women, and distrust of those who are descended from a mixed mating across caste or racial boundaries.

The fear of oblivion on the other hand lies at the heart of the levirate institution. In that institution we see, as John Mbiti has reminded us:

> the philosophical awareness of the individual that "I am because we are; and since we are, therefore I am." The existence of the individual is the existence of the corporate; and where the individual may physically die, this does not

relinquish his social-legal existence since the "*we*" continues to exist for the "*I*" . . . Viewed in this light, the elaborate kinship system acts like an insurance policy covering both the physical and the metaphysical dimensions of human life.[8]

Mbiti touches elsewhere the idea that an individual in African society is personally immortal for as long as he is remembered by relatives and friends who knew him in this life, and who have survived him.

Unless a person has close relatives to remember him when he has physically died, then he is nobody and simply vanishes out of human existence like a flame when it is extinguished. Therefore it is a duty, religious and ontological, for everyone to get married; and if a man has no children or only daughters, he finds another wife so that through her, children (and sons) may be born who would survive him and keep him (with the other living-dead of the family) in personal immortality. Procreation is the absolute way of insuring that a person is not cut off from personal immortality.[9]

We have then both in suttee and in the levirate principles which are connected respectively with the Hindu and the African conceptions of immortality. And for the Hindu the struggle toward perfection and immortality includes avoidance of pollution; whereas for the African that struggle includes escape from the danger of oblivion. Their respective attitudes to sex and procreation become part of an entire metaphysical system of thought. Their attitudes to mixed marriages are in turn profoundly conditioned by those metaphysically derived norms.

Power and Trans-Ethnic Marriage

The norms which govern family relations are profoundly relevant for intergroup relations. It follows therefore that the norms governing marriage itself have a bearing on attitudes to other races. The premise is relevant in comparing attitudes to marriage among Indians and Africans. Indians spiritualized marriage so much, making it so inseparable from the Laws of Manu, that marriage across caste and race was bedevilled by religious considerations. The militant matrimonial possessiveness implied by suttee, with all its connotations of monogamous extremism, at least below the Brahmin class, was also bound to reduce the toleration of racial exogamy.

By contrast, in spite of the levirate, marriage is a less sacred institution among Africans than among Indians. Even the coming of Christianity in Africa has not as yet sacralized marriage sufficiently to result in a cult of monogamy or fanatical indissolubility. Because marriage is less sacred in the attitudes of ordinary Africans, intermarriage is in turn less of an issue for them.

In the recent political history of Africa there has been a high incidence of trans-ethnic marriages, which cut across either a racial or a clear tribal boundary, among the African elite.

Black-white intermarriage includes Kenyatta's marriage to Edna Clarke during World War II. Kenyatta's Cambridge-educated son, Peter, is descended from that union. Another prominent African who married across the divide between black and white is President Leopold Senghor of Senegal. Afro-Arab or trans-Saharan marriages include the marriage of Kwame Nkrumah to Fathiyya. Nkrumah had children with this Egyptian wife. Also among Afro-Arab or Afro-Iranian marriages must be included the matrimonial experiments of Sheikh Abeid Karume, the First Vice-President of Tanzania and Chairman of The Revolutionary Council of Zanzibar.

Marriage across the tribal boundary would have to include the marriage of Milton Obote, a Langi, to Miria, a Muganda. In the Ugandan context the marriage was bound to have political connotations, implying commitment to national integration through encouragement of trans-ethnic marriages. Just as European kings had once sought to promote interstate alliances through intermarriage, so could Obote's marriage to Miria be interpreted as an attempt to promote interethnic fusion through a tribally mixed marriage.

Another trans-ethnic if fluctuating marriage was that of Idi Amin, the man who succeeded Milton Obote as President of Uganda. Not long after his coup Idi Amin referred to his choice of wives as a clear indication that he was not a tribalist. Though himself a Kakwa, he had one Lugbara wife, one Langi wife, one Musoga wife, and one Muganda wife. Amin explicitly supported the idea that national integration is connected with the biological mixture of tribal or racial stock. In the case of his Langi wife, Amin explained after the coup that he married her on the recommendation of his former boss, the then President Obote. Obote was himself a Langi, and sought to consolidate his relations with Amin by recommending a Langi wife.

In Amin's choice of wives we may also have a clue to understanding his image of Asians as a group unwilling to cross the racial boundary in marriage. Both Amin and the late Chairman Karume in Zanzibar did, in their own very direct and sometimes rather simplified ways, grasp the real relevance of marriage as an institution for processes of national integration. Both sought to demonstrate that there is a link between the boudoir and the nation, between political alliance and marriage partnership, between national fraternity and literal brotherhood. Part of the explanation of Amin's views on the Indian question may lie in the political concept which influenced his own choice of wives.

129

Of course, relations between groups are not consolidated on the basis of a single wife. But the idea of encouraging biological intermingling as an approach to national integration has a certain core of hard-headed practical calculation within it. It is true that in history nations have grown partly through literal interpenetration of kinship.[10]

We have tried to show that the idea of relating kinship to nationhood is only an extension of the principles of tribal cohesion. A tribe is sometimes defined almost in terms of being descended from the same parents. The Baganda have derived part of their sense of shared identity out of a system of myths whose center is the principle of shared descent. Kintu becomes the grandfather of all those who claim to be real Baganda, although a large proportion of them are Baganda by assimilation rather than biological descent. In his *Facing Mount Kenya,* Kenyatta analyzes the myths surrounding Kikuyu identity, with the centrality of the man Gikuyu, the "founder of the tribe".[11]

In many of these mythologies of tribal origin, problems regarding heirs, and questions affecting the choice of wives, worries concerning the fertility of the founder of the community become intertwined with the ancestry of collective identity. The principle of shared parenthood is so deeply embedded that family relations and tribal self-consciousness become almost indistinguishable.

The move from the idea that the tribe is descended from a shared father to the idea that the nation should build itself on a pattern of penetrating kinship relations is not such a big logical jump. General Amin's concept of the politics of intermarriage, as was that of Sheikh Karume, are in a sense profoundly African. They are an attempt to deduce principles of nationhood from principles of tribalism.

Sex, Security, and Citizenship

In July 1962—seven years almost to the day before his assassination— Tom Mboya of Kenya had this to say to the Kenya Indian Congress: "Cocktail integration is not enough. You must be prepared to revise some of your long-established conceptions. For instance, an integrated community can lead to inter-marriage between the members of that community—and why not?"[12]

The remark, simple in its own way, started widespread discussion in colonial Kenya. Mboya himself was glad of the controversy because he believed that trans-ethnic marriages—across both tribal and racial boundaries—were destined to increase dramatically in the following twenty years of Kenya's history. Mboya also believed that part of the problem had been precisely a deep unwillingness to discuss publically the question of racial intermarriage derived in part from a sense of embarrassment. It is true that different groups of people were indeed different partly because of cultural variation. It was also true that such cultural variation needed to be respected as far as possible. But if people had to live together in the same country, Mboya felt, they might need to speak more openly about those aspects of culture which could bedevil relations between different groups. In Mboya's own words:

The more people speak publicly about such matters, the better. There will be more inter-marriage during the next twenty years or so, and I welcome the prospect. We helped to break the myth that there is something wrong with the different races marrying each other, that inter-marriage leads to an extinction of values and civilized standards. The example of the West Indies should be enough to convince us that this is a false argument.[13]

Mboya felt, even at that stage, that while relations between Europeans and Africans, between white and black, had already been subject to long-standing probing and analysis, what still remained behind a shroud of mystery and embarrassed inhibition were relations between black and brown. The Asians too needed to find ways of accommodating themselves to a change of conditions in the African continent. In Mboya's formulation:

The Asian community which, in Kenya, is twice the size of the European and in Uganda and Tanganyika many times the size, does not receive the same agonizing appraisal from newspapers, presumably because the newspapers are mostly European-owned and the administrations have been subject to European influence. But their need to integrate swiftly and wipe out the memory of discrimination is probably greater than among Europeans, many of whom can leave East Africa if they cannot adapt to change. The majority of Asians here have no other home.[14]

Mboya was right in his assertion that relations between black and brown had received far less comment than relations between black and white; and that there was therefore a case for extra candor on the Asian question.

When General Idi Amin Dada took over power in Uganda nearly a decade later, and reopened discussion on the Asian question, he was in fact carrying the late Mboya's mission a little further. Perhaps the leadership in the debate in Uganda on the Asian question should not have been taken by the President himself, but by one of his ministers. Just as in Kenya controversial issues were sometimes brought to the forefront by Mboya, rather than by Mzee Kenyatta himself, so a similar policy in Uganda in the Second Republic should have been followed. On matters affecting profound areas of concern for some small group of citizens, the President should have remained in the background as the court of last appeal. A President should indeed help to promote certain policies if these are deemed to be in the national interest, but groups of citizens who find themselves under attack by the President himself tend to feel deprived of the right of appeal. It would have been in Uganda's interest for the debate on the Asian question to have been initiated by one of the ministers, and for the President to have lent a sympathetic ear to the Asian response without implying disloyalty to his own minister. But Amin's entire conception of citizenship was so bound up with the Asian question that he felt driven to take active leadership.

The real tragedy of the situation concerned precisely those Asians who took the plunge and applied for Uganda citizenship in good time. World sympathies in 1972 tended to focus on those Asians who decided to "go British". Time and again well-meaning western liberals before 1972 have blamed the 1968 Commonwealth Immigration Act of Great Britain on East African racial intolerance. They have failed to see that if the British government decided to allow one class of citizens unrestricted entry to Britain and apply a quota system to another class then the government had itself diluted the concept of citizenship with racism.

But could anyone blame those Asians who took British citizenship on the eve of East African independence? After all, the future in East Africa was very uncertain. Those Asians who opted for British citizenship were opting for an insurance policy, based on the assumption that the British passport was a surer guarantee of justice than an East African passport.

One must concede that independence for East Africa was indeed an ominous question mark. But it was a question mark which had to be confronted, for better or worse. The Asians who opted to take British citizenship had, in reality, three options at that time—they could remain in East Africa if all was well, they could migrate to England if that was more profitable, or they could ultimately return to the Indian sub-continent if the worst happened

The British Asians, receiving such special treatment, were better off than the majority of Africans in East Africa. It is true that independence was a gamble, but there was no insurance policy for the great majority of Africans. Who gave the Baganda an insurance policy that if things went wrong under Obote's regime they could claim citizenship of either Britain or some third country? Or the Ibo against things going wrong in the First Republic of Nigeria? Or the Luo of Kenya against the hazards of 1969? Or the Langi and Acholi of Uganda against the changing fortunes of the Second Republic? In others words, there are groups in Africa who have suffered more brutal victimization since independence than the Asians have sustained. And these groups had no British High

Commission to run back to, no India, Bangla Desh, and Pakistan as ultimate homes of retreat.

It is because of these considerations that the tragedy of the British Asians is a lesser tragedy than that of Asians who were African citizens. These latter made up their minds to establish roots in East Africa and apply for citizenship in good time. Those were the Asians who saw that ominous question mark hanging over their heads, but decided nevertheless to risk it all with black East Africans. Theirs was an act of faith—and it needed to be rewarded with reciprocal trust. And yet they got the backlash of the more general hostility to British Asians.

From the point of view of world order values, something can still be saved. It is important that those Asians who had opted for Ugandan or Kenyan citizenship should be classified simply as another Ugandan or Kenyan *tribe*. It is true that they have a disproportionate influence over commercial activity in the country, but then the Baganda have a disproportionate share of jobs in the Uganda Higher Civil Service; and northerners have a disproportionate presence in the Uganda armed forces as have the Kamba in the Kenyan armed forces and the Kikuyu in the higher ranks of the Kenya Civil Service. All these anomalies may have to be rectified. The Baganda share in the Civil Service and in the best schools of Uganda needs, in a humane fashion, to be made more proportional. The distribution of educational facilities in the country as a whole should become more equitable. The armed forces should become ethnically more representative both in Kenya and in Uganda. Commerce and shopkeeping should become ethnically balanced.

From the point of view of economic and political reorganization, the Asian question should be seen in the context of this accidental disproportion in the distribution of advantages among the different ethnic groups in the country. But in this case we are thinking of those Asians who are indeed citizens. The answer to such ethnic imbalances does not lie in blatant victimization. It lies in persuading citizens from other areas and other ethnic groups gradually to build up a share in these different spheres of national endeavor.

Conclusion

General Amin announced soon after the coup that the Uganda army was going to recruit more systematically from areas other than the north, so as to restore a balance in the ethnic composition of the security forces. General Amin's conception of the second university of Uganda, with campuses in less developed areas of the country, seemed also inspired by a desire to reduce the educational advantages enjoyed by some ethnic groups in Uganda. These two ambitions of Amin have yet to be realized, but they would be exercises in ethnic balance if they were.

The Asians should be treated as a tribe and in a similar way in each African country. There should be systematic attempts to Africanize commerce, but not in a manner which blatantly victimizes Asians. Just as educational advantages in Uganda could be distributed to communities outside Buganda more equitably without blatant injustice to the Baganda, so commercial activity could be made ethnically more representative without the risk of racialistic inequities against the Asians.

But differences in kinship culture between Asians and Africans may prove to be a more obstinate problem. Certainly the problem of intermarriage may have to await future effort after a long period of dialogue and reciprocal evaluation. The sexual habits of Africans may win the contempt of Indians; the sexual habits of Indians may reinforce African resentment. Indophobia is the tendency to react negatively toward Indians as a group. Cultural Indophobia is a reaction against certain aspects of Indian culture, of which the values and taboos surrounding sex may be an important component. Economic Indophobia derives sustenance from a real or presumed economic preeminence enjoyed by the Indians in situations like those in Uganda, Kenya, Zambia, Tanzania, Rhodesia, South Africa and other African countries with Indian minorities.

Economic Indophobia, although seemingly more important at the moment, may indeed be more transient. As African businessmen reduce the Asian predominance in commerce and trade, the African resentment of Indians on economic grounds may gradually decline. But the resentment of Indians based on their presumed social exclusiveness and other aspects of their culture may endure much longer in Africa, even if Africans extended to their Asian compatriots the full status of an African tribe.

The ghosts of cremated Indian widows of yesteryears, and the jealousies of dead Africans whose wives had been inherited by others, may continue to haunt Indo-African relations for generations to come.

Footnotes

1. "Positive Action in Africa" in *Africa Speaks,* edited by J. Duffy and R. A. Manners (Princeton: D. Van Nostrand, 1961) p. 50.
2. Consult Percival Spear, *India: A Modern History* (Ann Arbor: The University of Michigan Press, 1961), especially Chapters XX and XXIII. See also C.D. Darlington, *The Evolution of Man and Society* (London: George Allen and Unwin, 1969) especially pp. 357–362.
3. *African Religions and Philosophy* (London: Heinemann, 1969) pp. 144–145.
4. *Ghana: The Autobiography of Kwame Nkrumah* (London: Nelson, 1965), pp. 10–11.

5. *Ibid.*, pp. 21–22.
6. *Ibid.*, p. 10.
7. C. D. Darlington, *The Evolution of Man and Society*, p. 359.
8. *African Religions and Philosophy*, pp. 144–145.
9. *Ibid.*, p. 26.
10. This sexual approach to national integration is discussed more comprehensively, and with special reference to the Sudan, in my paper "The Black Arabs in Comparative Perspective: The Political Sociology of Race Mixture" (mimeo). A shorter version of this paper is published under the title of "The Arabs of Africa: Political Sociology of Race Mixture," *Patterns of Prejudice,* Journal of the Institute of Jewish Affairs, (London) Vol. 6, No. 1, Jan–Feb. 1972.
11. Jomo Kenyatta, *Facing Mount Kenya* (London: Secker and Warburg, 1959 Edition), pp. 2–5.
12. Tom Mboya, *Freedom and After* (London: Andre Deutsch, 1963), pp. 111.
13. *Ibid.*, pp. 111–112.
14. *Ibid.*, p. 112.

CHAPTER 7

Distance and Demonstration in Black-Yellow Relations

Two further concepts have been critically important in the history of race relations in the world, both emanating from the West. One is the concept of the *yellow peril,* designed as a warning to the white races to beware of the potential conquering power of China and Japan. The other is the concept of *the white man's burden,* inspired by a desire to conquer others. In the one case the whites were on the defensive, seeking to escape the peril posed by races far more numerous than their own. In the other, Rudyard Kipling provided the white races with a clarion call for imperial expansion and for the control of the non-white races of the globe, at the same time.

The two ideas together added up to a vision of the white man's conception of his place in the racial universe at that time. The concept of the yellow peril was of course specially focused toward the Asian continent, while the concept of the white man's burden came to be especially applied to the African continent. It was in relation to Africa that the white man felt particularly paternalistic, and it was especially to African peoples that the description "half devil and half child" was most often applied.

Yet the poem "The White Man's Burden" was composed by Rudyard Kipling on the eve of an Asian imperial event, rather than an African one, appearing in *The Times* of London on February 4, 1899, on the occasion of the American victory in the Spanish-American war. Kipling was to some extent seeking to invite Americans to join more fully in the grand task that destiny was supposed to have bequeathed to the white man to shoulder the burden of global service. We shall return to the significance of Kipling's poem in Chapter 18 on imperial mobility. Because the white man's self-definition in the context of the racial world was in these terms of protection against some races and commitment to conquering others, new bonds of solidarity developed between white America and imperial Europe. The white men did attain levels of shared missionary commitment in relation to Asia and Africa.

The experience of shared humiliation itself produced a counter-solidarity among Africans and Asians when conditions in the world favored a consciousness of this kind. The whole movement of Afro-Asianism drew inspiration from shared experiences as colonized or humiliated peoples. What the world witnessed was the phenomenon of *pan-pigmentationalism,* an affinity based on color. The first bonds between the yellow and black peoples in the modern period had their roots in this experience of *being non-white.* Later, two factors assumed historical significance—first, the geocultural distance separating black people from the Chinese and the Japanese, and second, the Sino-Japanese ascendancy to world prominence successfully breaking the whites' global power monopoly, which we call a "demonstration effect".

Geocultural distance is basically cultural divergence reinforced by geographical separation. If China and Japan had been a little nearer Africa, or if the Chinese and Japanese had settled in large numbers in Africa as the Indians and Europeans had done, the narrower geocultural distance thus caused could have transformed black perspectives on the yellow races. But the Chinese and Japanese were to Africans among the least familiar of the influential races of the world. In the absence of conflicting cultural perspectives seen in close proximity—of the kind which have bedevilled Indo-African relations within Africa—African attitudes to the distant Chinese and Japanese often focussed narrowly on the simple proposition that these were non-white races that had made good in the world.

The demonstration impact partly arises from the fact that the yellow peoples were the first to challenge the technological and military supremacy of the white races. Japan's victory over Russia in 1905 was a milestone in this regard. Nationalists not only in India, but also in West Africa and in black America, noted Japan's rise to world prominence with pride and awe. Even in the course of World War II—when disenchantment with Japan had set in—there remained the basic appeal of an Asian power technologically on a par with the white giants of the age. Japan's slogan of "Asia for the Asians" did—in spite of mounting evidence of Japanese brutality against fellow Asians—arouse widespread response among colored intellectuals in different parts of the world. The decision by India's Sobhas Surendra Bose to serve the Japanese cause on the outbreak of World War II was an intelligible decision to millions of non-white sympathizers.

At first, China's appeal to anti-colonial nationalists elsewhere rested on fundamentally different grounds from the appeal of the Japanese. The Japanese were respected for having become a world power inspite of the handicap of being non-white. The Chinese, on the other hand, were for quite a while merely fellow-sufferers—a race despised and exploited, even if not directly colonized. Japan symbolized the yellow man triumphant; China signified the yellow man victimized. Both symbols commanded widespread positive response among nationalists in Europe's colonies.

The Rise of Japan

Japan's role as an aspiring imperial power created some ambivalence. On the one hand, having an empire in the political climate of those times was often regarded as a claim to greatness. Japan could not hope to be the true equal of European powers without imperial credentials of her own. On the other hand, the whole ethos of Afro-Asian nationalism rested on a basic anti-colonialism. Many Afro-Asian nationalists were undecided whether to applaud Japanese imperial ambitions as the ulti- mate claim to equality with European powers or to denounce those Japanese imperial pretensions as a betrayal of the victimized non-white races of the world.

A major cultural factor behind Japan's dramatic rise was itself con- nected with Japan's geocultural distance from much of the rest of the world. The self-imposed isolation of pre-Meiji Japan, combined with the consequences of being an island civilization, resulted in a curious cultural interplay between *external arrogance* and *internal deference*.

External arrogance was that part of Japanese cultural identity which resulted in relative indifference or hostility to other nations. This was the arrogance which fed Japanese nationalism at its most militant. Internal deference, on the other hand, was the essential basis of hierarchy within Japanese society itself, and of major significance in Japan's economic transformation. The process of modernization could be analyzed in terms of the relative weight of three concepts in relation to each other— deference, discipline, and development. Much of the modernization of both Britain and Japan was connected with the place of deference in in- tergroup relations. The rapidity of the Industrial Revolution in England could so easily have resulted in a political revolution. But although there was a lot of social unrest and demands for reform as a result of the structural dislocations ensuing upon industrialization, Britain has continued to have more years under Tory rule than under Labour rule— owing to the place of deference in the class structure.

Deference in Japan was even more deeply institutionalized than in British culture. Japanese Confucianism, which had been substantially affected by Shintoism, Buddhism, and a feudal military society, put a special premium on each man's recognition of his own place in the social universe. "Social distinctions must be maintained if propriety and order are to be preserved. With each class, each age, each category go certain specific obligations. Correct relations among groups must be upheld if the society is to be harmonious and well-ordered."[1]

The critical factor in both Japan and England lay once again in the precise balance between *deference within* and *arrogance without*. Deference within was a basis of class relations; arrogance without was the source of nationalistic exertion. British industrialism owed a lot to deference as an organizational resource; British imperialism owed a lot to arrogance as a fountain of legitimacy. In Japan's case deference became a military resource in the face of external dangers to the nation. Japan, insecure as a result of the pressures of the western powers and the unequal treaties imposed by them, mobilized itself for major structural changes to strengthen her overall defenses.

The traditionalist response to the external threat was more blatant arrogance to outsiders as well as deference to the monarchy, expressed in the slogan *Sonno-joi* ("Revere the Emperor, Oust the barbarian!"). But the ideological strain which finally triumphed, and determined the course of the Japanese modernizing revolution, was the one which had these ambitions: "A Powerful Military Force—A Rich Country." Economic development became indistinguishable from military defence as imperatives for survival against the barbarians. The balance between the arrogance of nationalism and the deference of the class system was now at a more productive level. In some ways feudalism was modernized without necessarily being abandoned. It moved into the structure of the workshop from rural serfdom. This might be described as *the militarization of deference and its use in the economic field,* in effect, the consolidation of discipline. The Japanese in their thrust of modernization have remained among the most disciplined of all nations.

But Japan's arrogance was historically also militarized. Demeaning and unequal treaties with the West wounded Japanese pride. Japanese pride was first wounded before it became aggressive. The Japanese decided that ultimate security for Japan did not lie in diplomatic agreements with the West (contract approach) but in technological emulation of the West (power approach). This idea of borrowing and adapting foreign culture was not new, for the Japanese had responded to the Chinese influence earlier in their history in a way which was now basically repeated. The slogan in the confrontation with the West was, quite simply, "Western techniques and Japanese spirit."

The reign of Emperor Mutsuhito (1868–1912) came to be known as the

Meiji ("Enlightened Government") era, marked by selective westernization of Japan, as a route to military and economic parity with the West. In the words of Josefa M. Saniel:

> ... modernization was Japan's response to the nineteenth-century challenge posed by the threatening military and economic aggression from abroad at a time when Tokugawa Japan was beset with continued unrest. And after the fall of the Tokugawa *bakufu*, it was a response to the challenge of continued infringement of Japan's sovereign rights by "extra-territoriality" and "uniform tariffs"—provisions of her "unequal treaties" with the Western powers—for as long as Japanese feudal institutions persisted.[2]

The experience of enforced agreements with the West might well have left long-term scars on Japanese dignity and might have stimulated the quest for equality which characterized much of Japanese diplomacy during the Meiji period and beyond.

Included in Japanese reaction was Japanese arrogance toward outsiders. Even at such an early stage part of the Japanese quest for equality seemed to have had a racial dimension. It was a mixture of real dignity and militant arrogance. The white people were regarded as a people apart; and the Japanese felt humiliation in the face of Western arrogance. The Japanese have never been Pan-Asiatics in their nationalism. The nationalism of Japan has been profoundly inward-looking, concerned with the greatness of Japan, rather than the greatness of the colored peoples, or the Asian masses as such. Yet for part of that period western arrogance in China and Japan activated in the Japanese a response of racial defensiveness, reflected in Japanese diplomacy's struggle for parity.

There were indeed anomalies in the Japanese racial response. For example, a major element in Japanese desire for parity with the West became imperial expansion itself. In other words, Japan could not be a full equal of the western powers unless she became as imperialistic as they were. In the words of Michael Edwardes:

> The nature of Japanese hatred for the West was complex. ... Japan, by its own exertions and by the astounding metamorphosis she had forced herself to go through from the Meiji restoration onwards, had avoided occupation by one or more of the imperialists. Her leaders never forgot her narrow escapes. When Japan felt the impetus of imperial expansion herself—the natural consequences, Marxists would maintain, of her western capitalist structure—she was continually frustrated by the old colonial powers unless it suited the immediate advantage of imperial rivalries. Japan's position was that of an uninvited guest arriving late at the banquet, only to find that the choicest food was reserved for others.[3]

Edwardes argues that part of the Japanese hatred was a bitter response to the unwillingness of the western colonial powers to accept Japan as an associate in the game of imperial expansionism. External arrogance as a feature of Japanese attitudes profoundly conditioned the style of her expansionism. Behind that in turn was the old memory of extraterritoriality on Japanese soil itself, and the humiliation of Japan for nearly fifty years by this reduction of her sovereign rights. The Treaty powers of the West continued to refuse to allow their nationals to be subject to the jurisdiction of Japanese courts. Negotiations were conducted to end this reduction of Japanese sovereignty in 1871, in 1882, and in 1886, but extraterritoriality did not come to an end until 1899. The Western powers retained, even after that date, control over customs which did not come to an end until 1911. By that time Japan was beginning to consolidate her status as a great power. Her demonstrative appeal in this sense continued until World War II.

For a while after her defeat in 1945 Japan shared with China the fate of "the yellow man victimized", instead of "the yellow man triumphant". During the war itself Japan's positive image among Africans and Asians was seriously tarnished, though never completely shattered. But the way World War II ended raised questions similar to those which Prime Minister Indira Gandhi came to raise concerning the way the United States carried out the war in Vietnam—would those tactics have been used had the American enemy been European or white? Would the atomic bombs of Hiroshima and Nagasaki have been dropped on Germany, if she rather than Japan had been holding out?

The political psychology of such a decision is difficult to work out. Harry Truman was apparently unrepentant about the decision to the day he died in 1972. But whatever racial or cultural inhibitions Truman might have had about dropping such a bomb on a European enemy, there seem to have been weaker inhibitions operating on Roosevelt in ailment. According to Major-General Leslie Groves, who was in charge of the Manhattan Project which produced the bomb, President Roosevelt seriously considered dropping the first atomic bomb on Germany when he feared that the Battle of the Bulge in 1944 might result in a stalemate in Europe. The General disclosed this precisely in answer to the claim that the United States had demurred about dropping the bomb on a European enemy, but had used it on an Asian one.

Groves had pointed out the difficulties involved in changing the first atomic victims from Japanese to German. First, the bomb was not expected until August 1945; second, if for some reason the bomb did not explode, the Germans might discover what it was; third, the bomb was expected to be less effective in Germany with its solidly constructed buildings than in Japan; and fourth, there were no B-29 bombers in Europe to carry the bomb.[4]

But did the General suppress a fifth reason—conscious but never to be articulated—about different standards of "fair war" according to the race of the enemy? Perhaps no definitive answer is ever likely to emerge to this kind of question. All we know is that with Hiroshima, Japan was partially transformed in image from original aggressor to ultimate victim. She shared once again the destiny of large numbers of non-white peoples who had historically been used as raw materials for economic and military experimentation.

The Reemergence of China

While Japan was about to rejoin the ranks of the underprivileged briefly, China was taking revolutionary steps toward emerging from that status. China had more consistently been exploited by the West in the modern period than had Japan. The black world's bonds with China were therefore more consistently those of a "kindred spirit" than the bonds with Japan.

In 1959 W. E. B. Du Bois celebrated his ninety-first birthday in Peking. Du Bois was a black American who had become famous as a founding father of the Pan-African movement, and a citizen of Ghana since its independence. A black nationalist who was also a Marxist, Du Bois addressed the students and faculty of Peking University, on that occasion, in powerful lines of political rhetoric:

Speak, China, and tell your truth to Africa and the world. What people have been despised as you have? Who more than you have been rejected of men? Recall when lordly Britishers threw the rickshaw money on the ground to avoid touching a filthy hand. . . . Tell this to Africa, for today Africa stands on new feet, with new eyesight, with new brains and asks: Where am I and why?[5]

Du Bois was touching on an important theme in Sino-African relations—shared indigence and shared indignity, relating the poverty and underdevelopment of China and Africa, and their vulnerability to manipulation and humiliation by the West. Just the previous year W. E. B. Du Bois, addressing his fellow Blacks, touched upon the theme which he was later to treat more extensively in Peking: "Your nearest friends and neighbors are the colored peoples of China and India, the rest of Asia, the Middle East and the Sea Isles. . . . Your bond is not mere color of skin, but the deeper experience of wage slavery and contempt."[6]

In the privacy of their own thoughts each of Du Bois' listeners might have related his words to certain experiences in the history of Asia and

143

Africa. Certainly the concept of "wage slavery" must have had powerful historical associations to those who knew the origins of wages in Africa. When the white man came to the continent, large numbers of Africans were unwilling to let go of their traditional life-styles in pursuit of working for somebody else. A number of devices were invented by the white immigrants into Africa in order to provide additional incentives for Africans to work for wages. Preeminent amongst those devices was the simple expedient of imposing a poll-tax, or a hut-tax, on Africans, payable in cash and not in stock or harvest. That meant that Africans had to obtain cash, so that before they had learned the skills of selling some of their products in exchange for money they were forced to learn the necessity of selling their labor as a form of taxation.

Another solution to the problem of African labor linked Africa's experience to Asia's. In 1925 the labor situation in those parts of Africa which had significant white settlers had become quite acute, and there was serious discussion about seeking either Indian or Chinese indentured labor as a partial solution to the problem. In discussing the importance of the economic reconstruction of the Transvaal and Orange Free States in South Africa after the Boer War, the Rhodes Professor of Race Relations at Oxford has reminded us that: "Particular attention [was given] to railway and tariff policies and to labour questions, including the acute and prolonged controversies over the importation of Chinese labour in 1904 in order to restore a gold-mining industry at a time when native African labour was dispersed and difficult to recruit.[7]

In East Africa the choice lay between Chinese and Indians, and it is one of the accidents of history that when we use the term "Asians of East Africa" we do not mean Chinese, but Indians. Indians were imported to build the railway-line from Mombasa into the hinterland, while Chinese were imported to the Witwatersrand gold-fields of South Africa. Although India was near, and part of the British Empire, it was by no means automatic that labor should be coming from there. Apparently, however, the imperial power was less prepared to exploit her imperial subjects than to exploit colored races elsewhere: to be part of the British Empire was an insurance against excessive exploitation by the British. In this instance the concept of the white man's burden was taken seriously as an exercise in trusteeship, but a trusteeship applicable only to those who lived under the flag of a particular white power.

In 1922 legislation was passed by the British to protect Indians from being recklessly exported from their homes as cheap labor. But China was not part of the British Empire. Even Lord Lugard, one of the greatest of British colonial administrators, and one whose conception of the white man's burden had genuine liberal aspects, could argue in the

144

following terms in 1926:

There is the question of supplementing [African] labour by importing workers from overseas. The two sources of supply in the past have been India and China. . . . The Indian Immigration Act in 1922 has prohibited the indenture of Indian Coolie labour. There remains China. . . . The Chinese refuse to bring their wives with them . . . and there is the serious question of miscegenation. On the other hand, if the strict supervision exercised by a special official which is adopted in Malaya [over Chinese labour] is enforced, there are no grounds for humanitarian objections as far as the Chinese themselves are concerned.[8]

Twenty years later the Communist party of China was on its way to victory. In its civil war with the nationalists the tide was turned in 1947. That was also the year of India's independence. Two years later the world's most populous country became a communist state. The Chinese, who had been exported before as substitutes for defiant African labor, now dedicated themselves afresh to the Marxist fight against "wage slavery" at large.

In some ways their communist revolution was more relevant to the present societies of Africa than the Russian version of a communist takeover. It is true that the Soviet Union at the time of its revolution was much less of an industrial power than it has since become. But even at that time the Soviet Union differed economically from the bulk of Asia and Africa more than China did in 1949. The geocultural distance between the Russians and the Africans was in some respects even greater than that separating China from black Africa. Certain aspects of Chinese rural life provided an area of shared experience with peasants elsewhere. The Chinese communist revolution was a Third World revolution in a sense which the Russian could not, by its very definition as a second world, ever be.

Yet the very success of the Chinese revolution could create a new *distance* between China and the smaller countries of Asia and Africa. Following that revolution China began to consolidate her position in the globe, and to initiate a process of reemergence as a major power in the world. Before long the question was bound to be asked whether China belonged to the ranks of the weak and underprivileged, or was about to join the ranks of the powerful. For as long as China could be deemed to be part of the underdeveloped sector of the globe, relations between herself and Africa, experimental and inchoate as they were, could be deemed to be relations basically between *peers*. Of course, China was many times bigger than even the largest of the African states, but being on the defensive against the major industrial powers of the world bestowed on nonindustrialized countries generally comradeship in poverty. By the time President Julius K. Nyerere visited China for the second time, however, the differences between Tanzania and China were becoming pertinent. As Nyerere put it quite simply when addressing Prime Minister Chou En-lai in June 1968, "Mr. Prime Minister, your country is a nuclear power, mine is not."[9] When this disparity is related to another statement by Julius Nyerere, the implications are again hard to avoid. As the Mwalimu put it in another context:

> A poor nation which is an ally of such a powerful nation is, almost always, in danger of becoming a satellite of that rich and powerful state; its independence often becomes limited by the very action taken to defend it. It cannot hope to make the policy decisions of the alliance, yet it will be bound by them. It cannot be expected to influence the actions of its big partner; yet every action of its own will be affected by them.[10]

Nyerere spoke in these terms in discussing why Tanzania should not be tied to any of the major powers. At that stage the term major powers still tended to refer to the United States, the Soviet Union, Britain, and France—and to exclude China. But at the very moment that Nyerere was speaking, the position was changing. China was becoming a major power in her own right; and Tanzania was becoming the most important economic friend of China on the African continent.

Given this situation, was China in the process of evolving the role of "Big Brother" in such parts of the Third World? Was a neo-imperial destiny awaiting the new China comparable to that of pre-war Japan? Are we witnessing a birth of the yellow man's burden?

We hope to show that China's relations with Africa since the communist revolution have passed through three stages. We might describe these stages as, first, the stage of pan-pigmentationalism, or the affinity of color; second, the stage of pan-proletarianism, the affinity of shared indigence; and third, the beginnings of pan-socialism, the bonds of explicit leftward ideological commitment. Yet like most stages in political and diplomatic history, these three have not been distinct but have tended to overlap. The affinity of color is connected with kinship culture; pan-proletarianism is connected with economic culture; pan-socialism is preeminently an aspect of political culture.

Two East African countries lend themselves very well as case studies of this entire process, Kenya and Tanzania. Kenya was at one time expected to become the most revolutionary of all black African countries, simply because it was the one which went furthest in armed rebellion against colonialism. As the Kikuyu fighters rose in defiance of the White Man's Burden, the bonds of pan-pigmentationalism won them applause in different parts of Asia, and certainly in the new communist state of China.

Within three years of the success of the peasant revolution in China, a peasant revolt took place in Kenya. Much of the agitation behind the Mau Mau insurrection in Kenya was by people who were landless, living as squatters on European estates, and observing hungrily large tracts of land, uncultivated and unused, reserved exclusively for whites. As Donald L. Barnett put it in his introduction to Karari Njamaa's *Mau Mau from Within:*

> It is not only the brute fact of landlessness, land hunger and insecurity of tenure which conditioned the Kikuyu involvement in the nationalist movement and peasant revolt; it is also the fact that for a people who attach such sacred meaning to the land the areas alienated remained within their field of experience unattainable yet in considerable measure unused by its new [white] owners.[11]

The final outcome was the revolt of the rural dispossessed—and the long years of Kenya's state of emergency. The white man's burden had proved to be too heavy for the black peasants of the central lands of Kenya.

Did the Chinese peasant revolution cast its shadow across Kenya's peasant revolt? We are back to the issue of demonstration effect. Certainly many of the white settlers suspected communist instigation behind the insurrection, though because of Jomo Kenyatta's visit to the Soviet Union in the 1930's, this communist instigation was deemed to have come through Stalin's Russia rather than Mao's China. And yet there were aspects of the Mau Mau phenomenon which betrayed at least a certain awareness of the Chinese model. The very name "Mau Mau" has continued to have a touch of mystery about it. Rosberg and Nottingham traced the name to 1948, the critical initiation of the Chinese revolution. One of the leaders of the Mau Mau insurrection, Waruhiu Itote, came to be called "General China". The outbreak of violence in Kenya coincided with the lingering Korean war. Harold C. Hinton in his book, *Communist China in World Politics,* suggestively refers to a "General Korea" within the Mau Mau movement. The British were also involved at the time in fighting communist "terrorism" in Malaya. And Rosberg and Nottingham refer to British application in Kenya of "rehabilitation" methods based in part on experience in fighting ethnic Chinese in Malaya.

On the attainment of independence a pan-proletarian theme emerged, as China extended forms of material and moral support to the newly independent East African nation. Indeed, on the eve of independence forms

147

of special aid were being negotiated for Kenya by Jaramogi Oginga Odinga, who was shortly to become Vice-President of independent Kenya. The rhetoric of this period was that the peoples of China and Africa needed to help each other, in the face of the menace from the more powerful countries of the northern hemisphere. Among the poor of the world, some were less poor than others. And if China had certain services she could render to Kenya, that itself was an exercise in proletarian solidarity.

Then the government of Kenya began to drift ideologically to the right. Instead of building up socialism, as many had expected the country of the Mau Mau insurrection to do, Kenya under President Kenyatta proceeded to build a private enterprise system. Before long the alliance between Kenyatta and Oginga Odinga was broken. The latter became the chief voice of radical ideology in Kenya, and also the chief friend of the Chinese. The support that communist China gave to Oginga Odinga and his party, the Kenya Peoples' Union, was indeed an exercise in pan-socialism—but with a difference. In the Kenyan situation the Chinese were not supporting Mr. Kenyatta's government, but were extending moral, and to some extent material, aid to a group which was opposing Mr. Kenyatta's policies. Chinese operations in Kenya in that period were part of a general pattern of disguised Chinese ties with dissident groups in different parts of Africa. In defiance of normal methods of interstate relations, the Chinese were prepared to "offer themselves as the allies of oppositionists, rebels and power seekers". To use the words of Colin Legum, "In this field they have virtually no competition, neither the West nor the Russians will openly support movements against the *status quo*."[12] Kenya's experience illustrates precisely this passage from the ties of anticolonialism and pan-pigmentationalism, through the ties of Third World solidarity on the basis of pan-proletarianism, and finally to the support of leftist opposition groups as an exercise in pan-socialism proper.

In the experience of *Tanzania,* our second East African case study, the sequence is different. The Zanzibari part of the United Republic of Tanzania had earlier links with China. In the last phases of colonial rule Abdulrahman Babu, the Zanzibari Marxist, established fairly strong links with China, links of shared racial humiliation, shared indigence, as well as shared socialism. For the bulk of the Zanzibar Nationalist Party, the links with China constituted a marriage of convenience based on shared anticolonialism, rather than pan-socialism.

China's association with mainland Tanzania under Julius Nyerere finally matured into a legitimate form of pan-socialism between one government and another, both influenced in varying degrees by socialist values and radical perspectives. To that extent China's relations with Julius Nyerere were fundamentally different from her relations with Oginga Odinga. One was an alliance with dissidents in Kenya, the other was an alliance with the rulers in Tanzania.

Independence and the Sino-Kenyan Entente

The official end of the state of emergency in Kenya was in January 1960. That was also the year when the Lancaster House Conference in London agreed to an African majority in the Kenyan Legislative Council and eventual independence for Kenya under African rule. The Mau Mau had been defeated on the battlefield but had won the political war. African self-rule was at last on the horizon.

Meanwhile Maoism was analyzing the world in a new way. The developed countries, in Mao's thought, were the cities of the world, while the underdeveloped constituted the massive rural countryside. The revolt of the future was the revolt of the peasants in the countryside against the opulent luxury of the city. Here was a ruralization of Marxism, allocating the ultimate historic destiny to a rural revolutionary class rather than to an urban proletariat. This interpretation was to assume an ironic twist when China's friends in Kenya were more among the urban Luo than the rural Kikuyu.

1960 was the year not only when Kenya's settler hegemony was broken, but also when more than fifteen other African countries became independent. Communist China, a self-appointed leader of a global proletarian movement against the wealthy developed countries, was soon making a major diplomatic offensive to carry the message of revolution into Africa. And as Kenya approached independence, prospects for Sino-Kenyan cordiality seemed very good. At first, in her nonalignment, Kenya seemed quite willing to pursue the possibility of having relations with both Chinas, nationalist and communist. In August 1963 on the eve of independence, a Kenya delegation signed an agreement on economic and technical cooperation in Taiwan. Under the agreement Nationalist China was to dispatch a survey team to Kenya, to be followed by a farming demonstration team consisting of ten to twelve experienced Chinese farmers to help grow paddy rice, vegetables, and upland crops. But the communist Chinese soon established an edge over their rivals. Almost immediately after independence the Communists had sent a chargé d'affaires to Kenya, with an ambassador to follow.

Meanwhile the plot of competitions within competitions was thickening. The Russians extended aid to Kenya, announcing it within months of independence. And three days after the announcement of Russian aid an agreement between Kenya and communist China was disclosed by the two governments. The Chinese were offering a twofold plan, first a loan of $7.5 million free of interest, to cover the cost of equipment and technical assistance during the five years beginning in July, and second, a grant of some $2.5 million toward the relief of immediate financial stress. Jaramogi Oginga Odinga had a lot to do with the success of the negotiations. The *East African Standard* enthusiastically responded to the Chinese offer of aid:

> This practical gesture of Chinese friendship can be added to the Russian promises as the direct outcome of the visit paid to Peking and Moscow by the two Ministers, Mr. Oginga Odinga and Mr. Murumbi. There is a noteworthy difference between the two sets of proposals. Whereas the Russians are offering help with specific projects through credit for building, equipment and technical assistance—with the exception of a hospital to be provided as a gift and free equipment and staff for two years for the technical college—the Chinese are making equipment and technical help available for such projects as the Kenya Government itself may decide.[13]

The *Standard's* editorial went on to say that the Chinese approach was more consistent with the principle of Kenya's autonomy than the Russian terms were.

On balance the Russians have lived up to their promises much better than the Chinese have. The hospital which Kenyatta opened in Kisumu in 1969, accompanied by demonstrations and several deaths, was part of the package which the Russians promised to give to Kenya in 1964. In fairness it should also be pointed out that China's failure to live up to the promises made was in part due to the changing attitudes of Kenya's government toward her.

But in those early days after independence, prospects still looked very promising for Sino-Kenyan cordiality. A Kenyan delegation of ten members went to mainland China in August 1964. If the Chinese were supposed to be the leaders of a world peasant movement against the wealth of the developed countries, China's rural achievements gave them strong demonstration credentials. The fifteen-member delegation to China was led by Mr. Achieng-Oneko, later in detention but then Minister for Information and Broadcasting and Tourism, along with Mr. Sagini, who was then Minister for Natural Resources. One member of the delegation mentioned how impressed they had been by the Chinese system of farming and the textile industry; another paid tribute to China's ingenuity in land utilization.[14] The lure of demonstration was at play.

When the Chinese exploded their first atomic device, Kenya was the first African government to extend congratulations. Kenya's ambassador even talked about sharing nuclear knowledge as a form of sharing nuclear socialism. "I venture to say that no doubt the Chinese would make available this knowledge to African and Asian scientists in the interest of world peace." [15] China's demonstration impact ranged from rice fields to nuclear reactors, from rural mobilization to diplomatic rhetoric.

Domestic Cleavage and External Tension

But gradually domestic politics in Kenya began to disturb the still waters of Sino-Kenyan cordiality. In fact, Kenya is the clearest example in Africa of the interrelationship between domestic politics and external relations. On balance, it is clearly the domestic politics of Kenya that have determined her external relations, and not the other way round. The focus of Chinese attention was Jaramogi Oginga Odinga, a Luo leader. For as long as Oginga Odinga was the trusted Vice-President of the country, relations with China could remain cordial, even if not necessarily warm. In old travel books China was sometimes credited with oriental courtesy as part of her culture. But in reality China's diplomatic style has not always been characterized by any singular attachment to courteous niceties. Even when she decided to launch a major diplomatic offensive to carry the message of revolution into Africa, the effort soon became more offensive than diplomatic. One African country after another began to express some kind of disapproval of the activities of the Chinese embassy in its midst. It would not therefore have been surprising if Kenya's relations with China fell short of warmth, even if the government's relations with Oginga Odinga had not progressively deteriorated.

Oginga Odinga himself seemed to feel that what some people regarded as irritating in the Chinese was in fact their natural spontaneity. This is a question of cultural style. The Chinese made clear their feelings and allowed themselves to be naturally demonstrative, according to this interpretation. Mr. Odinga, invited to dinner by the American ambassador in Kenya, had been so pleased by the candid atmosphere of the dinner party that he decided to pay the Americans a compliment by saying that Americans as a people were basically like the Chinese, warm and spontaneous, but the Russians, in their cold diplomatic style, were just like the British. Ambassador Attwood of the United States was so moved by the compliment that he was not quite sure how to respond to it. [16]

But on balance the Chinese in their candor made more enemies than friends. Perhaps the Chinese shared with the Japanese a cultural arrogance toward others. It is true that the Chinese are not alone in their

151

intrigues in African countries. And the intrigues of the different embassies and their readiness at times to take sides in internal disputes between Africans have been known to exasperate African governments. In September 1964, Grace Ibingira, then Secretary-General of the Uganda People's Congress and Minister of State in Premier Obote's Government, warned some foreign embassies that were trying to influence political opinion in Uganda: "I wish to give public warning that if such activities continue I will personally instigate expulsion from this country of such officials from foreign embassies, and this is no idle threat.[17]

Even after we have made all these allowances, it remains true that the Sino-Kenyan dispute was an effect rather than a cause of the internal cleavages within Kenya itself. Gradually Oginga Odinga lost the Ministry of Home Affairs, the Vice-Presidency of the country, then the Vice-Presidency of the Party and finally broke away completely from the Kenya African National Union and formed his rival Party, the Kenya Peoples' Union.

In the meantime Kenya had experienced its first assassination. On February 24, 1965 the man who was regarded as Odinga's chief intellectual adviser on political strategy and tactics, Pio de Gama Pinto, was shot dead in the driveway of his own home by two gunmen who later escaped by car. Pinto, a Marxist, had apparently worked for Odinga in a variety of capacities, including that of serving as a liaison man with some friendly embassies. The politics of violent intrigue had begun to affect independent Kenya.

The question of external support for Oginga Odinga's internal activities continued to bedevil both domestic politics and Sino-Kenyan relations for quite a while. If former Ambassador Attwood's account is to be trusted, Mzee Kenyatta was uneasy both about external help to Tom Mboya from the West and to Oginga Odinga from the East. Attwood was called in to see Mzee Kenyatta in June 1964 to discuss the problem of the outside financing of Kenya's politicians. Kenyatta said that he realized that Mboya had been getting help from the AFL-CIO and other western labor groups to build up Kenya's trade union movement. Kenyatta wanted to be sure that such a system had stopped after independence. The Ambassador said he would make enquiries. He also expressed his agreement that all aid to independent Kenya should go through the government and not through individual politicians. The Ambassador then asked Mzee Kenyatta about Odinga's subsidies from the Chinese and the Russians. Mr. Kenyatta said: "I know about them, I have already called in the Ambassadors and told them to stop."[18]

The Spectre of Zanzibar

By that time the ghost of the Zanzibar revolution had begun to haunt the affairs of independent Kenya. In Zanzibar we have one further link between China's impact on Kenya politics and her growing importance in Tanzania as a whole.

It is not at all clear that the communist Chinese were involved in events immediately preceding the actual overthrow of the Sultan's regime in Zanzibar. What is clear is that for many years before the actual revolution, the communist Chinese had been backing some radicals in Zanzibar, especially Abdulrahman Babu. One of the ironies of the story of Zanzibar is that the original recipients of Chinese support were in fact members of the Zanzibar Nationalist Party (Z.N.P.), which was the main party overthrown at the time of the revolution. Babu was at one time Secretary-General of the Nationalist party. The Chinese provided a variety of support including a printing machine for the newspaper the *Mwongozi,* which for quite a while was the great voice of the Nationalist party, the radical party of Zanzibar. The Afro-Shirazi Party was easily the more conservative of the two parties.

In 1963 Babu broke away from the Zanzibar Nationalist Party, as pre-independence elections were on the horizon, and formed a new party, the Umma Party. I saw Babu at the Grand Hotel in Kampala shortly after he broke away from the Nationalists. I had known him for years, from the old imperial days in London when he was a journalist and I was a student. I asked him why he was forming a new party so late in the day when the chances of having any impact on the elections seemed to be negligible. Babu answered that his resignation and the formation of the new party were basically tactical. A few months later the Zanzibar Revolution exploded on the East African scene. Babu himself was away at the time. On his return to East Africa, it was again significant that one of the first people he was reported to have seen was the Chinese ambassador. And among the people who descended on the newly liberated island after independence were the Chinese, as well as East Germans and other advisors and assistants from communist countries.

The spectre of Zanzibar came to haunt the Kenya government later. When Mzee Kenyatta and Joseph Murumbi saw Ambassador Attwood of the United States in 1964 about the question of external finances coming into Kenya for individual politicians, they reportedly asked the Ambassador if the United States could provide the police with some planes to increase its mobility in case of a "Zanzibar" kind of uprising. The Ambassador claims to have promised to forward the request to Washington.[19]

The scare started fairly early. Not long after the revolution in Zanzibar mutinies took place first in Tanganyika (later mainland Tanzania) and then in Uganda and Kenya. The Zanzibar revolution had a demonstration impact on the mainland. The soldiers decided to try out their strength on the politicians. The region as a whole experienced a period of acute uncertainty until President Obote had the courage to set the example by inviting British troops to come and restore order. The fact that Zanzibar could act as a catalyst in this way profoundly affected the thinking of the heads of governments in the three countries, particularly in Tanzania and Kenya.

The Chinese Prime Minister, Chou En-lai, was scheduled to visit the East African countries shortly after, but Kenya and Uganda decided that the time was not opportune for such an appearance in their countries. The Chinese Prime Minister did visit Somalia, and in the course of his speech in Mogadishu he said: "Revolutionary prospects are excellent throughout the African Continent."[20] Chou En-lai returned to that theme when he visited Tanzania in June 1965. He reiterated: "An exceedingly favorable situation for revolution prevails in Africa." This time the Kenya government was even more indignant, as relations with China had by then cooled simultaneously with the cooling of relations between Mzee Kenyatta and Oginga Odinga. An official spokesman of the Kenya government vigorously answered the Chinese Prime Minister:

> It is not clear to the Kenya Government what type or what form of revolution he has in mind. But the Kenya Government wishes it to be known that Kenya intends to avert all revolutions irrespective of their origins or whether they come from inside or are influenced from outside. It will also be remembered that the Kenya Government recently banned the booklet entitled *Revolution in Africa* which attacked not only the leadership of our President, but also that of the President of Tanzania and the Prime Minister of Uganda. Finally the Government wishes to re-affirm its stand by the declared policy of non-alignment in world power politics.[21]

The old spectre of the Zanzibar revolution seemed once again to influence Kenya's reactions to Chinese taunts on revolutionary prospects. But we must not assume that it was only Kenya which regarded Zanzibar as a potential catalyst in its demonstration effects. It is quite possible that one of the major reasons behind President Nyerere's initiative to bring about a union between Zanzibar and Tanganyika was the fear of Zanzibar becoming another Cuba, affecting the stability of the mainland in some serious ways. Of course the union was also motivated by cultural and linguistic ties between Zanzibaris and Tanganyikans. The union was also a child to some extent of Mwalimu Nyerere's own Pan-

Africanism. But the swiftness, the sense of urgency with which it was brought into being, might have been due to a compelling desire for the ideological containment of the island. The rapid succession of the mutinies on the mainland so soon after the revolution in Zanzibar had deeply disturbed the Mwalimu. The authorities in Zanzibar might be easier to influence and advise, and even pressure, if Zanzibar was part of a union with Tanganyika than if it continued to be a sovereign revolutionary island a few miles from Dar-es-Salaam.

In Kenya the fear of Chinese money as an instrument of subversion continued to October 1969. President Kenyatta was still giving heated speeches about the dangers of foreign subversion through foreign subsidies on the eve of his fatal visit to Kisumu, Oginga Odinga's stronghold.

Curiously enough, relations between Kenya and China were maintained, in spite of recurrent demands by many Kenyan nationalists that the country should break with the communist Chinese. The Chinese themselves continued for a while to be indifferent to the sensibilities of others. When the country was plunged into grief on the assassination of Tom Mboya, Minister of Planning and Economic Development, the Chinese Embassy in Nairobi refused to fly its flag at half mast. It was a calculated symbolic defiance, expressing deep disapproval both of the Kenya government and of Mboya personally. Once again there followed demonstrations outside the Chinese Embassy. In fact, demonstrations in front of the Chinese Embassy in Nairobi have been a recurrent phenomenon in the turbulent story of Sino-Kenyan relations.

In May 1965 this spectre brought Kenya-Ugandan relations to a dangerous point of strain. On May 17, a convoy of forty lorries with Chinese weapons was stopped by the Kenya police. The lorries had in fact crashed through a road block at night as they were passing through Kenya from Tanzania to Uganda. The Kenyan authorities impounded the convoy and its cargo and took into custody the Uganda drivers. The fact that the lorries were passing through Odinga's home area aroused suspicion that they were destined precisely for that area. President Kenyatta was very angry. Even if the cargo was not going to the western region of Kenya, his government should have been informed about the passage of such dangerous goods through his country. He described the whole exercise as "an act of criminal folly," and refused to release either the convoy or the drivers without a personal explanation from President Obote. It would seem that the arms had in any case been ordered from China for the Congolese rebels. The order had been with the tacit cooperation of Uganda and Tanzania. President Obote had to make a special trip to Nairobi to reassure Mzee Kenyatta.[22]

To some extent, of course, the Zanzibar experience was not strictly relevant to the Kenya situation. After all, the prerevolutionary regime in Zanzibar had been a minority government both electorally and in terms of the racial composition of the leadership. But the present Kenya government is not a minority government in either of those senses. Nor is the Kenya government so weak as to be capable of being overthrown with the ease with which John Okello and his comrades overthrew the Zanzibari regime. Nevertheless, the relevant factor in the Zanzibar experience was the simple fact of external participation in revolutionary activities and the kind of planning which went with it. It is this kind of subversion which Kenya has been on guard against.

The great mistake of the prerevolutionary regime in Zanzibar was its supreme complacency on the eve of its own overthrow. There are times when a little nervousness on the part of a government is a good thing, since it means that the government is not excessively self-confident or excessively complacent. But, in spite of evidence that something was afoot, the government of Sheikh Mohammed Shamte and Sheikh Ali Muhsin remained supremely undisturbed barely a week before the coup. Some of the policy decisions their government took on the eve of the revolution were short-sighted enough to undermine the loyalty of the police on whom their own security might have depended. Talks about repatriating mainlanders back to Tanganyika were hardly calculated to consolidate the allegiance of mainland members of the island police force. The prerevolutionary regime on the island was simply too complacent.

The risk in Kenya in October 1969 was not excessive complacency but excessive alertness. When a guard is excessively on the alert there is a danger that he may mistake the rustle of every leaf in the night breeze for the footsteps of an intruder on the prowl. Too much complacency on the part of the government in guarding the nation is bad; but too much alertness may also have its risks. In the shadow of Chinese support for opposition groups, President Kenyatta's government was getting too strict with the Luo people. Oginga Odinga was detained; the opposition party was banned; and the curtain came down on yet another phase of Sino-Kenyan relations.

Race, Railways and Revolution

Among the most striking of the lines from Rudyard Kipling's poem, "The White Man's Burden" are these:

The ports ye shall not enter,
The roads ye shall not tread,

Go make them with your living,
And mark them with your dead.

We shall discuss more fully later this issue of imperial mobility. The whole idea of building ports and constructing the new means of communications into virgin lands was part of the whole imperial mission. East Africa too had its road builders and port builders. But of particular significance to the history of communications in this part of the world is, quite simply, the railway line from the Indian Ocean to Lake Victoria in the hinterland. It is indeed arguable that no single factor in the recent history of East Africa has been more important for regional integration that that railway line. The white man's burden contributed to the partial unification of Kenya, Uganda and Tanzania by building that track for the trains.

It now seems possible that one of the most important contributory factors to further integration between East Africa and Central Africa, would be a railway line—this time built by the Chinese. Kenya and Uganda were indissolubly tied because of such a track built by white endeavor; Tanzania and Zambia may also become deeply interlocked through Chinese engineering. The burden of the white man and the burden of the yellow man have both sought fulfillment in enhancing African mobility.

The Kenya-Uganda railway was part of a major imperial strategy in Britain, a factor which ought not to be underestimated. The railway had connections with an imperial strategy that included within it India, Egypt, Sudan, Uganda as well as what later came to be Kenya. Egypt was regarded as important partly because of the Suez Canal and access to India and Australasia. But, it was argued, whoever controlled Egypt had also to control the rest of the Nile valley. And so the Sudan was annexed as an extra protection for the British occupation of Egypt, as well as a logical extension of Egyptian hegemony. And because the waters of the White Nile had their origins in the heart of Africa, Uganda had to be annexed in order to complete British control over the Nile valley. And the way to Uganda from the coast was through what came to be known as Kenya, so that territory too had to be annexed in order to maximize access to the waters of Lake Victoria and the source of the Nile. The railway line from Mombasa to Lake Victoria was supposed to be a continuous line linking the Indian Ocean to the Nile and then onward to the Mediterranean and beyond.

The first construction staff for the East African Railway arrived at Mombasa in December 1895. In 1896 a viaduct was built at Makupa, linking the island of Mombasa with the massive mainland of eastern Africa. Having built a railway line, there was every case for making it pay. But how could it pay if on the way there were poverty-stricken villages, economically underdeveloped societies, and primitive systems of production? Out of such considerations grew the idea of encouraging white men to come and settle in Kenya, tame the wilderness, and transport the products along the railway line to the sea. Kenya came to be known by some of its white enthusiasts as indeed "a white man's country". The railway line had opened up new possibilities for the very concept of the white man's burden, with consequences which included the Mau Mau insurrection against the white presence, as well as the more positive result of greater regional integration in East Africa as a whole.

Throughout the rest of the colonial period there were some extensions of these railway lines. Tanganyika was more fully integrated after it ceased to be a German colony and fell under British administration as a mandate from the League of Nations. Other extensions of the railway line were added from time to time. But nothing after the initial construction matched in importance and potential consequence that other project which was born after independence to link Tanzania to Zambia, and thereby connect East Africa as a whole with Central and Southern Africa.

The preliminary survey for a railway line linking Tanzania and Zambia was to be paid for from the start by Britain and Canada. This was the feasibility study, which did indeed affirm that such a line was possible and potentially valuable. The African countries concerned applied to the International Monetary Fund for a grant to implement the project. The World Bank rejected it in 1964, arguing that development in Tanzania and Zambia might be better served by more pressing projects. In 1965 China stepped in, offering to build the 1060-mile railway. Action was swift. In August 1965 a feasibility study was conducted by the Chinese themselves on the Tanzanian section of the railway. A similar survey was concluded in Zambia by early 1968.

Rhodesia's Unilateral Declaration of Independence had consequences which increased the urgency for the railway line, especially from Zambia's point of view. Firmly tied during the colonial period to the economy of Southern Rhodesia, and relying for access to the sea partly on Portuguese territory, the Zambians were feeling a sense of imperial claustrophobia and they needed new openings to the north for a breath of political survival.

On September 5, 1967 an agreement concluded between China, Tanzania and Zambia was signed in Peking. The railway was estimated to cost up to something like $400 million, and China granted a loan which was interest-free for twenty-five years. Construction was scheduled to begin in March 1970, and was expected to take five years.

There is little doubt that the Tanzania-Zambia railway line is the most important single project in foreign economic aid undertaken by communist China so far. The project did indeed imply a significant sacrifice by the Chinese. As George T. Yu has put it:

> The estimated cost of $340–$400 million [for the Tanzanian-Zambian Railway] will double China's aid commitments to Africa. In view of China's own development needs, this cost is not negligible. China's own railway development, for example, has been poorly served. It has been estimated that China has added only 10,000 miles of railway since 1949 to the mere 12,500 miles which the regime inherited. It could be said that China will be deprived of the 1,060 miles of railway being contributed to Tanzania's and Zambia's development.[23]

The railway line has by no means been the only form of aid China has extended to Tanzania. The extent of her loans is second only to that of Britain. The range of projects handled by the Chinese has been from the Friendship Textile Mill to the multipurpose Ruvu State Farm as a contribution to improved methods of agricultural production.[24]

The aid to Tanzania does fall within the pan-proletarian conception, but it even more decisively falls within the pan-socialist conception of Chinese diplomacy. By the middle of the 1960's China was undergoing an agonising reappraisal of her policy in Africa. The initial phases had been based too systematically on assumptions derived from pan-pigmentationalism and pan-proletarianism. There was an indiscriminate commitment to promoting special relations with African countries. One dimension concerned the need to have more and more states recognize mainland China as against the nationalist Taiwan government. But the other side of the policy assumed that an Africa newly liberated from colonialism was eligible for solidarity with a country like communist China.

Concurrent with this phase was the strategy of supporting dissidents. To some extent the two strategies were mutually contradictory, but the Chinese pursued them simultaneously nonetheless. They sought to have relations with countries as ideologically diverse as Guinea and Tunisia. But they were also prepared to support opposition groups in those countries if they were more revolutionary in commitment.

By 1965 the Chinese were reconsidering this dual strategy. A certain diplomatic retreat began to take place, with a formal break of relations by Burundi in 1965, the Central African Republic in 1966, Dahomey in 1966, Ghana after the fall of Nkrumah also in 1966, and Tunisia in 1967. China's diplomatic relations with African countries fell from a maximum of eighteen in 1964 and 1965 to about a dozen in 1970. China was entering a period of diplomatic selectivity in Africa. She sought ties with countries that were self-consciously socialist at the level of governments and authoritative structures, rather than with dissident socialist groups in what were otherwise non-leftist countries.

Tanzania as the most influential of all the radical African states began to assume extra attraction for Chinese foreign policy, helping to radicalize even further Nyerere's own perspective on problems of development. This was the phase of Nyerere's rediscovery of China, and his whole strategy of self-reliance was profoundly influenced by a growing awareness of what China had achieved.

Initially Nyerere's desire to establish ties with China was influenced more by reasons of nonalignment than by reasons of pan-socialism. There was a growing feeling in Tanzania that too close an attachment to the West in trade and general economic relations compromised the commitment implicit in nonalignment. And nonalignment to President Nyerere became connected to some extent with his notions of economic independence and national self-reliance. The excessive concern shown by the West in the initial phases of Nyerere's relations with China only increased Nyerere's conviction that this was the right decision. His commitment was toward diversifying Tanzania's benefactors and friends, rather than toward dispensing with the West altogether.

But after a while, with Nyerere's rediscovery of China and her achievement, the pan-socialist dimension also entered the scene.

"Communism and Communication"—the first train to travel along the Tanzanian-Zambian railway-line may well have to proclaim that dual slogan in the future.

The idea of pan-socialism was providing a new arena of interaction between the black man and the yellow man in the bid to open up central and eastern Africa.

Conclusion

The strategy of this chapter so far has been from the general to the particular—from the broad lines of the history of Japan and China in a racial perspective to the specifics of Mao's policy for eastern Africa. We have sought to demonstrate in this that China's relations with Africa have moved in three circles of affinity: first, solidarity based on shared racial and colonial humiliation (pan-pigmentationalism); second, solidarity based on shared underdevelopment and indigence (pan-proletarianism); and finally solidarity based on socialism itself. We have focussed especially on Kenya and Tanzania, partly because these two countries have had a special status for policy makers in Peking and have manifested exceptionally significant factors inherent in the wider phenomenon of Sino-African relations at large.

The Chinese emergence as a world power poses for underdeveloped Africa questions which, though different, are not entirely unrelated to those which arose in the initial waves of Europe's penetration of the African continent. Issues concerning the responsibility of the developed toward the underdeveloped are a more modern and less bigoted version of the obligations of the more "civilized" towards the less civilized.

The white man's burden as a concept was tied to the more bigoted approach. But if there is a yellow man's burden, it seems, for the time being, to be far less racialistic than its predecessor. The Chinese, unlike the Japanese before World War II, are socialists. The Chinese may have their own opinions about the rest of the world, but their behavior toward black Tanzanians bears little of the discriminatory and directly invidious attitudes either of white arrogance or of Japanese chauvinism of an earlier period. Chinese chauvinism is clearly more controlled in interpersonal contacts, and far less institutionalized than its Caucasian or older Japanese equivalent. The yellow man's burden under the Chinese must therefore be regarded as an exercise where the yellowness of the more developed country is deemed by that country itself to be irrelevant to its technological superiority. The relationship is indeed between the more developed and the less developed, and not basically between the inherently better civilized and the inherently inferior. The place of race in Sino-African relations has remained more significant as a reaction to the historical role of the white races of the world, rather than as direct color consciousness on the part of the Chinese.

Given Chinese historic nationalism and chauvinism, there is no doubt that some degree of condescension is present in their inner orientation toward their new black friends. On the other hand, as an editorial in a British newspaper put it, "Africans can be relied upon to notice that the Chinese are not black either."[25]

Meanwhile the railway line that the Chinese are helping to build will not only serve the purpose of linking East with Central Africa but, temporarily, may also serve the purpose of loosening the ties among the East African countries themselves. In 1965 a correspondent of the *New York Times* predicted that China's evolving commercial relations with Tanzania would militate against East African unity. Referring to the working sessions that Chou En-lai and President Nyerere had been having at that time, Lawrence Fellows asserted:

It now seems almost certain that Tanzania is ready to impose almost a complete ban on imports from her neighbor to the north. . . . The Chinese have already begun to transport clothing, bicycles, sewing machines, canned goods, radios, toys and other items to Dar-es-Salaam for sale so as to raise funds to pay for development programs.[26]

Fellows exaggerated the divisive impact of China on East Africa, but his interpretation of the situation did have a core of plausibility. Chinese aid to Tanzania has necessitated from year to year "both the import of equipment to implement the aid program and the import of Chinese goods to help meet local costs." What is involved in this kind of interaction is a situation where special forms of aid to the less developed country entail special forms of imports from the more developed country. The local expenditure of some of the Chinese forms of aid entailed the importation of goods which were competitive with goods coming from Tanzania's own East African neighbors.

The railway has been reported to cost an estimated $340–400 million; Tanzania and Zambia were expected to contribute about 60% of the expenses by purchasing consumer goods. A basic issue concerned this massive important of Chinese consumer goods. For one thing, how would these imports affect the existing Tanzanian trade patterns with Europe and with East Africa?[27]

If then the ramifications of the new railway line between Zambia and Tanzania are adversely affecting the economic integration that previously existed between Tanzania and Kenya, the older railway line, constructed at the time of the coming of the white man, is now having its regional impact diluted by the new railway line being built by the Chinese. The Marxist dialectic has in its own inscrutable way begun to play havoc with the dialectic of regional communication. And yet these adverse consequences of the Chinese participation in East African development are bound to be of shorter-term importance than the exciting possibilities of expanding the African transportation network.

There is also the possibility that a major road right across Africa from Mombasa on the east coast to Lagos on the west may be built by the Japanese. The Japanese have been exploring this idea with vigor. If the road linking East Africa to West Africa were to materialize, history would indeed say that Africa's communication system received its most important contributions in the twentieth century from independent initiatives by, on one side, countries associated with the white man's burden and, on the other side, countries associated with the "yellow peril".

The biocultural distance between the yellow and the black races may not itself have narrowed. In fact, the Japanese, partly through their second economic miracle since World War II, have even obtained the courtesy title of "white" from the most racist of all contemporary regimes, that of South Africa. Japan's incredible reassertion of industrial preeminence since her Hiroshima has again consolidated her credentials as the first economic giant outside Europe and North America.

But although the biocultural distance between Africa and both Japan and China persists, these yellow giants have nevertheless been playing a significant role in reducing the distance between Africans themselves. The demonstration role of China and Japan now lies in their paradigmatic strategies of development. There was a time when the paradigms of capitalist and socialist strategies of development were the United States and the Soviet Union respectively. We may now be witnessing transformation of the yellow peril into *the yellow paradigm*. Japan and China may be emerging as a more relevant pair of models for much of the Third World than either the United States or the Soviet Union. The very fact that the biocultural distance between Japan and China is narrower than between America and Russia adds additional interest to the very divergent strategies that these two yellow giants have adopted. Though culturally close, one has become an impressive capitalist model, the other an influential communist paradigm.

The old debate between capitalism and socialism as strategies of development in Africa is in the process of being reopened with reference to the striking performance of oriental powers. The gradual shift away from western paradigms and models may itself become one of the most important contributions that the yellow powers will make toward a less Euro-centric and more symmetrical world culture.

Footnotes

1. Consult Robert A. Scalapino, "Ideology and Modernization: The Japanese Case," Chapter III, in David E. Apter (editor), *Ideology and Discontent* (New York: The Free Press of Glencoe, 1964) p. 94. See also Robert J. Smith and Richard K. Beardsley (editors), *Japanese Culture: Its Development and Characteristics* (Chicago: Aldine Publishing Co., 1962).
2. "The Mobilization of Traditional Values in the Modernization of Japan," chapter in Robert N. Bellah (editor), *Religion and Progress in Modern Asia* (New York: The Free Press, London: Collier-Macmillan, 1965) pp. 124–125.
3. Michael Edwardes, *Asia in the European Age, 1498–1955* (New York: Frederick A. Praeger, 1962) p. 278. Consult also Scalapino, "Ideology and Modernization: The Japanese Case," *op. cit.*
4. *The Times* (London) October 8, 1965.
5. The speech is reproduced in Du Bois's book *The World and Africa*, (first published 1946), (New York: International Publishers, 1965, enlarged edition) p. 312.

6. *Ibid.*, p. 35.

7. Kenneth Kirkwood, *Britain and Africa* (London: Chatto and Windus, 1965) pp. 28–29.

8. Sir Frederick D. Lugard, "The White Man's Task in Tropical Africa," *Foreign Affairs* (U.S.A.), October 1926. Consult also Maurice Freedman, *Family and Kinship in Chinese Society* (Stanford: Stanford University Press, 1970).

9. Information Services Division of Information and Tourism, Tanzania, Speech by the President Mwalimu Julius K. Nyerere at a Return Banquet in China, 21 June 1968 (Dar-es-Salaam: June 1968).

10. *The Nationalist* (Dar-es-Salaam) October 7, 1969.

11. Barnett and Njamaa, *Mau Mau From Within: Autobiography and Analysis of Kenya's Peasant Revolt* (New York: Monthly Review Press, 1967) p. 34.

12. Legum, "Peking's Strategic Priorities," *Africa Report* Vol. X, No. 1, January 1965, p. 21.

13. *East African Standard* (Nairobi) 21 May, 1964. For contacts with Nationalist China consult also *East African Standard* 15 August, 1963.

14. *East African Standard,* 24 August, 1964.

15. Du Bois, *The World and Africa,* p. 35.

16. Attwood, *The Reds and the Blacks* (London: Hutchinson, 1967), p. 242.

17. *Reporter,* East Africa's fortnightly magazine, September 11, 1964, p. 13.

18. Attwood, *op. cit.,* p. 241.

19. *Ibid.,* p. 241.

20. Editorial, "Revolutionary Prospects," *East African Standard,* February 5, 1964.

21. *East African Standard,* June 7 1965.

22. *East African Standard,* May 18 to May 25, 1965.

23. George T. Yu, *China and Tanzania: A Study in Co-operative Interaction,* China Research Monographs (Berkeley: University of California, Center for Chinese Studies, 1970), No. 5, p. 58.

24. Yu's analysis is useful in this regard and contains valuable comparative tables of aid and trade between Tanzania and other major countries. *Ibid.,* pp. 40–61.

25. *Manchester Guardian Weekly,* July 1, 1965.

26. *New York Times,* June 8, 1965.

27. Yu, *China and Tanzania,* pp. 44–45. See also *The Standard* (Dar-es-Salaam), September 26, 1969 and February 26, 1970. Consult also *The New York Times,* March 1, 1970.

CHAPTER 8

From Kinship to Citizenship

We have sought to demonstrate in previous chapters the interplay between kinship culture and racial identification, and between sex and group dynamics. We shall now examine more directly how kinship culture affects the struggle for our three world-order values—minimization of violence, maximization of social justice, and optimization of economic welfare.

In this connection we see the transition from rights of kinship to those of citizenship as a movement toward expanding empathy. Within nations, citizenship is a system of rights and obligations which attempts to fuse or balance the claims of the individual with the claims of the collectivity. In the global context of the future—whether or not a world government is achieved—societies and cultures may claim collective citizenship of the world in a bid to balance their distinctiveness with the claims of world culture. But before that can happen, the force of kinship culture in human affairs has to be understood and tamed.

In the context of our world order values, let us first examine how kinship culture relates to the phenomenon of purposeful and organized violence.

Violence and Masculinity

Images of valor, courage, endurance and maturity have, in different societies, been intimately related to the role of the male in social and military affairs. Sexual division of labor has been both a cause and an effect of a range of social symbols defining boundaries of propriety and congruence. Especially pertinent for politics and war is a historic link between manliness and capacity for violence. Nothing illustrates this more poignantly than the sexual ambivalence of at least one major prophet of nonviolence in modern history. In this ambivalence we see that link between masculinity and martial prowess.

In his psychological study of Mahatma Gandhi, Erik H. Erikson refers to Gandhi's tendency to see himself as half man and half woman, and his aspiration to acquire motherly qualities. Factors identified with Gandhi's bisexual state of mind range from his love for homespinning, traditionally women's work, to his self-description as a widow when a man dear to him died. We know that his renunciation of sexual activity, combined with a motherly interest in a young girl's physical development, added to the widespread speculation about Gandhi's psychological orientation with regard to sex.

> He undoubtedly saw a kind of sublimated maternalism as part of the positive identity of a whole man, and certainly of a *homo religiosus*. But by then all overt phallicism had become an expendable, if not a detestable, matter to him. Most men, of course, consider it not only unnecessary, but in a way indignant, and even irreverent, to disavow a small god-given organ of such singular potentials; and they remain deeply suspicious of a sick element in such sexual self-disarmament. And needless to say, the suspicion of psychological self-castration becomes easily linked with the age-old propensity for considering the renunciation of armament and abandonment of malehood.[1]

Erikson goes on to suggest in passing that increasing the mechanization of warfare would continue to decrease the equation of manliness with martial qualities. The move from the spear to the intercontinental ballistic missile amounts to some extent to the demasculinization of warfare. Face-to-face warfare makes greater demands on individual courage than does destruction by remote control. Gandhi's nonviolence, linked to Gandhi's sexual renunciation, was a simultaneous renunciation of both the spear and the penis. In Erikson's words: "Here, too, Gandhi may have been prophetic; for in a mechanized future the relative devaluation of the martial model of masculinity may well lead to a freer mutual identification of the two sexes."[2]

Africa still has many societies in which a combat culture of the spear flourishes. In such societies killing is a confrontation between individuals, and a man tests his manliness within a spear-throw of another. In such cultures martial and sexual qualities become virtually indistinguishable for the male of the species. Eligibility for marriage is sometimes tied to experience in killing—just as the war hero in developed technological societies continues to exert a sexual appeal. There are of course differences of scale in the killing between a culture of the spear and a culture of bombs falling from B-52's. And the purposes of the violence may be intelligible to one culture and bizarre to another. What we do know is that within the culture of the spear, the effort is more deeply personal. The bridegroom revels in having known moments of violence and danger.

Colin M. Turnbull, looking at a Dodo tribesman called Lemu, reflected on issues of this kind in a comparative perspective:

Lemu's shoulders were covered with rows of weals left by cicatrization. These are cut to show the number of people you have killed, and are an indispensable prerequisite to marriage. Lemu could look pretty fierce, if all you looked at was the rows of scars, his powerful body proudly bare except for the cloak flying in the breeze, and a string of ivory beads. His ears were pierced and lined with colored seeds, though, and he often wore a tuft of antelope hair on top of his head, and his smile and his eyes were warm and gentle like those of the rest of his people. His spear was for the protection of his cattle and his family, and it was difficult to think of Lemu wishing harm to anyone.

And then, bringing home this mysterious relationship between violence and sociability, Turnbull goes on:

He probably wished no harm at all even to those he killed, but faced with the choice of the life of a Turkana or that of himself and perhaps those of his wife and children, he made the same choice that most of us would make, without trying to justify it in the noble terms with which we justify our essays at mass murder.[3]

Lemu belonged to a combat culture still distant from mass destruction. He was also an African untouched either by Gandhism or by Euro-Christian inhibitions and tendencies. We shall return later to the softening and emasculating consequences of Christianity in Africa. What we should note from the outset is the interplay between martial and sexual prowess in man's ancestral heritage.

The interrelationship between sexual maturity and military manhood has had wider political consequences within Kikuyu political culture. Circumcision ceremonies involving the "shaping" of the penis were also ceremonies of initiation into the virtues of endurance and valor. The spear also featured more explicitly in initiation ceremonies of a traditional kind. Kenyatta tells us about the paramount resolution of young Kikuyu boys on being initiated by ancient custom. They used to say in courageous affirmation: "We brandish our spear, which is the symbol of our courageous and fighting spirit, never to retreat or abandon our hope, or run away from our comrades."[4] In the Mau Mau insurrection, the Kikuyu tendency to link sexual symbolism with martial symbolism continued in an even more elaborate fashion. Josiah Kariuki, who was later to be a minister in the Kenya government, took the Mau Mau Batuni oath in the 1950's to fight on the side of the rebels. He stood naked, his penis pushed through a hole in the thorax of a goat, while he solemnly swore not to hesitate in the obligation to kill should it be necessary. (Kariuki was assassinated in March 1975).

Some of the mixed symbolism of sexual and martial elements which were characteristic of Mau Mau became subjects of wide controversy, revolted some sections of international opinion, convincing them that the movement was not nationalistic but atavistic and primitive. Preeminent in controversial Mau Mau symbolism was the use of female menstrual blood, sometimes swallowed by the men in the oath ceremonies.[5] Some of the details of these ceremonies have in fact been disputed by those who took part in them. For our purposes it suffices that an elaborate intermixture between sexual and martial symbolism formed part of the foundation of the Mau Mau movement.[6]

Political Masculinity in an African Empire

The Kikuyu—as well as the Dodo, the Turkana, the Ik, and the like— are among the less centralized of the societies of eastern Africa. The Amhara, who ruled Ethiopia, are among the most centralized and elaborately institutionalized of the peoples of that part of the continent. The theme of masculinity as capacity to kill continues in the culture of the Amhara and the empire they ruled. The society is, on the one hand, deeply Christianized, and, on the other, continues to have a premium placed on martial virtues. Donald N. Levine tells about the place of the purposeful cultivation of ferocity in the process of socializing and educating young people. The Amhara youth develops skills in versification, especially of the kind which is declaimed in order to inflame the blood of the warrior. Young people memorize lines of aggressive assertion, many of which glorify the warrior and the act of killing.

"Kill a man! Kill a man! It is good to kill a man!
One who has not killed a man moves around sleepily."

Levine tells us of a walk he took with a provincial school teacher, a boy of about twenty, and another Ethiopian teacher in the countryside in Ethiopia one afternoon. Levine suggests that the mountain breeze and the rugged landscape might have gone to the head of the young teacher, for he suddenly exclaimed to his fellow: "We are Ethiopians. Let us kill something. Let us kill a man or a wild beast."[7] Levine sometimes sees too much in rhetorical bravado. But although hyperbolic in some of his interpretations, he is persuasive in the central thesis that "For the Amhara the virtues of the male are the virtues of the soldier."[8]

In some African societies the expansion of economic and political opportunities for young people has resulted in the decline of the prestige of the profession of combat as such. But in Ethiopia the prestige of the military hero continues to exercise considerable influence on the imagination of young people. A study some years ago of Ethiopian student conceptions of culture heroes disclosed that about 90 percent of the students tested "showed a preference for the 'military man' as their 'culture hero.' "[9] But that was before the coup of 1974.

Levine himself also conducted research among Ethiopian students and discovered that military virtues were the qualities most appreciated in Ethiopian historical figures of the past. But in spite of the persistence of martial sentiments in a large part of the student population, Levine discovered that those who reached the upper grades of the educational system "no longer look upon military activity as sanguinely as do their traditional counterparts."[10]

Across the border is Somalia. The Somali are radically different in political organization and social orientation from the Amhara. Politically and diplomatically there is also considerable tension between the Somali and the Amhara. But one cultural factor that they do have in common is esteem of purposeful ruthlessness as a manly virtue where the occasion arises. This is the central element within what I. M. Lewis calls "the martial character of the traditional Somali society where the display of force, however brutal and merciless, is associated with manly virility and contrasted with weakness, a quality which though despised is held to possess a certain, compensating mystical virtue."[11]

When the link between masculinity and aggressiveness is so close, almost any weapon of war becomes by definition a phallic symbol as well. The associations between combat and sexual conquest are so intimate that an easy psychological transition takes place between martial and sexual symbolism. The war dances in many African societies become also phallic dances. Many African dances fuse the aesthetic and the athletic. The grand leap, the stamping of the feet, the vigorous movements of the warrior's body, all acquire both sexual and martial suggestiveness. Sometimes fertility dances share movements with war dances. The symbolization of reproduction becomes interlinked with that of brave destruction. Such dances feature a range of elements from chest thumping to thunderous imitations of the copulation of beasts.

In many a context, the African dancer becomes himself a phallic symbol. In the words of Lawino,

It is danced in broad daylight
In the open
You cannot hide anything . . .
All parts of the body
Are shown in the arena!

Health and liveliness
Are shown in the arena![12]

The dancer, the warrior, the lover, become indistinguishable where the heritage of imagery draws no sharp distinction between valor and virility.

Compassion and Femininity

Almost inevitably the strong connection between masculinity and warfare is counterbalanced by a connection between kindliness and femininity. The example of Gandhi which we mentioned earlier is certainly a case in point. The great prophet of nonviolence found himself torn between serving as a father figure and acting as a mother symbol. At a more personal level Gandhi had played this second role for a young orphan girl named Manu. The girl had previously been adopted by Gandhi's wife Kasturba who, on her death bed, had asked her husband to take her place as a mother to Manu. Gandhi took this role so seriously that he assumed the task of teaching the girl about womanhood, and watching her physical development, and later actually sharing a bed with her as if Gandhi were another woman. The young woman's memoirs captured this strong maternalism in Gandhi's relationship with her when she entitled her book, *Bapu, My Mother.*[13]

Erikson points to a "persistent importance in Gandhi's life of the theme of motherhood, both in the sense of a need to be a perfect and pure mother, and in the sense of a much less acknowledged need to be held and reassured, especially at the time of his infinite loneliness." But to the extent that the loneliness might have been aggravated by a long period of sexual renunciation, we have in the story of Gandhi an illustration of the tense relationship between celibacy and masculinity, nonviolence and manliness.

The same problem arises with regard to Christianity. Is Christianity, in the ultimate analysis, a feminine religion? Does the centrality of forgiveness make the Christian God less manly than the Jewish Jehovah? Is the transition from the Old Testament to the New Testament a process of the emasculation of God? Does the centrality of love as a divine attribute make the Christian God less manly than Islam's Allah? Before he was assassinated and became a black martyr, Martin Luther King was sometimes denounced by some of his more militant black critics as "Martin Luther Queen". Underlying these questions is the prior question whether certain symbols are counter-phallic. The basic counter-phallicism of Christian mythology starts precisely with the virgin birth.

Pre-Christian Europe had considerable phallicism. The burden of infertility, which at that time was almost always blamed on the woman, resulted in a variety of phallic superstitions. Artificial insemination may be said to have originated with sterile women having sexual intercourse with a temple priest in a bid to get a child. Other attempts made by western women in those days to transcend the curse of barrenness were marked by phallicism:

> Down to the revolution there stood at Brest a chapel of St. Guignolet containing a priapean statue of a holy man. Women, who were, or feared to be, sterile used to go and scrape a little of the prominent member, which they put into a glass of water from the well and drank. The same practice was followed at the chapel of St. Pierre-à-Croquettes in Brabant until 1837, when the archaeologist Schayes called attention to it, and thereupon the ecclesiastical authorities removed the cause of the scandal. . . . At Antwerp stood at the gateway to the church of Saint Walburga in the Rue des Pêcheurs a statue, the sexual organ of which had been entirely scraped away by women for the same purpose.[14]

There had been so much phallicism in pre-Christian Europe that not even Christian prudishness could eliminate it entirely. The church compromised with elements of ancestral paganism, including the phallic themes of Christian cultures. In 1247 the Decree of Mans explicitly forbade phallicism, as did the Synod of Tours in 1396. But when in 1781 Sir William Hamilton visited Naples he found in Isermia phallic images being sold on the streets and placed in the church like candles today.[15] The candles themselves are not too far removed from phallic associations. Candles have been known to be used at a moment of weakness by otherwise dedicated women in a nunnery. Yet the nunnery itself, in its sexual renunciation, symbolizes the counter-phallic theme in Christianity.[16]

The coming of Christian civilization into Africa has included these counter-phallic themes. To a certain extent Christianity has softened African masculinity. Some might even argue that it initiated a process of demasculinization. The movement of "pacification" which imperialist powers helped to initiate reduced tribal confrontations. The idea of "loving thy neighbor", though still painfully unfulfilled in Africa, denuded warfare of some of its previous mystique.

"Turn the other cheek!"—This was the most feminine imperative of them all. Only a woman turned the other cheek upon being punished by her man. And even a woman attempted at times to shield herself with her arms. But the principle of turning the other cheek was part of the feminine baggage that came with Christianity.

Sexual richness which had been so much a part of an Africa before the onslaught of neo-Victorian prudery was now to be drastically circum-

171

scribed. The missionary schools were the great champions of a new prudish civilization. Suitably "modest" uniforms were devised for girl students; suitably "smart" uniforms came into being for the boys. The boys and the girls were usually in quite separate schools. Visits across the sexual divide were either strictly discouraged or rigidly controlled. Most African forms of dances were abolished altogether, for the movements were interpreted as "sinful". Phallic dances retreated before the accusing finger of the new self-righteous creed.

Behind it all was the virgin birth of the son of God when the male was dispensable, and the celibate life of Jesus when female sexual companionship was dispensable. The counter-phallic stream of Christianity had begun to erode the banks of Africa's masculinity. And so the traditionalist woman, Lawino, compares her Christianized husband, Ocol, with the real men of the tribe who had once faced death and emerged triumphant.

In battle
The hottest youths fight at the front,
Eager, angry, proud,
The youths think of their loves
And say,
It is the old ones
Who die in bed!
The spears of the foe
And the arrows
Rain like the hailstorms,
Your thumb is struck
In the small of the back,
And the spear
Cuts through the liver
And the heart.[17]

But what about Ocol, with his book knowledge and Christian inhibitions? Lawino suggests that Ocol's testicles have been put between two books and smashed. His manhood has been weakened. He cannot even play the drum of war or wield the shield. On the dancing arena, as in the battlefield, Ocol now an outcast.

You do not play the drum
Or do the mock fight;
At the funeral dance
Or at the war dance
You cannot wield the shield![18]

But, as we mentioned earlier in this book, the emasculating impact of Christianity on Africa simply increased Africa's cultural and psychological dependency. The kind of Christianity which was taught in Africa—"Turn the other cheek"—was needed more desperately by expansionist Europe than by vulnerable Africa. The strong need the softening influence of Christianity to curb their aggressive tendencies; the weak still need a warrior tradition to help their resolve to resist. Europe at the peak of her power needed feminine Christianity to restrain her; Africa in the depths of her weakness needed a residual martial determination to transcend dependency.

Kinship Culture and Women's Liberation

Perhaps changes in Europe and her western extensions are already under way, not necessarily in the direction of softening white men—but of hardening white women. In either case, sexual division of labor in white countries—both communist and noncommunist—is under a new challenge. Christianity may have lost the battle to soften the white man—but the white woman, asserting that new direction of change, does make her man share some of the chores of domesticity. In this new process the future of violence by white people may be affected. It is conceivable that the white man will become less aggressive to others as his woman asserts her own right to decide policy, although that is not yet fully clear. The masculinization of the white woman could reduce white racism as the white woman asserts the right to love a black man if she is so inclined. But it could work the other way if she is so powerful as to stop the white man's "illicit" relations with black women.

Initial indications on the American scene show a change in both directions. The parallel eruption of women's liberation and black militancy has resulted in more black men being married to white women *but* fewer white men being married to black women. Women's liberation in the United States has been primarily, though not exclusively, an assertion of white women against white males. As the sense of independence of white women has increased, so has their readiness to marry black men. As the militancy of black males has risen, so has their interest in conquering white women in defiance of old white taboos.

The white male, on the other hand, is on the defensive against both black nationalism and women's liberation. He can no longer have his pick of black females. The black female is also on the defensive, mainly because of a fundamental dilemma: If she is in love with a white man would she not let the black movement down if she married him? On the other hand, would she not let women's liberation down if she let such considerations interfere with her choice of a mate?

Nevertheless, the decline of the number of black women married to white males is less dramatic than the rise of black males married to white women. Black women married to white men fell from about 26,000 in 1960 to about 23,500 in 1970; black men married to white women rose from about 25,500 in 1960 to over 41,000 by 1970.[19] Clearly both the black movement and women's liberation are movements in the direction of greater social justice, but the fact that mixed marriages are so few in the American "melting pot" emphasizes the persistent strength of kinship culture in matters of matrimony.

The most promising mechanism for the transformation of kinship culture may lie precisely in the transformation of the role of women in society—an aspect of social and biocultural mobility. Mobility in relation to the sexes is partly concerned with interchangeability of roles. The whole movement toward sexual equality in western history has been in the direction of biocultural mobility: fathers playing nurse-maids to little babies, and feeding them at night while the mother sleeps; mothers competing in the job market, at least with other people's husbands. The biological differences between male and female naturally remain as rigid as ever; but the cultural roles devised for the two sexes in different societies have been moving in the direction of growing interchangeability. Even in the western world some residual emphasis for one sex as against another has persisted, yet no forms of differentiation apart from the strictly biological one are increasingly safe from challenge. The new feminist movement in the United States seeks to obliterate almost the last vestiges of cultural differentiation based on sexual differences.

Physical refinements and adornments too, are determined by a culture to emphasize biological variations. Until recently the fate of hair in western history had kept pace with the trend toward sex equality. Most societies, historically, have regarded manliness in terms both of dignified behavior by males in the face of difficulties and dangers and in terms of effective relationship with females. The beard has played a part in this cultural evolution. If you go back far enough in time, this may not have been unconnected with the change from the general mammalian copulation style of back-to-front to the more characteristically human style of face-to-face. C. D. Darlington has asserted that the directly psychological and social effects of face-to-face mating initiated evolutionary consequences which "will no doubt continue as long as Man exists." Facial beauty, as a major aspect of sexual attractiveness, therefore owes its origin to this major transformation of the sexual posture of man.[20] The beard became a symbol of masculinity in the male precisely because it was peculiar to the male. Among many ethnic groups in the Middle East, for example, the beard became part of the honor of man and a symbol of manliness.

It is especially in the changes of hair styles in Europe that we find the most direct correlation with the growth of sexual egalitarianism. When the differentiation between the sexes was at its sharpest in Europe, men grew beards and women had long hair. The beard became less and less common in the male population of the West, and long hair became less and less characteristic of western femininity, precisely when the relations between the sexes themselves socially were also becoming less sharply differentiated. More recently among the younger generation in the western world hair as an aspect of unisexuality has taken a different direction. It is no longer a question of women shortening their hair to a length comparable with that of men, but of men letting their hair grow to a length comparable with that of women.

As men have got round to letting their hair grow long, women have got round to wearing trousers. A group of long-haired men and women in trousers sitting together sharpens the visual impact of unisexualism at work. A related tendency is a growing toleration toward transvestism in western society. There was a time when transvestism was inevitably interpretated as indicating homosexuality. Recognition has grown that there could be a compulsion to wear the dress of the opposite sex without an accompanying compulsion to experience sexual intimacy with one's own sex. Of course, societies which have had elaborate traditions of dress have also tended to have elaborate differentiation in dress between the sexes. Some African societies have tended to be minimalist in attire. A few African communities had men going completely naked, while women had coverings in strategic places. The concept of transvestism among the Karamajong of Uganda would be difficult to define.

We have so far discussed unisexualism and transvestism as trends in the direction of biocultural mobility. What should not be forgotten is that the greater toleration toward homosexuality itself is an additional dimension in this tendency. The permissive society in the West has grown more tolerant of sexual deviants provided their deviance is not publicly displayed. Toleration of homosexuality between two consenting adults as an aspect of liberal freedom first conquered continental Western Europe, then won over England in the 1960's, and is now spreading in the United States. We shall return to these aspects of moral freedom. Permissiveness to homosexuals starts with discreet permission to two otherwise respectable males, and then grows to encompass toleration of special homosexual clubs and societies. The next step might well be a social acceptance of marriage between partners of the same sex. The concept of husband and wife is already a residue of biocultural differentiation between the sexes. But when society begins to accept solemn mating between members of the same sex, with automatic rights of inheritance should one die, and perhaps specified obligations attaching to a female husband or a male wife, biocultural mobility would have achieved its ultimate flexibility.

Finally, there is the phenomenon of transsexualism—an actual biological sex conversion in the human male or the human female. Surgical sophistication to facilitate sex conversion was attained earlier but not implemented, yet in recent times the world has grown to accept more readily the notion of a person growing up in a particular sexual role and later being helped to assume a different biological personality. Society has grown more tolerant of marriages involving transsexual personalities and it must be regarded as one further dimension in the complex theme of the biocultural mobility of the twentieth century.

These trends toward greater sexual toleration are all fundamentally relevant to the quest for social justice. Social justice involves the toleration not only of differences but also of previously unacceptable similarities. Women's liberation is a demand for the right to be similar to men in roles and functions. Gay liberation is a claim for the right to indulge in sexual sameness. Transvestism is a blurring of differences.

And yet the battle is far from concluded. Preeminent among the residual lines of sexual division of labor is the line separating those who fight wars from those who are initially exempted. The warrior class is still a male class. Nations send their sons to fight their wars, at least in the first instance. Even Israel makes her women equally liable to conscription without making them equally liable to service on the front line.

Because the men fight the wars, the men claim the right to decide between war and peace in almost all societies. The right to decide between war and peace requires high political authority. In a sense, men have become politically preeminent because they have been militarily preeminent. And they have been militarily preeminent because primordial kinship culture gave the club or the spear to the spouse with the greater muscular throwing power. Culture often changes in response to technological innovations. But there is one aspect of culture which has resisted cumulative technological revolutions—the simple cultural fact that it is men who fight wars.

If social justice in politics is a transition from kinship rights to the rights of citizenship, black males even in South Africa and the United States will acquire full rights sooner than white women. A residual sexual division of labor will persist—involving better social justice and control of large-scale violence. This world may even remain male-dominated generations after it has ceased to be white-dominated.

Perhaps relations between the sexes is the ultimate claim of kinship culture to determine distribution of power in man's political universe. On this front all one can hope for is at the most the economic and social liberation of women—which is still not the same thing as the equalization of the sexes in war and politics.

Kinship Culture versus Humanitarianism

For the time being the tensions between kinship culture and humanitarianism are wider than the issue of women's rights. And those tensions have been aggravated in the Third World by the whole experience of white racial domination.

There is evidence to suggest that the concentrated loyalties of the traditional kinship system are not easily compatible with the purely humanitarian impulse. It is almost as if there was a limit to how much responsibility a man can accept for his fellow man. If he accepts a large area of responsibility within a system of extended kinship obligations, he reduces, in the process, his readiness to accept responsibility for more distant human beings.

Within the kinship system, Africans know a level of human compassion and human obligation which is not even comprehensible to the western mind. The idea of a tribal welfare system, within which voluntary service and hospitality is extended to the indigent, the disabled, and the aged, provides a striking model of the instinct of social fellowship in man. We Africans all know of distant relatives we support, distant cousins who have a share in our salaries, distant kinsmen who call upon us as guests in our houses for days, sometimes for weeks. And yet it seems as if the very fact that we have a highly developed sense of responsibility toward our own kinsmen, a much more developed sense than is discernible in western society, has resulted in diluting our capacity to empathize with those that are much further from us.

The growth of individualism in the West has, curiously enough, resulted both in reduced collective responsibility within the immediate society and increased capacity to empathize with man much further away, even in other lands altogether. The western individualist would be capable of rising to the occasion when news of a natural catastrophe in Pakistan or Chile reached him. With the African it is the reverse; he is much more moved by the day-to-day problems of a distant kinsman than by a dramatic upheaval in a remote part of the world.

Qualifications need to be made here, especially in regard to the western response to humanitarian appeals, which bring us to the imperial factor behind African suspicions of pure humanitarianism. The growth of individualism in Western Europe did indeed result in the rhetoric and

177

sometimes even in the practise of humanitarianism. However the humanitarian impulse in a liberal Europe took the form of imperial expansion and a racialistic assumption of responsibility for the colored races of the world. Kipling's concept of the white man's burden was, in the rhetoric in which it was formulated, a case of civilizing humanitarianism. The concept of spreading the gospel as enunciated by Christian missionaries was in turn a case of Christianizing humanitarianism. Both these themes in the history of Western Europe are inseparable from the history of imperial expansion. In other words, the whole phenomenon of colonial annexation, an imposition of white power on colored races, was legitimated in history partly by reference to humanitarian and Christian principles. It may indeed have been significant, from the point of view of studying the relationship between individualism and humanitarianism, that the growth of liberalism in Europe coincided with the expansion of imperialism. An internal European renunciation of kinship and feudal obligations coincided with an external European assumption of responsibility for people much further away from their shores. Nevertheless, from Africa's point of view, it remains pertinent to measure European humanitarianism partly by the yardstick of the imperial experience.

More recently, there have been incidents since Africa's attainment of independence which have been defended on humanitarian grounds by the West, when in fact issues of racial solidarity on the part of the whites were discernible. A controversial example concerned the white hostages held by Congolese rebels in 1964 in their confrontation with their central government under Moise Tshombe. The hostages were later rescued by Belgian troops landing in what was then Stanleyville, using American planes in this venture. Much of Africa was indignant, but the West justified the Stanleyville operation on the grounds that it was a humanitarian act: the whites being saved from Congolese rebels were ordinary teachers, nurses, men, women, and children who gave service and dedication to the Congolese. They were now being used as hostages and pawns in a civil war between the Congolese themselves. Was there not a case that the western powers should, on humanitarian grounds, rescue these hostages?

But were the Americans and the Belgians really putting their humanity first and their nationality and racial identity second in that operation? Conor Cruise O'Brien, the former United Nations representative in Katanga, pointed out the relative indifference of European and American opinion toward Congolese suffering as contrasted with the indignant compassion which was aroused on behalf of white prisoners. O'Brien suggested that the "humanitarian" sensitivity displayed in the West at the time of the Stanleyville rescue operation was, in fact, little more than

an instance of racial solidarity. He indicated that Africa's own indignation against the operation had the same source as western self-
righteousness—the main difference was that Africans lacked the power
to send in paratroopers to rescue black victims from their oppressors in
Dixie and South Africa.[21]

Catherine Hoskyns has also pointed to the role of the western press.
She first admits that the Congolese did kill a number of Europeans and
Africans. She goes on to add:

> Having said this, however, it is also clear that press and diplomatic reporting
> did to a considerable degree distort the extent, the circumstances, and the
> political implications of these deaths. . . . The main distortions [included]
> . . . the suppression of any evidence of violence on the other side; and the
> much greater coverage given to acts of brutality against Europeans than to
> those against Africans. The result was to tarnish the genuinely humanitarian
> reaction. . . .[22]

African spokesmen themselves argued that the ultimate outcome of
the rescue operation was the loss of many more lives than those actually
saved. The paratroopers from Belgium shot their way to the hostages,
killing a number of innocent Africans. As the Foreign Minister of the
Congo (Brazzaville) put it in somewhat dramatic terms at the time:

> What humanitarian principles are at stake, when, on the pretext of saving
> lives of an insignificant number of whites, tens of thousands of blacks are
> massacred. . . ?
> . . . When we were younger, we learnt that in music one white note was
> worth two black ones. The famous humanitarian operation in Stanleyville
> has just proved to us that one white, particularly if his name is Carlson, if he
> is of American, Belgian, or British nationality, is worth thousands and thou-
> sands of blacks. . . .[23]

Even if we made allowances for rhetorical exaggeration, it remains suspi-
ciously true that no rescue operation of that scale would have been
launched by the United States and Belgium if the hostages had not been
white. The Belgians and the Americans were almost as susceptible to
considerations of racial solidarity as the African nationalists who so bit-
terly resented their intervention in Stanleyville. The whole affair was, in a
real sense, a conflict of racial sensitivities. It is partly because of incidents of this kind, reinforced by the whole doctrine of the white man's
burden in history and the place of humanitarian legitimation in imperialism, that the very term humanitarianism is sometimes suspect in the
eyes of African nationalists.

Not merely the virtues of humanitarianism have been compromised by
Caucasian abuse of its symbols, but also the virtues of nonviolence.

Black people were forced to retreat from a warrior tradition—only to be dominated. Implicit in concepts like that of Pax Britannica was the idea that the white races had a duty to disarm the rest of mankind. And so when the champions of imperial rule were at their most articulate in its defense, one argument they advanced was that imperialism had given the African, for example, a chance to know what life was like without violence. Claims of having abolished tribal warfare in Africa, and establishing a civilized pacification, were all claims for an imperial monopoly of the use of armies. In the total ideology of imperialism the warrior's right to initiate violence became a prerogative which only civilization and statehood could bestow.[24] What had happened to women in individual societies—as they were kept demilitarized—now happened also to colonial subjects. Lenin argued once that imperialism was "the monopoly stage of capitalism". What was perhaps more defensible was the thesis that imperialism was the monopoly stage of *warfare.*

Both anti-imperialism in Africa and black militancy in the United States might therefore be said to be, in some sense, a challenge against the monopoly of violence which white rulers had preempted for themselves. The Third Pan-African Congress held in Lisbon in 1923 already challenged the doctrine of the white man's exclusive right to initiate violence. The Congress first argued the link between Negro dignity and world peace. "In fine, we ask in all the world that black folk be treated as men. We can see no other road to peace and progress," the meeting affirmed. Also it asserted a connection between Negro dignity and the right to bear arms, though it linked the second assertion with the demand for general disarmament. The reasoning implicit in the demands of the Congress was that if the white man was going to insist that everyone else should be disarmed the white man must also renounce his own weapons. And so this Third Pan-African Congress called for: "World Disarmament and the Abolition of War; but failing this and as long as white folk bear arms against black folk, the right of blacks to bear arms in their own defense."[25]

The resurrection of the warrior tradition among black people was now a threat—but, as we shall indicate later, the pace toward that resurrection was still slow. But relations between races are not simply a matter of balance of weaponry; they are also a matter of balance of numbers between the groups themselves. What is not always grasped by observers is the simple fact that population figures, and the very image of being numerous, have often been at the heart of the struggle for racial dignity. In this regard, issues of economic welfare implicit in smaller families are up against the dictates of social justice and racial self-defense.

Numericalism and World Order

The phenomenon of *numericalism* in international politics is that collection of attitudes or general principles which puts a moral premium on numerical advantage. Its forms range from the moral complexities of majority rule to the status of China as the most populous country in the world. In the history of colonial liberation movements in the Third World it was the ethnic conception of "majority rule", rather than the orthodox liberal one, which was particularly crucial. And yet for as long as the nationalist movements had the support of the general populace as a whole, this distinction was merely academic. The nationalist leaders were "representative" by the canons of both liberalism and ethnic typicality.[26]

Any discussion of population control in relation to social justice has to take account of this numericalist ideological orientation among colored people. The importance of numbers for the dignity of colored people is not even limited to situations in which they are in a majority. The position of the blacks in the United States, where they are a minority, has been as much a part of the total picture of race relations in the world as the liberation movements in Angola, where they are the majority. Yet the black American has been no less conscious of the liberating potential of numbers than has the Afro-Asian nationalist in colonial situations. There was a time when militant American blacks saw the significance of their numbers in quasi-militaristic terms. Even as far back as the slave days black numerical superiority in individual situations occasionally turned a black man's thoughts toward a possible rebellion. And where it did not lead to rebellion, this was sometimes interpreted by black militants themselves as a sign of their inherent servility. As the defiant black man David Walker put it in 1829 in his *Appeal to the Colored Citizens of the World:*

> Here now, in the Southern and Western sections of this country [the United States] there are at least three colored persons for one white, why is it that those few weak, good-for-nothing whites are able to keep so many able men . . . in wretchedness and misery? It shows what the blacks are, we are ignorant, abject, servile and mean—and the whites know it—they know that we are too servile to assert our rights as men—or they would not fool with us as they do.[27]

More recently, the black American has sometimes seen the significance of population figures in electoral rather than revolutionary terms. While the Afro-Asian nationalist has linked numerical power to the ethic of self-determination, the American black has linked it to the liberating potential of the franchise. As Herbert Aptheker, a specialist on the history of the black American, put it:

> It never was right for the administration to "postpone" effective action on the Negro question because of so-called political expediency; today it is not wrong, it is unwise. This is shown ... in the fact that President Kennedy would have remained a United States Senator if but 75% of the Negro vote went his way in 1960 rather than the 85% cast for him.[28]

As the black movement has become more revolutionary, the importance of numbers has not diminished. Any suggestions to black Americans that they reduce their rate of reproduction are widely interpreted as a device to keep them numerically weak. The battle cry of black militancy might almost be paraphrased in the slogan: "Burn, baby, burn!—and then breed some more!" It is the dual strategy of engaging both in destructive acts which weaken the power of the white man and in creative acts which strengthen the power of the black man. Social justice and economic welfare are once again in conflict for the time being.

Sometimes the idea that history is on the side of colored people derives its credibility from their numerical preponderance. An oppressed people that is nevertheless a majority often cannot believe that the imbalance of power will last for ever. That is certainly the great feeling of the black population of South Africa. For the time being, they are no match for the connivance and technology of the Whites, or for their organizational power and industrial sophistication. The Blacks might not feel that history is on their side because their cause is just, for the cause of the Jews in Nazi Germany was also just, and yet the condemned Jews did not feel such optimism. Their sense of impending vindication arises quite simply out of a refusal to believe that a victimized majority can remain effectively victimized for any length of time. To ask the black people of South Africa to engage in vigorous family planning and birth control, while the white regime equally vigorously promotes immigration from Europe, is to seek to deny the preponderant Blacks even the solace of their preponderance.

The idea of numbers as an investment for the future goes beyond the security of whole races and social groups. It extends to the psychology of the individual father in situations of underprivilege, where the factors of infant mortality and low life-expectancy generally are critical. Parents who limit themselves to two or three children, while living in conditions of poverty and low life-expectancy, are taking a serious risk. By the time they themselves are so old as to need the assistance of their children, they may have lost one, two, or all three of them. Families which have lost several children are quite common in low-income countries. Having a large family then becomes an insurance policy for old age: an attempt to ensure that there is a son at the end of the road to help in feeding the family; or a daughter to help in tending the sick.

Leonard Doob defined modernization in terms of an expanding capacity to look to the future rather than the past. The argument is open to attack from a number of viewpoints, but it has areas of profound suggestiveness: saving, long-term investment, planning, all have important modernizing implications. Of course, all societies have some kind of planning, and some concept of the future. But the variety of uncertainties in underdeveloped societies tends to restrict planning to shorter periods. The hazards of the weather and disease are factors which make it difficult to plunge into calculations too far beyond the next harvest or two. Yet in their very desire to have many children, traditional families often manifest a consciousness of the future. Children are a primordial form of insurance, an idea connected to some of the defining characteristics of modernity.

In such African traditional societies the idea of having many children is connected both to the risks of infant mortality and to the hope of parental immortality. We have already discussed the nature of the risks of child mortality. But in some African traditional belief systems an additional insurance is necessary for the personal immortality of the parents. The period after death is quite often divided between an earlier period of "Death within Living Memory" and a later period concerning "Death beyond Living Recollection". John S. Mbiti has called the first period *Sasa* (the Now or the Recent) and the second period *Zamani* (the long ago). Mbiti recounts that death is a process by which a person moves gradually from the *Sasa* period to the *Zamani*. For as long as the individual is *remembered* by relatives and friends who knew him in this life, and who have survived him, he remains in the *Sasa* period. For as long as the deceased is remembered by name, he is not completely dead: in fact he combines death with life. He is a member of what Mbiti calls "the living-dead". "The living-dead is a person who is physically dead but alive in the memory of those who knew him in his life as well as being alive in the world of the spirits. So long as the living-dead is thus remembered, he is in the state of *personal immortality*."[29]

But what has this got to do with family planning and population control in Africa? Mbiti is not specifically concerned with this issue in his book, but what he has to say about dominant themes in African traditional religions is relevant for an understanding of African traditionalist attitudes toward these matters.

So long as the living-dead is thus remembered, he is in the state of *personal immortality*. This personal immortality is externalised in the physical continuation of the individual through procreation, so that the children bear the traits of their parents or progenitors. . . . This concept of personal immortality should help us to understand the religious significance of marriage in African societies. Unless a person has close relatives to remember him when he has physically died, then he is nobody and simply vanishes out of human existence like a flame when it is extinguished. Therefore it is a duty, religious and ontological, for everyone to get married; and if a man has no children or only daughters, he finds another wife so that through her, children (or sons) may be born who will survive him and keep him (with the other living-dead of the family) in personal immortality. Procreation is the absolute way of ensuring that a person is not cut off from personal immortality.[30]

The idea of ensuring for the future is, as we have indicated, modern. But the idea that the future consists of what happens to the dead after death is primordial. Large families in Africa become, therefore, symbols both of a forward-looking and a backward-looking traditionalism. The two issues of fear of infant mortality and hope for parental immortality jointly contribute toward a reluctance to engage in devices which circumscribe the creative potential of procreation.

Issues of cultural identity and spiritual values are thus inseparable from patterns of family sizes. And the whole debate about population emerges as being, once again, culture-bound. Respect for cultural distinctiveness may clash with considerations of increased economic welfare for families and nations. Kinship culture once again asserts its relevance for world reform.

Conclusion

We have attempted in this chapter to focus more comprehensively on the tensions between kinship culture and world order values. Cultural determinants of group behavior range from the clash between kinship loyalty and global perspectives in Africa to the interplay between violence and masculinity in the history of human cultures. Tensions between war and peace are related to a sexual division of labor; questions of social justice and economic welfare are affected by systems of descent. The transition from kinship to citizenship continues to be slow.

For the time being the phenomenon of expanding empathy in American society is best illustrated by white people, as the first signs of a Caucasian retreat from racism begin to emerge. Among black Americans, on the other hand, the phenomenon of the decade is that of *re-*

ceding empathy, as belated counter-racism among Blacks becomes radicalized in the ghettos. In southern Africa there is evidence of receding empathy among both white and black populations. The possibility of a violent racial confrontation before the 1990's cannot be ruled out.

Behind these racial situations there persist factors of kinship identification which are fundamentally domestic in their basic origins. A transformation of the racial and marital picture of the world would be inconceivable without a narrowing of cultural gaps between groups, and without changes in cultural values *within* groups. In the United States the cultural gap between white and black is more a consequence than a cause. The Blacks have had a different subculture mainly because they were not permitted full social integration from the start.

In Africa the cause of family planning and population control lacks, on the whole, adequate credibility. One or two African countries, strongly advised by technical assistance experts, have taken measures to promote some degree of propaganda in favor of population control. Among the East African countries Kenya has gone furthest in this sphere. But the majority of African countries seem to be at best lukewarm in their support, and more often sceptical and suspicious.

In situations of confrontation between Blacks and Whites, either in active combat or in terms of hostile attitudes, the issue of population links our two principles of the maximization of social justice and the minimization of violence. The inequalities in other spheres between white people and colored people have given the status of numerical superiority extra prestige among the more preponderant colored people. "We may be unequal to you in technology and education, in physical power and diplomatic sophistication—but when all is said and done there are more of us than of you!"

In 1958, Julius K. Nyerere of Tanzania cited Abraham Lincoln's romanticization of numbers to rebut those who shared Cecil Rhodes' dictum of "equal rights for all civilized men". Nyerere quarrelled especially with the "undignified assertion" of the colonial Tanganyika government that in the special circumstances of East and Central Africa universal suffrage would put the common good in jeopardy. He defended the idea of allowing "the common people" to have their own way—and quoted Lincoln's statement that "God must love the common people because he made so many of them." [31]

But to be citizens of the kingdom of God is not enough. It is also necessary that the common people should be citizens of the human community broadly defined. Yet they themselves may need to change—and expand the very concept of kinship beyond kith, toward man.

Footnotes

1. *Gandhi's Truth: On the Origins of Militant Violence* (New York: W. W. Norton, 1969) pp. 402–403.
2. *Ibid.* p. 403.
3. Colin M. Turnbull, *The Mountain People* (New York: Simon and Schuster, 1972) pp. 104–105.
4. Jomo Kenyatta gives a version of this story in his anthropological book about the Kikuyu, *Facing Mount Kenya* (first published in 1938) (London: Secker & Warburg, 1959), p. 199.
5. J. M. Kariuki, *Mau Mau Detainee* (London: Oxford University Press, 1963). Consult also my review of his book entitled, "On Heroes and Uhuru-Worship," *Transition* (Kampala), 1963.
6. Idi Amin, who later became President of Uganda, fought the Mau Mau insurrectionists as a member of the King's African Rifles. For the masculine image of Amin himself consult Mazrui, "The Militarization of Charisma: An African Perspective," paper presented at 9th World Congress of the International Political Science Association, Montreal, August 19 to 26, 1973.
7. Donald N. Levine, "The Concept of Masculinity in Ethiopian Culture," *The International Journal of Social Psychiatry*, Vol. XII, No. 1, 1966, pp. 18–20.
8. *Ibid.*, p. 18. Philip Attlee gives us a light-hearted fictional dramatization of his first encounter with the stone phalli of Michichi in Ethiopia. "The length of the grassy glade was broken by what seemed jutting, slanting, fallen, and erect stone cylinders. We paused to consider them in the bright moonlight. . . . All of the tapering cylinders were over five feet long, and the largest of them towered over twenty feet. . . . A tremendous gallery of erect male members, everyone loaded and ready to fire. All circumcized. For uncounted decades and centuries, they had been aimed at heaven, enduring seasonal rains and storms. . . . Men had long sought the Elephant's Graveyard and King Solomon's Mines, the Golden Fleece of Jason, and the fabled delights of the Old Man's Garden, where Assassins were trained. But this was the ultimate secret, the fierce and fecund heart of Africa, where all the unspent orgasms of the world were honored." See Attlee, *The Judah Lion Contract* (Greenwich, Conn.: Fawcett Publications, 1972) pp. 81–82.
9. This work was conducted by Dr. William Shack, an American anthropologist who worked in Ethiopia for a while, and is now at Berkeley. The study is cited by Levine.
10. Donald N. Levine *Wax and Gold: Tradition and Innovation in Ethiopian Culture* (Chicago: University of Chicago Press, 1965), p. 143.
11. I. M. Lewis, "The Politics of the 1969 Somali Coup," *The Journal of Modern African Studies*, Vol. 10, No. 3, October 1972, pp. 389–390.
12. Okot p'Bitek, *Song of Lawino,* (Nairobi: East African Publishing House, 1966) p. 34.
13. Manubehn Gandhi, *Bapu—My Mother* (Ahmedabad: Navajivan, 1949). Erikson, *Gandhi's Truth,* pp. 403–404.
14. Sidney Hartland, *Primitive Paternity,* vol. 1, pp. 63–64 quoted by Chapman Cohen, in *Religion and Sex* (London: T. N. Foulis, 1919), p. 108.
15. See George B. Vetter, *Magic and Religion: Their Psychological Nature, Origin, and Function* (New York: Philosophical Library, 1968), pp. 60–61.
16. Chapman Cohen, *Religion and Sex,* Consult also James H. Luba, *The Psychology of Religious Mysticism* (New York: Harcourt Brace Jovanovich, 1926). At a more popular level, consult also R. E. L. Masters, *Sexual Self Stimulation* and R. E. L. Masters, *Forbidden Sexual Behavior and Morality* (New York: Julian Press, 1962).

17. *Song of Lawino*, p. 164.
18. *Ibid.*, pp. 48–49. Material for this section of the paper has also been used for Mazrui, "Phallic Symbols in Politics and War: An African Perspective," paper presented on the panel "Biology and Politics," 9th World Congress of the International Political Science Association, Montreal, August 19 to 26, 1973.
19. See summary of special Census Bureau report on marriage, *New York Times*, February 14, 1973.
20. C. D. Darlington, *The Evolution of Man in Society* (London: George Allen and Unwin, 1969) pp. 55–56. Consult also Mazrui, "Political Man and the Heritage of Hair: An African Perspective," *British Journal of Political Science*, Vol. 00, No. 00, 1971.
21. See Conor Cruise O'Brien, "Mercy and Mercenaries," *The Observer*, (London), December 6, 1964.
22. See Hoskyns, "Violence in the Congo," *Transition*, Vol. 5, No. 21, 1965. This incident is discussed in a related but wider context in "External Events and Internal Racial Tension," chapter 4 in Ali A. Mazrui, *On Heroes and Uhuru-Worship* (London: Longmans, 1967), pp. 52–55.
23. South Ganeo, *United Nations Security Council Official Records*, 1170, December 9, 1964, pp. 14–16. Carlson was the American missionary who was killed by the insurgents.
24. Mazrui, *Towards a Pax Africana: A Study of Ideology and Ambition* (University of Chicago Press and Weidenfeld and Nicolson, 1967) pp. 196–71.
25. See George Padmore (editor) *History of the Pan-African Congress* pp. 22–23. See also Mazrui, *Towards a Pax Africana.*
26. These issues are discussed in greater detail in Mazrui, "Numerical Strength and Nuclear Status in the Politics of the Third World," *The Journal of Politics*, Vol. XXIX, No. 4, November 1967. The article is reprinted as Chapter 3 in Mazrui, *Violence and Thought: Essays on Social Tensions in Africa* (London: Longmans, 1969), pp. 50–81.
27. The *Appeal* is an important document in the history of black protest in the United States. It is reproduced in Herbert Aptheker, *"One Continual Cry": David Walker's Appeal to the Colored Citizens of the World (1829–1830) Its Setting and Its Meaning* (New York: Humanities Press, 1965), p. 129.
28. Herbert Aptheker, *Soul of the Republic: the Negro Today* (New York: Marzani and Munsell, 1964), p. 109.
29. John S. Mbiti, *African Religions and Philosophy* (London: Heinemann, 1969), pp. 25–26.
30. *Ibid.*
31. Nyerere, "The Entrenchment of Privilege," *Africa South*, Vol. 2, No. 2 (January/March 1958), pp. 86–89.

Section III

POLITICAL CULTURE AND THE SHADOW OF VIOLENCE

CHAPTER 9

Violent Change and Receding Empathy

In examining the relationship between violence and culture, we must also address ourselves to the violence which sometimes accompanies the process of cultural convergence itself. This is most likely to happen in situations of asymmetry between cultural donors and cultural recipients. The impact of the dominant power may be so great on the recipient country that the weaker country enters a period of agonizing instability, as her indigenous culture struggles to adapt itself to the pressures of the new culture.

For a while empathy itself recedes. Those who have been culturally dominated fight among themselves. Ethnocultural groups turn against each other; and their leaders rise and fall with the violent rhythm of social convulsions. The phenomenon *follows* colonialism. The imperial power arrived, created new political boundaries, planted new seeds of local ethnocultural rivalries, imported an alien but seductive culture of its own, and then left the new political chemistry to bubble out its own solutions. In this chapter we will examine these post-colonial tensions of political and cultural adjustment, especially as illustrated in Africa.

In trying to discern the ultimate prospects for Africa in the next two decades, two trends appear to be particularly likely—first, continuing political unrest; and second, increasing cultural revitalization. Political unrest includes problems of institutional fluidity, the military-civilian pendulum, the phenomenon of retribalization, and the changing fortunes of the different party systems. Africa will also witness a *cultural revitalization*. The basic Afro-Western cultural dualism which has already concerned writers and artists in much of Africa will now probably move on to produce an art of reintegration including, however, a reassertion of important elements in the indigenous heritage. The condition of the polity and its relative intolerance will also play its part in reactivating certain areas of cultural creativity.

The Pendular Model of Change

Much of the political upheaval in Africa is connected with two types of problems—problems of fragile institutions and of fragmented identity, the very essence of political underdevelopment. They are the heritage of imperialism's attempt to create new and larger communities in Africa and at the same time introduce a new political culture.

The problems of fragile institutions and fragmented ethnocultural identity are of course interconnected. Institutions are fragile partly because the political communities are newly created in their present form, encompassing units which have yet to recognize each other as legitimate compatriots. In all societies, conflict between groups is inevitable, and the nature of much of social life is concerned with ways of resolving a variety of different conflicts of interests, of values, and of beliefs. Political institutions are fragile if they lack the capability to withstand the strain of trying to resolve some of these conflicts. They are also fragile if they do not command enough faith among the people they are supposed to serve to make them politically authoritative.

Such institutional instability may best be understood through a pendulum model of social change. This model of course differs from one which looks at the process of transformation in unilinear terms, ferociously moving toward a single unalterable destination. Theories of social evolution, including the Marxist theory of historical materialism, postulate a movement by stages toward a particular ultimate destination. Indeed, some of the contemporary theories of modernization and political development betray neo-Darwinist assumptions about social evolution from a preconceived kind of underdevelopment and traditionalism to a closely specified model of development and modernity. In the case of political and intellectual movements the analogy which is sometimes pertinent is that of wave formation. Much of intellectual history itself is indeed a history of the rise and decline of intellectual fashions—with each succeeding wave owing something to the strength of what went before.

The pendulum model derives its pertinence to political Africa from a number of factors. One factor is the very nature of *sudden* political change. Most political shocks generate their own political reactions, and it is within the reactions that the springs of a swing-back tense up ready to be released. To change the metaphor, we might call this particular kind of swing-back the *counterrevolution syndrome.*

Another factor operative in the case of a former colony is the simple one of a profound dualism in the political culture of the country. We have, on the one hand, residual indigenous ways of political response, political reasoning, and political interaction. On the other hand, we have institutions created during the colonial period to serve a different kind of polity, and derived in their genesis from the experience of the metropolitan powers. The syndrome of ambivalence in a former colony takes the form of swings between rebellion and residual emulation. The values underlying the new institutions all come into conflict periodically with modes of political behavior from very different traditional experiences. Antinepotism as a principle of bureaucratic rationality, for example, might clash with the principle of kinship obligations as derived from traditional culture. The floating vote in mature democracies gradually achieves an optimum size which ensures a balance between stability and changeability. But in new societies the floating vote might constitute the bulk of the electorate swinging recklessly from the support of one party to another. Alternatively the very idea of a floating vote might simply clash with an indigenous notion of loyalty and prior commitment unchangeable by the vicissitudes of political campaigns.

The pendulum model of political change in Africa arises then both because changes are so sudden as to generate the counterrevolution syndrome, and because the whole personality of the polity in a newly liberated African country betrays a profound ambivalence between the values associated with newly created institutions inherited from the metropolitan power, on the one hand, and the residual modes of political response more deeply rooted in local traditions, on the other. Both syndromes—that of counterrevolution and that of cultural ambivalence—are likely to cause pendular swings especially in the field of establishing a new set of political institutions.

In other areas of national life the pendulum model may be totally irrelevant. Economic change could at all times be unilinear, though subject to temporary interruptions when there are obstacles in its way. Change in ideas and in methods of cultural creativity can be expressed in terms of wave formations. There are several interrelated reasons for the differences between institutionalized political change and other areas of social change. One reason concerns the nearness of politics to practice. Art and intellectual speculation can engage in flights of imagination, and these sometimes help the artist or the theoretical thinker to transcend the cultural dualism of his predicament. The range of choices is much greater where there is no need to be governed by the limitations of predictability. Novelists can therefore experiment with new modes of writing and even with the concept of the anti-novel; poets can range from discipline and rhyme to total aesthetic eccentricity; social thinkers may even build "models" or speculate about the future on a grand scale without the restraints of practical implementation.

But those who are called upon to write practical constitutions for their countries, designed to be implemented in day-to-day politics and intended to govern the behavior of men in their political and social activities, cannot indulge in too high a flight from the concrete floor of experience. Even a revolutionary constitution, if it is really designed to be operational and implemented in a particular society with all its habits and tendencies, has to curb the innovative instinct.

If, then, the invention of political institutions needs to take account of prospects for implementation, the choice of alternatives becomes limited. A particular regime may introduce highly innovative institutions. If there is a reaction against these institutions the tendency is not to plunge into another set of innovations but to grope back to the root of experience. When further disenchantment sets in, the subsequent reformers may once again be drawn toward that which was tried before but inadequately implemented, and see if the same basis could be used for further experimentation. The nearness of politics to practice must therefore be seen as one of the reasons why the pendulum effect is more discernible in the field of experimentation with political institutions than in the field of literature and general intellectual activity.

A related reason is that politicians themselves tend to have a narrower imaginative perspective than artists and academic thinkers. Those who become effective artists or great thinkers must be presumed to have a wider grasp of visionary possibilities than those who become great men of affairs. Great men of affairs may indeed often be men of vision. But their success in practical affairs demands constant contact with the realities of practical behavior. Poets may have limitless possibilities of how to play with words, but practical politicians are more circumscribed in their efforts to understand how to build institutions. Again the range of choices in the field of political institutions becomes more modest than in some other areas of social change. The temptations of relating to what has already been tried before is therefore a contributory factor toward the pendulum tendency in practical politics.

A third, more universal factor concerns the competitive spirit in man. In liberal democracies this competitive spirit is institutionalized in political parties which then compete for power and for political opportunities. Electoral swings toward radicalism or toward conservatism become part of the pendular phenomenon of the liberal polity.

However, in situations like that of post-colonial Africa the swings are not between supporting one party and supporting another, but are in effect swings between one political system and another. The pendulum effect in Africa is more fundamental, concerned not merely with support for a particular leader or party, which may fluctuate between elections.

Following the colonial experience, the pendulum effect in Africa, particularly in the 1970's, is likely to be in terms of swings between whole political systems.

Parties and Soldiers

Ghana led black Africa in ending colonial status and attaining independence. Ghana is also leading black Africa in the phenomenon of systemic swings. The Ghanaian experience may be a traffic indicator of the likely turn of events in much of Africa in the 1970's and the 1980's.

In the last stages of colonial rule in his country, Nkrumah of Ghana had been a believer in liberal competitive democracy. In June 1955, at the height of the opposition challenge, Nkrumah could still say at a rally of the Convention People's Party: "I have always expressed both in public and in private that we need a strong and well-organized Opposition Party in the country and the Assembly. . . . We must not forget that democracy means the rule of the majority, though it should be tempered by sweet reasonableness in the interests of the minority".[1]

The political culture of the imperial power was still exercising its captivating sway. In any case, it was important for Nkrumah to maintain the image of competitive parliamentary institutions both on the eve of Ghana's independence and in the first year or so of that independence. But Nkrumah's views on this matter gradually changed, and the road toward a one-party system was then taken. The opponents of the regime were harassed. Ideologues in Ghana soon turned their talents to the rationalization of the one-party system. The imported political culture was in the throes of modification.

Ghana enjoyed half a decade of the one-party system before the end came in February 1966 when Nkrumah's regime was overthrown, and the Convention People's Party was banned. The country fell under military rule, with civilian advisers, and party politics took an enforced pause.

Then in 1969 the world witnessed one of the most significant developments of the decade in Ghana. A constitutional political opposition came to life again, and quickly assumed its original power. In August 1969, K. A. Busia's Progress party polled 59 percent of the popular vote winning 104 seats or 75 percent of the National Assembly. Originally no less than sixteen parties had made an appearance, but mergers reduced the contest finally to five parties. Of these the major contest was between Busia's Progress party and Gbedemah's National Alliance of Liberals. The old Anglo-Saxon political culture was attempting a comeback in the central arena of Ghanaian politics. Ghana was once again back to a mul-

195

tiparty system—and the political philosophy behind it had reverted to that which Nkrumah expressed in 1955, quoted above. Then, in February 1972, the soldiers once again intervened in Ghana and Busia's liberally oriented government was overthrown. Africa's institutional experience had once again betrayed its pendular tendency.

In a different way Kenya has exhibited a similar tendency, changing to and from a one-party system, though the same regime has remained in power throughout these systemic swings. In 1964, the Kenya African Democratic Union, the original opposition party in the country, liquidated itself and merged with the ruling party. In one momentous decision the country changed from a two-party system to a one-party system. Then within the ruling party new tensions began to arise, and gradually a faction of the left of the party became a major source of challenge. By 1965 the leftist faction broke loose from the ruling party, and formed the Kenya People's Union. Since the original opposition, KADU, had been rightist, the very emergence of an ideological spectrum of "left" and "right" in a western sense, intermingling with primordial ethnic affiliations, was a process of tense political acculturation.

With the emergence of the leftist party, the vigor of Kenya politics entered a new phase. Then came the disturbing events in Kisumu in October 1969, referred to earlier, which led the government to ban the Kenya People's Union, and to detain its top leadership. Kenya was once again back to a state of single-partyism. The systemic pendulum was at work, as the clock of political revolution introduced alternating structural phases of public life. There was a time when many regarded the one-party system as inevitable in most African countries. If it is indeed inevitable in Kenya, the trend toward it has not been unilinear. If there is supposed to be a principle of inevitability at work, it is a principle which has found areas of technical accommodation with the realities of institutional reversibility.

The Kenya type of institutional swings presupposes a certain kind of flexibility in the regime in power. Kenya has yet to declare a one-party state *de jure;* alternative parties are not outlawed. In reality there are political difficulties in the way of any such formation of an opposition party. Kenya's laws in relation to the dominant regime have therefore permitted systemic changes while the same regime has remained in power. But where alternative parties are outlawed, and a country becomes a one-party state *de jure,* systemic changes may need more fundamental political disturbances than Kenya has yet experienced. The Ghanaian model of systemic change is a more likely one for repetition elsewhere than the Kenyan.

But, as we have indicated, Ghana has been a model not only of changes between one-partyism and multi-partyism, but also of a pendular tendency in military-civilian relations. Ghana and the Sudan are particularly illuminating in this regard, both countries having known alternating spells of military and civilian authority.

The limits of military intervention in politics is again a question of painful cultural readjustment. Local ethnocultural realities compete with imported western norms of apolitical soldiers. Yet both Ghana and Sudan do seem to be endowed with a *civic soldiery*. By the term "civic soldiery" we mean here a category of soldiers sufficiently socialized in the civilian ethos, and sufficiently sensitized to the virtues of civic order, to feel relatively inhibited about brutalizing ordinary citizens. In October 1964, General Aboud fell from power in Khartoum, a triumph of public opinion in northern Sudan, and an index of some degree of meaningful if transient national consensus. A series of demonstrations in Khartoum, some of which were led by university teachers, shattered the confidence of the military regime. It is not in every country that the military would bow to popular indignation. It is not in every country in Africa that popular indignation expresses itself in spite of possible reprisals from government forces. It is true that the vulnerability of the military regime was partly due to its own internal division. And yet the very division within the military forces seemed to have been partly connected with patriotic sentiment and with a reluctance to shed too much Sudanese blood in the streets of Khartoum.

The fall of Aboud in October 1964 was as creditable to Aboud and the military at large as it was to demonstrators in the streets demanding a return to parliamentary politics. In the conditions of Africa today and indeed of the Middle East, soldiers are to be given national credit when they are too inhibited to slaughter too many of their compatriots.[21]

But in 1969 a swing back to military power took place in the Sudan, and with more casualties than had been the case in previous swings. The restraining effect of the civic ethos was clearly still operative. The soldiery also seemed to be, to some extent, ideologically inspired, indicating an alliance with the radical and Marxist wing of civilian opinion. Then in 1971 the alliance ended when the Sudanese communists staged a coup—soon negated by Numeiry's countercoup. Many communists were killed. The tensions of adjustment were forcing Sudanese empathy further back.

In Ghana the civic ethos was also very much alive. The Ghanaian coup of 1966 was in many ways one of the most polished and sophisticated of all coups in the Third World. The regime took advantage of civilian disenchantment with Nkrumah's era, and quickly sought to jnvolve not only the civil service but other sectors of opinion in decision making. Party politics were banned, but popular dissent was given considerable latitude in newspapers and other publications. Important governmental decisions were subjected to public criticism and public evaluation while the soldiers remained in power. The National Liberation Council shared the glamor of political leadership in the country with civilian public figures, especially K. A. Busia who later took over as head of government.

The coup of 1972 in Ghana was also relatively smooth and bloodless, but inter-Ghanaian empathy may also be receding. Relations between ordinary soldiers and ordinary civilians in Ghana are again less tense and more cordial than is evident in some other African countries. There are parts of East Africa where villagers are frightened by the approach of an army lorry, where a car driver would think twice before overtaking a military vehicle. The Ghanaian regime is less terrifying. Yet the tensions of finding a new relationship between soldiers and civilians is another fundamental aspect of the incomplete political acculturation in Africa in the wake of the imperial retreat.

In this behavior of the soldiers lies the second major area of political tension in Africa—the problem of fragmented identity as the central dimension of the crisis of receding empathy. Let us now turn to this issue more attentively.

The Politics of Shifting Loyalties

Both colonialism and anticolonialism in Africa played two fundamental roles. They redefined the area of political activity and also redefined the boundaries of political loyalties. Political loyalties and political activity are closely related but could be differentiated analytically. There can be political loyalties even in situations where there is very little political activity. Yet a process of redefinition is a dynamic one, and loyalties can only be redefined in situations where politics is an active force.

Anticolonialism in Africa was the basis of *modern nationalism*. We are using the term "African nationalism" in this chapter in its original sense of a race-conscious, transterritorial and anticolonial bond among Africans in relation to their land and their rights. It was itself an intimate interplay between contiguity and consciousness, between geographical proximity and political perception. Africans, from east to west on their continent, were suddenly aware that they shared a continent and a colonial experience.

198

But in what way does nationalism in colonial Africa help to redefine the boundaries of political activity? The question is partly related to the issue of whether tribal communities are political communities at all. It is possible to look at politics as a product of differentiation. In situations where the political, the administrative, the mystical, and the ritualistic are undifferentiated, politics as a distinct activity might find it hard to flourish; some might even argue that it would not exist in such a community. The concept of politics in this sense becomes culturebound.

Some would argue that politics presupposes a discernible class of politicians. In new societies where no distinct class of people is identifiable as politicians, politics has no autonomous identity. The society might indeed have a system of government, but that is not the same thing as a system of politics. Those who hold this view would therefore insist that politics is essentially an aspect of modernization, arising out of structural differentiation and functional specificity. A society develops a polity when political activity becomes more easily isolated from, say, magic or criminal proceedings.

On the basis of such a definition of politics, one might look at African nationalism as the initial breeding ground of modern politics in Africa. That is why so many commentators during the colonial period regarded the growth of political consciousness as being virtually the same thing as the growth of nationalism. It was assumed that communities which were completely tribalistic—like the Masai in Kenya and Tanzania or the Karamojong in Uganda—were by definition nonpolitical. But communities which were producing nationalistic agitators—like the Ibos in Nigeria or the Kikuyus in Kenya—were ipso facto at a high degree of political consciousness. They were also the most responsive to the Western cultural stimulus. The study of nationalism in Africa was therefore the study of the beginnings of modern politics. And this in turn signified the emergence of westernized and semi-westernized political activists.

An alternative interpretation of the relationship betweeen nationalism and politics during Africa's colonial period would argue that African nationalism did not signify the birth but the nationalization of African politics. Politics within traditional communities had existed. The whole complex process of publicly determining *who gets what, when,* was something which went on all the time in traditional societies. Factions argued about resource allocation and there were methods of resolving conflicting claims. This was the essence of politics, and it was as present in traditional communities as it might be elsewhere.

Under this broader definition of political activity, what African nationalism did was to nationalize politics in each of the African colonial territories. Instead of *intra*-tribal intrigue within each ethnic community, nationalism released a consciousness of the territory as a whole as an arena of political argument, struggle and discourse. The initial stages of this nationalization of politics did not take the form of a direct struggle for independence but very often of more limited extensions of African political participation at the national level. In British Africa particularly the Legislative Council was a symbol of the new political culture, and political struggle by Africans was initially designed to increase African influence within it. Political participation was conceived in terms of extending the franchise and increasing African representation within that colonial legislature.

In those countries which had a significant white settler community, central politics started quite early. But central politics were not the same thing as national politics. The former were the politics of a central Legislative Council and of elite activity between government administrators and settler communities. In colonial Kenya, for example, the franchise was granted to the white settlers quite early, and was later extended to the Indian community and then to the Arabs. To the extent that this form of activity focused on some central legislative and administrative institutions of colony-wide significance, Kenya had centrally oriented politics from quite early. But the nationalization of politics came with the increasing involvement of Africans in the central system. This was the beginning of political reculturation. The growth of African agitation for participation at the center entailed a growing involvement of Africans in national issues and constituted the nationalization of politics in the country. The growing demands for increased African representation in central institutions later culminated in the cry for "Undiluted Democracy" and "One Man, One Vote". The full nationalization of Kenya politics was attained with the Africanization of power. A new method of exercising political power had now been inherited by Africa. A new universe of political ideas had come into being.

But what has happened since then? There has definitely been a decline of that phenomenon which we used to call African nationalism, concurrently with the weakening of the imported political culture. The original trends had been due to a particular type of colonial situation and to the African ambition to loosen the controls of alien power. The imperial withdrawal did not put an immediate end to those emotions, but it has meant a gradual decline of their influence on every day political behavior. Except in isolated cases, anticolonialism is a battle-cry of the past in most African countries.

The decline of African nationalism in many of these countries has also meant the decline of national politics. The political parties which had been the instruments of nationalist agitation have in many cases now lost their cohesion and sense of purpose. They have lost some of their old capacity to promote a sense of national involvement. In addition, the decline of political competition and suppression of political rivals has curtailed the openness of debate and public wooing for support on which politics as an activity must inevitably thrive. In some cases corruption and electoral malpractices have created widespread political cynicism in the populace, making it harder than ever to achieve a real sense of national involvement. Of many African states it would be true to say that the golden age of modern politics for their people coincided with the golden age of African nationalism. When the latter declined as a major determinant of political behavior, modern politics also declined as a nationalized phenomenon. Angling for presidential favors, or intriguing in some ultra-clandestine ways, has of course continued. So has some political activity in the villages and district councils. The imported institutions like parliaments, political parties, and a politically "neutral" military establishment lacked the deeper underpinnings of a comprehensive political culture to sustain them.

Be that as it may, it was not merely the boundaries of political activity which were redefined by the rise and then the decline of nationalism; it was also the boundaries of political loyalties. It is to these that we must now turn.

The most direct redefinition of loyalties which took place concerned the native strength of ethnocultural loyalties, on one side, and broader national loyalties, on the other. African colonial analysts often assumed that nationalism gained its recruits from the ranks of the detribalized. From these ranks came the leaders of the anticolonial agitation, the first distinct and definable class of politicians which modern Africa produced. These politicians were in the majority of cases westernized or semi-westernized, and it is partly this factor which tended to mark them out in the eyes of the spectator as a detribalized group.

Yet this analysis did not adequately differentiate between tribalism as a cultural system and tribalism as loyalty to an ethnic group. There were, in fact, two senses of membership of a tribe, both rooted in kinship culture. One was the sense of belonging; and the other the sense of participating. The quality of belonging simply asserted that one's ethnic affiliation was to that tribe; but the quality of participating implied a cultural affiliation as well, a sharing of the particular tribal way of life. When analysts talked about detribalization, they often meant a weakening of cultural affiliation, though not necessarily a weakening of ethnic loyalty. A person could become westernized and adopt almost entirely a western way of life, but still retain great love and loyalty to the ethnic group from which he sprang.

An alternative formulation of this distinction is to differentiate tribalism from traditionalism as different aspects of kinship culture. African nationalism garnered its leading recruits from the ranks of the *detraditionalized,* rather than from the detribalized. The educated and semieducated Africans who captured leading roles in the agitation movements had indeed lost some aspects of traditional modes of behavior and adopted others under the influence of western education and western control. But the erosion of traditionalism did not necessarily mean the diminution of ethnicity.

Among the most radically detraditionalized of all Africans would presumably be African academics. The Universities of Ibadan and Lagos even before the Nigerian coup of January 1966 were already feeling the internal tensions of conflicting ethnic loyalties. The University of Nairobi has at times experienced comparable difficulties. Like the Ibo of Nigeria, the Luos of Kenya produced, initially, more academics in East Africa than any other single community. This was not a simple matter of size, as there are other ethnic groups of comparable magnitude. No sociological or sociopsychological study has yet been undertaken to explain this kind of ethnic specialization in East Africa. Some might even say that it is too early yet to see much significance in it, as the sample of East African scholars is still rather limited. But the simple fact that the Luos supplied a disproportionately large number of academics within the University of Nairobi in its first few years caused tension. The institution is still torn by ethnic factors, but it is not as acute as it must have been at the University of Ibadan before the first Nigerian coup when there was a disproportionate Ibo presence in most categories of staff. The experience of both Kenya and Nigeria shows that even the most highly detraditionalized of all Africans, the scholars, have been feeling the commanding pull of ethnic loyalties. Kinship culture in such situations is once again politicized.

If one insists on looking at the colonial phenomenon of agitators as an outgrowth of partial detribalization, one must look at some of the events which followed independence in Africa as illustrations of partial *retribalization.* In Nigeria the latter phenomenon attained tragic proportions. The Ibos, for so long part of the vanguard of African nationalism, found themselves retreating since early 1966 into an ideology of the preeminence of ethnic interests. Their deepest political passions were now retribalized. The painful drama of conflict and civil war in Nigeria began to unfold itself.

In less stark terms, retribalization is also discernible in other parts of Africa. In Kenya, Luo ethnicity has probably significantly deepened since independence, partly in defensive reaction to the Kikuyu challenge and to some government policies. The political passions of some Luo freedom-fighters in the colonial struggle have now become to some extent dena-tionalized. The retreat of African nationalism has helped to rekindle some primordial flames. And the crisis of receding empathy has attained a new level of tensions.

The Arts and Creative Unrest

We have so far discussed the issue of fragile institutions and the frag-mented identity in their relationship to political instability. What ought to be borne in mind is that there are occasions when societies develop only after having had their psychic equilibrium upset by an intrusive rest-less urge. The restlessness might sometimes take the form of a wander-lust and produce explorers and adventurers in distant lands. Dame Mar-gery Perham captured this spirit of restless exuberance when she described Elizabethans, the great travelers who launched England on a maritime and later global career: "The Elizabethans tumbled out of En-gland like children after school."[3] In this metaphor is captured that urge to explore and discover which is so often an integral part of youthful rest-lessness.

Partly because of this it is perhaps safe to say that the 1970's in Africa are likely to be years of aesthetic revitalization. The first wave of rest-lessness in Africa led to the growth of the nationalist movements. Frus-trations at certain levels of society, especially of political intellectuals and others with educated ambitions, released the urge for change. Very often the psychic unrest of the individual is in fact a craving for upward mobility. African nationalism in the 1940's and 1950's, by its com-mitment to the elimination of foreign rule and colonial administration, opened up many positions which could temporarily allay psychic rest-lessness.

In French-speaking Africa the restlessness took the form of cultural creativity. Poetry, drama, novels, philosophical formulations about so-ciety, poured forth in impressive abandon. The French policy of assimilation and its assumptions about the cultural inadequacies of the African helped to provoke the creative response. Among aesthetic re-bellions in Francophone black-land was the old school of negritude and its commitment to cultural revivalism. Under the impact of French cultural arrogance, a psychic restlessness was released among those Africans who felt most keenly the humiliation of it all. The quest for aesthetic vindication was in fact an eruption of creativity.

Since independence there has been a decline of literary creativity in much of French-speaking Africa. A blanket of black authoritarianism has smothered that instinct in several places. And yet it would be a mistake to regard a literary pause as a pause in aesthetics at large. The performing arts in French-speaking Africa seem to have been strengthened since independence. A wave of aesthetic diplomacy has sent out dancers from Guinea and Senegal to other parts of Africa and indeed to other parts of the world. African ballet and the art of the drum have assumed a new sophistication in the playhouses of Dakar. While great writers like Camara Laye and Mongo Beti have retreated into relative silence, and either put away their pens or locked up manuscripts to await happier days for publication, in other areas of creativity artists seem to be throbbing with verve. Of course every arts festival in Africa is surrounded by the passion of artistic and political controversy, by boycotts and debates, by sneers. And yet somehow there does emerge in the midst of it all a hard core of cultural animation, a throbbing source of artistic life. The Dakar Festival of Arts in 1964 had its shortcomings and quarrels; the festival in Algiers in 1969 released its own froth of political emotions; but the festivals in their own way were a mirror of aesthetic revitalization in much of the black world.

In English-speaking Africa psychic restlessness under colonialism did not immediately erupt in the form of aesthetic creativity. Black response to British rule was more political and less cultural than to French rule. Because of this the leadership in Pan-African movements and in the anti-colonial struggle passed to English-speaking Africans. The Anglophones set the pace of colonial liberation and asserted more sharply than their French-speaking counterparts their separateness from the metropolitan power. The psychic restlessness took the form of organizational innovation and ideological militancy, rather than novels, plays and dances.

After independence something started to happen in English-speaking Africa too. That sense of cultural dualism, of a coexistence between what was imported from the West and what was indigenous to the local soil, has begun to be grasped even in Anglophone circles. Until its civil war, Nigeria took the lead in this cultural renaissance. The best African novelist in the English language, the best playwright in the English language in Africa, a galaxy of some of the most inspired poets of Africa, were all Nigerians. In addition the dance and the theatre had Ibadan throbbing with innovation and reckless provocation.

The Institute of African Studies of the University of Ghana in Legon has a mixed record in its contributions to African studies. But there is one area where its record is impressive, and that is in the field of dancing. A good deal of innovation, of the fusion of the traditional with modern techniques, of the utilization of modern instruments for ancient movements, all these have been bursting forth in innovative gusto from one single institute in Ghana's capital. Of course the experiments have had their shortcomings, but there is a clear commitment to the promotion of a Ghanaian presence in Africa's cultural world.

East Africa has been slow to respond to these challenges. In Uganda there was relatively limited psychic unrest, partly because the British had not been too brutal toward what they found of the ancient traditions. Much of Uganda's cultural preoccupations were oriented toward conservation rather than revivalism, by definition less innovative. In spite of that there have been tendencies in Uganda toward a new promotion of the arts and the creation of a Ugandan participation in Africa's renaissance. The National Theatre and Cultural Centre were set up partly with this in mind. The Heartbeat of Africa Dancing Troupe was again symptomatic of a groping for a new and larger stage to accommodate indigenous performers. These were the tendencies toward the nationalization of the tribal aesthetics. Uganda has also attempted aesthetic diplomacy by sending her dancers to tour other lands.

Meanwhile educational institutions are also exploring new ways of artistic participation and the promotion of the local renaissance. A School of Drama at Makerere was established some years ago. The question of whether African music should find a place in the curriculum has been debated; vocal reformers locally want greater commitment by the university to the idea of preserving and promoting what Uganda has to offer in the artistic field.

In literature too there is a growing restlessness in East Africa. Several literary magazines have grown up in Kenya, Uganda and Tanzania. Novels and short stories are coming out of the East African Publishing House. Epic poems and long narrative ventures in verse are being attempted. Even politicians have entered with gusto in this general area of aesthetic experimentation. Julius Nyerere is participating in the task of enriching the Swahili language partly through calling upon it to carry the load of literary masterpieces originally written in other languages. The subtle process of enriching a language consists in diversifying its uses and augmenting its versatility. Nyerere's translation of Shakespeare's *Julius Caesar* is a contribution both to local Swahili theater and to the effectiveness of the Swahili language as a literary medium.

Uganda is another country which has produced a major political figure in search of a literary role. Akena Adoko, Chief GenAral Service Officer of Obote's government and one of the most powerful political figures in government at that time, attempted a narrative in blank verse about the events of 1966 in Uganda when the central government had a military confrontation with one of the regions and when the leadership of the ruling party was threatened from within. Akena Adoko's *Uganda Crisis* is an important document about a critical year in the recent history of Uganda. But what is also significant from the point of view of this analysis is that the author aspired to make it a work of art, as well as a political document.

French-speaking Africa has of course a longer tradition linking active politics with the literary endeavors. Leopold Senghor of Senegal was a poet, Kéita Fodéba of Guinea a producer of ballets, Bernard Dadié of the Ivory Coast a novelist, and Cofi Gadeau a playwright, before they held office in their respective states. In English-speaking Africa literary engagement of this kind has been much more rare. There have indeed been cases of major political figures aspiring to be recognized as major political thinkers. Kwame Nkrumah's prolific and diversified output of political literature is one case in point. But major politicians actually writing creative or imaginative pieces is a rarer phenomenon in Anglophone Africa.

And yet the artistic ferment is not to be viewed purely in terms of the more conspicuous exercises of famous figures. Because the psychic equilibrium of African society has been disturbed, the dynamo of restlessness is active at different levels. The place of the individual is critical in all this. Very often the unrest which has erupted is a case of individual response. Cultural factors are at play in restless vigor, not merely among the literate but also among migrant laborers, urban unemployed, ambitious clerks. A sense of social redundancy has in some cases already afflicted African societies, as jobs in the higher sectors have been filled up, and many whose education has generated certain expectations as to their rightful role find themselves frustrated. But this very redundancy arising out of bad manpower planning assumes the potentialities of social transformation.

Manpower projects are fallible at the best of times. But if it were possible to devise an educational system which calculated accurately how many people would be needed for which types of jobs by which year, the education system would develop a profoundly conservative tendency. It would be the modern equivalent of the mediaeval belief that God so planned the world that each man "belonged to his appointed place". The dynamo of restlessness would for a while be diffused and the competitive spirit neutralized.

In Africa the problem assumes an extra dimension because collective tendencies in traditional life are in many cases still strong, and the growth of individualism has been interrupted in part by a quest in the new states for national cohesion or sociopolitical conformity. The demands for obedience in many political systems in Africa, and the attempt for extra control of the educational system, of the press, and of other areas of potential intellectual self-assertion, all carry the risk of arrested individuation.

The first great individualists are in any case not the masses but particularly outstanding figures in an emerging elite. This has been the experience elsewhere in the world most of the time and has been the experience in Africa as well. The first modern individualists in Africa were to be found within an emerging intelligentsia. When their ambitions found fulfillment with the departure of the foreign ruler, there was a tendency for many of these individualists to develop a concern for *conformity*. Social and political conformity becomes an assurance for the status quo, and the status quo includes the preservation of the positions of power already achieved by those who were once great individualists.

But the competitive spirit of those who are out of power, or who are coming up in the generation ladder, is likely to find new innovative outlets. It is not just a revolution of rising expectations which erupts into innovative vigor. That other revolution of rising frustrations which began in the second half of the 1960's has potentialities of creative unrest in its own right. The cultural ferment in literature and the arts is only one manifestation of this unrest.

The Arts and Cultural Miscegenation

In the arts and literature, unlike politics, cultural dualism need not be restrained by the dictates of practical operation and implementation. The field is wide open for different endeavors in cultural integration, for fusion and counterfusion, for stylistic interplay between divergent artistic media. Cultural dualism in Africa is the dualism, as we indicated, between the imperial cultural impact and the indigenous traditions. But the indigenous traditions themselves are in turn diverse, creating cultural pluralism. Cultural dualism might therefore be described as extranational and cultural pluralism as intranational. The dualistic dimension becomes connected with the issue of racial identity. A desire to assert an African essence, to discover a black meaning of things, becomes an aspect of the consolidation of racial identity. The movement known as negritude has been one manifestation of this, but other areas of black assertiveness also are an outgrowth of the phenomenon of dualism. Pride in African culture and the African heritage lies at the heart of the crisis of racial identity.

Cultural pluralism also generates experimentation of its own kind, linked to problems of national, rather than racial, identity. How can the particularistic ethnic heritages of individual communities be amalgamated into a new national heritage?

At Makerere University in Uganda the problem concretized itself partly in the issues of the localization of the history syllabus. It was easy enough to argue that the teaching of history at Makerere should cease to be Anglo-centric or even Euro-centric, and become more concerned with major themes of historical development in Africa. Then consideration had to be given to due emphasis on Ugandan material, posing a politically sensitive problem. Uganda material for the teaching of history was preponderantly derived from the history of three ethnic communities, the Baganda, the Banyoro, and the Banyankole. The disproportionate attention paid them by historians was partly connected with the centrality of Buganda in the affairs of Uganda, partly tied to the mystique of monarchies, and partly also tied to the accident that highly institutionalized traditional states tended to afford more obvious sources of information about the past than segmentary societies might do. For a department of history at Makerere to give disproportionate attention to Buganda in its syllabus would be likely to be interpreted as a continuing attempt to exaggerate the significance of the Baganda in the nation's affairs. In 1968 a new head of the department of history therefore decided to embark on a comprehensive program of intensive research in those areas which had previously been neglected by historians. There developed a clear commitment in the department to the cause of constructing a Ugandan historical course with some semblance of ethnic balance in the presentation of the nation's past.

Meanwhile the Department of English at Makerere has been renamed the Department of Literature and now hopes to include, among its offerings, a variety of oral literature drawn from the different communities of Uganda. Again a conscious attempt has to be made to create balance in representation. Fusion of the different literatures might not be possible, but balanced structures of presentation might be the initial stage of a national heritage.

The creative unrest released by cultural dualism is older than that generated by cultural pluralism. As we indicated, in Francophone Africa much of the nationalist movement during the colonial period was cultural in impetus, and motivated by a desire for racial vindication.

But after independence it is no longer enough to prove that the African genius for cultural creativity is as rich as that of Europe. It becomes necessary to discover areas of cultural unity in the richness of each African territorial entity. The 1970's are likely to go further in responding to the challenge of cultural pluralism than the 1960's. But in literature a preoccupation with cultural dualism so characteristic of the products of the 1950's and the 1960's is likely to decline as a theme in the actual works, though not necessarily as an inspiration behind the very urge to create and innovate. In other words, novelists might no longer be obsessed with culture contact and conflict of values as between the imported and the traditional—but much of the urge to write novels and excel in creativity might still bear the stamp of racial pride and owe some of its inspiration to the legacy of colonialism and aesthetic duality.

Conclusion

In the next two decades, a pendulum model of political change is likely to prevail, as African countries swing between one type of institutional arrangement and another. Each new stage is nevertheless likely to be at a higher level of progression than the one which went before—the model is not simply of a swinging pendulum in a static glass case. The nation is not stationary. Each return to a pattern of social arrangements should carry the benefit of previous failures with it, and enact experimental improvements for the new stage.

Concurrently with the swinging changes of politics, the decades of the 1970's and 1980's will witness a creative unrest in the continent, groping for solutions, for self-recognition, and innovating. The decline of literature in French-speaking countries is likely to be reversed, and in any case the performing arts even in Francophone Africa have continued to flourish with vigor. Both literature and the performing arts in English-speaking Africa are likely to reach new levels of attainment, in response both to dualism and pluralism within the cultural destiny of their societies.

There may be occasions when political instability might be too acute to sustain cultural creativity. And yet it is impossible to be sure what kind of instability in politics is likely to be totally countercreative in culture. Chinua Achebe, one of Africa's leading novelists, and a strong supporter of the Biafran cause while it lasted, wrote in the middle of the Nigerian Civil War:

> something apart from life. . . . I can create, but of course not the kind of thing I created when I was at ease. I can't write a novel now; something short, intense, more in keeping with my mood. . . . what I am saying is that there are forms of creativity which suit different moments. I wouldn't

consider writing a poem on daffodils particularly creative in my situation now. . . . But there are plays—about the Biafran war. I have seen two really excellent plays and an opera, the title of which is the name of one of the weapons that Biafran scientists developed. It's a jolly good opera. And there is a lot of poetry by young people, all concerned with this thing.[4]

There is hope, if even the most acute recession of empathy like a civil war not only fails to extinguish the urge to be culturally expressive but, on the contrary, creates different longings for expression. It may well be that in the long run the whole trauma of the Nigerian Civil War will have as one compensating factor its own contribution to the cultural ferment of Nigeria.

When a nation's psychic equilibrium is shattered to that degree, the potentialities of creative unrest in the years which follow might be difficult to calculate. Conceivably they might even be limitless. For Africa as a whole the instability and political agonies, those very recessions of empathy of the 1970's and 1980's, might well turn out to be the pangs of mother culture in the throes of creative labor.

Footnotes

1. *The Evening News* (Accra), June 14, 1955.
2. See "The Multiple Marginality of the Sudan," chapter 8 in Mazrui, *Violence and Thought* (London: Longmans, 1969), pp. 174–176.
3. *The Colonial Reckoning* (London: Collins, 1961; New York: Knopf, 1962).
4. See Bernth Lindfors' interview with Achebe, "Achebe on Commitment and African Writers," *Africa Report,* Vol. 15, No. 3, March 1970, pp. 17–18.

CHAPTER 10

Violent Change and Emergent Empathy

Although the minimization of violence is one of our ideals, we should remember that violence has positive as well as negative effects—as any revolutionary would tell us. Although theories of violence and theories of revolution are by no means identical, recent political thought often *derives* the legitimation of violence from its orientation toward a social revolution and systemic change.

It is because of this persistent—but by no means inevitable—linkage between violence and revolution as rallying political ideas, that contemporary perspectives on violence have been influenced so profoundly by Marx and his successors. Marxism has entered the main stream of world political culture substantially because of its orientation toward revolutionary change.

The basic assumption behind this revolutionary school of violence rests on the presumed efficacy of violence as a method of achieving *sudden* or *rapid* change. However, what have tended to be overlooked are the functions of violence on an *evolutionary* scale of change. In other words, there are certain positive changes in societies which are achieved not by a sudden eruption of violence, but by the slow process of having to *cope with violence* over several decades or generations.

We might here then distinguish between the *transformative* functions of violence and the *integrative* functions of violence. The transformative functions are those which help to bring about sudden or rapid systemic change. It is these functions which have produced a tendency to equate political or social violence with revolution.

We are concerned, however, with the much slower integrative functions of violence. The role of violence in the evolution of nationhood and the enlargement of social empathy is a process which takes several generations. The role of violence in *regional* integration, across several states, is also an area of gradual rather than sudden change.

Before we look more closely at the relationship between violence and the integrative process, one further factor should be borne in mind: violence is not merely a *cause* of change, revolutionary or gradual, it is even more often an *effect* of other social factors. Political violence is often an outcome of other social realities; it can emerge out of an interplay between cultural and economic factors. Perceptions of relative deprivation, for example, are conditioned by the interplay between a culturally influenced scale of values and the actual pattern of resource allocation in a given society.

Violence and National Integration

At one level of argument it may indeed be true that internal conflict within a country is inherently disintegrative. Yet, paradoxically, no national integration is possible without internal conflict. The paradox arises because while conflict itself has a capacity to force a dissolution, the *resolution* of conflict is an essential mechanism of integration. Jointly looking for a way out of a crisis, seeing your mutual hostility subside to a level of mutual tolerance, being intensely conscious of each other's positions and yet sensing the need to bridge the gulf—these are experiences which, over a period of time, should help two groups of people move forward into a relationship of deeper integration. Conflict resolution might not be a sufficient condition for national integration, but it is certainly a necessary one.

In our discussion of the process of cultural convergence in Chapter 3, we defined the four stages of coexistence, contact, compromise and coalescence. Much of the interethnic violence in post-colonial Africa is the violence between the stage of interethnic contact and the future stage of interethnic compromise.[1] This means that violence can be an indicator of the stage of national integration achieved. Here we must draw a distinction between primary violence and secondary violence within the territorial state. The most basic form of violent conflict, judged in these terms, is that which concerns the territorial survival of that state. When one group is so resolutely opposed to another that it resents having to share the same frontiers, political cleavage is at its most profound. It affects not only explicitly integrative issues, but also raises the question of whether a ruler chosen from one particular ethnic community has a right to exercise authority over any other. Problems of integration and political legitimacy become intertwined, although the initial cause of the cleavage is a fracture in the integrative section. In short, primary violence is violence concerning the boundaries of a given political community.

Secondary violence, on the other hand, may be defined as that which does not threaten the integrity of the state, but arises from conflict over its internal organization, the formulation of public policy, or the distribution of public goods. Secondary violence is concerned not with the *boundaries* of a political community but with its *purposes*. One of the greatest dangers confronting Africa is that cleavage over secondary policy issues is very often ethnic in origin, and involves fundamental questions of group identity. This means that, once secondary violence occurs, it frequently has primary implications as well, although these need not necessarily lead to the dissolution of the state. Dissatisfaction with the workings of the political system may very rapidly create separatist tendencies which, in turn, may lead to secessionism, if the realities of economic and political geography favor such a radical solution.[2]

There are clear indications that party politics in Nigeria before the first coup were generating increased secondary violence, and yet containing the dangers of primary violence. It is not always remembered that *politics*, viewed as a process of continuous definition and redefinition of areas of agreement and disagreement, is an integrative function in its own right. Certainly it is an important vehicle for the move from mere contact to real compromise.

If the pre-coup regime in Nigeria achieved nothing else, it certainly contributed to the spread of nationally oriented political activity. The defensiveness of the north against the south had originally taken the form of separatism which raised the specter of primary violence. Following independence however the northern strategy became that of *infiltrating* the south. The interest of the north in consolidating its federal power was perhaps the most significant integrative factor in Nigeria's history until that time, although, paradoxically, it also led to a heightening of ethnic and regional consciousness which was potentially disruptive.

The nationalization of politics in Nigeria was growing faster than the country's capacity for compromise. Another way of formulating this hypothesis is that political activity was helping to spread direct ethnic contact, but the system had not acquired the compromise capability to cope with the resultant tensions of that ethno-economic contact. In that kind of situation, to spread political activity over a widening field of national affairs was to increase the area of conflict potential. Such conflicts may indeed be perfectly compatible with national integration, but the system's ability to resolve conflicts had not become sophisticated enough in Nigeria to cope with the tensions of increased interaction between its sub-units.

If the Nigerian eruptions had been concerned with, for example, whether the country should be socialist or adopt a private enterprise system, or should have an alliance with the West or remain nonaligned, these might well have been issues of secondary importance even if the emotions generated amounted to actual violence. To kill because one

213

hates socialism is less fundamental than to kill because one hates the tribe or race of one's opponent. Tribal or racial violence is the violence of identity; violence between the left and the right is usually the violence of policy. Violence on policy issues of this kind is secondary violence; violence on identity and national survival is primary violence.

Tribalism in Africa is unlikely to disappear within a single lifetime. Pessimistic as it may seem, the first signs of disappearance might have to be sought in the changing motives of political violence—from primary to secondary. Secondary violence is violence between partialized identities, and that itself is a move toward national integration.

Inter-African Demonstration Effect

Domestic violence in each African country has consequences beyond its own borders. Are these effects disruptive only or also integrative? And how do they relate to the crisis of receding empathy we discussed before?

In discussing receding empathy, we examined the decline of continentally oriented nationalism in Africa. But the decline of African nationalism has not necessarily meant the decline of all its after-effects. That old interplay between contiguity and political consciousness is still very much at work. And in situations of social violence, geopolitical contiguity facilitates sociopolitical contagion.

This simple proposition is itself a useful tool for understanding some of the major political trends in contemporary Africa. For example, a major factor is that the very multiplicity of army coups in Africa, in rapid succession, has itself been due to the reality of Pan-African identification. What happens in one African country can give rise to imitative tendencies in another African country and this presupposes a capacity to empathize. The degree of this capacity in Africa has sometimes varied in proportion to the degree of trans-national integration between specific African states.

The experience of East Africa in 1964 was a particularly dramatic illustration of this point. On January 12 a revolution took place in Zanzibar. Within ten days, army mutinies had taken place in Tanganyika, Uganda and Kenya. The mutinies in all the three countries on the East African mainland were put down by British troops. What matters from our point of view is the compulsive power of imitation which the whole experience demonstrated.[3]

A major factor was the degree of integration which had been accomplished among the three countries, mutually contiguous and with years of similar administrative experience. The territories had emerged into independence with their own regional common market and with "an impressive range of common services which had no counterpart in the [European Economic Community]." The East African Common Services Organization was responsible for a number of shared services and institutions, ranging from Railways and Harbours, Post and Telecommunications, to a common body for tax and customs collection.[4]

Even more relevant for the growth of mutual identification was the degree of social and cultural intercourse which had developed. Apart from the usual related tribes along the border there was the interrelationship among the three educational systems, culminating in the shared apex of Makerere College. Similar syllabuses in schools and consultations among educational authorities resulted in broadly similar socializing influences on East African children within the educational pipeline. Few of those who later joined the armed forces had gone very far in that pipeline, but exposure to similar educative influences, even when limited to the primary and secondary school levels, was a significant contribution to social integration in East Africa.

Language provided an additional area of fusion. The spread of Swahili in East Africa has been one of the most impressive cultural phenomena in the region in this century. Swahili has been changing from a communal to a regional language. In Tanzania, it has all but become supreme, and is being called upon to replace English in certain areas of national life. In Kenya, Swahili has not yet fully conquered the country, but it has spread far in the last thirty years. In Uganda it is on its way toward conquering all towns and cities; it has been crucial in the trade union movement, and professionally important in the Ugandan sectors of the East African Common Services. Kenya's export of manpower to her neighbor in the northwest has also been a form of linguistic penetration.

It is particularly significant that Swahili has enjoyed a special position within the security forces of Uganda. These forces came to symbolize both culture contact and the profession of violence. Both the police and the army in Uganda have used Swahili as their official language. This remained the most formal role that Swahili was being called upon to play in Uganda since it was eliminated from Uganda schools in 1930's under the pressure of the Luganda-speaking region of the country. Within the ranks of the King's African Rifles in all three countries, Swahili remained the language of command and of trans-tribal discourse. It therefore contributed to some shared habits of newspaper reading, which was important in a region with a tradition of both newspaper chains and trans-national readerships. Exposure to affiliated mass media is itself a contributory factor in social integration. When combined with the other elements of cultural interplay among the three countries, it helped to create the kind of conditions which made a Pan-African demonstration effect in this region more immediate at a moment of critical impact.

In addition, the three countries, though having had separate armed forces as they approached independence, had nevertheless known areas of common military experience. There was, first, the common British training for the army, reinforced institutionally by the whole concept of the "King's African Rifles." Second, the pool of recruitment was not the individual country but the region as a whole, not merely mixing tribes but also nationalities among the three countries. As Uganda approached independence there were a number of Kenyans in important positions in the police. The army in Tanganyika started mainly with recruits drawn from elsewhere in East Africa. And it is significant that the Zanzibar revolution which sparked off the mutinies appeared to have been spearheaded by a Ugandan, John Okello, who had known service in the Zanzibar police. This mixing process in the security forces helped to accentuate the capacity for imitation under a suitably powerful stimulus.[5]

Finally, there was the consultative involvement of the East African High Commission and its successor in some defense matters affecting the region as a whole. The East African Defense Committee was, in a modest sense, the defense arm of the Commission. The small Royal East African Navy, militarily insignificant, was nevertheless an effective stimulant of interterritorial discussions and debates on the fundamentals of regional defense.

Although East Africa had achieved a particularly high degree of integration, it was by no means the only instance of a discernible demonstration effect in military matters commensurate with the degree of mutual identification. At the risk of oversimplification, we may begin by noting that Francophone Africans identify with each other more readily than they identify with other Africans. There is a bond of linguistic identification even between former French and former Belgian Africa. It is a measure of the impact of the metropolitan languages on identification processes in Africa. And where there has been such a bond of a shared European language between African states, the demonstration effect has been facilitated. The first series of coups in the Africa of 1965–1966 was in French-speaking Africa. Excluding Algeria, there were four coups in French-speaking Africa before English-speaking Africa followed suit. On November 25, 1965, the relatively long-established regime of Joseph Kasavuvu in the Congo was overthrown, and General Joseph Mobutu took over the government. On December 22 there followed the coup in Dahomey. On New Year's Day in 1966 the Central African Republic marked the occasion with a coup, to be imitated two days later by Upper Volta. W. F. Gutteridge might have been exaggerating, but there was certainly some evidence for his assertion that:

The effectiveness of Mobutu's employment of the retrained and reorganized Congolese Army to overthrow a disorganized political regime provided a model and an example. To African soldiers aware of the French tradition in which they were trained, the lesson was easily assimilated from him and from one another.[6]

The specter of a Euro-centric world culture was once again in combat with other social forces in new African nations. It was not until January 15, 1966, that the first military coup in English-speaking Africa took place when the regime of Sir Abubaker Tafawa Balewa was overthrown in Nigeria. It is not clear whether Kwame Nkrumah in Ghana became a little more worried about his own political survival as a result of the Nigerian coup. If he did not, he ought to have. Perhaps no two countries in West Africa had been more conscious of each other as "rivals" in some matters than Nigeria and Ghana. And rivalry of that kind arose precisely because of a mutual acceptance of each other as comparable entities. A spirit of "keeping up with the Joneses" often presupposes a capacity to empathize with the Joneses—"If they can do it, why can't we?" These close mental links between Nigerians and Ghanaians should perhaps have been a warning that after Nigeria's, the next coup was likely to be in Ghana. It was not, of course, inevitable. The demonstration effect could have been neutralized by other factors. But it seems very likely that the Nigerian coup was an important precipitating factor behind the fall of Nkrumah in February 1966. By a twist of historical irony, this was itself a manifestation of Pan-Africanism, a demonstration that, at a certain level, Nigerians and Ghanians did have a sense of shared identity after all.

There are occasions when the reaction produced in a neighboring community is not emulation but retaliation. Nor need these reactions be across national boundaries; they might be across regional or ethnic frontiers. This is an area of demonstration effect in which the phenomenon of retribalization might have special relevance. The facts surrounding the immediate causes of the Nigerian Civil War are still rather unclear, but one version of the September massacres of the Ibos in northern Nigeria in 1966 is that they were preceded by the killing of Hausa tradesmen in the East. A radio report probably exaggerated the scale of killing of northerners by easterners, but the rumors reactivated a wounded ethnic pride in the north, with ghastly consequences for Ibos in that region.

Instability and the African Anti-Models

On balance, however, the politics of retribalization have more often given rise to a counterdemonstration impact than to a demonstration effect as such. Where ethnic loyalties have assumed explosive dimensions in one country, the repercussions in a neighboring country have often taken the form of "a lesson to be avoided". For example, when the Congo exploded, on attainment of independence, into violent ethnic rivalries, the costly repercussions of it all had a sobering effect on the Congo's neighbors. Many of these were on the threshold of independence and saw how meaningless independence could become in the wake of ethnic conflicts and international intervention. Julius Nyerere of Tanzania hastened to reassure his countrymen and the world that the presence of an effective political party in Tanganyika was a safeguard against the risk of having another Congo in his country.

Kenya looked even more clearly like a potential Congo. As independence approached, a resurgence of tribal feeling crystallized into two major political parties, the Kenya African National Union, associated at the time preeminently with the dominant tribes of the Kikuyu and the Luo, and the Kenya African Democratic Union, associated with the smaller tribes scattered across the rest of the country. There was also briefly a more exclusive ethnic party, headed by Paul Ngei, a Kamba leader. The debates in the country as independence approached revolved around the issue of centralization as against devolution of authority. In the background was the Somalia issue involving the question of whether the Northern Frontier District of Kenya should indeed remain part of Kenya or be ceded to Somalia on the principle of ethnic self-determination.

In Kenya, too, the lesson of the Congo was fortunately not far from the consciousness of politicians. In fact, the danger point came more immediately before independence than after it. A certain momentary stability descended on the country after the British had withdrawn, culminating in the dissolution of the smaller party, KADU, and its absorption by the major party, KANU. There was a genuine fear of pushing ethnic rivalry too far, and behind this fear the Congo as an anti-model was highly relevant. The concept of "anti-model" is here defined quite simply as a convincing example of what to avoid.

From the point of view of ethnic resurgence, Nigeria comes after the Congo as a frightening anti-model for the rest of Africa. It has been a clearer case of retribalization than the Congo ever was. There was a time when Nigeria provided an elegant contrast to the disintegration of the Congo. Foreign newspapers such as the *New York Times* carried articles attempting to understand why Belgian policy in the Congo had so disastrously failed while British policy in Nigeria had emerged triumphant. And the leading Pan-Nigerian nationalist, Nnamdi Azikiwe, an Ibo, paid tribute to Britain's bequest of stability under the rule of law.

It really did seem as if a sense of Nigerian identity had begun to take shape. But it was soon demonstrated that national integration was a reversible process. What had been achieved in the evolution of national consciousness in Nigeria was partially lost with the resurgence of a more militant ethnic consciousness. As we indicated, the most Pan-Nigerian of all Nigerians were in fact the Ibos. When the Ibo officers carried out the first coup in January 1966, the cause of one Nigeria seemed for a brief period to have taken another step forward. And then, within months, things began to change. Partly through the new regime's mishandling of northern sensibilities following the murder of prominent northern leaders, a sense of wounded pride gathered momentum in the northern region as well as among northerners in the armed forces. The stage was set for the counter-coup of May 1966 and the stiffening ethnicity which culminated in Biafra's bid to secede. A ghastly civil war ensued.

For quite a while the rest of Africa was reluctant to discuss too openly the Nigerian civil war. There was a particularly marked reluctance to concede legitimacy to Biafra, a clear case of a counterdemonstration impact. The fear of a successful secession on the basis of ethnic withdrawal made much of Africa shrink from open encouragement of the Ibos. Multi-ethnic states were the order of the day in Africa, and few governments were inclined to encourage ethnic self-determination. At the meeting which brought the Organization of African Unity into being, a Kenya delegation—of Odinga, Koinage, Kiano, and others—had affirmed that "the principle of self-determination has relevance where *foreign domination* is the issue. It has no relevance where the issue is territorial disintegration by dissident citizens."[7]

This view was widely accepted in much of Africa and helped to determine the nature of the Organization of African Unity and the principles underlying it. When therefore the Nigerian civil war broke out, the OAU, after prolonged pause for reflection, set up a special consultative commission on the Nigerian civil war, which included within its terms of reference a reaffirmation of the territorial integrity of Nigeria. In its fear of secession, Africa was fearful of fragmented empathy. But Africa was also fearful of the equation between smallness and vulnerability.

Milton Obote of Uganda captured the ideological essence behind African attitudes when, in 1960, he reacted to Buganda's attempted secession with the words "African nationalism hates small states."[8] This attempted secession was during the colonial period. But the British authorities supremely ignored Buganda's attempts to break away from Uganda, so that the nation emerged in entirety into independence in October 1962. Yet four years later, Bugunda's strong identity was once again shaking the territorial survival of Uganda. A confrontation between the central government and the Buganda region, accompanied by

219

the suspension of the constitution, led to the worst crisis the country had faced since independence. In May 1966 Buganda attempted what might be called an inverse secession. Instead of saying "we are pulling out," as the Ibos had done in Nigeria, the Kabaka's government in the Buganda region said to the central government of Uganda, "You get off Buganda soil." As Kampala, the national capital, was surrounded by Buganda and was itself ostensibly on Buganda soil, this was separatism with a difference.

It was an attempted expulsion of the nation from the region instead of an attempted withdrawal of a region from the nation. And Kampala, surrounded by the region, but politically tied to the rival side of the dispute, was momentarily converted into an African "West Berlin". Because Buganda did not have the power to impose a blockade on the city, in the ensuing confrontation between the central government and the Kabaka's government, the center emerged triumphant. The Kabaka fled into exile in Britain and his region was put under a state of emergency and strict central control.

All these factors helped to give the Nigerian crisis added meaning to countries like Uganda, though the division of opinion between supporters of Biafra and those of Nigeria among Africans elsewhere did not always coincide with the division of opinion between centralizers and regionalists.

By the beginning of 1968, African reluctance to interfere in the Nigerian civil war was cracking. It was partly the strain of uncertainty, partly the reports of federal ruthlessness in prosecuting the civil war, and partly the fact that the war had been internationalized by the participation of Britain, the Soviet Union, the United Arab Republic and, less openly, France. All these made it inevitable that African reservations about the federal position should at last be openly articulated. Tanzania led the way with the recognition of Biafra in the spring of 1968, and she was soon followed by Zambia, Gabon and the Ivory Coast.

Yet when the Organization of African Unity met at the summit level in Algiers in September 1968, the meeting backed the Nigerian government's efforts to reunify the country, suggested a criticism of the four African countries who had recognized Biafra, and urged the separatist Ibos to rejoin Nigeria. The fear of a triumphant secessionist precedent had once again prevailed at this highest African decision-making body. The counterdemonstration impact of a divided Nigeria was still very much at play.

The fear of precedents has not been limited to challenges to existing regimes. The issue of territorial integrity is connected with problems of national integration; the security of regimes with problems of political legitimacy. A successful secession is a step away from the goal of national integration; a successful overthrow of a government or assassination of a leader is often deemed to be a step away from the ideal of consolidating political legitimacy. The fear of political assassination is therefore an important area of counterdemonstration in inter-African politics.

The Organization of African Unity was formed in the shadow of the assassination of President Sylvanus Olympio of Togo. At the time there was strong suspicion in some quarters that the killing had resulted from a series of subversive activities in which President Nkrumah's government was implicated. For a short while after Olympio's death Africa had been seriously divided. Apart from the dubious Mobutu "takeover" in the Congo in 1960-1961, the overthrow of Olympio's regime in January 1963 was the first clear coup d'état in sub-Saharan Africa. Its immediate impact on relations among African states was angrily divisive. Nigeria's Foreign Minister at the time, Jaja Wachuku, was quick to express his suspicions. He regarded Olympio's assassination as "engineered, organized and financed by somebody". He warned that Nigeria would intervene militarily if "the contingent of armored Ghanian troops lined up on the Ghana-Togo border" attempted to cross the border. French-speaking Africa was also divided both on the question of possible subversion at large and on whether or not the new regime of Nicolas Grunitzky was to be recognized. A suggestion of the politics of retribalization in relation to boundaries was, in the case of Togo, implicit in the fate of the Ewe tribe divided between Togo and Ghana.

By the time the heads of African states met at Addis Ababa in May 1963, the passions which had been aroused by the assassination had subsided a little but the general suspicion about subversion from neighboring countries had not. Of the seven principles promulgated by the Charter of the Organization of African Unity, four reflected a general preoccupation with respect for borders and their sanctity against violation or interference. But the fear of assassination was also present. The fifth principle of the Charter, explicitly affirmed "unreserved condemnation, in all its forms, of political assassination as well as of subversive activities on the part of neighboring states or any other states".

The fear of the assassin's bullet might therefore be said to be another major area of violent contiguity—a proximity to violent events near enough to entail the risk of imitation and too near in this case for political comfort.[9]

Violence and Regional Integration

The four stages of coexistence, contact, compromise, and coalescence are, as we indicated, applicable to regional as well as to national integration. But the factors which initiate change from one stage to another are different in a multistate region from what they are within a single territorial state. Whereas in relations within a single country it is the stage between contact and compromise which has a high potentiality for conflict, in relations between states it is very often the stage between compromise and coalescence. We have noted in this regard that the two most ghastly wars experienced by the human race so far started off as European wars.

Sometimes the tensions arise because the structure of compromise assumes a cooperative framework for competitive relationships. There are times when such a situation has a greater potential for acute and divisive rivalry than a complete absence of cooperation would have. Indeed, there are times when such family rivalries evoke greater passions than rivalry with a distant enemy. It is conceivable that Canadians, for example, feel more strongly against American economic dominance in Canada than they do about the more remote danger of communist China. It was certainly true that President de Gaulle when he was in power was more suspicious of "Anglo-Saxon" intentions within the Atlantic Alliance than he was of Soviet policies.

If we turn to East Africa and the East African community, we find again that few things have contributed more to, say, Ugandan national consciousness than Uganda's competitive relationship with its immediate neighbors. The East African community itself encourages territorial competition for a share of the economic cake of the region as a whole. The awareness of conflicting interests has been deepened. Each country has not only grown more protective of its own interests as *opposed* to the interests of the others—it has sometimes developed a more enduring psychological complex and suspicion of the motives of others. It is this consideration which converts regional economic cooperation, as a stage of compromise, into a breeding ground for economic nationalism within each member state in certain circumstances. The degree of nationalism varies with each nation-state, usually in relation to the benefits which each derives from the cooperation. Sometimes the greatest beneficiary is the least defensive and the least militant in her economic nationalism. Within the East African Community Kenya has therefore tended to be less defensively nationalistic in economic matters than either Uganda or Tanzania.

But in the case of Canada's relationship with the United States it is conceivable that Canada is the greater net beneficiary in the economic relationship between the two countries, whatever might be lost in terms of political autonomy. Though it is possible that Canada would stand to lose more than the United States by a complete economic break, Canada is the more defensively nationalistic of the two.

East Africans for quite a while now have had dreams of combining into a single federal state. Among the experiences which have given them that idea is precisely the sharing of an economic community for a while. And yet it is meaningful to ask whether the spirit of economic rivalry fostered among the constituent members of the East African Economic Community has itself harmed the cause of an East African federation. The competitive habits and protective militancy which were nourished by the existence of an economic union might conceivably have pushed the federal cause further away from realization for the time being. What this means is that a period of compromise relationships has generated enough tensions to push East African relations backward toward contact rather than forward toward coalescence. The compromise relationships may indeed later generate enough integrative momentum to cross the boundary at last into coalescence. But in the initial phases the tensions of compromise relations are of such a kind that they pull a regional entity backward toward bare contact and then forward again. It is almost like Lenin's concept, duly inverted, concerning two steps forward and one step backward. Occasionally it becomes indeed two steps backward and one step forward.

The role of conflict and violence in regional integration is again somewhat different from its role within a territorial entity. The absence of a common government in a multi-state region is one vital differentiating characteristic when we are comparing such a region with a multi-ethnic state. Compromise relationships within a multi-ethnic state are stabilized more effectively, as the state moves toward national coalescence, than they can be in a multi-state region. That is one reason why it is easier in a multi-ethnic state to move from compromise to coalescence than it is in a multi-state region.

It has often been pointed out that Hobbes's theory about "the state of war" is vindicated in the international system much more than in the behavior of individual nations. As we know, Thomas Hobbes had postulated that in the absence of a common government, men act in relative distrust of each other, taking precautions against each other, all too often aware that it is each man for himself in the social jungle.

It is not at all clear that men do in practice revert back to aggressive individualistic behavior as soon as they know that government and political authority have broken down. There continues to be a restraining factor, possibly arising out of habitual social conformity. In any case, it is rare that individual societies exist without either individual institutionalized government or alternative structures of authority. In individual states we may as a generalization continue to reaffirm that politics is an activity which relates to national government, but in the international sphere politics has continued to be an activity which relates to the *absence* of a supra-national government.

It is because of this vital distinction that the place of conflict in regional integration fundamentally differs from its role in national integration. Methods of conflict resolution in a region which has no shared structures of authority have to be more subtle, often more fragile and less effective, than methods of conflict resolution within a multi-ethnic state.

Partly because of this, violence itself plays a different role in the integration of a multi-state region. We might say that violence and economic interaction are the two most effective agencies of interpenetration in the politics of *regional* political systems. The role of economic interaction as a form of penetration, in trade exchange and labor migration, has been treated in different places extensively. We might now therefore concentrate on violence as a penetrative agency.

Violence is a penetrative agency in interstate relations because it loosens some of the inhibitions against interference in other people's affairs, and because it tends to create a compulsive case for seeking allies in a power struggle within each of the states. A power struggle in the Sudan, for example, might bring in the support of Egypt as a way of tilting the forces within. A power struggle within southern Sudan might involve Uganda, as contenders within southern Sudan either seek allies or campaign to avert the maturation of alliances between their enemies and some third party. A power struggle in Egypt might result in involving the Sudan to the south, as well as Libya to the west, and the Arab Fertile Crescent to the east.

If we look at the Nile Valley as an emerging regional system, we see the interpenetration between domestic politics in the Sudan and the Egyptian presence to the north, over some issues. The Ugandan presence to the south of the Sudan, with regard to other issues, has also become increasingly manifest.

Some of the initial areas of interaction between Egypt and the Sudan were indeed economic—in addition to the all-powerful factor of the Nile passing through the Sudan before it entered Egypt to give Egypt its life. But preeminent among the forces of interpenetration in recent years have remained the phenomena of conflict and violence. Aid in military situations, diplomatic support in moments of political wrangles, have both contributed to deepening a shared political experience between Egypt and the Sudan in the years of independence.

Further south, a civil war raged in southern Sudan from 1955 to 1972, opening up opportunities for penetration by others into Sudanese affairs. While in domestic politics it is not conflict but conflict *resolution* which promotes national integration, in regional integration conflict itself could, by being penetrative, also be in some cases integrative. The Valley of the Nile might be converted into a regional political system not simply by the flow of its waters, but also by the flow of blood.

Though not always consistently, Milton Obote, as President of Uganda, aspired to keep out of his neighbors' quarrels. But he sometimes used a curious yet fundamental argument for this policy—that Uganda itself was constantly on the brink of her own internal quarrels. Obote assumed that until Uganda attained its own national cohesion, she could not afford to be involved in other people's adventures. His statement was defensible as a moral assertion but it was unsound as a political proposition. Obote argued:

> Uganda's foreign policy can only be a reflection of Uganda. If Uganda is divided into tribal, religious or ethnic factions, no Government of Uganda will be in a position to project any other image except the image of a country dissected by tribal, religious, ethnic and other considerations. For the people of Uganda it is academic and dishonest for them to aspire to influence international relations ahead of their being able to bury their sectional interests. After all, Uganda in international relations presupposes that Uganda itself has an identity—that is, one image—but . . . Uganda is amorphous. . . .[10]

In the political assumptions of his analysis, Milton Obote was wrong. It is precisely in situations of amorphous national identity, and imminent social violence, that quarrels of one country spill over into another—and transnational interpenetration is facilitated by intranational cleavages. The fluid identities of both the Sudan and Uganda, with overlapping tribal communities, have been part of the process by which the two countries have profoundly affected each other.

There were occasions for concern lest there be a Ugandan factor in Sudanese conflicts. Obote himself kept repeatedly reassuring the Sudanese government that in spite of ethnic ties, he did not intend to make Uganda a base for the liberation movements of southern Sudan. At times Obote fulfilled this promise; at other times he fell short of fulfilling it. A Ugandan factor was never entirely absent in the Sudanese civil war.

The question arising as the 1970's began was whether there would be a Sudanese factor within Uganda's own power struggles. After all, if the border tribes traversed the two nations, it was not simply a question of the Ugandan sector of the tribe helping the Sudanese sector, but also of whether the Sudanese sector of the tribe would help the Ugandan sector

225

in potentially similar circumstances. Are there, then, southern Sudanese in the Ugandan army?

The Kakwa, the tribe of General Idi Amin, the man who succeeded Obote in January 1971, traverses the border between the Sudan and Uganda. Indeed, the bulk of it is in the Sudan, though it overflows into both Uganda and Zaire. The question which arose following the coup in 1971 was whether General Amin would find it necessary or expedient to ignore the territorial boundary declared by modern states, and recognize instead the reality of ethnic bonds. Would General Amin seek to have Kakwa in his army, irrespective of whether they were Sudanese Kakwa, Zairean Kakwa, or Ugandan Kakwa?

Speculation also included the question of whether General Amin had in fact started to recruit from among southern Sudanese even before the army coup of January 1971. Was this in fact one of the issues which was beginning to bedevil relations between General Amin as head of the army, and President Obote as Commander-in-Chief?

Southern Sudanese were themselves engaged in a civil war, as we indicated, against the government in Khartoum. The Anya Nya, the southern Sudanese separatist movement, had been in the field for a number of years. Did the coup of January 1971 in Uganda afford southern Sudanese a greater atmosphere of hospitality? Has there been an interpenetration between southern Sudan and Uganda in their respective fighting forces?

The Commonwealth correspondent of *The Observer* (London), Colin Legum, in one of his rash reports about the Ugandan situation, prematurely claimed that a number of southern Sudanese had been promoted not long after the coup in Uganda. The Ugandan Government of the Second Republic corrected the excesses of Legum's report, pointing out that the only officer of Sudanese extraction who had been promoted had in fact been in the Ugandan army for a number of years. The new government of Uganda repudiated the innuendo that southern Sudanese had assumed critical areas of decision-making in the Ugandan armed forces. Subsequent decisions narrowed the gap between reality and Legum's claims. But for our purposes the question is whether there is indeed a Sudanese factor, however modest, which has now become significant in the balance of forces within Uganda. There is evidence that about 600 southern Sudanese were employed soon after the coup, and many of them became part of Amin's own "palace guard". There is evidence also of further recruitment of Sudanese into the Uganda Army. If there is now a Sudanese factor in the Ugandan crisis, just as there was a Ugandan factor in the Sudanese civil war, the situation is one more illustration of the role of violence in creating opportunities for interpenetration between contiguous nation-states. In the African situation the violence reactivates certain primordial loyalties among peoples with the same ethnic or linguistic ancestry, who have nevertheless been previously divided by artificial colonial boundaries and find in the experience of post-colonial tensions a resumption of militant solidarity. By reactivating those primordial bonds across artificial territorial boundaries, the violence may itself be laying the foundation for deeper forms of integration in the region as a whole. The artificiality of the boundaries then acquires a greater conspicuousness, and the realities of ethnic interconnections might once again be given due credence in the tensions of regional integration. The forces of expanding empathy find a strange ally in violence itself.

Conclusion

We have attempted to show in this chapter that it is not merely on a scale of revolutionary change that violence plays critical roles, but also along the scale of gradual and evolutionary social mutation. We began by dividing the functions of violence into two broad categories—the transformative functions, related to revolutionary experience; and the integrative functions which take longer to reveal their effects and whose positive consequences are often unintended by those who initiate the eruptions.

As we know, the revolutionary schools of violence have borrowed substantially from Karl Marx and his successors. In the Third World an important thinker in recent times has been the late Frantz Fanon, psychologist from Martinique, who fought for Algeria's independence with the National Liberation Front. Within a few years Fanon has become a leading thinker of the revolutionary school of the Third World, with special reference to movements connected with anticolonialism and antiracialism. For Fanon, colonialism itself is once again a form of structured violence, and must precipitate counterviolence: ". . . colonialism is not a thinking machine, nor a body endowed with reasoning faculties. It is violence in its natural state: and it will only yield when confronted with greater violence."[11]

Fanon, drawing substantially from African and West Indian experience, also pays attention to the passionate dances and possession by spirit which have sometimes characterized the shadowy phases of black life. These tumultous moments of abandon of dancing and song had been known to escalate into fratricidal combat. Fanon sees in this very phenomenon the stuff of which real violence is ultimately made. And he wants these emotions politicized, and given a sense of direction.

We have seen that this same violence, though kept very much under the surface all through the colonial period, yet turns in the void. We have also seen that it is canalized by the emotional outlets of dance and possession by the

227

spirits; we have seen how it is exhausted in fratricidal combats. Now the problem is to lay hold of this violence which is changing direction. When formerly it was appeased by myths and exercised its talents in finding fresh ways of committing mass suicide, now new conditions will make possible a completely new line of action.[12]

Purposeful violence to Fanon therefore becomes a purifying experience for those whose energies were before misdirected, and those who suffered under the disruptive impact of colonialism.

Although Fanon was not an African in the usual sense, he was of African descent. He also devoted his own energies to a major African and colonial war, perhaps the most important in the African continent: the Algerian struggle for independence. If the Third World is conceived as a tricontinental entity, consisting of Africa, Asia and Latin America, we might say that Africa's most important contribution to revolutionary militancy in the Third World is the political thought of Frantz Fanon. It is conceivable that Fanon is on the way toward entering the main stream of world intellectual culture.

Latin America's contribution is, in the final analysis, the political thought of Che Guevara. As a theorist Fanon is more original than Guevara, but both knew the experience of being involved in insurrection, the fear and excitement of violence, and the overpowering symbolism of blood which is politically spilt. And both were aware that guerrilla tactics are the tactics of the underprivileged, the underarmed, the underfinanced, the undernourished. But behind this band of ill-equipped fighters is the invincibility of the people. To use Guevara's formulation:

The guerrilla band is an armed nucleus, the fighting vanguard of the people. It draws its great force from the mass of the people themselves. The guerrilla band is not to be considered inferior to the army against which it fights simply because it is inferior in fire power. Guerrilla warfare is used by the side which is supported by the majority but which possesses a much smaller number of arms for use in defense against aggression.[13]

As for Asia's contribution to the militancy of the Third World, the most towering figure must for the time being remain Mao Tse-tung. The people of the Third World are the majority of the human race. Mao played up the question of numbers, not only in the moral sense that "the majority are right", but in the military sense that the masses are powerful. As the *Peking Review* put it in April 1960:

There was a theory current for a time among some people in China before and during the War of Resistance to Japanese Aggression, which was known as the "Weapons-Mean-Everything Theory"; from this theory they concluded that since Japan's weapons were new and its techniques backward, "China would inevitably be subjugated." Comrade Mao Tse-tung in his work *On the Protracted War* published at that time refuted such nonsense. . . . Comrade Mao Tse-tung pointed out that the most abundant source of strength in war lay in the masses, and in the people's army organized by awakened and united masses, the people would be invincible throughout the world.[14]

But violence as an integrative phenomenon has as yet found no major prophets. For the very reason that violence, as a phenomenon within the process of either national integration or regional integration, plays its part independently of the intentions of those who initiated the violence, this area of experience has yet to find a Fanon or a Che Guevara or a Mao Tse-tung. Violence on the evolutionary scale has the dullness of gradualism, and the banality of unintended consequences. It connotes no anger against class privilege, no militant indignation against imperialism. It is the sum of these slow human experiences in a given society which forces men to find ways of resolving their conflicts, and of reducing their propensity to be brutal to each other. As for the violence of regional integration, ranging from the record of Europe as a continent at once deeply integrated and deeply divided, to the experience of the Nile Valley seeking to emerge as a regional political system from the very experience of violent interpenetration, we have again the dynamics of evolutionary gradualism. Out of the blood and ashes, the torment and anger, a region at last finds its own identity—and history assembles the generations together at last.

Footnotes

1. These stages of integration were previously worked out in Chapter 5 in Mazrui, *Violence and Thought: Essays on Social Tensions in Africa* (London: Longmans, 1969) pp. 103–105.
2. This distinction between primary and secondary violence is derived from that worked out in relation to the Ugandan situation in Mazrui, "Leadership in Africa: Obote of Uganda" *International Journal* (Toronto) Summer 1970. The distinction was elaborated further in Mazrui, "Social Cleavage and Nation Building in East Africa," paper presented at the Seventh World Congress of the International Political Science Association, Munich, September 1970. It also featured in John D. Chick and Ali A. Mazrui, "The Nigerian Army and African Images of the Military," paper presented at the Eighth World Congress of the International Sociological Association, Varna, Bulgaria, September 1970. By extension one might also perhaps speak of tertiary violence, using this as a residual category to cover those forms of violence which have—in the short run at least—no overtly political objectives or repercussions.
3. See Ali A. Mazrui and Donald Rothchild, "The Soldier and the State in East Africa: Some Theoretical Conclusions on the Army Mutinies of 1964," *Western Political Quarterly* Vol. 9, No. 2, March 1967.

4. For a comprehensive account of the background to the East African Community see Joseph S. Nye Jr., *Pan Africanism and East African Integration* (Cambridge, Mass: Harvard University Press, 1966).

5. For a history of the King's African Rifles see Moyse-Bartlet, *The King's African Rifles* (Aldershot: Gale and Polden, 1956).

6. See his introduction to David Wood's *The Armed Forces of African States,* Adelphi Paper No. 27 (London: Institute for Strategic Studies, April 1966), p. 2.

7. "Pan-African Unity and the N.F.D. Question in Kenya," a memorandum presented to the African Summit Conference, Addis Ababa, 1963. Cited by Nye, *Pan Africanism and East African Integration,* p. 40.

8. *Uganda Argus* (Kampala), February 3, 1960.

9. For discussion of the politics of assassination in Africa see Mazrui, "Thoughts on Assassination Africa," *Political Science Quarterly,* Vol. 83, No. 1, March 1968.

10. Makerere Institute in Diplomacy, Speech by H. E. The President of Uganda, Dr. A. Milton Obote, August 30, 1968. (mimeo), p. 28.

11. *The Wretched of the Earth,* translated by Constance Farrington (New York: Grove Press, 1963), p. 48.

12. *Ibid.,* p. 46.

13. *Guerrilla Warfare,* (New York: Vintage Books, 1961 and 1968).

14. "Long Live Leninism!" *Peking Review,* April 1960.

CHAPTER 11
Violence and Civil Order

In one sense, *collective violence* is the most explicitly political of all forms of social eruptions. And yet, in trying to understand violence, all dimensions of culture have to be taken into account—kinship, economic factors, the impact of ideas, as well as the conditioning exerted by political culture. Additionally, we have to distinguish among different forms of violence. Of special concern to us in this study are the three categories of deviant violence, social violence, and international violence.

Deviant violence is of the kind which is committed as a result of individual criminality or individual aggression, and has no *conscious* social or political purposes. A bank clerk killed in the course of a bank robbery, a woman poisoning her husband, an alcoholic killing himself, a reckless driver maiming a child, all these are instances of what we describe as deviant violence.

Social violence, for our purposes, concerns issues of conscious societal implications. An assassination, a riot in protest against hunger, intercommunal strife in a given country, political insurrection, civil war, are all instances of social violence. The word "social" in this instance encompasses political phenomena within individual societies. Indeed, social violence is, as a rule, highly politicized and virtually indistinguishable from political violence at the domestic level. The term "political violence" is sometimes broad enough to include the extra national dimension, when two states find themselves in active combat. But social violence in our sense tends to limit itself to the domestic national dimension—ethnic clashes, military coups, demonstrations against specific government policies.

International violence takes us into the realm of war in the more general sense. The range is from border clashes between states to strategies of nuclear annihilation.

Let us take all these three levels of violence, attempt to understand their interrelationship, and seek to determine the kinds of solutions needed to cope with them in the rest of this century.

Social Structure and Deviant Violence

One thing to be noted from the outset is that the three levels of violence are not in the real world neatly separated from each other. To what extent is deviant violence and the whole phenomenon of criminality determined by the nature of social arrangements? To what extent is international war the outcome of political and economic conflict and class confrontation within the individual countries participating in that war? These are difficult questions to answer.

In a certain sense both world federalists and Leninists look forward to the withering away of the sovereign nation-state, but for different reasons. World federalists have tended to see the whole trend of international change as an imperative to tame and ultimately eliminate the principle of sovereignty in international affairs. Their call is for the pooling of nationalities into a global source of sovereign initiative. Leninism, starting from different premises, nevertheless seems to move in the same direction. The state according to this school is seen as an aspect of the economic culture of a given society. True communism is born when it is no longer enough to uphold the principle of "from each according to his ability, to each according to his work". In the communist phase proper, the relevant principle at last asserts itself as being "from each according to his ability, to each according to his needs". This is the stage when, in the famous phrase, "the state withers away"—and instead of men being governed, things are administered. As Engels put it: "The government of persons is replaced by the administration of things and the direction of the process of production."[1]

But why should the state wither away? Because it has outlived its purpose. What would be the purpose of an instrument of class domination in a society which has become classless? The whole definition of statehood dictates the withering away of the state—since the state is looked upon as an instrument of class oppression, and class oppression is regarded as finite. But is that the exclusive purpose of a state? What about such simple functions of the state as apprehending and punishing criminals? How is *deviant* violence to be handled? Lenin sometimes sounded somewhat naive about this issue before he assumed real power. On the one hand, Lenin denied that he and his kind were Utopians. He said: "We are not Utopians and we do not in the least deny the possibility and inevitability of excesses on the part of individual persons and by individual persons. Or the need to suppress such excesses."

On the other hand, Lenin argued that no special machinery would be needed to control crime by individuals. "This will be done by the armed people itself, as simply and as readily as any crowd of civilized people, even in modern society ... interferes to prevent a woman from being assaulted."[2] In this argument Lenin concedes that crime is "inevitable", but says there are ways of controlling it apart from the state. We shall come to this issue of the spontaneous popular control of crime with regard to problems of civic violence in Uganda and in the United States in recent times.

Lenin also uses another argument which is, to a certain extent, inconsistent with his concession that crime is "inevitable". This second argument implies that crime may not be "inevitable" after all—but the psychology of individual criminality is inseparable from the sociology of class exploitation. He is positing deviant violence once again with the economic culture of a given society, and relates it to issues of economic equity and social justice: "The fundamental social cause of excesses, which consist in violating the rules of social life, is the exploitation of the masses, their want, their poverty." When class exploitation is removed, individual crime and excesses will inevitably begin to "wither away". "We do not know how quickly and in what order, but we know they will wither away." What then is the point of the state at that stage? There would be no classes to oppress, no criminals to prosecute. The state itself, according to this reasoning, must wither away.[3]

This kind of analysis does link deviant behavior to class relations, and to that extent it links deviant violence to social violence. When we distinguish deviant violence from social violence what we have in mind are not simply the causes but also the conscious purposes. The causes both of crime and of social violence may be indistinguishable sociologically. But the differences between the conscious purposes of a person who burgles a house to steal a radio and an army general who shoots his way to power are profound, in spite of superficial similarities. The general's bid in a coup is an action of more explicitly social and political intention than the sneaking burglar's venture into the house.

Both the Leninists and champions of world government sometimes prescribe reforms in a language which is not adequately relevant to the problems of developing countries. At least this is the case when they recommend the weakening of nationhood and statehood, because the problems of developing countries sometimes lie precisely in the commitment to create nationhood and consolidate statehood. The Leninists and Marxists generally view statehood in terms which imply class oppression. They are not consistent on the desirability of states continuing to exist in situations where they are not under the control of the workers. But, in any case, there is in Marxism a profound distrust of the concept of the state as well as a disparagement of the meaning of national ties as against the idea of trans-national class solidarity. In the words of the Manifesto of the Communist International at its Congress of 1919: "The workers not only of Amman, Algiers and Bengal, but also of Persia and Armenia will gain the opportunity of independent existence only when the workers of England and France have overthrown Lloyd George and Clemenceau. . . ." Yet the problems of developing countries, particularly those in Africa, include the compelling need to forge a sense of nationality over and above ethnic and class differences, and to consolidate authority and statehood.

When Lenin's vision of the classless society of the future encompasses the idea of the popular control of crime by the masses themselves, he is, in some ways, portraying a situation which already exists in countries like Uganda and which has been important in the history of countries like the United States—and yet which needs to be stopped by a further consolidation of authority and statehood.

Violence and Fluid Institutions

Both Uganda and the United States have a record of a variety of forms of violence. Both countries have deep internal cleavages, with some propensity toward dangerous confrontation. But both countries have, in addition, a substantial tradition of rustic self-reliance and a readiness on the part of simple folk to make arrangements for their own protection. This is the basis of the spontaneous control of crime by the people themselves.

Yet out of this mixture of social phenomena two types of social eruptions have emerged—civic violence and political violence. Civic violence arises when the citizens themselves, out of a sense of outraged civic conscience, take the law into their own hands and inflict punishment on transgressors or suspected transgressors. The whole tradition of vigilantism in the United States, the ugliness of lynching, the tradition of hue-and-cry in Uganda, the recurrent cases of outraged villagers beating suspects, sometimes to death—all these are instances of civic violence at work in society.

Political violence, on the other hand, is directed not at suspected thieves and other presumed social transgressors but concerns the nature of political arrangements under which a society is governed and organized. Sometimes the issues which give rise to political violence may be issues relating to an ad hoc policy by a regime in power. Rioting against a war in Vietnam, for example, would be a case of political violence within the United States concerned with an ad hoc policy. Where political violence is directed at specific issues of policy, it is secondary political violence.

Primary violence in politics, on the other hand, concerns matters of identity and fundamental authority rather than simply questions of ad

234

hoc policy. Violence arising out of the racial revolution in the United States is evidently primary in the sense of its being concerned with the very idea of integrated nationhood. Violence between ethnic groups in Africa, arising out of an inadequate acceptance of each other as compatriots, is again primary violence—concerned with national identity and the fundamental basis of political authority.

A major thesis that should concern us in this analysis is that civic violence, at its most prevalent, is to be found in situations of *fragile statehood,* while political violence, at its most dangerous, is to be found in situations of *fragile nationhood.* The experience of Uganda merges with the experience of the United States in a joint illumination of this area of social reality.

The concept of statehood which is at stake here has points of contact with the Weberian definition, in spite of the inadequacies of that definition. Weber asserted that, sociologically, the state could not be defined in terms of its ends. The maintenance of law and order, the preservation of society, the promotion of the well-being of the community, the control of suppression of deviant behavior may all be very central to the purposes of the state. Yet, Weber points out there is scarcely any task which some political association has not taken in hand, and there is no task which one could say has always been exclusive and peculiar to those associations which are designated as political ones. To Weber, the modern state could be defined sociologically only in terms of the specific means peculiar to it, namely the use of physical force.

Weber goes on to quote Trotsky's belief that, "Every state is founded on force." Weber concedes that force is not the normal nor the only means of the state, but he regards it as a means specific to the state.

> Today the relation between the State and violence is an especially intimate one. In the past, the most varied institutions—beginning with the sib—have known the use of physical force as quite normal. Today, however, we have to say that a state is a human community that (successfully) *claims the monopoly of the legitimate use of physical force* within a given territory. Specifically, at the present time the right to use physical force is ascribed to other institutions or to individuals only to the extent to which the State permits it. The State is considered the sole source of the "right" to use violence.[4]

Weber's definition of the state has elements of ethnocentrism, but in its basic outlines it has significant analytical utility. Societies which have a widespread incidence of civic violence, in the sense of citizens taking the law into their own hands and inflicting punishment, are societies in which statehood has not, as yet, consolidated itself. Even now, statehood in the United States has fractures of fragility, and the incidence of civic violence has by no means been eliminated. But in the case of the American experience one of the major reasons why civic violence has been retreating is the simple fact that political violence has been advancing. The upsurge of the civil rights revolution and black militancy, the readiness of black people to take risks in retaliation against acts perpetrated on their fellows, have been among the latest forces which have deterred the whites from a tradition of racial lynching in the United States. The rise of new forms of political violence—special urban riots, militant disruption perpetrated out of black grievances—have manifested deep crises of identity in the nation, and, at the same time, they have led to the elimination of one of the uglier forms of civic violence—lynching—in the American tradition.

Vigilantism in the United States arose as a response to a problem not too unfamiliar to some villagers in Uganda—the absence or inadequacy of an effective law and order infrastructure in areas away from major concentrations of population. In the American case the frontier played an important role in the evolution of the vigilante tradition. The normal foundations of an evolved society were as yet inadequately laid in a frontier region. The sheriffs were indeed sometimes there and attempts were made in places to observe due process as far as possible. The whole machinery of enforcing the law was often painfully inadequate, and a good deal had to depend on the civic readiness of the citizen if the society as a whole was to be protected from outlaws. Ideologically, vigilantism in the United States was also connected with the whole ethos of individualism and private initiative. American liberalism, American capitalism, the rugged self-reliance of the frontier, and the tradition of private violence for civic ends have all been interconnected in the American ethos.

In Uganda, on the other hand, civic violence is animated more by collective ideals than by an ethic of individualism. There is a more obvious link between civic violence and kinship culture in Uganda than is sometimes observable in American history. Villagers rise in shared indignation against thieves, and beat them up, sometimes to death, to this day in Uganda. But the same vigilantism, the initiative of citizens to punish criminals themselves, has been a manifestation of two widely divergent cultural ideologies. In the American case, a distinctive characteristic is the readiness to take action privately where the machinery of the state is inadequate. There were indeed occasions when vigilantism paralleled the structure of law enforcement, and did not simply compensate for its inadequacies. In such case, the motives were again sometimes connected with long-standing American distrust of governmental power. Taxpayers in local communities sometimes devised voluntary ways of law enforcement as a contribution to the security of the society which did not entail any further financial strengthening of institutionalized authority.

The tradition of responding to the cry of "thief" in Ugandan villages, and joining the multitude to chase a suspect, and participating in inflicting punishment, is within the stream of primordial collectivism, rather than liberal individualism. The same impulse which makes a neighbor help another in building his house leads to help in punishing the one who has broken into the house. The paramount animating value in the Ugandan situation is not the value of private initiative, but the value of collective security, rooted in the tradition of kinship obligations.

Both in Uganda and in the United States, the phenomenon of the control of crime at the grass-roots by citizens themselves has to be related to this all too familiar issue of fragile statehood. Authority has yet to be centralized adequately, and violence has, therefore, remained decentralized. Those who are in favor of the abolition of statehood might do well to remember that the alternative could all too readily be decentralized violence.

Civic violence of this kind falls within our definition of social violence. But the civic violence may itself be a response to deviant violence by lawbreakers. Certainly in Uganda the sense of retribution against thieves is often in direct response to the violence of the thieves themselves. Burglars and robbers in the country have been known to be singularly indifferent to life. Old women have been robbed of a few shillings and then slashed to death. Whole families have, on occasion, suffered heavy brutalization in the course of surrendering a few items of property in their homes. These violent transgressors are locally known as the *kondos*—robbers who do their job with an easy resort to violence and strike terror in many communities.

Both before and after the coup which overthrew President Obote, the Uganda government, bewildered by the callous disregard of such robbers, has groped for legal and penal solutions. There is a temptation in a country which has limited resources to seek an answer in the severity of punishment. It is not always remembered that the certainty of punishment, arising out of an efficient law-enforcement infrastructure, is often a greater deterrent than mere severity of punishment in a situation where only a few ever get caught. Nevertheless, it is not very difficult to understand why the Uganda government felt it had to raise the punishment for robbery with violence from mere imprisonment to death.

Voices did protest, arguing that by making robbery with violence a capital offense, the thief would be more tempted than ever to destroy all witnesses after the theft. Having brandished the weapon and threatened death in order to get the loot and having thereby exposed himself to capital punishment, the *kondo* might then feel more secure if he murdered those whom he had already robbed.

It is still not clear whether the Uganda government's decision in 1968 to make robbery with violence a capital offense has, in fact, increased the incidence of murder, rather than decreased the incidence of robbery with violence. It is conceivable that the measure has had both effects. There may indeed be fewer robberies than there might have been without the new law, but also more murders of those who have been robbed.*

But if the central government has felt this sense of desperation, so have the villagers now and again. To take an example almost at random, in the villages of Kibuzi, Bugadu, and Busana in Bugerere County in Uganda, several robberies had terrorized the villagers and a number of people had been tortured or killed by *kondos*. The villagers had first attempted a system of organizing guards at night, but these had been overpowered. A number of villagers unable to bear the torment of fear in this area migrated to other villages. But the tension mounted too high, and the villagers broke loose on those they suspected as *kondos* and proceeded to wreak vengeance.[5]

What all this means is that certain forms of social violence are in response to deviant violence. How then can this spiral be prevented from escalating too high? How, to change the metaphor, can the circle be broken?

It is sometimes argued that severity and oppression do not themselves deter thieves. The discussion here hinges on the issue of whether those who are already inclined to deviate from the norms of the society are necessarily deterred from that course by the prospect of punishment. Is it conceivable that the criminal inclination is not only indifferent to the sanctity of norms but also to the prospect of penalty? Can punishment, therefore, ever be a deterrent?

This whole line of reasoning looks at the deviant in order to judge the impact of punishment on *him*. But in a situation where respect for authority has yet to be consolidated, the issue is not simply what sort of authoritative decisions are likely to impress the deviant, but also what type are likely to influence the population as a whole. The task of inculcating respect for the law among the ordinary villagers assumes in some ways a significance which is even more fundamental than the task of inspiring

---

* The Kenya government was also briefly tempted to resort to a similar solution of capitalizing robbery with violence. Such a proposal was seriously considered and defeated. But President Kenyatta then decided in favor of capital punishment after all. For an earlier analysis of such violence in the Continent consult Colin Leys "Violence in Africa," *Transition*, No. 21, 1965, pp. 17–20.

fear in the lawbreaker.[6] In this regard both institutional effectiveness and cultural conversion are needed.

If then we seek to minimize violence, it becomes imperative to look at the interaction in countries like Uganda, for example, between deviant violence by transgressors and civic violence by outraged citizens in defense of their rights. The answer seems to lie in purposeful state consolidation, with a gradual monopolization of the legitimate use of physical force. Yet what should also be borne in mind is that Weber's concept of the "monopoly of the legitimate use of physical force within a given territory" could as easily be a definition of "the sovereign" as of "statehood". In the history of state formation, consolidation of statehood and centralization of domestic sovereignty have been almost indistinguishable as political concepts. John Austin's definition of sovereignty, because of its guarded qualifications in true British empirical style, comes near to capturing the essence of the concept:

> The superiority which is styled sovereignty and the independent political society which sovereignty implies, is distinguished from other superiority, and from other society, by the following marks or characters— 1. the bulk of the given society are in a *habit* of obedience or submission to a *determinate* and *common* superior . . . 2. that certain individual or certain body of individuals, is *not* in a habit of obedience to a determinant human superior. . . . and this habitual obedience is rendered by the bulk of its members to *one and the same* superior, the given society is either in a state of nature, or is split into two or more independent political societies. . . .[7]

These categories are Weberian ideal types. But civic violence and the popular control of crime by citizens themselves give an indication of a situation where sections of a given country have not as yet felt confident enough to abandon the self-reliance imposed by that philosophical fiction which we sometimes call "a state of nature".

The Nation-State and Civil Order

Those who advocate the abolition of state sovereignty as a way of minimizing *international violence* have to ask themselves whether that abolition might not increase the incidence of social and deviant violence within the units concerned.

Within the concept of the nation-state we have so far analyzed mainly the question of statehood and the consequences of its fragility. But the other part of the concept of the nation-state is the concept of nationhood. Again, both Uganda and the United States are examples of fragile nationhood with the potentialities for domestic violence.

White lynchings in American history are cases of civic and sometimes

political violence; black riots in the ghettos in more recent times are
cases of economic protest and political violence. The street riot in the
United States gradually became, in the 1960's, an urban institution. The
ideas of Malcolm X and also of Frantz Fanon began to influence black
militants in the United States. Fanon's ideas about purification through
violence helped to provide a moral foundation for violent protest.

In the case of black-white relations in the United States, fragile
statehood and fragile nationhood had at one time deeply interrelated
consequences. The lynching of a black rapist or suspected rapist was
both civic and political—manifesting both inadequate statehood and im-
mature nationhood. It also touched deeply taboos of the kinship culture
of white America.

Underlying lynching in the United States was a persistent assumption
by Whites that among the best and most desired prizes craved by the
black man was the possession of a white woman. Gunnar Myrdal's
classical work *An American Dilemma,* published in the 1940's, included
what he called "the Rank Order of Discrimination". Myrdal interviewed
white southerners and asked them to list in order of importance what
they thought the Blacks wanted most. The order formulated by white
southerners was:

1. Intermarriage and sex intercourse with whites.
2. Social equality and etiquette.
3. Desegregation of public facilities, buses, churches, etc.
4. Political enfranchisement.
5. Fair treatment in the law courts.
6. Economic opportunities.

Myrdal then turned to the black people themselves to enquire what
their ultimate ambitions were and in what order of priority. The ambitions were the same as those attributed to them by white southerners,
but with one fundamental difference: the black people listed those ambitions in the reverse order of priority.[8]

The assumption by Whites for so long that to the black man sex took
priority over economics did have some self-fulfilling prophetic impact for
a while. Large numbers of Blacks were at one time profoundly affected
by the big taboo which surrounded interracial sexuality. But this black
preoccupation with interracial sexuality was not the cause but the effect
of white sexual fears. Whites took this area of relationships so seriously
that large numbers of Blacks began to wonder whether they should not
take it seriously as well. The radicalization of the black movement in the
United States, however, has in part meant its own desexualization. In the
eyes of black militants, questions of power now take precedence over

questions of intimacy. Equality of economic opportunity which had been the real primary ambition of Blacks when Gunnar Myrdal was doing his research for *An American Dilemma* has now reasserted itself in neo-Marxian black movements.

Black Americans are now challenging the monopoly of violence which white rulers had previously preempted for themselves, either through informal constitutional structures, or in the form of private initiative. The new violence of black militancy in the United States seems to derive its ethos, not from the rugged individualism of the frontier tradition of the United States but seemingly from the proud collective solidarity of tribal Africa. The violence which is being urged by militants in America, or which continually breaks out, has the stamp of collectivist self-assertion rather than simply individualistic self-reliance. But American political culture continues to cast its shadow. To the Blacks what is at stake is whether the term "the right of the people to bear arms" in the U.S. Constitution could indeed mean the right of the *oppressed* people, domestically, to do so. It is arguable that armed militancy by the Blacks accords better with the Constitution than does the kind of self-help advocated by the National Rifle Association to vindicate individual weapon-play in the country. After all, black violence, if it is designed to increase black freedom, might easily be demonstrated to be, in the words of the Constitution, "necessary to the security of a *free* state".

Black violence in the United States is clearly a dependent variable—manifesting a rebellion against a tradition of inequality and denial of social justice. The older white violence, which precipitated the black response, was a dependent variable in the other sense we mentioned, a manifestation of inadequate centralization of authority and inadequate sense of shared citizenship between Blacks and Whites.

We are back here to the proposition formulated earlier—*that the control of certain forms of domestic violence depends not on the abolition of the nation-state but on the consolidation of both nationhood and statehood.* Nor can rioting in the American ghettos or tensions between the Tutsi and the Hutu in Burundi be controlled primarily by international agencies. There seems to be no escape from the need for effective domestic instruments to control certain types of disorder; and effective forms of national identification to make smaller units of groups recognize each other as fellow citizens within the same country.

Conclusion

If the world between now and the end of the century seeks to create an order in which violence is minimized, nation-building and state formation in many of the newly independent countries remain critical preconditions for such a world order. Nation-building in itself involves in effect five major processes.

First, the process of *intellectual and normative convergence* is ultimately the acquisition of shared ideas, modes of expression, general mores and view of one's place in the universe. Second, the promotion of *economic interpenetration and exchange* between subgroups is in part a commitment to the idea of economic interdependence. In other words, the economic dimension of nation-building is the process by which the different subgroups within a country develop a conscious vested interest in the national economy and in the structure of national economic relationships. But these changes in turn will help to modify or even transform the economic culture. Third, the dimension of *social integration,* which means that process by which the gaps between the elite and the masses, the town and the countryside, the privileged and the underprivileged, are gradually narrowed. Fourth, the routinization of *conflict resolution,* which is preeminently linked to political culture. It involves building institutions and consolidating procedures at different levels of society to enable clashes of interest, divergences of values and opinion, and disputes over rights and duties, to be resolved with minimal social disruption or violence. And fifth, the acquisition of *shared national memories,* a consciousness of having undergone some important experiences in the past *together* develops cultural convergence. When this fifth dimension interacts with the first process of intellectual and normative fusion in African conditions, what we have is the gradual merger of tribal sub-identities into a new national identity.[9]

Of these five processes which make up nation-building, the fourth is particularly critical for state formation as well: building institutions for effective conflict resolution. In essence this is the whole problem of political legitimacy—which in turn is the older problem of political obligation in social philosophy. It is an issue of determining the right boundaries of authority and the right procedures and mechanisms for resolving clashes between individuals, between groups, or between either and the central government.

But although the idea of routinizing conflict resolution is the most central of the processes of state formation, it should always be remembered that the other four dimensions of nation-building are also relevant for state formation to some degree. It is possible to have a country which is deeply integrated as a nation, but where the central institutions have not as yet acquired adequate political legitimacy. Certain periods of Japan's history seem to indicate a profound sense of internalized national identity going hand in hand with an inadequate acceptance of the governmental institutions below the imperial pinnacle. Nevertheless, although the issue of political legitimacy should not be confused with the issue of national integration, there are definite areas of interdependence between the two worth bearing in mind.

To summarize then, state formation and nation-building are themselves preconditions for the minimization of violence in the world order. In important respects nation-building and state formation are processes which need indigenous initiative. But the world community must be infrastructurally involved in maximizing mobility and promoting economic interrelationships and exchange precisely in those countries which are still struggling to consolidate nationhood and statehood.

Footnotes

1. See *Anti-Duhring* (Moscow: Foreign Languages Pub., 1962).
2. V. I. Lenin, *State and Revolution* (1917). Consult Lenin *Selected Works,* Vol. VII (New York: International Publishers, 1935).
3. *State and Revolution* (1917).
4. Max Weber, "Politics as a Vocation," originally a speech at Munich University, 1918.
5. *Uganda Argus,* April 17, 1969.
6. These issues are discussed more fully in a companion paper entitled "Civic Violence and Political Violence in Uganda and the United States" (mimeo).
7. Austin, Lecture VI, *The Province of Jurisprudence Determined* (1832).
8. Gunnar Myrdal, *An American Dilemma,* Vol. I (New York and London: Harper and Row, 1944), pp. 60–61. Consult also *Violence in America: Historical and Comparative Perspectives,* a report to the National Commission on the Causes and Prevention of Violence, June 1969, prepared under the direction and authorship of Hugh Davis Graham and Ted Robert Gurr for the President's Commission (New York: The New American Library, 1969).
9. These processes are discussed in a related context in Mazrui, *Cultural Engineering and Nation-Building in East Africa.* (Evanston, Illinois: Northwestern University Press, 1972), esp. pp. 277–293.

CHAPTER 12

Violence and International Order

Although international order may appear to be something distinct from civil order, the two are in fact intimately connected. Certainly the causes of international violence have a wide area of overlap with the causes of domestic violence.

A major premise of this analysis is that world order is secondarily a matter of reorganizing international relations but primarily a matter of restricting domestic arrangements. There is too ready an assumption among reformers that anti-aggression pacts between states, or world disarmament, or the setting up of an interstate police force, would be the appropriate initial stage of a more viable world order. We postulate that, first, social violence is a dependent variable, often reflecting the state of the other two social realities of economic welfare and justice. Second, much of the international violence which the world has so far experienced is basically an externalization of domestic deficiencies and tensions. An alternative way of framing the hypothesis is to assert that the problem of world peace is, in the initial stages, a problem of domestic cultures and of relations between social groups in individual countries and of values governing those groups. *It could be said that all international wars have been, so far, externalized civil deficiencies, both cultural and social.* To solve the problem of international conflict therefore necessitates an attempt to tackle the causes of domestic tensions and domestic pathologies.

On balance the prevalent view in Africa is that violence is a dependent variable. To describe it as a precondition for either social justice or economic welfare is, in a sense, to mistake cause for effect. Violence is often a consequence of the violation of social justice or denial of economic welfare, or it is at least a manifestation of deficiencies in those two areas. It can never be convincingly argued that men are denied social justice or economic welfare because men are violent. But it can be argued that there is violence because men are deprived of social justice or denied economic welfare.

Much of the violence of the twentieth century is the violence of popular causes. The revolution of identity in world affairs is in some respects a revolution of political consciousness, one that has a high sensitivity to deficiencies in the political system. From the struggle in Vietnam to the student uprisings in Europe, America, and Japan, political consciousness is at a level that is at once violent and morally inspired. The violence is the symptom of the social malaise; the moral fervor is often a prescription of how to cure it. The youth are preoccupied with the crisis of relevance in cultural values and social mores. Their tendency to take to the streets in rioting bands of noisy youthfulness, and their uglier tendency to resort to arson and physical brutality against those who disagree, must all be seen as symptomatic. The problem is not the violence; it is what has gone wrong either in relationships between generations or, alternatively as the youth themselves assert, what has gone wrong in the heritage of the society as a whole. It is because of these considerations that social violence might be regarded as a dependent variable, while the denial of social justice and economic welfare are more basic social determinants. An interpretation of warfare in the world in terms of either pursuing interests inconsistent with economic welfare or inconsistent with social justice would by no means be too far removed from the real causes of human strife. Men often fight because there is hunger or economic ambition in the world or because of injustice in human relations. They are not unjust or ambitious simply because they fight. The direction of social causation has to be clearly understood.

Imperialism as Frozen Warfare

Our concept of domestic primacy in global issues refers to two domestic factors—culture and social stratification. To the Marxist idea of class struggle as a cause of war we have added the concept of primordial culture self-awareness.

Let us first elaborate on the issue of class stratification before we examine culturally derived aggressiveness. Class struggle normally arises because of unequal distribution of economic benefits and denial of social justice. The intensification of class struggle could mean civil war. In Lenin's own words:

> Whoever recognizes the class struggle cannot fail to recognize civil wars, which in every class society are the natural, and under certain conditions, inevitable continuation, development and intensification of the class struggle. All the great revolutions prove this. To repudiate civil war, or to forget about it, would mean sinking into extreme opportunism and renouncing the socialist revolution.[1]

Cecil Rhodes, the founder of modern Rhodesia, had occasion to say in 1895:

> In order to save the forty million inhabitants of the U.K. from a bloody civil war, we colonial statesmen must acquire new land to settle surplus population, to provide new markets for the goods produced by them in the factories and mines. The Empire, as I have always said, is a bread and butter question. If you want to avoid civil war [in the U.K.] you must become imperialists.

Lenin was to quote these remarks of Rhodes with great relish, as a method of explaining why Marx's prediction that the poor of the capitalist countries would get poorer until they became revolutionary had not in fact been fulfilled. The Leninist answer was that the exploitation of the British Empire abroad had saved the British worker at home. By helping to satisfy the workers' standard of living and sense of dignity in England through the British Empire, the internal divisions in the metropolitan power were prevented from widening for the time being.

Following World War II, the British Empire in Asia disintegrated, and barely ten years later the process of disintegration started in Africa as well. Now the logic of Marxism would point toward a British vulnerability to a domestic proletarian revolution. The British Empire as a diversionary tactic to keep the workers quiet had now been neutralized. The lower classes should now at last perceive their underprivileged position and revolt against it once and for all. Kwame Nkrumah argued in this situation that the confrontation in the metropolitan countries could still now be averted by the new phenomenon of neo-colonialism, the possibility of exploiting other people abroad without actually ruling them. To that extent therefore the phenomenon is serving the same purpose as the old imperialism of Cecil Rhodes—it is delaying the ultimate class confrontation within the metropolitan countries themselves. In the words of Nkrumah, only when neo-colonialism in turn comes to an end will "the monopolists" in the metropolitan countries "come face to face with their working class in their own countries, and a new struggle will arise within which the liquidation and collapse of imperialism will be complete."[2]

This is, then, a state of civil war in suspended animation, awaiting the right signal to activate it. If a civil war can be frozen or be in suspended animation, so can an international war. Imperialism itself has come to be seen increasingly as a case of frozen warfare between the imperial power and its victims.

If then imperialism is frozen warfare, and is at the same time, according to Cecil Rhodes and Lenin, a diversion from the risk of domestic war in the imperial power itself, imperialism is basically an externalized civil war.

Imperial Retreat and Domestic Fragmentation

Malinowski defined war as "armed conflict between two independent political units, by means of organized military forces, in the pursuit of tribal or national policy."

The definition has been criticized on the basis that not all the features enumerated are always present in a war, and that in any case the classification of certain instances might pose problems. Is a civil war conducted by two "independent political units"? It is also possible for two political units in combat to have started as independent and then for one of them to lose its independence before the war is ended.

Raymond Aron has defended Malinowski's definition on the grounds that the marginal cases (which may or may not involve independent political units or organized military forces) do not invalidate the definition but are simply fresh evidence of "the graduation always found in social phenomena . . . On the borderline, civil war and international war merge together as do the clash of armies and guerilla warfare. We must not overlook this area of doubt on the borderline . . . but it does not make it impossible for us to begin by considering the phenomenon in the 'perfect' state."[3]

Both Malinowski and Aron in this analysis take international war as "the perfect case", and regard civil war as borderline manifestations of bigger instances of warfare. But what we have discussed so far is, in a sense, a reversal of the order of fundamentality. Civil cleavage in our analysis is the "perfect" case, while international wars are either an extension or an externalization of a civil war. When an international war is an extension of a civil war, the civil war itself is also raging. The Vietnam case was an instance of a civil war which, possibly at the initiative of the United States, had been extended to encompass conflict between the domestic communists in Vietnam and the foreign giant supporting the opposing side in that southeast Asian country. When a civil war is externalized, the domestic cleavage is frozen, and violence is exported.

The weakness of the orthodox Marxist position on war is its insistence that the most important cleavages are those which concern class. Marxism does not do justice to *cultural* cleavages and that is why it sees the impact of imperialism on the imperial powers mainly in economic terms. But *tribalism* in Africa, *racialism* in the United States, and other varieties of *militant ethnicity* elsewhere have in the modern period been at least as profound forms of internal cleavage as the class dimension. The restructuring of domestic arrangements in the days ahead has

248

therefore to take this factor into account, and might at times involve *creating* new classes in order to mitigate ethnic tensions. *Primordial culture aggressiveness manifests itself precisely in militant nationalism and tribalism.*

If international wars are externalized domestic deficiencies, one would expect a new resurgence of domestic ethnic and class tensions when international wars are reduced. Does the present world situation lend support to such a thesis? Has there been a decline of international conflict, and has this decline resulted in widening domestic cracks? Active wars between states may not have been conspicuously reduced since World War II, though the United Nations, the character of postwar diplomacy, the nature of the cold war and the danger of nuclear conflict, may have helped to keep in suspended animation interstate conflicts which might in previous ages have been readily activated. Nevertheless the range of wars which have broken out is from the Korean War to the series of Middle Eastern conflagrations, from Indo-Pakistani conflicts to the football war of Central America in 1969.

At least let us concede that the incidence of interstate warfare has not spectacularly declined in the last thirty years. The question still remains whether any other change has taken place to reactivate domestic tensions in this area. The answer has to be in the affirmative. The change is the disintegration of empires. If imperialism amounted to frozen aggression, and was therefore an externalization of domestic deficiencies, the disintegration of the empires should witness a process of re-internalizing those tensions.

In fact this is indeed what has happened. On imperial withdrawal not merely have the former colonies begun to face the danger of fragmentation, but also the former imperial powers of Europe themselves. Both class and cultural cleavages have erupted anew. Within the United Kingdom a residual Welsh nationalism had indeed persisted in the history of the country all along, but the reduction of Great Britain to an island power in Europe has been an important contributory factor to the intensification of Welsh nationalism. An even more surprising development has been the dramatic rise of Scottish nationalism. The United Kingdom, which had for so long been considered one of the most deeply integrated of all nation-states, is now facing a real threat of post-imperial fragmentation. The troubles in Northern Ireland are also related to the phenomenon of widening religio-cultural cleavages within the former imperial country, following her reduction in stature in world affairs and the shrinkage of her national purpose. Economic and cultural factors have remained intertwined.

Empires disintegrated partly as a result of the triumph of egalitar-

249

ianism as a moral imperative in international political culture. But the triumph of egalitarianism is dysfunctional to some extent for those countries which had previously succeeded in externalizing their domestic cleavages. That egalitarian triumph has reduced opportunities for externalization because it has discredited territorial expansionism. In addition the triumph of egalitarianism reinforced those internal cleavages which derived their strength from a sense of relative deprivation. Fragmentation within the boundaries of the imperial powers themselves is, in other words, a special case of the global triumph of self-determination.

Yet even within the ranks of imperial powers some distinctions ought to be recognized. Those imperial powers which were deeply divided internally in their colonial period, found later a measure of unifying relief. One major example is France, which experienced a greater fragmentation in the course of trying to hold on to Algeria than in relinquishing her imperial role. Decolonization for France became to some extent a step away from the brink of disintegration, whereas for Britain, it seems to have meant a step toward such a brink. What had happened in France by 1958 was that domestic cleavages were no longer easily camouflaged by a sense of imperial mission. The discrediting of expansionism, and the long drawn-out costs of the war in Algeria, neutralized the efficacy of external aggression as a diversionary tactic to contain internal tensions. On the contrary, the Algerian War opened up French wounds more deeply in the special circumstances which surrounded its long and painful duration. Yet even in France—where at least the myth of global grandeur of a neo-imperial kind has yet to die in spite of the passing of Charles de Gaulle—signs of new forms of post-imperial sectionalism are beginning to be discernible, ranging from industrial unrest to cultural and regional sub-nationalism in Brittany and Provence.

Holland is another country which experienced the agony of divisiveness on the eve of decolonization, rather than as an aftermath. Indonesia's unilateral declaration of independence following the ouster of the Japanese shook the Dutch profoundly. The government and the imperial wing of Dutch opinion tried its best to regain the Dutch Indies and initiated a war with Indonesia. But there was enough internal bitterness within Holland itself to lead to moments of activated domestic conflict and anguish.

Henri Baudet has traced the great divisive events in the Netherlands in that period—from the proclamation of the Republic of Indonesia in August 1945 to the conference of Hoge Velowe in the spring of 1946; from the discussions at Linggadjati, Malino, Dentassar, to the first military action; and then through the summer of 1947 and the cease-fire and Renville talks in the following year to the second military action; and ultimately by way of intervention by the U.N. Security Council to the final transfer of sovereignty: Baudet observed: ". . . throughout this long drawn chain of events the Netherlands' air was disturbed and agitated by the continual violent actions in and outside Parliament which felt involved in the great drama in one way or another, by demonstrations, mass meetings, petitions from right and left."[4]

The Dutch situation in relation to Indonesia was therefore somewhat comparable to the situation of the French in relation to Algeria. The period prior to relinquishing imperial sovereignty was so divisive domestically that when sovereignty was indeed at last formally transferred, the sense of relief in Holland and France was temporarily unifying at home. The frozen aggression of an imperial role had toward the end of the colonial period ceased to disguise internal tensions and had only served to deepen them. So the loss of empire momentarily mitigated some of the consequences of that deepening cleavage. But basically that loss was bound to release afresh certain forms of sectionalism in the former imperial countries. In Holland the issues are back to class struggle; in Belgium, former ruler of the Congo, they have crystallized in linguistic and cultural cleavages.

Even in the former colonies the elimination of imperialism as frozen aggression has had the effect of reopening some domestic areas of conflict. The nationalist movements in Africa, for example, had included within them the beginnings of a process of detribalization, as members from different tribal groups joined together in militant opposition to colonialism as permanent aggression. But since the imperial withdrawal there have been signs of a partial political retribalization in many parts of the continent. In Nigeria, as we know, retribalization attained tragic dimensions. We have discussed the agonies of Rwanda, Burundi, and Uganda. In Kenya, Luo ethnicity has probably significantly deepened since independence, partly in defensive reaction to some government policies, and in the absence of the diversionary unifying formula of opposition to an imperial presence.

Again if imperialism was the externalization of domestic cleavages in both the imperial powers and among the different groups within the colonized countries, the end of empire is in effect a process of redomesticating a cleavage. Bangla Desh, Ulster, and Biafra therefore all become symbols of this return to the tensions of contiguity and primordial local disparities.

Nationalism as militant cultural self-recognition is, therefore, often a medium of externalizing internal cleavages. This applies to mature nationalism in developed countries as well as emergent nationalism in new states. On balance, it is probably true to say that Americans are a more nationalistic people than Britons. If this is true the reason might well be because the United States has been more pluralistic internally than Great Britain and hence less internally secure. Complex heterogeneity multiples the number of possible conflict situations between groups. The need for devices which would help the resolution of those conflicts becomes greater than ever.

Technology and International Terrorism

The link between local violence and international violence lies not merely in the causes but, increasingly, in the methods and strategies of conflict. The 1960's witnessed two innovations which may be of long-term significance in the connection between civil and international tensions. One innovation was skyjacking and its use in capturing international attention for local causes, the other the abduction of foreign ambassadors as hostages for a variety of political causes. Both tactics as modes of combat are relatively rudimentary and still sparingly used. But they have potential for further elaboration as a method of internationalizing local or regional issues or embarrassing local tyrants.

Raymond Aron has analyzed contemporary warfare in terms of a triad of violence, symbolized by the hydrogen bomb, the tank, and the sten-gun. The most comprehensive of these three types of warfare is, of course, nuclear war, with its power of massive destruction over widely dispersed areas. The age itself is called the nuclear age, yet a nuclear war as such is still outside direct human experience, Hiroshima and Nagasaki having been nuclear conclusions to an otherwise conventional war. On balance, it is fear of nuclear war, rather than its experience, which has affected the age so far.

By contrast, warfare symbolized by the tank has been very much part of the post-World War II period. The tank signifies what is sometimes called conventional warfare, though what is conventional is itself subject to the mutations of time. The most important outbreaks of conventional wars since World War II include the Korean War, Vietnam, the Suez adventure of 1956 when Israel, Britain, and France attacked Nasser's Egypt, the June war of 1967 between Israel and Egypt, the clashes between India and China and India and Pakistan, the Nigerian and other civil wars.

A third type in Aron's triad of violence is guerilla warfare and terrorist movements. These are symbolized by the sten-gun, the stealthy steps in the stillness of the forest, the sudden spurt of fire on an unsuspecting target heard from southern Africa to Indo-China. In this domain we see the strategies of David confronting Goliath.

The newest versions of this last type of warfare include political piracy and political kidnapping in a new style. Of special interest in this regard are some of the tactics and dramatic "terror games" elaborately played by the Palestine commandos, especially since 1970. Early in 1970 they planted bombs in aircraft. One blew up in mid-air, killing a number of people, many of whom had nothing to do with the issue of Palestine. Later, in September 1970, Palestine commandos hijacked three planes—two American and one Swiss, but failed in their attempt on an Israeli plane. One of the American aircraft was taken to Cairo where, after the passengers had been permitted to disembark, it was blown up in one dramatic explosion. The passengers of the remaining two planes were for a while held in Beirut and Amman as hostages as demands were made for the release of other Palestinians held prisoner in different parts of the western world. The Palestinians, partly because of Israeli retaliation and partly because of their own divisions, have sometimes been forced to suspend such tactics. But in the years ahead the tactic may reappear—either over Palestine or over South Africa, or conceivably over some Latin American problem.

What the world was witnessing in September 1970 was guerilla warfare transferred from the forests to the skies, internationalizing guerilla warfare. As in the case of guerilla tactics in a domestic situation, the purpose of aerial terrorism is to manipulate fear as a mechanism of combat. The grand design is to undermine morale, not only among the soldiers but also civilians. An atmosphere of general insecurity, promoted by spectacular acts of destruction or specially dramatized acts of brutality, is contrived in order to drive the enemy into a desperate readiness to seek a settlement.

Aerial terrorism is, in some important respects, symbolic both of the communications revolution and of the conversion of the world into a global village. The news aspect of the communications revolution makes aerial terrorism a useful device for attracting world attention to a particular grievance. The travelling aspect of the communications revolution has meant heavy air traffic and therefore a wide choice of plans for hijacking. The passengers are men and women in influential countries of the world, who are now forced to worry about the implications for their holidays or for their business of this whole new phenomenon in the skies.

The publicity gained by aerial terrorism relies in part on the sensationalism of *political piracy,* the forceful takeover of a vessel at sea or in the air for publicity, carrying out political revenge, or preparing for a political deal. In 1961, for example, a Brazilian seized control of a Portuguese ship on the high seas in a dramatic assertion of solidarity with the colonized peoples of Angola and Mozambique. This was political piracy in the tradition of tactical publicity.

The recent phenomenon of political abduction, especially of foreign diplomats in Latin America and elsewhere is a form of political piracy. The abduction of foreign diplomats has involved the diversion not of aeroplanes in mid-air, but quite often of cars in the street. The kidnapping of diplomats of other powers is distinctive of recent times; but the kidnapping of specific domestic individuals as a form of political vengeance or as a prelude to civic justice is part of an older tradition of political behavior. In Africa—north and south of the Sahara—abduction of this kind has on the whole tended to be preeminently a Francophone style of gamesmanship and intrigue. Of course, there has been abduction in the politics of English-speaking Africa, but Francophone Africa has had a more consistent "tradition" of kidnapping than other parts of the continent. Sometimes France herself has been implicated in this phenomenon. In the course of the Algerian war, for example, there were cases of dramatic abduction conducted with the full connivance of French authorities. Then there was the kidnapping of Ben Berka, the Moroccan radical, from a street in Paris in 1965—a kidnapping and suspected killing which again compromised the French police itself.

In 1967 Guinea's foreign minister was held by the Ivory Coast, after a whole Guinean delegation returning from the United Nations had been virtually hijacked from a plane at the airport.

The most dramatic abduction in the history of modern Africa involved Moise Tshombe, once self-styled President of breakaway Katanga and later Prime Minister of the Congo as a whole (now Zaire). In July 1967 the plane on which he was travelling was hijacked, and brought to the capital of Algeria. The government of the Congo requested Tshombe's extradition so that he could face the death sentence for treason which had been passed on him in his absence. The Algerian Supreme Court decided that Tshombe was extraditable. It was then left to the Algerian government itself to decide whether or not Tshombe was to be extradited.

Curiously enough, even in regard to the abduction of Tshombe, the issue of Israel and the Arabs was somewhere in the background either as a direct political factor or by analogy. Just a month before Tshombe was abducted, the Arabs had sustained a humiliating defeat in the June war against Israel. There was widespread speculation at the time of Tshombe's abduction as to whether the Algerians, then holding Tshombe in their power, would attempt, in diplomatic circles, to extract extra support against Israel from the Congolese government in exchange for Tshombe's extradition to the Congo.[5]

By analogy the Jewish question was also present in that the kidnapping of Tshombe was interpreted as an opportunity for an African Nuremberg. Tshombe and his henchmen were now to be considered for possible charges of crimes against the African race. The real analogy to Tshombe's judicial abduction was not Nuremberg but another event connected with the Jews—the kidnapping of Eichmann by Jews and his trial in Israel. Eichmann, who had helped Hitler to exterminate hundreds of thousands of Jews, was outwitted in a dramatic abduction from Argentina and made to face trial in Israel more than fifteen years after the death of Hitler, within the legal jurisdiction of a state which had not been in existence at the time he had committed the crimes.

The abduction of Eichmann, the kidnapping of foreign diplomats in different countries, the hijacking of Moise Tshombe's plane to Algiers in 1967, and the hijacking of civil aviation planes by Palestine commandos in 1970 and later, all these fall into place as a pattern of political combat, at once very old in its links, and very new in some of its recent manifestations.

Of course, there are differences between the abduction of Eichmann and Tshombe, the abduction of foreign diplomats in Latin America, and the hijacking of planes for purposes of holding hostages. The abductions of Eichmann and Tshombe were specific—they concerned particular individuals wanted for acts of betrayal or brutality by those who regarded themselves victimised. This kind of abduction is at a high point of specificity. The kidnapping of foreign diplomats is less specific because the kidnapped have no direct link with the grievances for the dramatization of which they are being diverted from their daily routines. A German or Japanese diplomat in Latin America could hardly be regarded as having a very immediate bearing on the clash of views between a Latin American government and its domestic antagonists. The men abducted are nevertheless purposefully chosen as specific individuals.

The hijacking of airplanes by Palestine commandos is general in regard to the passengers, but *specific* in regard to the vehicle, the nationality of the plane being the critical variable. The hijackings of September 1970 illustrated this quite clearly. The grievance of the Palestine commandos against Americans included not only the general American sympathy with Israel, but also the American initiatives in persuading Egypt to start negotiating for an ad hoc settlement with Israel, without necessarily taking Palestinian rights into account.

The specificity of the nationality of the plane implies that hijacking of this kind is not simply a matter of kidnapping individuals but also a matter of violating territory. Hijacking is an instrument of the weak; it enables a couple of Palestinians to engage in an activity which is almost tantamount to the violation of the territorial jurisdiction of, say, the United States.

255

International Tension and the Manipulation of Fear

To ask: Does terrorism attract the right kind of publicity, misses the whole point of the exercise. Does it not succeed only in alienating world opinion? In a propaganda campaign to win sympathy in the more influential parts of the world, the Arabs are no match for the Jews. Quite apart from the greater sophistication of Jewish communities in the Western world, and indeed of Israel itself as compared with the more underdeveloped capacities of the Arab world, there is also the question of sheer access to the influential media of the international system. C. Eric Lincoln refers to stereotypes which black Americans have about different categories of Whites—"The Anglo-Saxons are diplomats and statesmen; the Italians are criminals and racketeers; the stupid Irishmen are cops; the Germans are good scientists; the Jews are the brains of the white race."

Lincoln draws attention to the disproportionate Jewish presence among writers and intellectuals in the United States. He also refers to the financial resources which enable the Jews to exercise considerable influence on mass media:

> The Jews are believed to have a stronger hold on public opinion through their control of mass communication. They are said to own the radio and television stations, along with many magazines and newspapers. They hire Gentiles to "front" for them so as not to antagonize the public; but on crucial issues such as the Suez Canal, they control the thinking of the people. And they use this power to forward the Zionist cause.[6]

It is quite clear that black American images of Jews include, in some cases, strong anti-Semitic tendencies. The images can, therefore, become hostile stereotypes. But one cannot escape the issue of comparative Jewish access to the media of communication. Indeed, without such access Israel itself might never have been created. From the point of view of racial equality, there is little doubt that the Jews have been among the more oppressed peoples of the world. But from the point of view of economic equality, there is equally little doubt that, on balance, the Jews have been among the privileged groups of the human race. When we divide the world into the haves and havenots, it is quite clear where world Jewry belongs—and it does not belong in the ranks of the indigent.

Zionism as a movement to create a national home for the Jews would not have gotten very far if it had lacked access to immense financial resources for its implementation as a movement. Even the establishment of a political party in one country needs considerable financial support. The establishment of a movement to create a home for the Jews, and the necessary economic resources for their transportation, and the necessary propaganda and financial power to create a national climate favorable to such a move, was something which only a group happily privileged in monetary influence could have undertaken. We might, therefore, say that discrimination against the Jews in Europe helped the creation of Israel in two ways. One way was in arousing the conscience of Europe in the twentieth century to the need for some form of protection for this racial minority. But a way with a longer history behind it was the role of medieval European anti-Semitism in forcing Jewish minorities in the western hemisphere over the years to specialize in business techniques and financial enterprises. This enabled them to acquire an impressive base of economic and political initiative.

If Jewish access to the media was effective enough to result in the very creation of Israel, it remains effective enough in the western world to create a climate of opinion favorable to the Israeli cause. Any competition by Palestine commandos for sympathy is handicapped from the start by the massive disproportion between them and Israel in terms of access to mass communications.

The purpose of aerial terrorism is, therefore, not a quest for sympathetic publicity but an attempt to arouse popular anxieties. That is why terrorism is so often an instrument of the weak. Sympathy does sometimes help in mobilizing international opinion, and could result in changes in a particular situation. Sympathy for Biafra and the starving Ibo, for example, was escalating at a pace which might sooner or later have resulted first in the French recognition of Biafra followed by the blessing of French-speaking Africa. This, in turn, could have transformed the Nigerian situation, and perhaps have made it possible for the war to end in favor of the Biafran side.

A related question to be borne in mind in the case of both Biafra and Israel is the sympathy aroused by a David versus Goliath confrontation. Such a confrontation has potentialities for sympathetic exploitation in propaganda by the smaller unit. Thus Biafra, quite apart from being more sophisticated than the federal side in techniques of propaganda, was substantially aided in mobilizing international sympathy by the innate tendencies of empathizing with the underdog.

The same kind of image can be teased out of the human imagination by the predicament of Israel. The image is of Israel as a courageous and industrious immigrant community, defying a hostile environment of nature and of neighbors, and surviving with honor. Other communities elsewhere, anxious about a hostile environment, have drawn inspiration from the Israeli predicament. A minister of defense in South Africa once extolled Israel in the following terms: "They stand alone in the world, but they are full of courage." The South African publication *Die Burger*

has drawn similar inspiration from Israel's example of triumphant loneliness: "We in South Africa would be foolish if we did not at least take
account of the possibility that we are destined to become a sort of Israel,
in a preponderantly hostile Africa, and that fact might become part of
our national way of life . . ."[7]

White Rhodesians in June 1967, following the swift victory of Israel,
gave clear evidence of empathic identification with Israel. Israel was
small; the Arab countries and their populations were large. And yet the
Arabs had proved to be militarily impotent in the face of Israel. By the
same token, Rhodesia was small; the African continent was large and its
population impressive. And yet Africans were militarily impotent in the
face of Ian Smith's government. The white Rhodesians did identify
themselves as "the Israelis of Africa" surrounded by hostile, but less distinguished, neighbors.

In the face of these handicaps in the propaganda game for sympathy, it
is rational for the Palestinians to pursue a strategy of maximizing anxiety
rather than promoting popularity. Terrorism alienates much of world
opinion even further away from the Palestinian cause. But the Arab
cause could be less popular and yet nearer to fulfillment at the same
time. The Palestinian commandos are forcing more and more people—
ordinary travellers and passersby—to develop a vested interest in a solution of the Middle Eastern problem. They may hate the tactics that are
being used; they may dislike the Arabs more than ever; they may be
drawn closer to Israel in sympathy; and yet all these tendencies are not
inconsistent with their growing desire to see this whole Middle Eastern
mess sorted out once and for all. In this sense, the Palestine commandos
agree that the world is a global village. The sten-gun approach in
domestic contexts conventionally limits terrorism to internal enemies;
but the sten-gun approach in the skies globalizes guerilla tactics. The
Middle Eastern problem has never been purely local. Moreover, the
original cause of the present problem—the creation of Israel—was an
act of the international community rather than an outcome of the
domestic balance of forces between local Jews and local Arabs. If the
creation of Israel was itself an act of the international community, the
consequences which have followed can never be shrugged off as merely a
regional difficulty. The world was involved in the mess from the start.
The indiscriminate terror tactics of Palestinian commandos are
gradually becoming effective in reminding the world that it was still part
of the mess. Even the choice of the Olympic games as a context of terror
in 1972 served that purpose of globalizing the struggle.

What is likely to happen in the present situation is that the Israelis,
with greater organizational and technological sophistication, will remain

militarily victorious but not at peace. They may even be tempted to expand a little further in a quest for a greater sense of security. Expansionism historically has often been inspired by strategic considerations and the need for extra precautions in the defense of national interests and safety.

But there is nothing like concrete military experience as a training ground. For the foreseeable future it is unlikely, man to man, that an Arab soldier or pilot could be as well disciplined or as sophisticated as his Israeli counterpart. But there is a minimum of skill and sophistication which would then begin to make numerical superiority for conventional combat relevant once again. The hard experiences of coping with Israeli attacks, of learning to be alert, of perfecting the skills of weaponry and manoeuvre, could all help to diminish or reduce the organizational and technological gulf between the Arabs and the Israelis. Before the end of the century the balance of forces in the Middle East might have become fundamentally altered. Any attempt to exterminate the Jews physically would immediately extra-regionalize the problem. After all, if apartheid in South Africa is an issue that is of global rather than continental implications, so must be any victimization of the Jews in the Middle East. But there are solutions to the Palestine problem far short of the annihilation of the Jews—and yet solutions which, at the moment, stand no chance of being accepted by the Israelis. Preeminent among the alternatives is the repatriation of Palestinian refugees to their homes within Israel. There are 1.5 million refugees already who come from within the boundaries originally intended to define Israel. The population of Israel would be drastically transformed by such an influx.

Until those institutional changes are brought about, we may simply witness an increasing utilization of techniques of international terrorism for purposes of solving what might otherwise have been more localized issues. The abduction of foreign diplomats and the phenomenon of political piracy in the skies might well be heralding the intensification of links between civil disturbances and international tensions in the years ahead.

Africa and Vietnam

It is not merely terror which the weak invoke when confronted with the strong. It is also political protest as a claim to a share in deciding human destinies. In this regard, the Vietnam war was a homogenizing experience in its own right, dramatizing certain human values simply by violating them so conspicuously. The whole symbolism of David against Goliath was captured at its most poignant in that bizarre experience of a superpower at war with brave military midgets.

From Africa's point of view, the brief role of one political leader encompassed within itself the varied implications of such a war for millions
distant from the battlefield. That African leader was Kwame Nkrumah.
And we might, in a reversal of sequence, start with his death.

It was the end of April 1972. I was stepping out of a hotel in Washington, D.C.. A Russian friend of mine, also visiting the United States,
approached and asked: "Have you heard?"

"Heard what?"

"Kwame Nkrumah is dead."

I was deeply moved. I was moved by the death of Nkrumah and by the
situation in which the news was broken to me. Here was a Soviet national, informing an African that another African had died. Nkrumah
had died in Roumania; the Russian was telling me this in the capital city
of the United States. The world had indeed become a village in the course
of that brief conversation outside the Statler Hilton Hotel, and it was
precisely this concept which made the war in Vietnam an issue of concern
to Kwame Nkrumah while he lived.

Kwame Nkrumah's last days coincided with the United States
resumption of the bombing of North Vietnam, though he was spared
President Nixon's worst excesses later in the year. It is probable that
Nkrumah retained his interest in the tragedy of Vietnam right up to his
death in April 1972. In 1965, when he was President of Ghana, he was involved in discussions with other members of the British Commonwealth
on a possible initiative to break the impasse in the Vietnamese situation.
Britain herself was at the time interested in the possibility of mediation
by a collective Commonwealth initiative to help the combatants in
Vietnam toward the negotiating table.

But before long Nkrumah became the leading voice for a new bid,
Ghana's High Commissioner in the United Kingdom became Ghana's
special envoy to Hanoi in pursuit of this goal. To help the atmosphere,
Ghana under Nkrumah suggested that the United States should stop
bombing North Vietnam. But President Johnson rejected the proposal,
apparently regarding it as one more exercise in impudence and presump-
tion by that flamboyant President of a little West African state.

Nkrumah's initiative was illustrative of two factors. One was his belief
that Africa had been kept out of decisions affecting the world for far too
long. The contraction of the world in size in the twentieth century, and
the possibility of the great powers destroying the human species itself,
had made it more than ever justifiable that Africa's voice should be heard
on the global issues of the day. War itself was preeminently critical if a
major power was engaged in it. The possibility of local war, with partici-

pation by the United States, escalating into a major war inevitably made each such a local war a matter of potential concern for Africans, as well as for other inhabitants of this planet.

It was partly because of these considerations that Kwame Nkrumah would not limit, in principle, African participation to those affairs which were of direct regional relevance to Africa. On the contrary, the African presence in world politics had to be felt beyond the issues of immediate concern to the African continent, especially if major powers were involved in those issues. Nkrumah in this represented an important school of African thought—influential as a political position far beyond Nkrumah's own country.

The second factor was Nkrumah's version of nonalignment. To him, nonalignment was not a neutrality in major debates, but the right of independent participation in international affairs. Combined with that desire to pursue an independent foreign policy was an ambition to help in preventing small wars from escalating into major conflagrations. Again Nkrumah captured an important Third World aspiration; in many ways his views remain profoundly representative of the Third World.

The Vietnamese war was the second conflict, rather than the first, which involved communist China, and which Nkrumah sought to prevent from escalating. The previous conflict was between India and China. In 1962 China invaded Indian territory. The situation appeared to be of the kind that might evoke a collective Commonwealth response. Britain granted military aid to help Nehru's government in India in the face of the Chinese challenge. President Nkrumah of Ghana immediately wrote to Prime Minister Macmillan of Britain in the following terms:

> Are you sure that by giving support, whatever this is, to one side against the other, you will be able to increase the chances of bringing an end to hostilities? Assistance by way of arms and equipment to any country engaged in a conflict with another, in my view, is likely merely to occasion a counter offer of assistance to the other parties to the dispute. The balance of military strength therefore remains the same but the dispute is made much more difficult of solution through the involvement of outside powers.[8]

In his reply Macmillan said that he found it difficult to understand Nkrumah's objection to British sympathy and support for India. Macmillan argued that when the territory of a Commonwealth people was invaded, it was surely right and natural that Britain should be sympathetic and helpful. Back came President Nkrumah's reply:

> The Commonwealth is not a military alliance and it would be most detrimental to its progress if the impression was created that Commonwealth

members did not judge each issue independently on its merits, but instead automatically sided with a fellow Commonwealth country when the country was engaged in a dispute with an outside power.[9]

It was basically this same desire for an independent foreign policy, and the same commitment to the proposition that local wars should be prevented from escalating into major conflagrations, which made Nkrumah take the most pathetic trip of his career. In February 1966 the President of Ghana left for Peking to ease the calamity of Vietnam and bring the combatants to the negotiating table. The Americans had so far proved obstinate. Certainly Johnson's refusal to stop bombing North Vietnam had made conciliatory moves more difficult. Nkrumah was now going to discuss some of these issues with Chairman Mao Tse-Tung, Prime Minister Chou En-Lai and other communist Chinese leaders. The very position Nkrumah had taken within the Commonwealth in 1962 when Britain was extending military support to India helped his credentials in discussing issues with the communist Chinese.

But his absence from his capital, Accra, helped Nkrumah's own domestic opponents. He was overthrown in a military coup on February 24, 1966, while he was still in Peking. The enormous banquet which the Chinese hosts had arranged for the visiting Ghanaian President turned out to be one of the most painful diplomatic occasions in modern history. The limelight of the world was on Peking following Nkrumah's overthrow behind his back. The banquet was already set, to cancel it would imply a recognition that the coup was successful. There was no time to make alternative arrangements. The banquet had to go on. It was a quiet affair—a massive meal with hundreds of guests and silently suppressed embarrassment.

Not even the Ghanaian Embassy in Peking was prepared any longer to let Kwame Nkrumah through its doors. The tragic vicissitudes of African politics had interacted with the Vietnamese tragedy—and facilitated the fall of the most internationalist of all African statesmen.

Would Nkrumah have fallen from power had he been in Accra? Would his presence in the capital have stiffened resistance and foiled the bid to capture power? Indeed, would his presence have served as a disincentive to any such bid by his local soldiers? This sounds like a great unanswerable question of history. What is clear is that his absence from Accra made it easier for those who were carrying out the coup, even if the ease did not constitute the difference between a successful coup and a failure. That being the case, it is not unreasonable to claim that Nkrumah's interest in the solution of the war in Vietnam was a contributory factor to the nature of his fall from power. He lost domestic power partly because he had internationalist concerns.

Nkrumah's views were basically representative of some of Africa's foremost aspirations. On the eastern side of Africa Nkrumah's greatest admirer was at the time the Prime Minister of Uganda, Dr. A. Milton Obote. Indeed, Obote believed that on February 24, 1966, it was not merely Nkrumah who was intended to fall from power. Obote himself was likewise scheduled to be the victim of a military coup. The Ugandan soldiers refused to be instigated in that direction on that occasion, and Obote was able to turn the tables on his opponents. He suspended the Constitution, took over executive power, and was later to declare February 24 as "Heroes Day" in honor partly of Kwame Nkrumah, and partly of his own soldiers who had refused to overthrow their Prime Minister.

But why should Obote have been a target for overthrow by external manipulation? Obote believed that $1 million found their way into the hands of one of his strongest opponents in Uganda, to facilitate his own overthrow. But why should this have been deemed necessary and worth a million dollars?

Again the ghost of Vietnam hovered in the background. On April 17 the previous year, Uganda had become the first noncommunist country to join the Soviet Union in a formal denunciation of American aggression in Vietnam. At the time Soviet diplomats were believed to be campaigning in other African countries for similar endorsements of their position on Vietnam. Ghana under Nkrumah and Mali under Modibo Kéita were already rallying behind a general diplomatic disapproval of American policies in Vietnam. But in eastern Africa there had appeared to be no strong anti-American position until the joint Soviet-Ugandan declaration. In 1965 Julius Nyerere had yet to perfect the independence of his foreign policy. Milton Obote's government stole a march over other East Africans when a Ugandan delegation, in a joint report with the Russians, affirmed that Uganda and the Soviet Union condemned "the aggression of American imperialism against the peoples of Vietnam and the whole of Indo-China."

In drawing attention to this significant declaration, the *New York Times* also drew the attention of its readers to the following: "Uganda, which is in Eastern Equatorial Africa, has been the gateway for shipments of Communist arms to the insurgents in the Eastern Congo. There have been armed clashes between Ugandan troops and the mercenary-led forces of the Congolese Premier, Moise Tshombe."[10]

This Vietnamese stand by Uganda was part of a process of radicalization which Milton Obote had begun to initiate in the course of 1965. It was as if Dr. Obote wished to forge a new image of his country and find a place among the radicals of the continent.

There had been two ways by which an African country could win a reputation for radicalism—either through militant socialism in domestic policy or militant nonalignment in foreign policy. By the definitions of the Third World, "militancy" in foreign policy has tended to mean a slight anti-Western orientation. Uganda under Milton Obote in 1965 was beginning to radicalize both its internal and foreign policy, but the pace was faster in the latter than in the former. Sometimes the militancy of pronouncements in foreign affairs was almost in compensation for the slower rate of domestic radicalization.

In interpreting the event, western commentators saw the declaration as what the *New York Times* called "gain for Moscow", in the sense that it might be the beginning of rising support for the Soviet position among the African countries. But who was the loser? The United States was the most direct target of denunciation. On the other hand, western commentators also saw the increasing Soviet involvement in the Vietnamese issue as something which might reduce the more "ominous" Chinese presence. In the words of the *New York Times:* "Most Western diplomats here [in Moscow] agree that the increase of Soviet influence in Vietnam at the expense of Peking would be a good thing. It is widely believed that the Soviet leaders would favor a negotiated settlement and that they are exerting a cautiously moderating influence on Hanoi."[11]

Any African support for the Soviet position could, therefore, be interpreted as being partly at the expense of Peking. Yet in the course of the same year, Milton Obote of Uganda paid his respects to Mao Tsetung in a visit to communist China. Obote had already established quite early his reluctance to be a pawn in the cold war at the expense of communist China. Although both Chinas had been represented at the independence celebrations of Uganda, it was not long before preference manifested itself in the fundamental decision to confirm diplomatic relations with Mao's country and also in the more symbolic decision to protect Ugandan audiences from American anti-Chinese propaganda. In June 1963 an American film called "The Manchurian Candidate" was banned in Uganda. No reason was given at the time, but a year later it was admitted that the film was banned because it was anticommunist and anti-Chinese. The plot of the film reportedly concerned an American soldier captured and brainwashed by the Chinese communists.[12]

But while symbolic gestures toward the communist Chinese had been made by Obote from the very beginning of Uganda's independence, the more dramatic radicalization of foreign policy in 1965 created new apprehensions in certain circles both domestically and internationally.

Uganda had already a tradition of neo-McCarthyism, by which those who showed sympathies for the eastern bloc were interpreted as ungodly and fellow travelers. Fears that Obote might be taking the country toward socialism, and endangering certain traditional institutions in Uganda, were activated. Obote's tour of communist countries in that year seemed to confirm some of these apprehensions. Possibilities of mutual sympathies between Ugandan conservatives and opponents of Obote, on the one hand, and western embassies and other western interests on the other, were emerging. Domestic enemies of Obote were beginning to calculate the likelihood of getting external western support should there be a confrontation between themselves and Obote at home. The radicalization of Obote's foreign policy was deemed to be an opportunity which could be exploited by Obote's domestic opponents as a way of securing western assistance. The $1 million which Obote claimed found its way into the hands of one of his opponents, as well as the admission by the regional King Mutesa of Buganda that he had asked the British for troops should there be a military confrontation between himself and Prime Minister Obote, added up to a pattern of interrelationships between domestic and international considerations in that 1966 crisis of Uganda which looked even more ominous on the day Kwame Nkrumah was overthrown.

An earlier factor which might have contributed to Obote's position on Vietnam was American involvement in the neighboring Congo (now Zaire). Just as in Saigon the Americans seemed to be maintaining in power a puppet regime, so in Kinshasa Americans were helping to consolidate the political survival of Moise Tshombe. Obote saw a direct parallel between the Saigon regime and the regime of Moise Tshombe, "the imperialist stooge".

The parallels of this form of American military involvement assumed greater relevance for Uganda when Congolese planes bombed the villages of Goli and Paidha in West Nile District on February 13, 1965. The Congolese planes had been provided by the United States government—just as the United States government had continued to provide military aid to the government of South Vietnam.

Following the bombing of the two Ugandan villages in West Nile District, Prime Minister Obote gave a television address on the same evening: "We blame the Government of the United States—the Government that claims to be the greatest democracy in the World, but a Government that does not respect democracies."

Just as the Vietcong and North Vietnam were a David in collision with a gigantic Goliath, so was Uganda similarly cast in the role of a small power having to defend itself against the aggressive tendencies of a colossus. Dr. Obote went on: "We have been attacked without provocation on our part. I cannot say whether we are going to retaliate . . . We must all be prepared to throw sand, and sacks of sand, in the eyes of the mighty."[13]

The Uganda Government then arranged a national demonstration for Tuesday afternoon, February 16, 1965. There were ministerial appeals to employers to release their workers for the great march to the American Embassy and for the rally of protest which was to follow. Ugandans were up in arms—metaphorically at least—and the demonstration was supposed to indicate the depth of Ugandan indignation at being "Vietnamized." Even a wounded soldier in a West Nile village was elevated to a symbolic state hero. As Obote put it: "Our one officer has already spilt blood for all of us. It will be our duty to redeem that blood."[14] Although the expression of indignation turned out to be not quite as spontaneous as was intended, the march on the American Embassy was the most significant exercise in diplomatic protest that independent Uganda had undertaken up to that time. The march took place, as we indicated, in February. By April, a Ugandan delegation in the Soviet Union was denouncing in strong terms "The aggression of American Imperialism against the peoples of Vietnam and the whole of Indo-China."*

Once again the image of David against Goliath portrayed by the entire Vietnam experience had an impact far beyond Uganda. The whole problem of southern Africa, exhibiting as it does a case of white technological superiority, would normally rule out the possibility of a successful black insurrection against white supremacy. The liberation movements against apartheid would normally have appeared doomed to eternal futility but for the success of such movements as the National Liberation Front of South Vietnam and the support from the relatively small brotherly country, North Vietnam. Pitched against the might of the United States, a guerilla movement in Vietnam had nevertheless reduced a gigantic Goliath to a stalemate. We might therefore argue that the Vietnamese experience opened up new areas of hope for African liberation movements in southern Africa.

Conclusion

The French had been defeated in Vietnam, capitulating in humiliation at Dien Bien Phu. Their defeat in Vietnam intensified their desire to be victorious in Algeria. The morale of the French army suffered a severe setback in the Vietnamese experience; and this setback might itself have contributed to the obstinacy with which the French fought the Alterian

---

*General Idi Amin attempted to carry on certain aspects of the internationalist tradition of his predecessor. The general spoke out a number of times against American policies in Vietnam.

war for so long. Again, a mighty white power, France, was ultimately reduced to a standstill in Algeria. Fortunately, because of de Gaulle's foresight, the French in Algeria avoided the kind of humiliating defeat they had encountered in Indo-China. Neither the National Liberation Front of Algeria nor the French Army had been militarily defeated by the end of this experience. They turned to the task of negotiating a settlement. The ghost of Vietnam had hovered over Algeria for quite a while, initially intensifying French resistance to compensate for Dien Bien Phu, but later facilitating de Gaulle's own pragmatic approach to the solution of this last of France's colonial wars.

We might, therefore, say that Vietnam first affected the destiny of a north African situation, in Algeria, and more recently affected the morale of Southern African Freedom Fighters. In north Africa, Vietnam had an impact on the oppressing power, France. In southern Africa, Vietnam has enhanced the optimism of the oppressed, the liberation fighters. David pitched against Goliath continues to be an image of devastating revolutionary potential.

If the weak can defeat the strong in war, should not the weak also be permitted a say in diplomacy at the global level? Nkrumah's bid in Peking in 1965–1966 might well have been a case of David on a peace mission to save two Goliaths from each other. Nkrumah's friend, Obote, later also asserted the right to be concerned. Two figures in modern African history had attempted to give Africa a say in a sensitive arena of world affairs. Their efforts were but a beginning—a prelude to the next phase of Africa's diplomatic involvement in the *barazas* of the global village.

But equally significant was of course what went on in Indo-China itself. The connections between civil and international strife, the lessons of terror as an instrument of the weak, the interplay between economic and cultural variables, were captured in that most remarkable of all localized wars.

Vietnam for a while even overshadowed the Middle East as the most internationally sensitive of all crisis areas. But both areas together brought to a focus the varied issues which link warfare to the inequalities of the technological age. Over the years almost all world order values have been subjected to ultimate tests in the jungles of Vietnam and the deserts of the Middle East.

Footnotes

1. Lenin, The War Program of the Proletarian Revolution (1916) *Collected Works* Vol. 23 (Moscow: Foreign Languages Publishing House, 1960), pp. 816–821. Also available in Lenin, *Selected Works in 3 Vol.,* Vol. 1.

2. Nkrumah, *Neo-Colonialism: The Last Stage of Imperialism* (London: Nelson, 1965) p. 256.

3. International Sociological Association, *The Nature of Conflict* (*Studies on the Sociological Aspects of International Tension*) (Paris: UNESCO Publication, 1967), pp. 177–203.

4. Henri Baudet, "The Netherlands after the Loss of Empire," *Journal of Contemporary History*, Vol. IV, No. 1, January, 1969, p. 130. See also Arend Lyphart, *The Trauma of De-Colonization: The Dutch and West New Guinea* (New Haven: Yale University Press, 1966). These issues are also discussed in my paper "Scotland and Biafra: Problems of Post-Imperial Fragmentation," First Lecture to launch the new Center for International Race Relations, University of Denver, 1969. The lectures were published in Mazrui, *Post-Imperial Fragmentation: The Legacy of Ethnic and Racial Conflict* (Denver: University of Denver, 1969).

5. These points are discussed more fully in Mazrui, "Moise Tshombe and the Arabs; 1960–1968," *Race,* January 1969. Reprinted as Chapter 11 in Mazrui, *Violence and Thought: Essays on Social Tensions in Africa* (London: Longmans, 1969) pp. 231–254.

6. C. Eric Lincoln, *The Black Muslims in America* (Boston: Beacon Press, 1968) pp. 165–169.

7. Cited by Colin and Margaret Legum, *South Africa: Crisis for the West* (London: Pall Mall Press, 1964) pp. 107, 108. On the other hand, Afrikaaner nationalism has often suspected sections of the local Jewry in South Africa of having leanings toward Communism. See for example Muriel Horrell (Compiler) *A Survey of Race Relations in South Africa* (Johannesburg: South African Institute on Race Relations, 1965) pp. 22–24.

8. For the full text of Nkrumah's letters see *Ghana Today,* November 7, 1962. For a brief statement of Nkrumah's neutralist position generally see "Dr. Nkrumah States the Neutralist Case," *Africa Report,* Vol. VII, No. 8, August 1962.

9. *Ghana Today, Ibid.*

10. See Henry Tanner, "Soviet Pressing Africans to Back Stand on Saigon: Uganda Joins in Scoring U.S. 'Agression' as Russians Affirm Tie to Hanoi," *New York Times,* April 19, 1965, pp. 1, 2.

11. *Ibid.*

12. This information was obtained in a conversation with a person intimately connected with the picture house concerned in Kampala. The film was shown to a private audience at Makerere University College, Kampala.

13. See *Uganda Argus* (Kampala), February 15, 1965.

14. *Ibid.*

Section IV

ECONOMIC CULTURE AND THE LURE OF DEVELOPMENT

CHAPTER 13
Economic Modernization
and Domestic Equity

Another key process in the transformation of the world within the next thirty years will be, quite simply, the process of *modernization*. The term "modernization" itself is much abused by looseness of usage and is at times in danger of losing all claims to socioscientific utility. But there is a relevant residual meaning of the term which is, in brief, change in a direction which is compatible with the present stage of human knowledge and which does justice to the potentialities of man as an innovative being. Societies oblivious of the stage of human achievement already accomplished, or reluctant to benefit by the potentialities of man as an innovating being, are basically premodern.

Particularly significant for these societies will be the ambition to modernize their economic culture. This process has three basic dimensions. The preferred world of the 1990's will have gone furthest in, first, *the modernization of economic techniques and processes;* second, the *modernization of economic motivation;* and third, the *modernization of social stratification* both domestically and internationally.

The modernization of economic techniques and processes amounts to the modernization of what Marx would call "productive forces". The machinery, skills, and organization of production would need to be transformed in many societies to make them conducive to optimum economic performance and social returns. The need for good roads, the mechanization of agriculture, the promotion of technical education, the inauguration of viable industries, the promotion of intersectorial or regional economic integration, all fall within that category of socioeconomic change which in this analysis might be described as the modernization of economic techniques and processes.

The second major area of modernization, and one which in practise cannot easily be differentiated from the first, is the modernization of economic motivation. Economic performance is not simply a question of

271

whether a person in India or the Ivory Coast is capable of acquiring the skill to drive or even repair a tractor and mechanical plow. The acquisition of skills falls within that first dimension of modernization—the process of fostering economic techniques and new processes. What is at stake in this second dimension of economic modernization is whether that person in India or the Ivory Coast is *motivated* to use that tractor, and whether the sociocultural climate within which that man lives and works favors the use of such devices in a manner which would yield optimum economic advantage to the individuals concerned.

The nineteenth century was the great period of interdisciplinary approaches in social studies. Economics had not as yet asserted its complete independence from the other social sciences. Political economy was a hybrid discipline respectable as an approach to the understanding of social problems. Underlying political economy was a further hybrid phenomenon—the beginnings of *economic psychology.* The whole theory of the profit motive as a major concept in trying to understand economic behavior was basically a contribution of economic psychology. As the study of economics tore itself away from the other social sciences, it became more scientific but less social. Economics today is still a hybrid subject in some fundamental sense, but in the quest for the scientific the most "eligible" partner for economics now is perhaps mathematics rather than either politics or psychology.

And yet to understand social man, social science has to be both scientific and social. A partial retreat to some nineteenth century concepts might be in order. Economic psychology assumes relevance when we try to understand the motivation of man in economic situations. Concepts like profit motive as against other forms of motivation, and social attitudes toward work and self-improvement all acquire a new significance when we are trying to comprehend why it is that some societies respond more quickly to the challenge of development than others.

The third area of modernization if we are to reach something approaching the preferred world in the 1990's is the modernization of stratification. It is an assumption of this analysis that the complete abolition of classes is utopian and unattainable. Tribalism can and has been abolished in some parts of the world. It is even conceivable that nation-states are transitory, though the evidence seems to suggest a certain defiant obstinacy in the nation-state; it threatens to be part of our world for many centuries to come. But even if it were true that nation-states are indeed a transitory phenomenon, we should not assume that other group categories in human organization are similarly on the way out. A nationless world might be more easily conceivable than modernization in relation to social and economic equity.

In the next chapter we shall explore further the international aspects of structural reform and economic equity. In this chapter our focus will be on the domestic dimension. For illustration of the problems involved we shall draw especially from both East African and American experience in the economics of ethnicity. At stake is both social justice and economic welfare, ominously beclouded by interethnic violence.

The interaction between economic issues and race relations has been manifesting itself in new ways in East Africa, as well as in the United States. In East Africa controversy has continued about the future of merchants and traders of Indian and Pakistani origin. We discussed this problem earlier in connection with the social and sexual exclusiveness of the Asians as a factor behind General Amin's decision to expel them from Uganda. But the exodus started earlier than that. Since 1967 many East African Indians with British passports have packed up and left the region. In their insecurity, they left East Africa to go and settle in Britain. But their very departure in large numbers sparked off controversy about colored immigration in the United Kingdom, and the British government finally capitulated to popular racial feelings in Britain and imposed restrictions on Britain's own citizens of non-European origins. As the deadline for the imposition of restrictions approached, more East African Asians panicked—grabbed their suitcases, and rushed for planes to take them from Nairobi to London. This is when heated racial controversy first broke out between Britain and East Africa on the Asian question. Were the Asians victims of African racialism as African governments sought to replace them with Africans in their jobs and businesses? Or were the Asians victims of British racialism as the United Kingdom started a policy of first- and second-class citizenship with different rights of entry into the "mother country"? Certainly British kinship culture had started differentiating between "real kith and kin", recognizably white, on one side, and the new "brown pretenders", on the other.

Meanwhile, in the United States the civil rights movement and black militancy were entering a new phase, in which a prime question was the future economic role and economic status of black Americans. In Kenya and Uganda, the governments were trying to create a fairer deal for the black populations by helping them to become more effective in business enterprise. Was there a similar trend in the United States? Are we witnessing in both East Africa and the United States an attempt to solve racial disparities by promoting black capitalism? Are the tensions of conflicting kinship cultures to be moderated by a transformation of economic relations?

A critical question underlying the interaction between economic roles and race relations is the deceptively simple difference between a *class* system of stratification and a *caste* system of stratification. The British in the colonial period had in fact created something approaching an ethnic caste system in East Africa, especially in Kenya—with Europeans at the top, the Asians in the middle, and the Africans at the bottom. This is what Donald Rothchild has called a "three-tier socioeconomic structure":

> ... the Europeans held the most important places in the public and private sectors of the economy; the Asians predominated in the middle-level positions, as artisans, clerks, professionals, merchants and tradesmen; the Africans filled out the picture by performing unskilled tasks on the farms and in the homes and factories.[1]

The difference between a class system and a caste system is partly related to the degree of social and occupational mobility in the given society. If the stratification is so rigid that it is difficult for an individual to change the socioeconomic category to which he belongs, and if the rigidity is quasi-hereditary, then the category is more like a caste than a class. Rigidity in stratification is maximized when stratification is mainly or wholly based on hereditary factors. A stratification based on race becomes therefore basically a caste system rather than simply a class structure.

While a class system can theoretically be divorced from kinship and become more purely an aspect of economic culture, a caste system domestically is always both a kinship category and an economic arrangement. This is because a caste system tends to include *endogamous* closure. It becomes difficult for members of one caste to marry into another. At the very minimum, endogamy is an accompanying rather than a defining characteristic of caste. It is unlikely that a caste system would be freely exogamous, and approve of general intermarriage. Nevertheless, a caste system which theoretically permits general intermarriage would not be a contradiction in terms, provided it is clear which stratum the children belong to. The ultimate definition of caste for our purpose is a rigidity of stratification which is wholly or mainly based on hereditary factors. The system of descent usually involves descending miscegenation. Occupational specialization by caste provides the other component of this rigidity.[2]

Black Economic Power: The Search in East Africa

The British colonial administration in Kenya might therefore be said to have evolved a caste system within which the Europeans were the landed and political aristocracy, the Asians were the reservoir of professional, clerical, and commercial personnel, and the Africans afforded manpower in the lower reaches of the occupational structure. While it was possible for some types of jobs to be manned by either a European, an Asian, or an African, the caste rewards were made distinctive by differential salary scales. Colonial Kenya had European scales of pay, Asian scales of pay, and African scales of pay in a descending order of benefits and attractiveness.[3]

As independence approached, the elaborateness of this caste system was rapidly abandoned. Policies of Africanization were pushed in order to place Africans in important political and administrative sectors. Independence had of course to mean African ministers; then it had to mean African permanent secretaries heading the administrative side of government; then it had to mean, in at least some countries, African military commanders to direct the armed forces. But was that enough?

By the end of the 1960's the African had now experienced not only what it was like to be a subsistence farmer, but also a plantation owner of cash crops in the former White Highlands. The African's range of occupational experience now included proletarian, clerical, ministerial, administrative, and professional categories. What was still rare was for an African to be a highly successful businessman with a major shop on Kenyatta Avenue in Nairobi. This residual handicap of a former caste status was what the policies of commercial Africanization in Kenya and Uganda sought to eliminate. The ambition reached its most dramatic proportions when President Idi Amin of Uganda took the Indian bull by the horns and gave a ninety-day explusion order.

The ambition in Kenya as in Uganda is still to replace the old colonial caste system of ethnic stratification with a modern class system of economic competition. Zambia has shown similar inclinations, but there is a serious danger that the African governments might go too far even if they do not go as far as General Amin. From an indigenous point of view, the real danger is the replacement of one caste system with another, as different tribal communities specialize in different economic roles.

To avert such a danger, it becomes important to develop in the African a business capacity which would be able to stand up to non-indigenous competition without the necessity of imposing a complete occupational closure on the system and either exclude non-indigenous *citizens* or discriminate against less privileged tribal groups. The discrimination against those Asians who did not take up local citizenship but preferred to invest in British citizenship might be sad but not necessarily immoral. Nor can discrimination against noncitizens be described as a caste system. The danger of replacing one caste system with another in Kenya and Uganda would only arise when there is a serious long-term possibility of rigid ethnic stratification, with certain tribes or certain races relegated to the bottom while others enjoy hereditary succession to privilege.

Uganda and Kenya have continued to differ from Tanzania in their approach to the economic transformation of their peoples. On July 4, 1966, Uganda's National Assembly approved the National Trading Corporation Bill setting up a new body to accelerate African participation in trade and commerce. This was the culmination of a number of different experiments and appeals by the Uganda government to achieve greater indigenous involvement in these sectors of the economy. A month before the passing of the bill setting up the new body, the Minister of Commerce and Industry told a meeting of the National Economic and Social Advisory Council that a situation had to be created in which Africans could be helped to become commercially effective. "They must learn commercial tricks and trade tricks, and be ready to burn their fingers." It was easy to open a shop, but it needed perseverance to keep it open.

The Uganda government continued to grope for methods by which Africans could learn, in the words of the old minister, "commercial tricks and trade tricks and be ready to burn their fingers". The National Trading Corporation was intended to facilitate this process of experimentation with African involvement in commercial activities.

In 1967 there was a slight unease among non-African businessmen. Tanzania had already chosen a socialist approach to development and had nationalized certain industries. In Kenya and Uganda there seemed already to be increasing militancy in the process of Africanizing commerce. Consequently, the Uganda government decided that reassurance was needed for non-African businessmen. Addressing the Uganda Chamber of Commerce at its Annual Meeting Mr. C. J. Obwangor, then Minister of Commerce and Industry, urged the businessmen not to regard the National Trading Corporation as a threat to them: "It is not this Government's intention to see that all non-African businessmen go out of business. Far from it, it is the intention to see that there is a proper balance between Africans and non-Africans in the distributive trade." The Minister asked the businessmen to cooperate in achieving greater racial integration in commerce. Private enterprise had a challenge to meet. "I do look for an attitude of energy, vigor, and of willingness to take reasonable risks," Mr. Obwangor asserted.

As part of this process of economic resocialization, the Uganda government under Milton Obote sometimes put faith in commercial education and training. This policy has continued since Amin's coup of January 1971. Training in accountancy, book-keeping, secretarialship, and even personnel management does not of course constitute an induction into entrepreneurial behavior. But such education is perhaps a supportive factor in the whole growth of economic readjustment and psychological reorientation. As early as May 1966 the Minister of Education announced that new steps to expand the range of commercial education in Uganda were being undertaken. Some of these steps affected the new role of the Uganda College of Commerce which was already in existence but whose scope was under review. Discussions between the government and Makerere University College later led in July 1, 1968 to the introduction of accountancy at degree level at Makerere, supported by legal studies with a special orientation toward business law. Since then a full course leading to the degree of Bachelor of Commerce has been instituted.

To some extent this is an attempt to utilize the mystique of education as a way of giving an extra boost to the reputation of commercial activity. The craze for education in East Africa is already striking, and its acquisition is the order of the day, but the attraction of commercial activity itself is as yet uncertain. The skills asked for in commercial education continue to be purely supportive rather than fundamental to the creation of an African commercial class. Nevertheless the new faith in training for business and private enterprise is part of the East African groping for effective means of economic resocialization.

Kenya's policy in this sphere of national life, though pursued with greater moderation, has been basically similar to that of Uganda. To some extent Kenya's problem has been more severe. After all, some kind of successful "middleman economic activity" by Africans had a longer history in Uganda; prosperous African farmers and merchants were known well before independence. In Kenya, however, the growth of an African prosperous class was much more manifestly a post-independence phenomenon. Cash crop farming in Kenya had been dominated by Europeans; distributive trade was overwhelmingly in the control of Europeans and Asians. A resettlement scheme in the Kenya Highlands helped to give an increasing share in agriculture to Africans, but there was still a good deal to be done. Progress in the commercial sector was in many ways less spectacular than the resettlement schemes. Here again then there was an early commitment to the Africanization of commerce and to the creation of an effective African business class. The government *Sessional Paper No. 10 on African Socialism* was in part an undertaking to Africanize the rudimentary capitalism which Kenya had already created.

At first the methods used were mainly those of *appealing* to immigrant businessmen to involve more and more Africans in their activities. But Asian kinship culture was in the way. Many Asian businesses were essentially family businesses which did not lend themselves very easily to acquiring partners outside the family circle. In addition the very idea of creating an African commercial class was inevitably a matter which could undermine seriously the livelihood of some of the poorer shop-keepers among immigrant communities. This was like inviting certain Asians to commit commercial suicide. A third reason why the initial loose appeals to Asians to help African businessmen did not yield immediate results was the simple fact that Africans were seldom effectively competitive in commerce even when given a little push. This last brings us back to the whole problem of attempting a transformation of African economic culture as a prerequisite for the creation of an effective African commercial class.

Partly because of these considerations the Kenya government had by then become increasingly militant in its policy of trying to push Africans into effective business behavior. One method used was simply to reduce the opportunities open to non-Africans in the hope that the gaps left would draw in those Africans who might otherwise have been too timid or too disorganized to be fully competitive. Out of this grew the whole idea of the Trade Licensing Act, designed to Africanize trade by licensing businesses more systematically and limiting the duration of licenses to one calendar year. The minister had a right to refuse a non-citizen a license if he was convinced that a business could be done by a citizen. It is true that measures of this kind were in principle intended to be nonracial, and those immigrant people who had already taken Kenya citizenship were not to be penalized, but ultimately the purpose was indeed to achieve a greater Africanization.

The opportunities themselves could only be created by a deliberate elimination of some Asians and Europeans from these businesses. This side of the Kenya government policy was designed not to increase African competitiveness but to decrease the competition that the African has had to face from others. It was hoped by policy-makers that the security which these new African businessmen would enjoy might gradually have a healthy demonstration impact on other aspiring Africans. The later generations of African merchants might be forced to manifest a more meaningful faith in risk-taking than this overprotected first generation was called upon to do.

The Kenya government has also been utilizing other methods of economic transformation intended to increase the number of African traders without necessarily ousting their rivals. For example, the Ministry of Commerce has helped distribute shares of an occasional Asian-owned industry, widely and at cheap rates. The industry itself might offer the shares to the Ministry for this kind of distribution to attract significant African participation into what has previously been a large family business. The Kenya government seemed convinced that one could only learn to invest by investing. Africans had therefore to be encouraged to take the risks of buying shares and familiarize themselves with this exercise. At times Kenya policy has echoed that of Sweden in the 1950's—the ideal of trying to create "an ownership democracy".[4]

Black Economic Power: The Search in the United States

In the United States, the Nixon administration declared a commitment to the promotion of "black capitalism" though the degree of determination with which this policy was pushed was modest. President Nixon established soon after taking office in 1969 the new Office of Minority Enterprise within the Department of Commerce, charged with coordinating all government programs to help black businessmen; getting white businessmen more actively involved in helping black enterprise; and disseminating information about available government programs and sources of assistance.

There are indeed a number of government or government-supported programs already in being in the United States designed to boost minority enterprise. In April 1969, when Nixon established the Office of Minority Enterprise, he observed that "by one count there are now 116 such programs, operated by no less than 21 different departments and agencies. These are largely uncoordinated." The new Office was to address itself precisely to the problem of coordination.[5]

In the first Nixon administration the program which was reputed to have had the most effect was the Small Business Administration (SBA), whose work was consolidated under the leadership of Mexican-American Hilary Sandoval Jr.. SBA emphasized loans to black people to start their own business—a program which was given the name of "Project Own". In the first eight months of 1968–1969 (July through March) SBA made 2,197 loans to minority businessmen, apparently worth $64 million. At the same stage the previous year SBA had given only 1,124 loans worth $19 million.[6]

Throughout Nixon's first term as President his administration continued to retain a theoretical commitment to the promotion of "black capitalism" in the United States, but was not prepared to make available the immense financial resources necessary if such a major economic restructuring of the society was to be accomplished. However, testifying before the House Select Committee on Business in July 1969, the U.S. Secretary of Commerce, Maurice Stans, claimed that the efforts of the new Office of Minority Business Enterprise would before long show concrete results. He specifically mentioned negotiations to persuade large car and oil companies to channel new "auto dealerships and gas station franchises" to members of minority groups.[7]

After Nixon's reelection the policy of promoting minority enterprise seemed to be still better suited to Nixon's call for a spirit of self-reliance than almost any of the welfare programs, which Nixon in any case distrusted.

In East Africa one of the difficulties which African businessmen encounter is, as we indicated, the sheer lack of a managerial tradition suitable for business organization. The problem is partly cultural. A similar difficulty seems to be encountered in the struggle to create effective black enterprise in the United States. The SBA publicly undertook to provide managerial training as well as loans for prospective businessmen.

How rational is this policy of trying to integrate the Blacks more fully into American capitalism? For those who are against ultimate separation of the Blacks into a separate national entity, there may be only two alternatives to the American dilemma. Either the United States must become rapidly socialist or black Americans must become *effectively* capitalist. While either could restore parity of esteem between the races, the trauma of instant socialism might be more difficult for the country as a whole to bear than the agonies of making the Blacks more effectively competitive in an economically competitive system. But black economic effectiveness requires more than control of the ghetto shops. The Blacks have to enter the *main* stream of American economic civilization. To put it crudely, one out of every ten American millionaires should be a black man, and by comparable millions.

The idea that racial parity in America might lie in black capitalism is by no means new in the history of the black man in the United States, with its Anglo-Saxon sociocultural heritage. Britain and the United States between them either invented or perfected capitalism both as a system of thought and as a structure of economic organization. Certain conclusions follow from this system of thought. For the Blacks in America to become the equals of the Whites it is not enough to embrace Jesus and the white man's religion. They should also embrace Adam Smith and the economic ideology of Anglo-American civilization. The best formulation of this is John Hope's, who later became President of the Atlanta University System. At a conference on the theme of "The Negro in Business" in 1898 Hope said:

> We are living among the so-called Anglo-Saxons and dealing with them. They are a conquering people who turn their conquests into their pockets. . . . Business seems to be not only simply the raw material of Anglo-Saxon civilization, but almost the civilization itself. . . . To the finite

vision, to say the least, the policy of avoiding entrance in the world's business would be suicide to the Negro.[8]

Two years after the Atlanta conference, Booker T. Washington took the lead in organizing the National Negro Business League. The slogan of "Negro business" became a crusade—and Washington's oratory bridged the gulf between the Bible and Adam Smith's *Wealth of Nations*. His annual address as the president of the League was apparently delivered in the form of a "Business Sermon", based upon the Biblical text: "To him that hath shall be given." In Washington's view, "these lines spoken by the Master strike the keynote for individual success and equally so for racial success."[9]

The National Negro Business League undertook to establish the Colored Merchants Association (CMA) grocery stores throughout the United States. The first CMA was established in Montgomery, Alabama, in 1928, and was soon followed in a number of other cities. In addition there was an expansion of business education in black colleges. The number of black colleges giving business courses rose from six in 1900 to more than twenty on the eve of World War II.[10]

So far, black attempts to enter the full stream of American capitalism have failed. One reason might indeed be what the late Howard sociologist Franklin Frazier called the "fundamental sociological fact that the Negro lacks a business tradition or the experience of people who, over generations, have engaged in buying and selling."[11] A similar sociological fact is, as we indicated, encountered in East Africa in the struggle to awaken in the African a profit motive sharp enough and a managerial sense developed enough to make him a match for the European and Indian businessman. The governments in Kenya and Uganda are still seeking an answer partly in business and managerial education—comparable to the attempts of black colleges in the United States to cultivate a business sense in the black man through business education. What is at stake is partly a cultural revolution—the modernization of motivational patterns among black people, as an approach toward modernizing the system of stratification.

In spite of the past failures of full-blooded black capitalism, such a policy stands a better chance in the years ahead. A fundamental change in the status of the black man has taken place in the United States. Black Americans have been promoted from the status of a lower *caste* to the status of a lower *class*. The change in immediate comforts is negligible. But there is probably a major change in potential social and occupational mobility: and that is precisely what differentiates class status from a caste status in such a context. Two decades ago certain positions in American society were to be left "uncontaminated" by Negro participation. Now it is no longer clear what are the limits of black potential in the United States, solely from the point of view of racial credentials. We already know that the Supreme Court of the United States is no longer beyond the reach of black aspirants in law, nor if the polls are to be believed, is the theoretical possibility of a black President of the United States any longer automatically dismissed by the American electorate.

The old American caste system suppressed the Negro in many spheres of experience, strongly enforcing taboos of Anglo-Saxon kinship culture. For example, Hollywood did not dare to offend the American market by permitting a black man to kiss a white woman on the cinema screen. Even this aspect of the old American caste system was broken through by Sidney Poitier's affection for a giggly white co-ed in *Guess Who's Coming to Dinner,* although this film still paid homage to the screen taboos of the American caste system. In the words of one reviewer: "Audiences accepted this couple because the film featured Katherine Hepburn's comeback and Spencer Tracy's last performance, and because Director Stanley Kramer had the mixed couple express their affection by fond glances rather than by fondling each other."

The reviewer goes on to discuss an even more daring film, if a less artistic one. Black ex-fullback Jim Brown and "white sex-pot" Raquel Welch co-star in *100 Rifles,* complete with a bedroom scene.

> However, they did soften the impact a bit by smothering Raquel in brown make-up and having her portray an Indian. Thus, during their bedroom scene, it is a brown hand rather than a white one that we see frenziedly gripping Jim's muscular back. The impact is further softened by the fact that both these two are sordid sex symbols from whom we expect shocking behavior. Both stars are limited in that their assets are purely anatomical. If their survival depended upon acting ability, both would be doomed.[12]

The film reviewer may have been right in his ominous prediction about a continuing disapproval of miscegenation on the screen in the United States. Nevertheless he predicted a "deluge of films with such themes" shortly. Another Jim Brown film, *Kenner,* has been released—this time the white co-star has been permitted to portray a white character. Zero Mostel is making a film about a Harlem white shopkeeper who falls in love with a middle-aged black woman. "Even Sidney Poitier has moved beyond the angelic affair of *Guess Who's Coming to Dinner.* He has just completed a film in which he has an affair with a white girl, portrayed by Joanna Shimkus." Reviewer Dennis Hunt concludes with the compelling question: "Are American filmgoers ready for all this?"[13]

It might well be that a "deluge" of such films might be more than white America can as yet bear. There might even be a significant reaction. But a caste system is in disintegration when the old taboos of kinship culture are being brazenly challenged.[14] Now, as the ultimate taboos of the caste system are rapidly being eroded, the black American finds himself moving from the untouchability of a lower caste to the more flexible status of a lower class. This constitutes the modernization of social stratification in the United States.

Conclusion

We have attempted to deal in this chapter with the problem of economic solutions to racial problems, with special reference to attempts being made in East Africa and the United States to create an effective black entrepreneurial class. In East Africa a policy of Africanization has now resulted in strong moves to eliminate or drastically reduce Asian dominance in important sections of trade and commerce, from General Amin's expulsion order to Kenya's Trade Licensing Act. British colonial policy in places like Kenya had promoted what amounted to a caste system, with Europeans at the top, Asians in the middle, and Africans at the base of the socioeconomic pyramid. As independence approached many Africans managed to move from the base to the pinnacle, but the middle of the pyramid continued to be primarily non-African. The policy of Africanization of commerce is in part designed to darken the shade of the middle of the pyramid and make it less conspicuously different from the black bottom and the black pinnacle.

In the United States, black militancy is groping for ways to open up new opportunities for black Americans. One economic theme in the picture is an old one—the quest to make black Americans fully share in the material benefits of the country's capitalist civilization. One way of making them share is to create for a section of them the possibility of being effective competitors in the business world of the United States.

It is perhaps ironic that it should be Indians in East Africa and "Anglo-Saxons" in Britain and the United States who formed some of the forces of opposition to the restructuring of the societies concerned. The caste system has after all found one of its striking models in Hindu civilization in India; while the class system insofar as it is related to capitalism has often been symbolized by Britain as the initiator of the nineteenth century wave of industrialization and the United States as the twentieth century leader of the liberal capitalist civilization. The so-called Anglo-Saxon nations are in some ways virtually the inventors of capitalism as a self-conscious system of thought and economic organizations. Adam Smith and Lord Keynes stand out as leading contributors in their different ways to the capitalist heritage. They are giants in the Anglo-American stream of economic ideas.

In Kenya and Uganda, the rule of an Anglo-Saxon power, the United Kingdom, both bequeathed to the country the ethos of capitalism and imposed on the country a caste system based on racial gradation. British colonial policy imposed on Kenya, especially, in East Africa the caste pyramid. After independence, the struggle to change the structure of society in East Africa came into conflict with local Indians. Many of the East African Indians were not quite as subject to Hindu-based caste regulations and taboos as their counterparts were in India, and yet the whole Asian community found itself occupying the role of a middle caste in a colonially derived structure of stratification. The struggle against this colonial legacy then began to hit Indian merchants and shopkeepers in the streets of Nakuru, Nairobi, and Mbale. A conflict of kinship cultures was working itself out, and the pursuit of social justice and economic welfare was generating the tensions of its own contradictions.

Within the United States, the so-called Anglo-Saxon civilization again excelled itself, both in giving the country capitalism as its socioeconomic ethos and ethnic stratification as a racially based caste system. As we pointed out in the chapter on monogamy and descent, the Germanic streak among Europeans tends to be among the most racially exclusive. Let us again repeat that it might not be purely by accident that both the Nazi civilization and the Afrikaaner civilization in South Africa sprang from ways of thought of Germanic stock. White America today includes too many ethnic strands to be described as Germanic. But there is little doubt that the basic civilization of white America, complete with its prejudices, is part of the stream of racial exclusiveness which took its worst form in Nazi Germany, continues today to be manifested in Afrikaaner-dominated South Africa, created racially segregated British colonies, supported a policy of "White Australia", invented in 1968 in Britain two categories of citizenship differentiated by racial considerations, and imposed on the United States a long history of racial bigotry. The Anglo-Americans are both among the most liberal people in history and among the most racially exclusive. Both the liberalism and the racial exclusiveness might in part have been connected with the capitalism that evolved in Britain, the British Empire, and the United States.

But the place of the black American in his nation's life is undergoing significant changes. We advanced the hypothesis that full black salvation in America would come either if America went socialist and achieved social justice through socialist equality, of if black Americans went capitalist and obtained an equitable share of the benefits of American civilization. The prospects for black capitalism have improved as a result of a change which might at first look imperceptible but which is critically relevant. Black Americans have moved, or are in the process of being promoted, from the status of a lower caste to the status of a lower class. The old kinship taboos of the American caste system, including endogamous tendencies and disapproval of "miscegenation", are being increasingly challenged, defied, or defiled. And it is becoming increasingly clear that no special job or position in the United States will in the years ahead be regarded as out of bounds for black Americans on purely racial grounds. Occupational and social mobility, even if for the time being merely hypothetical, has helped to convert the status of black Americans from that of the lower caste to that of the lower class.

The cultural heritage of India and the cultural heritage of the Anglo-Saxon powers merged for a while when capitalism and the caste system interracted in racially mixed situations in Africa and the United States. These two heritages are now undergoing traumatic transformation under the impact of black assertiveness in both Africa and the United States. The lessons of that experience are likely to be of profound relevance for both modernization and intergroup relations as problems of world order.[15]

Footnotes

1. Rothchild, "Citizenship and National Integration: The Non-African Crisis in Kenya," unpublished typescript. A companion piece by Rothchild is his article "Kenya's Minorities and the African Crisis over Citizenship," *Race,* Vol. IX, No. 4, April 1968, pp. 421–437.
2. Such a definition overlaps with Weber's but with important differences. See, for example, Max Weber *On Charisma and Institution Building,* Selected Papers edited by S. N. Eisenstadt (Chicago: University of Chicago Press, 1968) pp. 178–186.
3. Consult also Tamotsu Shibutani and Kian M. Kwan, *Ethnic Stratification: A Comparative Approach* (New York: Macmillan, 1965).
4. This part of the chapter has borrowed from the following works, Mazrui, "Socialized Capitalism in East Africa," *African Quarterly,* Vol. VI, No. 3, December 1966, Mazrui, *Post-Imperial Fragmentation: The Legacy of Ethnic and Racial Conflict (A Publication of the University of Denver, Vol. I, No. 2, 1969–1970), and* Mazrui, *Cultural Engineering and Nation-Building in East Africa,* (Evanston, Illinois: Northwestern University Press, 1972) pp. 209–228.
5. See Robert P. Hey, "What help for black capitalism?" *Christian Science Monitor,* May 5, 1969, pp. 1 and 8. Consult also Theodore L. Cross, *Black Capitalism: A Strategy for Business in the Ghetto* (New York: Atheneum, 1969).
6. The 1969 figures constitute, according to Hey, 28 percent of all SBA's loans, and 13 percent of the total value.
7. See "Nixon is accused of failing to promote 'Black Capitalism'," *Herald Tribune,* July 25, 1969.
8. Quoted by Abram L. Harris, *The Negro as Capitalist* (Philadelphia: American Academy of Political and Social Science, 1936), pp. 49–52.
9. *Report of the Eleventh Annual Convention of the National Negro Business League* (Nashville: A.M.E. Sunday School Union, 1911) p. 11.
10. See E. Franklin Frazier, *Black Bourgeoisie* (New York: Collier Book, 1968, pp. 136–

137. Although excessively polemical in parts, this book is a major contribution. I am grateful to it for some insights and for bibliographical guidance.

11. *Ibid.*, p. 139.

12. Dennis Hunt, "Jim Brown and Raquel Welch in Bed: Yet More Interracial Naughtiness," *The Daily Californian,* May 16, 1969, p. 21. See also the light biography of Sidney Poitier by Carolyn H. Ewers entitled *Sidney Poitier: The Long Journey* (New York: The New American Library, 1969).

13. *Ibid.*

14. For an analysis of America's entry into the 1960's with widespread laws against miscegenation see Arthur Krock, "Miscegenation Debate" *New York times Weekly Review,* September 8, 1963. For the Gallup Poll in which for the first time the American electorate envisages the possibility of voting for a black President see *New York Times,* April, 1969. Of interest also from the point of view of the endogamous inhibitions is Calvin C. Hernton's *Sex and Racism in America.* (New York: Doubleday, 1965).

15. In discussing black capitalism this chapter has again borrowed heavily from Mazrui, *Post-Imperial Fragmentation: The Legacy of Ethnic and Racial Conflict.*

CHAPTER 14

Economic Modernization and International Equity

In the last chapter we discussed the modernization of stratification and motivation in relation to American and East African experiments. The move from caste relations to class relations does in part overlap with Sir Henry Maine's concept of transition from status to contract as an index of modernized human relations. And the purposeful creation of black capitalism in East Africa and the United States—out of the ashes of colonialism and slavery respectively—could become a powerful human saga under the title of "From Bondsmen to Bourgeoisie". Underlying it all is, once again, the universe of economic culture and its consequences for the distribution of power.

Caste and Class in International Relations

On the international scene, the question of economic mobility remains critical for both social justice and economic welfare. Here too there is an important difference between an international class system and an international caste system. A class system in the international sphere consists primarily in differences in per capita income. Nations become graded on a scale which moves from indigence to affluence. Potentialities for mobility within the system, that is, the capacity to increase per capita income and perhaps even close the gap between this or that country, are within the bounds of possibility. But an international *caste* system is again a more rigid phenomenon. Just as in the case of a single society a caste system perpetuates itself by relating gradation to unchangeable hereditary factors, so in the international system gradation is rigidified by trying to base economic specialization on unchangeable climatic and geophysical factors. This underlay the imperial vision of a "partnership" between the colonies as sources of raw material and the metropolitan countries as manufacturers. When European countries were negotiating the Treaty of Rome in the second half of the 1950's that doctrine of interdependence, of "partnership", was implicit in the French vision of "Eur-Africa" on which the French based their case for the association of French Africa with the European Economic Community.[1]

There had indeed been a time when western capital, seeking raw materials in the colonies, served as an instrument of development in those very colonies. There emerged something approaching a genuine interdependence between the metropolitan center of industry and the colonial periphery of producers of raw materials. A caste system is indeed a system of interdependence, with specialization of roles, but including within that specialization a clear hierarchy of advantage. Lord Lugard, perhaps the greatest British administrator in tropical Africa, saw the economic relationship between Europe and Africa as being essentially one in which tropical raw materials left Africa to go to Europe and then some of them returned to Africa "converted into articles for the use and comfort of its peoples".[2]

Presumably it was even best that cocoa should be converted into chocolate in Europe and then returned to the Ghanaian chocolate consumer at the cheapest price possible in the short run. In the assessment of metropolitan interests, such an arrangement would be preferable to the initiation of processing industries in the countries which produced the raw materials, considering that in the short run the locally produced might be more expensive than the imported.

Such a scale of values nationalists in Africa have regarded as an extension, perhaps in a glorified twentieth century version, of the old idea of allotting to the African the role of a "hewer of wood and drawer of water." And such a division of labor is again basically a caste division. The British political economist, Thomas Soper, once retorted: "If wood is wanted and people are prepared to pay for it, I fail to see what is lost by being a hewer of it."[3]

According to this reasoning, producing tropical products can, after all, be an instrument of development in its own right. Yet even if the terms of trade were to remain favorable for primary producers, and Europe were to continue to buy cocoa from Ghana, there would still remain a serious imbalance because there is little meaningful "interdependence" left between the producer of cocoa in Africa and the buyer in Europe. Europe could presumably live without buying chocolate, but could Ghana live without selling cocoa, if her economy depended overwhelmingly on cocoa?

In fact, the worsening terms of trade were aggravating the caste gap. The French vision of a "Eur-Africa" was, as an economic assessment, anachronistic from the very moment it was propounded in the 1950's. This was because a significant shift had already taken place in the relationship of reciprocal dependence between Africa and Europe. Indeed, by 1941 Lord Lugard himself was already drawing attention to this shift and invoking the authority of international statisticians in the League of Nations and the findings of the Royal Institute of International Affairs. The main staples of industry such as iron, cotton, and petroleum were, Lugard noted, produced by the older dominions and India "and not by the colonies". It was also from them that the chief food supply of the world was derived—wheat and other cereals, meat of all kinds, dairy produce, animal and vegetable oils and fats. The conclusion to which Lugard drew attention from the findings of the experts was that except in the case of rubber, colonial areas accounted for "only about 3% of the world's production of raw materials."[4]

Since then indications have been that Europe's internal production has continued to grow more rapidly than its needs for imports, and some of the previously imported raw materials can now be produced within the frontiers of at least the West as a whole. Barbara Ward Jackson, in a study of the economics of underdevelopment in relation to the richer countries, drew attention to the emergence of such items as artificial rubber, new fabrics for textiles, petrochemicals, and "conceivably even ersatz chocolate". She noted specifically that the western world's "pull of development" on the outside world has declined in magnitude since the early days of the West's industrial expansion.[5]

Consequently the greatest problem that a newly independent Africa has to face now is the problem of an *increasingly independent Europe.* Europe's independence is not complete, especially in relation to such sources of energy as oil, uranium, and bauxite, but on the whole Europe now needs Africa far less than she once did. Within the context of that problem, the old imperial vision of "the abounding wealth of the tropical regions" has now been deflated into "the dangerous poverty of the underdeveloped areas".

We have already analyzed ethnic stratification in single societies as being basically caste relations. In the international sphere too ethnicity touches the issue of caste stratification. Westerners themselves have become vaguely disturbed more recently about the implications both of the distribution of wealth in the world and of the relative coincidence between this distribution and racial differences. Radical opinion in the West sometimes sees the problem in terms of blind economic forces dividing the world into a white bourgeoisie and a colored proletariat. The blind economic forces which are stratifying the world in this way include, of course, falling prices of primary commodities and trade imbalance generally. Arnold Smith, the Canadian diplomat who became the first Secretary-General of the Commonwealth of Nations, said on taking office, "the division of humanity between the white and the other races, which coincides too closely for comfort with the division between the affluent industrialized peoples and the poor underdeveloped peoples is, I think, the most difficult and potentially dangerous problem in the world."[6]

It is not of course completely true that the division between the rich and the poor coincides with the division between the fairer and darker races of the world. Much of Latin America must be included in the poorer sector of the world. And Latin America is usually conceived of as a white continent, with some Indian and Negro mixture. But it is true that almost all the rich countries of the world are white, and almost all the non-white countries are poor. It is therefore possible for nationalists in Africa for example to think of their continent as "a proletarian continent" with all the connotations of revolutionary potential.[7]

But even nonradical opinion in the West has had its own way of responding to the implications of racial disparities. The year 1960 saw the independence explosion in Africa when sixteen new states came into being. Writing the following year for the *New York Times,* James Reston claimed that Britain believed in a continuing dialogue between the West and Russia for reasons of future protection of the white races against the pressure of races far more numerous. Looking at the same long-range future a French official, talking to Reston, had forecast that "the great conflict at the end of the century will not be ideological, but racial."[8] This French prediction of the racial conflict in the years ahead was similar to what was predicted by the American black nationalist, W.E.B. DuBois, in an article in *Foreign Affairs* much earlier in the century. DuBois had argued that the racial problem was going to be a persistent theme in the turmoil of the twentieth century.[9]

Both ethnicity and climate are relatively rigid criteria of stratification. A system of international division of labor which sentences large sections of the colored population of the world to a form of economic activity whose returns are on the decline, must be regarded as no less premodern than domestic caste arrangements.

The process of modernization therefore must aim at facilitating mobility in the international system of stratification. Foreign aid and foreign investment are, as we indicated, important instruments in the modernization of economic techniques and processes. But foreign aid and foreign investment could have the effect of perpetuating the caste system if they promote forms of economic specialization detrimental to the long-term interests of the less developed countries. When aid and investment do result in such specialization, they are abetting caste perpetuation. Increased international economic mobility partly requires a commitment to the principle of optimum diversification of productive activities in each society. The old imperial idea of a partnership between primary producing colonies and manufacturing metropolitan centers was a vision of economic complementarity. But the fostering of diversification in the poor countries, with renewed emphasis upon industrialization alongside modernized agriculture is a policy which might involve a vision of economic competitiveness between the older countries and the new. Economic competitiveness is often a determinant of social mobility in a single society. Effective competitiveness makes it possible to have a relatively fluid class system in a given society. But where the vision is economic complementing between primary and secondary producers, there is a danger that the old imperial division of labor with its caste implications will detain the world in its premodern stage of international evolution.

Stratification is perhaps the central meeting point of problems of potential violence, economic welfare, and social justice. The stability of a caste system derives from a high degree of acceptance of the system by those who live in it, are affected by it, and form part of it. In premodern societies a caste system retains its assured existence if it is adequately sanctified by a long tradition of acquiescence and neo-religious resignation. A caste system on the international plane would also have been assured adequate stability if the poor continued to accept their lot, and wealth were regarded as a legitimate prerogative of the wealthy. But the transformation of expectations in the world, the impact of the international demonstration effect, the manifold implications of the communications revolution and greater awareness of the potentialities of human advancement, have all introduced profoundly destabilizing factors into the international system of economic gradation. To use the popular phrases of the age, the revolution of rising expectations, when confronted with the rigid obstacles to rapid change, might indeed degenerate into a "revolution of rising frustrations". The division of the world into a rich northern hemisphere and a poor southern hemisphere has therefore been regarded as a point of perilous cleavage in the current economic arrangements of the world.

Horizontal and Hierarchical Specialization

We have defined an international caste system in terms of division of labor. But here a fundamental distinction needs to be made between a horizontal division of labor and a heirarchical division of labor. A horizontal division is basically between equals, either all underdeveloped or all developed. The division of enterprise between them does not contain a principle inherently disadvantageous to one side, nor a relationship of deference or obedience between one side and another.

A hierarchical division of labor, on the other hand, leads to a caste system when it is rigid. Sentencing the countries of the tropics to a life of primary production indefinitely while the western hemisphere is industrialized and diversified would amount to a hierarchical division of labor. Certainly the old partnership in the imperial order between producers of raw materials in the colonies and manufacturers in the metropolitan powers amounted, in terms of real disparities between the two sides, to a hierarchical order.

In thinking about developments in the next thirty years in the economic arrangements of the world, it might make sense to promote within the less developed world a horizontal form of division of labor, while at the same time ending the pre-existent hierarchical division of labor between the northern and southern hemispheres. The promotion of intraregional division of labor on a horizontal basis might help serve the cause of regional integration, while the promotion of interregional competitive relations between the developing and the developed countries should help introduce areas of economic equality in the relations between the north and the south.

The promotion of horizontal division of labor among the developing countries themselves should help to increase their own need for each other and their capacity to trade with each other. It has been pointed out all too often that African countries, for example, are economically competitive rather than complementary, making any proposals for closer economic union in Africa more difficult than ever to implement. Those Africans who have sometimes said "We would rather establish an African Common Market than be associated with the European Common Market" have therefore appeared to be somewhat naive. Even within the East African Community of Kenya, Uganda and Tanzania, only a small proportion of the volume of trade of each country is, in fact, with the others. Most of East Africa's trade remains with other countries abroad.

Let us therefore accept the supposition that the competitive nature of African economies generally makes closer African economic union either more difficult or less meaningful. If, at the same time, we further assume that Africans are nevertheless vaguely desirous of closer union, we might recommend to them a systematic *creation* of, initially, artificial economic interdependence between the African countries themselves. A more modest ambition which could be pursued is to avoid making African economies any more competitive in the future. This need not mean making the economies complementary. The countries could produce different things but not necessarily for exchange among each other. Yet even this has its problems. As Julius Nyerere of Tanzania told the East African Legislative assembly in May 1963, if his country avoided duplicating her neighbors' industries she would "end up with nothing because everything we want you will be able to find in Kenya or Uganda."[10]

All the same, if British imperial policy in central Africa made the old Nyasaland, Northern Rhodesia, and Southern Rhodesia increasingly interdependent, that policy had at least established that the economies of some African countries could, as a deliberate act of policy, be made more complementary. Zambia after independence has had a hard time trying to break her relationship of interdependence with Rhodesia after U.D.I.. The systematic creation of a division of labor among the three members of the old Central African Federation had long-term consequences for those countries themselves.

Could a similar act of policy foster greater interdependence between other developing states within Africa and other states in the Third World at large? The East African Community's allocation of specialized industrial "monopolies" to each country as attempted first by the Kampala Agreement and then by the Treaty of East African Cooperation is the kind of venture which could augment complementarity between African economies and increase intraregional trade between countries within the same region. In reality the workings of the East African Community are not adequately smooth, and the other provisions of the Treaty do not always help in fostering a real division of labor among the member states. But the principle underlying the allocation of industries within the East African Community bears some resemblance to this proposed quest for a purposeful creation of a horizontal division of labor among the less developed countries of the world.

But in their relations with the developed world the task should remain one of increasing the competitiveness of at least a region as a whole within the southern hemisphere in its economic interaction with countries in the nothern hemisphere. Horizontal division of labor intraregionally and collective competitiveness between a less developed region and countries in the developed world are two desirable reforms worthy of being pursued in the last three decades of the twentieth century. Such a policy would make less developed countries more dependent on each other, on the one hand, and less vulnerable to the economic power of the economically mighty, on the other.

Even economic complementarity among member states of the Third World should, from the point of view of ultimate welfare arrangements and even social justice, be transitional. We have already partly defined the process of modernization in terms of recognizing the potentialities of man as an innovative being. The society of the future should therefore

293

aim for optimum diversification of creative opportunities within each society. Kwame Nkrumah once said that Africa could not hope to "improve the skill and ingenuity of her peoples by keeping them solely as workers in rural areas."[11]

Marx, Engels, and even Lenin distrusted the whole idea of division of labor partly because it was inconsistent with the vision of human versatility. The Marxist concept of *alienation* is partly definable in terms of frustrated human creativity. Division of labor within single societies, particularly as it forced factory workers to specialize in narrow areas of skill, amounted to sentensing man to a life of perpetual incompleteness. It is partly because of this that the Marxist utopia of the classless society includes within it the ideal of optimal versatility in human endeavor. And so it is that Marxism envisages that utopia in terms of every man being able to "hunt in the morning, fish in the afternoon, rear cattle in the evening, criticize after dinner without ever becoming hunter, fisherman, shepherd or critic."[12]

The Dependency Complex

The third dimension of economic modernization lies, as we indicated, in the realm of social psychology—the modernization of motivation. In an article published in 1968, Udai Pareek enumerates three motivations important for planned social change: the achievement motive, the extension motive, and the dependency motive. Development, he argues, is a function of those three motives, although dependency motivation contributes negatively. "In other words, for effecting social change achievement motivation and extension motivation should be developed, and dependency motivation should be drastically reduced."[13] In relating the dependency complex more directly to economics, we must examine two factors to which Pareek does not address himself. One is the balance of efficacy among the three motives of achievement, extension (or empathy), and dependency; and the second is the question of whether the three motives operate in the same way in international behavior as in the behavior of individuals in a single society.

The negative motivation of dependency has been examined by clinical psychologists but has received less attention from social psychologists. Murray did indeed discuss "psychogenic need" and "succorance" as being near to the concept of dependency. Behavioral characteristics are enumerated by Murray as the wish to have one's needs gratified by the sympathetic aid of an allied object; the wish to be protected, loved, advised, guided, and indulged; the desire to remain close to a devoted protector and, if possible, to have a permanent supporter.[14]

Pareek is more explicitly concerned with the wider social implications of the dependency motivation. He regards the concept in the social sphere as being derived from the general paradigm that a particular societal system generates a correspondence motivation, and further that a feudal system generates dependency motivation. "Dependency motivation in social behavior is expressed through lack of initiative, avoidance syndromes (shifting responsibilities to others, exaggerating obstacles), excessive fear of failure, seeking favors of superiors, over-conformism, and aggressive rejection of authority (which has been called counter-dependency)."[15]

Pareek argues that dependency motivation is very high in feudal society where rewards are related to the individual's closeness to an authority figure, and where hierarchical gradations are the very basis of the system. We have already discussed certain aspects of the colonial division of labor as being basically a caste system with a feudalistic element of dependency and authority. The imperial system did to some extent imply an international feudal system complete with readiness to raise armies from the colonies to fight the wars of imperial authority.

With the breakdown of the formal feudalistic arrangements which were implicit in imperial relations, dignified assertiveness has emerged among the lower strata of the international system. The quest for equality and self-reliance has been an important feature of the post-colonial ethos. But it would be a mistake to conclude that the dependency motive which arose out of imperial relationships has as yet disappeared. Even the demands for aid totally without strings tend to connote a dependency complex. I had occasion to argue once at a public meeting in Kampala that foreign aid completely without strings was an insult to human dignity, and that free aid should be avoided unless the situation is one in which no conceivable reciprocal service is feasible between donor and recipient. The truth is that aid is hardly ever granted totally without strings; and if it were, it would definitely denote a lack of equality between donor and the recipient. A relationship of absolute charity is a relationship of inequality.

No two developed states ever give to each other major economic gifts without an attempt to arrive at some form of reciprocity; and the more nearly equal the negotiating states are the tougher the bargain about reciprocal concessions and benefits. There can be no major transfers of economic advantages from, say, France to Britain without a close calculation of what the French will get in return. Even in relations between the United States and Britain, though less equal than relations between Britain and France, the idea of what one party gains from a special favor it does for the other is never absent. When a developing country demands to be given aid completely freely, with no strings attached whatsoever, it

295

is demanding absolute charity—and absolute charity is not a normal relationship between real peers.

Of course, the very fact that one is receiving aid is an admission of at least a temporary inequality. But the more one gives in return for that aid the less it is aid. Strings attached to aid help to make the exercise a mutual transaction; the donor is not entirely a benefactor but also a beneficiary. The recipient of the aid is not entirely a beneficiary but becomes in his own right a benefactor by extending some reciprocal favor to the donor. The real issue between equals in matters of aid is not whether there are strings but what kinds of strings, and the whole business of scrutinizing strings and negotiating about them is an assertion of parity of esteem.[16]

As we mentioned earlier, aggressive political sensitivities can in fact be a symptom of "counter-dependency". Neo-colonialism is sometimes a real threat, but there are times when conspiratorial "neo-colonial" theories are animated by a desire to shift responsibility to others. This can be an indication of the dependency complex. The problem of development in new states, therefore, includes both the gradual erosion of the dependency complex and the growth of the achievement motive in the developing countries, and the growth of empathy in the international behavior of the developed countries. The dependency motive may itself be a variable which is dependent on other social and economic factors. Perhaps the dependency complex will automatically decline as residual imperial habits themselves lose their efficacy, and as greater self-confidence emerges in developing countries with the rise of status and the realization of certain ambitions.

Achievement and Empathy Motives

Let us now look more closely at those two other motivations relevant to socioeconomic change—achievement and empathy or extension. Achievement motivation is defined in terms of a psychological urge to excel in areas of competitive endeavor. David C. McClelland calls this psychological impulse "n-Achievement". He has argued that a high level of achievement motivation in a nation produces more people prepared to take risks and therefore more people who engage in entrepreneurial activities. He has discerned this relationship even in tribal and preliterate societies studied in Africa, Asia, South Pacific, and in North America among the Indian tribes.

Despite many flaws in the collection of such cross-cultural data, they confirm the hypothesis that the n-Achievement level of a society is a variable significantly related to entrepreneurial economic activity in a culture, despite wide variations in social structure, in climate, means of subsistence, and level of technological development. The data also hint that tribes with high *n* Achievement are readier to adopt more efficient but also more complex and difficult means of earning a living, while the tribes with the lower *n* Achievement appear to be more tradition-bound, particularly in the religious sphere. It does, indeed, seem possible that Weber's observation of the connection between Protestantism and the rise of Capitalism may be a special instance of a much more general phenomenon.[17]

Even in modern society, McClelland argues, economic development is correlated to the availability of sufficient numbers of people who have a strong need to be agents of change, derive satisfaction from personal accomplishments, and have developed skills and traits which make it possible for them to achieve these goals. It is clear that one form which this kind of motivation has taken in the evolution of western societies is the symbol of "rugged individualism". The creation of an entrepreneurial culture in a given society therefore implies a certain degree of individuation.

Pareek's concept of the extension motive, on the other hand, is socially rather than individually oriented. "Extension motivation is reflected in the need to extend the ego to society."[18] What is involved in the extension motivation is a capacity by the individual to socialize the self. And this in turn is the secret of empathy. The individual sees his own pride and sense of achievement partly in terms of the pride and achievement of his social group. At its most developed, empathy is what McClelland has called "concern for the common welfare of all".[19]

Pareek argues that the recent histories of countries which have struggled against colonialism and imperial rule have illustrated a high level of extension motivation. An analysis of the songs, stories, and other mass media material during those periods in such countries showed such a level. "Extension motivation is reflected in regard for other persons, cooperation with others for the achievement of a common goal, faith and trust in members of the group, and involvement in goals which concern not only oneself but society at large."[20]

We have indicated that Pareek does not adequately deal with the relative balance between those two motives in their impact on behavior. The two motives are not in effect mutually exclusive but are often both present in the behavior of most people. The balance of the motives in the population of a given society is a critical variable in determining the impact of motivation on the economic performance of that society. We have also indicated that Pareek does not concern himself with the place of motivation in international behavior, and the extent to which achievement, empathy, and dependency influence economic interaction at the international level. Our hypothesis is that the modernization of motivation in the world entails, first, a calculated increase of achievement motivation in developing societies in their domestic economic behavior, and second, a calculated increase of empathic or *extension* motivation in developed societies in their international economic behavior. We shall take these two aspects of the proposition in turn.

In the domestic behavior of many premodern societies in Asia and Africa a preponderance of the extension motive, sometimes in conflict with the achievement motive, results from an interplay between kinship culture and economic culture. The extension motive in Africa, for example, arises out of the collectivist sensitivities of individuals in their traditional setting. The approval of the tribe, clan, or extended family is a powerful influence on the behavior of the individual, and disapproval of the traditional group of identification serves as a powerful deterrent for that individual. The extension motive has raised serious economic problems, among them trying to get people to save. Earnings are expended on kinship obligations, on entertainment and hospitality, on ostentatious weddings, expensive funerals, and initiation ceremonies. Many a struggling businessman has at best a blunted profit motive—torn as he is between the desire to make money for himself and the desire to let his kith and kin benefit by what his enterprise yields. As we indicated earlier, these are some of the issues which economic reformers in Kenya and Uganda have had to confront.

To the extent that empathy lies at the heart of the extension motive, it is quite often socially more ethical than the profit motive. Nevertheless, this commitment to some degree of altruism is not unconnected with fear of disapproval. The canons of hospitality and kinship obligations are maintained partly out of conviction, and partly out of a wish to be respected—but ultimately because of a desire to maintain a sense of belonging to a social group and to avert the burden of disapproval. Precisely because the extension motive in traditional contexts encompasses within itself this web of complex impulses, it is a motive which defies any attempt to compartmentalize economic interests from other forms of interests. The economic factor refuses to be isolated from the complex of general motivation at large.

As we intimated in the previous chapter, what is needed in African economic enterprise is a capacity to accept the tautology that "business is business", which seeks to assert the autonomy of the economic factor and the independence of economic culture from kinship culture. Many aspiring African businessmen have yet to be socialized into a complete acceptance of the tautology "Business is business". They might succumb to family pressures for special concessions or prices in business relations—often reducing the whole economic exercise to a noneconomic venture. The extension motive here operates as hypersensitivity to kinship obligations and special loyalties. Sometimes ministers in East Africa have complained that African businessmen leave their shops at the slightest social pretext, to attend a funeral or an initiation ceremony. Far too often customers relying on African shopkeepers have had to divert their custom to the more persistently business-like behavior of their Indian counterparts. Surprisingly, the Indians in East Africa found a better relationship between kinship culture and economic culture than did the Africans. The marginality of the Asians enabled them to rally kinship solidarity behind economic effectiveness.

The African businessman sometimes attends an initiation ceremony or funeral during business hours rather reluctantly. He is unwilling to invoke the excuse of "pressure of business" and, even more important, his kin refuse to accept such an excuse as legitimate. To sacrifice greater loyalties to one's people for the sake of an extra penny earned at one's shop is usually a very serious charge for most members of African social groups. What we discussed in the last chapter was an attempt in East Africa to lend greater respectability to the achievement motive.

A related factor in this tension between personal achievement and the spirit of the extended ego is the attitude to work and the motivation which leads to hard work. Once again economic culture and work norms are inseparable. Why should one work hard? For the satisfaction of personal improvement or for the prestige of having tribal hangers-on? Or should one work hard only for limited targets—and then relax to enjoy the ancestral village? Underlying all these questions is the persistent struggle to modify the balance of efficacy between the achievement motive and the empathetic or extension motive in African traditional behavior.

The Psychology of International Behavior

When we look at the balance of these motives in general international behavior, we find a reversal of motivation is needed. The first point to bear in mind is the asymmetry in motivation as between the aid-giver in the contemporary world and the aid-receiver. The developing countries find themselves confronted with major areas of deficiencies in the productive and welfare processes of their countries. They negotiate with the richer nations for aid in order to try and correct those deficiencies. On the other hand, the motivation behind the giving of aid among major powers is *political* rather than economic; aid is an aspect of their foreign policy and political diplomacy. Sometimes the political dividends occur in the metropolitan countries themselves. Aid given to or withheld from

Israel is a matter of importance in the domestic politics of the United States.

Of course, the asymmetry implied in the motivation between the donor and the recipient is exaggerated here. There are often elements of economic calculation in the motives of the aid-giver and political considerations behind the behavior of the developing country seeking aid. Although the picture is not as neat as our analysis might suggest, there is no doubt that the balance of motive in the giving of aid is basically political, while the balance of motive in seeking aid is ultimately economic.

In pursuit of the preferred world of the 1990's it becomes important to look more closely at the politics of aid-giving because here might lie another area where motivation might need to be modernized in at least a special sense.

Political motives in international behavior are ultimately reducible to that central concept of national policies—the pursuit of the national self-interest. The realist school of international analysis has much evidence to support it from the experience of the international system in the past. The question which arises is whether the modernization of diplomatic behavior necessitates either the elimination or the transformation of the concept of national interest as the ultimate impulse behind state behavior.

Both the realist school of international analysis on the one hand, and the champions of world government, on the other, accept to some extent the basic Hobbesian interpretation that sovereigns in their relations with each other are indeed in a state of potential war since they recognize no common superior with authority to settle disputes between themselves, and since they insist on at least a theoretical equality between one sovereign and another. But the Hobbesian element in the philosophy of world governmentalists, is, curiously enough, more pessimistic than the Hobbesianism element in the realist school. The world governmentalists see the absence of government as a state of war in a more *imminent* sense. That is why they feel a sense of urgency about filling the international gap of anarchy with viable institutions of authority.

On the other hand, the realist school of international analysis, as symbolized by Hans Morgenthau, while regarding the international "state of war" as being a state of potential war, by no means considers it a state of imminent war or even unavoidable war. To some extent the realist school is an attempt to internationalize Adam Smith's conception of the invisible hand. Just as in single countries the pursuit of self-interest by individual members of society is guided by an invisible hand toward the cumulative welfare of the society as a whole, so in the international system does the pursuit of the national interest by individual states permit a healthy system of interstate relations and harmony between sovereign powers. Transgressions are indeed possible both domestically and internationally, but the realist school of international analysis would not regard that as a nullification of its belief in international harmony in spite of the pursuit of the national interest. As Stanley H. Hoffmann has put it:

... the "realist" theory combines a Hobbesian image of naked power politics with an attempt to show that states are nevertheless not condemned to a life that is "nasty, brutish, and short"; "realism" thus puts its faith in voluntary restraint, moderation, and the underlying assumption of possible harmony among national interests. . . .[21]

If then both the realists and the world governmentalists believe that the present international system is one of nations acting basically as "rugged individualists", the great transformation of motivation required here is, on the one hand, a reduction of the self-oriented achievement motive among nations and, on the other hand, the strengthening of the empathetic motive. The process is the reverse of that which is required for a motivational revolution in developing societies. Paradoxically, the modernization of the international system entails the application of certain tribal values to the human race as a whole. Marshall McLuhan has talked about retribalization in a global sense—the conversion of the world into a village as a result of the communications revolution. International mobility, the use of satellites for television, the transistor revolution, the growth of literacy and the homogenization of cultures—all these can indeed be seen as trends toward the globalization of face-to-face relationships and the universalization of certain village values.[22]

Needless to say, to describe the impact of the communications revolution as a process of retribalizing the world on a global scale is itself a massive exaggeration. But there are important elements of truth in this line of analogy. What needs to be added to this picture of a brave new world is the need for economic retribalization in the international sphere—the globalization of kinship obligations among human kinsmen scattered far from each other's immediate societies.

Conclusion

We have attempted to demonstrate in the last two chapters that a comprehensive approach to economic reform in the world has to rely on a three-dimensional process of modernization. A dependent dimension is the modernization of economic techniques and processes. The transfer of skills and of machinery, the construction of viable institutions and infrastructure for production are the essential elements in this first process. We shall look at this dependent process once again in a later chapter more fully. But success in the modernization of techniques and processes depends in turn upon two other processes—the modernization of motivational patterns and the modernization of stratification, both profoundly *cultural.* The modernization of stratification entails optimizing socioeconomic mobility both domestically and internationally. It means the replacement of a relatively rigid caste system with a highly flexible class system of gradation.

We know that social mobility is important domestically as a precondition of adequate income distribution. But a similar mobility in the international gradation is necessary if areas of possible confrontation between the developed and the developing countries are to be reduced in number and in potential explosiveness. We have indicated that a neat confrontation between the developed northern hemisphere and the underdeveloped southern hemisphere is unlikely, but there are already areas of tension between sectors of each hemisphere, arising partly out of economic disparities and exploitative relationships. In any case it should be noted that poverty has the potential of being used as a basis of militant mobilization against the privileged. The imperative of minimizing areas of potential violence in the preferred world of the 1990's demands therefore the restructuring of economic relationships in the world in the direction of reduced revolutionary potential. To anticipate a revolution is itself a revolutionary precaution. The act of anticipating a revolution by providing the changes necessary to avert it could hopefully amount to substituting a peaceful revolution for a violent one.

But the restructuring of the economic arrangements of the world has also a direct bearing on increased social justice and welfare. Indigence and indignity are interrelated phenomena. By definition the poor cannot be sufficiently free in the positive sense, nor can they be adequately dignified in the presence of the more affluent.

It has been a basic premise of our argument that complete equality is an impossible utopia, and the pursuit of social justice and increased welfare should not take the form of seeking to abolish classes altogether but of maximizing mobility among domestic classes and among different economic gradations of state. Aplying this to the relationship between the developed northern hemisphere and the underdeveloped southern hemisphere, we have advanced the recommendation that within the southern hemisphere there should be increased promotion of economic complementarity among its members, through the calculated pursuit of a horizontal division of labor. But in the relations between the poorer regions and the rich the policy should be directed against the prevailing hierarchical division of labor. In other words, the poorer regions should be internally complementary to each other but externally competitive with the developed world.[23]

On the question of modernizing motivational patterns, we have used the distinction between achievement motives and extension motives. Achievement motives are oriented toward a need for self-accomplishment, while the empathetic or extension motive takes the form of the extended ego from individual well-being to social concern. In the traditional behavior patterns of the developing world we have recommended that the quest should be toward the promotion of greater achievement motivation as a way of optimizing risk taking, increasing preoccupation with personal accomplishment, and creating an entrepreneurial culture. The traditional extension motive of concern with the welfare of the kinship group should by no means be abolished altogether, but should be moderated by some degree of personal economic ambition and commitment.[24]

In the international sphere, on the other hand, the extension motive as the capability of one nation to emphathize economically with another needs to be nourished to greater efficacy. The national ego of one society has all too often been inadequately capable of extending itself to empathize with another in terms of mutual economic obligations. The task at the international level of motivational pattern is therefore, in some ways, the reverse of the task at the domestic level in developing societies. What needs to be moderated and reduced domestically as a basis of behavior needs to be nourished and expanded in international behavior – and vice versa.

The promotion of the extension motive in international behavior might need a more systematic utilization of the communications revolution to strengthen current trends toward global empathy. Greater awareness in developing societies of the wealth and potentialities of the rich nations has been an important contributory factor toward the revolution of rising expectations. Rising expectations in turn have a part to play toward the evolution of the achievement motive. The demonstration effect of the developed on the developing world becomes a major product of the communications revolution. But there is at the moment an imbalance in this transmission of information. A greater awareness within the developed world of levels of poverty, indigence, and underdevelopment in the southern hemisphere might in turn initiate in the northern hemisphere a revolution of diminishing complacency. Awareness of wealth among the poor should make the poor more ambitious, and awareness of poverty among the rich should help to make the rich less indifferent. The two processes of rising expectations in the southern hemisphere and diminishing complacency in the northern, promoted in part by the impact of global communications, should result in a more balanced villagization of human perspectives. When man succeeds in recapturing selectively the ethos of kinship obligations, and applies the ethos not to small-scale societies but to human relations at the global level, the process of retribalizing the world in the direction of egalitarian interdependence will indeed be well under way. The preferred world of the 1990's should be, in the ultimate analysis, a world under the influence of such a vision.

Footnotes

1. For a discussion of this see Uwe Kitzinger, *The Challenge of the Common Market* (Oxford: Blackwell, July 1962), p. 93.
2. Lugard, *The Dual Mandate in British Tropical Africa* (Edinburgh and London: W. Blackwell 1926), pp. 60–62.
3. "Africa and the Common Market" *The Listener,* August 10, 1961.
4. See Lugard, *Federal Union and the Colonies,* Federal Tract No. 7 (London: Macmillan, 1941), pp. 7–8.
5. See Barbara Ward, *The Rich Nations and the Poor Nations* (New York: W.W. Norton, 1962), pp. 31–34. See also Mazrui, *Towards a Pax Africana* (Chicago: U. Chicago P., 1967), pp. 90–92.
6. See *Manchester Guardian Weekly* July 1st, 1965, p. 5.
7. See for example President Sékou Touré's article "Africa's Destiny," in James Duffy and Robert A. Manners (editors), *Africa Speaks* (Princeton: D. Van Nostrand, 1961).
8. James Reston, "The Problem of Race in World Politics" *New York Times,* December 13, 1961.
9. DuBois, in 1925, was repeating something he had said even earlier. See W.E. DuBois, "Worlds of Color," *Foreign Affairs,* April 1925. Reprinted in Philip W. Quigg (editor) *Africa: A Foreign Affairs Reader* (New York: Frederick A. Praeger, 1964), pp. 32–52.
10. See *Proceedings,* The Central Legislative Assembly, May 1963. Mr. Nyerere was of course indulging in a rhetorical exaggeration. Consult also Mazrui, *On Heroes and Uhuru-Worship* (London: Longmans Green, 1967), pp. 71–72.
11. See *Ghana Today,* February 28th 1962.
12. *German Ideology* (1846)
13. Pareek, "Motivational patterns and planned social change," *International Social Science Journal,* Vol. XX, No. 3, 1968, p. 467. See also Pareek, "A Motivational Paradigm of Development," *Indian Educational Review,* Vol. 2, No. 2, 1967, pp. 105–11.
14. C. S. Hall and G. Lindzey, *Theories of Personalities* (New York: Wiley, 1957).
15. Pareek, *op. cit,* pp. 470–471.
16. See Mazrui, "The Functions of Anti-Americanism in African Political Development," *Africa Report,* Vol. XIV, No. 1, January 1969, pp. 14–15. On the dependency complex in a colonial situation consult also O. Mannoni, *Prospero and Caliban: The Study of the Psychology of Colonisation,* translated by Pamela Powesland (London: Methuen, 1956). See also Pareek "A Motivational Paradigm of Development," *op. cit.*
17. *The Achieving Society* (New York: The Free Press, 1961), p. 70.
18. Pareek, "Motivational Patterns and Planned Social Change" *loc. cit.,* p. 469.
19. McClelland, "The Impulse to Modernization," in M. Weiner, (editor) *Modernization* (New York: Basic Books, 1966), pp. 28–39.

20. Pareek, *op. cit.,* p. 469.
21. Stanley H. Hoffman, (editor) *Contemporary Theory in International Relations* (Englewood Cliffs, N.J.: Prentice-Hall, 1960), p. 37.
22. See H. Marshall McLuhan, *Understanding Media: The Extensions of Man* (New York: McGraw-Hill, 1964).
23. John Galtung of the International Peace Research Institute in Oslo has also used the term "feudalism" in relation to certain aspects of the international system, but seemingly in a sense different from ours.
24. Achievement motivation subsumes the old profit motive, while extension motivation often includes what I have called elsewhere the *prestige motive.* See Mazrui, "Is African Development Plannable?" *On Heroes and Uhuru-Worship* (London: Longmans, 1967), pp. 137–139, and Mazrui, *Cultural Engineering and Nation-Building in East Africa* (Evanston, Illinois: Northwestern University Press, 1972) pp. 209–228.

CHAPTER 15

Toward Counterpenetration by the Third World

Ever since the energy crisis hit the headlines of the world press in 1973, a new agonizing reappraisal of interdependence among nations has been under way among scholars and men of affairs alike. Discussions have gone on between the European Economic Community and the Arab oil producers concerning the possibility of exchanging European technology for Arab oil in a bid for mutually induced economic development. The American government has explored ways of strengthening relations between western Europe and the United States in search of a new economic basis for the Atlantic partnership. The United Nations has studied the problem of raw materials in relation to international trade, and one eminent statesman after another has called for a new definition of international interdependence.

But also central to all these debates was an ancient moral problem— that of equality, at once simple and taxing, at once topical and perennial.

In the last chapter we distinguished between two *types* of division of labor—horizontal and hierarchical. In this chapter we distinguish three *stages* of interdependence—primitive, feudo-imperial, and mature. We define *primitive* interdependence as the relationship existing in conditions of rudimentary technology and limited social horizons. In most parts of the developed world, primitive interdependence within individual societies is a matter of the past, with only a few residual elements surviving to the present day. But there are small societies in the Third World still characterized by limited and narrow social horizons, and by rudimentary and primordial technology. To the extent to which members of those societies are mutually dependent for their needs, these societies exhibit precisely what we mean by primitive interdependence.

The second type of interdependence we designate as *feudo-imperial* interdependence. The epithet seeks to combine some characteristics of feudalism and some attributes of imperialism. A central characteristic of this kind of interdependence is *hierarchy,* and hierarchy takes us back to the premise of inequality as discussed in the last two chapters.

The third stage of interdependence combines sophistication with symmetry. The sophistication comes from enhanced technological capabilities and expanded social and intellectual awareness; the symmetry emerges out of a new egalitarian morality combined with *a more balanced capacity for mutual harm.* The different parties in the interdependence must not only need each other but their different needs ought to be on a scale which makes possible serious mutual dislocations in case of conflict. The energy crisis revealed the vulnerability of the developed industrial powers. The crisis also revealed the potentialities of *counter-penetration* by Third World countries into the citadels of industrial giants. Are we on the way toward *mature* interdependence between primary producers and industrial states? Only a combination of an *egalitarian ethic* and *reciprocal vulnerability,* within a framework of wider technological and intellectual frontiers, can provide the foundations of mature interdependence.

In this chapter we propose to demonstrate that relations among nations in the world as a whole have been primarily feudo-imperial in the first three quarters of the twentieth century, deprived of both the kinship solidarity of primitive interdependence and the sophisticated symmetry of mature interdependence. One of the most important question marks in the last quarter of the twentieth century is whether the human race is at last about to evolve a genuine pattern of mature interdependence before this momentous century comes to a close.

Behind these issues is the all-powerful variable of technological change. We propose to illustrate briefly that technological change within individual western societies influenced the transition first from primitive to feudo-imperial interdependence, and then much more recently from feudo-imperial to the beginnings of mature interdependence. Thus, the modernization of economic techniques and processes carried modernizing implications for stratification as well.

Again the question arises whether technological change on an *international* scale could in turn facilitate a new leap forward from feudo-imperial relationships between the developed northern hemisphere and the underdeveloped southern hemisphere to a transformed interaction on a mature plane in the last quarter of the twentieth century. The energy crisis might have once again opened up new possibilities as it revealed the inner vulnerability of feudo-imperial relationships as they have existed until now in international affairs. A new form of solidarity among the underprivileged might be on the way, a solidarity needing to perfect a comprehensive strategy of counterpenetration into the ranks of the powerful, rather than resorting to the tactic of mere withdrawal from the international capitalist system.

In the last two chapters we discussed the entrepreneurial culture in positive terms, implying that it is something which black people and the Third World in general might well cultivate. In this chapter we propose to link that recommendation to the strategy of counterpenetration. A strategy of withdrawal from the international capitalist system might give the Third World greater *autonomy* internally, but less *power* over the destiny of the rest of mankind. Counterpenetration, on the other hand, can be a claim to ultimate global power.

Technological Change and Social Imbalance

But first let us note the technological roots of the present imbalance. The most basic factor behind Europe's rise to imperial preeminence was, as we noted before, the technological revolution in Europe. The rise of new techniques of production and the utilization of new forms of energy and mechanical implements set the stage for European expansion and colonization. And behind that technological revolution were prior changes in *values* as inaugurated by the renaissance.

A basic paradox revealed itself before long. The industrial revolution in Europe prepared the way for domestic equality within each country, at the same time establishing a basis for major international disparities between the western world, on the one hand, and much of the rest of the world, on the other. Technology within Europe and North America from the eighteenth century onward was helping to lay the foundations of a more internally egalitarian western world; yet that same technology, by increasing the inventive and productive capabilities of western societies way beyond those attained by others, initiated a process of massive disparities of income and power among the nations of the world. Let us take each part of this paradox in turn and examine it more fully.

Domestically, technology served as an equalizing process partly by destroying the traditional legitimation of hierarchy. The industrial revolution in England produced new challenges from the middle classes against the ancient privileges of the landed aristocracy. Pressures began to mount for social and political reform as trade, commerce, and expanded manufacturing capabilities produced new levels of wealth among the bourgeoisie. The previous revolution of the seventeenth century in England had decided the issue as between king and parliament, in favour of parliamentary preeminence. But by the eighteenth and nineteenth centuries the issue was who controlled parliament itself. The 1832 Great Reform Bill put forward a new basis of parliamentary composition, and therefore of legislative power. As the nineteenth century

309

entered its second half, pressures were mounting for expansion of the franchise to include the new urban proletariat. This group was enfranchised before long, and the enfranchisement of rural workers followed as the century came to a close.

The industrial revolution was at the heart of these electoral and political reforms. The massive migration of people from the countryside to the cities, the growing restlessness of the newly urbanized, the pressures and social ills of new concentrations of populations, and the rise of political consciousness among the masses all prepared the way for the process of social equalization in industrial societies. Workers began to sense the need for organization, and the principle of collective bargaining entered the economic arena.

The full consolidation of labor unions in the West took much longer, going right into the twentieth century. For a while legislation was used to discourage organization among workers, and to stigmatize strikes as conspiracies, sometimes even as treason. Nevertheless, the momentum of proletarian self-consciousness was now under way, and both the labor movement and rudimentary socialist parties began to take shape in the second half of the nineteenth century in much of the western world.

This was of course also the period which saw the emergence of egalitarian thinkers like Karl Marx and Friedrich Engels. New sensibilities concerning the plight of the impoverished, increased awareness of the possibilities of income distribution, growing reluctance to see rank and status as immutable, were all part of this process of technological equalization.

But the industrial revolution was at the same time pushing western Europe and later North America further and further ahead in global terms. The western world was increasing its social and economic distance from the rest of mankind, whilst narrowing rank and status within western societies.

Three types of technology were particularly important in the rise of the West to global preeminence—the technology of production, the technology of communication, and the technology of violence. The new technology of production gave rise to the industrial revolution in the first place, indeed defining the boundaries of that revolution. The technology of communication, with new experiments in seafaring in Europe, enhanced later by the invention of the steam engine, went toward strengthening the West's capability to penetrate the rest of the world. The western world's capacity to move around, traverse oceans, cross deserts, and penetrate jungles all provided part of the necessary precondition for empire building.

As for the technology of violence, this gave the western world the edge in military sophistication. New weapons entered the battlefield, new powers of destruction and subjugation. Against the military might of the Maxim gun, the sword of Asia and the spear of Africa finally capitulated. Western Europe was triumphant, creating empires larger than any others known in history. Western Europe's superiority in the technology of violence reinforced the advantages of the technology of communication and of production, ensuring the preeminence of the western world as a whole in following generations. The same technology which was a force for gradual equalization within the western world itself was also serving the purpose of strengthening the West's domination over the rest of mankind.

Meanwhile, economic growth in the United States was laying the foundation for new levels of affluence and power. The American experience came to demonstrate even more sharply the paradox of technological change as a force for both domestic equalization and international disequilibrium.

In rhetoric, at least, the United States was one of the earliest modern experiments in the doctrines of both interdependence and egalitarianism. Federalism as a system of government was preeminently a doctrine of interdependence among coordinating elements. The American federal experiment brought into the arena of modern political institutions an innovative exercise in institutionalized interdependence. The original thirteen colonies later recruited additional constituent elements into this partnership, creating an enduring if sometimes convulsive pluralistic polity.

But the United States was also born on a wave of egalitarian rhetoric. The American Declaration of Independence asserted the conviction that all men were created equal, proceeding to draw an elaborate social contract theory from that premise of primeval equality.

Yet a major theme of inequality has persisted in the American political system from its inception to the present day. This theme touches the issue of race relations. At the time of the Declaration of Independence, the United States already had an elaborate system of both plantation and domestic slavery. Black men continued to be imported into the country for a few more decades after the American affirmation of human equality.

Yet once again it was neither America's political rhetoric, nor even the wider and older Christian morality, which created conditions for termination of the slave system. It was, in fact, technological change. As the industrial revolution got under way, new techniques of production were invented, and new skills of trade and exchange between the United States and the western world were attained. Western Europe was finding the old triangle of trade involving slaves from West Africa to the Americas, and other merchandise between the Americas and Europe, no longer efficient. The rise of humanitarian concern in Europe was substantially stimulated by the emergence of new methods of production and general technological improvements. Ultimately, it was neither John Locke nor Jesus Christ who created a responsive constituency in Europe and the Americas for the abolitionists; it was the discovery that prosperity no longer needed slavery in the old sense.

The new technology, assisted to some extent by the new science, began to rescue the black man from at least the most degrading of the different fates to which he had been subjected—that of an outright slave, available for capture or purchase, for both exploitation and humiliation. Here again, within the plantation system of the Americas in the wake of the industrial revolution in the western world, was an illustration of how technological change helped the equalization process.

But this same technology which helped to end the slave trade also helped to expand imperialism. The black man's status within the Americas showed a slight improvement after abolition, but the black man's status within the African continent was exposed to new levels of penetration and subjugation as a result of the western world's mastery of the new technology. The different European states carved out large chunks of the African continent, just as they had carved out substantial parts of the Asian continent. Human history entered its most elaborate stage of feudo-imperial relationships.

The United States did not venture far into the game of outright annexation of territory. There was territorial expansion within the North American continent, and also colonization of the Philippines. But in general the United States preferred economic imperialism without territorial annexation. Latin America acquired formal independence from Spain and Portugal, but became increasingly subject to penetration and manipulation by the United States for generations. The Monroe Doctrine, ostensibly intended to keep European powers from meddling in the affairs of the American hemisphere, became in effect a force to legitimize intervention by the United States in the affairs of Latin America without a direct planting of the star-spangled banner on Latin American territory. The relationship between the United States and the Latin American states was certainly akin to both feudalism and imperialism. A system of clients and patrons, of vassals and masters, even of Latin American barons paying tribute to Washington monarchs, dominated relations between the southern states of that hemisphere with the colossus to the north. The different political regimes in Latin America were sometimes the functional equivalent of barons in a feudal system, exacting contributions from their own rural populations as part of the tribute to the monarchical center of the hemisphere. Individual barons rose in favor, sometimes to decline and fall, partly through the manipulation of a strong monarchical center.

Feudalism in Europe's history fluctuated between periods of strong barons, manipulating the king, and periods of a strong king, playing baron against baron, dispensing favors while receiving tribute. In the relationship between the United States and Latin America the barons could not be too strong, lest either their own cavalry or peasants should be externally equipped with a capability to overthrow them. The imperial factor tended to centralize the nature of this international feudal system.

At the global level the United States grew, becoming the richest and most industrially developed country in the world. The distance between the United States and a country like Niger or Tanzania in affluence and technological sophistication illustrated that powerful tendency of modern technology to widen international disparities beyond anything conceived a few generations ago. These levels of affluence had repercussions on a global plane. The northern hemisphere as a whole consumed a staggeringly disproportionate share of the scarce resources of the world, conducted the bulk of the international trade, used vast amounts of raw materials, controlled much of the world's finance, and enjoyed the highest standard of living yet attained by man. The Third World was overshadowed in both living standards and outright power.

To some extent it did appear like a form of interdependence. Primary producers, contributing raw materials and oil and other sources of energy to the manufacturing and industrial plants of the northern hemisphere, received in return processed goods and products of a highly sophisticated technology. It was claimed that this was a sound basis for partnership between the poorer societies of the world in Asia, Africa, and Latin America, and their more affluent neighbors to the north. Copper from Zambia and Chile, coffee from Brazil and Uganda, oil from the Middle East and Venezuela, tea and jute from Pakistan, rubber from Malaya, uranium from Niger, cloves from Zanzibar, and cocoa from Ghana, all these provided a pattern of contributions from the southern hemisphere to the life-styles and methods of production of the people of the north. Back from the north came radios and bicycles, typewriters and train engines, knives and forks, padlocks and tractors. A partnership was presumed to have grown out of the natural processes of economic and industrial change. It was indeed a system of interdependence, but the interdependence was once again feudo-imperial. The richer countries seemed to be getting richer still; the poorer seemed to remain in indigence. "Nothing prospers like prosperity"—so the international system of the world seemed to affirm. An old adage discovered a new and

ominous vindication. In the international sphere, as in domestic arrangements, it appeared to be once again true that nothing succeeds like success. The northern hemisphere, under the impetus of technological success, was widening more than ever the gap existing between itself and the
less fortunate sectors of the human race.

Primitive Interdependence among Third World Countries

Against this background of feudo-imperialism and the hegemony of
the northern hemisphere, there began to develop within the southern
hemisphere of the world in the first half of this century rudiments of
primitive interdependence among the underprivileged. A form of nationalism emerged which was in fact transnational. Issues of color were
particularly important because western feudo-imperialism had for so
long included a fundamental racial theme. Within the African continent
there developed bonds south of the Sahara based mainly on a growing
recognition of a shared black destiny. East Africans began to discover
more and more about the fluctuating fortunes of West Africans, and to
develop the rudiments of empathy. West Africans discovered East and
South African Blacks, sharing some of the emotions generated by racial
confrontations.

Pan-Africanism developed as a movement, sometimes uniting only
black people south of the Sahara, sometimes uniting black people both in
the African continent and in the black diaspora, and sometimes forging
links between black Africans and the Arabs of the Sahara. Therefore,
Pan-Africanism has always been a transnational force. Because it was
based on a broad mutual recognition among Africans and Afro-Americans as kindred spirits under a racialistic system of domination, some
trend toward primitive interdependence developed. As in the case of
primitive interdependence on a small scale within individual primordial
societies, Pan-Africanism assumed a basic equality among the members
of that solidarity.

There were occasions when one group would regard itself as specially
suited to provide leadership for Africans or for black people. Certainly,
there was a time when black Americans, because of their levels of
literacy as compared with Africans and because of their basic westernization, regarded themselves as the rightful source of leadership for black
people everywhere. Even such an enlightened egalitarian as W. E. B. Du-
Bois, with all his deep socialistic inclinations, entertained for many years
the idea that black Africa needed black Americans as its leaders and carriers of the torch of modernity. DuBois had a theory somewhat related
to Mitchell's doctrine of the Iron Law of Oligarchy. Mitchell discerned

314

in the behavior of organizations a strong tendency toward the emergence of leadership and power provided by a small oligarchy within a system. DuBois believed that not only human organization but all human major enterprises had ultimately to rely on the "gifted tenth". This "gifted tenth" would provide the higher skills of foresight, leadership, and sometimes innovation. At least until the outbreak of World War II, DuBois tended to believe that among the black people the gifted tenth was ultimately to be discovered disproportionately within the black diaspora, rather than within the African continent itself.

But as the movement for independence shifted into the African continent, with leaders like Kwame Nkrumah and Jomo Kenyatta beginning to capture world attention, the doctrine of the gifted tenth in black affairs had to be drastically reexamined. Each African country might produce its own leaders and privileged groups, but no section of the black world any longer claimed a positive feudo-imperial hegemony with regard to other sections. At the time black Americans regarded themselves as the rightful bearers of the torch of progress in the black world, the emphasis in the relationship between them and the rest of the black world carried a serious risk of feudo-imperialism. But the second half of the twentieth century witnessed a levelling off, a new sense of egalitarianism between one black group and another. This was true in relative, rather than absolute, terms. Different black groups were still capable of feeling a sense of superiority over other groups, but in confronting the basic reality of domination by the western world, black people rediscovered primitive interdependence on a modest scale and used that as a basis for political liberation.

But it was not merely black people who had been humiliated and dominated by the white races in the last two to three centuries. It was also other *nonwhite* peoples, ranging from Indians to Arabs, Chinese to Filipinos. Again, finally, Asians and Africans arrived at the bond of being jointly nonwhite. Afro-Asianism emerged as a movement, seeking to assert the principle of equality among nations regardless of race.

The quest for equality regardless of race necessitated an alliance based on race. Black, brown, and yellow joined in one more transnational movement based ultimately on panpigmentationalism, an affinity based on color of the skin. Once again a form of primitive interdependence did lie behind the impetus for Afro-Asian solidarity.

But there was a parallel movement at the same time not based on color. This was the nonaligned movement. There were times when the nonaligned movement was virtually indistinguishable from the Afro-Asian movement, but the special alliance between President Tito of Yugoslavia, Prime Minister Nehru of India, President Nasser of Egypt, and to a lesser extent President Nkrumah of Ghana, converted from quite early the nonaligned movement into an interracial and transpigmentational force in world affairs. While Afro-Asianism continued to be influenced by issues of racial equality, the nonaligned movement was more concerned about relations between the major powers and the small countries in other areas of international life, ranging from military bases to patterns of voting in the United Nations. Once again, an element of primitive interdependence was at the heart of the nonaligned movement from the beginning, with considerable egalitarian solidarity among those countries that were militarily weak in the twentieth century.

The birth of Third World transnationalism came as a result of a marriage between these two pan movements—Afro-Asianism and nonalignment. Solidarity between Africans and Asians continued, but based less and less on the sentiment of being colored peoples and more on the recognition of shared economic and diplomatic weakness.

The nonaligned movement was also changing its emphasis, away from preoccupations about keeping out of the cold war and refusing alliance with the major powers, toward a struggle to try and create a new economic order in the world. Issues of race continued to be relevant for as long as southern Africa continued to be dominated along racial lines. A nonaligned conference was held in Lusaka, Zambia, partly to dramatize the commitment of the movement in support of the remaining wars of national liberation. But both the 1970 conference in Lusaka and the 1973 conference in Algiers clearly revealed that the nonaligned movement had become more committed to the cause of economic justice in the world than it was in the old days of Tito, Nehru, Nasser, and Nkrumah, and less fundamentally preoccupied with issues of keeping out of military alliances since the superpowers themselves were now pursuing a policy of détente.

As Afro-Asianism became deracialized and nonalignment became demilitarized in emphasis, a new synthesis emerged based on the concept of *the Third World*. This synthesis provided a transition from panpigmentationalism, an affinity based on color, to panproletarianism, a solidarity based on shared indigence and underdevelopment. While Afro-Asianism had by definition limited itself to two continents, the Third World also encompasses Latin America. The Third World is thus a tricontinental phenomenon, forging a primitive interdependence among underdeveloped countries in Asia, Africa, and Latin America. The interdependence is once again transnational, relatively rudimentary for the time being, provisionally influenced by an egalitarian ethic among the constituent countries, and increasingly conscious of the possibilities of cooperation in the future.

Third World transnationalism has found expression in a variety of submovements, ranging from a radical left-wing tricontinental movement to such governmental international organizations as the United Nations Conference on Trade and Development (UNCTAD). Increasingly, there had also been developing a few alliances of primary producers, ranging from the Organization of Petroleum Exporting Countries to new informal arrangements among producers of copper.

Basically, most of these primary producers are competitive and vulnerable to tactics of divide and rule. And yet, in their relationship to consumers of their primary products, a sense of primitive solidarity has been growing, however fragile and inchoate for the time being.

The doctrine of equality among Third World countries is also fragile and uncertain. Technological imbalances are important not only in relationships between the northern hemisphere and the southern, but also in relationships among Third World countries themselves. Nations like Brazil and India are technologically in a different category from countries like Libya and Uganda. The weight and leverage exerted by the technologically and demographically more powerful Third World countries carries the risk of feudo-imperial influences within the Third World itself.

Brazilians have had a vision of their own, first in Latin America and then in the Third World, similar to DuBois's conception of "the gifted tenth". The Brazilians have seen themselves as a potential superpower, which could begin by establishing a constituency of influence within the Third World.

For a while Brazil seemed to have even entertained the idea of sharing a feudo-imperial role with Portugal in Africa. A Portuguese colony like Angola seemed briefly to be developing into a condominium, under the joint hegemony of both Portugal and Brazil.

There were occasions when third parties sought to influence Portugal's policies in Africa through the intervention of Brazil. Brazil's former Ambassador to Washington, Robert D'Oliverra Campos, claimed soon after the Spring 1974 coup in Portugal that the government of President John F. Kennedy had offered to finance substantial economic projects in Angola, Mozambique, and Guinea-Bissau in 1963, fearing to see in "Portuguese Africa" a repetition of the chaos which had befallen the former Belgium Congo on attainment of independence. According to Campos, the United States was reluctant to approach Portugal directly, fearing a negative reaction from Lisbon so strong that it could shake the

317

Atlantic alliance. The Kennedy initiative, if Campos's report is correct, failed partly because Brazil was unsure about the wisdom of the American initiative, and partly because Portugal had been predictably unenthusiastic once the danger of a Congo-type collapse had receded.

By 1963 Brazil was already sensing the broad difficulties of feudo-imperialism in the modern period, but continued to play a basically supportive role behind Portugal for the time being.

By the end of the 1960's the process of Brazil's shift from serving as a co-imperial power in an informal sense to serving as a Third World partner in Africa began to be discernible. The Brazilians were still reluctant to be associated with African liberation movements as such, but nevertheless they now sought to establish new economic relations not only with the countries still under Portuguese control but also with those in the independent sector of the continent. On the one hand, Brazil's economic and technological development was widening the gulf between itself and many other countries within the Third World. On the other hand, the new policies pursued by Brazil in the Third World emphasized a spirit of egalitarian solidarity, seeming to lay the foundation of a new Third World transnationalism.

The Arab world was also exploring possibilities of enhanced solidarity with African states and with the Muslim world. Some of these movements could conceivably split the Third World along continental, religious, or ideological lines. But they could also be seen as an additional manifestation of the new mood of transnationalism among the poorer and weaker countries of the globe.

The interdependence continues to be fitful and inconclusive. The Arab oil producers had been reluctant to concede to fellow Third World nations special concessions in oil prices. In the case of the African states, the only support promised by Arab oil producers was at the most development aid and subsidies from a new Arab fund for Africa, but even this aid fell far short of meeting the extra costs of increased oil prices.

There was briefly a possibility of special concessions to Muslim countries from Arab oil producers, but the Islamic Summit Conference of Lahore in 1974 failed to realize such a spirit of economic generosity and solidarity between the haves and the have-nots. What all this means is that the struggle for effective and operational Third World transnationalism has only started. There are enormous obstacles in the way toward fulfillment, ranging from a residual dependency complex among those Third World countries still dominated by the former metropolitan masters to excessive greed among those Third World countries that had become staggeringly rich without evolving a commensurate scale of Third World solidarity.

The Strategy of Counterpenetration

But Third World transnationalism requires not only a new relationship among Third World countries but also a new relationship between the Third World and the dominant northern hemisphere. What should the nations of Asia, Africa, and Latin America do in the face of the continuing hegemony of the northern hemisphere? How is the economic and political dependency to be broken?

An important school of thought in the Third World has opted for the strategy of *disengagement*. Under this strategy the Third World countries should seek to explore the maximum possibilities of self-reliance. In situations involving a shortage of capital, they should investigate how well they can use their own surplus of labor. In situations involving a shortage of advanced skills, they should use intermediate technology, and further develop traditional expertise in their own midst. There should also be exchange of information and consultation among Third World countries on these modest technological approaches toward solving their problems. It may make sense to move from the hoe to the plow before one attempts to utilize the tractor. Both the People's Republic of China and the Republic of Tanzania have been among the countries to explore the possibilities of self-reliance, both by substituting labor-intensive for capital-intensive techniques and by substituting intermediate technology for the more alluring advanced technology of the western world.

The doctrine of *disengagement*, as defined and elaborated upon in the Third World, has also placed special emphasis on the need for at least partial disengagement from the international capitalist system. The reasoning is to the effect that the international system of trade and investment is for the time being so structured that full integration of a Third World country within it cannot but lead to exploitation. The movement of both foreign investment and so-called foreign aid from the developed world to the developing countries entails exploitative relationships ranging from distorted patterns of economic development within Third World countries to enforced purchasing of advanced equipment from the developed world.

The integration of, say, an African country into the international capitalist system could all too easily result in strengthening self-seeking elites in that country, in the emergence of luxurious consumption patterns, in the distortion of the economy to serve external investors and external tourists rather than local people, in the underutilization of local skills and labor, and in a deepening economic and political dependency between that African country and its benefactors in the northern hemisphere.

In the face of such possibilities, some Third World policy-makers and

319

political and economic theoreticians have begun to urge the strategy of disengagement as a method of maintaining autonomous viability and capacity for genuine self-sustained human development within Third World countries.

In fact, an alternative strategy is already revealing its potentialities, but it has yet to command the attention of theoreticians and economic and political analysts. We call this strategy *counterpenetration*. It involves not a withdrawal from the international capitalist system but a readiness to infiltrate that system and make it more vulnerable to Third World pressures. If Saudi Arabia had disengaged from the international capitalist system, it would not be enjoying today the immense economic influence it now has at the international level—out of all proportion to its size or to the level of its technological skills. But, by being substantially integrated through its own resources into the international capitalist system, Saudi Arabia gradually built within that system an immense economic leverage.

Until the energy crisis of 1973 onward, it had been too readily assumed that a country had to be economically developed in order to be economically powerful. Countries measured their international leverage largely in terms of technological and demographic size, and seldom in terms of primary economic products.

It was easy to assume that while the poor in individual industrial countries of the western world had managed to acquire power domestically by organizing for collective bargaining, the poor countries at the international level could not threaten economic action against the north even remotely comparable to a strike action by workers in industrial nations against employers.

The growth of labor unionism in industrial countries was substantially the growth of a system of collective economic "blackmail". Strike action was a form of economic boycott, an assertion of the right to withhold the needed resource of labor from an employer as a way of influencing him toward making concessions.

But at the international level it continued to seem impossible that primary producers could ever acquire a capacity to threaten "economic blackmail" against the northern hemisphere even remotely comparable in impact to the threat of strike action in individual countries. Transforming this old interpretation of the world's economic realities was the energy crisis, and the readiness of the Arabs to use that crisis as a means of exerting international pressure. All of a sudden it looked as if oil as energy could indeed be comparable at the international level to labor as energy at the domestic level. New possibilities of international collective bargaining were now discernible on the horizon. The special session of the United Nations General Assembly, requested by the President of Algeria and held in the Spring of 1974, emphasized afresh the growing realization among primary producers that they had acquired a little more leverage than they thought they had before the energy crisis. The triumph of the Third World at that conference of the United Nations, in the face of strong opposition from the United States which was championing an alternative strategy of economic reform, was a measure of the new self-confidence among Third World countries.

In reality their power against the northern hemisphere varied enormously from nation to nation. Saudi Arabia and Iran might have become substantial actors on the international economic scene, but countries like Chad, Malawi, and Haiti were still doomed to the status of the periphery.

Producers of oil might be among the new economic giants of the globe, but this did not necessarily make producers of cotton or cocoa similarly influential. The spectrum of power and leverage within the Third World was indeed wide.

But even though we have made allowances for these immense variations, the fact nevertheless remains that a new mood of political international effectiveness has developed for these countries, and different subsections of the Third World are exploring possibilities of establishing cartels of their own in a bid for improved economic justice.

The strategy of counterpenetration therefore requires not a withdrawal from having any links with the economies of the mighty northern hemisphere, but an exploration into the possibilities of making that hemisphere reciprocally dependent in a new way.

In fact, the immense wealth of some Third World countries could be used to establish *counter-national* corporations—immense trading companies, financed by, say, Libya or Venezuela or Indonesia or Saudi Arabia, and located in the heartland of the industrialized nations of the world. The oil princes could buy up shares in some existing western multinational corporations, and gradually tilt the balance of influence within those corporations. In some cases, a major American company could perhaps be bought up completely by Third World oil producers, or at least be subjected to majority control by such Third World countries, with important consequences for the international system of investment.

In the wake of the severe energy strains in Britain in the winter and spring of 1974, speculation started about inviting Arab money not only for private industry in Britain but also for the country's nationalized industry. The British Gas Council, the Coal Board, British Railways, and the Electricity Board were reported to be planning "a massive onslaught on the international lending market which could swell their coffers—and the country's foreign reserves—by more than 500 million pounds in six months". The specialists of the merchant banking world were engaged in delicate explorations.

> This has given rise to speculation that the Banks could put the two sides together and raise cash for the nationalized industries straight from Arab sources, and bypass the traditional supply routes. Arab cash is rumoured to have played a big part in recent large Euro-currency loans for State industries and is also said to account for a lot of recent activity in the gold market. The Arabs are impressed by the new guarantees given to official holders of Sterling which make our currency one of the most secure in the world and also recall that we are one of the few nations never to have reneged in our debts.*

At the time it was pointed out that some Arab countries were already more interested in experimental investments of this kind than others. Kuwait was regarded as inclined in that direction, while Saudi Arabia was still cautious. But whatever the outcome of such explorations and experiments, they did raise the possibility of Third World cash penetrating not only private firms and factories within the developed industrial countries, but also some state-owned industries. Involved, once again, was the possibility of counter-penetration on a scale which would begin to make sections of the industrial world almost as vulnerable to economic pressure from the Third World as sections of the Third World are already deeply vulnerable to manipulations by the developed world.

The stage might be set here for the beginnings of *mature* interdependence. Certainly some negotiations between the Arab countries and the European Economic Community had envisaged new relationships involving the exchange of skilled technology and expertise from western Europe for energy resources from the Arab world, in pursuit of parallel development in both regions.

But there are other possibilities of counterpenetration. The most directly human resources are the pockets of Third World populations within the industrial countries. West Germany's development moved increasingly in the direction of importing large numbers of southern Europeans into German industries. While southern Europeans are not members of the Third World proper, their relative underprivileged status makes them potential allies with other immigrant workers in the European Economic Community from outside Europe itself. There are significant populations of Algerians and other north Africans, as well as black Africans, involved in French economic life. The number of these

*John Phelps, "Will Arab Cash Be Married to Britain's State Need?" *Evening Standard* (London), April 8, 1974.

peoples is still relatively modest, and the energy crisis has interrupted the flow of such migrations into the heartland of industrialized Europe. But the phenomenon could constitute the beginnings of human counterpenetration, as employment of migrant workers from other parts of the world creates conditions at once exploitative in the short run and potentially revolutionary in the years ahead.

But the most important pocket of the Third World within the heartland of the northern hemisphere is the black American population. Black Americans can be regarded as the second largest black nation in the world, but a black nation which is at the same time part of the most powerful country in the world. The political consciousness of black Americans has increasingly included sensitivity to Third World status, and expanding empathy with the peoples of Africa, Asia and Latin America.

The impact of black Americans on United States foreign policy is still very modest, but the potentialities emerge as considerable once we contrast that modest influence of American Blacks with the immense influence of American Jews.

In October 1974 the United States government ordered a nuclear alert in connection with the Middle Eastern crisis. The alert was worldwide, carrying the logic of readiness to initiate a nuclear war rather than risk the destruction of Israel. For the time being it is inconceivable that any United States administration should order a nuclear alert in defense of the rights of black people in southern Africa. This points up the enormous difference between American readiness to commit great economic and military resources in defense of Israeli rights as against a conspicuous lack of similar commitment in defense of black South Africans or black "Rhodesians".

The United States Senate continued to link the issue of Jewish emigration from the Soviet Union with the issue of what type of economic relationship Americans should have with the Russians. The proposal to extend most favored nation treatment to the Soviet Union floundered repeatedly in the United States Senate against the rock of the controversy concerning Jewish emigration from Russia. The American senators correctly asserted that the Jews in Russia were denied a particular right to emigrate without paying a tax. But these were not American citizens being victimized by the Soviet Union, nor were they Israelis endangered by the Arabs, they were citizens of Russia by birth and descent, in no way constituting a treaty obligation that the American Senate had to take into account.

The Blacks of South Africa were often denied not only the right to emigrate to other lands, but even the right of movement from one part of the same country to another, or from one section of the same city in South Africa to another. Elaborate pass laws had been in operation for generations. Movement across racial boundaries, in terms of either marriage or of visits among relatives and friends, had been drastically curtailed for generations.

Yet it remains inconceivable for the time being that an American Senate should ever threaten strong economic sanctions against South Africa on the issue of the black people's right to move around within their own country, let alone to emigrate to a distant land. The rights denied to many Blacks in South Africa are far greater in number and in substance than the simple right to emigrate withheld from Russian Jews. The American Senate has not as yet produced the equivalent of Senator Henry Jackson, totally dedicated to the freedom of movement of black people within South Africa, and immensely influential among fellow senators on an issue of this kind.

In short, although black Americans are four times the number of Jewish Americans, their impact on American foreign policy is less than one hundredth of that so far exerted by Jewish Americans. When four black Americans begin to count for as much as one single Jewish American of the present period, it might at last be conceivable for an American President to order a nuclear alert in defense of beleaguered Zimbabwe or South African freedom fighters, and conceivable also for an American Senate to threaten economic sanctions against the government of South Africa if freedom of mobility from one part of Johannesburg to another was not fully conceded. The American Revolution had been born on the slogan of "no taxation without representation". The Soviet policies concerning citizens who wanted to go elsewhere and change their national status was based on the doctrine of "no emigration without taxation". The Russian rationale was that every citizen had received substantial benefits from the country which had educated him, and a decision to change citizenship and establish new loyalties entailed payment of a tax back to the mother country. American Jews had been influential enough to arouse powerful disapproval of such a doctrine within the governmental structure of the United States. American Blacks have yet to attain a similar level of political leverage to influence the policies of their own mighty country in the direction of a better deal for racial kinsmen in other parts of the world.

When American Blacks finally attain a level of influence which gives every four of them equal weight to one American Jew, the value of the black American enclave for the Third World would rise dramatically. This black enclave in the mightiest nation in the world would become a powerful instrument of counterpenetration, valuable not only for black Africa but for the Third World at large.

Toward Mature Interdependence

What emerges from these considerations is the simple proposition that counterpenetration might well be an indispensable mechanism for the ultimate transition from feudo-imperial relationships to mature interdependence.

The contradictions of technological imbalance will continue, but technological and economic superiority could still be outweighed by other strategies pursued by the Third World and its enclaves. Once again the potential of black Americans is particularly illuminating. This largest of the Third World enclaves in the dominant northern hemisphere continues to be, by United States standards, part of the national technological periphery. While Jewish Americans are disproportionately overrepresented in technological, economic, and intellectual achievements within the United States, black Americans are still underrepresented in the structures of economic, technological, and intellectual power within their own country. American universities at their best include a rich intellectual contribution by Jewish Americans, but those universities are still struggling to give a fair representation to black Americans. Scientific giants among Jewish Americans include no less a genius than Einstein himself; the black American contribution to scientific and technological innovativeness remains modest by comparison.

In the face of this technological and intellectual imbalance, how effectively can black Americans ever hope to intercede on behalf of the Third World? Again, there is a case for exploring alternative possibilities. We could illustrate by examining the two parts of Eisenhower's concept of a "military-industrial complex". Dwight Eisenhower, as he was retiring from the presidency, warned his countrymen against the power of the military-industrial complex within the United States. This was the alliance between the industrial giants and the powerful system of technological consumption within the American armed forces. American industry provided some of the technology of violence suitable for the preeminence of the United States in world affairs. A combination of decision-makers within that part of American industry oriented toward satisfying military needs and that part of American government oriented toward making military decisions provided an alliance capable of exerting disproportionate influence on the political system as a whole. It was to this hazard that President Eisenhower drew attention in his farewell message to his countrymen.

The domestic alignment of forces as formulated contained two major elements—the industrial domain and the military domain. What is the place of black Americans in each of these?

Clearly, in the industrial domain, the technological and economic underprivileges suffered by black Americans prevented them from exercising an effective say at the highest levels of this structure of power. The industrial section of the military-industrial complex was overwhelmingly Caucasian. The black American factor in such a structure was bound to be negligible.

The question now arising is whether there can be a significant black American presence in the military component of that military-industrial complex. Can black Americans exert influence within the complex as a whole by acquiring a new role within its military component? We recommended in Chapter 13 that black Americans should have a fairer share of their country's capitalist cake. But can black America enhance its economic influence by first increasing its military leverage?

The emergence of a volunteer army under the Nixon Administration raised afresh the possibility of a disproportionate black American presence within the American armed forces. In situations of ecnomic underprivilege, there is a serious possibility that black Americans will seek professional fulfillment within the armed forces in the absence of adequate alternative careers. The armed forces in a number of countries have recruited disproportionately from the less privileged sectors of society precisely because they provide opportunities not easily available in alternative areas of national endeavor.

But once the underprivileged infiltrate the armed forces to a significant degree, a new possibility arises—that of exerting an unexpected level of influence on the national system as a whole as a result of being overrepresented within the armed forces. This has certainly taken place in parts of Asia and Africa. A number of African countries during the colonial period, and immediately after, recruited overwhelmingly from ethnic groups which were otherwise economically and educationally handicapped. But these ethnic groups, now placed within the avenues of power of military establishments, began to acquire a new level of political effectiveness. The ethnic groups constituting a majority of the armed forces might, at the national level, be only small minorities in thesproportionate presence within the armed establishment converted them into effective contenders for power.

In the wake of a volunteer army in the United States, the question must arise whether the armed forces would become conspicuously black, as the underprivileged seek fulfillment within them. This is not merely a case of black Americans serving as cannon fodder, front material to be used as the first casualties in war. Black Americans had been used as cannon fodder in some previous wars. The emerging possibility in the wake of both the black revolution in the United States and of the volunteer army is that the combination of a new egalitarianism in the nation and black presence in the armed forces will bring more and more black Americans into the highest levels of decision-making within the armed forces as their numbers in the ranks increase. An American military establishment which is even one-third black could transform significantly the power of black men within the totality of the governmental establishment. After all, black Americans are only a tenth of the total population. When the power within the armed forces becomes more than three times disproportionate, it may significantly change the balance of influence within that alliance which Dwight Eisenhower had called the "military-industrial complex".

The proportion of Blacks within the armed forces could conceivably be even higher than one third, and might even go up to a half, if the United States permits it. The chances are that enough alarm would be caused within the white sector of the population to prevent an overwhelming black presence within the American armed forces. Precautions would be invoked quite soon to make them more ethnically representative, thus preventing a devastating counterpenetration by black men into the military-industrial complex of the mightiest nation in human history.

In spite of the probability of such preventive action by the Caucasian sector of the American population, it might still be worth the while of black America to explore how far their presence within the military sector of the military-industrial complex would be permitted to grow. Since Blacks are still out of the industrial section because of technological and economic handicaps, the case is strong for attempting to penetrate more fully the military half of that equation. Even an American military establishment which was merely one-third black could provide a convincing new level of counterpenetration by this fundamental enclave of the Third World. It might then be said that, just as colonialism had set the stage for white penetration into Africa, the slave trade had set the stage for black penetration into the Americas. It was precisely the enforced export of black men into the New World which created that enclave. Historic justice might now dictate a new level of political effectiveness by that enclave in the destiny of the country of its enforced adoption.

But, whatever the outcome of this scenario, it does provide at least a potential illustration of counterpenetration as a mechanism for re-

327

storing parity and equality of advantage, and therefore a mechanism for promoting a more mature patrn of interdependence.

Conclusion

The contradictions of technological change continue. Saudi Arabia is still technologically a backwater in terms of skills, even if it is in the forefront of the production of energy for technological creativity in other countries. A mature interdependence would entail a better relationship, based in part on effective mutual vulnerability, between the technologically superior northern hemisphere and the sources of primary products to the south.

The world might indeed be on the verge of that ultimate transition from feudo-imperial interdependence to this more mature balance. Within the southern hemisphere primitive interdependence might still be struggling to maintain at once a sense of solidarity and a sense of equality among the constituent parts. As the century moves through its last quarter, primitive interdependence in the Third World might remain to serve the function of creating mature interdependence between the Third World and the developed states. With that arrival in maturity, that fulfillment in human interaction, the link between the problem of equality and the tensions of interdependence might at last be entering a utopia of compatibility. Karl Marx and Jean-Jacques Rousseau, turning in their graves, might concede that mankind in the last quarter of the twentieth century has at last found a formula which could prevent division of labor from becoming basically exploitative, permitting human interdependence without culminating in institutional hierarchy. The contradictions of technological change, even if still not resolved, might at least be changed sufficiently to prevent them from playing havoc with the imperatives of social justice and equality among nations.

Section V

INTELLECTUAL CULTURE AS A MEDIUM OF DISSEMINATION

CHAPTER 16

Language and World Culture

In an earlier chapter we have defined intellectual culture in terms which make it a residual category, encompassing ideas on science and the arts, on logical calculation and aesthetic assessment. The intellectual culture of a society defines its framework of reasoning and the limits of its creative and innovative potential.

But to the extent that intellectual culture is a fund of ideas, and ideas are capable of circulation, we have here a basic medium of cultural convergence, initiating that critical process of acculturation. Linguists talk of "loan words," as one language borrows from another. But loan words are sometimes an indicator of "loan ideas," as one culture borrows ideas from another.

In this chapter we shall address ourselves to the relevance of language for world culture. We shall pay special attention to the English language as the most important linguistic medium that mankind has so far produced. But we should bear in mind that the English language has acquired this importance not only because of the role which the major English-speaking powers have played in world history, but also because mankind now feels the need for shared global languages much more than it has ever done before. Both English and French meet a new need in the world—and mankind is using them as tools which happen to be at hand. Once again our perspective on this issue will be African, as we examine a global phenomenon through regional lenses.

In 1960 seventeen African countries became independent and launched Africa's entry into world politics, on however modest a scale. The black diplomats arrived at the United Nations equipped with two major metropolitan languages, which they had inherited from the colonial era—English and French. They entered a United Nations which already had five official languages—the others being, of course, Russian, Chinese, and Spanish. The importance of language in diplomacy received a new emphasis when these black diplomats from the last of the continents to be liberated moved into the corridors of the United Nations, and sought to have their views heard and their values understood.

The Universe of Languages

The linguistic picture of the globe at that time was, according to some calculations, as follows. Chinese had the largest number of speakers. There were of course wide differences between the various forms of Chinese, but the calculations at the time were that over 600 million people spoke some form of Chinese. The overwhelming majority of them were themselves Chinese.

The second language by number of speakers was English, with 510 million speakers, of whom 260 million were native speakers.

Third in number of speakers was Russian, with 220 million, 200 million of those were native speakers, the additional 20 million being found mainly in eastern Europe.

Spanish was fourth with approximately 130 million speakers in Latin America and Spain, and perhaps another 10 million outside, with special reference to the Philippines.

Fifth in importance among the languages of the globe in terms of users was French, with 50 million users in France itself, and another 50 million elsewhere.

In reality some of the figures were calculations of populations in countries where a language was the official language, and where it might be deemed to be on the ascendancy in the schools. Not even the 100 million people of Spanish America are all Spanish-speakers. But on balance the proportions might be regarded as fair indications of the numerical importance of these five languages recognized by the United Nations.[1]

In a lecture delivered to the Royal Commonwealth Society in March 1963, Sir Paul Sinker, Director General of the British Council made an observation very pertinent to our concerns in this chapter: "When we turn to consider the question what is or is not a world language, the significant feature is not the home market but the export market. The significant figure is that of the other users. The export figures are the vital ones." Sir Paul noted that French and English, on the basis of the users distributed in different parts of the world, were the two main languages that had been exported. They had a ratio at the time of something like one to one of outside users to native users. However, the export of English in absolute terms was something like five times that of French.

We distinguish four types of languages, beginning with world languages. For our purposes, world languages are those which have not only been exported beyond their home country, but beyond their continent or immediate region. World languages are intercontinental languages and include three of the five U.N. languages—English, Spanish, and French. In addition, to qualify as a world language, a tongue must command at least 100 million speakers, or 5 percent of the population of the world, whichever is higher, and must have been adopted by at least ten states as a national language.

The second category to be differentiated is that of regional languages. Regional languages, for our purposes, are international but basically intraregional and often intracontinental. Among the five U.N. languages, the most clearly regional is Russian—limited in its impact to the Soviet Union and her immediate neighbors. It is true that the Soviet Union itself traverses both Europe and Asia. But for our purposes in this analysis the Russian language is clearly intraregional, and therefore a regional rather than a world language.

In addition to Russian, other regional languages are Arabic, German, and Swahili. Swahili is certainly the most international of all indigenous African languages. Curiously enough, it is even more of an export language than either English or French in terms of ratio of the racial or native speakers to non-native speakers, though of course it is not as widely exported as those two world languages. The native speakers of Swahili are perhaps little more than 350,000, yet the language is spoken at different levels of fluency by another 40 million people. In terms of distribution among different African states, Swahili is more of an international language than Hausa, its nearest indigenous rival in the continent. Swahili is both the official and national language of Tanzania, the national language of Kenya, and is widely spoken in Uganda, Rwanda, Zaire, Burundi, and on the borders of Zambia and Malawi.

The fifth U.N. language, Chinese, technically falls into our third category—the category of national languages, by definition, languages that are adopted as official or national only in their place of birth. Chinese is a national language in that sense, although it has more speakers than English. The consolidation of Taiwan as a separate state would make the claims of Chinese to be a regional language even more irresistable. Other national languages include Hindi, Persian, Urdu in Pakistan, Bengali in Bangla Desh, Bahasa in Indonesia.*

A fourth category of languages is what might be called communal languages. These are basically sub-national languages, spoken by minority groups within individual nations, and not accorded official status. Both Asia and Africa have a multiplicity of communal languages.

We see problems of world order in terms of trends towards the con-

*This last could be described as a regional language for those who regard it as basically the same as Malay—the official language of Malaysia.

vergence of human values and the expansion of human capacity for empathy. Within that context, the issue of communication between human beings is evidently of paramount importance. In another chapter we shall discuss intellectual and physical mobility as indispensable aspects of these processes through which the human race is approaching something that might be called a world culture. What should be borne in mind in this chapter is the importance of language as a medium of cultural convergence and as a major factor in intellectual mobility itself.

Language and the Intellect

President Senghor of Senegal has often discussed the concept of what he calls "The Civilization of the Universal" or sometimes "The Universal Civilization." Senghor supports the concept of negritude as an attachment to the civilized values of the black man, on the one hand, and to the civilization of the universal, the shared heritage of mankind, on the other. In a rather fundamental sense President Senghor's philosophy does capture the whole idea of a world federation of cultures. It seeks to emphasize the distinctive black component of the cultural heritage of man, while also defining the shared pool on a global scale.

From his point of view as a colonized child of the French language, Senghor recognized quite early the importance of French as a medium through which his own countrymen of Senegal, and indeed all those black people who had been ruled by France, could make their contribution to world civilization more explicit. To use Senghor's own words: "It is a fact that French has made it possible for us to communicate to our brothers and to the world the unheard of message which only we could write. It has allowed us to bring to *Universal Civilization* a contribution without which the civilization of the twentieth century would not have been universal."[2]

In this enthusiasm for his own version of world cultural federalism, Senghor is sometimes carried away by beautiful sentimentality about the French language.

> . . . if we had a choice we would have chosen French. Firstly, it is a language which has enjoyed a far reaching influence and which still enjoys it in great measure. In the eighteenth century French was proposed and accepted as the universal language of culture. I know that today it comes after English, Chinese and Russian in the number of people who speak it, and it is a language of fewer countries than English. But if quantity is lacking there is *quality*.

Senghor goes on to assure us: "I am not claiming that French is superior to these other languages, either in beauty or in richness, but I do say that it is the supreme language of *communication:* 'a language of politeness and honesty', a language of beauty and clarity. . . ."[4] We may allow Senghor his enthusiasm for French. He is much more persuasive when he tells us French had made it possible for him and his kind to communicate to the world the unheard of message which only he and his kind could convey. The language of the outside world has given the black man a medium of contribution to the civilization of that wider world.

We discussed before the problems of uneven creativity and its implications for parity of dignity among human groups. The slower performance of Africans in science and technology has contrasted with the more impressive performance of others either today or in historical times. Yet the issue of language also may be indispensable in this quest for the effective rise of African man to parity of achievement with other races.

It is arguable that for Africa the experience of colonialism itself was at once a political bondage and a mental liberation. The colonial impact might well have been the greatest liberating factor that the African mind had ever experienced. At the heart of this mental liberation was the world of new ideas—unveiled particularly well through the medium of the metropolitan languages which conveyed those ideas.

Of course once the stream of African thought was let loose, it was beyond the powers of the colonizers to determine the direction of its flow. Nor could the process of intellectual liberation be reversed.

The most formal of these processes of liberation lay in formal education itself. For generations African villages had gone through their traditional activities, not fully aware of the full potential of their own minds within those villages.

Full many a gem of purest ray serene
The dark unfathomed caves of ocean bear:
Full many a flower is born to blush unseen,
And waste its sweetness on the desert air.[4]

Not every village need have had "a mute inglorious Milton"—nor indeed a mute inglorious "Newton." Not every village buried a genius beneath ancestral rural ways. Yet even today among the modestly clad Karamajong or Masai we do not always have the means of knowing how many potential doctors, physicists, historians, or writers, walk around disguised behind that relative physical nakedness.

But while formal education is an obvious factor in mental liberation, what is not obvious is the precise role of foreign languages in releasing the African mind. White racist myth has alleged that the African is not an intellectual animal—that he is by nature incapable of coming to grips with ideas at a high level of abstraction. However, Nkrumah's book *Consciencism,* unlike almost anything else written by him before or after, was definitely a work of the intellect at its most intellectual. To the extent that it was written by an African, or by an African assisted by other Africans, the book was indeed a refutation of that myth. Central to our point, however, is the simple fact that *Consciencism* was written in the English language. Nkrumah could not have reached that precise level of intellectuality and abstraction on such a theme if he had opted to write it in his native Nzima language.

Of course no language is *inherently* incapable of coping with abstract thought. But science is an expanding universe, and so therefore is the language that goes with it. Left behind scientifically, African languages gradually became incapable either of coping with or of stimulating new areas of reflection and analysis. It was not the African mind which was defective; it was to some extent African languages.

In a paper published in 1966, Mohamed Hyder, now Professor of Zoology at the University of Nairobi, posed the question in stark terms: Is it possible to write a serious scientific paper in Swahili on the subject of "The Effect of Thyroid Stimulating Hormone on the Radio-Active Iodine Uptake Beef Thyroid Tissue *in vitro*"? His answer was that if a serious attempt were made to develop a "technical limb" to Swahili, this was indeed possible. The title of the paper would, it is true, include terms like "thairodi, homoni, ayodini, redioaktivu and vitiro." However, Dr. Hyder went on to assert:

> There is no good reason why this development of a "technical limb" . . . of Swahili through the swahilization of such terms should weigh heavily on our conscience. Examination of any technical or scientific journal in English, French, German, Russian or Chinese shows clearly that such technical terms are really international in usage. Look up the word "thyroid" or "radio active" in any one of these languages and you will find that apart from the token digestive processes exerted on them, they are practically the same the world over.[5]

In a Présence Africaine lecture delivered in November 1961, Pierre Alexandre, the French linguist and Africanist, made a similar point:

> It would be wrong to say that African languages are a barrier to the teaching of science and technical subjects. The syntactical structure of those known to me would not provide any major obstacle to the pursuit of logical reasoning. The absence of technical terminology in the vocabulary is all the more easy to remedy since, in fact, the international technical terminology is based on an artificial assembly of Greek and Latin roots. The Parisian who speaks of a "telegramme" rather than "far-off writing" is expressing himself in Greek, in the same way as a Duala who speaks of "telefun."[6]

Having them demonstrated the feasibility of creating technical and scientific limbs to African languages, the question which remains is the desirability of embarking on such an adventure. From the point of view of the possibility of creating a world federation of cultures, there may be a case for converting a few African languages into effective scientific media, but not at the cost of eliminating the world languages which have already entered Africa. Languages like Hausa, Swahili, and Yoruba in Africa may command enough speakers in terms of millions of people to make it worthwhile. But the majority of African languages have too few speakers to warrant a serious undertaking to convert them into scientific and technological languages. In any case, an attempt to attain linguistic self-sufficiency for every linguistic group in the country would be an extreme form of cultural autarky.

The case for converting Hausa and Swahili into languages capable of sustaining the weight of scientific and technological thought is quite strong. And if Africa is to make an adequate contribution to that federal level of our system of federated cultures, at least one or two African languages ought to be made fully versatile across the whole span of human reasoning. However, the spread of English and French as world languages is itself a great step toward a global system of federated cultures, and their renunciation by African countries would be a retrograde step. A few African languages could be expanded and developed to the maximum levels feasible, without necessarily renouncing the linguistic heritage of Western imperialism. What may be needed is a systematic taming of the metropolitan languages to suit local conditions. This would be an exercise in linguistic domestication, as the alien beasts from England and France are familiarized with the African domestic scene and gradually acclimatized.

Toward Decolonizing Rudyard Kipling

In a previous chapter we discussed Rudyard Kipling's poem, "The White Man's Burden" as symbolic of that massive historical phenomenon, Euro-American imperialism. There is no doubt that Kipling was the poet of militant expansionist patriotism, and was, in some sense, a hero of both the British and the American wings of Anglo-Saxon militancy. He married an American woman, Caroline Balestier, and lived for a few years in Vermont. As Louis Untermeyer has observed: "It is probable that Kipling would have remained in America, where he wrote several of his most popular works, if a quarrel with his brother-in-law had not driven him back to England."[7]

In sentiment Rudyard Kipling belonged to the second half of the nineteenth century and the first decade of the twentieth. The Anglo-Saxons were deemed both a "race" and a linguistic group. There was optimism that the race would dominate the world, a prediction not borne out by history. But there was also optimism that the English language would conquer the world, a prediction well on the road towards fulfilment. The militancy of Rudyard Kipling's rhetoric and poetry were animated by the forces of enthusiasm implicit in both those prophecies. In 1868 Sir Charles Wentworth Dilke published his two-volume study, *Greater Britain,* after his travels in the United States, New Zealand, Australia, Ceylon, India, and Egypt. "Everywhere I was in English-speaking, or in English-governed land." He detected the resilience of "the essentials of the race" and the power both of the English language and English laws. He was particularly impressed by the potentialities of America as a field for the dissemination of English values. To use a more recent metaphor, Sir Charles Dilke saw the United States as the microphone and loud-speaker for the British heritage. In his own words: "Through America, England is speaking to the world . . . Alfred's laws and Chaucer's tongue are theirs whether they would or no."

Sir Charles shared the view that Britain could claim the glory of "having planted greater Englands across the seas" and here he was capturing a sentiment made even more immortal by Kipling's lines:

Winds of the World, give answer! They are whimpering to and fro—
And what should they know of England who only England know?[8]

Across the Atlantic in the United States Josiah Strong, a Congrega-tionalist minister, even more explicitly associated the destiny of the Anglo-Saxon "race" with the destiny of the English language, and saw the latter as the carrier of Christian ideas and as the medium for "Anglo-Saxonizing mankind." Strong heartily quoted the German philologist, Jacob Grimm, in his predictions about the English language:

. . . the English language, saturated with Christian ideas, gathering up into itself the best thoughts of all the ages, is the great agent of Christian civiliza-tion throughout the world; at this moment affecting the destinies and moulding the character of half the human race. . . . It seems chosen, like its people, to rule in future times in still greater degree in all the corners of the earth.[9]

Strong took up this solemn prophecy about the infinite conquering power of the English language. The racial chauvinism detracts from what would otherwise be a prediction still very far from being invalidated. In his own exaggerated way, Strong saw the potentialities of the English language as a factor in world-order problems and tied this to Tennyson's vision of a future "Federation of the World." Half chauvinist and half genuine prophet, this Congregationalist minister in the United States asserted that "the language of Shakespeare would eventually become the language of mankind." He then asked whether Tennyson's noble prophecy about the end of war and the beginning of world federalism would not find its fulfilment in Anglo-Saxondom's extending its dominion and influence:

Til the war-drum throbs no longer, and the battleflags are furl'd
In the Parliament of man, the Federation of the world.[10]

The British certainly extended their sway across much of the globe as an imperial power; and the United States rose as the most powerful nation in the history of mankind. But then other forces in the world began to conspire against the political domination or hegemony of both the British and the Americans. American hegemony took longer to be fully on the defensive, and to start beating a retreat to some limited extent following challenges which ranged from the war in Vietnam to the nationalism of Charles de Gaulle. In fact, the American decline in world stature is still in its early stages, but the British decline is more firmly demonstrable.

Africa was among the last sectors of the British empire to be liberated. The year 1966 marked the virtual end of British colonialism in Africa, except for the continuing legal fiction of British power over rebellious Rhodesia. But while 1966 marked the end of the British empire, it witnessed at the same time newer reports about the expansion of the English language. An East African magazine reported in December 1966 that the English language had already become the primary language of science in the world as well as of aviation and sports, and increasingly of literature and the theatre. As the magazine put it: "When a Russian pilot seeks to land at an airfield in Athens, Cairo, or New Delhi, he talks to the control tower in English." The same weekly magazine estimated that by 1966 70 percent of the world's mail was written in English, and an even bigger percentage of cable and wireless transmissions. Sixty percent of the world's broadcasts were already in English. And more and more countries were introducing English as a compulsory second language in schools.[11]

What the world picture as a whole indicates is not only the significance of French and English as the two most important languages of international politics, but also the simple fact that English continues to outstrip French even in diplomatic importance.

Even within the European Economic Community there is anxiety among champions of the French language now that Britain has become a

339

member of the Community. The British themselves, far less nationalistic about their language than the French, have indicated a readiness to let French continue to hold a special position in the councils of Europe. But English has often spread and conquered in spite of Britain's own lack of interest in that spread. The European Economic Community may fall under the spell of the English language whatever reassurances are given the French.

In May 1971 President Pompidou was asked why he insisted on the importance of the French language. His answer, which became more elaborate as the time of British entry approached, conceded first the idea of equality of languages, but then intimated that French had to remain the first among equals in Europe. President Pompidou wanted to safeguard the special role of French within the bodies of the European Economic Community and the working parties of experts. Why did he want to do so? "Because the language reflects a certain way of looking at the world."[12]

In some ways the conquest of continental Europe by the English language would be an even more dramatic victory for the language than its triumphs in Asia and Africa. After all, within Europe the overpowering rivalry of French and German as appropriate languages of science and culture for so many years would normally have been expected to present an intractable obstacle to the new hegemony of a language from outside the continent. English has indeed been replacing German as the second language in places like the Scandinavian countries.

English may push back French in Europe in one sweeping invasion, and beat French into a retreat behind the Maginot line of France herself. If that were to happen such an event would be even more impressive than the acquisition of English by Indians and Nigerians, who were more vulnerable because they were colonized and were also more vulnerable because their languages had not as yet acquired the kind of scientific and modern technological capability which French and German had already imbibed prior to the English challenge on the continent. But French has continued to resist the encroachment of English. President Pompidou's worry about the linguistic implications for the European Economic Community of the British entry was an illustration of a continuing vigilance by France to protect the interests of French.

And yet English, even at its most victorious, can only be a foreign language in Europe. England and Ireland are destined to be the only European countries that have English as the official language. Everywhere else English will be playing a secondary role within the European continent.

In Africa, however, the position is different. Thomas Soper, Deputy Director of the Overseas Development Institute in London at the time, estimated that two thirds of black Africa was English-speaking and one third was French-speaking. What Soper meant was that two thirds of the population of black Africa was under a system of government which had adopted English as the official language, or one of the official languages, whereas about one third or less was under systems of government which had adopted French for that purpose. In terms of the number of independent states in sub-Saharan Africa, there are indeed about as many French-speaking governments as there are English-speaking. But in terms of population the picture is different. Nigeria alone has more than the population of former French Africa put together, but then out of the 150 million or so Commonwealth Africans, about half are Nigerians.

Against this must be balanced two factors. First, French-speaking Africa does not consist merely of former French Africa. It includes former Belgian Africa—Zaire, Rwanda, and Burundi—with a population of over 20 million. Second, there may be more people who actually speak French in French-speaking Africa than there are people who speak English in English-speaking Africa. This calculation is impressionistic, based partly on observations in major centers of population, and partly on the sophistication in the command of French maintained by the French-speaking elite. It is certainly true that many African users of French have a more sophisticated command of it than African users of English have of that language. Even if the calculation of language populations is uncertain, the schools in English-speaking Africa are unquestionably producing educated Africans more rapidly than the schools in French-speaking Africa are. There is a greater commitment towards promoting education in Commonwealth Africa, and towards disseminating it widely. Former French Africa still inclines towards an elitist conception of education, and the expansion of the primary and secondary sectors of education in even such a richly Francophone country as the Ivory Coast does not compare with the expansion of pre-university education in, say, Kenya and Ghana. Again all these are impressionistic assessments, but at least they do add up to the phenomenon of dual Franco-English cultural and linguistic penetration into the African continent. And of the two languages there is no doubt at all that English is the more dominant in the affairs of the continent.

Strong's prediction concerning the conquests of the world by the English language is coming into conflict with another prediction made famous by Rudyard Kipling himself. We have indicated before that Kipling belonged to that school of militant Anglo-Saxon patriotism which saw the world falling under the influence of those that spoke "the tongue that Shakespeare spake." But it was also Kipling who bequeathed to human thought the witticism captured in the verse:

Oh, East is East, and West is West, and never the twain shall meet,
Till Earth and Sky stand presently at God's great Judgment Seat.[13]

However the English language itself is helping to contradict the prediction that "never the twain shall meet." The language of Shakespeare, even more so the language of Kipling, has established points of contact, avenues of meeting, between Americans and Pakistanis, Australians and Nigerians, Jamaicans and New Zealanders. Thanks to Kipling's own language East may still be East and West may still be West, but it is harder than ever to predict that "never the twain shall meet."

Kipling himself can be regarded as a more up-to-date representative of the language in some ways than Shakespeare. Looking at the history of English as a whole, it is true that among the poets it was Shakespeare and Alexander Pope who contributed most to the phraseological heritage of English. But Kipling was the nearest modern equivalent to Shakespeare and Pope as a contributor to popular English. In the words of George Orwell: "Kipling is the only English writer of our time who has added phrases to the English language. The phrases and neologisms which we take over and use without remembering their origin do not always come from writers we admire." Orwell refers to phrases coined by Kipling which "one sees quoted in leaderettes in the gutter press or overhears in saloon bars from people who have barely heard his name." He cites "East is East, and West is West," "The female of the species is more deadly than the male," "Paying the Dane-Geld" and, of course, "The white man's burden."[14]

Orwell sees in Kipling's capability to enrich the language a capacity to capture the urgency of things. One did not have to agree with the philosophy put forward by Kipling, but a phrase may capture an area of importance, even if there is a divergence of values. "White man's burden" instantly conjures up a real problem, even if one feels that it ought to be altered to "black man's burden."[15]

Orwell's modification of the concept in the direction of the oppressed, the black man, had been touched on earlier by other users of English. Edmund D. Morel, founder of the newspaper *West Africa Mail,* and founder of the Congo Reform Association in defence of the rise of the Congolese against the King of the Belgians, wrote a book entitled *The Black Man's Burden,* in 1920. Taking a point of view diametrically opposed to that of Kipling, Morel nevertheless echoed the rhetoric of his more jingoistic compatriot.

It is [the people of Africa] who carry the "Black Man's Burden." They have not withered away before the white Man's *occupation*. . . . The African has survived, and it is well for the white settlers that he has. . . . [But] in fine, to kill the soul in a people—this is a crime which transcends physical murder.[16]

We are taking Orwell's analysis of Kipling a little further, to illustrate the importance of linguistic dissemination and the power of words. Orwell asks "But how true is it that Kipling was a vulgar flag waver, a sort of publicity agent for Cecil Rhodes?" Orwell, himself basically an anti-imperialist, conceded that it was true that Kipling provided rhythmic legitimation of British jingoism and British imperialism. Kipling also helped to romanticize the values popular with the ruling classes of Britain. In the stupid early years of this century, the blimps, having at last discovered someone who could be called a poet and who was on their side, set Kipling on a pedestal, and some of his more sententious poems, such as "If," were given almost biblical status.[17] What Orwell did not realize was that the very poem "If" captured the imagination not simply of the blimps and jingo imperialists, but of African nationalists far away from Britain. On the eve of an election in Nairobi, before a massive crowd waiting to hear his last speech before the great day, Kenya's Tom Mboya stood there and recited to that African audience the whole of Rudyard Kipling's poem "If." The whole concept of leadership unflappable in the face of adversity, unwilling to pass the buck, ("Here the buck stops"), unwilling to collapse under the weight of pressures, and characterized by the supreme British virtue of the "stiff upper lip," seemed captured in those lines from a supreme British patriot:

If you can keep your head when all about you
Are losing theirs and blaming it on you,
If you can meet with Triumph and Disaster
And treat those two imposters just the same,
If you can talk with crowds and keep your virtue,
Or walk with kings—nor lose the common touch,
If you can fill the unforgiving minute
With sixty seconds' worth of distance run,
Yours is the Earth and everything that's in it,
And—which is more—you'll be a Man, my son.[18]

There in Nairobi was this immortal son of Kenya, worn out by the exertions of campaigning, nervous about the election the next day, confronting an eager audience of fellow black people listening to his words of wisdom. Mboya was later to communicate to posterity the following paragraph:

. . . I read out to the great crowd the whole of Rudyard Kipling's poem *If*. When facing the challenge of nation-building, nobody can claim to have played a manly part if he (or she) has not ". . . filled the unforgiving minute with sixty seconds' worth of distance run."[19]

Across the border in Uganda Rudyard Kipling had had a similar impact. J. W. Lwamafa, Minister and Member of Parliament, commemorated President A. Milton Obote's ten years in Parliament with the observation:

He is essentially a man of crisis—he has a unique flair for solving them, but once solved, he will never wait for applause, he simply moves on to the next problem as if nothing had happened. No one reminds me more than President Obote of Rudyard Kipling's poem (which, by the way, I have got framed and hangs in my office) and more particularly the verse, 'If you can keep your head when all about you are losing theirs . . .'.[20]

Kipling, the poet of "The White Man's Burden," had turned out also to be the poet of "The Black Man's Leader." The man who had contributed significantly to the phraseological heritage of the English language was also serving African politicians' inspirational purposes within their own domestic systems. The cultural penetration of the English language was manifesting its comprehensiveness. That was in part a form of colonization of the African mind. But when Rudyard Kipling is being called upon to serve purposes of the Africans themselves, the phenomenon we are witnessing may also amount to a decolonization of Rudyard Kipling. It was Kipling himself who said in 1923: "Words are, of course, the most powerful drug used by mankind."[21]

The drug of words may hypnotize men away from rationality. But there are times when drugs are used for medicinal and curative purposes. And there are times when one drug is used to neutralize the hypnotic effects of another. In these latter two cases the story of the English language and its role in the world may include the remedial functions of mitigating man's inclinations towards cultural autarky.

The Emergence of the Afro-Saxons

By the year 2000 there will probably be more black than British people in the world who speak English as their native tongue, quite apart from the millions more who already speak English as a second language. Already black Americans alone who speak the language as their mother tongue are the equivalent of half the population of Great Britain. And then there are a few more million black speakers of the language scattered around the Caribbean and the northern fringes of South America.

Within the African continent the only black native speakers of the language who are politically significant are members of the ruling community of Liberia descended from black Americans. There are also a few black native speakers of English in places like Sierre Leone. But at least as important a phenomenon is the growing number of educated African families that use English as the language of the home. A number of African children, especially in West Africa but also increasingly in East Africa, are growing up bilingual in English and their own African language because their parents are highly educated and speak English to each other. These considerations make it likely that by the end of the twentieth century there will be more black native speakers of English than there are speakers of it in Great Britain. And the speakers of it in Great Britain itself should, by the end of the century, include a few million black Englishmen.

English-speaking Commonwealth Africans may well be joined by the inhabitants of what was once Portuguese Africa. It is possible that Angola and Mozambique, following the precedent of Indonesia, might decide that there is a case for changing their metropolitan language from Portuguese to either French or English. That Portuguese and French are both Latin languages may tend to pull the people of Angola and Mozambique towards French. On the other hand, in so momentous a decision they might as easily shift towards English. After all, they have many more neighbours who are English-speaking than French-speaking. Also, many of the top leaders of the liberation movements have acquired English as an additional language, partly because of their work in Dar-es-Salaam, the headquarters of liberation movements, in Addis Ababa, the headquarters of the Organization of African Unity, and in New York, the venue of the United Nations.

It is feasible for all the inhabitants of the continent of Africa to become speakers of English, and yet for English to remain a foreign language there. What then would make English indigenous to Africa? One criterion would be that substantial number of indigenous Africans, placed in positions of policy makers, acquire the language as their first language.

But what is a "first" language? Is this a chronological "first"—the language one spoke first as a baby? Or is it a functional primacy, "the first in importance" in the total life of the individual—the language that comes to dominate one's life? English is already becoming the first language in the functional sense of dominating the lives of many Africans. Significant sectors of the ruling elites of African states conduct much of their public thinking, and in some cases, much of their private lives, in the English language.

In addition it looks probable that English will become increasingly the first language chronologically of many African children. One sense of "first" tends to lead on to the second sense of "first" in the succeeding generations. For me, English is my first language in terms of dominating my life, both public and private, but it was not my mother-tongue chronologically. To my children, on the other hand, English is the first language in both senses.

My own case is complicated by the fact that the mother of my children speaks English as a native language, and not simply as a functional first language. But the home of my former neighbours in Kampala, Dr. and Mrs. Sekabunga, is bilingual because both English and Luganda are used. There are signs that, in the case of their children, English is gaining the upper hand, partly because at school they get only English, while at home they get both English and Luganda. The functional primacy of English among the parents leads on to the chronological primacy of English among the children.

There is a third category of family in Africa growing in number—it results from "intertribal" marriages among the educated. As the father and mother come from different African linguistic groups, they resort to English as the language of the home. English thus becomes the other tongue of their children with a clear ascendancy over the indigenous languages of both the father and the mother. The emergence of black people who speak English as a native language, chronologically first, is what we term the emergence of Afro-Saxons in the world.[22]

We may be moving towards a situation where English-speaking nations are either white or black—but with virtually no English-speaking nations in Asia in the sense of nations under the control of people to whom English is the mother tongue. At the moment we do have English-speaking nations among black populations in the Caribbean and in Liberia. As the elite of former British Africa pass on their English in the home to their children, and convert their children into genuine black Afro-Saxons, we may expect more nations in Africa that have not only adopted English as the language of government and business, but where English is the language of the home within the ruling elites.

For a number of historical and cultural reasons, Africa was more exposed than Asia to both Christian and linguistic penetration from the West. It is not of course true that African societies constituted a tabula rasa, a blank slate, on which a new mission from the West was to be impressed. The French policy of assimilation certainly assumed a kind of cultural void in Africa, which French culture could fill. It is true that this kind of reasoning was false to its very roots. And yet the smallness of African cultural units, and the degree to which these cultures were often preliterate, made them more vulnerable to the Western impact than were the larger and more militantly traditionalist communities of Asia.

In Asia outside the Phillipines, the English language is likely to continue indefinitely as a language understood only by a minority of the population in each country. In India, the proportion of those who understand English has not been increasing since independence. The quality of spoken English among large sections of Indians who enter universities has in fact declined. The competition of Hindi is one basic factor behind the deterioration of Indian English. In Africa, on the other hand, English is still on the ascendancy. It is conceivable that a majority of people in each so-called English-speaking African country will be able to conduct a conversation in English by the end of the century. Of course, the populations of African countries are much smaller than those of Asian countries. But combined with a demographic resistance to the total Western impact has been the phenomenon of depth among Eastern religions and cultures, and the resultant cultural impermeability among the larger Asian communities.

Should English be de-Anglicized?

If, then, significant numbers of black countries are going to be breeding grounds for Afro-Saxons, the English language itself must sustain closer scrutiny. Is it a language that can be made to bear the experience of the black man? Is it a language that does justice to that experience, and is compatible with the dignity of the new races which are adopting it?

Because of these issues, a number of proposals have been made to reform the English language, the most ambitious of which would amount to its de-Anglicization in the sense of its universalization. An immediate consequence would be to reject the Queen's English as the standard of right and wrong. In Africa, something approaching West African English has already emerged, with usages and tendencies that would be regarded as idiosyncratic by the standards of British English. From British Honduras in the western hemisphere to Papua-New Guinea in the Pacific, forms of language derived originally from English as Creole, Krio, Pidgin, and others, have emerged, all extreme forms of the de-Anglicization of the English language.

Curiously enough, the extreme de-Anglicization of the English language may be the logical result of its universalization, and yet it threatens to nullify that universalism. The considerable variations in usage in different parts of the world could be so great that the very universalism that decreed the de-Anglicization would be negated by the multiplication of dialects. Versions of English would emerge, some further from each other than French is from Italian, or Portuguese is from Spanish. In this sense English can remain universal only if, at the same time, it retains its links with the original version of the Anglo-Saxons themselves. Some kind of standard English might be necessary for the world, and the strongest candidate is the English of the Anglo-Saxons. Divergence from this standard to suit the needs of the new users of the language cannot be helped and to some extent is desirable. Partial de-Anglicization may indeed be implicit in the logic of universalism, but the total de-Anglicization would negate the principle of universal intelligibility.

Yet partial de-Anglicization needs to be promoted by the new users of the language in response to their needs. Militancy for the de-Anglicization of the English language sometimes goes to the extent of demanding a change of name for the language. A delightful controversy broke out in the *East African Standard* (Nairobi) in 1965. Kenya still has a population of Englishmen who regard as among their rightful areas of social influence that of trying to maintain good standards of the Queen's English in this former colony. M. S. Robinson, an Englishman, complained about the degeneration of English in the newly independent Kenya, with particular reference to the impact of broadcasting on linguistic usage. A non-British Kenyan, S. Meghani, disputing this monopolistic approach to the English language, replied that if Robinson did not like the way other people spoke English, he should also remember that others might not like the way he did. "English as spoken by an Englishman is not at all pleasant to listen to . . . let alone easy to follow." Challenging the claims of the English people to the English language, S. Meghani wrote:

> It is not all wisdom on the part of a tiny English population in this wide world to claim that English, as represented and pronounced by Americans, Canadians, Africans, Indians and the people of Madras State is not English. It may not be the Queen's English, but then what? Has the Englishman the sole right to decide upon the form and style of a universal language?

He then asserted that the whole trouble lay in the name which the language continued to bear, a misnomer since English had by far outgrown its origins: Strictly speaking, English cannot be called "English" at all, since it is a universal language belonging to all. "It is difficult to understand why it is still known under that horrible name; it should have had another name."

Within a few days back came a reply from another native speaker of the language, seemingly from the British Isles. This new correspondent confessed that he held the view that civilization was bounded on the north by the Thames—and woe to those overtolerant individuals who would substitute the Trent—on the west by the Tamar and the Severn, and on the south by the English Channel. He then went on to support the suggestion that English as spoken by Meghani and "others of similar linguistic and cultural attainments," including the Voice of Kenya radio announcers, should bear some other name. The new writer thought that was the most sensible suggestion he had heard for a long time:

> As one who holds that the English language is an autochthonous product of that civilization [bounded on North by the Thames and on the South by the English Channel] I feel that your correspondent's suggestion should be acted on immediately or, as he would probably prefer to put it, implemented forthwith. There is however no need to coin a new name for the "universal" language. There is a time-honoured one—"pidgin-English."[23]

A more modest ambition among linguistic reformers is not the de-Anglicization of English, but its deracialization. Adoption as the official language of black states is certainly one step in the direction of deracializing it, but that is by no means enough. The English language, partly because of its origins as a language of white-skinned people, has accumulated a heritage of imagery which invests black men with negative connotations. The "black market" was a market of illicit merchandise; blackmail was an exercise in the exploitation of fear; the blackleg was an adventurer who betrayed collective bargaining by the workers; the "Black Hole of Calcutta" was a miserable instance of the agony of suffocation. If the English language is now to mature into a language of black people, the black users of the language cannot afford to be complacent about the cumulative negativeness of the concept of blackness in English imagery. Of course, users of phrases like "blackmail," "black heart," "black mark on the record of an individual," are not always conscious of the neo-racialistic implications of their usage. But the very unconsciousness of these manifestations of color prejudice could be deemed to aggravate the situation, rather than mitigate it. Prejudice is the more deeply rooted when it springs from automatic spontaneity, without conscious reflection.

The English language has invested blackness with three basic meanings—first, that black was evil; second, that black was void; and third, that black was death. These three areas of negative associations have in fact multiple sub-associations. The association with death, for example, also makes black the color of grief. Conversely, if war is death, white becomes the color of peace.

The Europeanization of Christianity increased these negative connotations of black in the English language. Nothing has captured the association of black with evil more sharply than Blake's poem, "The Little Black Boy." The poem exclaims with a startling revelation: "And I am black but O! My soul is white." John Bunyan and other Christian writers have made suggestions about washing a black man, or an Ethiopian, white as a way of conferring upon him salvation. But John Dryden, the master of the heroic couplet in the late Restoration Period in England, put limitations on the degree of whiteness which could ever deserve hell. To John Dryden the agony of purgatory was the predicament of he who was "too black for heaven, and yet too white for hell."[24] The saturation of the English language with this metaphorical negativeness associated with the color black imposes on the new black users of the English language the obligation to tame and domesticate the language, in the direction of greater compatibility both with black dignity and black experience. This is the process that we have designated as the deracilization of the English language, in some ways a proposition to be accompanied by that *partial* de-Anglicization we have referred to.

The third process that flows on logically from the partial de-Anglicization and the deracialization of the English language is the more positive aspiration to Africanize it. African writers have a special role in this undertaking, as they help to expand the body of African literature, and seek to enrich their version of English with African similes, African proverbs, and African metaphors. Those of their books which find their way into the new systems of education in African countries may help the trend towards the Africanization of English. African fiction in English produced in West Africa is already well on the way towards this kind of commitment. The characters in the novels of Chinua Achebe do not use the Queen's English, they use credible English. As a conscious artist Achebe has himself illustrated how he has sought artistic credibility by maintaining contact with the world of simile and metaphor in West Africa. In his novel, *Arrow of God,* the Chief Priest is telling one of his sons why it is necessary to send him to the mission school:

> I want one of my sons to join these people and be my eyes there. If there is nothing in it you will come back. But if there is something there you will bring home my share. The world is like a Mask, dancing. If you want to see it well you do not stand in one place. My spirit tells me that those who do not befriend the white man today will be saying *had we known* tomorrow.

In an article published later Achebe suggests the following alternative for the same little speech:

> I am sending you as my representative among these people—just to be on the safe side in case the new religion develops. One has to move with the

times or else one is left behind. I have a hunch that those who fail to come to terms with the white man may well regret their lack of foresight.

The author goes on to say that these two speeches have the same material. "But the form of the one is in *character* and the other is not."

Achebe himself revels not only in the distinctiveness of West African English, but also in the very fact that writers like him are not native to the language. He inclines to the view that that very fact, at least for the time being, would put the stamp of distinctiveness on African usage:

> So my answer to the question, Can an African ever learn English well enough to be able to use it effectively in creative writing? is certainly yes. If on the other hand you ask: Can he ever learn to use it like a native speaker? I should say, I hope not. It is neither necessary nor desirable for him to be able to do so.

Achebe captures the essence of combining the Africanization of the English language with a continuing commitment to the role of English as a world language:

> The price a world language must be prepared to pay is submission to many different kinds of use. The African writer should aim to use English in a way that brings out his message best without altering the language to the extent that its value as a medium of international exchange will be lost. He should aim at fashioning out an English which is at once universal and able to carry his own experience. . . . But it will have to be a new English, still in full communion with its ancestral home but altered to suit its new African surroundings.[25]

Achebe's formulation would be well within our conception of a subfederation of Anglophone cultures, each sector of the English-speaking world maintaining its own distinctiveness without departing so far from mutual intelligibility as to render the language no longer useful as a universal currency.

In Asia, English is to some extent on the defensive. Malaysia since federation has sought to make all communities speak Malay, starting as a compulsory subject in all the schools and finally becoming the sole official language of the country. Experiments in providing university education in Malay are certainly under way. In India, a similar tendency is observable to reduce education in English and increase the utilization of Hindi for primary education in at least some parts of the country. It has been estimated that within forty years a third of the urban population and one fifteenth of the rural population may become literate in English, but that literacy in Hindi may be equal to that in English for people in the towns and five times as great in the country. The greatest growth in

351

literacy, so it is estimated, will be in indigenous Indian languages. If fact, literacy in languages other than both Hindi and English by the year 2000 could account for more than half the total literates in India. The concept of "Indo-Saxons" is basically more remote than the concept of "Afro-Saxons."

African linguistic education contrasts strongly with the Asian. There is less of a push in Africa to promote indigenous languages as media for literacy, though some attempts in that direction are under way in Tanzania. There is also less linguistic nationalism generally in Africa than has been observable in places like Malaysia, India, and Bangla Desh. In Africa utilization of English is expanding, whereas in Asia it is declining. African governments are introducing English at an earlier phase in the educational pyramid than the British themselves had done. As Geoffrey Moorehouse put it:

> On both sides of Africa, moreover, in Ghana and Nigeria, in Uganda and in Kenya, the spread of education has led to an increased demand for English at a primary level. The remarkable thing is that English has not been rejected as a symbol of colonialism; it has rather been adopted as a politically neutral language beyond the reproaches of tribalism. It is also a more attractive proposition in Africa than in either India or Malaysia because comparatively few Africans are completely literate in the vernacular tongues and even in the languages of regional communication, Hausa and Swahili, which are spoken by millions, are only read and written by thousands.[26]

It is these considerations favoring the growing ascendancy of the English language among black people that continue to confirm the likelihood of an expanding population of Afro-Saxons.

Winston Churchill once wrote a mammoth three-volume study entitled *A History of the English-Speaking Peoples*. Churchill lived at a time when the English-speaking peoples were overwhelmingly white, and he was basically writing about the Anglo-Saxons. A future Churchillian historian writing a similar study might have to pause and reflect whether the English-speaking peoples did not include a population of Afro-Saxons greater in number than the population of Australia, New Zealand, and Great Britain, added together.

And when a William Wordsworth of the future asserts his people's love of freedom, he might reflect upon the increasing ambiguity of these immortal lines:

> We must be free or die, who speak the tongue
> That Shakespeare spake; the faith and morals hold
> Which Milton held.[27]

352

Those who speak the tongue that Shakespeare spake will by the end of the twentieth century include the descendants of Julius K. Nyerere, President of Tanzania, and translator into Swahili of Shakespeare's *Julius Caesar* and *The Merchant of Venice*. Those holding the faith and morals which Milton held might be deemed to include the descendants of A. Milton Obote, former President of Uganda, who adopted the name Milton in admiration of the author of *Paradise Lost* and some of his moral principles. The Afro-Saxons are not only here to stay; they may be here to multiply.

Conclusion

We started by pointing out the four categories of language: world languages, intercontinental in what they encompass; regional languages, which are international but not intercontinental; national languages, which are enclosed within the boundaries of particular states; and communal languages, which include a variety of sub-national tongues. A major premise of our analysis is that the future of the concept of federated cultures necessitates the facilitation of trends towards the emergence of world languages.

The world languages at the moment are, by our definition, English, French, and perhaps Spanish. All the other languages of the world belong to the other categories, although Portuguese is on its way towards commanding the 100 million speakers which would qualify it. These world languages are overwhelmingly drawn from European culture and European historical experience. As they stand they can be made to bear the experience of others. And much of the analysis of this chapter has been oriented towards demonstrating the issues involved in decolonizing Rudyard Kipling, partially de-Anglicizing the English language, de-racializing it, and finally Africanizing it to serve the pressing demands of the black continent. A language born from other cultures might be invited to serve the destiny of societies distant from its origins. But the preponderance of the Western heritage in the collective pool of human civilization would still need to be reduced and mitigated. A global language policy cannot, therefore, rest simply on the principle of promoting English, French, or Spanish. Ways need to be devised to increase the impact of other languages on the European sector of world civilization. One possible approach is again recommended in the relevant appendix to this book—A Global Language Policy for a Global Cultural Heritage.

Footnotes

1. I have used the figures provided by the British Council in 1963. See the address by Sir Paul Sinker, Director General of the British Council, delivered to the Royal Common-

wealth Society in London, on March 14, 1963. A condensed version of the lecture is published under the title of "The Future of the English Language Overseas," *Oversea Quarterly,* Vol. III, No. 6, June 1963, pp. 171, 173.

2. Senghor, "Negritude and the Concept of Universal Civilization," *Présence Africaine,* Vol. 18, No. 46, Second Quarter, 1963, p. 10.

3. *Ibid.,* p. 10.

4. Thomas Gray *Elegy Written in a Country Churchyard.*

5. M. Hyder, "Swahili in the Technical Age," *East Africa Journal,* (Nairobi), Vol. II, No. 2, February 1966, p. 6.

6. Pierre Alexandre, "Linguistic Problems of Contemporary Africa," *Présence Africaine,* Vol. 13, No. 41, Second Quarter, 1962, p. 21.

7. Untermeyer, (editor) *A Treasury of Great Poems: English and American,* (New York: Simon and Schuster, 1955), pp. 1046–1047.

8. Kipling, "The English Flag." For the quotations from Dilke see Sir Charles Wentworth Dilke; *Greater Britain: A Record of Travel in English Speaking Countries during 1866-7* (London: Macmillan & Co. 1868) Vol. I, pp. vi–viii.

9. Cited by Josiah Strong, *Our Country* (New York: Baker & Taylor 1885), pp. 178–179.

10. Strong, *Ibid.* The lines from Tennyson are from his poem "Locksley Hall" (1842) Lines 1-7, 8.

11. See section on "Education," *Reporter* (Nairobi), Dec. 30, 1966, p. 13.

12. See *The Daily Telegraph* (London) May 27, 1971, p. 4.

13. *The Ballad of East and West.* The rest of the stanza goes thus:
    "But there is neither East nor West, Border, nor Breed, nor Birth,
    When two strong men stand face to face, though they come from the ends of the earth!

14. Orwell, "Rudyard Kipling," *Decline of the English Murder and other Essays* (London: Penguin Books in association with Secker & Warburg, 1965), pp. 56–57.

15. *Ibid.*

16. E. D. Morel, *The Black Man's Burden* (London: B. W. Huebsch, 1920) pp. 7–11.

17. Orwell, "Rudyard Kipling," *loc. cit.,* pp. 50–51.

18. Kipling: "If."

19. Tom Mboya, *Freedom and After* (London: Andre Deutsch, 1963), p. 114.

20. *Thoughts of an African Leader,* compiled by the editorial department of the *Uganda Argus* (Kampala: Longmans Uganda Ltd., 1970), p. 68.

21. Speech, Feb. 14, 1923. See *The Times* (London) Feb. 16, 1923.

22. My Dyason Lecture Series in Australia in 1972 on "Africa, the West and the World" borrowed heavily from this section. Consult also Ali A. Mazrui, *World Culture and the Black Experience* (Seattle: University of Washington Press, 1974), Chapter 3.

23. See Letters to the Editor, *East African Standard* (Nairobi), Feb. 15 and Feb. 19, 1965, p. 4.

24. Dryden, "The Hind and the Panther."

25. Chinua Achebe, "English and the African Writer," *Transition,* (Kampala), Vol. 4, No. 18, 1965, pp. 29–30.

26. Geoffrey Moorehouse, "Tongue Ties," *Manchester Guardian Weekly* (London and Manchester) July 16, 1964, p. 5. The estimates of likely proportions of literacy among Indian languages are also from Geoffrey Moorehouse's two articles to the *Manchester Guardian Weekly* in that year.

27. William Wordsworth, "London, 1802."

CHAPTER 17

Education and World Culture

Of special importance in the homogenization of the intellectual culture of the world is the role of modern education. The impact of the West on the rest of the world has been particularly critical in this regard. The technological triumph of the western world gave its system of education almost universal prestige. Cultures which previously trained and socialized their children in radically different ways saw themselves drawn irresistibly toward the western approach to education.

Once again western imperialism played a part in diffusing and disseminating the central elements of this approach. Some modifications were made in different colonies and dependencies. But on balance the great bulk of the intellectual elite of the world had, by the second half of the twentieth century, emerged from a style of education inherited from western experience. It is true that the West had itself originally learnt aspects of those techniques from other cultures. But that fact simply reinforces the role of modern education as a medium for global cultural convergence in the intellectual sphere.

In black Africa the impact of education was often closely related to the impact of Christianity. We discussed earlier the role of universal religions in the evolution of world culture. But, except in Ethiopia, Christianity came to black Africa rather late. By the nineteenth century the West was itself going secular, but western missionaries in Africa were committed to the task of both "westernizing" and "Christianizing" Africa. The stage was set for one of the great cultural paradoxes of modern African history.

Two interrelated processes were involved—*socialization* and *acculturation*. Socialization is common to all societies. It is the process by which a society transmits its values to the next generation through multiple influences on the young. Socialization could also be exercised on adults as a process of modifying or transforming the intellectual orientations acquired in younger days.

While socialization can and often is within a single culture, acculturation is a trans-cultural phenomenon by definition. We define acculturation as the process by which an individual or a group acquires the

355

cultural characteristics of another through direct contact and interaction:

> From an individual point of view this is a process of social learning similar to that of adult socialization in which linguistic communication plays an essential role. From a social point of view *acculturation* implies the diffusion of particular values, techniques and institutions and their modification under different conditions.[1]

It is indeed worth accepting this distinction between values, techniques, and institutions when we are exploring what Africa has borrowed from the West. The modern school itself is an institution so borrowed. The style of instruction, the general ethos of the school, and the curriculum help to determine what values and techniques are transmitted within those walls.

Techniques require an infrastructure of supportive values. This is particularly clear in economic behavior. As we indicated earlier, certain commercial techniques from the West can only be transferred to an African society if there are supportive entrepreneurial values in the host society to sustain the techniques. Britain and France did not try to transmit either all their values or all their techniques to the colonies, even if this had been possible. Only some Western values and some Western skills were promoted in African schools. But did these partial values match the partial skills? Given the skills which were being sought, were the African schools fostering the right normative orientations? It is our contention that a profound *incongruence* lay at the heart of the imported educational system in African colonies. The wrong western values were being provided as an infrastructure for the wrong western skills. We might call this gap between norms and techniques the *technocultural gap* of the western heritage in Africa.

A major reason for the gap in the field of education lies in the paradoxical role of the missionary school in Africa. On the one hand, the missionary school was supposed to be the principal medium for the promotion of "modern civilization" in Africa. On the other hand, western civilization on its home ground in Europe had become increasingly secular. The best schools in colonial Africa were often religious schools. The missionaries were bringing into Africa a religious feature of western civilization, Christian values, in a form which most westerners had already rejected in the course of their own modernization. Sacred values, sometimes fanatical and prudish, were central to colonial educational systems—and yet the ultimate imperial aim was at the same time for these schools to produce African men and women with modern secular skills necessary for the new society of the twentieth century. A heritage based on a technocultural gap was thus bequeathed to Africa, formulated in a new kind of clash between the City of God and the City of Man.[2]

The Origins of Cultural Schizophrenia

This paradox of the missionary school has had long-term consequences for Africa. It may even lie at the heart of widespread *cultural schizophrenia* in Uganda and elsewhere. We define cultural schizophrenia as the tense ambivalence which arises out of the interplay between dependency and aggression in the process of acculturation. The conquering culture produces fascination and repulsion, emulation and defiance, among its recipients.[3] Christianity soon showed itself unable to withstand adequately these pressures. First, the Christian ideal had to compete with vast opportunities for material advancement that were beginning to open up, especially for the young men. Second, once a man became literate a whole new world became accessible to him. If he was naturally curious, he could find out answers to puzzles by reading literature other than the Bible, which often tended to undermine the faith. Christianity is still taken more seriously in Africa than in Europe, but it has had problems even in Africa. It is not surprising that by the early 1920's complaints about "the demon of materialism" operating among the school population were already becoming widespread among the missionary educators. Increasingly the hope of material gain became the average schoolboy's basic motivation.

Outside of the schools, not only did the Christians try to destroy African cultures but their manner of introducing the new faith could only lead to its own decline without substituting adequate alternative values. Cultural schizophrenia was aggravated when attempts were made to Christianize even African deities. As Okot p'Bitek put it:

Somehow, the Christian missionaries managed to convince themselves that the central Luo really believe in a high god called Lubanga, who after creating the world withdrew from it, and though still supreme, takes no interest in his creations. As Russel put it, "The essence of the Christian message as presented in Uganda has, I would say, been something like this. You believe in a high god, but you believe that that god, having made the world, had no further interest in it and is not concerned with your troubles and joys . . ." Rev. John Taylor, Secretary of the Church Missionary Society wrote, "undoubtedly, it was the influence of the mission and their adoption of this or that name to designate the God of the Bible, which helped to crystallise the concept of the supreme creator even among those who did not become Christians," and he warns, "If God remains 'outside' much longer, Africa's this-worldliness will turn to materialism."[4]

357

There have been attempts, in recent years, to interpret the Bible and religion in a more realistic style that does not make God turn his back on the world. But in many cases this has come too late to avert effectively either the tensions of cultural schizophrenia or the triumph of unmitigated materialism among the new Africans.

The technocultural gap has continued to haunt educational systems in Africa. Secular skills were given a religious infrastructure. And when the infrastructure was rejected, there were no alternative supportive values for the new secular ambitions. Many schools taught the virtues of obedience instead of the ethic of initiative; they taught fear of God instead of love of country; they taught the evils of acquisition instead of the strategy of reconciling personal ambition with social obligation. Religious indoctrination was paramount, political education was anathema—yet the schools were also intended to help create viable modern societies.

Even those tribal communities that responded well to the western stimulus discovered the constraints of the technocultural gap. In this regard it is worth looking at the case of the Baganda in historical perspective, and then go on briefly to compare once again the Baganda with the Japanese.

In Buganda, the palace was both the central political institution and the central educational institution. A system of social mobility hinged, in part, on this dual role of the court. The system of education was profoundly socially oriented, at least to the extent of being interlinked with the survival of the social system. Because the Kabaka's court was the pinnacle of both the political and the educational systems of traditional Buganda, social commitment and service to the king and nation were embedded in the educational system. Personal ambition and patriotic performance were inextricably intertwined. The Ganda traditional educational system was indeed élitist, but there were strong expectations of honorable service from the élite.

> The Royal family alone was regarded as superior to and separate from other classes in virtue of their birth. With this single exception, any member of a clan could rise to the highest position in the land, if he succeeded in making himself conversant with state affairs, was brave in warfare and shrewd in council. As a rule either the sons of the chiefs . . . or those who had been brought up as pages became chiefs, and took the lead among the people partly owing to their birth and surrounding, but partly owing to their superior training which as pages they had received.[5]

It was the king's and to a lesser extent the chiefs' courts which were thus the most important school for those interested in important public positions. Consequently almost every chief of Buganda who had children chose some for service in the palace "that they might learn good behavior. And after it happened that when there were chieftainships to be distributed, the Kabaka thought first of his pages, and not of others, because . . . the palace was the school."[6]

What the British colonial administration did in Uganda was to replace the palace, as the educational institution, with formal schools. They also introduced the art of reading and command of the English language as critical qualifications for attaining high official positions in the land. It is in this sense that Governor Johnston's assurance to the country in 1900 marks a turning point in the development of education in Uganda. The Governor said then: "So far from wishing to shut the Baganda out of the Government of their own country, I want to encourage them to enter into that Government. I want their boys to learn English so that they make take the place of the Indian clerks in the Government offices . . ."[7] The road to offices and the key to advancement was thus to be through the English language. The process of desocializing the educational system was under way. Soon there was a passion for learning how to read and write; especially how to read and write English among all those who could have contact with the schools—to the detriment of any other subjects. Those who would have been pages and from there advanced to become leaders, now saw that within the context of the new "palace" the English language replaced court etiquette and the need to please the Kabaka as means of advancing in life. This led to a number of important developments, especially that the educational system remained élitist but lost its original patriotic commitment and practical orientation.

A comparison between the Ganda and Japanese versions of westernization reveals significant differences in levels of acculturation. It may well be that the Baganda borrowed more of the *values* but fewer of the *techniques* from the West than did the Japanese. A number of factors may go toward explaining the difference between the responses of the two peoples. One was the direct colonization of Buganda as against a looser, far more informal external threat experienced by Japan. True, Japan's experience after World War II, was similar to Buganda's. The American occupation had an impact more nearly comparable to the British colonization of Buganda. Japanese assimilation of western values following the American occupation was therefore at least as rapid as anything that the Baganda underwent under the British. But until that actual occupation by the Americans, the Japanese borrowed more techniques than values from the West.

Another major differentiating characteristic which may account for the different levels of acculturation is language. That the Japanese modernized primarily through the Japanese language and did not become linguistic converts to an alien idiom, accounted for the slower pace of value acculturation as distinct from technical acculturation. The prestige of the English language in Buganda and the extent to which it was used as a medium of instruction and education for the élite, as well as for the aspiring élite, profoundly conditioned the orientation of the leaders. In the words of one observer:

> ... a good many of the élite have, for half a century, been educated in the very type of institution best calculated to produce the maximum socialization impact—the English "public school" type of boarding school, after which the Baganda schools were modelled. The leading Buganda government officials and the leaders of the most important political parties are overwhelmingly "old boys" of the two élite boarding schools—one Anglican and the other Roman Catholic.[8]

Fallers also referred to "more subtle levels of cultural change at which it is possible here only to hint"—clothing as a manifestation of acculturation.

> One of the striking characteristics of Buganda is the ability to wear Western clothing with a real feeling for style. Over much of Africa, Western clothing is worn like an uncomfortable, ill-fitting uniform, but Baganda men and women have penetrated sufficiently into the inner recesses of Western style that many of them can wear Western clothes with real taste.[9]

As regards clothing there may be little difference between the Japanese and the Baganda. Since the American occupation, the Japanese have assimilated western clothing styles with more thoroughness and completeness than anything achieved anywhere else in the non-western world. The multitudes in Tokyo are overwhelmingly attired in a western style and basically according to western tastes. But the retention of their own language as the primary medium of intellectual discourse and transmission of values remains a major difference between the Japanese and Baganda.

Religion also accounts for the greater value acculturation of the Baganda as compared to the Japanese. Christianity has had a greater impact in Buganda than in Japan. The Baganda have embraced the western version of the Christian religion with a deep sense of inner response. So important has religion been in Uganda that it seems to have played a greater role in the politics of the nation than it has done in most other countries of Africa. The Christianization of Buganda must therefore be counted as a critical additional level of difference in acculturation between the Baganda and the Japanese.

But the achievements of the Japanese in technical acculturation have been far more impressive than anything in Uganda. It is not quite clear what the ultimate explanation for this particular differential is, but several factors no doubt have a bearing. Relative size could explain both why small Buganda was conquered faster by the values of the West than big Japan and why she could make less impressive use of western techniques than Japan. Small size facilitates the process of value assimilation because of the rapidity of diffusion in a small area and population. Successful adoption of techniques in such massive areas as industrialization and economic reorganization requires a greater scale of operation. Japan had a bigger base on which to build a modernized economy, and more impressive resources to mobilize for the endeavor.

Further, because of colonial control the direction of change in Buganda was far less in the hands of the Baganda than it was in the hands of the Japanese in Japan. The precise modes of the economic response by the Baganda had to be related to the high dictates of policy of the imperial power. The range of activities engaged in by the populace had also to be subject to the broader aims of British overrule.

The Japanese educational system did remain élitist, but social commitment and patriotic obligation survived the modernization of the educational system. The Japanese were in a position to transform the educational system themselves, and to choose the relevant forms of indoctrination to accompany the transmission of the new skills. They were in a position to innovate educationally, and experiment with new forms of technical and vocational training. They were spared too painful a clash between the pursuit of modernity and the pursuit of piety.

Even after independence Buganda cannot have quite the flexibility and educational choice enjoyed by Japan. After all, Buganda is part of a country, rather than a country by itself. But independence has opened up new opportunities for reappraising the educational system of Uganda as a whole. Yet in that very reappraisal we have come full circle. Some of the questions which independent Africa as a whole has to ask herself are exactly the same questions which colonial policy-makers asked for Uganda at the beginning of the century. The ultimate differences may not lie in the questions asked but in the answers given.

There are also new questions. How is the educational system to cope with the crisis of cultural schizophrenia? How can it handle the tensions of intellectual dependency?

If one were worrying about education in an exclusively white country, the emphasis in educational reform might have to be toward promoting greater toleration of alien cultures and alien groups. In an exclusively black country, one might have to contend not with the problem of intolerance but with the problem of the dependency complex. The educational system in an African country might need to handle the crisis of a sense of psychological inadequacy, sometimes manifesting itself in indiscriminate imitation of western culture, sometimes in aggressive hostility toward that culture. Both cultural aggression and cultural imitation in the black man could be symptoms of an inner dependency complex, still struggling with itself.

What of a country which is racially mixed? Kinship culture again asserts its relevance. There are times when equal attention might need to be paid to, on the one hand, the task of inculcating greater toleration in white children and, on the other, the task of overcoming dependency in colored children. But racially mixed societies are not at the same stage of integration, and the relative sizes of the problems might vary considerably.

As a generalization, we might say that the central problem in South Africa for the time being is not so much black dependence as white arrogance. If one were hoping to see educational reforms in South Africa, the first emphasis might be toward transforming the attitudes of the white children in the direction of greater toleration and understanding of groups other than their own. The problem of the dependency complex in black children, though certainly very much there, is for the time being secondary in a society whose stratification arises primarily from the racial assertiveness of the Whites.

A look at American society reveals different emphases. There is indeed still the lingering problem of white arrogance as an aspect of the American racial scene. On the black side there are two problems—the residual dependency problem and the intermediate problem of anomie. The residual dependency problem may be manifested in "Uncle Toms", a breed of people who are taken or mistaken to be blind imitators of western or Anglo-Saxon norms, and who feel uneasy about being abandoned by the Anglo-Saxon world. It may take more subtle forms than that of blatant imitation, and could sometimes be an aggressive reaction to what is taken to be white abandonment of the black man. Aggression among Blacks in the United States may also be due to anomie, a stage subsequent to dependency. It comes in the agony of rejecting the cultural and protective embrace of Anglo-Saxon liberalism, and then seeking to assert one's inner autonomy in relations with one's former superiors.

This latter kind of problem, is, in a way, the most acute manifestation of a crisis of identity. It is not necessarily the Uncle Toms and securely independent black men in the United States who are devoid of identity. Most of these do have an identity, that of imported black people assimilated culturally in certain directions, and accepting certain expectations in the society into which they have been born. The Uncle Toms are secure in the identities they have. The militants might not like those identities, but it may not be the Uncle Toms who are suffering from a crisis. Very often, it is the militants because they are in an intermediate position between shedding an old dependent personality and acquiring a new autonomous self-conception. In between this leap from the role of an Uncle Tom to a new, autonomously satisfying, alternative self-image, lies that painful period of anomie.

What challenges do these interethnic and interracial problems pose for educational systems? One point which needs to be grasped immediately is that the problem of relations between races has points in common with problems of relations between religious denominations, as in Ireland, or between tribal groups, as in Kenya and Uganda. The educational problems of plural societies may be strikingly similar, regardless of whether the pluralism derives from racial, religious, or ethnocultural differentiation. Some of the basic values which need to be transmitted within the educational system might remain unchanged across this whole spectrum of social pluralism, though there may be additional values unique to a particular country which need to be fed into the socialization process over and above the more general precepts. The link between these and world order values can be critical, as we shall indicate.

On close examination it may well turn out that there are at least three politically significant values which can be inculcated in an educational system and retain relevance regardless of the nature of differentiation in the plural society, and indeed regardless of the regime in power. We might call these values "The Three T's of Training in Nationhood". The T's I have in mind are first, Tolerance; second, Toil; and third, Teamwork. They are themselves to be seen as supplementary perhaps to the three traditional R's of basic education—Reading, Writing and Arithmetic.[10]

Tolerance and Toil

By "Tolerance" I do not mean the promotion of a sense of "brotherhood". The idea of human brotherhood is a religious idea, and people respond to it more positively when they are listening to a sermon in a church than in their day-to-day lives. It is just not realistic to expect people who are otherwise rivals and strongly in competition, without any blood or cultural affinity, to regard each other as brothers nevertheless. Only a few religious individuals, deeply animated by human amity, can transcend notions of ethnic and cultural identification and embrace the human family as a whole. The majority of people can only be asked to tolerate those who are different from them. It is not realistic to expect them to treat total strangers and total aliens as brothers.

The Christian imperative to "love thy neighbor" is a tall order. Even a literal neighbor may be quite demanding—if he plays his record-player too loudly at night, or if his children are boisterous and tend to scream, or if he has a habit of dropping by to borrow eggs never to be returned.

The critical issue for a society is not how much brotherhood there is, but how much tolerance. There is no special credit in being favorably disposed toward your own brother. The real test comes when, in spite of being unable to regard a stranger as your brother, you still succeed in tolerating his unusual and idiosyncratic ways. The educational system should allow for this critical variable in human relations. In childhood especially, notions of kinship and brotherhood are beginning to consolidate themselves and there is a risk in trying to expand them too far.

Our societies need, above all, the capacity to tolerate people of different cultural backgrounds, or different regions or identities, or different political views. Our societies need to be guided not necessarily by the values of liberalism in their totality, such as individualism, nor indeed by the institutions of liberalism, such as certain types of parliaments and certain types of multi-party systems. But our societies do need to be governed by the liberal rules of the game—which simply say "Live and let live" and permit competing viewpoints and competing interpretations of reality to survive together. The liberal rules of the game prescribe toleration of difference and of pluralism.

Tolerance is, in fact, the most difficult of these three values to be inculcated in children. Children are notoriously intolerant at times, and can be painfully and brutally cruel. What kind of approach should be adopted to foster and build up their capacity to tolerate others is perhaps one of the most important and yet intractable problems in the whole field of child education.

Intellectual toleration can be nurtured by a system of education which puts a special premium on debating as an activity. The idea of getting schoolchildren to debate among themselves on a variety of fundamental issues has great potential as a teaching device to promote toleration of differing viewpoints through exposure to radically polarized viewpoints. Every school in Africa must do its best to have a vigorous debating society, with debates several times a term, instead of once or twice a year. By all means combine these debates with the idea of inviting controversial speakers to address current affairs societies, and answer student challenges and expostulations, but controversial speakers should supplement confrontations between students themselves over intellectual issues.

In this regard, there are important differences to be borne in mind between student power in a developed society and student power in an underdeveloped country. Social reformers and student militants in a developed country are confronted with entrenched values, difficult to dislodge or affect without a massive challenge. Therefore, it sometimes makes sense in a developed society for young people to demonstrate in the streets in favor of certain positions, ranging from issues connected with race relations domestically to issues of foreign policy abroad. The young people may be demonstrating against race prejudice in the United States or Britain, or against class inequalities in Japan, or against a war somewhere. But behind these policy issues are the entrenched values of a society that has stabilized itself in certain spheres, combined with entrenched institutions of mature political and economic systems. To make a dent on this complex of structures requires, at times, more than a speech. It requires a demonstration of vigorous dissent, and often more than that.

In African countries, the real problem is not of entrenched values, for these nations are still groping for those social directions we mentioned earlier. There is a mutability of political preferences, some uncertainty as regards ideological positions. Amid these fluid values, demonstrations are not necessarily the appropriate mode of youthful assertion. More than demonstrating, debating should be promoted as a device to help these young people find their own intellectual bearings. Debating becomes a useful technique in a situation of fluid values, partly because it helps to sharpen the faculties of deciding between different values, and gradually developing a sophisticated evaluation of different alternatives. Debating is also a critical training in the art of toleration.

The imperative of Toil, like the other two T's, is subject to cultural variations. As we indicated earlier, attitudes to work are conditoned by certain cultural factors. The incentives to work in traditional Africa were often in the following order: first, the search for the individual's own basic needs and those of his immediate family; second, the individual's contribution to the welfare of neighbors and kinsmen if this was customarily expected; and only third, the individual's interest in accumulating more things for himself and aspiring to self-improvement as distinct from self-maintenance.[11]

The ordering of priorities is quite significant. It is not correct that the traditional African subordinated his own basic needs to those of his community. His own basic needs came first, the needs of his community and kinsmen second, and the need for personal advancement *third*. The incentive to work hard varied accordingly. Working for personal maintenance made good sense; working hard to meet one's normal or cus-

365

tomary obligations to one's kinsmen also made sense; but working hard for some undefined target of self-improvement was in many cases less clearly understood.

The phenomenon of "target workers" in Africa—who came to the cities to satisfy certain specific needs and then went back home, or who worked fewer hours as soon as they were paid more per hour—has been interpreted by various economic anthropologists as indications of the low priority which self-improvement has in traditional African values, if it is regarded as an indefinite process of upward mobility.

The role of schools in dealing with such a scale of values might vary according to the dominant orientation of the government in power. Kenya might be inclined to foster and encourage the ethic of self-improvement, since the government is committed to the goal of creating an indigenous entrepreneurial culture and private enterprise system. Tanzania, on the other hand, might be inclined to preserve the traditional scale of priorities—which put communal work before self-improvement.

But how does the educator know how long Kenya's policies or Tanzania's policies would last? We are back to the difficult problem of trying to decide which values are likely to survive a military coup or an electoral swing. Perhaps educators could investigate ways of transmitting the ethic of work in a manner which attempts to reconcile working for society with working for one's own improvement. The very process of acquiring an education poses the dilemma of education for effective citizenship as against education for personal ambition.

What should be remembered is that the harder it is to acquire an education, the more it will be regarded as a passport to a future life of leisure. Many African children walk long distances every day, and take heavy part-time work, in an endeavor to acquire an education. Because they have acquired their education the hard way, they tend to feel at the end of it that they have now "arrived" and deserve to rest. Thus the educated become, alas, an élite of leisure.

Teamwork and Nationhood

The third "T" of Training in Nationhood is the imperative of *Teamwork*. It is important that, at all levels of education, there should be opportunities for teamwork, ranging from encouragement of basketball and soccer to encouragement of student political societies and social organizations. Not long after the Ugandan coup, a journalist asked me if, in the present situation in Uganda, there was a case for banning student activities on the Makerere campus and other educational institutions. My answer was that the banning of extracurricular student activities would affect the quality of their education. I argued that education was not simply what went on in the classroom, but it was also the experience of being socially engaged and intellectually committed. But behind it all was the further experience of teamwork and collaboration, even in situations where one team has to compete and even quarrel with another.

The aim in this entire exercise could be the inculcation of the rules of national integration. Africa is confronted with ethnic pluralism and cultural diversity; interaction among different tribes could generate considerable stress and tension. The quest is for a system which would permit these groups not only to tolerate each other—which is the first precondition—but also to work with each other in pursuit of shared goals. And even when the groups are in competition, the competition itself should be subject to rules of fair play.

Among the least violent societies in the world is the British. How much of the British tradition of fair play is derived from the place of games in British public schools?

In 1966, Eric Dunning, a sociology lecturer at the University of Leicester, wrote a book entitled *The Making Of Football: A Sociological Study*. (By "football" he meant Rugby.) The history of football went back to the twelfth century and perhaps even earlier. Prior to the nineteenth century the game was rough and loosely organized, but then important changes began to take place. The game began to assume greater sophistication, greater complexity, and greater formal organization. Leadership in this transformation of the game was given by seven great public schools of England—Charterhouse, Eton, Harrow, Rugby, Shrewsbury, Westminster and Winchester, the only public schools which were in existence throughout the period of the game.

From 1840 to 1860 the rules of the game were committed to writing for the first time, and the boys were called upon to exercise much greater self-restraint in their play than had ever been demanded before. Eric Dunning tells us:

> Football became a "mock-fight" which provided as much as possible the pleasures of a real fight without its risks and dangers, a struggle regulated in such a way that the contestants had much less chance than formerly to inflict serious injury or to use physical violence on each other in earnest. Pleasure in playing was enhanced, henceforward, by the fact that the "battle" was not fought by brute force alone, but by force transformed by specific skills. Football became at once spontaneous and highly controlled. Ample room was left for inventiveness and the expression of individuality, but barriers—in the form of explicit rules—were set up to ensure that the excitement of the battle did not carry too far.[12]

Dunning compared the evolving system of the English public school in its games with what was happening in Prussian schools. The Prussian schools at the time were highly authoritarian institutions, in which the equivalent of football was "drill", a regimented activity in which a master barked out the orders and the boys mechanically complied.

Drill reflected the authoritarian structure of the Prussian schools—indeed, of Prussian society as a whole. Duelling in the German universities provides a further contrast. It represented a far more open outlet for aggressive urges—death, serious injury and disfigurement were its frequent accompaniments. Football in the English public schools represented a far more constructive means of channelling aggression.[13]

Because the British public schools provided the ruling élite of the country, and because many of the political norms and institutions evolved out of the history of the British élite, the country's entire political culture was affected in a variety of subtle ways by the principles of restraint, teamwork, and fair play which were partly acquired on the football fields of Winchester, Eton, Rugby and Harrow.

Into their colonies the British introduced some of the games which had helped to shape their own social and political styles. The most popular game in Africa became soccer. The rules of the game were not internalized overnight, nor has soccer always been effective in averting more ferocious forms of aggression. On the contrary, battles have been fought in Kampala over a referee's decision or a linesman's verdict. But the policy-makers of British imperial rule knew what they were doing when they sought to divert the "natives" with a game of soccer on an afternoon or two every week. The virtues of self-restraint, obedience to rules, team spirit on each side, a spirit of fair play toward the opponents, and respect for the referee—these were virtues which were as relevant in politics as they were in sports. They took time to acquire. They had to be taught, and the sports stadium was one school of citizenship.

The experience of British public schools illustrates that transmission of values is not necessarily a matter of lectures in the classroom or sermons in a chapel. It can be done through media far less obvious—like a game of football, "Sixth Form versus School", in nineteenth century Eton.

Perhaps more work needs to be done about how best to transmit, in African conditions, the three imperatives of Tolerance, Teamwork and Toil. Debating societies and games need to be studied more closely in their sociological and psychological implications. They have too often been taken for granted as mere diversions for young people—"after all, all work and no play. . . ." Some school games may be better suited for training in tolerance and teamwork than others. If so, which are which? Educational research could pay renewed attention to the study of sports and games, and their comparative efficiency as media of socialization and promotion of national values. If certain games, as yet untried in African schools, are better for citizenship training than those which are already popular, there is a compelling case for promoting experimentation with the new games. In some situations the gymnasium may be a more effective school of values than an ideological institute can hope to be.

The Three T's and World Order

These three politically significant values if inculcated by the educational system could retain relevance regardless of which government is in power. They could also serve as carrier values or Trojan horses by which world order values might infiltrate educational systems. If these are carrier values for our world order performances in what way do they carry out their assignment?

The great strength of these carrier values is that they emphasize the interconnection of the world order values we have in mind. The principal of tolerance certainly has great relevance both for the minimization of violence and for the promotion of social justice. The term *tolerance* in this case would have to be defined in a way which encompasses mutual recognition of human worth, as well as the capacity to withstand the stresses of human differences. The two elements together should interact in the direction of increased social amity and fair play, and away from the direction of imminent social violence.

Toil, if it is conditioned by considerations of mutual recognition of human worth, could increase productive capability and help to maximize economic welfare. Well-organized toil also has a propensity to reduce areas of human frustration, increase a sense of human creativity and fulfillment, and therefore divert constructively the forces of human aggressiveness. It can, indeed, often be said that *boredom is bloodthirsty.* The sense of functional redundancy could activate the desire for violent experimentation. Boredom at the barracks in African countries has sometimes resulted in military coups. Boredom in American ghettos has sometimes resulted in black rioting and looting. The bored husband in diverse societies has sometimes resorted to beating up his wife.

The urge to terrorize that arises in the frustrated human mind can sometimes be neutralized by opportunities for constructive work. Work can, therefore, be a cleansing process both for the individual and for the society in which he lives. The association of work with cleanliness is something which has occurred to social analysts before. For example, in 1860 the Russian writer, Nikolai Alexandrovich wrote about work and cleanliness among certain Protestant denominations.

At first glance the juxtaposition of the words work and cleanliness seems strange. One can imagine that the only connection between them is a bath at the end of one working week to renew oneself for the next. There is however something still more fundamental about which I would like to say something. . . . Among [the Protestant peoples] labor gives rise to cleanliness. Both one and the other are inexplicably connected; for labor is the honor of the *moral* man and cleanliness of the physical. It is the honor of his body.[14]

As we indicated earlier, Tanzania has attempted to link work with general political health and with the promotion of a good society. The work ethic has been used as a slogan for national mobilization. But less clearly articulated as a function of work is the task of averting a sense of social redundancy in the population. By helping to mitigate the risk of this sense of redundancy, the imperative of toil helps to reduce the risk of violent eruptions in the society. Tanzania is already one of the least politically violent countries in Africa. The work ethic of the régime may help to maintain that distinctive feature of the country.

The third carrier value postulated, teamwork, emphasizes interconnections with other ambitions. Teamwork is an assertion of interdependence; and in the economic sphere it could be part of the strategy of maximizing economic welfare. Hierarchical interdependence could increase economic welfare more for the higher level of the hierarchy than the lower level.

Precisely because it is hierarchical, the division of labor is implicitly a denial of social justice. The idea of dividing the world between those who hew wood and draw water and those who are engaged in more sophisticated human enterprises and who consume higher levels of human luxuries is basically a hierarchical division of labor.

A horizontal division of labor, however, asserts parity of esteem as a foundation of social justice, while promoting a more efficient organizational basis for productivity. Teamwork as a carrier value in this analysis should, therefore, aim at promoting the horizontal interdependence. Our own example of systemic inculcation of teamwork is drawn from the English society, which, however, is a system of deference and hierarchy. Much of the teamwork inculcated in British public schools, while emphasizing the principles of fair play, nevertheless also emphasizes the legitimacy of hierarchy on which British society is based. The example of England offers many insights as to how the promotion of tolerance, toil and teamwork could result in one of the least violent political cultures in the world, and one of the most tolerant, in at least some respects. But the ultimate refinement of the transmission of a spirit of teamwork should aspire to horizontality and parity of esteem, rather than a hierarchical division of privilege and function.

Teamwork, in turn, by emphasizing the dimension of interdependence could help to reduce propensities toward violent relations between those interdependent units. Calculated horizontal interdependence can be a safeguard against the possibility of war between countries, as well as violence between groups. After World War II, for example, Germany and France were so suspicious of one another that they united to form the European Coal and Steel Community, a proposal originating with the then Foreign Minister of France, Robert Schuman, in May 1950. Two major ambitions underlay the plan. Economically it was hoped to achieve more efficient production and more rational distribution. Politically, Schuman expressed the hope that "the solidarity in production thus established will make it plain that any war between France and Germany becomes not merely unthinkable but materially impossible". Uwe Kitzinger has argued that French motives were "mixed": "Like the whole notion of the European federation itself, the Schuman Plan arose out of a concern over Germany's revival and over economic policy no less than over foreign policy at large."[15]

What emerges from this illustration is yet another example of the relevance of *teamwork* as a value capable of helping to minimize the threat of collective violence. Bringing the three carrier values together, it might therefore be said that *toiling on the basis of teamwork is itself a foundation for tolerance.* The interdependence between the values themselves is fundamental to their efficacy.

Education and the Dependency Complex

While the inculcation of the three T's might promote integrative inclinations in plural societies on at least a minimal level, and while they may help in carrying world values, they are not enough by themselves to overcome the crisis of dependency among black people in Africa, the Caribbean, and the Americas. The crisis of dependency has two main manifestations: aggressive dependency and submissive dependency. The black movement in the United States has moved from a stage of submissive dependency to a stage of aggressive dependency; some parts of English-speaking Africa are also entering the initial phases of aggressive dependency; but much of French-speaking Africa is still in a mood of submissive dependency.

We drew attention earlier to the work of Udai Pareek and his analysis of the dependency complex in relation to motivational patterns and planned social change. We noted that there were points of comparison with Murray's proposed "psychogenic need" of "succorance". The behavioral characteristics include:

"... the wish to have one's needs gratified by the sympathetic aid of an allied object; to be nursed, supported, sustained, surrounded, protected, loved, advised, guided, indulged, forgiven, consoled; to remain close to a devoted protector; to have a permanent supporter."[16]

Other manifestations analyzed in relation to dependency inclinations include high deference, negative attention-seeking, and positive attention-seeking.

Negative attention-seeking is a step toward the aggressive manifestation of the dependency complex. At its more developed it becomes an aggressive rejection of authority—what has been called "counter dependency". Black militancy in the United States often falls within this category. Again it is intimately linked with problems of alienation and even of anomie.

O. Mannoni has discussed submissive dependency at its most elaborate among the people of Malagasy. In part, Mannoni sees this as a quest to recreate feudal relationships:

If left to themselves, the majority of Malagasys would, it is certain, spontaneously and even unthinkingly strive to recreate a feudal type of society. They would call it a republic or a democracy, but their need for dependence would drive them almost inevitably to organize a society composed of clienteles grouped about patrons in the way they like best. They would lack the courage to face the terrors of a genuine liberation of the individual.[17]

In the case of the black Americans, it was not a literal feudal order from which they emerged—it was a slave society. And the slave society could induce in the slaves depths of dependence even more acute than those perpetrated by feudalism.

Mannoni's analysis of the Malagasy does not adequately distinguish between aggressive dependency and submissive dependency. Moreover, Mannoni often assumes that the aggression arises when the protector is no longer able or willing to provide comfort to his ward. But, in fact, the aggression can arise out of a desire for liberation which outstrips the *will* to be liberated. The desire for liberation could be, at the surface of attachment, more shallow than the real will. It could be an intellectualized emotion or "freedom" rather than an activated instinct for self-autonomy.

The militant black American may be at once resentful of the heritage of dependency at the intellectual level and simultaneously held down by the neo-feudalistic psyche which still controls him. Mannoni comes nearest to capturing this particular dilemma when he says:

If the collapse of dependence merely breaks the bonds without putting anything in their place, then clearly the man who finds himself suddenly independent in this way will no longer be able to tolerate guidance, but will yet be unable to guide himself. He will then fall prey to Pascalian despair, existentialist anguish, dereliction. The paths to freedom are more tortuous than this vertical drop into independence or Kunkel's straight path back to dependence.[18]

In much of black Africa submissive dependency is more prevalent than aggressive dependency or counterdependency. The causes of submissive dependency include the processes of conquest, the processes of conversion, and the processes of acculturation. Cultural schizophrenia is less pronounced at the submissive than at the aggressive stage of dependency.

Becoming a conquered people is not in itself enough to create a dependency complex. In the classical world the Greeks retained their sense of superiority, and even succeeded in partially Hellenizing the Romans, their conquerors. There is a difference between conquest by quantitatively superior military forces and by qualitatively superior fighting capability, that is, a more advanced military technology. In a book addressed to Africans, Dame Margery Perham said:

> Let it, therefore, be admitted upon both sides that the British Empire like others, was obtained mainly by force. Even where there was no serious fighting, news of victories nearby, or *the fear of stronger weapons,* was often enough to persuade tribes to accept the rule of the white strangers. . . . African tribes, backward, disunited, weak, were helpless before Europe, *especially since the perfection of the machine gun.*[19]

After a while, Pax Britannica was maintained through what has been called "an economy of force". A few hundred British officers exercised power over millions of Indians in the Indian sub-continent and a minimal British presence in Africa managed to contain and pacify large areas of the continent. The beginnings of a military inferiority complex among Africans lay deep in the mode of the original conquest. In 1964, two years after independence, when some Ugandan soldiers mutinied, Prime Minister Milton Obote felt compelled to invite British troops to come back. So great was the legend of their invincibility that they disarmed the mutineers and recovered the armoury at Jinja without a single shot being fired, the local mutineers capitulating like lambs. It is, of course, conceivable that the British reputation has now sufficiently waned for greater resistance to be shown by local soldiers in the face of a British military challenge. But for our analysis what needed to be noted was simply the reaction in 1964, two years after Uganda had attained sovereign statehood. The dependency complex among the soldiers, derived from deep within imperial history, and the assumption of high military technology and power, was so acute that 450 Scottish guards imported

373

into Uganda did not have to fire a single shot to restore order. The soldiers were also flown into Tanzania where the mutiny was much more serious and encompassed two battalions. From all accounts, there were only a few casualties, though three of them were fatalities. The rest of the Tanzanian force submitted without further resistance to a force much smaller in size.

The other two causal factors behind the dependency complex in Africa are related through the educational system: conversion to Christianity and acculturation to western education and western styles. As we indicated, the missionaries in Africa took a leading role in creating an educational infrastructure for African societies and therefore the dependency complex became extra strong. Christian values, which in the western world had already been challenged by the growth of liberalism and individualism, were in Africa transmitted unmodified. Values of submitting to authority, accepting one's place in the grand design of God, and showing deference toward superiors, strongly conditioned many a missionary school in an African town or village. The missionaries themselves acted almost like rural feudal lords in their own domains, exercising influence and extending the comforts of paternalism. In the words of the Kenya leader, Oginga Odinga: "The missions dominated African education. The government, by neglecting to provide state schools, left the field to the various denominations, which presided over their schools and congregations as though over small empires."[20]

As the role of the government in education increased, a curious paradox began to be discernible: the spirit of political conformity and political deference seemed to be more prevalent among those students produced by missionary schools than among those produced by government schools. In other words, deference to governmental authority was itself better inculcated by Christian religious teachers than under government arrangements. The main reason may simply have been that government schools were less well geared for the task of direct political indoctrination than religious schools were for the task of religious teaching. And religious teaching could be conducted in such a way that deferential political attitudes might be acquired therefrom. While in British Africa there was some form of indirect political indoctrination, arising from the books chosen for schools, the Anglocentrism of much of the syllabus, and the general mystique of the Empire and the Crown, there were few lessons in direct political education as such. Yet missionary schools could give lessons about giving unto Caesar that which was Caesar's, through formal classroom situations, without offending the more liberal side of British susceptibilities. Missionary schools became better instruments for the creation of the dependency complex than direct government schools.

A study of schoolchildren carried out in Tanzania after independence revealed that "government direction of social improvement is seen as more important by those who have only attended religious schools than by those in government schools." The students who had been "isolated from secular influences—tend to show a lower sense of personal efficacy than do students whose schooling had occurred in government schools."[21]

The School and the Psyche

To break the influence of religious submissiveness in African schools after independence, policies of secularization are indispensible. Sometimes it is too readily assumed that putting the schools under government control and financing would be enough of a secularizing measure. Unfortunately this is not the case. Missionary schools continue to be a focus of religious denominations even after they have been taken over by the government:

> Today all schools [in Tanzania] are responsible to the national government, but in organization and general tone strongly reflect the nature of their founding agency. In our sample, schools founded by a religious society are attended almost exclusively by students of the corresponding religion, whereas the government schools are heterogeneous in religious composition.[22]

The aim of secularization should therefore emphasize heterogeneity in the composition of students, rather than simply nationalization of policy and control. For as long as the overwhelming majority of a particular school are, say, Catholic, the mere control of the school by government is not enough of a secularizing agency. The life-style of the school and the nature of interaction would make it a reinforcing agency for Catholic upbringing at home, rather than a mechanism for secular socialization.

In countries which are both multi-ethnic and multi-religious, there should be a purposeful policy to ensure that each school not only mixes races and tribes but also religions. The theory of cross-cutting loyalties as a mechanism for integration provides the basis for this recommendation. If some black families are Catholic and some are Protestant, and some white families are Catholic and some are Protestant, integration in schools should not only aim to mix Blacks with Whites but also to mix, at the same time and in the same school, black Catholics with white Catholics and black Protestants with white Protestants. The fact that these categories in such a school overlap and cut across each other would itself reduce the dangers of a neatly reinforced confrontation. On some issues White would team up with White against a black opposition, but on others white Protestants would team up with black Protestants against Catholic opposition. The fluidity of alliances afforded by criss-crossing pulls of this kind would themselves be a step away from a petrified and rigid ethnic confrontation.

Another precondition for the promotion of interethnic amity is the application of the principle of *cultural parity* to the curriculum. Where groups have different cultural backgrounds it is imperative that the educational system should not betray too sharp an evaluation in favor of one cultural heritage as against another. The eruption of black studies in the United States is itself one indication of the quest for cultural parity in the educational system of that country. But black studies has to be an intermediate measure, to restore balance, rather than a permanent innovation. After all, there are no "white studies" as a distinct area of academic pursuit in the United States. To single out black studies as a separate entity does itself imply an *absence* of cultural parity. Full cultural parity would only be achieved when the educational system has integrated more coherently a respect for the black heritage into one curriculum, instead of isolating it as a separate quaint preoccupation. And yet, in the face of previous lags and imbalance in the educational curriculum, black studies remain an important improvisation pending a more integrated restoration of balance.

In Africa, cultural parity also requires important reforms in curricula and syllabuses. The inherited assumption that not enough African history has been recorded to be usable in school syllabuses has already been vigorously challenged. Courses in African history are provided increasingly, though the pace of Africanization of syllabuses has been considerably slower in former French Africa than in former British Africa. The introduction of creative writing by Africans as part of the course in literature is another innovation of the last few years. Books by African writers are being introduced with increasing emphasis in African schools. Basically, in much of English-speaking Africa, there is a vigorous pursuit for cultural parity, though many educational reformers among Africans would argue that not enough has been achieved. Francophone Africa, in submissive dependency within the educational system, continues to be decisively Franco-centric.

Finally, there is the problem of the staffing of schools. In the United States, the use of Jewish teachers in many black schools has raised special problems of tension. At times, this has resulted in black anti-

Semitism. In New York the crisis of 1969, with the teachers' strike and the demands of black ghettos for local communal control of schools, highlighted a problem which has continued.

A situation where a disproportionate number of teachers belong to a different community from the students they teach has potentialities for creating either submissive dependency or aggressive dependency. In the United States, aggressive dependency among black children in schools has, from all accounts, been rising. The situation has become critical with regard to women teachers, who feel increasingly insecure among boys of different ethnic origins. Cases of juvenile brutalization of women teachers, even of rape by assertive sixteen-year-olds ravishing their teachers, were reported in the first few months of 1971.[23]

In much of Africa the massive use of expatriate teachers continues to consolidate submissive rather than aggressive dependency. The very conspicuous presence of expatriate teachers in schools reinforces certain aspects of the image of the white man as a father figure with certain skills. The accumulation of layers of this kind of perception might later result in an aggressive rejection of the white presence as a form of counterdependency. Cultural schizophrenia would then have entered a more disruptive stage.

Two policy recommendations are particularly urgent. One concerns the headmaster. As rapidly as possible African secondary schools should have African headmasters, particularly in those schools which have a disproportionate number of white teachers. The idea of a black man right at the top of authority could make considerable difference in mitigating the tendency toward paternalistic attachment which the presence of white teachers might occasion. A black headmaster, clearly active and in authority, helps to reduce the dangers of socializing the children into a persistent dependency orientation toward the white man.

The second policy recommendation concerns the primary schools. Unless it is desperately necessary, there should, in fact, be no white expatriates teaching in black primary schools. First, the primary age is a particularly impressionable stage in the socialization process. It is important that at this stage the child should be spared conditioning influences which would adversely affect his orientation toward the expatriate world. Second, it is imperative that the teaching at the primary level be by indigenous teachers because of the very structure of primary education. At the primary level the child typically has one teacher in any particular year, or at any rate one main teacher. There are continuities here with the role of the parents, emphasized by the very fact that the teacher remains the same. As Talcott Parsons has argued in relation to the American educational system:

> The first major step in socialization, beyond that in family, takes place in the elementary school, so it seems reasonable to expect that the teacher-figure should be characterized by a combination of similarities to and differences from parental figures. The teacher, then, is an adult, characterized by the generalized superiority, which a parent also has, of adult status relative to children. She is not, however, ascriptively related to her pupils, but is performing an occupational role—a role, however, in which the recipients of her services are tightly bound in solidarity to her and to each other. . . . The process of identification with the teacher which has been postulated here is furthered by the fact that in the elementary grades the child typically has one teacher, just as in the pre-Oedipal period he had one parent, the mother, who was the focus of his object-relations. The continuity between the two phases is also favored by the fact that the teacher, like the mother, is a woman. But, if she acted only like a mother, there would be no genuine reorganization of the pupil's personality system. This reorganization is furthered by the features of the teacher role which differentiates from the maternal.[24]

Given this high potentiality for socialization into dependency, it is imperative that African primary schools should rapidly Africanize their entire teaching staff, as well as vigorously pursue the principle of cultural parity in the curriculum afforded the young minds.

Conclusion

Educational techniques have not only been important historically for the emergence of world culture but can be used more effectively now to promote ethnic amity and world order values. In much of the United States the problem is no longer simply that of coping with inculcating toleration in young white children, but also of finding ways to cope with the consequences of generations of dependency among black people. The most dramatic eruptions among Blacks in the United States are either in the form of anomie, as values totally disintegrate, or in the form of aggressive counterdependency. The distinction between the two is not very sharp in situations of racial militancy. The major difference is that anomie need not become aggressive, but could take the form of despair and total withdrawal. But counterdependency, by definition, takes a militant stand against the domination from which it has not itself fully escaped.

Wherever plural societies exist, three values at least need to be promoted. We have called these the three T's of nationhood and global responsiveness, the values of Tolerance, Toil and Teamwork. They are designed to foster a capability for tolerating differences, a commitment to social application and endeavor, and a readiness to collaborate with others in pursuit of shared goals. Children at school could be introduced to these values through a variety of devices, ranging from debating societies to sports and games.

We have also discussed cultural schizophrenia and the acute phenomenon of dependency within Africa, which is still more submissive than aggressive, especially in Francophone Africa. We have suggested that certain changes need to be made not only in the curriculum, but also in the structural organization of the schools. In the curriculum the paramount principle has to be that of cultural parity, designed to emphasize equality of worth and value in the inherited cultures of the different groups represented in the school. On the structural side attention has to be paid both to the composition of the student body and the composition of the staff. Heterogeneity in the student body should be the ambition in each case—where possible of a criss-crossing kind based on diversity of faiths as well as diversity of ethnicity.

On the staff side, heterogeneity should also be a guiding principle where the composition of the students is truly mixed. But in African conditions the guiding principle should be Africanization of all headships of secondary schools as rapidly as possible, and the Africanization of the entire teaching staff of primary schools as rapidly as possible. The teachers in African schools should attempt to be tribally and religiously heterogeneous, even if they are pigmentationally homogeneous.

In the United States a modification of the policy is in order. Black schools should, as far as possible, aim for heterogeneous staffing, with a black headmaster, conspicuously authoritative and active. It would not do to have a black headmaster mistaken for just a figurehead, an Uncle Tom placed there for appearances. His authority over his staff should not be too subtle. White schools should attempt to have at least one or two black teachers, and, where realistic, a black headmaster. The images which have to be transformed in black children are fundamentally different from those which need to be transformed in white children. It therefore makes sense in white schools to permit a black headmaster where one is available and suitable; but a white headmaster in a black school should, for the time being, be avoided.

While the introduction of such educational techniques needs to be seriously considered, it ought always to be remembered that the school is, in the final analysis, only one agency of socialization, only one factor in identity formation among young people. Society as a whole must engage in similar self-analysis for reform if the positive effects of a rational educational system are not to be neutralized by countervailing influences from the social world beyond the classroom.

Moreover, in addition to infiltrating the cultures of individual societies the world over, these three values of tolerance, toil and teamwork have somehow to determine the relations *between* or *among* those various cultures. Out of those carrier values may emerge the principles of cultural toleration, the principle of purposeful cultural activation, and the principle of cultural interdependence. Tolerance comes into play because of the need for parity of esteem among the different cultural heritages of the world—a readiness to respect someone else's culture even if one fails to understand it. Toil comes indirectly as a counterpoise to cultural inertia. The heavy weight of tradition could suffocate human innovation, and create a sense of resistance to new influences. To that extent cultural inertia in individual countries could be a major stumbling block to the evolution of a world culture. There has to be some minimal responsiveness to mutual cultural interaction if the world is to become at once rich in what it has to offer and rich in what each segment has absorbed from others.

Teamwork and interdependence constitute the process of interaction itself. Starting from the premise that cultural enrichment is an exercise in pluralistic teamwork, the different cultures should facilitate mutual exposure. Cultural interaction is a stage above mere cultural toleration. The latter is an exercise in mutual respect, and is, as it were, the minimum degree of relationship that should exist between cultures. Cultural interaction is readiness to borrow from each other and to learn from each other.

Only a small fraction of each culture need be borrowed by another. In this connection, what we have in mind is not cultural homogenization but cultural *convergence*. The area of mutual borrowing is the interaction, and is to be controlled by the principle of teamwork and interdependence. The rest of each culture is to be subject to the principle of tolerance. What one person is not prepared to borrow from another, he should at least be prepared to respect and tolerate in the other.

The quest underlying all this is for some degree of a homogenized intellectual culture as a precondition for adequate world reform. This is not a plea for the abolition of pluralism in the world. Pluralism cannot be abolished even if there was a policy recommendation to that effect. The modern school can now move from its historic role as the carrier of western culture to a new commitment involving parity of esteem and more symmetrical cultural convergence.

Footnotes

1. See G. Duncan Mitchell, *A Dictionary of Sociology* (London: Routledge and Kegan Paul, 1968). See also Dent Ocaya-Lakidi and Ali A. Mazrui, "Secular Skills and

Sacred Values in Uganda Schools," Conference on "Conflict and Harmony between Western and African Education," University of London, March 27–30, 1973.

2. Consult also Ali A. Mazrui, "Moral Puritanism Under a Military Theocracy: The Sacred Origins of Uganda's Second Republic." Lecture delivered at Makerere Main Hall, July 20, 1972. (Mimeo.)

3. See also Mazrui, "The Soldier, the Socialist, and the Soul of Development," paper presented at conference on "Dependency and Development", sponsored by Canadian African Studies Association and Carleton University, Ottawa, February 15–18, 1973. The terms "dependency complex" and "cultural schizophrenia" are not used here in a clinical sense, but in a looser sense of psychological approximation.

4. Okot p'Bitek, *Religion of the Central Luo* (East African Literature Bureau, 1971), pp. 49–50.

5. John Roscoe, *The Baganda* (London, Macmillan, 1911), p. 246.

6. P. M. Lwanga, *Obulamu Bw'Omutaka, J. K. Miti, Kabazzi* (Life of the Clan Head, J. K. Miti, Kabazzi) (Kampala, 1954), p. 3, cited by Tom Watson, *History of Christian Missionary Society High Schools in Uganda, 1900–1925: The Education of a Protestant Elite.* Unpublished Ph.D. Thesis, 1962, Makerere University Library, Kampala.

7. Johnston to Jackson, 24 January 1900. In Watson, *Ibid.* See also Dent Ocaya-Lakidi and Ali A. Mazrui, "Secular Skills and Sacred Values in Uganda Schools," *loc. cit.*

8. Lloyd A. Fallers, "Ideology and Culture in Uganda Nationalism," *American Anthropologist,* Vol. 63, 1961, pp. 677–686.

9. *Ibid.*

10. These three T's were first discussed in my address on "The Educational Implications of National Goals and Political Values in Africa," given to the first biannual conference of the International Association for Teacher Education held at Makerere from March 29 to April 2, 1971. See also Mazrui, "Educational Techniques in Plural Societies," *International Social Science Journal,* Vol. 24, No. 3, 1972, pp. 149–165.

11. See Mazrui, *Cultural Engineering and Nation-Building in East Africa* (Evanston, Illinois: Northwestern University Press, 1972), Chapter 14.

12. Dunning, "The Concept of Development: Two Illustrative Studies," in Peter L. Rose (editor), *The Study of Society: An Integrated Anthology* (New York: Random House, 1967), pp. 884–885.

13. *Ibid.,* p. 885.

14. See Mel'Gunov, "Respect for Work and Cleanliness," first published in *Nashe Vremya,* No. 31, August 14, 1960, pp. 493–496. I am grateful to Philip Shashko's revival of the manuscript in his "Nikolai Alexandrovich Mel'Gunov on the Reformation and the Work Ethic," *Comparative Studies in Society and History,* Vol. 9, No. 3, April 1967, pp. 256–265.

15. Kitzinger, *The Challenge of the Common Market* (Oxford; Blackwell, 1962), p. 10.

16. See S. Hall and G. Lindzey, *Theories of Personality* (New York: Wiley, 1957). Consult Udai Pareek, "Motivational Patterns and Planned Social Change," *International Social Science Journal,* Vol. 20, No. 3, 1968, pp. 470–471.

17. Mannoni, *Prospero and Caliban: The Psychology of Colonisation,* translated by Pamela Powesland (London: Methuen and Company, 1956,) p. 65.

18. *Ibid.*

19. Margery Perham, *Africans and British Rule* (London: Oxford University Press, 1941), pp. 53–54, 60. The emphasis is mine.

20. Oginga Odinga, *Not Yet Uhuru* (New York: Hill and Wang, 1967), p. 63.

21. See Kenneth Prewitt, George von der Muhll, and David Court, "School Experiences and Political Socialization: A Study of Tanzanian Secondary School Students," *Comparative Political Studies,* Vol. 3, No. 2, July 1970, p. 213.
22. *Ibid.*
23. See, for example, *The Observer* (London), April 4, 1971.
24. See Talcott Parsons, "The School Class as a Social System," *Harvard Educational Review,* Vol. 29, 1959, pp. 297–318.

CHAPTER 18

Mobility and World Culture

Of the three social changes which need immediate acceleration in pursuit of cultural federalism—the enhancement of mobility, world language, and an educational policy designed toward achieving a more equitable distribution of *creativity*—we have yet to discuss the first. Let us now turn to the issue of mobility.

We shall stress two forms of mobility—physical and intellectual. By physical mobility we simply mean the capacity of men and equipment to move around physically in the world, and beyond the world. By intellectual mobility we mean the whole revolution of communicated ideas—including the "mobility" of news and transmission of ideas through the radio, television, airmail editions of newspapers, and circulation of books and pamphlets. Physical mobility does indeed entail violence by remote control, involving long-distance warfare and the risk of universal annihilation. Intellectual mobility, on the other hand, tends to globalize awareness about shared dangers for the human race, however modest this dissemination of awareness may have been so far. Intellectual mobility is also intimately linked to the linguistic trends and educational ambitions basic to cultural federalism.

In terms of their impact on world history, physical and intellectual mobility are symbolized by two entities—a ship and a poem. The ship is the *Mayflower,* which took disgruntled Puritans to populate a new world; the poem is Rudyard Kipling's "The White Man's Burden". The *Mayflower* signified the capacity of individuals to rally together, migrate thousands of miles away from home and create a new civilization, for better or for worse. Kipling's poem, on the other hand, signifies not so much colonization in the oldest sense of creating settlements away from home, but colonialism in the sense of establishing political rule elsewhere. Both the *Mayflower* and the concept of the white man's burden remain two of the most significant instances of mobility in world history. Their relevance for the globalization of world culture has not always been fully grasped. It is to this mobile duality of a ship and a poem that we should now turn.

The Mayflower and World Culture

The populating of newly discovered America was the most dramatic fulfillment of the principle of nomadic self-determination, the right to move around territorially, so far accomplished. Before the advent of colonial rule in Africa, it was possible in some regions for a small clan or an extended family, dissatisfied with the parent tribe, to move physically and establish itself elsewhere. This concept of nomadic self-determination was not entirely absent from European political thought at the time. John Locke's idea of "tacit consent" presupposed that a person, dissatisfied with his rulers, had the means to move on to some other land. Locke argued that remaining in the same society and accepting the protection afforded by it implied accepting the legitimacy of the system. The man who therefore remained a member of society A must be presumed to have tacitly consented to the government exercised within it.

The Anglo-Irish philosopher, Edmund Burke, so defined a country as to assume the mobility of cultural collectivities. Burke's definition of a country would have found ready supporters in the Africa of such tribal and clan mobility. Burke asserted: "Our country is not a thing of mere physical locality. It consists in a great measure in the ancient order into which we are born. We may have the same geographical situation, but another country, as we may have the same country in another soil. The place that determines our duty to our country is a social, civil relation."[1]

The voyage of the Mayflower became an important exercise in nomadic self-determination—a grand precedent which was followed later by many other adventures in intercontinental mobility. Burke's idea that a country is not a territory but a way of life found an important illustration in some of these migratory groups. Burke himself later came to defend the American colonies against George III mainly in terms of his vision that the colonists were Englishmen abroad and the colonies themselves an extension of England. The territory might be different, but the way of life was intended to continue.

But regardless of whether this particular interpretation of the significance of the colonies is tenable, the mere fact that the Mayflower symbolized a new era of nomadic self-determination converted the whole episode into one of the great dramas of human history.

In the four centuries before the twentieth, the greatest transplantation of peoples in human history took place as millions of Europeans left their home lands, crossed oceans, and made for themselves new homes in overseas lands. These immigrants brought with them what has been aptly called their "cultural baggage"—their language, religion, folk habits, and experience and attitudes of government.[2]

North America, South America, Australia and New Zealand, and South Africa all represent important demonstrations of human mobility as a major factor in the history of the last 500 years.

In the case of black people exported to the Americas, the movement westward was involuntary. But there was a case of nomadic self-determination in the subsequent "back to Africa" black movement in the New World. One such movement was, of course, the unsuccessful but ideologically influential one led by Marcus Garvey. The black people of the New World were a people who had been exported to the Americas by the most blatant of all denials of freedom—outright enslavement. But the dilemma about migrating back to Africa or remaining in the United States was at times based on a meaningful set of alternatives, especially in those recurrent periods when Liberia actively tried to recruit immigrants from the United States. It would therefore be true to say that the Blacks of America who did return to their ancestral home in Africa had in the main exercised some kind of nomadic self-determination.

Meanwhile the United States itself grew, prospered, and came to bestride this narrow world like a colossus. Nomadic self-determination within America itself had taken the form of the civilization of the frontier. The readiness of individual colonists to move westward was itself an impressive migratory phenomenon. And because it was a movement of individuals, rather than of tribes, it may have played an important part in shaping the myths and values which have conditioned both the political and economic dimensions of American culture. Frederick Jackson Turner's epoch-making essay on *The Significance of the Frontier in American History* captured the essential elements of this approach to the understanding of America. Turner, as we know, argued that American democracy itself was fundamentally the outcome of the experience of the American people in dealing with the West and in taming the frontier. The wilderness moulded the colonial settler. It found him in European dress, with European industries, tools, modes of travel, and thought. It took him from the railroad car and put him in the birch canoe. The whole tradition which later came to be called "rugged individualism" owed its impetus to the movement westward of the American frontier, to the taming of the wilderness and the fostering of self-reliance in rugged conditions.

American democracy was born of no theorist dream. It was not carried in the *Susan Constant* to Virginia nor in the *Mayflower* to Plymouth. It came out of the American forest, and it gained a new strength each time it touched

385

a new frontier. Not the constitution, but free land, and an abundance of natural resources open to a fit people, made the democratic type of society in America for three centuries. . . . The advance of their frontier has meant a steady movement away from the influence of Europe, a steady growth of independence on American lines. And to study this advance, the men who grew up under these conditions, and the political, economic, and social results of it, is to study the really American part of our history.[3]

In short, mobility as a creative process in the New World did not end with the trans-Atlantic experience of the *Mayflower*. Across the wilderness of America itself mobility entered a second creative process.

In their patriotic moments, Americans often like to believe that their greatest impact on world civilization lies in the evolution of democratic precepts and liberal ideals. It was Chester Bowles who contended in the optimism of the New Frontier that the American Revolution was a small revolution intended for all mankind.[4] In fact, eighteenth century America was often insecure and had a strong tendency to look up to old world Europe. As Thomas Jefferson put it: "Every man has two homes—his own and France." But as the United States grew into a world power, so did her self-confidence. Two centuries after Jefferson, Max Lerner could say: Every man has two countries—"his own and America."[5]

Lerner's assumption of the universal significance of the United States was by no means entirely misplaced by the second half of this century. But the impact of the United States on world civilization is not to be attributed to American political innovativeness, but quite simply to American mobility. Certainly America's impact on world culture is not primarily in the area of political ideology. In fact, the most important American contribution to the standardization of world culture lies in the area of popular culture. American popular songs, American modes of dress, and American expressions in popular speech are being disseminated over the face of the earth on a scale unknown in the history of mankind. This cultural onslaught in not being accepted without resistance. It has given rise to a special form of cultural anti-Americanism, particularly among America's own allies in western Europe.

Because of the mobility of Americans as individuals, and of the mobility of American ideas through her technological lead in communications, there has developed an American omnipresence in the postwar world. And because of that omnipresence, aspects of American styles of behavior are entering cultures which used to be very different in tone and style. The whole world is now becoming somewhat flamboyant simply because it is becoming somewhat Americanized.

Yet it would be a mistake to assume that America's cultural influence is exclusively at this level. Since America is the most highly developed nation in the world technologically, with a capacity for the sophisticated utilization of science even in simple areas of domestic life, styles of living as well as styles of entertainment all over the world are feeling the American impact. Its gadgetry is slowly conquering the rest of the globe—partly because of the simple fact that life does indeed become more comfortable by an imaginative use of gadgets and gimmicks as innovatively produced by American genius. The United States has gone further than any other country in domesticating technology, making it help not only the scientist in the laboratory, nor only the factory worker in the plant, but also the homemaker in the kitchen.

The Wings of Mission and
The Winds of Change

The Age of Mobility was inaugurated by the *Mayflower,* but it was fostered by the imperial mission. Rudyard Kipling's "The White Man's Burden" provided a connecting poetic link between imperialism as an agent of change and mobility, and the United States itself as a child of the era of migration. Kipling's poem first appeared in *The Times* of London, on February 4, 1899. This was on the occasion when the United States emerged triumphant from the Spanish-American War. In May 1898 Commodore Dewey defeated a Spanish fleet in Manila Bay. The annexation of the Philippines followed, in the face of some significant opposition in the Congress of the United States. The imperial mission, which had already been under way for quite a while among Europeans, was now manifesting itself more blatantly among Americans. Kipling's poem was in part addressed to white Americans as they stood on the threshhold of becoming—like their European parent nations—an imperial power.

Take up the White Man's Burden—
Send forth the best ye breed—
Go bind your sons to exile
To serve your captives' need;
To wait in heavy harness,
On fluttered folk and wild—
Your new caught sullen peoples,
Half-devil and half-child.

The American government was certainly entering into this mood of legitimation in terms of civilizing the natives and raising their moral stature and material standards. President McKinley denied emphatically any colonial mission in the Philippines—and salved his conscience by affirming that: ". . . there was nothing else for us to do but to take them all, and to educate the Filipinos, and uplift and civilize and Christianize them, and by God's grace do the very best we could by them, as our fellowmen for whom Christ also died."[6]

Considerations of access to markets and raw materials were important in American thinking. Once again imperial strategy was connected with ease of mobility to economically relevant parts of the world. But these considerations were in turn legitimated in missionary terms, as new ports had to be built, new bases established, new roads constructed. Were they constructed for trade or for service to the inhabitants of the areas concerned? Rudyard Kipling had no doubt that the new ports, the new roads, the toil and sweat of imperial officers, were ultimately not for the greater glory and benefit of the metropolitan power, but for the greater salvation and service of those underdeveloped societies.

> Take up the White Man's Burden—
> No tawdry rule of kings,
> But toil of serf and sweeper—
> The tale of common things.
> The ports ye shall not enter,
> The roads ye shall not tread,
> Go make them with your living,
> And mark them with your dead.[7]

Physical mobility as a value has therefore been central to imperial thinking in both its economic and its strategic manifestations. The military aspects of physical mobility included the need for bases in the earlier phases of this modern era, but this need has in turn been subject to the changing nature of weaponry and the expanding capabilities of violence by remote control. Both strategic and economic considerations have been at the heart of Euro-American expansionism in modern history.

It is possible to look at imperialism in terms of a basic imbalance between the mobility of the conquering power and the mobility of the subject peoples. Imperialism as an imbalance in weaponry has already received considerable attention elsewhere. But expansionism and imperialism as phenomena of the comparative capacity for mobility have yet to be adequately analyzed.

The English people during the Tudor period came to realize that the sea was more than just the outer limit of their island; it was a promise of more worlds beyond. First came the waves of discoveries with British sailors competing with other sailors from elsewhere in Europe. The balance of achievements was mixed. Columbus and Vasco da Gama achieved greater immortality in many ways than did Sir John Hawkins. But in general the maritime mobility of the English during the Tudor period marked the great starting point of their expansionism. The *Mayflower* in this context is to be seen not only as a prelude to colonization but also as a prelude to colonialism.

If we turn now to look at the African continent, we see in this era that much of the interior of the continent remained isolated precisely because Africa was not as yet a beneficiary of the mobilitarian revolution. Movement of populations in Africa had, as we indicated, been a continuing phenomenon for generations. The Luo moved across eastern Africa gathering in different centers and evolving as different sub-units of the Nilotic population. The history of the Bantu as a whole is less clear than that of the Luo, but the movement of the Bantu section of the black people across different parts of the continent again signified some degree of internal intracontinental mobility. Scholars still debate where the Bantu originated. Was it in the Congo? Was it in West Africa? Was it elsewhere? The answers are yet to arrive, but the pattern of distribution of peoples in Africa sharing physical characteristics and linguistic links does indicate an impressive intracontinental mobility.

What all this tells us is that parts of Africa were not as isolated from each other as earlier assessments had indicated. The fact nevertheless remains that among the three historic continents of the ancient world— Asia, Africa, and Europe—it was Africa which had been in many ways the most insular and the most isolated. North Africa was, it is true, part of the Mediterranean civilization, affected directly by the changing fortunes of different empires in Europe and the Middle East. North Africa had in turn some links with West Africa and with the Nile Valley. But on balance the mobilitarian revolution which was sending Europeans to discover new continents, and establish links with far-flung, previously unknown societies, did not inspire Africa.

In a fundamental sense, it was therefore imperialism itself and the doctrine of the white man's burden which brought new possibilities of mobility into the interior of Africa. The African seaboard had, for a long time, enjoyed maritime intercourse with other parts of the world, but the interior of Africa did not achieve its optimum links with the outside until imperialism facilitated this process. Imperialism as a presence in Africa has therefore to be seen not merely in terms of power defined militarily, but also defined by relative mobility. The mobile capability of the colonizing countries had given them, ipso facto, greater capabilities of political penetration as well.

Imperial expansion sometimes shared the cumulative tendencies of the snowball. An annexation of one part of the world led to a new strategic interest in another part of the world, partly in order to safeguard the previous annexation. India was, by the nineteenth century, the brightest jewel in the British imperial crown. The route to India came to be through Suez after the canal was built; it was therefore important to take no chances about who controlled Egypt. The British therefore occupied Egypt when a suitable pretext arose. Because the life of Egypt was inseparable from the Nile, the question arose whether Egypt could be effectively controlled if the rest of the Nile were not also controlled—the doctrine of "The Unity of the Nile Valley". The Sudan had to be controlled also, jointly with Egypt, partly because it constituted another portion of the Nile Valley. Because the Nile itself started from the lakes further south in Africa, Uganda, in turn, had to be under British control. Because the way to the lakes from the important port of Mombasa was through what came to be known as Kenya, it had to be annexed too. The strategy of expanding mobility, to the extent that it was also a strategy of expanding access, dictated its own logic of mounting imperial annexation.

This question of access, of a mobile presence in a given area, was therefore a major motivating factor behind European expansionism, as the experience of the Philippines, mentioned earlier, also reinforced. The whole debate about the control of the Indian Ocean, which has more recently affected British thinking, is a new illustration of efforts to maintain access for maritime mobility. As the then British Foreign Secretary, Sir Alec Douglas Home, put it:

> In the future some [black] African country may have the strength to contribute to the defence of these ocean routes—but not yet. The only protection that can be given is Britain operating from Simonstown, plus the South African Navy equipped for navy patrol. It is possible to make sure that the [British arms sales] to South Africa would be confined to the equipment necessary for naval patrolling.[8]

It is quite clear here that the old logic of maximum access to and maximum mobility in areas of strategic military or economic interest continued to condition profoundly the behavior of Britain under the Conservatives in their postimperial postures. In the absence of effective naval power among the black states of eastern Africa, Britain and a white-dominated South Africa had to protect the Indian Ocean against such menacing aliens as the Russians. The mission of the white man had assumed a new guise.

Nonalignment and New Norms

This connection between strategy, bases, and imperialism helped to establish a counterconnection between opposition to bases and the doctrine of nonalignment. There has been a feeling among smaller nationalist powers that being used as a base implied a relationship of inequality. Charles de Gaulle grasped this point in relation to NATO bases in France. There could be American bases in Europe but it was not conceivable to have a European base in the United States. An American base in Panama was not reciprocated by a Panamanian base in the United States. Even less conceivable was the prospect of a Malaysian base in Britain, to reciprocate a British base in Malaysia. There was something about the bases themselves and their location and distribution which implied a relationship of glaring inequality.

In addition, there was and continues to be the inequality which arises out of having a military alliance with a power much bigger than oneself. The attraction of nonalignment for the small countries as they achieved independence in the 1950's and 1960's did not rest merely on the ideal of peace and the desire to be disengaged from preparations for war; it rested even more on the ideal of equal dignity as an ambition for the newly liberated. To be part of an alliance led by massive powers was to be overshadowed by those powers. An alliance involved an element of self-denial and self-discipline, but if a country was a very small member of an alliance led by giants, the "self-denial" and "self-discipline" might not be so self-imposed after all. Nonalignment helped to give small powers at least the *appearance* of independent initiative. To the extent that it involved fewer formal ties with big powers, nonalignment became an external extension of domestic self-government and an additional badge of independent status.[9]

If nuclear power has made bases less fundamental as a guarantee of access, it has also helped to make political ideas more important as factors in international diplomacy. The ideological war between the communist East and the noncommunist West was at its most heated in the 1950's. Under John F. Kennedy's vision of the New Frontier, ideological hysteria as a motivating factor behind American foreign policy was put under some control. Nevertheless, the relevance of ideology for diplomatic relations and international quests for friends and allies retained a validity greater than it had ever had before the rise of the Soviet Union.

Religious wars, as we pointed out earlier, flourished at one time, and diplomacy connected with religious convictions remains an aspect of the modern scene, with a long history behind it. But secular ideologies are factors in interstate relations, as foundations for diplomatic accord and diplomatic competition, as criteria for determining beneficiaries of aid and sometimes even of trade. This whole phenomenon was given additional vigor by some of the more important changes in the world which have taken place in the second half of this century. The concept of the cold war itself, emerging as it did out of the fear of a hot war between the giants in a nuclear age, greatly facilitated this type of diplomatic contest. It is partly these considerations that provide a link between the history of physical mobility and physical access, on the one side, and the history of intellectual mobility and circulation of ideas, on the other.

Global competition to influence the thinking of nations has taken more elaborate intellectual forms in this century. The flow of information and propaganda, of political salesmanship generally, through books, radio programs, visiting professors and graduate students, and international conferences have reached a scale unprecedented in history. Here again, as we intimated earlier, the long-term consequences of the *Mayflower* merge into the long-term consequences of the white man's burden. The dissemination of American concepts of education, of American technology and gadgetry, of American popular culture, has been one of the great forces toward cultural homogenization in the world. It could even be argued that the United States is giving the world higher scientific standards and lower cultural standards simultaneously. American science and technology is definitely helping to deepen the sophistication of the rest of the world in the scientific field. By contrast, American styles of social life—from Coca Cola to the cult of violence with stereophonic sound—may be an exercise in global cultural dilution.

This is not because the United States has not produced great culture. It is simply because, for reasons which are partly the fault of the recipient countries and partly the result of the form of America's global presence, the United States has been more effective in selling its low culture than in disseminating its more impressive creations. Great American literature is almost unknown outside the western hemisphere, but the more crude cowboy films have become a feature of world civilization. With the war cry "High Science and Low Culture", Americans have burst forth to Coca-colanize the world!

And yet as a contribution toward building a shared pool of human heritage, the trend still has positive aspects. What is wrong is the imbalance in the cultural interaction between the United States and other societies. The United States teaches more than she learns. This imbalance in cultural interaction is bound to have aspects which are akin to cultural imperialism. The American impact on styles of culture in the world has therefore inevitably generated some degree of resistance.

Cultural Donors and Cultural Recipients

America is a superdonor, not only in the economic but also in the cultural sense. In the face of the communications revolution, no country is an island unto itself. The idea of cultural autarky, a withdrawal into total cultural self-reliance, was last attempted in a major way by Japan before the Restoration, as we indicated in an earlier chapter. Some Middle Eastern sheikhdoms have also at times attempted cultural autarky, as witness the Yemen until the revolution.

But the villagization of the world is making autarkic exercises less and less possible. Different societies have been forced to respond to cultural influences from outside themselves. The spread of universal religions, with special reference to Christianity and Islam, was one major world move which reduced the capabilities of many societies for sustained cultural autarky.

But the second half of the twentieth century did arrive with a basic imbalance in cultural interaction between the West and the rest of the world. And the lack of parity, as we indicated in discussing the American phenomenon, resulted in both emulation and resentment as concurrent reactions among cultural recipients. Coca-colanization even in Europe, though often vigorously denounced and satirized, is at the same time often embraced.

The answer to the imbalance is not to prevent the free circulation of ideas and intellectual styles, but to seek ways of maximizing the circulation of ideas from the culturally underprivileged to the culturally dominant. While the villagization of the world has so far meant that no country can be a pure donor, always giving and not receiving, it has not yet made it impossible for a small country to be almost a pure recipient, never extending its cultural influence beyond its own borders. The western countries were destined by history to become the super cultural donors of all time. But the western world has been receiving influences from the Middle East especially, and the Orient, and to a lesser extent Africa, for many centuries.

The really unacceptable anomaly is that of the pure cultural recipient. A major imperative for cultural world federalism is therefore the elimination of this category, so that each society may succeed in donating something to the total pool of human heritage.

Yet that solution has to maximize cultural currents, rather than seeking to stifle one stream as a method of giving a chance to another. Of all the forms of mobility, the one which should be least controlled is precisely this area of intellectual mobility. The free flow of ideas, the interplay between different interpretations of reality, the dialogue between points of view, the freedom to write and to publish, the freedom to read, the freedom to teach and the freedom to learn, the freedom to listen to broadcasts and to participate in widening the areas of knowledge—these elemental forms of intellectual circulation would need to be maintained and expanded.

393

If the twentieth century has revealed nothing else, it has revealed the great interdependence between nations and continents in scholarship, science, and ideas. When a source of ideas in one part of the world is suppressed, it becomes a matter of concern to peoples in other parts of the world sharing an interest in that particular intellectual fountain. Great books should be able to move from boundary to boundary. Intellectual mobility must continue to mean the free dissemination of knowledge and the right of men to benefit therefrom. This free flow of knowledge and ideas extends beyond territorial frontiers. If there was a total suppression of the study of economics in one English-speaking section of the world, the study of economics in, say, Uganda or Australia would suffer. Uganda and Australia must therefore have a vested interest in the freedom of economic scholarship as it exists in Britain and the United States. By the same token the study of medicine in India and Jamaica would suffer if all medical journals in Britain and America were suddenly suppressed.

The difficult element lies simply in the fact that while Uganda, Jamaica, and India might suffer deeply if the British and American fountains dried up, Britain and the United States would suffer much less if Uganda and India withdrew entirely from the intellectual and scientific race. The lack of symmetry in cultural ineraction retains its position as a gloomy cloud hanging over human arrangements.

Conclusion

We have attempted to show in this chapter how physical mobility and intellectual mobility have been among the great agents for cultural homogenization in the world, and therefore a means toward that ideal of a world federation of cultures. Preeminent among these forces have been the consequences of the *Mayflower* as the most momentous migration of peoples in the annals of humanity, and the repercussions of imperialism and the mission of the white man's burden. Intellectual horizons were widened as physical distances seemed to contract with communications. The age of cultural autarky was coming to an end. The luxury of cultural autarky was becoming impossible.

But an imbalance has persisted in cultural interaction, and any effort toward restructuring human arrangements has to take into account the lack of symmetry in human interaction.

It seems safe to assume that the overwhelming majority of the population of the world has not travelled much more than a hundred miles from its place of birth. Mobility as a human resource is inequitably distributed.

The West as a whole is by far and away much more mobile than the non-West. And cultural federalism must remain profoundly inegalitarian for as long as mobility is so inequitably shared out.[10]

Footnotes

1. "Appeal from the New to the Old Whigs," Burke, *Works,* Vol. V, (London: World Classics Edition, 1907), p. 94.
2. T. Walter Wallbank, Alstair M. Taylor, and Nels M. Bailkey, *Civilization: Past and Present* (Chicago: Scott, Foresman and Company, 1962), pp. 596–597.
3. Turner, "The Significance of the Frontier in American History" (1893) in Turner, *The Frontier in American History* (New York, H. Holt & Co. 1920).
4. Chester Bowles, "A Revolution Intended for all Mankind," *New York Times Magazine,* December 10, 1961.
5. Max Lerner, *America as a Civilization: Life and Thought in the United States Today* (New York: Simon and Schuster, 1957), p. 934.
6. Cited by Michael Edwardes, *Asia in the European Age, 1498–1955* (New York: Frederick A. Praeger, 1962), p. 162.
7. Kipling's poem occurs of course in a variety of different publications. But in the context of its relationship with imperialism generally, refer to the poem as placed in Louis L. Snyder (editor), *The Imperialism Reader: Documents and Readings on Modern Expansionism* (Princeton, N.J.: D. Van Nostrand, 1962), pp. 87–88.
8. *The Times* (London), July 23, 1970.
9. This point is discussed more fully in Mazrui, *Towards a Pax Africana: A Study of Ideology and Ambition* (Weidenfeld and Nicolson and the University of Chicago Press, 1967), especially Chapter 8.
10. Consult our Appendix on the Model of A World Federation of Cultures for one possible approach to the solution of this problem.

Section VI

CULTURAL CONVERGENCE AND ENLARGEMENT OF EMPATHY

CHAPTER 19
Toward Shared Tastes and Images

Kenneth E. Boulding has argued that the people whose decisions determined the policies and actions of nations did not really respond to the objective facts of that situation but to their image of it:

> It is what we think the world is like, not what it is really like, that determines our behavior. . . . We act according to the way the world appears to us, not necessarily according to the way it "is." Thus, in Richardson's models it is one nation's image of the hostility of another, not the "real" hostility, which determines its reaction. The "image" then, must be thought of as the total cognitive, affective, and evaluative structure of the behavior of the elite, or its internal view of itself and its universe.[1]

Boulding emphasizes the phenomenon of the psychological accumulation of impressions and its relevance for the evolution of world views of individuals. Images grow, are modified, interconnect with other images, but, in any case, often have deep roots in the earlier history of the mind.

> It is always in some sense a product of messages received in the past. It is not, however, a simple inventory or "pile" of such messages but a highly structured piece of information-capital, developed partly by its inputs and outputs of information and partly by internal messages and its own laws of growth and stability.[2]

The search for consensus in human affairs must therefore include a search for shared images. And the most important image for any human being is the self-image, a person's conception of himself in relation to others.

Our own view of man inclines toward regarding him as basically self-centered. The basic issue is how near to that center he permits others to approach. And are there occasions when his images of others merge with his own image? We are back here to the issue of empathy. As we indicated in the introduction, we believe mankind is on the verge of a great empathetic leap. We also referred to Theodore Lipps' definition of empathy as an act of sympathetic projection into objects or persons distinct from the agents. Our own idea of empathy is a combination of Theodore Lipps' and Sigmund Freud's. And if empathy is, in Lipps' terms, "objectivated *enjoyment* of self", the phenomenon of *images* has to be related to the experience of *taste*. Empathy becomes an exercise in both moral and aesthetic contemplation.

Underlying both dimensions are psychological factors. That is why in our approach we would prefer to fuse Lipps' idea with Freud's concept of *narcissistic identification*. Narcissism is Freud's term for self-love, which does not recognize those characteristics in others which one shares with them. But under normal circumstances two people in love are deemed to be, in some sense, involved in an act of self-recognition. Their love is partly based on their capacity to see in each other characteristics they share. As Calvin S. Hall put it in his definition and simplification of Freudian psychology:

> Narcissistic identification is responsible for the ties that exist between members of the same group. Members of a fraternity share at least one common characteristic: membership in the same organization. Whenever two or more people have something in common, whether it be a physical or mental trait, an interest, a value, a possession, membership in the same club, citizenship, or whatever, they tend to identify with one another. Two people might identify with one another because they both want the same thing, yet fight with each other over possession of the desired object. It may sound paradoxical to speak of an affinity between enemies or rivals, but there can be no doubt that such affinities do exist. Enemies sometimes become friends, and competition sometimes turns into cooperation. The policeman identifies with the thief, and the thief with the policeman.[3]

The linkage we have attempted to establish between the primarily psychological concept of narcissism promoted by Freud and the primarily aesthetic concept of empathy as formulated by Lipps is a conscious attempt to reintroduce into discussions on world order the aesthetic dimensions in relation to psychology.

In our own approach to aesthetics we define the term not merely in relation to concepts of beauty, but also to concepts of good and bad taste. In some spheres of human relations, the revolution in values is a shift from values rooted in morality to values rooted in taste. The physical dimension of toleration is at the heart of this transition from a culture of moral reprobation to a culture of aesthetic assessment.

In intergroup and international relations, however, the shift may well be from a culture of judgments based on taste to a culture of judgments based on duty and morality. There was a time when aggression by one country against another was at worst a matter of "bad diplomatic taste". Whether one got along with people of other races, whether one was capable of admiring them or only of despising them, was again, very often, a matter purely of taste. The shift in intergroup relations and international relations is away from a reduction of all judgments in terms of taste and toward judgments in terms of duty, obligation and moral censure.

We might here, perhaps in an oversimplified way, reduce human judgments to three areas—legal judgments, moral judgments, and judgments of taste or aesthetics. Legal judgments are those which are subject to enforcement and judicial process. They presume a system of procedural interpretation whereby no man need be judge in his own cause. Legal judgments also imply sanctions following due process. Moral judgments are derived from concepts of right and wrong, are rooted in social approval and disapproval, and imply the duty to do what is right and avoid doing what is wrong. Moral judgments differ from legal judgments in relation to due process, sanctions, and enforcement. Where moral judgments are made by due process and are enforced by a system of sanctions, they have been converted into legal judgments. Judgments of taste are, by contrast, judgments of what is beautiful and what is ugly, sometimes what is good and what is bad—but not really what is right and what is wrong. When judgments of taste include concepts of "bad" and "good" they share some area of terminology with both moral and legal judgments.

In the next chapter we shall discuss more fully the bearing of all these kinds of judgments on world order and social change. What needs to be noted for the time being is the place of images in the global scheme of things. We shall then discuss the role of changing tastes in the process of changing images.

Images and Attitudes

It is quite clear that the image which, say, a white American southerner had of the black man helped to condition the white man's attitude to his black neighbor. Stereotypes are notorious as elements in the formation of attitudes, as well as in the rationalization of those attitudes. The socialization of children everywhere inevitably includes a process of cumulative image-building, including the acquisition of stereotypical conceptions of other races, other tribes or other nations.

Images are not always a conceptualization of concrete objects, but sometimes of abstract attributes or qualities, like honor or dignity or insult. The image of what constitutes *manliness* has been a major factor in the history of violence in different societies. Of special interest in this

401

regard are both the similarities and the differences between experience in Africa and America.

There is a continuing conviction in American and African folk and romantic thought that manliness postulates a capacity to defend oneself physically. On this point the Constitution of the United States and the tribal ways of the Kikuyu have been in accord. The Second Amendment of the American Constitution guarantees "the right of the people to keep and bear arms." Jomo Kenyatta tells us of the paramount resolution of young Kikuyu boys on being initiated by ancient customs: "We brandish our spear, which is the symbol of our courageous and fighting spirit, never to retreat or abandon our hope or run away from our comrades."[4]

An important difference, however, is that the right to be violent in the American ethos is much more clearly individualized than such a right is in much of Africa. It is true that the Second Amendment, Article 2, of the Bill of Rights, has been interpreted in collective terms. The Article says: "A well regulated Militia, being necessary to the security of a free State, the right of the people to keep and bear arms, shall not be infringed." The phrase "a well regulated Militia" is cited as evidence that this right is in terms of the nation as a whole defending itself at a time when this was best done through a militia. The term "the right of the *people*" is interpreted to refer to a collective right. It is the right of the American people and not of the individual American to bear arms in order to defend the security of a free state. Nevertheless, in spite of these interpretations and of substantial judicial opinion on its side, the excesses of individualism and self-reliance in the United States have helped to give the National Riflemen's Association a base of influence which has surprised many observers. The Association, in an American ethos, is capable of complaining in the following terms: "One is forever being told, 'You don't need to protect yourself; that's the job for the police.' What kind of talk is this for America? Are we becoming a nation of defeatists, devoid of personal pride and content to rely entirely on our police for protection?"[5] In Africa, on the other hand, the right to be violent is more subject to collective considerations. Homicide by one man often involves his extended family, or his clan, or the whole tribe. And the idea of revenge or compensation is subject to collective deliberation.

Behind the violence in both Africa and America is a history of rugged conditions which have fostered the growth of certain attitudes to brutality and cleavage. When Malcolm X was murdered in Harlem in February 1964, the African National Congress of South Africa issued a statement from Dar-es-Salaam condemning the conditions in America which made such violence happen and happen again. The statement criticized the United States for having the characteristics of a sick society that thrives on "political gangsterism".[6] This, in effect, was not an unusual image of American society. Much of the outside world was tempted toward a similar conclusion when Ruby, in broad television daylight, killed Oswald in Dallas, Texas, in connection with the assassination of President John F. Kennedy. Two dramatic killings of that kind following each other did heighten the sense of a country on the brink of moral disintegration. And when, in 1968, first Martin Luther King, Jr. and then Robert F. Kennedy were assassinated, the image of America as a country of guns and extremism received a new emphasis.

What should not be forgotten is that the view of America as a society which hovers on the brink of anarchy is an old view in intellectual history, though it has undergone significant modifications over the years. Nor must it be forgotten that some conceptions of America in intellectual history bear a strong comparison with some conceptions of Africa. In other words, the attributes which constituted or were deemed to constitute the American model or anti-model in political or social organization were the same attributes which thinkers sometimes discerned in Africa as a human model.

Of special comparative interest in this regard is the interplay between the image of *innocence* and the image of *violence*. At first glance these two concepts of innocence and violence might be regarded as fundamentally divergent, but in fact they have been closely related in much of social thought down the centuries. The connecting link between violence and innocence in social thought is the idea of *anarchy* itself. Anarchy as an absence of government is sometimes regarded as, ipso facto, a state of war. To that extent it is a context for social violence. On the other hand, the optimistic stream in political and social thought has held that there can be societies without government or rulers. For societies to exist without organized coercive mechanisms a specific kind of innocence should be deemed to prevail. When government becomes necessary it could mean only one thing—in the words of Thomas Paine "government, like dress, is the badge of lost innocence."

Here we must distinguish between two senses of innocence. In one sense, innocence means "not guilty"; the other, even if related sense, is "simple and unsophisticated". We might call this latter sense the innocence of "not knowing", as distinguished from the innocence of "not guilty".[7]

The innocence of not knowing, by implying simplicity and lack of sophistication, became inevitably associated with a certain sense of the term primitiveness. And this is where characteristics of America prior to colonization and of Africa prior to colonialism became closely connected in European political thought. But the image of America as a continent of subsophistication did not end with the colonization of the continent but took another form in intellectual history. The meaning of America in terms of simplicity influenced important streams of American romantic thought within the United States itself. To that extent the American self-image in relation to Europe has important points of comparison with at least one school of African self-characterization in relation to Europe.

Primitivism and the Modern Patriot

The image of America as an epitome of the state of nature is the oldest in political and social theory. And the America in question here was the America which was as yet untamed by the immigrants from Europe. When Thomas Hobbes described "the state of war" which resulted from having no government it was to the wilderness of America that he turned for illustration. Hobbes said:

> It may peradventure be thought, that there was never such a time of condition of war as this; and I believe there was never generally so, over all the world: but there are many places where they live so now. For a savage people in many places of America . . . have no government at all; and live at this day in that brutish manner, as I said before.[8]

Locke also turned to America as the ultimate example of untamed wilderness but saw an essential humanity still present even when there was no significant civilization at all. Locke did indeed regard America as a state of nature, but he felt that if a European from a well-established civil society went to America he would find in the Indian "savage" an inner core of human trustworthiness. As Locke put it: "The promises and bargains for truck . . . between a Swiss and an Indian, in the woods of America, are binding to them, though they are perfectly in a state of nature in reference to one another. For truth and keeping of faith belong to men as men and not as members of society."[9]

It is with Rousseau that this image of natural man in America conforms particularly with ideas about natural man in Africa. Rousseau idealized the noble savage in his romantic philosophy. His noble savage is sometimes indistinguishable from the rugged individualist. Rousseau argues that inequality was born out of interdependence.

> So long as men remained content with their rustic huts, so long as they were satisfied with clothes made of the skins of animals and sewn together with thorns and fishbones, adorned themselves only with feathers and shells, and continued to paint their bodies different colors, to improve and beautify their bows and arrows, and to make with sharp edged stones fishing boats or clumsy musical instruments; in a word, so long as they undertook only what a single person could accomplish, and confined themselves to such arts as

404

did not require the joint labor of several hands, they lived free, healthy, honest and happy lives, so long as their nature allowed, and as they continued to enjoy the pleasures of mutual and *independent* intercourse.[10]

Rousseau is here putting forward the view that individual independence is the ultimate guarantee not only of freedom but even of equality. The ethos of the frontier in American political thought, and the vision of the rugged, self-reliant individualist, have areas of comparison with this view of Rousseau. Rousseau goes on to say:

But from the moment one man began to stand in need of the help of another; from the moment it appeared advantageous to any one man to have enough provisions for two, equality disappeared. Property was introduced, work became indispensable, and vast forests became smiling fields, which man had to water with the sweat of his brow, and where slavery and misery were soon seen to germinate and grow up with the crops.[11]

Of course, there are important differences between the concept of the noble savage and the concept of the rugged individualist. Rousseau's ideal of equality is too intimately related to a distrust of private property to be fully comparable to the predominate ethos of the American frontier. But there is an echo of a shared distrust of social complexity in both visions. Rousseau argues that it was not the coming of gold and silver which corrupted man; it was the coming of new and complex methods of production and of consumption. He says: "Metallurgy and agriculture were the two arts which produced this great revolution. The poets tell us it was gold and silver, but, for the philosophers, it was iron and coal, which first civilized man and ruined humanity."[12]

It is, in fact, one of the ironies of cultures that America, based from its agrarian cradle on a rugged individualist tradition, should have evolved into the most technologically developed country in the world. To that extent, Americans might be deemed to have lost a little of their rugged innocence under the softening and encircling complexities of modern life. But the real heroes of American mythology in their own identity crisis, and certainly in preindustrial America, are those who were still simple, self-reliant and nontechnical.

The parallel theme of the "noble savage" was to constitute an intellectual tradition which, for the black man in Africa and parts of the new world, culminated in the movement of négritude. It was Aimé Césaire, the West Indian poet, who eulogized his black brothers by describing them as:

"Those who have invented neither power nor the compass;
Those who have tamed neither gas nor electricity;
Those who have explored neither the seas nor the skies . . ."[13]

Jean-Paul Sartre describes this as "a proud claim of nontechnicalness". Certainly this revelling in simplicity echoes aspects of Rousseau's romantic primitivism.[14]

Négritude writers in Africa attribute spontaneity and a sense of natural authenticity to the African man prior to Europeanization. Similar notions are discernible in American romantic thought. But in this case the America we are talking about is, in part, the untamed wilderness of Indian America and, in part, the America subjugated and changed under the influence of immigrants from Europe and elsewhere. Négritude thinkers argue that there was a spontaneity and innocence in Africa which derived its authenticity from being pre-European. Modern American romantic thinkers, on the other hand, discern a spontaneity and innocence in Africa which derives its genuineness from being post-European. As a contemporary American historian, Henry Bamford Parkes, has put it:

> To a much greater degree than elsewhere, society in America was based on the natural man rather than on man as moulded by social rituals and restraints. . . . By European standards this American attitude often seems unrealistic, Utopian, and naive. . . . His naivety was, in fact, an expression of genuine innocence. He was simpler than the European because his life was freer, more spontaneous, and less frustrated.[15]

Connected with these thoughts of innocence and spontaneity is inevitably the concept of the Garden of Eden in relation to both American romantic thought and African romantic self-images. In an article in *Encounter* David Lodge said: "In a large quasi-metaphorical sense all significant American literature is utopian in spirit, and saturated in the midst of Paradise Lost or Regained, either celebrating the potentialities of the American Adam, or brooding over where he went wrong."[16]

What is pervasive in American self-images is perhaps the notion of America as a second Eden in an almost literal sense. Man fell from grace and sin entered the world. That sin came to attain its most cunning complexities in European man, and the quest for a second Eden started among a few of the saved ones of Europe. The subtle complexity of European man as contrasted with the open and candid innocence of purified man in the New World has continued to affect American interpretations of themselves and of their roots. Henry Bamford Parkes maintains this view:

> The European was psychologically much more complex than the American, and therefore capable of deeper and more subtle insights and of profounder

spiritual and aesthetic achievements; but he was also more corrupt, with a greater propensity toward the negative emotions of fear and avarice and hatred. He believed in the depravity of human nature because he knew it in his own experience.[17]

The founding of modern America therefore becomes a case of paradise regained. The whole idea of a "new world" in the western hemisphere becomes connected with notions of spiritual rebirth. And even today in popular self-images Americans compare themselves with Europeans and regard the American experiment as the moment of man's political and social rejuvenation. In notions of paradise regained the dominant theme is not nostalgia but thanksgiving. Americans regard themselves still as among the blessed of the earth because they created a new paradise out of a wild hemisphere.

In African romantic thought, on the other hand, the dominant mood is indeed nostalgia, rather than thanksgiving. As a colleague and I had occasion to say in a joint article:

Négritude is apt to drift into an exaggerated portrayal of traditional precolonial Africa as a Garden of Eden. Perhaps this is part of a larger African phenomenon. Perhaps it is a curious aspect of the planting of Christianity itself in Africa that there is an absence of conviction that man before the invention of colonialism was ever evil.[18]

The mood is of an innocence which is eternally lost. All that can be done now is to make the best of a bad job, try to save some of the values of old Africa, and find a synthesis between these and the influences which have come with colonialism and modernity.

There are occasions when the Garden of Eden idea in Africa is literal rather than metaphorical. There is a belief that Adam was a black man, a theme that seems to be shared by the black Muslims in the United States. The most scientific knowledge available today may conceivably be on the side of black Muslim theology. It is not certain that the first man was black, but there is a good deal of evidence to vindicate the claim that the first man was *African*. The anthropological findings of Dr. Leakey would seem to suggest that East Africa might well have been the cradle of mankind. So the black Muslims have a firmer basis of scientific knowledge in support of their "genesis" than some of the old armchair biologists of eighteenth century Europe had for their versions of racialist genesis. The Garden of Eden as a symbol of the birth of humanity and the Garden of Eden as a symbol of the moment of absolute innocence converge in the romantic ideas of significant sections of black peoples.

Diminishing Innocence and Expanding Violence

Yet the themes of innocence and violence continue to interact. There are occasions when African nationalism itself rebels *against* the myths of precolonial innocence. To be inherently innocent is to cease to be ordinary. And so egalitarian nationalists like Julius Nyerere of Tanzania have been known to protest in terms like these: "It would be absurd to imply that . . . pre-colonial Africa was an ideal place in which the noble savage of Rousseau lived his idyllic existence. The members of this social unit were no more noble than other human beings. . . ."[19]

Ezekiel Mphahlele, the South African writer, is more specifically rebellious against the pristine assumptions of négritude. He believes that when négritude assumes too much innocence, it cannot at the same time attribute to African man the capacity for natural spontaneity; for to be spontaneous sometimes implies reacting in violent ways. At a conference in Dakar a few years ago, Mphahlele explosively said:

> I do not accept . . . the way in which too much of the poetry inspired by négritude romanticizes Africa—as a symbol of innocence, purity and artless primitiveness. I feel insulted when some people imply that Africa is not also a violent Continent. I am a violent person, and proud of it because it is often a healthy state of mind.[20]

Innocence in the sense of "not guilty" is denied here because it implies an incapacity for violence. Innocence in the sense of "not knowing" would imply such a high degree of primitiveness and childlike irresponsibility that it would no longer be adequately compatible with an image supposedly rooted in cultural nationalism. It is these considerations which make it difficult to combine a claim that the African has a genius for spontaneity with a claim that the African springs from a tradition of innocence. Depending upon its consequences, spontaneous violence is not always innocent.

In America the price of spontaneity has also been a high toleration of violence in the social structure and its historical background. The tradition of the frontier with its demands for fighting preparedness has continued to affect American attitudes to violent self-reliance. And American theorists of identity have a good deal to do with these American self-conceptions. It has been estimated that 20,000 Americans are killed every year by guns; since 1900 more Americans have been killed by domestic firearms than have died in all American wars.[21]

Among black Americans today the interplay between the myth of violence and the myth of innocence has entered a new phase. In the slave days innocence was part of the limitation of slavery; and white America, at its most humanitarian, invested the American Negro with the innocence of a child. At its least humanitarian, white America attributed to the American Negro the innocent irresponsibility of a domestic animal. Innocence in slave conditions of that kind was an assertion of diminished responsibility. And diminished responsibility was an aspect of diminished humanity. But black spontaneity included moments of violence. And black violence, in the form of slave uprisings or moments of individual breakdowns, met with penalizing white ruthlessness. The whip or the lynching rope are an intimate part of black experience in the United States.

As the civil rights movement gathered momentum after World War II, new forms of violence were beginning to take shape in American race relations. The Nation of Islam was perhaps partly attracted toward Islam by the concept of a *jihad*, a holy war, against Christian oppressors. But then new organizations took shape with an even more explicit commitment to the utilization of violence for social change. The street riot became an urban institution and the ideas of Frantz Fanon began to influence black militants in the United States. Fanon's ideas about purification through violence constituted a reorganization of the relationship between innocence and violence. The purification becomes renewed moral vigor, a rebirth for him who fights colonialism with weapons of blood. Fanon emphasizes that the rebirth after ousting white dominants is not to be a retreat to primitive innocence. In Fanon's words as quoted by Stokeley Carmichael and Charles V. Hamilton: "No, there is no question of a return to nature. It is simply a very concrete question of not dragging men toward mutilation. . . . What we want to do is to go forward all the time, night and day, in the company of Man, in the company of all men. . . ."[22]

What is accepted in certain schools of black power is apparently the belief that injustice is itself a form of institutionalized violence, and can only be ended by counterviolence. Thus, the principle of reciprocity is invoked.

But the new violence of black militancy seems to derive its ethos not from the rugged individualism of the frontier but from the proud solidarity of tribal Africa. The violence which is being urged, or which continuously breaks out, has the stamp of collectivist self-assertion rather than mere individualist self-reliance. In the case of the blacks, it could indeed be said that what is at stake is whether or not the clause "the right of the people to bear arms" in the Second Amendment of the American Constitution allows for a definition which accepts the arming of the Blacks. Perhaps this section of the Bill of Rights can no more be used by black militants to legitimate armed self-assertion than it can be used by the National Rifle Association to vindicate individual weapon play. But the latter is perhaps more distant from the permissiveness of the Second Amendment than the former—if for nothing else than the fact that black assertion is more easily demonstrated as "necessary to the security of a *free* State" than individual gun-play for pleasure, personal financial gain, or even manly self-defense, can ever claim to be.

Whatever the correct interpretation may be, we do have in the history of both America and Africa compelling illustrations of how stereotypes have conditioned intergroup relations and how images of "manly" self-reliance as against simple innocence have conditioned general attitudes to violence. What is needed is the ameliorating effect of that empathetic revolution we have referred to—so that stereotypes become not merely similar but *reciprocal*. This brings us back to the whole process of cultural convergence in human affairs.

Arts and Sports

In an important sense, two disparate factors in the world share the distinction of being the successors to religion and imperialism as central agents of cultural diffusion.

Until this century it was indeed the proselytizing religions, combined with sheer imperial expansion by certain nations, which helped to make mankind more culturally homogeneous. As we have noted, Christianity and Islam especially, because of their intercontinental spread and greater commitment to proselytizing, have helped to narrow the divergences in values which had previously separated world cultures. Of course, the differences are still enormous between Christian Uganda and Christian Holland, but they would have been greater still if western imperialism and Christianity had not jointly exerted an influence of cultural diffusion. But with the rise of secularism in the world and the disintegration of empires, new factors have been competing for the status of being agents of further cultural diffusion.

The two disparate factors now helping to fill the void, and which themselves were partly the outgrowth of imperial and missionary expansionism, are the arts and sports. They are indeed very different as agents, and signify different influences on the world, but share the leisure area of interaction. It is not merely what men jointly know that helps to integrate them. It is also what men jointly enjoy in their leisure moments.

Games are subject to the same rules, regardless of the societies in which they are being played. A soccer team preparing itself in Nigeria for possible confrontation with Brazil, the boxer from Uganda wanting to challenge a boxer in Scotland, cricket players in Jamaica undergoing training for a match in New Zealand, all have to learn the same rules, be aware of the boundaries of fair play and the shared canons of skillful performance. Thus, the first laws ever to be voluntarily embraced by men from a wide variety of cultures and backgrounds are the laws of sports. As religion has spread, it has had to give in to local variations. Christianity has often had to turn a blind eye to the presence of polygamy in its midst; Islam has had to accommodate itself to cultures which are incapable of exercising alcoholic abstinence. Additionally, the rules of religion demand comprehensive adherence and are, in some sense, anti-pluralistic. One cannot be a Christian and a Hindu at the same time in the normal course of events.

But the rules of sports limit themselves to the game in hand, to the few hours in which man challenges man in a nonviolent confrontation. Then, after the game, each can return to his own cultural context without experiencing pangs of conscience for having obeyed the same rules as a total cultural alien for two hours in a sports stadium. If, then, we are ever to write the history of the globalization of rule observance, we would have to include among the pioneering instances the capacity of people from widely different backgrounds to obey the same rules in a structure of competition.

Finally, the globalization of sports has given us the world champion. Through this medium, we are approaching the experience of choosing among men from very different countries the leading exemplar of one particular physical virtue. Sports to this extent is a much fairer exercise in choosing the best specimens than, say, beauty competitions, which are much more subject to aesthetic prejudices and where ultimate achievement is a matter for the private judgment of a panel of judges, rather than a measurable performance in terms of goals scored, or speed of running, or height of jumping.

The impact of art is of a different order. Music as an agent of cultural homogenization begins to narrow the gulf which separates the different aesthetic worlds of the human race. It may, of course, be regretted that the most global of all music so far is pop music. A program of Listeners' Choice on Radio Uganda has sharp areas of similarity with Listeners' Choice in Stockholm and Chicago. Of course, the aesthetic world is still very diverse, and the drums of Congolese music are decidedly different from the Indian *sitar,* or the Arab *ud.* But there is a form of music which is beginning to be enjoyed, at least to some extent, by sectors of societies which are otherwise very different from each other and very distant. This is a modest achievement and not without significance.

After all, aesthetic values are often the most conservative of all values in their response to foreign influence. It is often far easier to be converted to the ethics than to the aesthetics of a conquering power. An African is often more easily converted to western Christianity than to western

411

classical music. And the chances are that even formal monogamy will become part of African life sooner than we can expect high western opera, or ballet, to enter the lives of African peoples. As between societies which are otherwise very different, agreement between right and wrong, good and bad, is often easier to achieve than agreement on what is beautiful and what is ugly.[23]

Vulgar art, like vulgar morality, is easier to diffuse than high culture because it appeals to the lowest common denominator. Pop music, in its very lack of sophistication, is much less demanding than Mozart and Bach—and therefore more capable of being spread to cultures distant from those of its origin. In that phenomenon we might have the beginnings of aesthetic homogenization.

Aesthetics and the Body

The body has always been important in art as well as in morality. What we are suggesting is that even that part of the life of the human body which used to be controlled by moral considerations is now more firmly entering the world of aesthetics.

In this simple proposition lies a new and potentially important area of African contribution to world civilization. For it is preeminently in Africa that art and sex, aesthetics and sensuality, have refused to be kept too far apart. There was a time when this fusion earned Africa *negative images* in the world of white Christianity. Now the crisis of relevar ce in the Western world has become partly a quest to reestablish contact between aesthetics and sensuality. The most dramatic example is in fact in modern drama and the groping for sexual candor on the stage. Other branches of literature seem to be also groping for a point of fusion between aesthetic appreciation and sensual responsiveness. This quest partly manifests itself in the themes which are treated, in the erosion of taboos about subjecting sex to artistic treatment, but also experimentation in sensual styles, as well as sensual scenes.

The crisis of relevance in the western world has now resulted in the abolition of the post of Lord Chamberlain in England, an institution which had served for many generations to censor the English stage. In 1968, London could at last see, without the red pencil of the Lord Chamberlain, displays of the human body in all its nakedness in such presentations as the American play, *Hair*. There was a time in Africa's recent experience when the authority of the Christian missionaries was used to cast disapproval on certain kinds of African dancing. Now African dancers themselves from countries like Guinea and Uganda, have found acclaim for their sensual movements in previously stuffy theaters of the western world. Occasionally the women dancers from Africa were mistakenly called upon to cover their breasts, but on the whole bodily performances previously regarded as immodest had attained a new acceptability in the cultural revolution of the 1960's. The place of the body in the arts, the bridging of the gap between aesthetics and sensuality, have themselves become an aspect of that other revolution by which moral taboos concerning the human body are transformed into issues of taste.[24]

The utilization of the body in performed art has been linked with the potential of folktales as material for African drama by Bob Leshoai, a South African literary figure and more recently Head of Theatre Arts at the University of Dar-es-Salaam:

> Great portions of the story can be told simply in mimed action and music and dance. The body, in African dancing, is capable of being used to express and convey ideas that would be quite difficult to express adequately in speech. For example, swaying of the hips, the movement of the shoulders, the tempo of the stamping feet and the twitching of the nostrils can say so much to an infatuated suitor as to leave no doubt in his mind about the girl's attitude to him. This is a combination of movements which speak more fluently, adequately and unequivocally than the spoken word. Body movement in African dances is as important as hand movement in the Indian dance.[25]

Here again the gap between aesthetics and sensuality, art and the body, is narrowed. Sometimes the narrowing takes the form of utilizing more than one of the five physical senses in art appreciation. Paul Bohannan has lamented the inevitable reluctance of American museums to let African specimens be handled. Bohannan points out that tactile sensations are as important in learning about African sculpture as are visual sensations. He suggests that learning is made easier through touching:

> The memory of it, like the sensation of it, comes through the muscles and the sense of touch as well as through the eyes. Dahomean brass sculpture is tactilely sinewy and tough and not at all delicate as it appears to the visual sense: actually of course, the combination tells a great deal about Dahomean culture. Some African wood carving is in heavy earthbound wood; other is in wood so porous and so light as to seem almost spiritual. To make such remarks is *not* so much to interpret African art (which they do not) as to prepare one for the fact that there is more in it than the artist put there and the something more is derivative of the cultural view of the human condition.[26]

Sculpture in western civilization had for long been permitted a certain liberty in portraying the human body in naked frankness. But the other western arts had remained relatively inhibited, until the gulf between art and sensuality became so great that it was swept into the crisis of relevance currently afflicting western civilization.

The old images of the African in western romantic thought are now reasserting a new meaning for Western civilization itself. The African has indeed often been conceded a nearness to nature as we indicated earlier in this chapter. But in the context of modern problems, and the unrest which is affecting intellectual values in educational institutions from Canada to Japan, this old interpretation of the African now possesses a new pertinence. To use the words of Jean-Paul Sartre, the French philosopher: "In concerning himself first with himself, the Negro proposes to gain nature in gaining himself." Sartre than proceeds to cite Aimé Césaine: "They abandoned themselves, possessed to the essence of all things, ignoring surfaces but possessed by the movement of all things."

The nearness to nature which is attributed to the African becomes associated with that spontaneity we discussed; spontaneity finds expression sometimes in responsive sexuality; and sexuality connotes the nakedness of things. The entire life-style of the black man is romanticized into one constant work of natural creation. To quote Sartre again:

> Techniques have contaminated the white worker, but the black remains the great male of the earth, the sperm of the world. His existence—it is the great vegetal patience; his work—it is the repetition from year to year of the sacred coitus. He creates and is fertile because he creates. The sexual pantheism of these [black] poets is without doubt that which first strikes the reader. To labor, to plant, to eat, is to make love with nature. . . .[27]

This kind of analysis refines the link between the body and creativity. We know the body is connected with physical creativity; emerging in Sartrean analysis is the body's connection with aesthetic creativity. Bringing art back to the body may be a way of bringing it back to real life. It was again Paul Bohannan who said:

> In order to appreciate the African aesthetic, then, we must first recognize a few points in our own. Probably the most important one to note is that even in the mid-twentieth century, Americans have an unshakeable conviction that "art" is something special—a little off to the left of life. Art is, we are taught, a separate world; it is done only by special kinds of people who are not very "practical." Such an opinion cannot be held by a people who have no word for "art" and none for "society" or "reality" . . . Art permeates African culture, which in turn permeates African art. Art is not set aside from "real life"—it cannot be among the people who do not make such distinctions.[28]

The link then between the aesthetic and the sensual, the spiritual and the physical, was a link between art and life.

Conclusion

In some ways the western world is now called upon to recapture the values of ancient Greece by embracing the spirit of African culture. Oscar Wilde lamented that already, by the end of the nineteenth century, the trends in western art were moving from the sun of reality to the shadows of make-believe. While he was in jail, Wilde longed for what he called "the great simple primeval things, such as the Sea, to me no less of a mother than the Earth". He complained that while the nineteenth century called itself a utilitarian age it nevertheless did not know the uses of things, that his age had forgotten that water could cleanse, that fire could purify, and that the earth was mother to us all. It was different with the Greeks:

> It seems to me that we all look at Nature too much, and live with her too little. I discern great sanity in the Greek attitude. They never chattered about sunsets, or discussed whether the shadows on the grass were really mauve or not. But they saw that the sea was for the swimmer, and the sand for the feet of the runner.[29]

Wilde was suggesting that athletics were, in a sense, the real aesthetics of nature. The Greek preoccupation with athletics profoundly affected their culture and their concepts of form. The Olympic Games were in this sense a living art gallery. It is worth noting that athletics have also affected Africa's aesthetic experience. In many African societies the distinction between athletics and dancing is indeed blurred. In other societies in Africa the preoccupation with representational perfection has connections with a grand awareness of primeval physical attributes.

Ife is credited with the first known metal sculpture in Nigeria. The representational quality of Ife bronzes was so strikingly physioplastic, and so technically impressive, that western discoverers of Ife styles soon found themselves comparing them with Greek sculpture. J. Newton Hill was by no means the first to put his finger on this Afro-Hellenic equation.

> The Ife casters established standards even as the Greeks did. Their heads conformed to an accepted predetermined proportion; so, too, did the heads of the Hellenic sculptors. There were *idealistic* measurements to which Greek and/or Ife sculpture had to conform. As the perfected Greek marbles represented the sculptor's image of man, so, too, did the Ife heads represent the perfected image of an Ife man.

Hill concedes that it may seem strange to attribute equally intellectual approaches to the art of the Greeks and the sculpture of Ife. But he argues that this could only be strange to those who were new to the early history of West Africa, more specifically to the era from 1000 to 1870. Hill saw the classical style of Ife as marked by, first, a methodical balance of practically all compositional units; second, the observance of rhythmic placements of nearly all facial units including eyes, ears, as well as animal adornments and crowns; third, a precision in measurement producing symmetry following a geometrically homogeneous formation; fourth, decorative designing which employed many of the symbolic units in Yoruba mythology; fifth, technical proficiency in casting; and sixth, physioplastic naturalness.[30]

These experiences of mutual aesthetic discovery between Africa and the West have come through either the voluntary mobility of westerners going into Africa, or the involuntary export of black people to the western world. Behind both phenomena lies once again the imperative of mobility as a medium of cultural fusion. Some English army officers and a few French painters were cast by history into the role of aesthetic discoverers within Africa. General Pitt-Rivers, Torday, Picasso, and Les Fauves were among the participants in this new exploration. Paul Bohannan has warned us:

> No one should jump to the idea that Picasso's women who look two ways at once, or anything else about his work, is a copy of something he discovered in African art. There was little direct, stylistic influence, although some can be discovered by latter-day critics. Rather, what happened was that with the discovery of African and other exotic art, the way was discovered for breaking out of the confines that had been put on European art by tradition—perspective, measured naturalism, and anti-intellectual sentimentality.[31]

Bohannan continues that African figurines could give the "modern" artists courage to foreshorten, to emphasize by changes of scale, to adjust scale to message:

> Looking at African art made such artists see what some of the earlier great painters had already known—El Greco stretches his human figures—that one sees passionately quite differently from the way one sees mensuristically. To get inside the vision, it was necessary to get outside the inherited canons of art. And African . . . art was one means of taking such a journey.[32]

In reality, Africa is less homogeneous in its art than the previous comparison with ancient Greece might imply. But the preoccupation with physical attributes, the centrality of movement, the athletic touch in some art forms, raise new possibilities of fusion between the Greek legacy, basically abandoned in this sphere by the West until recently, and the African heritage.

This certainly opens up at least one important area of African cultural donation to a de-hellenized West. In the quest for cultural symmetry as between donors and recipients, the longer history in Africa of the contact between art and life, aesthetics and sensuality, opens up a domain of reciprocal feedback. And with such reciprocity in tastes, the domain of mutual images may also undergo a more positive transformation.

Footnotes

1. Boulding, "National Images and International Systems," *The Journal of Conflict Resolution*, Vol. III, 1959, pp. 121–122. For a fuller exposition of the theory see Boulding, *The Image* (Ann Arbor: University of Michigan Press, 1956).
2. *Ibid.*
3. Calvin S. Hall, *A Primer of Freudian Psychology*, (The New American Library, 1954) pp. 75–76. The date of the publication of Freud's paper "On Narcissism: An Introduction" is significant. It appeared in 1914, the year of the outbreak of World War I. Stanley Edgar Hyman sees in this paper another effort by Freud to enter into the domain of "metapsychology". See Hyman, *The Tangled Bank: Darwin, Marx, Frazer, and Freud as Imaginative Writers* (New York: The Universal Library, Grosset and Dunlap, 1966) p. 368.
4. Jomo Kenyatta, *Facing Mount Kenya* (first published 1938) (London: Secker and Warburg, 1959) p. 199. The initiation ceremonies have been simplified since then.
5. Quoted in the *New Republic* (U.S.A.) December 14, 1963.
6. *East African Standard* (Nairobi), February 23, 1965.
7. See the chapter "Romantic Self-Images: British and African" in Mazrui, *The Anglo-African Commonwealth: Political Friction and Cultural Fusion* (Oxford: Pergamon Press, 1967).
8. Thomas Hobbes, *The Leviathan* (Everyman's Edition, NY: Dutton, 1965) Chapter 8, p. 65.
9. Locke, *Second Treatise of Government*, Blackwell's 1956 edition, Chapter 2, p. 9.
10. Rousseau, 'On the Origin of Inequality,' *Social Contract and Discourses* (Everyman's Edition) 1955, p. 199.
11. *Ibid.*
12. *Ibid.*
13. *Return to My Native Land* (Paris: Présence Africaine, 1939).
14. Sartre, *Black Orpheus*, translated by F. A. Allen (Paris: Présence Africaine, n.d.), pp. 42–45.
15. Parkes, *The American Experience* (New York: Vintage Books, 1959) p. 10.
16. Lodge "Utopia and Criticism: The Radical Longing for Paradise," *Encounter* (London) Vol. 33, No. 4, April 1969, p. 74.
17. *Parkes, op. cit.*
18. Mazrui and G. F. Engholm, "Rousseau and Intellectualized Populism in Africa," *The Review of Politics*, Vol. 30, No. 1, January 1968, p. 24.
19. Julius K. Nyerere, *Freedom and Unity: A selection from Writings and speeches, 1952–1965* (Dar-es-Salaam: Oxford University Press, 1966), p. 12.
20. "Negritude and Its Enemies: A Reply," in Gerald Moore (editor), *African Literature and the Universities* (Ibadan: University Press 1965) p. 25.

21. Consult Carl Bakal, *The Right to Bear Arms* (New York: Paperback Library, 1968).

22. Fanon, *The Wretched of the Earth* (New York: Grove Press, 1963) pp. 253–55. Cited by Carmichael and Hamilton, *Black Power: The Politics of Liberation in America* (New York: Vintage Press, 1967) pp. xii.

23. This point is discussed more fully in Mazrui, "Aesthetic Dualism and Creative Literature in East Africa," *Cambridge Review* (England), Vol. 92, No. 2193, October 23, 1970, pp. 11–20.

24. There is still enough prudish restraint in the West, however, to ensure steady protests against the more glaring "excesses" of this liberalizing trend. See, for example, a report entitled "Harvest of Porn Brings Backlash," in *Sunday Nation* (Nairobi), 19 March, 1972.

25. See Bob Leshoai, "Theatre and the Common Man in Africa" *Transition*, No. 19, 1965, p. 46.

26. Bohannan, *Africa and Africans* (Published for the American Museum of Natural History by the Natural History Press, Garden City, N.Y., 1964), pp. 150, 152.

27. See Sartre, *Black Orpheus*, pp. 45–47.

28. Bohannan, *Africa and Africans*, pp. 152, 150.

29. Oscar Wilde, *De Profundis* (New York: Vintage Books, Random House, 1964) p. 158.

30. See J. Newton Hill's chapter on "Art" in David Brokenshaw and Michael Crowder (editors), *Africa in the Wider World: The Inter-Relationship of Area and Comparative Studies* (Oxford: Pergamon Press, 1967), pp. 49–51.

31. Bohannan, *Africa and Africans*, p. 156.

32. *Ibid.*

CHAPTER 20

Toward Shared Emotions and Values

When discussing such cosmic issues as world peace, science and the arts, disarmament, international trade, and the world's monetary system, there is a danger of forgetting the individual. Just as the proper study of mankind is man, the proper evaluation of the quality of human life is indeed the life of the individual man. We must therefore remind ourselves of what progress may have been made so far before we can be sensitive to what remains to be done to enhance the qualitative aspects of the life of the individual.

Toward Depoliticizing Disgust

The nineteenth century was, in the western world, the century of the liberation of the individual. That was the century which produced greater mobility from the countryside to the city, the extension of the franchise to the working classes, the abolition of slavery, and the flowering of the novel as an art form preeminently designed to study individuals either in isolation or in interaction.

John Stuart Mill in his classic essay *On Liberty* made the distinction between the self-regarding acts and the other-regarding acts of an individual. The self-regarding acts are those which ultimately should concern only the individual, since in the final analysis they harm nobody else. The other-regarding acts, on the contrary, are those acts done by an individual or by a group of individuals, which have direct adverse consequences for people other than themselves. In Mills' words: ". . . the only purpose for which power can be rightfully exercised over any member of a civilised community, against his will, is to prevent harm to others. His own good either physical or moral, is not a sufficient warrant."[1] Society has to curb its own collective indignation or collective disgust and let the individual be himself even if it is an evil self, provided he does not thereby harm another.

In many ways John Stuart Mill was ahead of his time. The implication of his essay *On Liberty* was a plea not only for intellectual freedom in the sense of freedom to give and receive ideas, not only for political freedom in the sense of freedom of expression, political debate, and political competition, but also for moral freedom in the sense of freedom to make moral choices and to determine one's moral conduct. What John Stuart Mill was asserting was that the individual had a right to be immoral if he wished to be, provided it was a form of immorality that would not harm others directly. His concept of harm was very much that which later came to be designated in American judicial rhetoric as "clear and present danger." This was to be sharply differentiated from concepts of harm rooted in allegations of "corrupting the young" or "degrading the standards of the race or of society." The danger in the moral misbehavior of a particular individual had to be more than a bad influence on other adults. The adverse consequences had to be more tangible than hurting the feelings of society.

Out of the distinction between self-regarding and other-regarding acts emerged the whole debate on how far a person's sexual behavior should be subject to the constraints of society. A man and a woman, unmarried but living together—if they harm nobody directly, has society a right to act against them? How about a man and a man living together in sexual intimacy, both adults and in full possession of their faculties, with due consideration for the freedoms of others? Should these two be permitted to cohabit provided there is no evidence of a "clear and present danger" to some third party? On balance, the 1860's was the great era of debates in England concerning intellectual and political freedom. But England had to wait until the 1950's and 1960's to debate the freedom of the individual to be moral or immoral without undue restrictions being imposed by the law upon him. Constitutionalism and homosexuality became a subject of debate in the popular press, in Parliament, and by special commissions of inquiry, preeminently the Wolfenden Commission. Homosexuality between females was already permitted, but homosexuality between men was illegal. Was the illegality an invasion of the rights of the individual?

Church voices were heard arguing that the issue of sin was a matter for the church and not for the state, that what was immoral need not be at the same time illegal. The sexual deviant, or even the would-be suicide, could legitimately be an object of strong moral reprobation without the necessity of dragging him before the courts of prosecution as a criminal.

What was emerging was precisely the concept of a permissive society, to supplement the concept of a free society. The free society had been the creature of the nineteenth century and its liberalism, the freedom conceived then having been political and intellectual freedom. The permissive society goes beyond political and intellectual freedom—and ex-

420

tends the right to an autonomous moral identity. Preeminent among the preconditions is the depoliticization of moral disgust among those who disapprove. Society can frown without legislating and prosecuting.

The Scandinavian countries had already arrived fairly early at the idea of "free love", but the 1960's saw the extension of the permissive society to other parts of the West. Sexual "deviants" received a degree of toleration never before conceded to them in that part of the world. The laws against homosexuality were abolished in England and toleration extended across the Atlantic where the beginnings of a social acceptance of marriage between partners of the same sex began to appear. Certainly the concept of husband and wife is a residue of a biocultural differentiation of roles between the sexes. At last a challenge was being posed to this very tradition itself.

In October 1970 the American magazine *Newsweek* published a report which was itself profoundly symptomatic of such permissiveness. A church in California under the leadership of the Reverend Troy Perry, catered to Christians whom other churches did not want or found it difficult to accept. Forty percent of the parishioners in Los Angeles were baptised Roman Catholics, and another 40 percent, like Reverend Perry himself, were Evangelical Protestants. "But all have joined his fold because they desire a conventional religious life—and a minister with a personal interest in homosexuality." Perry was himself an ordained Baptist preacher, and was married and the father of two children "before he discovered his real sexual preference."

A whole reexamination of Christianity was under way in this group, and links were being established with similar Christian groups in San Francisco, San Diego, Phoenix, Chicago, and other growing congregations in cities as distant from each other as Boston and Honolulu. They raised such questions as: Was Jesus a homosexual? If not, did his religion at least imply an acceptance and toleration of love even if it was homosexual? The central emotion of Christianity is indeed *love*. How "prudish" was this Christian conception of love supposed to be? Although some religious historians have maintained that Jesus was a homosexual, Reverend Perry did not agree with them, according to this report: "But had Jesus lived in this age he at least would have been labelled a homosexual. After all, he never married, ran around with twelve guys, and was even betrayed by a kiss from another guy."[2] But the real point that the Reverend Perry wanted to make was that the logic of Jesus' teaching implied an acceptance and toleration of homosexuality, despite Biblical prohibitions. "As far as Christ is concerned, love in any form is permissible."

Even more startling was the report about marriage services conducted

421

in Reverend Perry's church. At the time of publication Reverend Perry had performed ceremonies for thirty-six homosexual couples, eight of them lesbians. "We substitute the word 'spouse' for 'husband' or 'wife'," the pastor explained. "Do you accept John Smith as your lawfully wedded 'spouse'?—do you in turn accept Tom Jones as your lawfully wedded 'spouse'?"

A legal point which the magazine drew attention to concerned the implications of California law on such marriages:

> California law recognises all marriages between partners who can show a certificate from an ordained minister proving that their marriage has been solemnised in a church ceremony. This law does not stipulate that the partners must be a man and a woman, only a "husband" and a "wife".[3]

What is often overlooked is that the permissive society is beginning to shift the whole domain of sexual behavior away not only from legal considerations, but also from moral considerations, and into the domain of taste and aesthetics.

This is where we take issues of taste beyond the arts and sports, as discussed in the last chapter, and connect them with wider values. We might distinguish between behavioral aesthetics and performance aesthetics. Behavioral aesthetics concerns questions of ugly and beautiful forms of human indulgence, without implying moral reprobation or disapproval. Bigamy in the West is still illegal; but not marriage between a man and a man. Bigamy remains within the realm of enforced sanctions, while marriage between a man and a man in Reverend Perry's church is to some citizens immoral, but to others merely a matter of taste. Sex before marriage might have been at one time in the West a question of legal control and sanctions; then it became a question of strong moral control under the church. Sex before marriage by the 1950's and certainly by the 1960's, was becoming not a matter for moral judgment but a matter of taste. Toleration of the individual in a self-regarding act could very rapidly reduce ethics to aesthetics.

Performance aesthetics, on the other hand, concerns the more usual issues of appreciation of art and nature in their respective forms of beauty and meaning. But nature here would be nature as enhanced and tended by human contrivance. A beautiful garden, a well-organized park, a display of multicolored birds at a zoo, are all instances of performance aesthetics in our sense. The performance in this case is by man, either utilizing color and sound and material, or utilizing living elements of nature for aesthetic effect. The range of performance aesthetics is from

Makonde sculpture to Beethoven's Ninth Symphony, from the Taj Mahal to *Hamlet*.*

Empathy and Imagination

There is a direct relationship between permissiveness and empathy. Societies capable of high moral disgust toward individual behavior reduce the area of empathy between individuals. Societies which are shocked by sexual deviance pollute the pool of the reflection of Narcissus. Victorian England with its high principles prevented moral critics from recognizing themselves in the behavior of others. Prudishness often keeps hypocrisy company on the high road to self-righteousness. The capacity to see one's self in the other man is reduced. Indeed, in this sphere of the high moral reprobation of the individual behavior of others there is a conscious attempt to create a moral distance between the object contemplated and the subject contemplating.

Oscar Wilde, the tragic English dramatist of the nineteenth century, was one such victim of Victorian prudishness and dissociation from empathy. He served a term of imprisonment on being convicted of homosexuality, falling in the process from a pinnacle of social applause and dazzling intellectual preeminence to the dark nadir of ostracism and social shame. While serving his sentence, Wilde wrote *De Profundis,* addressed to his former lover, Lord Alfred Douglas. Douglas had once written to Wilde to say, "When you are not on your pedestal you are not interesting." In *De Profundis* Wilde reminds Douglas that in those very words he created a distance both from the true temper of the artist and from what Matthew Arnold called "the secret of Jesus":

> Either would have taught you that whatever happens to another happens to one's self, and if you want an inscription to read at dawn and at night-time and for pleasure or for pain, write up on the wall of your house in letters of the sun to gild and the moon to silver *"Whatever happens to another happens to one's self"* and should anyone ask you what such an inscription can possibly mean you can answer that it means "Lord Christ's heart and Shakespeare's brain."[4]

Wilde here was in fact discussing the phenomenon of empathy in our sense, combining in it the aesthetics of Lipps and the psychology of Freud. The fusion of aesthetics and psychology is nothing less than the imagination itself. And it is the imagination that must form the spring-

---

* There is a third category of aesthetics apart from behavioral and performance—natural aesthetics. This is quite simply the appreciation of the beauty in nature and the cosmos which is independent of human manipulation and enhancement.

board of the empathetic leap. Oscar Wilde continued:

> Christ's place indeed is with the poets. His whole conception of Humanity
> sprang right out of the imagination and can only be realised by it. What God
> was to the Pantheist, man was to him. He was the first to conceive the
> divided races as a unity. Before his time there had been gods and men. He
> alone saw that on the hills of life there were but God and Man, and, feeling
> through the mysticism of sympathy that in himself each had been made in-
> carnate, he calls himself the Son of One or the son of the other, according to
> his mood.[5]

Wilde's conception of the poetic imagination of Jesus Christ in relation
to the fusion of man and God and of man and life, is what the concept of
empathy in our sense is all about. The capacity of nations to see
themselves in others, of races to identify the shared humanity of all, of
individuals to judge each other if they must by the yardstick of taste and
not of the inquisition—all are captured in some sense in the golden rule of
Jesus Christ and further beautified by the sensibility of an English
dramatist serving a sentence for homosexuality in Her Majesty's Prison,
Reading, in the year of his Lord 1897.

In a sense Jesus Christ was an intermediate moral stage toward Karl
Marx's precept that "the supreme being for man is man." Oscar Wilde
tells us that before Jesus there had been gods and men, but with Jesus,
God and man fuse, and the son of God and the son of man find abode in
the same person. But Karl Marx, the humanist, takes the stage further
and deifies man. What Marx deifies is not a particular man, not a king,
nor an emperor of Japan, not a prophet, but the human person as such.
As Robert Tucker has reminded us:

> Marx's atheism . . . meant only a negation of the trans-mundane god of
> traditional Western religion. It did not mean the denial of a supreme being.
> Indeed, denial of the trans-mundane god was only a negative way of
> asserting that "man" should be regarded as the supreme being or object of
> ultimate concern. . . . [as Marx himself put it] the criticism of religion ends
> with the precept that the supreme being for man is man. . . .[6]

With Karl Marx, perhaps more than with any other thinker before
him, history moved from a God-centered system of values to a man-
centered system of values. Things were right and wrong, virtuous or vicious, not in relation to the grand design of the Almighty, but in relation
to the purpose and well-being of man. It was as if the whole Judeo-Chris-
tian tradition were drastically tilting the balance between the commandment "Thou shalt love the Lord, thy God" to the commandment
"Thou shalt love thy neighbor as theyself." Love as a central emotion
was again conscripted for higher ends. The latter commandment was

assuming not only greater importance than the former; it was beginning to push the former out of the realm of relevance. This was the grand secularization of culture.

Bernard Murchaland in a symposium about the debate on "The Death of God" said:

> Every culture is undergirded by a substratum of religiosity. . . . What is happening now is that the religiosity of Western culture is expiring and at last appears as what it truly is, namely, the paraphernalia of faith in God. . . . We have "desacralized" the world, forgetting that ultimately culture is a consecration of the world.[7]

The very debate about the death of God concerns this profound theme of desacralization in western culture. Nietzsche had started the debate in its new form by contributing the very phrase itself: "God is dead. God remains dead. And we have killed him. How shall we the murderers of all murderers comfort ourselves? What was holiest and most powerful of all that the world has yet owned has bled to death under our knives."[8] In Nietzsche's provocative image, an old saint digs for roots in the forest, while from the mountain Zarathustra descends with fire. "Can it be possible? This old saint in his forest has not yet heard the news that *God is dead?*"

Nietzsche was moving from the concept of the Supreme Being to his own preferred concept of Superman. He was indeed thrusting destiny into human hands, but was looking for a Superman to control the steering wheel: "Can you create a god?—Then be silent about all gods! But you could create a Superman. Perhaps you yourselves cannot, my brothers! But you can recreate yourselves to be the fathers and forefathers of the Superman: let that be your best creation!"[9] The impact of Nietzsche on mid-twentieth century theological thought was deep, and not always conscious. It affected schools of thought ranging from nihilism to existentialism. In the words of Dietrich Bonhoeffer, God "spoke to us and now is silent, all that we touch now is his corpse."[10]

The secularization of culture in the West was moving not only from Supreme Being to Superman, but also from Superman to man. The process had for its fountain the Renaissance itself. A theme of *homocentrism,* the centrality of the person, seemed to augur at long last a "transvaluation of values" more fundamental than even Nietzsche's conception.

What we would emphasize in this analysis is not only the tripartite distinction between values as ethics, values as aesthetics, and values as law, but also the hypothesis that the trend in the transvaluation of values is toward a diminishing area of morality, and expanding areas of law and

425

aesthetics. The old domain of ethics implying rules of behavior which may or may not be codified in law is losing out both to the realm of pure taste and to the realm of law. Personal moralistic emotions are on the retreat. Those issues of ethics and virtue which were "other-regarding" would now be in any case codified. Those issues of ethics which were self-regarding are on their way toward dilution into questions of taste.

The expanding area of law has now to include welfare legislation and social services. Those self-righteous days when the poor were helped out of charity by the rich were in fact the days of a broad area of model behavior not necessitated by law. With the expansion of social welfare and social services, the domain of voluntary charity from the rich to the poor is contracting, as the domain of enforced distributive justice expands.

In domestic arrangements we might therefore say that the process of the secularization of culture at once reduces the penalties of vice and the opportunities of voluntary virtue. Lovers out of wedlock find wider boundaries of freedom; well-meaning millionaires find narrower horizons of charity. The United States, that last bastion of voluntary charity, is beginning to put the squeeze on charitable foundations. New tax laws seek to expand the sources of revenue for the state, in the wake of greater demands for welfare legislation and urban renewal—and those same tax laws reduce the options of charitable initiatives by voluntary organizations. Once again the phenomenon of expanding legislation, expanding areas of aesthetic choice, and diminishing areas of virtuous initiatives, together add up to the new trend in the secularization of culture. This is now true more of the western world than of any other, but the loosening social controls in tribal communities in Africa and the growth of impersonal forces in the wake of urbanization would seem to suggest that in this secularization of culture the West is once again anticipating a global trend. If world culture means a convergence of values and emotive responses, the trend toward the morally liberated individual is a fundamental aspect of that process.

The Sacralization of International Relations

While the trend in domestic arrangements is in the direction of secularization, the trend in international politics is, by contrast, in the direction of a new sacralization. There was indeed a time when international politics was sacralized in the most literal of senses—it was profoundly influenced by religious factors. Wars were fought for religious reasons and diplomacy conducted beneath the supervising eye of an "omniplomatic" god. But Europe, weary after the Thirty Years' War, gradually moved toward a secular diplomacy, almost in the direction of diplomatic aesthetics and propriety. Morality as a factor in international politics began to recede and power and good taste moved to the center as determinants of the behavior of states.

It is of course an exaggeration to suggest this style of politics was absent until after the Thirty Years' War. It was after all Machiavelli who first put into immortal formulations the whole dictum of secularized diplomacy. Machiavelli's advise to the Prince was based not on authority and theological prescriptions but on the concrete experience of history and observable political behavior. Machiavelli as a political theorist took a great step toward isolating state policy from religious, metaphysical, and ethical principles. By so doing Machiavelli initiated a grand process of desacralization in policy making.

Machiavelli was not so naive as to exclude the role of religion and morality as rationalizations of the pursuit of national self-interest. He cited the example of an early invasion of Africa in the name of religion—the invasion by Ferdinand, King of Aragon, who later became King of Spain as a whole. Ferdinand extracted money from the Church in order to pay his soldiers, and the Church got in return the solace of knowing that Ferdinand's conquests were in the name of God. As Machiavelli put it:

> [Ferdinand] found out a way of maintaining his army at the expense of the Church and the people; and by the length of that war he established such order and discipline among his soldiers, that afterwards they gained him many honorable victories. Besides this, to adapt him for greater enterprises (always making religion his pretence) by a kind of devout cruelty he destroyed and exterminated the Moors than which nothing could be more strange or deplorable. Under the same cloak of religion he invaded Africa . . . and began many great things which always kept the minds of his subjects in admiration and suspense, wondering what the next event of his machinations would be.[11]

Machiavelli was the first great rationalizer of hypocrisy and false pretenses as a cornerstone of high policy in diplomacy and politics. He still allowed room for virtue and morality, but these were to be in the area of public relations and rhetoric. The real calculations which lead to decisions are to be conducted on an *amoral* basis, sometimes verging on cynical immortality. In Machiavelli's terms:

> A prince therefore, is not obliged to have all the . . . good qualities in reality, but it is necessary he have them in appearance; nay, I will be bold to affirm that, having them actually, and employing them upon all occasions, they are extremely prejudicial, whereas, having them only in appearance, they turn to better account; it is honorable to seem mild, and merciful, and courteous, and religious, and sincere, and indeed to be so, provided your mind be so rectified and prepared that you can act quite contrary upon occasion. . . .

427

> Nevertheless, it is of great consequence to disguise your inclination, and to play the hypocrite well.[12]

More than 450 years later another diplomatic realist, Kenneth W. Thompson, reminded his readers that nations were more inclined than individuals to follow their own interests; the imperatives of national security and survival forced the statesmen to distinguish between personal and public responsibilities:

> There is no clearer and more poignant example than Lincoln's subordination of his private views on slavery to the goal of the preservation of the Union. Nations always pretend to have a purer devotion to morality than they actually have. They are not as pure in their actions as they claim to be in their intentions. Moral pretension arises from the claims of a nation that it has acted not from self-interest or national security but in obedience to some higher purpose like "civilization" or "justice."[13]

A more controversial exponent of the realist school of international relations is Hans J. Morgenthau. Certainly his initial position in *Politics Among Nations* had strong echoes of the Machiavellian tradition of diplomacy:

> The main signpost that helps political realism to find its way through the landscape of international politics is the concept of interest defined in terms of power. This concept . . . sets politics as an independent sphere of action and understanding apart from other spheres, such as economics, ethics, aesthetics or religion. . . . A realist theory of international politics, then, will guard against two popular fallacies: The concern with motives and the concern with ideological preferences."[14]

The concepts of interest and power as determinants of behavior are in this context, preeminently secular. And much of the diplomacy of Europe in the eighteenth, nineteenth, and first half of the twentieth centuries went a considerable way toward bearing out this realist school of international relations.

Three trends of the twentieth century began to reintroduce the sacred dimension in international politics, though still on a modest scale. These three trends are, first, the rise of internationalist ideologies; second, the rise of the United States as a superpower; and third, the emergence of the new countries of Asia and Africa. The most important of the internationalist ideologies is communism, and its success in the Soviet Union heralded a new period of moral commitment in diplomacy. It is true that Stalin, after a period of hesitation, embarked on a policy of socialism in one country. But Stalin never completely broke away from the consequences of ruling the first country to be conquered by a new internationalist ideology. The imperative of proselytism and evangelical commitment was indeed regulated under Stalin but also permitted to affect profoundly policy calculations. The triumph of communism in China in 1949, and the creation of a communist eastern Europe, added new layers of moralistic diplomacy to the arena of world politics.

A separate element in the remoralization of world politics was the rise of the United States, born out of a transvaluation of political values. Here was a country that became quite early, moralistic in its political rhetoric, and deeply influenced both by moral bombast and by puritanic self-righteousness. The American phenomenon was not a simple case of an internationalist ideology; it was a case of a power steeped in the idiom of pioneering fervor. The Russians regarded themselves as missionaries not because they were Russians but because they were communists. After all, even the Czars had been Russians. But Americans regarded themselves as missionaries not because they were liberals but because they were Americans. Their evangelism was nationalistic first and foremost, rather than derived from the liberal tradition which they shared with Western Europe.

Within the nationalistic evangelism of the United States was a genuine charitable streak. With a naive belief that every man was a potential American if only he were given the opportunity went a readiness to expand the opportunities of others. The United States has probably more charitable institutions and foundations than any other country in history; it has spent more on other nations and societies than is likely to be done by any other country for generations to come.

But this very belief in the potential Americanness of the rest of the human species, and the readiness of the United States to provide the opportunities for this Americanization of the world, made a contribution toward the resacralization of diplomacy. It is true that the United States is now undergoing that long-awaited "agonizing reappraisal" with which John Foster Dulles had threatened Europe in the 1950's. At the end of November 1971 the Senate of the United States made the historic decision to attempt a grand retreat from the policy of massive American aid to other parts of the world. The Senate decision was facilitated by President Nixon's own tactics following the expulsion of Taiwan from the U.N., and the attempt by Nixon to appeal to American chauvinism in his denunciation of the ingratitude of those who received American aid and were ready to vote against the United States in the world body. But even after we have made allowances for the isolationist tendencies shown by the United States in its military, fiscal, commercial, and aid policies under Richard Nixon, we may still be driven to conclude that some precedents in diplomatic styles set by the United States are not completely reversible. The very diplomacy of aid, whatever the United States herself may decide to do, has become part of the world political system. The Marshall Plan and the subsequent methods of helping the Third World, ranging from funding world development to sending out Peace Corps men and women, have influenced other rich countries in the world. The United States has helped to establish and consolidate a tradition of economic aid and technical assistance, and has itself played an important part in putting pressure on its allies to be active in this sphere.

For example, on November 3, 1971 the *Uganda Argus,* carried this headline: "U.S. Senate rejects foreign aid bill but British Queen makes promise" referring to the speech of Queen Elizabeth II opening a new session of parliament with a promise to maintain all economic and political friendships and alliances, while seeking a new relationship in Europe. The tone of the report was that no alternative aid could make up for losses sustained by the Third World following the U.S. Senate's decision to scale down the administration's original $3.6 billion to $2.5 billion. Nevertheless, the survival of this kind of diplomacy as part of the world scene can now withstand post-Nixonic changes in American contributions toward it. We cannot therefore escape the conclusion that the rise of the United States itself as a superpower, no less than the rise of internationalist ideologies, was a major factor in the resacralization of international relations.

The Emergence of the Third World

The third major trend which has resulted in this resacralization is the emergence of new states in Asia and Africa. By the time the United Nations celebrated its twenty-fifth anniversary in October 1970, the organization had become more a weapon of war against certain forms of international immortality than a mechanism of peace between nations. As more and more countries from Africa and Asia joined the world body, the liberating role of the United Nations became more pronounced. The new members of the world organization were regarding it not so much as designed to ensure peace and security—as the big powers had intended it to be in San Francisco—but as primarily concerned with human rights at large. The actual framers of the Charter in 1945 had first declared their determination to "save succeeding generations from the scourge of war" and then only secondarily to "reaffirm faith in fundamental human rights, in the dignity and worth of the human person, in the equal rights of men and women and of nations large and small."[15] Judging by their policies, attitudes, and stands, the new states of Africa and Asia would have reversed this order of affirmation.

This had an important bearing on qualifications for membership in the

United Nations as viewed by, on the one hand, countries like the United States which, until 1971, continued to oppose the admission of communist China and, on the other hand, countries like Tanzania which have sought South Africa's expulsion from the world organization. Those who used to be opposed to communist China's admission interpreted Article 4 of the United Nations' Charter as restricting membership to those countries which were "peace-loving". This whole emphasis on peace was more characteristic of the big powers' conception of the United Nations' role than it was of the view of the new and smaller states. Those who have sought South Africa's expulsion have indeed sometimes used rationalizations connected with international peace and security, but the main case against the continued membership of South Africa in the world organization has been deemed to lie in her racialistic political system at home.

In this trend toward the resacralization of diplomacy, we may say that the United Nations has been particularly important in casting a shadow of global disapproval on two phenomena which have been regarded as legitimate for hundreds of years before—colonial subjugation and institutionalized racial predjudice.

On colonialism itself the United Nations' record must already be pronounced as one of success. In the course of the 1950's, if not earlier, the world body had already become the main forum of censure against colonial policies. The colonial powers at first resisted these challenges from world critics. Even those countries being administered on behalf of the world organization as trusteeships had a difficult time persuading the administrative power to speed up the process of liberation. In 1954 a United Nations' Visiting Mission to Tanganyika recommended that a timetable should be drawn up for Tanganyika's independence by 1974 and certainly not later than 1979. This timetable was rejected by the administering authority, the United Kingdom, as unrealistic, and the report as a presumptuous attempt to hurry up an administering authority in its responsibilities for trusteeship.

The impact of the United Nations on decolonization went of course beyond its own trusteeships. Sometimes the United Nations was implicated directly in other issues as well, as in the case of the argument between Indonesia and the Dutch over the control of West Irian. The United Nations interpreted the situation in favor of Indonesia—partly on the assumption that the Dutch were more alien in that area than the Indonesians.

In the Congo of Lumumba and Kasavubu the United Nations did try to be a mechanism for maintaining the territorial integrity of a newly independent African state, as well as to keep the big powers from having a direct confrontation within the Congo. The U.N. Congo operation had its failures, among them the failure to save the life of Patrice Lumumba. But the operation did succeed in frustrating Katanga's bid to secede— and thereby helped to consolidate the principle of territorial integrity in postcolonial Africa.

The record of the United Nations as a liberating force became in 1965 one of the factors which inclined Harold Wilson's government in Britain to favor the application of sanctions against Rhodesia, however ineffectual they might have turned out to be. There was a genuine fear in the United Kingdom that unless Britain acted firmly against Ian Smith, the initiative for action against Rhodesia would pass to the world body. A bipartisan policy in England in favor of a strong stand against Ian Smith was inspired precisely by this fear of a "red army in blue berets," intimating Russian participation in subduing the Ian Smith regime under the banner of the United Nations.

The regime of Ian Smith has lasted much longer than might have been anticipated in 1965. And here then it is worth making the distinction between white minority rule and colonial rule. The United Nations does indeed have an impressive record in facilitating the end of colonial rule; but its success in ending white minority rule in those countries where this still exists has been much more modest. An alternative way of formulating this conclusion is to say that while the United Nations has to its credit important achievements in the fight against colonialism, the history of its participation in the fight against racialism has been characterized more by frustrations than by accomplishment.

And yet the battle still continues, and is an aspect of the resacralization of diplomacy in the world. When the United Nations Organization was formed in San Francisco in 1945, South Africa was in fact the most influential African state present there. But history has come to indulge her ironic sense of humor once again. South Africa, which had been one of the architects of the world body in San Francisco in 1945, was destined to become one of the primary targets of the Organization's moral war. If the world body continues to survive it will not be a very long time before at last an African becomes the Secretary-General of the Organization. It is conceivable that when that time comes South Africa will already have been squeezed out of the world body, or will be considering withdrawing of her own accord rather than having to deal with a black Secretary-General.

The United Nations' influence has declined in the world in the last ten years; but the African influence within the world body has increased dramatically. Now that communist China has entered the United Nations, it is conceivable that the Organization will receive a new lease of diplomatic life.

For the time being its mission in the fight against colonialism is virtually complete. That is in fact its most solid achievement. Its mission against racialism in southern Africa is underway but the difficulties are great. Its mission against underdevelopment through its specialized agencies may well be vastly strengthened before the end of the 1970's in spite of the present uncertainty concerning the American contribution. But meanwhile, the United Nations remains at its most helpless in dealing with problems of war—either a war within a member state, like the Nigerian Civil War, or the massive danger of nuclear annihilation. Clouds of uncertainty continue to hang over the destiny of the world body and of the human kind it is supposed to serve. What is certain already is that the United Nations has been both a symbol of the resacralization of international relations and an instrument for promoting that fragile new morality in world politics.

There is no doubt that the moral tone of international politics and the degree of commitment to moral causes implied by that tone are still delicate. All we can say is that the rise of new internationalist ideologies, the rise of the United States as a superpower and the emergence of the new nations of Asia and Africa, have all converged as important forces behind the birth of a new pax humana in world affairs.

Conclusion

We have attempted to demonstrate two paradoxical trends in human relations, each profoundly important for the phenomenon of empathy and for the role of culture. In relations among individuals and among groups domestically, we have argued that judgments on human behavior are moving from ethics to aesthetics. Large areas of the individual's active life, which before were fit for moral approbation or moral disapproval by others, have in the last few decades become areas of discretion according to *taste*. The range is from premarital sex to suicide, from milder forms of drug taking to homosexuality, from pornography to flamboyant modes of dress. Involved in all is the depoliticization of certain negative emotions as society restrains itself from giving legislative forms to its own disgust.

In relations between states, on the other hand, the trend has been from the diplomacy of propriety to the diplomacy of principles. The diplomacy of propriety was again an exercise in discretion according to taste, with styles deemed as more civilized or less, in terms implying behavioral ugliness and behavioral attractiveness rather than good and evil. An aesthetic judgment in our sense is of the kind which, for example, disapproves of a person turning up at a formal dinner party in shorts and an open shirt. He may incur serious censure from the other participants. But the judgment passed on him is fundamentally different from what we pass on someone who rapes a girl of fourteen. The latter judgment is still within the moral domain. What we have suggested here is that premarital sex according to Victorian morality belonged roughly in the same category as the raping of a girl of fourteen; premarital sex by the 1960's had moved from that category to the aesthetic category by the standards of which we also judge the man who turns up at a formal dinner party in shorts and an open shirt.

There is a third category to be borne in mind—that of legal judgments, distinct both from moral judgments and from aesthetic ones. In domestic relations what is happening is an expanding area of legal judgments and legal obligations, an expanding area of aesthetic judgments, but a contracting area of moral judgments per se. Forms of personal behavior which do not become outlawed specifically very rapidly become matters of taste. On balance we are still talking about trends and tendencies, rather than about a world already aesthetically revolutionized. But the trend in domestic relations between individuals and between groups is toward expanding aesthetics, expanding law, and contracting morality.

Why is it that in interstate relations the trend is toward expanding international morality? The essential difference once again between the international domain and the domestic may hinge on the simple fact that the international dimension does not have law in the same sense as the domestic. There are no legal sanctions, as we know all too clearly, that can be applied against transgressors in the international system. There are no jails to which offending nations might be sent; and even economic sanctions and boycotts have been applied so half-heartedly that as often as not they have strengthened the transgressor instead of weakening her.

Because the international arena does not have enforceable law, and because there is no legislature to bring international law up to date in conformity with changing norms, there cannot be at this level the equivalent of the domestic phenomenon of an expanding legal framework. In domestic relations, as we have indicated, morality is losing both to law and to aesthetics. But in international relations there is no law by which the new values of human obligation might be transformed into a really authoritative allocation of values.

Both the domestic and the international trends we have discussed illustrate changes in the boundaries of empathy itself. In domestic relations law is expanding in those areas which manifest new social responsibilities and popular welfare. Behavioral aesthetics are expanding because of a new social permissiveness toward individual preferences. The widening frontiers of taste are in fact widening frontiers of toleration.

The world of the 1990's ought therefore to aim for the maturation of these two trends—increased social and welfare legislation, diminishing moral self-righteousness with regard to the private behavior of others, and widening horizons of personal choice and personal taste.

In the international system, on the other hand, the world of the 1990's should aim to consolidate the trend toward a new international morality, susceptible to the obligations of the strong toward the weak, the rich toward the poor, and of each toward a concept of pax humana and a man-centred system of values. Perhaps by that time a new concept of international law might also have been helped to mature, allowing for possibilities of enactment and enforcement. If that were indeed to be realized the international system could for a while manifest an expanding area of law, an expanding area of morality, and a diminishing area of sovereign taste. Trends in relations between individuals will thus for a while continue to be, in important and defensible ways, different from trends in relations between national entities.

Behind both trends remains the impact of culture on emotive responses. It is, of course, culture as a system of values that encompasses these changing balances among aesthetics, ethics, and law. And in the notion of empathy and its connection both to psychology and to aesthetics as areas of emotive experience, we have a sense of culture that is narrower than the whole system of values, but one which could at the same time be richer and more symbolic of human creativity than other sectors of the normative world. Our concept of human empathy remains profoundly cultural in its roots, and our evaluation of world trends springs from an interpretation of changing cultural patterns behind both individual and national behavior. To a certain extent, the problems of world order are concerned with the interplay between the sacred and the secular in man's emotions and judgments, and these in turn find their origins in the world of values and cultural perspectives.

Once again the high road to a viable world order must carry signs to guide the pilgrim toward the penultimate stage of normative convergence.

Footnotes

1. John Stuart Mill, *On Liberty,* especially Chapter IV concerning "The Limits to the Authority of Society over the Individual."
2. "The Homosexual Church," *Newsweek,* Department of Religion, October 12, 1970, p. 57.
3. *Ibid.*

4. Oscar Wilde, *De Profundis,* with an introduction by Jacques Barzun (New York: Vintage Books, Random House, 1964), p. 100.
5. *Ibid.*
6. Robert Tucker, *Philosophy and Myth in Karl Marx* (Cambridge: Cambridge University Press, 1961), pp. 11, 22.
7. Bernard Murchaland, "Editor's Introduction: The Meaning of the Death of God," *The Meaning of the Death of God: Protestant, Jewish and Catholic Scholars Explore Atheistic Theology* (New York: Vintage Books, Random House, 1967), p. 11.
8. Friedrich Nietzsche, *Joyful Wisdom,* translated by Thomas Common (New York: Frederick Ungar, 1960), pp. 107–185.
9. Friedrich Nietzsche, "Ecce Homo," *The Philosophy of Nietzsche* (New York: Modern Library, n.d.), p. 18.
10. Dietrich Bonhoeffer, *Letters and Papers from Prison* (London: SCM Press, 1953), Letters dated April 30, 1944, June 8, 1944. Cited by Murchaland, *op. cit.,* p. 70.
11. Machiavelli, *The Prince,* Chapter XXI.
12. *The Prince,* Chapter XVIII.
13. Kenneth W. Thompson, "Toward a Theory of International Politics," *American Political Science Review,* Vol. 49, No. 3, September 1955, pp. 739–742.
14. Hans J. Morgenthau, *Politics Among Nations* 2nd Edition (New York: Alfred A. Knopf, 1948, 1954), pp. 3–7.
15. From the lines of re-affirmation opening the Charter.

CHAPTER 21

Toward a Shared Humanity

We have sought to demonstrate in this book that in the last two millennia, starting with the world religions, the human race has been experiencing a process of normative convergence. Values, tastes, emotional responses, and intellectual perspectives, have all been moving toward a shared center of discourse. But since the beginning of the second half of this last millennium Europe has been outstripping the rest of mankind in technology and general readiness to experiment and innovate in different arenas of human experience. Europe's imperial expansion, coupled with its escalating technological superiority, left a dominant imprint of its own personality on that shared portion of the human heritage. It is this disproportionate European presence in the federal level of world culture that has resulted in the whole phenomenon of cultural dependency in the rest of the world.

We distinguished in the introduction between structural dependency and cultural dependency. Much of structual dependency is *economic*. How is the Third World to transcend these two levels of domination by the northern hemisphere?

On the structural and economic front, a particularly suggestive episode in international politics was the October war in the Middle East. Let us first examine strategies of transcending structural and economic dependency before we return to the problem of cultural subjugation.

Structural Counter-Penetration

The October war in the Middle East in 1973 was fought at two levels—military and diplomatic. From the point of view of the Middle East, both levels were perhaps equally important. The relatively modest military successes of the Arabs were politically important beyond their military significance. They certainly helped to restore Egyptian and Syrian morale, and contributed toward destroying the myth of Israeli invincibility.

But while these military factors were quite fundamental to the Middle East itself, it was the *economic* war waged by the Arabs which fired the imagination of the Third World. From the point of view of the rest of Asia, Africa and the Middle East it was neither the tank battles in the Sinai nor the air battles over the Golan Heights which were basic to their own destiny. It was, as we have indicated earlier, the utilization of oil as a political weapon, with all its implications for relations between the affluent industrial world and the primary producers of the southern hemisphere.

From the economic point of view, the term "October War" is somewhat inaccurate. The Arab *economic* war for the restoration of Arab lands lasted for several months longer than the Arab *military* challenge to Israel.

What the economic war revealed were two potentially critical strategies toward creating a new economic order in the world. One was the strategy of counter-penetration by the Third World into the dominant northern hemisphere. The other was the strategy of *inter-penetration* between the different sections of the Third World itself. It is to these two strategies that we must now turn more fully, with a special emphasis on Afro-Arab relations as an illustration of tensions and amity within the Third World itself.

As we indicated earlier, an important school of thought in the Third World has opted for the strategy of *disengagement*. Under this strategy the Third World countries should seek to explore the maximum possibilities of self-reliance and of "emancipation" from the international capitalist system.

But here one must distinguish between domestic and international capitalism. There are Third World theoreticians who assume that by eliminating capitalism in their own countries they would necessarily *"disengage"* from the international capitalist system. What they overlook is that a country can abolish private enterprise and even private property at home and still be wholly dependent on the vagaries of trade with the capitalist countries and the fluctuations of the capitalist monetary system.

The Soviet Union, domestically socialist in at least economic organization, has been groping for ways to strengthen its links with the capitalist system. The Soviet Union has negotiated the involvement of Japanese firms in the exploitation of the mineral resources of Siberia, and has sought Japanese expertise in related economic endeavors.

The Soviet Union has also been keen on expanding trade with the United States. To attain the status of most favored nation has been one of Russia's economic ambitions in the process of consolidating détente with the United States. Even the grain deal between Russia and America in 1971-2 was envisaged with American private enterprise. In that grain deal Russia's commercial skills in the art of "maximizing returns" were impressively revealed. What all this meant was that a superpower like the U.S.S.R., committed to domestic socialism, could still find it moral and prudent to strengthen its links with international capitalism.

A similar trend is discernible in the economic attitude of the People's Republic of China. It is true that China pursued a policy of isolation for over twenty-years, yet that isolation was not entirely by choice. The United States took the leadership for that period to ostracize the People's Republic. When, under Richard M. Nixon, the United States at last decided to end its policy of ostracism, and to court Mao's China instead, the latter did not effectively resist the overtures. Since then China has begun responding to economic explorations from the Japanese, the western Europeans as well as the Americans. China has yet to move as enthusiastically as Russia toward strengthening links with international capitalism, but the trends are in that direction.

If then "disengagement" from the international capitalist system is difficult for even such socialist giants as Russia and China, it is bound to be an elusive dream for the bulk of the Third World. Is there an alternative strategy?

We come back to the strategy of counter-penetration. The Arab oil producers will shortly have 5000 million pounds available for investment abroad. Should they use it for investment in the Third World or in the northern hemisphere? The answer is *both*. The negotiations concerning Arab investment within the European Economic Community would be in the direction of counter-penetration. Arab investment in the United States will also increase. So of course will Iranian investment.

Japanese counter-penetration into the United States is an illustration of how a former appendage of American capitalism has become a serious economic rival to the United States. Japanese businessmen have recently been manipulating aspects of the American economy almost as cynically as American businessmen once manipulated Japan. The strategy of counter-penetration in Japan's relations with the West has been dramatically and convincingly vindicated so far.

As compared with Japan's position, the Third World's capabilities for counter-penetration are still modest, but the oil producers may help to create the kind of leverage which could one day transform the economic order of the world. To disengage from the capitalist system would be an act of economic abdication. Libya, Iran, Nigeria and Saudi Arabia are much weaker outside the system than within it. It is their potential influence within the system which much of the rest of the Third World really needs. Parts of the northern hemisphere are beginning to feel the countervailing power of parts of the south.

As the Arab world celebrated the first anniversary of the October War two trends were already discernible among the industrialized nations. One was a campaign to get the petro-dollars recycled. Britain led this campaign, eager to persuade the oil producers to invest their surplus capital precisely in countries like the United Kingdom. There was some success already. Both Iran and the Arab world were evolving aggressive commercial enthusiasm, and had begun fundamental explorations for new investment opportunities. Chancellor Helmut Schmidt of the German Federal Republic announced in November that a Middle Eastern government had bought a substantial share of the Daimler-Benz corporation, the manufacturer of not only Mercedes cars but also some military vehicles. It later transpired that the government concerned was Kuwait, which had acquired a 14 per cent interest. A few months earlier Iran had acquired a 25 per cent interest in the steel division of the massive Krupp Enterprises. Other industrial and commercial enterprises in the western world which had entered, or were reported to have entered into discussions with oil producers, included Lockheed Aircraft Corporation in the United States, Pan-American World Airlines, and Grumman Aerospace Corporation. Iran has helped in salvaging Pan-American from economic disaster.

But precisely because the oil producers were beginning to take seriously the western invitation to recycle and reinvest their dollars, a second trend was also discernible in the West—a groping for ways to "contain the threat of inappropriate foreign investment". At a news conference early in December 1974, U.S. Secretary of State Henry Kissinger indicated that the Administration wished to study "the implications of substantial investments" from oil producers into the United States, "how we can keep track of them", and the identification of the "dangers against which we must guard".[1]

More specifically, the American government was getting concerned that some oil producing countries might attempt to take over financial control of critical defense industries. The anxieties were partly an outgrowth of an offer by Iran in the summer of 1974 of a loan to help financially troubled Grumman Aerospace Corporation. Iran's offer originally envisaged the acquisition of a potential equity position in the company. A controversy flared up, influenced by the fear that some oil producing countries might attempt to take over control of industries which were critical to American defense needs. The Defense Department resolved the Grumman case by insisting that Iran should be given equity control of this traditional producer of fighter planes for the American Navy. A full-scale study was ordered a few months later by the Ford Administration about the wider implications of this new wave of foreign investments into the United States. A distinction was beginning to be made behind the scenes between investment from military allies like western Europe and Japan and investment from nonaligned Third World countries with different political and economic imperatives. In the words of a report in *The New York Times:*

> In contemplating a possible invasion of Arab oil money, the Defense Department finds itself trying to walk a line between an over-all Administration policy of welcoming foreign investments and a desire to protect the defense sector against foreign control. In the past year, there have been some rumblings of discontent in the Congress over foreign investment in American industry—faint echoes thus far compared to the cries in Canada and Europe over alleged domination by American investments . . . At a news conference last Friday, James R. Schlesinger, Secretary of Defense, said his department would examine any attempt by a foreign government to acquire a major or controlling interest in an American contractor doing classified work "with great caution and on a case-by-case basis.[2]

If the strategy of counter-penetration has achieved nothing else so far, it is beginning to make Americans appreciate a little the fears of those who have previously expressed anxieties about American economic presence in other lands. Such a fundamental re-examination by the United States about the role of foreign investment in world affairs could itself have far-reaching implications.

Yet that is only the beginning. The long-term potential of counter-penetration lies in creating conditions which would help to force the creation of a new international economic order.

What should be borne in mind once again is that counter-penetration consists of more than just the recycling of petro-dollars into the developed world. An even more fundamental aspect of counter-penetration is *the conversion of Third World resources from their old role as sources of dependency to a new role as sources of power.* Part of this conversion is merely a change in level of political consciousness and economic astuteness. For as long as the Arabs did not realize that their oil was a potential source of immense power, their oil became a pretext for their own exploitation by others. But as the oil producers attained new levels of economic awareness and political consciousness, they first began demanding a bigger percentage of profits from the Euro-American oil companies. As they got away with bigger and bigger percentages of the profit, and as the consumption of oil in the developed world increased, a de-

441

vastating new realization dawned upon the consciousness of oil producers. It they were united, they could transform their dependency into power. The Organization of the Petroleum Exporting Countries—originally conceived primarily as an instrument for pressuring the foreign oil companies—was soon to enter the main stream of world economic diplomacy. Without the actors realizing it, the age of counter-penetration by the Third World had begun.

In addition to these two aspects of counter-penetration (recycling petro-dollars and converting primary resources from dependency to power), the strategy of counter-penetration also requires a sensitivity to the implications of the international monetary system. The immense foreign reserves in the hands of the oil-producers should be used to force changes in the international monetary system in the direction of easing the burdens of the developing countries. The potentialities of this monetary power in the hands of oil-producing countries was illustrated in December 1974. A major oil company almost casually revealed that Saudi Arabia no longer wanted to be paid in sterling for her oil. Until then Saudi Arabia received about a quarter to a third of her oil revenue in the form of British sterling. The new anti-sterling decision created consternation in London. The British pound descended to an all-time low in western money markets, and the stock exchange in London reverberated with gloom. The Bank of England had to supply millions in support of the pound. The only silver-lining in the cloud was the possibility that Saudi Arabia would continue to invest in Great Britain, though no longer accepting pounds for her oil. The future of sterling as a world currency was briefly under a cloud simply because a small Arab country was reconsidering its financial options. The world caught a glimpse of the potential power of the oil producers to force major changes in the international monetary system.

Finally, as we indicated in a previous chapter, counter-penetration also has a demographic element concerning distribution of population. The brain-drain from the Third World into the northern hemisphere could one day become a source of Third World influence within the north—comparable in principle to the role played by Jewish intellectuals and businessmen in Europe and North America in defense of Israeli interests. Given that Israel has been so dependent on the United States especially for economic and military support, and has therefore been deeply penetrated by America, the Jewish presence within the United States is a case of demographic counter-penetration.

As for the more humble migratory patterns from poorer countries to richer countries, like Jamaicans in Britain or Algerians in France, these too might one day serve comparable purposes. The world of the future has to include inter-locking population centers—Blacks in the Americas and Europe, Whites in Africa; Jews in North America and the Middle East; Arabs in Africa; East Indians in the Caribbean; and perhaps one day Chinese in Australia after all. Some population exchanges will be symmetrical, like the Blacks in the white world "in exchange" for Whites in the black world. Other demographic migratory patterns might be less symmetrical—like the Chinese in Malaya. Where there is lack of symmetry, or where the immigrants are more privileged than the indigenous peoples, tensions are inevitable. But, inspite of General Idi Amin and his expulsion of Asians, the central long-term meaning of demographic dispersal for the world is the emergence of an inter-locking population system between now and the end of the twenty-first century. Demographic counter-penetration from the Third World into the northern hemisphere would be only one aspect of such a system.

Inter-penetration: Cultural and Economic

Clearly it is not merely relations between the Third World and the northern hemisphere which are fundamental to the quest for a new economic and political order. In matters of migratory patterns, as well as in other areas of international life, relations among different parts of the Third World itself are equally fundamental.

The bulk of economic interaction in the world so far has been between northern industrial nations themselves (upper horizontal relations). Next in importance has been interaction between the industrial north and the less developed southern hemisphere (vertical relations). The least significant has been interaction within the southern hemisphere itself (lower horizontal relations).

Because of this latter deficiency, the bonds among Third World countries have been weak. Until recently, there was only a weak sense of interdependence and little awareness of each other's problems. A strategy of increased mutual economic penetration between Third World countries, ranging from trade to technical assistance, could raise their level of interdependence and enhance the possibilities of organic solidarity among developing countries.

In the economic domain, we define *organic solidarity* as a form of partnership based on interlocking economic systems. We define *strategic solidarity* as an alliance for purposes of collective bargaining with a third party. The developing countries have already discovered the virtues of strategic economic solidarity against the industrial north. Most of Third World economic dealings are with the industrial north rather than with each other. By "ganging up" against the industrial powers in forums like the General Assembly session on raw materials, or the United Nations'

Conference on Trade and Development, the Third World has begun to develop some skills of strategic solidarity. But only effective inter-penetration between Third World economies could create a solid organic form of interdependence.

At the cultural level some parts of the Third World have interacted for a much longer time. In some cases this cultural interaction could prepare the way for a fuller economic partnership in the years ahead. But there are intermediate problems. Pre-eminent among those transitional problems is the lack of symmetry in that old cultural interaction. Modern Africa has borrowed much more from the European heritage than Europe has borrowed from the African. Similarly, Africa has been more deeply influenced by the Middle East than the Middle East has been influenced by Africa. This lack of balance and symmetry carries risks of dependency and resentment.

From Africa's point of view, the next most important external region after Europe in terms of its total impact on the life of the African continent is certainly the Middle East. Europe and the Middle East together over the centuries have exerted an influence over the lives of black peoples at once disruptive and creative, at once pacifying and transformative. Both these regions have played major roles in creating the possibility of a world culture in our own lifetime. The Middle East played its role partly through the emergence of universalistic religions there. Western Europe, in turn, played its role partly through the emergence of modern technology. The Middle East helped to shape the spiritual side of modern Africa through the dissemination of the Semitic religions of Christianity and Islam. Europe, on the other hand, asserted its leadership in modern science and technology, and through these helped to transform the Africa of our day.

Both Christianity and Islam are Semitic religions to the extent to which they both initially emerged among Semitic peoples, the Jews and the Arabs. Islam in Africa was spread by the Semitic peoples themselves in the main, helped by indigenous Africans. Christianity, on the other hand, was spread in Africa through the initiatives of a third party—the European.

We might therefore say that Islam came to Africa first-hand, straight from the Arabs. Christianity, by contrast, came in second-hand, under the banner of European expansionism, instead of Jewish reformism.

These, of course, are generalizations, and deliberately overlook such exceptions as the ancient status of Christianity in Ethiopia, or the recent propagation of Islam by Muslims of Indian extraction. These exceptions are details which do not invalidate the general rule.

Both the Middle East and western Europe played a part in dominating or subjugating portions of Africa. Both the Middle East and western Europe played a part in enslaving some of the peoples of Africa. Both the Middle East and western Europe in addition played a part in transforming the cultural universe and ways of life of the black continent.

The Semitic peoples of the Middle East split into two. One wing migrated and became part of the western world. These were the Jews, struggling over the centuries to be accepted as westerners. The other wing of the Semitic peoples, the Arabs, migrated and Arabized much of North Africa, and helped to Islamize other parts of the African continent.

In the past, the Jews struggled to be accepted as Europeans; in the future, many Arabs will struggle to be accepted as Africans. Anti-semitism in Europe for many centuries in the past was prejudice against the Jews. Anti-semitism in parts of Africa south of the Sahara might at times be prejudice against the Arabs.

Anti-Arabism and pro-Israeli sentiments in parts of black Africa are not always easy to understand. After all, from the point of view of global stratification in our own era, it is the Jewish sector of the Semitic people that has, in the main, now become part of the affluent and developed classes of the world community. Although geographically Israel is part of the Middle East, in culture and scientific civilization Israel is more immediately part of the northern hemisphere of the world, a member of the relatively affluent. Certainly the great majority of world Jewry are resident in the developed parts of the world.

By contrast, the great majority of the Arab sector of the Semitic peoples are clearly among the underprivileged. They are part and parcel of the Third World.

And yet, in many African countries, a residual sense of dependency with regard to the Arabs continues to condition social and political behavior. Here we must distinguish again between these two stages of intellectual and mental dependency. One stage might be called a *submissive dependency complex,* a signifying excessive deference toward external standards, a keeness to imitate the dominant culture, a compulsive subservience to the inner commandments of the conquering civilization.

An *aggressive dependency complex,* on the other hand, comes at the moment of rebellion against the dominant culture, but in a form which falls short of genuine self-confidence. Aggressive dependency today in Africa manifests itself in forms which range from refusing to talk to a white man because he is white, to a readiness to kill a white child because he is white. Aggressive dependency sometimes signifies a profound lack of adequate social direction, an experience of alienation, yet with a clear cause for one's grievances, a clear villain to blame for one's self-hatred.

There was a time in some parts of Africa when submissive dependency toward the Arabs was the order of the day. Many people patterned their life-styles in imitation of the Arabs, whether these people were Muslims or not. Indeed, the word *ustaarabu* in Kiswahili, which originally meant the imitation of Arab ways, then became equated with civilization itself. There are still many African Muslims who manifest symptoms of dependency toward the Arabs.

But, on the whole, in parts of black Africa, the shift has been toward aggressive dependency in relation to the Arabs. This is a state of mind which is undecided as to whether to admire or despise the Arabs, to love them in comradeship or hate them as enemies.

Many black Africans have found it possible to be aggressive against the Arabs, but not yet the will to be aggressive against the western world. Indeed, even black aggression against the Arabs is, in some cases, an outcome of African submissiveness to the western world. Until recently, there was a strong anti-Arab tendency in much of the western world. Many black Africans echo their sentiments in sheer imitation. Many were taught in colonial schools about the Arab slave trade by people who came from countries that had themselves participated in the slave trade on a much larger scale. In the colonial days African children listened to missionaries talking about Islam's links with slavery, and believed what they said, in spite of the fact that Christendom practised slavery for five hundred years longer than Islam. In other words, there are times when anti-Arabism within black Africa is simply a manifestation of black pro-westernism. Many black Africans have become aggressive against the Arabs partly for genuine reasons of history, but also because they are still submissive toward the sentiments, emotions, prejudices, and inclinations of those who once ruled them from Europe.

But the frustration had deeper causes in history. The most central problem was the lack of symmetry in the interpenetration between the Middle East and Black Africa. The Middle East was more "the giver"; black Africa more "the receiver". Black Africa had been penetrated culturally and economically—but had not managed to accomplish adequate counter-penetration. Black dependency was bound to result in black frustration. That is not a healthy relationship between two parts of the Third World. It is a relationship which threatens to affect the future, as well as the present.

Economic Partnership versus Political Alliance

A major distinction which has to be drawn in Afro-Arab relations is between a political alliance and an economic partnership. When African states broke off relations with Israel in 1973, they were consolidating a political alliance with the Arabs. At the very minimum a political alliance involves "sharing enemies". Black Africans, in asserting solidarity with the Arabs, treated Israel as a common enemy for the time-being.

What many African critics of the Arabs tended to forget was that the Arabs had already paid back this particular debt well in advance. Just as most black African states have no diplomatic relations with Israel, most of the Arab world has had no diplomatic relations with South Africa and Rhodesia.

Black Africa has decided to treat Israel as a common enemy only recently, while most of the Arab world had treated South Africa as a common enemy for many years before now. When black African states broke off relations with Israel, they were not extending political credit to the Arabs which the Arabs had then to pay back. On the contrary, black Africa was paying back an earlier political debt incurred when most of the Arabs decided to treat the racist governments of South Africa and Rhodesia as shared enemies well before black Africa turned against Israel.

Arab countries like Algeria, Egypt and Libya were supporting black liberation movements in Southern Africa years before black Africa recognized Palestinians as a people with a grievance at all.

But in October 1973 the political alliance between black Africa and the Arab world ceased to be one-sided. Both sides decided to "share enemies".

Yet when Africans ask for cheaper oil and development aid from the Arabs they are trying to move beyond the solidarity of a political alliance. They are demanding the establishment of an economic partnership. They are saying to the Arabs: "Let us not merely share enemies; let us also share energy. To some extent, let us merge economies."

This is not a bad argument, but the case for such a proposal does not rest on Africa's break with Israel. The case for an economic alliance between the Arab world and black Africa rests on the proposition that a political alliance can best be consolidated by an economic partnership.

We should remember that the United States and western Europe have been engaged in a similar debate among themselves. The Atlantic Alliance was intended to be a military and political alliance; it was not designed to be an economic partnership. France has argued that questions of security should not be mixed up with questions of trade and monetary stability. The Atlantic Alliance was an exercise in *sharing enemies* rather than *merging economies*.

Henry Kissinger, on the other hand, has taken the position that a political or military alliance could best be consolidated by an underlying economic partnership. Kissinger has urged Europe to bear in mind the health of the American economy when Europe formulates trade and fiscal policies to serve purely European interests. An alliance based merely on common enemies could be very unstable. The Kissinger argument is similar to Africa's position in her relations with the Arabs. Africans are asking the Arabs to strengthen the Afro-Arab political alliance by a decision to explore the possibilities of an inter-regional economic partnership between the Arab world and black Africa.

But progress may be slow. The North Atlantic Treaty Organization has been in existence for over twenty years, and yet it is only now that an attempt is being made to make it an economic partnership to some extent. The Ottawa meeting of NATO in June 1974 showed at last some recognition of the relevance of economic issues for such a political and military alliance. And the new NATO Declaration of Principles adopted in 1974 narrowed the gap between the French position and the Kissinger position regarding the relationship between shared security and shared prosperity. Disagreements among the political partners in NATO did not result in the immediate break-up of the alliance. On the contrary, twenty years of patience are now just beginning to bear fruit.

Similar discussions and compromises are needed between Africa and the Arab world. There is indeed a case for a two-tier pricing system for oil. The developed world should be charged one price, the developing a lower price. But these privileges should be open to countries like India and Bangladesh, as well as to African countries. It is not remembered that India had supported the Arabs in the Middle East for twenty years before the majority of black African states were converted to the Arab side. Why then should Kenya or the Ivory Coast receive better treatment from the Arabs than India? The two-tier pricing system should apply to the Third World as a whole, and not merely to Africa south of the Sahara. The developing countries generally have a good case against the oil producers.

Finally, in this strategy of counter-penetration there is need to use petro-dollars for investment in, say, irrigation schemes in the Sahel or the Sudan, as well as in Daimler-Benz and International Business Machines (IBM). The oil exporting Third World countries must be the vanguard of the third development decade, and of part of the second. They are in a position to demonstrate that what could not be accomplished under western economic leadership in the 1960's can be accomplished with the imaginative initiatives of the organization of petroleum-exporting countries in the 1970's and 1980's. The Third World's under-privileged status in relation to the industrial north could at last be transcended, as the Third World itself creates a genuine organic and symmetrical solidarity among its own members in the south.

But what is likely to be the balance between vertical counter-penetration (from the south into the north) and horizontal interpenetration (among Third World countries themselves)?

For a while the oil-rich Third World countries will be tempted to invest much more in the industrialized countries than in less developed nations. This is partly because of the tempting short term returns of investing in western Europe and North America and partly because the industrialized countries can in any case *absorb* more capital than can the less developed economies.

But investment by the Third World into the Third World will nevertheless grow and expand. So will foreign aid from resource-rich Third World countries into resource-poor, less developed economies. There are already strong indications of such a trend, in spite of all the scepticism one finds in the West. In the words of the Washington Correspondent for the *Financial Times* of London:

For the very poor [countries], there is no alternative to charity. The O.P.E.C. countries are starting to face up to their responsibilities here, although their reaction has been slow and they often show a preference for the Islamic poor over the rest. All the same, their development aid is already up to the target level set by the United Nations—something which cannot be said for the rest of the industrial world and particularly for the United States, which is not only the world's richest nation but its meanest. As yet O.P.E.C. aid may be insignificant in terms of the size of the difficulty the oil price rise has created for the very poorest countries such as India and the Central African nations, which have neither oil nor many other marketable commodities. But the fact that they are making some kind of an effort helps them maintain the political support of the rest of the Third World, and there is some fragmentary evidence that they may already be doing rather more than appears in any of the figures.*

When the oil-rich Third World countries are compared among themselves, some differences in orientation are inevitable. The conservative oil-rich regimes are likely to invest more into vertical counter-penetration than into horizontal inter-penetration. Kuwait, Saudi Arabia

* Paul Lewis, "Getting Even", New York Times Magazine, December 15, 1974, p. 84.

449

and Iran will either favor western Europe and North America or give priority to fellow Muslims. Algeria and Libya, on the other hand, may prefer Third World solidarity to Euro-American profits. They may still help fellow Muslims, but also show sensitivity to the needs of other developing societies in Africa and Asia. Therefore, while conservative regimes like Kuwait and Saudi Arabia enhance the process of vertical counter-penetration, radical or militant regimes like Algeria and Libya should in time accelerate the process of horizontal inter-penetration among Third World countries themselves.

But neither kind of regime is likely to limit itself to only one direction of investment and general economic activity. Destiny has placed on the shoulders of the oil-rich developing countries a historic role in the transformation of the world's economic order.

Toward an Ideology of Global Reform

But how is the Third World to find the political will for such action? We are back to the general implications of cultural conditioning under the experience of imperial domination.

We also indicated that the Third World could not develop the will to rebel against structural dependency in the field of economic, political, and military relationships, unless a major change of values were to take place in the Third World in the direction of strengthening the political will. The tendency among Third World decision-makers to use the northern hemisphere overwhelmingly as a reference point for the destinies of their own societies has in part been an outcome of cultural conditioning. The will to resist has been weakened by the cumulative impact of a Eurocentric educational system, an emasculating and demilitarized version of Christianity, a set of European languages which are so prestigious in the Third World that leaders are chosen on the basis of their competence in them, and a motivational dependency which looks to the life-styles of the western world for models of personal existence and national change. A process of partial deculturation is needed in much of the Third World, away from the heavy weight of metropolitan culture. And yet the purpose of the new world order we have in mind is not simply to rebestow on the Third World a sense of cultural autonomy but also to maintain a federal level of shared values and norms for the human race as an infrastructure for human consensus. In the general ideological domain, what trends need to be encouraged?

A simple but fundamental point which needs to be grasped is that the coming divisions for the human race are not between a capitalist west and a communist east but between a technologically developed north and an underdeveloped south. This is a theme that has received increasing attention in the last few years. Détente between western and eastern powers, culminating in the new era inaugurated by Richard Nixon's visits to Moscow and Peking in 1972, underlies the diminishing division of the world in the old cold war terms of east and west. But the north-south potentialities of confrontation are still there, perhaps made all the more ominous by the emergence of oil power.

There is a tendency at times to regard such a confrontation as unreal mainly because the southern hemisphere of the world is unlikely to be monolithic enough to pose a serious challenge to the affluent northern hemisphere. Indeed, the atmosphere of détente among developed countries, the explorations for new trading arrangements between the United States and the Soviet Union and before long between the United States and China, the explorations for mutual and balanced reduction of troops in Europe, and the discussions concerning a new Atlantic Charter that would strengthen relations between the United States, the new European community and Japan, are all indicators of the possibility of a monolithic northern hemisphere, confronting a disastrously fragmented southern hemisphere.

And yet the confrontations themselves need not in any case be so neat. We already know that Latin America in an underprivileged situation is up against its colossus of the north. We already know that underdeveloped Africa is watching with increased anxiety the consolidation of inter-European ties and their potential economic consequences for the African continent. And we know that relatively underdeveloped China is anticipating its future role in the communist world by challenging the credentials of the Soviet Union and asserting its own autonomy of Moscow's leadership. The three units of confrontation—the United States versus Latin America; Africa versus western Europe; and China versus the Soviet Union—already involve a great majority of the human race. The issue is whether these subconfrontations between segments of each hemisphere would deepen before the end of the century into dangerous cleavages.

A normative reorientation of the world should ideally promote socialism in the whole of the northern hemisphere and nationalism in the whole of the southern hemisphere. While socialism and capitalism might at one time have been conflicting ideologies, northern socialism and southern nationalism could in the years ahead be complementary ideologies. If all the affluent societies of the north acquired a socialist conscience of global dimension, that conscience might help to tame and soften the inclination of the north to dominate and exploit the rest of the world. Of course socialism could coexist with imperialism, as certain aspects of the behavior of the Soviet Union, especially in eastern Europe,

451

would demonstrate. But that is because much of the northern hemisphere has continued to have a disproportionate inclination toward nationalism. It is Russian nationalism, rather than Soviet socialism, which is at the root of Russian imperialism. Similarly, nationalism in Britain and France was the great source of imperial expansion while it lasted. And the nationalism of the United States has been a major factor behind the American self-image as the policeman of the world, with all the consequences of such self-appointment for the rest of the world.

What we are advancing here is the theory that socialism in the northern hemisphere is the great ideological change needed to increase responsiveness to the poorer and weaker sectors of the human race. Cultural convergence has already gone some way in the northern hemisphere in the direction of increasing socialistic sensibilities, even if these sensibilities are not always given that name in certain western countries. The impact of Marx and Keynes, themselves different in striking ways, has nevertheless initiated in much of the west movements toward a concern for the needy, fairness in the distribution of the national cake, and a consolidation of egalitarian norms in the national political cultures. Cultural convergence in the northern hemisphere has certainly gone some way toward preparing the ground for the socialization of the affluent north. But there is still room for considerably more socialization before adequate responsiveness to global issues is reached.

One strategy which might help to push the western world a little closer to socialism is, once again, counter-penetration. Investment from the Arab world especially is both welcome and suspect. To the extent to which it is needed by countries with acute balance-of-payments problems, that investment will be welcome. But to the extent to which the West fears the potential manipulative power of the Arabs, investment from them will gradually result in a modification of the free enterprise system in the West. The United States is already re-examining its policy of an open door for foreign investment. The idea of unrestricted free enterprise will be further eroded as Americans learn to see more clearly the political consequences of being economically penetrated. The fears expressed by the Department of Defense may be only the beginning of an agonizing reappraisal. Fear of Third World investment may increase state control of the economy in countries like the United States and West Germany. Increased state control of the economy, and reduction of independent private economic initiative, may in turn help to prepare the way for greater responsiveness to socialism in those countries. In short, counter-penetration by the Third World into the northern hemisphere may in time help the cause of socialism in the north. When finally that stage is reached, counter-penetration should have served a large part of its role as a mechanism for the creation of a new international economic order.

But while the northern hemisphere needs more socialism, the Third World itself first needs to generate its own *nationalistic* momentum. The emotions required for the rebellion against dependency will have to look for their ultimate sustenance to the still relatively dormant reserves of dignity and national pride, especially among the colored peoples of Asia and Africa. Moreover, as we have indicated in previous chapters, many Third World countries have yet to consolidate their sense of national identity or create adequate national institutions. Nation-building within the Third World is a major imperative, in the face of fragmented politics, violent ethnic tensions, and fluid loyalties to long-term national interests. Whatever additional values the Third World needs, it also needs a sense of nationalism with which to build nations, and by which to rebel against the encroachments of a Euro-centric cultural universe.

There are times when nationalism in the Third World does not wear a socialistic face. This quite often is a situation where the socialism is subordinate to the nationalism. The government in less developed societies has quite often to take initiatives in the absence of adequate private sources of endeavor. Existing industries may be put under public ownership as a way of eliminating the element of foreign dominance, rather than as a method of ending capitalism as such. Gamal Abdel Nasser's first dramatic nationalization measure was the nationalization of the Suez Canal in 1956. But Nasser nationalized the Suez Canal not for reasons of socialistic egalitarianism, but for reasons of nationalistic assertiveness. In the face of a humiliating letdown by the World Bank, the United States and Great Britain, when loans promised were withdrawn following Nasser's purchase of arms from Czechoslovakia, the Egyptian ruler turned round and at long last put under Egyptian ownership an international waterway passing through his country. The radicalization of Nasser as a revolutionary was through Arab nationalism, rather than socialism—although important aspects of the rhetoric and organization of domestic arrangements in Egypt did borrow considerably from socialistic schools of thought.

Nasser's radical successor in the Arab world, Col. Muhammad al-Qaddafi of Libya is again a major exponent of militant Arab nationalism, with some revolutionary rhetoric. Tripoli and al-Qaddafi have developed into a Mecca for revolutionaries and freedom fighters, almost all of them ultimately motivated by nationalistic rebellion even if quite often using borrowed Marxist rhetoric.

In Tripoli's main hotels and government buildings, Palestinian guerrillas and black Rhodesian and South African militants rub elbows with Africans from Portuguese colonies, Filipino Muslims, agents for the Irish Republican Army, and Moroccan dissidents dedicated to overthrowing King Hassan. It would also not be unusual to meet a representative of the Eritrean nationalists fighting Emperor Haile Selassie of Ethiopia, or even a member of a militant Iranian urban-guerrilla group.[3]

A number of African leaders have also arrived at some degree of socialistic radicalization through economic nationalism. President Julius Nyerere of Tanzania is a case in point. A series of humiliations arising from his older expectations about western economic aid gradually led Julius Nyerere toward the path of economic self-reliance as a principle to accompany Tanzania's socialism. The Arusha declaration sought to awaken Tanzanians to a realization that their own most important resource was human labor and their strategy for development should therefore be based on the efficient utilization of that labor instead of on the persistent supplication for capital from others.

In reality, the doctrine did not mean economic autarky, but it did mean a combination of genuine economic nonalignment (balancing the West with China) and greater domestic efforts, with communal exertion through *ujamaa* villages. Nyerere then is indeed an example of wounded economic nationalism leading on to greater radicalization. Once again a Third World socialist has been born out of nationalism.

Socialism and Cultural Schizophrenia

But socialism carries significant risks when it is too blindly embraced as a method of rebelling against the West's intellectual dominance. The most influential schools of socialism in the modern world are the different Marxist approaches. The most disguised form of Europe's cultural dominance could so easily be the Marxist heritage. Because the governments of the western world have on the whole been anti-Marxist, cultural nationalists in the Third World have often forgotten that Marx himself was a European. It is not unusual to find African intellectuals who, on the one hand, are militantly hostile to Europe's cultural infiltration into Africa and, on the other, tend to express that hostility in Marxist terms. To be an African cultural nationalist and a Marxist at the same time is a contradiction not only from the point of view of Marxism, but also from the point of view of African cultural nationalism. Embracing Marxism is a process of deAfricanization in this sense.

This question has haunted the ideological life of Julius Nyerere from quite early. In his more moderate days, Nyerere's cultural nationalism still had the upper hand. He was indeed already fascinated by the concept of socialism, but was keen to link it to indigenous African traditions.

> We in Africa have no more need for being 'converted' to socialism than we have of being 'taught' democracy. Both are rooted in our own past—in the traditional society which produced us.[4]

This is the language of a cultural nationalist even more than that of a socialist. It was therefore not surprising that this was a period when Nyerere was criticized in Soviet literature for putting his main ideological stress on the "African originality of views and outlook".

Nyerere had explicitly rejected the Marxist concept of "class struggle" as being inapplicable in Africa. In 1965 he was criticized by Soviet writers for what in the Soviet Union is sometimes referred to as "distributive socialism"—the idea that exploiting relationships can be eliminated by perfecting the system of distribution of the goods produced. Even as late as 1966 Nyerere—as a partisan of "African socialism"—was unfavorably contrasted with "revolutionary democrats . . . carrying out radical, social and economic reforms".[5]

In this refusal to be drawn into Marxist preconceptions, Nyerere had domestic as well as distant critics. There were Tanzanians who preferred the language of historical and dialectical materialism, and insisted on discerning a continuing "class struggle" in Tanzania whatever policies Nyerere pursued. These were usually more severe cases of cultural schizophrenia than Nyerere himself had ever been.

But Nyerere continued to be aware of the "danger of being bemused by this new theology, and therefore of trying to solve our problems according to what the priests of Marxism say is what Marx said or meant". Nyerere sensed that compliance with Marxist postulates was itself a form of ideological and cultural dependency. To be so captivated by Marxism was indeed an exercise in voluntary captivity.

> If we do this we shall fail. Africa's conditions are very different from those of the Europe in which Marx and Lenin wrote and worked. To talk as if these thinkers provided all the answers to our problems, or as if Marx invented socialism, is to reject both the humanity of Africa and the universality of socialism. Marx did contribute a great deal to socialist thought. But socialism did not begin with him, nor can it end in constant reinterpretations of his writings.[6]

It is not clear whether Nyerere has escaped entirely the lure of this Marxist opium of the intellectuals in the Third World, but at least he is one Third World leader who is aware of the hazards. To rebel against Europe by embracing one particular intellectual tradition of Europe is a contradiction in terms. The danger is the greater since Marxism is a *system* of thought, rather than simply a series of propositions. Borrowing individual concepts from Marxism is indeed defensible, and certainly from our perspective of an evolving world culture. But embracing Marxism as a system of perspectives and ideas carries the danger of deepening the intellectual dependency of Asia and Africa.

The case of Latin America is ambivalent in this regard. Is Latin America part of Europe's cultural tradition, or is Latin America an object of European domination? Perhaps part of the answer may lie in terms of assessing the de-Europeanizing impact of the Indian population in important parts of Latin America. Certainly for the Indians at the very least, Marxism is as alien as Jeffersonian liberalism. Both are drawn from intellectual traditions fundamentally divergent from the indigenous inheritance of native Latin Americans.

However, the proportion of Caucasians in the population of Latin America is so great, and the identification of many Latin Americans as descendants from Europe so firmly embraced, that we could say that Marxism is definitely much less alien to Latin America than it is to Asia and Africa. To that extent, a Latin American Marxist is less a victim of intellectual dependency than an African Marxist or an Indian or Chinese Marxist.

China's approach has been to tame Marxism to the realities and heritage of China. But Mao's China certainly encumbered its own capacity for intellectual innovation by joining a stream of European revolutionary thought. It may be that a gradual re-emergence of China's own universe of culture will reduce the massive intellectual strategy which for a while smothered Chinese nationalism with a European-dominated revolutionary movement. China's rebellion against the Soviet Union, and the beginnings of her cultural self-discovery, may gradually redress the balance in the intellectual personality of the most populous state in the world.

We have ourselves in this book borrowed quite often from Marxist propositions and perspectives on society. This is partly because the warning against embracing Marxism as a system is quite compatible with a readiness to utilize individual propositions out of that system, in combination with ideas drawn from elsewhere.

But when all is said and done, Marxism does provide a supreme language of social and political *protest*. The nature of both the theory and ideology of Marxism is oriented against the status quo and against those who wield power and authority in formal institutions. The revolutionary nature of this system of thought provides a telling language against injustice and dominance, and thus captivates the imaginations of those who are profoundly disturbed with the state of the world. As it happens, protest is a fundamental factor in the whole process of cultural convergence. Since protest is an eruption arising out of disturbed values, it is also an indicator of changes in norms and principles across time. Normative convergence, to the extent that it involves a moving equilibrium of values, releases different forms of protest, both in defense of continuity and in defense of reform. Our concern with cultural integration must therefore include an awareness of the very functions of protest. It is to these that we now turn, placing the phenomenon in historical perspective.

The Functions of Protest

Protest is connected with persuasion, reform, systemic growth, and social integration. The three most important periods of protest in human history are perhaps the second half of the eighteenth century, the second half of the nineteenth century, and the second half of the twentieth century. The second half of the eighteenth century included movements which culminated in the first modern anti-colonial war in history, the American War of Independence. That period in time also saw the explosion of the French Revolution, with its long term historical consequences in the domain of egalitarian ideas. In the second half of the eighteenth century also came the initiation of the Industrial Revolution in England, starting from the 1760's, and escalating into the innovative outburst of the following century.

Then there was the second half of the nineteenth century with the strengthening of socialistic ideas, the emergence of Marx and the Communist Internationale, the expansion of the franchise to urban workers in England, the consolidation of the labor union movement in Europe, the revolutionary ferment in Europe, and the Civil War in the United States. The leadership of Europe and North America in the realm of political innovation had already started. Protest as a manifestation of this intellectual ferment was also a manifestation of the expanding European dominance of the world.

Then came the second half of the twentieth century. Protest as an upsurge of new ideas was engulfing the rest of the world. The anti-colonial movements of Asia and Africa were reaching a moment of consummation, empires disintegrated, new sovereign states multiplied, and a new nationalistic assertiveness exploded on the face of the world engulfing ethnic groups, setting young against old, women against men, oppressed against oppressors.

What these subcenturies of protest released in the past were social upheavals which sometimes escalated into international wars, and certainly spilled over into the following centuries. The Napoleonic Wars shook the foundations of Europe as Europe staggered into the nineteenth century. The rise of social movements, nationalism, and imperial expansion in the second half of the nineteenth century released forces which later culminated in the First World War. And this, in turn, had consequences which interacted with periods of economic depression, disturbed peace in Europe more deeply, accentuated Germany's sense of humiliation in the new political stratification of Europe after the Treaty of Versailles, and initiated the ferment of factors which pulled the world toward the second global conflagration. The First World War helped to facilitate the decay of the Czar's empire, and the first communist state came into being while the war still dragged on. And as the world was about to enter the second half of the twentieth century, the most populous country on earth, China, proclaimed its own Marxist identity.

But when we look at protest at the *micro* level of individual protest, rather than at the *macro* level of social movements, we see that it arises out of three emotional states. It arises either out of, first, offended dignity; second, imperilled identity; third, frustrated ambition. Offended dignity can be either inclusive of the person protesting or extended in empathy. When a Swedish socialist is angry because an Ibo mother is starving, or because a Vietnamese child is maimed, this might be a case of offended dignity at the empathetic level. The Swedish socialist is offended because he identifies with the Ibo mother or the Vietnamese child as creatures from the same species, and revolts at what seems to him to be humiliation of a human being. Here a moment of shared humanity is indeed reached in that very act of protest. The distinction to bear in mind here is, primarily, between personal dignity and empathetic dignity. Personal dignity is offended when the Swedish socialist is himself insulted in the streets of Stockholm, or when his ambassador is asked not to return to the United States after his Prime Minister has offended the dignity of the White House. But the Swede's empathetic dignity can only be genuinely offended if he has evolved a capacity to link his own self-respect with a respect for others.

Imperilled or disturbed identity can also be either personal or empathetic. It is personal when the man himself or his immediate social group are imperilled in relation to things which are important to their self-recognition. But when the empathetic identity of a person is disturbed, what is happening may well be far from himself and his immediate social group. Dignity and identity become intricately intertwined. In the context of the sensibilities of black people in history, this inter-relationship between dignity and identity is something of a paradox. After all, when a man seeks his own identity, he is usually seeking those qualities which distinguish him, or ought to distinguish him from other men. But when he is concerned with asserting his *human* dignity, he is referrina to those qualities which he *shares* with other men. Nevertheless, dignity and identity remain welded together at the center of black nationalistic thought because of the special history of humiliation and denial of distinctiveness which the black peoples have undergone.

As for protests arising out of frustrated ambition, this is more often self-regarding, but by no means always. The ambition can be in terms of realizing a major altruistic moral cause. The ambition can be a quest for restructuring the entire universe of values in a given society.[7]

But what is the precise relationship between protest and normative convergence and cultural change? One role of protest in this regard is the role of maximizing the need for persuasion. The protestor at certain levels needs to articulate a new set of values, or defend an old set which has been endangered. Protest is a device which often calls for a re-examination of the postulates of the society. When it is conducted at the level of militant dialogue rather than actual confrontation, protest helps to compel attention to issues which need further examination. A society is saved from the danger of complacency and inertia if possibilities for protest are active within the system. A society is also forced to defend its identity and avert too rapid an erosion of its values if its conservative protestors are allowed a field of articulation.

Social persuasion, social analysis, and self-examination pre-eminently flourish in societies which permit symmetrical protest. Symmetrical protest is of the kind which may come either from the side of conservation or from the side of reform and transformation. There are societies which permit only asymmetrical protest—protest from those who are against deviation or dissent. A lack of symmetry on the other side is unlikely. In other words, there are hardly any societies which permit protest only from dissenters and reformers and stifle protest from conservatives and orthodox supporters of the system as it exists. The nature of human organization is such that it is the voice of dissent, rather than the voice of conservation, which is particularly vulnerable to suppression. A society which does permit symmetrical protest facilitates, to some degree, optimum self-analysis and persuasive interaction between its members.

Protest combined with reform may well be the mechanism which restores equilibrium between the changes already brought about and the further changes necessary to complete the balance. The situation is not dissimilar from what C. D. Darlington said about the nature of scientific discovery. Lecturing in 1953 Professor Darlington once said:

> Scientific discovery is a process like pulling out a stuck drawer. If it sticks on one side you have to pull it on the other side.

459

The person swearing, under his breath, in annoyance as he tries to pull out the other side, is in fact engaged in a protest. He is trying to restore some kind of balance. The drawer is stuck, perhaps because it is too old and inefficient in its ways. The protestor pulls on. Having succeeded in letting in fresh air on one side, he now seeks to complete the freshening process on the drawer as a whole.

Darlington, has, for a long time, been the self-proclaimed foe of complacency, a believer in the need for constant social reawakening. Lecturing in 1948 he said:

> We need a Ministry of Disturbance, a regulated source of annoyance; a destroyer of routine, and underminer of complacency, an *enfant terrible;* or will nothing short of another war serve us?[8]

But if Darlington represents the patience of a reformer, Michael Oakeshott represents the pragmatism of a conservative. In a famous sentence Oakeshott has asserted:

> In politics, then, every enterprise is a consequential enterprise, the pursuit, not of a dream, or of a general principle, but of an intimation.

Oakeshott cites one important movement of protest in British history, the Suffragette Movement and its quest for the rights of women. He argues that the arrangements which constitute a society capable of political activity, whether these arrangements are customs or institutions or laws or diplomatic decisions, are *to some extent* internally coherent, but they always include certain elements of incoherence. The pattern may be a little out of shape, but the very nature of the pattern "intimates" what kind of change would help to add greater coherence to that pattern. Where that intimation really comes from the very structure of the social arrangements already achieved, that intimation amounts to a sympathy for such a change.

> Political activity is the exploration of sympathy; and consequently relevant political reasoning will be the convincing exposure of a sympathy, present but not yet followed up, and the convincing demonstration that now is the appropriate moment for recognizing it.

This is where Oakeshott uses the question of the legal status of women in English society. Their status had been for a long time in comparative confusion, because the rights and duties which composed it "intimated rights and duties which were nevertheless not recognized." Oakeshott regarded it as irrelevant to have based the case for the technical enfranchisement of women on arguments about natural right, or justice between the sexes, or some general concepts of feminine personality.

. . . on the view of things I am suggesting the only cogent reason to be advanced for the technical 'enfranchisement' of women was that in all or most other important respects they had already been enfranchised. Arguments drawn from abstract natural rights, from 'justice', or from general concepts of feminine personality, must be regarded as either irrelevant, or unfortunately disguised forms of the one valid argument; namely, that there was an incoherence in the arrangements of the society which pressed convincingly for a remedy. In politics, then, every enterprise is a consequential enterprise, the pursuit, not of a dream, or of a general principle, but of an intimation.[9]

From the point of view of our analysis here we might regard protest as one of the most important forms which this intimation takes. In a transitional phase in society protest is sometimes a cry we use to awaken the society to the incoherence which has occurred in its social arrangements. It is a cry which demands, either explicitly or implicitly, that this incoherence should be corrected. The view of social change as a moving equilibrium is therefore as much Oakeshottian as it is Hegelian and Marxist. The major difference is that the Marxist equilibrium demands a revolution to restore compatibility between the forces of production already transformed by development and the slower and more rigid relations of property within the superstructure—whereas Oakeshott's equilibrium is more modest, demanding piecemeal correction as the intimation of incoherence becomes irresistible.

As for the function of protest in growth, it lies precisely in the growth of systemic capabilities. We have already referred to changes which have come about in the world as a result of expanding mobility, escalating technological development, increasing population, and cultural transformation. A society, if it is to remain a society, has to maintain a capability for absorbing these changes effectively. The demands for changes which need to be made in social arrangements are often articulated through protest as a medium of reform. The institutionalization of protest in ways which make conflict-management feasible and efficient is one important dimension of the whole process of systemic growth and political development.[10]

This leads us to the place of protest in the process of political integration. We discussed earlier that the quest for empathy in much of the Third World has to begin at home. Societies are deeply divided internally on ethnic, religious, class, and regional lines. The purpose of national integration is not to end such divisions, but to tame them in a manner which would make them compatible with the quest for minimum violence, maximum social justice, and optimum economic welfare. The search for enlarged empathy in Africa needs to begin with empathy between tribe and tribe, region and region, the political ins in relation to the political outs. Protest is both a symptom of some of these problems in the body politic and potentially part of the cure. The struggle to discover a shared humanity in people who otherwise appear so different from oneself is a struggle of competing perspectives and values. To that extent, it is a struggle important both for the growth of new nations and the promotion of world cultures. Let us take each of these two dimensions in turn.

Protest and National Consciousness

John Stuart Mill opens the sixteenth chapter of his *Representative Government* with a definition of "nationality". He argues that a portion of mankind may be said to constitute a nationality if they are united among themselves by common sympathies which do not exist between them and any others—sympathies which enable them to cooperate with each other more willingly than with other people.

Mill goes on to say that this feeling of nationality may have been generated by various causes. He includes a shared language and a shared religion as among possible causes in this or that group of people. But to him the strongest of all causes is a shared political experience in one's past, shared with one's neighbors and those who live in the area which is being identified as constituting the nation. Out of this shared political experience, Mill sees what he calls "the community of recollections; collective pride and humiliation, pleasure and regret".[11]

It is clear that Mill regards the forging of communal emotions as being an indispensable part of the creation of nationhood. This is a proposition with considerable evidence in its favor. It is true that the emergence of nationhood does indeed sometimes require the capacity to accept a certain government as being the legitimate government of the population. What we have here is that old issue of vertical identification, as the ruled identify with the rulers.

But at least as important in the creation of a nation is, of course, horizontal identification, the capacity of people for collective response and reciprocal empathy. Shared emotive experiences are often at the heart of this process of horizontal identification. In analyzing the development of nationhood it therefore makes sense always to inquire into the nature of shared emotion and the conditions which make the sharing feasible.[12]

The process of building up a capacity for shared feelings has, until this century, taken many generations to acquire. But the communications revolution of the modern world poses the question whether the process can be compressed to such an extent that two generations could share a pool of emotions and perspectives which had previously taken many centuries to accumulate and internalize.

The second dimension which arises in the modern period is the possibility of manipulating emotions on a scale more sophisticated than ever before. Cultural engineering as a manipulation of cultural symbols is therefore a rearrangement of cultural stimuli and the responses these provoke.

Since, as we have indicated, protest as a social phenomenon has potentialities for reform, persuasion, systemic development and social integration, the manipulation of situations of protest can have significant possibilities for nation-building at large.

We discussed in Chapter 20 aspects of interaction between emotions and values. Pre-eminent among the feelings behind protest is *anger*. Offended dignity, imperilled identity, and sometimes even frustrated ambition have all too often been the springs of social or individual indignation. Anger is a political emotion *par excellence*. It is certainly an emotion which has intimate connections with the kind of political attitudes which lead to great movements of change and passionate re-examination of social directions. Anger has a particularly close relationship both with the emotion of *pride,* especially self-pride or self-respect, and the emotion of *animosity.* Both these latter two emotions have great potential for political behavior and political expression.

It is arguable that great moments of reform and revolution, even of war, tend to have links with the three emotions of anger, pride and animosity. These are deep drives, pregnant with a variety of consequences.

Of these three emotions, anger—partly because it is an activating emotion—is perhaps the most specifically instrumental. It tends to give meaning and life to other emotions of political consequences. Wounded pride is in fact another name for wounded dignity. And this in turn generates animosities. The sustained feeling of anger can then sustain feelings of animosity.

Among black peoples the deepest anger has arisen out of a sense of wounded racial pride. Race consciousness among black people is thus intimately fused with offended self-esteem. The experience of indignity has resulted in the explosion of indignation. The fountain of black nationalism is indeed black anger.

Within Africa itself the anger became partially assuaged with independence. But in North America black anger remains part of the potential revolutionary ferment. The American system is then tested as to whether it can accommodate black protest, or respond to the demands implicit in that protest, and restore a new equilibrium in the so-

463

ciety. In Oakeshottian terms, a persistent intimation is seeking attention—so that the incoherence in American social arrangements can at last be corrected.

But within African countries protest can now take other forms, as tribes cease to get fair shares of the national cake, or dissenters seek to assert their preferences, or soldiers exploit grievances against politicians. Symmetrical protest in Africa is not yet a reality. Dissent is a difficult exercise, except when it is accompanied by counter power. Protest as a mechanism of national integration is therefore denied adequate fulfillment in African conditions. After all, national integration is, in an important sense, the growth of a country's capability not only to expand empathy among its people but also to resolve conflicts amongst its people, short of armed confrontation. The acquisition of the experience of conflict resolution does itself require enough openness to permit conflict to take place, and solutions to be sought without violent strife.

The first basic resting place in the process of national integration might well be the attainment of the capacity for symmetrical dissent. This might well be the beginning of a fundamental equilibrium between the forces of conservation and the forces of reform. A capacity to sustain symmetrical dissent and balanced protest is the first precondition of a self-regulating system. And social justice itself, if it is to be constantly maintained, would need a system where the incoherences of the Left and the incoherences of the Right are permitted equal access to the avenues of "intimation". It is because of this that protest becomes a mechanism of reconciliation deeply relevant to the search for a shared humanity.

It is true that a system of symmetrical protest runs the risk of disturbing the idea of an increasingly socialistic northern hemisphere as against an increasingly nationalistic southern hemisphere. A free market-place of contending values could swing ideological trends in other directions. But that is a risk which has to be taken. After all, the whole purpose of seeking to encourage socialistic trends in the north and nationalistic trends in the south is a quest for human well-being. Such a purpose would receive a serious setback if the struggle to build socialism and nationalism was to be conducted in a manner which suppressed voices of dissent.

But the whole idea of a free market allows for an extra push in defense of certain values as against others. In an ideal situation, the push in the southern hemisphere must remain in the direction of consolidating nationhood, integrating conflicting subgroups, and acquiring the political will to rebel against both cultural and structural dependency. The ideological push in the north should encourage the invisible hand which has been moving much of the northern hemisphere toward greater social responsiveness to the underprivileged, first in their own society, and hopefully later in societies distant from their own.

In this latter development we have a pre-eminent example of the role of international protest as a vehicle of cultural diffusion, as a medium toward ameliorating social ills. Let us now turn to these aspects.

International Protest and Cultural Diffusion

Here again the important breakthroughs in the evolution of the functions of protest have probably taken place in the second half of the nineteenth and the second half of the twentieth centuries.

In the second half of the nineteenth century we have the beginnings of socialist internationalism. The degree to which this phenomenon heralded transnational movements of social reform and even social revolution is only now beginning to be fully understood. In some schools of Marxism it is constantly maintained that class consciousness is a greater determinant of human behavior and a more fundamental basis of human motivation than national or racial consciousness. The idea of "workers of the world" constitutes the great international dimension of Marxist socialism.

Yet, there is here a confusion which verges on being a case of mistaken identity. Solidarity between socialists or radicals is not the same thing as solidarity between workers. Socialist consciousness may indeed be an international phenomenon, and yet class consciousness among dockers still remains basically parochial.

When the Communist Manifesto proclaimed "Workers of the world unite," it was at best simply saying "Socialist revolutionaries of the world unite." In socialistic rhetoric there is, at times, a tendency to use the term "working classes" when in reality what is meant is "socialist intellectuals". Certainly the duties which Marxism sometimes seems to impose on ordinary workers betray a confusion between radical intellectualism and militant proletarianism. Take for example Karl Marx's inaugural address for the Working Men's International Association, established on September 28, 1864, at a public meeting held at St. Martin's Hall in London. Marx concluded his address with again the clarion call "Proletarians of all countries unite." Did this mean factory sweepers in Manchester and railway porters in New York? Did it include textile laborers in Bombay, garden boys in Accra? If so, Marx was assuming a high level of intellectual sophistication among these different sections of workers. For in that same speech Marx assigned to the "working classes" what he called:

... the duty to master for themselves the mysteries of international politics; to watch the diplomatic pacts of their respective governments, to counteract them, if necessary, by all means in their power; when unable to prevent, to combine in simultaneous denunciations, and to vindicate the simple laws of moral justice which ought to govern the relations of private individuals, as the rules paramount for the intercourse of nations . . . . Proletarians of all countries unite!

Evidently this language was not addressed to dock workers of Liverpool or coolies of Bombay, or African miners in the Copper Belts in southern Africa. Nor was the duty being imposed on these people likely to be of the kind which ordinary workers could undertake. To "master the mysteries of international politics", as Marx put it, is an undertaking for intellectual radicals rather than discontented road sweepers. What all this means is that the beginnings of international protest lay in the responses of intellectuals. Such people spearheaded transnational movements, first in the northern hemisphere, with important consequences for the trend toward socializing it.

Marx did understand the relevance of class consciousness for revolutionary assertiveness. He did rightly see that a growing self-awareness among the working classes could be a matter of great political consequence. What Marx did not understand was the revolutionary potential of trans-class empathy, pre-eminently exemplified in the intellectuals. No other social category of people has a greater capacity to empathize with the oppressed of a class other than its own, and of nations far from its own, than the intellectual class. Even when intellectuals feel for other intellectuals the international dimension is far more clearly perceived than is the case with any category in any other social class.

No business tycoon in India or Africa, for example, is likely to react in a passionate protest if a fellow business tycoon in the United States were to get into trouble with the authorities. No railway porter in Germany is likely to have the remotest idea of what is happening to railway porters in Nigeria. This is partly because the occupation of the railway porter is not one which is likely to have a transnational impact. Nor is the status of a Nigerian tycoon likely to command the protective anxiety of German millionaires much further away. But with intellectuals it is different. The advantages they have had in education have given them advantages of communication, and of disproportionate access to mass media and literary sources of information. These have developed in the intellectuals a disproportionate consciousness of what goes on in other parts of the world, and their sense of anxiety about what is wrong with the world.

This phenomenon of revolutionary trans-class empathy is a phenomenon which Marx, for some reason, did not fully grasp. And yet

466

it is curious that he should have failed to undertstand it, considering that he himself was an intellectual and not a member of the proletariat. It was Lenin, a couple of generations later, who saw more clearly the limitations of the working classes in terms of revolutionary commitment, and regarded the birth of socialism itself as inseparable from the activities of intellectuals.

In Lenin's own words:

> The theory of socialism . . . grew out of the philosophic, historical, and economic theories elaborated by educated representatives of the property classes, by intellectuals. By their social status, the founders of modern scientific socialism, Marx and Engels, themselves belonged to the bourgeois intelligentsia.[14]

This revolutionary trans-class empathy as exemplified in intellectuals has been, in the second half of the twentieth century, one of the important mechanisms for the dissemination of new ideas of social justice, first in the northern hemisphere, and then beyond. It has been intellectuals more than any other group in the richer western countries of the world who first developed a sensitivity to the problems of the poor countries of the world, and sought to propagate new values capable of reforming their own countries in the direction of a greater sense of responsibility for the agonies of the Third World. Utilizing their literary skills, engaging the sympathies of the mass media, putting pressure on their politicians and statesmen, intellectuals of Europe and North America have been in the vanguard of the movement for greater social justice on a world scale, and for improved standards of economic welfare among men.

It is true that intellectuals can also be reactionary. What is being suggested here is not that all intellectuals are capable of revolutionary transclass empathy. The proposition is different—it is simply to the effect that among those with a highly developed capacity for empathizing with groups other than their own, intellectuals are disproportionate in number. The socialization of the northern hemisphere would have been considerably retarded had not the northern intelligentsia generated ideas and causes which went beyond mere Oakeshottian 'intimations'.

As the intellectual influence of northern writers and scholars extended beyond their own borders, they helped to globalize some of these values. World culture as a phenomenon has indeed been helped in part by the dissemination of values which protest itself accomplishes.

The death of Lumumba in what was then the Congo could mean demonstrations in Paris and New York. The war in Nigeria could mean militant organization for relief in capitals as diverse as Oslo, Dar es Salaam and London. Suppression of dissent in Greece could result in a demonstration in Cambridge and a cable of protest from Kampala.

Poems in different parts of the world have also entered the mainstream of the culture of protest in different ages. One might look at an East African magazine like *Zuka* and find a poem by Jonathan Kariara and another by Charles Owuor, both bearing the same title, "Vietnam". Lines from the two poems can be interspersed without disturbing too much the mood of a deeply shared depression.

Women sat reclining
Monuments of peace
Sculptured by death.
The river heaved, eased
Flowed on . . .
Quiet,
depressing quiet
somber quiet of a cathedral
as mutilated human bodies
sleep the sleep of ages . . .
In the field the dead women
Sighed
Remembering the dull thud
Of the metal fist
Of the interrogator . . .
No more no more
Betrayal
The useless pain of snatching
Life from the fertile flood.*

Members of the younger generation have been among those who have shown a profound dissatisfaction with the world as they have encountered it. The student movement has now subsided at least in North America, but even in North America student sensibilities remain an exciting illustration of the empathetic leap.

Protest highlights a disturbed conscience. And when it is carried out in a manner which commands attention and publicity, the moral postulates on which it stands become part of the slow diffusion of a new normative consensus. And even those who react against protest find themselves seeking new rationalizations, new reasons, for the preferences they have embraced.

It is all these factors which go to make protest, both domestic and

* Jonathan Kariara, "Vietnam," and Charles Owuor, "Vietnam," *Zuka* No. 2, May 1968, p. 11.

international, an important mechanism in the slow and intermittent reconciliation between the world of yesterday's traditions and the world of tomorrow's values.

Conclusion

We started this chapter by examining the global implications of the Middle East war of 1973. We indicated that from the perspective of the Third World, the economic war which was inaugurated last October by Arab oil producers was more fundamental than the military operations, no matter how dramatic the tank battles in the deserts might have been.

The utilization of oil as an instrument of political leverage revealed new potential power for the southern hemisphere. The old hierarchy of the globe was beginning to sense its first real threat since the industrial revolution in Europe.

Two complementary strategies need to be systematically employed by the Third World. One is the strategy of *counter-penetration,* designed to make the northern hemisphere more responsive to economic pressure from the south. The other is the strategy of *inter-penetration* between different parts of the Third World itself. The latter strategy would seek to create complementarity between Third World economies, and thus consolidate their organic solidarity.

What ought to be remembered is that Third World inter-penetration could be deeply divisive if it lacks balance and symmetry. The growth of anti-Arab sentiment in some parts of black Africa is partly due to the simple fact that interaction between Arabs and Africans has not been on an adequately equal basis in the past. In some countries the antagonism goes back to the days of a slave trade in which the Arabs participated conspicuously. There have also been situations of Arab cultural arrogance and intolerance in places as far flung as Zanzibar and Chad, Southern Sudan and Northern Nigeria.

In relation to black Muslims, the Arabs can at times be unbearably paternalistic; in relation to other black people, the Arabs can simply be insensitive.

Yet the October war and its economic parallel did open up new areas of solidarity. This solidarity is still strategic rather than organic, an exercise in sharing enemies rather than merging economies. But a few years ago it was inconceivable that black Africa as a whole could, however temporarily, break off relations with Israel almost unanimously. In 1973 this became feasible, partly because of a significant shift in the politics of the Organization of African Unity, and partly because of the energy crisis and its implications for African states. The Arabs began to sense an increasing need for the political support of the Third World generally;

the Africans in turn began to sense greater need for Arab economic support.

The changes in relationship are still new and fragile. There is still an ominous lack of balance and equality in that relationship. It is still much more of a political alliance than an economic partnership, much more of a strategic alignment than of an organic one.

But when all this has been said, it remains true that the October war might have started a process of fundamental significance not only for Afro-Arab relations, not even merely for the Third World, but conceivably for the broader ambition of trying to create a new and fairer economic order on earth.

We have also discussed in this final chapter, once again, the phenomenon of normative convergence and cultural diffusion, and attempted to indicate the ideological trends which need to be encouraged for the future. We have returned to the theme of cultural and structural dependency afflicting much of the human race, in the shadow of Euro-American omnipotence. We remain convinced that cultural dependency is more fundamental, since it affects the will to resist among those who are dominated. The imported heritage has to be partially indigenized. Christianity in an African situation has to come to terms to some extent with African ancestral predispositions and contemporary African gropings for cultural autonomy. French and English as imported languages have to submit to a process of de-racialization and partial indigenization. But in addition these media, ranging from education to ecumenical conferences, can be used by Africans as points of entry for their own contributions in the future toward the emerging world culture.

We have also addressed ourselves to the desirability of fostering trends in the northern hemisphere toward socialistic values of greater fellowship, reduced privilege, and sensitivity to the oppressed. But it has to be socialism animated not only by international solidarity, but also by domestic tolerance. Alexander Dubcek's version of "socialism with a human face" goes some way toward meeting this criterion. To the extent that cultural convergence is at play here, it may well be a convergence between socialism and liberalism. The northern hemisphere needs a socialist ethos within a liberal infrastructure of tolerance. It has also to be a socialist ethos responsive to counter-penetration by the Third World, just as Russia has begun to respond to some penetration by the U.S.A. and Japan.

The southern hemisphere needs the values which would give meaning to the new territorial entities they have inherited from the days of subjugation. They need to create nations partly out of nationalism. But in addition they need to create nations with personalities of their own, rather than entities which are poor imitations, frail approximations, of their supposed counterparts in the northern metropolitan countries.

The socialization of the metropolis and the nationalization of the periphery could produce the kind of ideological complimentarity necessary for the coming decades. Human bewilderment at this particular phase of the history of the species does not lie merely in the question "who am I?"—not even in the deprived southern hemisphere—but also in the question "who is my fellow?"

There is a crisis of empathy. It arises partly because mankind is on the verge of a great empathetic leap. History and technology between them have promoted a level of mutual awareness in the second half of the twentieth century unprecedented in the evolution of human society. But this monumental fact has to be given a new focus.

The world needs to change, but first it needs the will to change. And the will to change needs an infrastructure of increasingly converging moral preferences. We have defined some of our own preferences in broad terms in this book—a moral struggle against violence, a political pursuit of social justice, economic innovations to make expanded welfare more feasible. But these are principles which need more detailed elaboration. And the decision concerning priorities requires massive human consensus. This is the inescapable refrain of our song—the song of man as the architect of a new world of cultures.

Footnotes

1. See *New York Times,* December 8, 1974 and December 10, 1974.
2. *New York Times,* December 10, 1974. Consult also Paul Lewis, "Getting Even: A Redistribution of the World's Wealth," *New York Times Magazine,* December 15, 1974, pp. 13, 76–93.
3. John Cooley, "Tripoli, Libya, cradles hotbed of 'liberation' groups," *The Christian Science Monitor,* September 14, 1972.
4. Nyerere, "Ujamaa: The Basis of African Socialism," *Présence Africaine* (Paris) Vol. 18, No. 47, 3rd quarter, 1963.
5. "Tanzania: Soviet Views on the Arusha Program," *Mizan: Journal of Sino-Soviet Policies* (London) Vol. IX, No. 5, September–October, 1967, p. 197. See also William Tordoff and Ali A. Mazrui, "The Left and the Super-Left in Tanzania," *The Journal of Modern African Studies,* Vol. 10, No. 3, October 1972, pp. 442–445.
6. Julius K. Nyerere, *Freedom and Socialism: A Selection from Writings and Speeches, 1965-1967* (Dar-es-Salaam, Oxford University Press, 1968) pp. 17 and 22–3.
7. For an earlier version of my views on the social functions of protest see "Postlude: Toward a Theory of Protest," in Robert I. Rotberg and Ali A. Mazrui (editors), *Protest and Power in Black Africa* (New York: Oxford University Press, 1970), pp. 1185–1196.
8. Cited by Richard Holmes, "A Dynamic View of History" review of C. D. Darlington's book *The Evolution of Man and Society.* The review was published in *The Times Saturday Review* (London), September 6, 1969.

9. Oakeshott, *Rationalism in Politics and other Essays* (London: Methuen and Company, 1962) p. 124. This point is discussed in similar terms in Mazrui, "Postlude: Toward a Theory of Protest," in *Protest and Power in Black Africa, op. cit.*

10. For one insightful discussion of modernization in terms of systemic capabilities see, Eisenstadt, *Modernization: Protest and Change* (Prentice Hall, Englewood Cliffs, 1966). See also M. L. Lipsky, "Protest as a Political Resource," *The American Political Science Review,* Vol. LXII (1968), pp. 1144–1158.

11. *Representative Government* (1861), Chapter XVI.

12. Consult Ali A. Mazrui, *Cultural Engineering and Nation-Building in East Africa* (Evanston, Illinois: Northwestern University Press, 1972), especially the Conclusion.

13. See Selected Works, in two volumes by Karl Marx and Fredrick Engels (Moscow: Foreign Languages and Publishing House, 1962) pp. 384–385.

14. Lenin, "What Is to Be Done? *Selected Works,* Vol. 1 of 3 volumes (Moscow: Foreign Languages, 1960), p. 149.

A Model World Federation of Cultures

This model is given the modest status of an appendix mainly because we believe that several different structural arrangements are feasible and perhaps equally valid for a World Federation of Cultures. In the book as a whole we have sought to put forward a *perspective,* rather than a model. We have endeavoured to draw attention to the relevance of intellectual, economic, political, and kinship aspects of culture to problems of world order. But what rearrangement in the world can be accomplished in order to promote this World Federation of Cultures is a question which admits a number of structural answers, each of which is valid in its own right. Our model therefore claims no special preeminence in fullfilling our own perspective. The perspective is more important than the model.

A primary problem to be resolved in devising world institutions which are based on cultures is to devise an appropriate method of representing cultures. The distinctiveness of our perspective on world order is not in the nature of institutions devised, but partly in the functions served by those institutions and partly in the principles of composition and membership of those institutions.

A major component of culture is language. This component would need to be mobilised for purposes of world reform.

A World Structure of Five Languages

Henry Kissinger once envisaged a five-sided structure of peace involving the United States, the Soviet Union, China, Western Europe, and Japan.

Our own structure of peace will be based partly on five languages—English, French, Russian, Arabic, and Chinese. We have in these five a combination of two types of languages. First, there are those which have already fulfilled the criteria of a world language. English and French already have well over the minimum of one hundred million speakers, have already been adopted as national languages by more than ten states, and have extended well beyond their continent of birth.

The second category is of languages which are not yet world languages but deserve to be promoted and developed for such a role in the near future. Russian, Chinese, and Arabic fall into that category.

The case for promoting Russian further is partly derived from the sheer exigencies of power. The Soviet Union is already one of the two super giants of the twentieth century, with immense power and influence in Eastern Europe and parts of Asia. The country has made remarkable progress in certain areas of technological and organisational innovation, and some of its models of social and economic organisation are influential and have entered the stream of world culture. The Russian language is already the mother tongue of more than the minimum of one hundred million speakers and has been adopted as at least the second language of education and culture by nearly ten states.

In some ways, Spanish is more of a world language than Russian, at least in terms of its adoption by many more states than Russian as the *first* language of national business. Spanish has also spread beyond its continent of birth and has more than the minimum of one hundred million speakers.

But precisely because Spanish is a Western European language in a world already heavily Eurocentric in a western sense, and because we have already adopted two other Western European languages as world languages, the case for Spanish is weaker than that for Russian. Russian—though also a European language—comes from a significantly different cultural tradition. And a World Federation of Cultures has to take pluralism, as well as convergence, into account. In our new world Spanish would have to be demoted into a regional language.

The case for elevating Chinese to a world language is perhaps even more obvious. The very fact that one out of every five human beings speaks Chinese is a major consideration. The language is not widespread and has certainly not crossed continents except with overseas Chinese and some western scholars. But the sheer weight of the number of those who speak Chinese—greater than the number of those who speak English and French put together—makes the case for making Chinese one of the world languages of tomorrow irresistible.

There are additional considerations in favour of such a move. One concerns China's past contributions to world culture, ranging from Chinese science and philosophy over several hundred years to Chinese cuisine today.

Third, there is the People's Republic of China as a major model of political and cultural engineering, with all its potentialities as a whole new civilisation in the world. For the time being communist China's experiment still shows Eurocentric intellectual dependency. Marx and Lenin are revered, whereas China's own greatest philosopher, Confucius, is militantly denounced. European socialist masters are worshipped, while the population is urged to curse its own cultural heritage. The Chinese communists are caught between genuine innovativeness and residual intellectual dependency.

But in this ambivalence they are no different from much of the rest of the Third World. What is more significant and distinctive is China's determined attempt to transcend many of its problems through the energies of its own people and to mobilise a fifth of mankind in the quest for new social directions. The Chinese language deserves to be elevated to a world language partly in order to make this monumental experiment more accessible and more comprehensible to the rest of mankind.

As a candidate for elevation to a world language Arabic is less obvious. But among Third World languages Arabic has special credentials. The development of Arabic into a world language would partly be in recognition of its dual identity as a language of both Asia and Africa and partly in recognition of the impact of the Middle East as a whole on world culture. As we have indicated previously in this book, the Middle East played its part in the evolution of a world culture partly through the emergence of universalistic religions and partly through the impact of Arab scientists and mathematicians on the eve of Europe's emergence.

Both Christianity and Islam were born in the Middle East. Had Hebrew been as widespread as Arabic in the modern world, perhaps Hebrew would have had a stronger case than Arabic for elevation to a world language. Much of the spiritual universe of mankind owes something to the impact of Hebraic values and systems of thought. Even Islam bears the marks of Hebraic and Judaic influence. But given that Hebrew today is the mother-tongue of little more than two million people, its case for global status is much weaker that that of Arabic, with more than a hundred million speakers spread over a much larger area.

Moreover, both Islam and the Arabic language are Afro-Asian cultural phenomena—whereas the great majority of Christians and Jews are part of the already dominant European civilization. If our world federation of cultures is partly a quest to reduce the Eurocentrism of today's cultural arrangements, the language of Islam has a stronger case than the language of either Christianity or Judaism.

From Africa's point of view, Arabic has additional attributes worth taking into account. The majority of Arabic-speakers are part of the African continent and are represented as members of the Organization of African Unity. Although technically Arabic is not an indigenous language of Africa, it is the mother tongue of millions of indigenous people in the continent from the Sudan to Mauritania. The great majority of African Arabs are not immigrants from the Arabian peninsula but indigenous people who have been assimiliated into the Arabic language and culture.

Linguistic Representation of Cultures

We propose that at the global level of a World Federation of Cultures, representation should be not only on the basis of nation-states but also on allegiance to a particular world language and on regional location. A combination of linguistic, national, and regional principles would together constitute the basis of representation at the global level of our institutions.

We discussed previously not only world languages but also the other three types of languages—regional (e.g. German or Swahili), national (e.g. Persian or Japanese), and communal (e.g. Gujerati or Luganda).

In our new world we require that every child in the world should learn three languages—a world language, a regional language, and *either* a national language *or* a communal language.

Those countries in the world which for the time being have not adopted English, French, Russian, Chinese, or Arabic for any official purposes domestically would have to declare their allegiance to at least one of them. This would be important from the point of view of their educational system and the degree to which they promote that language in their schools. But it would also be important because their representation on world bodies would be partly by reference to their being within the global territory covered by a particular world language.

It is an assumption of this model that sharing a language helps to reduce the culture gap among a people. When for example Russians are called upon to learn Spanish as their choice of a regional language, and a growing number of Russian children emerge from schools equipped with skills in Spanish, it may be presumed that Russian sensibilities to the problems of Spanish America would enter a more sophisticated phase.

Spanish Americans need not choose Russian as their own world language in reciprocity. They may decide to adopt another world language like French. That would be up to them. If they did adopt Chinese or English or French or Arabic, Spanish Americans would be no better informed about Russians than they are at the moment, but the Russians would be growing more familiar with Spanish America than they are at the moment. The process of comprehension would by no means be symmetrical, but it would still serve the purpose of our World Federation of Cultures. If Spanish Americans were busy learning a little more about the Middle East after adopting Arabic, for example, or about France and French-speaking Africa after adopting French, the cultural order of the world would be served even if they remained as ignorant of the Soviet Union as they had been before.

Each world language would have a General Assembly. The General Assembly for French-speakers would serve certain functions to promote intellectual, technological, and educational collaboration among the countries that have adopted French as their world language. But in addition the General Assembly of French-speakers would serve as an electoral college to elect delegates of the French-speaking World Community for the global institutions at the center of our Federation. The members of the General Assembly of French-speakers would be elected on a national basis, preferably by a popular vote. Each country would have, say, one member for every 10 million of its population. Countries with less than 10 million will have only one member.

On bodies as varied as the General Council for Security and Political Affairs and the Agency for Migration and Economic Opportunity, representation would in part be by this global linguistic affiliation.

At this initial stage no choice of a world language need be definitive. Brazil and others would have time to rethink by the end of the century. Firm commitment to a world language would not be required of any country until the year 2000.

The United States would now have to seek admission into what has so far been the British Commonwealth. Again the Commonwealth would now constitute the basis of the General Assembly of English-speakers, as a transitional stage. George Bernard Shaw's play, *The Apple Cart,* published in 1929, anticipated the thesis of the United States seeking readmission into the British Commonwealth. The King of England was appalled and frightened by the prospect, according to Shaw.

The original Gaullist idea of the French Community, and the subsequent Senegalese notion of *Francophonie,* would in turn form the nucleus of the General Assembly of French-speakers.

The distribution of the five world languages for the time being would itself offer special opportunities for studying the interaction between regionalism and linguistic affiliation.

The Arab League might form the nucleus of the World Assembly of Arabic-speakers and COMICORN the nucleus of a World Assembly of Russian-speakers. A new body would have to come into being as the global forum for Chinese-speakers.

French provides a special relationship between Africa and Europe. The majority of *individual* French-speakers are in Europe; the majority of French-speaking *countries* are in Africa. The transitional General

Assembly of French-speakers would, in the initial stages, be overwhelmingly Afro-European. This would afford special insights into a new interaction between Europe and Africa, hopefully more egalitarian than the original French version of "Eurafrica" as symbolised by the associated territories of the European Economic Community under the original Treaty of Rome.

It is the General Assembly of English-speakers which would be from the start the most ecumenical—absorbing diverse representatives from Europe, North America, Africa, Asia, and Australasia.

Also in the transitional phase pending the end of the century there should be a dramatic reform of the functions of UNESCO. Each of the three General Assemblies of World Languages should be sending representatives to this World Council on Science and Culture. The principle of membership of UNESCO, its scale of operation, and of course its resources would have to be drastically transformed if UNESCO is to serve as the transitional mechanism for the promotion of a more symmetrical world culture. The details of this transformation can be worked out only after consultation with the new General Assemblies of the five languages. In other words, the Assemblies have to be brought into being before their precise relationship with a transformed and radically elevated UNESCO could be worked out. In the words of a report by a consultative group which met in Paris in December 1972 to review and appraise UNESCO's contribution to the second United Nations Development Decade:

> The present work of UNESCO in the cultural field focusses on three areas: cultural studies, cultural development and cultural heritage. Each plays a part in the general process of development. There is, moreover, an interplay between the national and international aspects in each of these cultural fields. A world culture is emerging in our time, but it is a world culture which is overwhelmingly Euro-centric. Europe's predominance during the last historical period combined with Europe's expansion to the Americas and her annexation of large parts of Africa and Asia, have resulted in an imbalance in *cultural dissemination*. The rest of the world learns European languages, sings European songs, debates about European ideologies, reads European books in a manner which is not reciprocated. And "Europe" in this cultural sense includes Europe's extensions, the Americas.

The report of the UNESCO-sponsored consultative committee then refers to the need for a new emphasis in acculturation processes:

> The right approach to the cultural problems of world is not to attempt to keep Western influences out, but to help create parity of esteem between cultures. And parity of esteem requires reciprocity of influence.

478

The report then confronts the issue of the role of UNESCO. Some of the work done by UNESCO—from its eight-volume project on the History of Africa to its promotion of technical assistance—clearly has a bearing on the wider enterprise of seeking cultural parity. But the Report on the Consultative Committee still had to pose the questions:

Should UNESCO play a greater part in redressing the balance? Should UNESCO play a bigger role in making available to Europe and the Americas the cultures of the rest of the world? UNESCO has started this work but should the scale and the skills needed now be expanded?

This author—who was a member of that consultative group—certainly believes that there is room for a vast expansion of UNESCO's activities if the world we have in mind is to be realized. There is also room for expanding UNESCO's own concept of culture in the direction of emphasizing its interrelationship with UNESCO's other endeavors in the scientific, technological, and educational fields.

Actors and social reformers who could be mobilized in support of such changes include many of those who sympathise with UNESCO's aims in cultural dissemination and educational reforms. Educators are particularly relevant here. Other potential actors behind a movement for such changes would include those who sense a profound unease about the phenomenon of international dependency in this northern-dominated world and are groping for ways of reducing the weight of inequality and imbalance.

In the meantime consideration would need to be given to the role of the other bodies of the United Nations, including the Security Council, the General Assembly, and the Economic and Social Council. But the most drastic transitional transformation within the world body would hinge on a redefinition of the role of UNESCO as a mechanism for educational change, dissemination of science, and promotion of a world culture based on egalitarian principles. This would become the World Council on Science and Culture.

Regional Representation of Cultures

The second principle of representation in the world bodies would be by regions. Of course geographical contiguity does not mean cultural congruence. Some regions are more clearly culturally determined than others. On balance, for example, the Middle East has a massive regional identity either by reference to Islam, which would include Turkey and Iran in the Middle East, or by reference to the Arabic language.

Western Europe is also culturally homogeneous to some extent, though not sharing one language. On the other hand, the African continent is not culturally homogeneous if countries both north and south of the Sahara are included. A good deal of attention might have to be paid to the problem of defining regions. The problems can in some cases be very difficult. But they need not be insurmountable. There may be occasions when a particular country might be given a choice in a national referendum to determine whether it belongs to one region or another. For example, North African countries might have to decide whether they belong to the Middle East or to the African continent for the purpose of this representation. It would be conceivable for some of them to regard themselves primarily as African, while others opted to join the ranks of fellow Arabic speakers elsewhere in the area. Irredentism on a regional scale or secessionism on a regional scale, as particular countries seek to change their regional affiliation, might be a recurrent issue. But the World Federation of Cultures might simply have to decide on periodic referenda—possibly every twenty-five years—for those who are ambiguous or ambivalent in their regional affiliations. The issue would simply have to be resolved by resort to a popular decision in the ambivalent country.

The regional principle is chosen partly because the spread of cultures is affected by geographical contiguity. There was a time when culture, like water, flowed downwards—from the dominant group to the dominated group. We referred earlier to the cultural imbalance in the world, with the heavy weight of European civilization in the central pool of the human heritage. One purpose of the new restructuring of institutions in the world is to negate the proposition that culture flows downwards along the political slope, as inevitably as water does.

In reality, as we have indicated elsewhere, there have been cases when rulers have been acculturated to the values of the ruled, rather than the other way around. The case of the Romans gradually imbibing Greek civilization is noteworthy. The Swahili language in Zanzibar was well on the way towards conquering the ruling Arab elite. Turkish and Islam were adopted by the invaders who descended on Anatolia. We might therefore say that the culture, unlike water, is capable of flowing upwards—from the politically lower groups to the politically dominant. What the new Federation of Cultures would have to seek is an arrangement whereby the economically and politically less powerful sectors of the world might help to facilitate the flow of cultures towards the common pool of humanity.

Their say in issues concerning education in English or French would itself be a process of decolonizing these languages and making them more responsive to the contribution of users distant from the originators of the language.

In addition the representation of these groups by regions would increase the impact of their values and perspectives on policies which determine the direction of the world. There is therefore a case for suitably modifying and strengthening such organizations as the Organization of African Unity, the European Union and European Assembly, the Arab League, a new organization for the Indian subcontinent and Ceylon, and perhaps even a Sino-Japanese complex. Canada, the United States, and the non-Latin Caribbean may also form a new region.

The three world order values of maximization of welfare, maximization of social justice, and minimization of violence are themselves values which are subject to modifications according to the cultural perspectives of those seeking to realize them. We have mentioned before that the most culture-bound of all these values is the value of social justice. What is social justice to a German in Bonn need not be social justice to a Karamajong in Moroto; what is social justice to an American Indian in Peru need not be social justice to a Korean peasant.

But economic welfare is more easily shared as a value. And both the Korean and the Peru Indian may know the difference when they have more to eat, or newer clothes to wear, or a better house to live in. The quantification of economic welfare is a more manageable ambition than the quantification of social justice.

Violence also is a concept subject to some extent to ideological and cultural differences. Concepts like structural violence have already entered even into the general discourse of the existing world languages. What is violence? The answer varies to some extent according to the ideological position of the person defining it. Ideology is an aspect of culture or subculture.

The General Assembly of the United Nations may now need to have a new principle of membership. Each region would have a minimum number of seats *as a region,* chosen by the regional organization like the Organization of American States or the European Community. Additional seats would be allocated on the basis of population in each region. But the U.N. seats would rotate among member states of each regional organization on a three-year basis.

Whatever the precise mechanisms used, the world does need a more equitable distribution both of creativity and its dissemination. It is because of these considerations that we see world order in terms of a federation of human cultural contributions, combining a global pool of shared achievement with local pools of distinctive innovation and tradition.

481

National Representation of Cultures

The nation-state would not disappear in this global federation of cultures. As we indicated in previous chapters, there are countries in the Third World which need to consolidate both their nationhood and their statehood if they are to realize the values of reduced violence and enhanced welfare and justice. Such nations are sometimes threatened by excessive cultural diversity at the domestic level—and their primary quest is for a new collective national culture. Many individual countries in Africa need a domestic federation of cultures. They already have multiple tribal cultures. What they lack for the time being is a coherent federal level of national culture.

Our blueprint for a brave new cultural world must therefore give recognition to nationhood as a unit of culture, real or prospective. Representation on regional institutions should be on the basis of nation-states. In addition, global institutions should also find ways of combining national representation with linguistic and regional credentials.

The newly emergent national cultures should themselves be guided in their evolution by world-order values. A principle of kinship culture specially relevant to world order values may well be the status of women. The national unit of culture would have special responsibility in handling this kinship factor, but regional and linguistic institutions would need to reinforce this trend towards a new politicization of women. There should be a systematic attempt made to increase the proportion of participation by women in these bodies. It may therefore be stipulated as a condition that representatives from, say, the World Community of Arabic-speakers should be no more than two thirds male. Ideally the proportion of men to women in the world bodies of decision-making should as far as possible be on the basis of parity. But for historical and other reasons complete parity should not be insisted upon, and certainly not within this century. A safeguard to ensure that at least one third of each decision-making body consists of women would be an important contribution towards the partial demasculinization of the whole process of determining priorities for the world.

We should at least remind ourselves that any world which concedes to culture the status of a determining factor behind politics, business, and war, is a world which must concede to women a much greater role in determining directions than they had enjoyed before. The role of women as agents of the processes of socialization among young people is only one fundamental idea referred to earlier. The disjunction between infant-socialization and adolescent-socialization, the move from the world of maternal transmission in the home to the wider world of masculine dominance created a disjunction in the socialization process which could be mitigated by making the future world less dominated by the male.

Issues of what is virtuous and what is vicious, what is honorable and what is dishonorable, what is desirable and what is not, could be modified to a significant extent in situations where women help to shape political and economic directions of whole societies.

In a previous discussion we had distinguished between the *enfranchisement of women,* which merely means the acquiring of the vote, and the *politicization of women,* which means their readiness to enter the next level of political effectiveness—the holding of political office. It is one thing to be given the power to vote for somebody else; it is quite another to be a candidate for whom votes are cast.

One major way of politicizing women is simply to insist on a minimum number of women in major institutions of decision making; especially those concerned with security, war and peace. It is because of this that our Model World Federation of Cultures has insisted on at least a ratio of one woman to two men.

Let us now turn to the institutions themselves that would seek to regulate the world in the direction of maximising cultural interplay along lines which could help to enhance economic welfare, promote wider agreement on social justice, and help to diminish violence in all those senses held valid by the global institutions concerned.

A. World Council on Science and Culture

A world which is governed on the basis of a federated system of cultures has to put a special premium on education and training. The whole quest for cultural convergence and a shared pool of values necessitates some convergence among processes of education and socialization. Membership on the council would be first, by affiliation to a world language; second, by region; third, by cooptation by the council itself for reasons of special expertness on specific aspects of education; and fourth, by state.

The World Council on Science and Culture would succeed and drastically expand the work of UNESCO. The council would have several bureaus. Among these would be the following:

(i) Bureau on Educational Methods. This would seek to promote research in the direction of improving educational methods, and of distributing the skills which come with newer expertness. The research into and distribution of these skills would of course take into account the modifications that might be necessary as methods evolved in one part of the world are tried out in another part of the world. Cultural differences

would be taken into account in promoting effectiveness of teaching according to the latest available expertness.

(ii) The Bureau on Language in Education. This bureau would concern itself especially with the issues arising out of the directive that every child at school throughout the world would be required to learn three languages—one world language, one regional language, and one national or communal language. The practical implications of this directive would have to be faced in terms of availability of teachers, teaching materials, shared syllabi, and other issues arising out of this general linguistic tripartite system.

(iii) Bureau on the Arts and Fine Culture. This bureau would seek especially to promote greater awareness in different parts of the world of what has been artistically achieved in other parts of the world. Examples are the promotion of travelling theaters, mobile dancing teams, special radio programs of good music from one part of the world for utilization on radio stations in other parts of the world, translation of plays and books from one linguistic heritage to another, promotion of international seminars and workshops for artists and others professionally involved in the arts and fine culture. Of course, this Bureau on the Arts and Fine Culture would have areas of overlap with the other bureaus. A wide area of collaboration might, for example, be needed between this bureau and the Bureau on Language in Education. Translation of masterpieces from one linguistic heritage to another is one case in point. It may also sometimes be necessary to ensure even within one linguistic group that the literature of one region reaches another. For example, African literature in English should be more widely available to American school-children just as American literature in English should be more accessible to African school-children. The language is the same but the regional context is different; and these last two bureaus could collaborate in promoting adequate literary intercourse not only between linguistic areas but also within linguistic areas.

(iv) Bureau of Technology. This sub-section would keep itself fully informed about technological developments in different parts of the world, and about specified technological gaps. The bureau would be concerned with the dissemination of information about certain technological innovations from one part of the world to another, and would facilitate the transfer of skills and training. What is involved here is not simply the dissemination of sophisticated technological know-how. Even more pressing in some of the less developed countries is information about what has sometimes been called "intermediate technology," tried out in one part of the less developed world, and capable of being utilized

elsewhere, if only the information were made available and the moderate skills required were transmitted effectively.

The Bureau of Technology would be called upon to pay special attention to the problem of determining which technological innovations are feasible or applicable to which cultural conditions. Continuing research would be needed into that fundamental process of interaction between social and cultural variables on one side and technological skills on the other.

(v) Bureau on World-Order Training. This bureau would concern itself with what in individual societies might be called political education, but which in this case would be education towards realizing a world where economic welfare is enhanced, social justice expanded in extent and narrowed in definitional diversity, and violence is reduced. These three imperatives themselves of economic welfare, social justice, and diminished violence, have values which are in turn preconditions for them. These also might be part of the whole process of World Order Training. The Bureau would do research into the best methods of political education oriented towards this more desirable world, taking into account once again the sub-units of ideological and cultural systems that go to make up the human race. The necessary skills for this introduction of world order material in the educational systems of the different countries would have to be somehow transmitted to teachers through suitable educational institutions scattered round the globe.

B. *World Council on Mobility and Communication*

We have already indicated the fundamental relevance of mobility and communication for the whole ambition of relative cultural homogenization in the world. The interplay of different perspectives, the free market of ideas, the competition of ideologies for converts, the primordial intercourse between cultures, all do presuppose some degree of mobility and considerable communication. Our Model World Federation of Cultures must again pay special attention to these processes of human interaction.

The World Council on Mobility and Communication would also have a number of bureaus and special agencies. Particularly important would be the following departments of the World Council on Mobility and Communication.

(i) International Agency on Physical Mobility. An Agency is a wider unit which may have several bureaus under it. This Agency would include an International Bureau for Land and Sea Transportation; an Aerial Control Bureau; and an International Bureau on Space and interplanetary travel. The composition of the Agency will again include, first,

linguistic delegates; second, regional delegates; third, national delegates; and fourth, coopted experts.

All these bureaus under the Agency on Physical Mobility would include among their responsibilities a special working relationship with the Inspectorate Agency under the Political and Security Council as described below. If there is any one area of physical mobility which has to be closely controlled, it is the kind of mobility which would infringe the principle of regional security. At its most obvious the control would affect movements of large shipments of military equipment and movements of military personnel from one region against another. But there would be other areas of mobility less obvious which would need nevertheless to be carefully scrutinised. If the principle of regional autonomy in military matters is to be safeguarded and no one region endanger the security of another, such care is indispensable.

But apart from such tasks of control and limitation of mobility, the bureaus would be concerned with *facilitating* mobility on land, sea, air, and space in a manner which promotes intercultural contacts while protecting the rights of the different users and potential beneficiaries. The bureaus would include an investigating machinery in cases of alleged infringement of the mobilitarian principle. The Bureaus would also facilitate negotiations and compromise, and provide their good offices for that purpose. When contending parties are unable to reach agreement, the bureaus would refer the issues concerned to the relevant bodies for the resolution of such conflicts. The relevant bodies might be regional institutions, or the Political and Security Council or the Economic and Social Council, or the World Court.

Obviously physical mobility needs to be subject to more restrictions than mobility of ideas. But even in the case of physical mobility, the aim should be towards expanding frontiers and loosening of controls.

(ii) International Agency on News and Intellectual Media. This agency would seek to facilitate the dissemination of news in different parts of the world. Copyright for all books would be lodged with the Agency. The Agency would encourage the circulation of published material, and at the same time protect the international rights of writers, inventors, and artists.

A special responsibility of the Agency would be to license the international agencies. No institution which seeks to establish an international coverage of news for client newspapers would be permitted to operate without a special license from the International Agency on News and Intellectual Media. A condition for the issuing of such licenses would be the principle of balance of coverage of the world, determined either in terms of minimum number of correspondents assigned to a particular region, or in terms of a minimum number of stories and reports written up about each region of the world.

The news agencies themselves would in addition be required to devise conditions of their own to govern the relations with their customers in individual countries. Each newspaper using the services of an international news agency would have to pay for a minimum quantity of news about each region of the world, regardless of whether the newspaper prints that news or not. In other words, *The Times of India* for example would be required to pay for a minimum of news about Latin America, every year, regardless of whether *The Times of India* in fact manages to use that news or not. The system of payment to international news agencies would cease to be based either on a principle of whatever is used, or on a principle of a flat subscription. It would have to include special subscriptions for each region of the world, designed to encourage and promote a balanced coverage of world news in domestic newspapers throughout the globe.

(iii) International Agency for Migration and Wider Economic Opportunity. This Agency would deal with some of the issues connected with social justice and economic welfare, but in a special relationship with at least two other institutions or sets of institutions. Questions of economic opportunity and fluidity of class structure are related to issues of national development. It is quite clear therefore that on some questions the Agency for Migration and Economic Opportunity has to keep in close working relationship with the Bureau of National Development as mentioned below under the Economic and Social Council. National development as an activity is of course closely tied in with those five sub-processes of nation building which were specified in the chapters on Violence and Civil and International Order. Nation-building as an activity entails infrastructural changes designed in part to promote economic interpenetration between different strata and regions, to facilitate cultural homogenization, and to consolidate structures of conflict resolution within the domestic domain. Political and economic culture would be centrally affected in the work of the International Agency for Migration and Wider Economic Opportunity.

A distinctive problem under this International Agency on Migration and Economic Opportunity would be the issue of movement of population, especially across national and regional frontiers. The problem of the brain-drain would have to be closely examined.

In this sphere, this International Agency on Migration and Economic Opportunity would again have to be in a working relationship with the

Bureau of Population Control under the Economic and Social Council. On the issue of redistribution of population there may have to be a tax for those countries which annually have a deficit of immigrants as against emigrants. But not all movement of population is concerned with redistribution in numbers as such. Sometimes the brain-drain operates in a manner which might aggravate population pressures in countries which are already densely populated. This tax on deficit of immigrants as against emigrants would therefore have to be applied with certain safe-guards in mind. There may be countries where it would make better sense to apply the tax in a reverse order of relationship between immigrants and emigrants. And yet the tax here proposed would recognize such a situation only in terms of exemption from the other tax. In reality there would only be one type of tax—that imposed on situations where people coming into the country are fewer than people going out of the country. But if a particular country is under population pressure, it could apply for exemption from this tax.

On the precise question of the movement of skilled manpower, a different kind of "human tax" would have to be devised. Any country which imports a skilled person from another country has to allow in its immigration quota for the next year the importation of two unskilled individuals from the same country other than the members of the family of the skilled immigrant. Careful figures of movements of qualified people would have to be kept both by donor countries and by recipient countries. If Britain were to accept the immigration of one doctor from India in 1993, it would, as a condition of that acceptance not only have to accept his immediate family, but also expand its quota of immigration from India for the following year to include two additional unskilled or semi-skilled Indians into Britain.

Again conditions in different countries may vary and they may well be reasons sometimes for applying to the International Agency on Immigration and Economic Opportunity for an exemption from this kind of requirement. It depends on the pressures of the specific countries in terms of population and economic plight.

The Agency would have to facilitate healthy acculturation where advice and resources are needed for new immigrants to settle down to their new homes. Yet the Agency may also have to devise rules and regulations which protect new immigrants from discrimination on the basis of their original culture in their new homes.

C. Political and Security Council: Structure and Functions

(a) Membership: The Council would consist of three types of delegates—national delegates on the basis of one state, one vote; regional delegates, based on population; and language delegates chosen by both population and number of states affiliated to the world language. Each region would decide through its own regional institutions how its regional delegates to the Political and Security Council are to be appointed. Each linguistic General Assembly would also have its electoral by-laws. But the number of delegates for each region would be strictly commensurate with globally determined criteria.

(b) Sub-Departments and Specialized Agencies:

(i) General Secretariat for Security and Political Affairs. This would be in charge of coordinating the work which falls under the Political and Security Council and would take such executive initiatives as are needed under the statutes and regulations of the Council.

(ii) Security and Conciliation Agency. This would be in charge of making arrangements and facilitating global mediation in interregional conflicts when invited to do so by the parties concerned or when instructed to do so by the Political and Security Council.

It would also be in charge of mediation in intraregional conflicts but only on the invitation of the relevant authoritative institutions of the particular region concerned or on the instructions of the Political and Security Council.

Third, the agency would be in charge of making arrangements for global *intervention* in interregional conflict on being instructed to do so by the Political and Security Council. A decision in favour of global mediation needs only a simple majority of the Political and Security Council; but a decision for global intervention would need a two-thirds majority of the Council. Intervention in this case carries the use of force and readiness to impose a solution upon the combatants.

Fourth, the agency would be in charge of making arrangements for global intervention in an *intra*regional conflict, but only if the conflict has serious extraregional consequences as defined under the statutes governing the limits of intervention. Preeminent among intraregional conflicts which have extraregional consequences would be racial wars where the races in conflict come from different regions and where there is a serious danger that a continuation of the conflict could seriously inflame racial antagonisms elsewhere. A violation of the principle of racial sovereignty in this sense, or a contravention of the principle of regional jurisdiction, would immediately be of concern to the global Political and Security Council, and might necessitate direct intervention. But the Political and Security Council might first have to assess whether or not the conflict within a single region could in fact be adequately handled by the regional institutions themselves; and might also have to assess whether the nature of the confrontation would fall within the

defined boundaries of "intraregional tensions with extraregional consequences." Where serious doubt exists, a ruling might be invited from the
World Court as to whether a particular conflict falls within that
definition. But in the heat of an emergency only the Political and Security
Council itself could decide whether or not to refer the issue to the World
Court. The Council would have the option to take direct action unless a
prior procedural vote forces it to refer the matter to the World Court be-
forehand.

(iii) Military Inspectorate. This would be in charge of maintaining a
check on the balance of armaments in the world, and ensuring that no
single state maintains a level of armed forces or weaponry which is of
extraregional concern. The quantities and types of weapons which are of
extraregional concern have to be worked out closely by the Military Inspectorate and confirmed by the Political and Security Council. By such
calculations, it may well appear that no African country at the moment
has a military capability which is of extraregional concern. There may
still be latitude for African countries to move up in their military capability before they reach the minimum permitted by such an arrangement. On the other hand, Britain and France, as well as the Soviet Union
and the United States, have already attained a level of military capability
which is clearly well above intraregional maxima. Such countries would
therefore have to disarm downwards to the level permitted.

In the 1990's the situation would be such that no single *state* is permitted a capability which is of extraregional concern. But the final ambition
in the field of armaments is to arrive at a type of world order in which no
single *region,* even when unified for collective action, has a military capability which is effective enough to cause a serious threat to another
region. Of course calculations based on military capabilities of individual
states still permit for the possibility of alliances within regions—alliances
which could conceivably threaten other regions. By the 1990s, the
military capability of no African state should be high enough to threaten
a country outside the region; but the military capability of a united
Africa could still pose such risks.

In spite of this situation, however, the immediate aim for the 1990's is
simply to bring down the level of weaponry and armed forces per *state* to
a maximum based on a *principle of intraregionality.* The figures and
specifications would be worked out by the Military Inspectorate and
sanctioned by the Political and Security Council. The measurements of
the principle of military intraregionality would be subject to review at
regular intervals, as military technology advances.

The Military Inspectorate would consist in part of military technocrats, equipped with expertness and advice on the whole range of military technology. But the Inspectorate would also include under its wing the global police force, used as a nucleus both in enforcing decisions on arms limitations and also in intervening on being instructed by the Political and Security Council either in interregional conflicts or in those intraregional tensions with extraregional consequences as previously defined.

(iv) Commission for Constitutional Review. This would receive recommendations on constitutional changes in the whole structure of global authority, and refer such proposals to the relevant bodies. All changes in the different branches of the global authoritative structure would need to have, in addition to support within those branches, the final two-thirds approval of the Political and Security Council. Thus changes in the functions of the Economic and Social Council would need not only a two-thirds majority within that Council itself, but also a confirmation by the Political and Security Council. But changes in the functions or organization of the Political and Security Council would need a two-thirds majority only of this Council itself, unless there is an issue which invades the rights of the other Councils—in which case the World Court might have to be involved in giving a ruling.

Constitutional changes concerning the division of powers as between global institutions and regional institutions would need a two-thirds majority not only in the Political and Security Council but also a two-thirds majority in a number of regions whose total population amounts to two-thirds of the population of the world.

D. Economic and Social Council

(a) Membership: The Economic and Social Council would also have national, regional, and language delegates. This criss-crossing tripartite system of representation should favour special approaches to bargaining and normative convergence.

But in addition there would be a system of economic weighting, based on per capita income both negatively and positively. Countries with a per capita income of *less* than $200 a year would have an *extra* vote. Countries with a per capita income of more than $1500 a year would also have an extra vote. These figures are simply illustrative. The principle involved is one which would, on the one hand, recognize that there should be a level of tolerable poverty below which a country deserves to have a greater say in the distribution of the world's resources. But this principle is in turn married to another principle which rewards those who have succeeded in raising the standard of income of their countries and the standards of living of their people above a certain stage. The latter

491

reward would be a recognition of the simple proposition that affluence beyond a certain point in the restructured world could mean greater capability to contribute to the common pool of human welfare, partly through taxation by the global authorities and hopefully through voluntary commitment to a principle of aid and distributive justice. In that case it would make sense for those who are rich beyond a certain point to have their economic power recognized by an additional vote, in the same way in which those who are poor below a certain point would have their economic need recognized by being given the capacity to exert extra voting pressure in favour of change.

(b) Sub-Departments and Functions:

(i) Taxation Authority for General Development. The Economic and Social Council would determine types and levels of taxation to be levied on states and regions. There would be a tax based on gross national product for each country. Such a tax is designed mainly to augment global revenues for general development.

But in addition the Taxation Authority, on instructions from its mother Council, would levy certain taxes designed not so much to augment revenues only but also as instruments of social control and social manipulation. A population poll tax, for example, would be collected from those countries in which infant mortality has fallen down to 50 or less per 1000 or whose level of life expectancy has arisen. There may also be a case for levying taxes on countries which have a deficit of immigrants as against emigrants each year. This particular taxation would be oriented towards creating a structure which favours greater personal mobility in the world.

(ii) Bureau of National Development. This would be concerned with the task of facilitating economic growth and development in member countries, with special reference to the poorer and less developed member states. The help extended would range from loans for special development projects to outright grants for critical infrastructural improvements within the process of nation-building.

(iii) Bank of Reconstruction and Economic Normalization. This would have special responsibilities for countries which are going through a particularly difficult period, either because of a natural calamity or because of the ending of civil war, or because of general economic dislocations as a result of worsening terms of trade. While the Bureau of National Development would be concerned primarily with less developed countries, the Bank of Reconstruction and Economic Normalization may have special responsibilities for the economic difficulties of developed states. Britain or Japan in need of loans to facilitate changes

directed at economic adjustments might then look to the Bank for this kind of service.

(iv) Bureau of Health and Environmental Control. This would pay special attention to those health hazards which are of international or interregional concern. It would have responsibility for ascertaining outbreaks of epidemics, and ensuring that they are controlled and contained. An outbreak of smallpox, for example, would immediately fall under the jurisdiction of the Bureau of Health and Environmental Control, which would then mobilize its resources to contain the danger.

But this Bureau would also be entrusted with the general problem of pollution of the atmosphere, the rivers, and the seas. Special regulations governing the utilization of shared human resources, like the atmosphere and the oceans, would have to be devised and enforced. Sanctions, mainly of an economic kind, might also have to be formulated in cases of wanton violation of international health regulations by individual states.

The Bureau of Health and Environmental Control would need a Health Inspectorate of its own, but in close collaboration with the regional Inspectorates in this general sphere.

(v) Bureau of Population Control. This would be in charge of keeping complete records of population figures in the world from year to year, and calculating tax liability in regard to population growth. As indicated in the sub-section entitled "Taxation Authority for General Development" countries would become subject to population taxation only after life expectancy in the particular society has hit the fifty-year mark, or alternatively, only after the rate of infant mortality has fallen down to 50 in 1000. The Bureau of Population Control would submit its calculation of national liabilities in this regard to the Taxation Authority for General Development. Within the countries themselves the tax would be applied to every member of a nuclear family—parents and children—regardless of age. Contrary to the proper balance between population control and social justice, the present taxation system in most countries of the world grants eligibility for tax reductions the more children one has, at least up to a certain point. But under the proposed restructuring of the taxing system, having more children in those countries which are so liable would increase the tax burden.

The Bureau of Population Control would also be in charge of assessing the impact of demographic variations on relevant resources in the world. In the early stages the most relevant resources from the point of view of population growth might still be food supplies and their distribution, and issues of natural conservation. But after a while calculations may have to be made on availability of healthy living space in individual areas, on the possibility of encouraging mobility from densely populated parts of the world to more sparsely populated areas, and on the feasibility of converting previously unhabitable or barren sectors of the world's surface into areas suitable for productive human habitation. There may even come a time when the availability of enough oxygen in the atmosphere becomes a factor to be borne in mind both in assessing tolerable levels of population growth and in determining suitable types of fuel for industry and transportation and for technological utilization of oxygen at large.

(vi) Bureau of Culture and Conservation. This Bureau would deliberately bring together issues of national conservation with issues of human culture. This is partly because natural conservation is linked to questions of cultural continuities in human society, and partly because human culture involves processes of conservation, as well as of change.

Ecological problems are of three types:

(a) Aesthetic ecological problems. What is at stake under this category is the preservation of those aspects of the natural world which are aesthetically satisfying to man. The attempt is to defend the planet against those who would deface it, or recklessly despoil it, and leave it a much uglier place than they found it. The preservation of wild life in Africa, or of beautiful woods in the United States, or usable beaches in Europe, all fall roughly within the aesthetics of ecology.

(b) Economic ecological problems. These are those ecological issues which are likely to have adverse economic consequences over a period of time. Examples would include the survival of a fishing industry in a certain lake exposed to pollution; or the balance between consumption of wood and cultivation of new trees in a forest in order to ensure a continuing supply; or the quest to discover modes of industrial production and fuel which do not endanger the atmosphere with pollution or fill the rivers with waste matter. All these are ecological problems which have clear and direct economic implications. They may sometimes be an overlap between economic problems of ecology and aesthetic problems of ecology. But it is still worth distinguishing between motives which seek to preserve the beauties of the planet from motives which seek to safeguard the world's economic well-being not simply in the short run but also over an extended period of time.

(c) Survival problems of ecology. What is at stake here is human survival itself. Ecological problems which affect human survival range from the dangers of radiation and nuclear fall-out to questions of relating oxygen supply to population growth.

Both aesthetic ecological problems and economic problems of ecology are connected with cultural factors in human societies. But there are other cultural enterprises to be promoted.

The Bureau of Culture and Conservation would concern itself with fostering cultural exchanges between countries. Other functions would include raising funds to preserve important historical monuments in countries which would otherwise have to let them dissolve into oblivion, and facilitating those aspects of cultural life which stand a chance of becoming part of a world culture.

These different sub-departments of the Economic and Social Council, while designed to strengthen each other in a joint endeavor to meet the economic and social problems of the world, are in fact bound to clash on a variety of fronts in the course of fulfilling their duties. This is a fact of organizational life. The Bureau of National Development, for example, is likely to have recurrent clashes with the Bureau of Culture and Conservation. In East Africa the issue of conserving wild life under the Bureau of Culture and Conservation could conceivably come into conflict with certain issues of economic development under the Bureau of National Development.

Partly in order to coordinate these endeavours and smooth out areas of conflict, the Taxation Authority for General Development would also function as the Secretariat of the Economic and Social Council as a whole.

Conclusion

We must again emphasise that this whole idea of a World Federation of Cultures is primarily a perspective on human arrangements rather than a blueprint for a particular set of new institutions. The above set of institutions do not exhaust the range of structures which are compatible with the principle of global cultural federalism.

Specially important in the above model is the principle of triple representation—by nationality, by region, and by language. A particular bureau may have functions which are not directly cultural, but the principle of triple representation should foster the process of cultural interaction and normative convergence. On an issue as mundane as, say, a new tax increase on alcohol there would be brought to bear considerations and perspectives which are rooted in national, regional and linguistic civilizations.

An infrastructure would thus be provided for a new and more equitable process of cultural interaction. Man might at last find it possible to back conscience with consensus and find a new political will out of a shared universe of culture.

We have sought to indicate in this study a perspective on world order that puts a special premium on cultural integration. Our preference for culture is partly derived from the conviction that a shared pool of values is what consensus is all about. The reform of the world in the direction of greater social justice, enhanced economic welfare, and diminishing prospects for violence requires human consensus behind some core values. The world of tomorrow can either be tamed through outright force or through shared values. And the shared values are what cultural convergence is all about.

But we referred earlier to the paradox of violence emerging precisely out of cultural integration. Violent eruptions in places like Zanzibar, Rwanda and Burundi, societies small enough to offer opportunities for discerning the dynamics of human relations, have in fact revealed the tension-generating defects of cultural integration.

But the ideal world order we are pursuing is not only one of reduced violence, but also of economic welfare and social justice. The cases of Zanzibar, Rwanda, and Burundi reveal the agonies of violence. But why did violence take place? Mainly because the stratification systems within those countries were no longer viable. Cultural integration was therefore helping to reveal more glaringly the injustice of a stratification system that was too unequal. The Arabized Waswahili of Zanzibar therefore rose up against their cultural kins, the Swahilized Waarabu. The rebellion was in part a rebellion against a system of inadequate social justice and asymmetrical economic welfare. It was a rebellion against dependency.

The successful Hutu rebellion against the Tutsi oligarchy in Rwanda, and the unsuccessful Hutu rebellion against the Tutsi militariat in Burundi, were again convulsions connected with the pursuit of social justice. But all three have been very expensive rebellions in terms of the violence which accompanied them, as compared with the modest returns of egalitarianism achieved in Zanzibar and Rwanda. And even these returns are very fragile, tending at times in the direction of a reversed hierarchical tyranny.

But cultural homogenization on a world scale has happier egalitarian prospects, mainly because of the scale of the unit of integration. It would be unlikely that consensus would be obtained on a world scale behind a system of gross inequalities between nations, states, races and cultures. Cultural homogenization globally must therefore carry the seeds of human equalization. The consensus which would emerge would be a consensus behind a global stratification system which is not too glaring.

We have sought to indicate in this study that in fact the beginnings of world culture are already at hand, but for the time being it is a system of hierarchy in the cultural domain rather than a system of cultural federalism. Cultural hierarchy converts one culture into the dominant culture of the world, and yet the culture is drawn primarily from a specific subsection of the human species. The world community at the moment bears comparison with a multireligious state which nevertheless has a single established church. England is a multireligious state, which has chosen one of its denominations, the Anglican faith, as the dominant church of the polity.

The world is a multicultural entity but seems to have chosen for the time being overwhelmingly Western culture as the established cultural church of the human species. Again we are up against dominance and dependency.

The great change which needs to be made in the days ahead is to substitute the principle of an established church with a principle of cultural ecumenicalism. In our sense this would mean a World Federation of Cultures, with the constituent cultures coordinating their status and with the joint pool borrowing from a number of regionally and linguistically-based cultural contributions.

The principle of regionalism, combined with a creative utilization of the languages of the world, could gradually help to cope with the imbalance of contemporary arrangements and solve the problem of uneven creativity and uneven dissemination. Mobility in both the intellectual and physical domain could be critical in directing the human species towards that globalized community of cultures.

INDEX

DATE DUE

FEB 10 '83	